ACTORS OF THE SPAGHETTI WESTERNS

JAMES PRICKETTE

COVER ART BY CHARLES ANTHONY MCLENDON

Library of Congress Control Number:		2011963628
ISBN:	Hardcover	978-1-4691-4428-3
	Softcover	978-1-4691-4427-6
	Ebook	978-1-4691-4429-0

This book was printed in the United States of America.

To order additional copies of this book, contact:
Xlibris Corporation
1-888-795-4274
www.Xlibris.com
Orders@Xlibris.com
104939

Foreword by Thomas Betts, WAI!

DEDICATION

To my wonderful sister-in-law, Joan who actually go this publishing ball rolling for me. And of course to my daughter Carrie and my son Matthew, who were always in the wings routing me on.

Acknowledgments

As personal acknowledgements lets begin with my wife, Helen, who never faltered in her confidence or support in this project. Next are my friends within the Spaghetti world of films: Thomas Betts, editor of genre Fanzine *WAI! Westerns All'Italiana* and now Blogspot!; William "Bill" Connolly, editor of Fanzine Spaghetti Cinema and now Blogspot; William and Ruth Staats, both now deceased but were true friends who without them the LVC section couldn't possibly have taken place; Kasimir Berger; Bridget Madison, who without her love and perseverance in pushing her father's name and accomplishments none of his chapter section would have been possible either. Barbara Van Cleef, truly a remarkable woman that I am proud to have known. A special nod goes to Denise Van Cleef another truly astounding woman, who with her lovely daughter Kate for just being there in the wings. Lastly, I wish to thank my editor and publishing staff for their enduring help, confidence, and overall knowledge of their craft. I sincerely thank you all.

And to others, all of who are truly devoted to the European film genres and who continually will lend a helping hand when needed are listed herein below:

Sebastian Haselbeck of *spaghetti-western.net* website
Cenk Kiral of *fistful of Leone.com* website
Craig Ledbetter, former Editor of *ETC* Fanzine, now the website
Michael Malloy, Author and Cinematographer

A special thanks to you guys as well . . .
Ciao

CONTENTS

FOREWORD

European action films during the 1960s and 1970s took many forms. There were *Peplum* films, which most of us know as Sword and Sandal films, *Spaghetti* Westerns; Crime films; Spy films, and just plain Adventure films. Many of the same actors appeared in some or all of these film genres and usually progressed from one to another as the fads began or faded away. Many of us here in the United States were drawn to these films by some of the major actors therein who were Americans, now working there in Europe. Sometimes the mere names of these actors tended to lend more of a Hollywood feel, or an authoritative realism to these 'B' movies. Some of those actors were on the rebound from failed or fading Hollywood careers, while others were just starting out in film work with in these European movies. At any rate these actors could now see their careers spread back not only in to the United States but worldwide as well.

Since a large majority of these productions wound up relegated to the smaller cities and towns of Europe for the blue-collar workers to enjoy, these were not heralded and released in the United States as being the latest Italian, Spanish, French, or German blockbuster films. Actually if they appeared at all in the United States, they were shown in small towns and drive-in theaters. If you were an action film fan during this era in time, some of these actor names are familiar to you: Clint Eastwood, Guy Madison, Wayde Preston, and Chuck Connors who also had been big TV stars in their day. Other names you knew somewhat in passing but little about the actor such as Mickey Hargitay, Mickey Knox, or Richard Harrison. These were actors who had actually begun their careers in Europe and was now enjoying a cult following back in the States. Lee Van Cleef and John Ireland were film stars from the '40s and '50s but because they couldn't find work in Hollywood, wound up in Europe where their names were being featured in these films and advertisements. Van Cleef, like Eastwood and others became international stars solely because of the films they made in Italy and Spain.

Many of these names are also familiar to younger readers, thanks to the advent of the video players, and mainly the DVD formats which have given a whole new viewing audience a chance to see these heroes of yesterday. Films such as these are simply not made anymore since the decline of the European cinema which began about the mid 1970's. That type of production has become way too costly to make now days and regretfully, those action heroes of that era are now a dying breed.

What is the career history behind these actors that we consider cult heroes of the era? Who really were these guys that we used spend our allowances on to see up there on the big screen or at the drive-in theaters of our youth? Who they are and how they came to appear in these films is now covered by my longtime friend James Prickette. A dedicated collector / researcher of the films, and actor associated materials for decades now. He's gone through his files and put together a book on twenty-two of some of the more popular actors of that era. Within is possibly everything you've ever wanted to know and more on these guys. So sit back relax and remember those days of excitement as we watched some real heroes of the big screen in action.

Tom Betts
Editor and Chief of *WAI!*
(Westerns All'Italiana)
Fanzine & Blogspot

INTRODUCTION

The spaghetti Western movies affectionately deemed so by fans and critics alike, pertains to a unique era of Western filmdom. This genre phenomenon, as it is also known, began in Europe, primarily in Italy during 1964 and lasted approximately some ten years into the 1970s.

In these chapters we'll discuss some of the better-known actors who were associated with this phenomenon and who were responsible in part not only for its beginning but also for the total success of these new types of Westerns of the era. While some of those actors reached international fame, others made fortunes as well. Then there were some simply enticed by the prospects of newfound stardom or perhaps even a revitalization of an old dwindled past career. Some might have just relished the idea of being a part of the action once again, working and making a living in their chosen field of endeavor. Yes, monetary fortunes were to be made by some. Others would squander it away much as they had done in past times. At any rate, many a career-minded actor would have the opportunity here to make it or break it as they say.

Out of this European film culture would derive many talented film directors and other film professionals. One of these men, a young director named Sergio Leone, would come to revolutionize the film industry worldwide. He was a man full of dreams; and his love for the then American commonplace shoot-'em-ups, as a staple of the theater-going audiences both here and abroad during that 1960s era, was about to be changed forever. Leone sought to reengineer the old-school Westerns as we once knew it to a more stylish "horse opera" theme in sound and appearances. His would be a tribute to both past and present films and screen idols of a livid Western culture in films. His dreams would now push him to greater heights in achievement.

In the early days prior to 1964, some twenty-five Westerns had already been made from overseas sources. A few of them were insignificant efforts already made or in production at the time. Most of those were utilizing only a small handful of actors who had already proven themselves as key box-office draws in Europe through the epics genre of films. Most were being made down in Spain, where labor was cheap and the weather warm mostly year round. Horses were easy to come by here, as were Mexican-look-alike extras that were also plentiful. Near a small town called Almeria, in southern Spain, there the sparsely populated, arid, dry desert lands resembled those of the American southwest and Mexico of the 1800s. Spanish films had already been made in the area before, with features coming forth since the 1950s. Now the Euro Westerns would have their turn to evolve in the sun, into a new age genre.

Many a fine and some equally talented directors, like Leone, coming from the epics would also join this new Western phenomenon—those like Sergio Corbucci, Sergio Sollima, and Duccio Tessari, to name just a few of the early ones. However, none would generate quite the impact that Leone would come to make on the Italian film industry as a whole. Born January 3, 1929, in Rome, and coming from good solid film professionals stock, he would grow up no stranger to the business. His mother, Francesca Bertini, was a renowned screen actress. His father was Vincenzo Leone, a film director himself who is credited with more than fifty films of his long pioneering association within the European silent film industry.

For Sergio's first Western, he used the Americanized name "Bob Robertson." This was in fact a nod to his father who had used the pseudonym "Roberto Roberti" for early film credits within his own career. Other fine young professionals would come to join Leone in his efforts. One such man was Ennio Morricone, who also had used a pseudonym (Dan Salvo) for an earlier Western he'd composed the music for called *Gunfight at Red Sands* (1963). It had been directed by one Ricardo Blasco and starred a young American *Peplum* (epics) actor, Richard Harrison. This early film of Morricone's was actually the second Western for our Mr. Harrison. His previous oater had been a Spanish-Italian co production effort directed by Joaquin Romero Marchent called *The Ruthless Ones* (1963). This film, however (being released internally in Spain), was not released to the rest of the world until 1966, and then with a title change to *A Gunfight at High Noon*. By that time the new Western revolution was well on its way to being a phenomenon for the industry.

Morricone's slick handling of his first-time joint coordination efforts with Leone turned out a truly amazing musical score; then there was Morricone's pupil Bruno Nicolai doing a jam-up job with the conducting.

But Morricone was about to add something else to the pot, one Allessandro Allessandroni, a musician friend who was a prolific whistler to boot, along with his backup choir group he'd founded back in 1961. Morricone requested that he add eight more singers to the group and perform his famous twangy guitar sounds for this new Leone Western film soundtrack. But specifically, he wanted to use Allessandroni's unique whistling techniques also on the track. His choir group would now become known as *I Cantori Moderni* (The Modern Choristers); then add in American actor Clint Eastwood portraying the gunslinger character "Joe" and we now had a true spaghetti Western in the making. True enough, the reworked storyline; Leone admitted was borrowed from the Japanese film *Yojimbo* for his new production, now to be called *A Fistful of Dollars*. This story borrowing did cause some release issues in the end, but finally it was able to hit the screens there in Italy where it received great appreciation from the theater going public, as well as kudos from the producers and other filmmakers of Europe.

Per contract, Leone owed producers Colombo and Papi a sequel in the same vein. This he would do, but not with them since he believed they had held too many restraints on him. Instead, Leone managed to void the contract deal with his lawyer friend Alberto Grimaldi, who now would become Leone's producer. He formed his own company, calling it *PEA* (*Produzioni Europee Associate* SRL), and was able to wrangle co production monies with Spanish and West German film producers. From that time on he was considered to have practically invented the film co productions with Spain. This movie would now be made under the banner of *PEA*, Rome; *Arturo Gonzalez Productiones Cinematograficas, Madrid; and Constantin Film Produktion GmbH,* Munich.

Fistful had now set the stage, and now the monies were in place. For Leone's next effort, it would come to be realized as *For a Few Dollars More.* Leone was being given full range to call the shots and had the money to do with the film pretty much as he wished without the undue restraints of Colombo and Papi. Leone created his film for a late 1965 Italian release. When viewed, it opened the floodgates that had been holding back the floods. Now the spaghetti Western phenomenon began full steam ahead. The rest is pure history for the Italian cinema.

These films with their virtual nonstop action and the close-ups were a true cinema art form especially the use of same frame shooting (shooter and victim), which was a unique style in itself, previously avoided in all American films considered too violent. Then topped with their wild and weird sounds comprised of big band music, lots of horns, flutes, whips cracking, and that twangy guitar and intense whistling by Allessandroni, who also was an accomplished vocalist, guitarist, and composer himself, all tended to set the wheels in motion as the Italian horse opera was truly born.

That combination of Leone's astute direction and Morricone's thrilling music, executed so proficiently by Nicolai and Allessandroni's group, now coupled with Eastwood's unforgettable role as the laconic bounty killer, sprinkled in with an international cast, the Western film world was soon to be taken aback. The thrill was in going, seeing, and hearing for oneself; the true age of the Western film genre was reborn, Italian style.

Within these following pages, we wish to enlighten the general public as to the origins, the accomplishments, and finally a clearer overlook on the subject of the Italian Western phenomenon and the men who made them. Herein we discuss some of the better known, as well as a few of the lesser known actors who were all in some way directly responsible, along with the Italian filmmakers for the success of these new action Westerns. These were men and women from all walks of life brought together for one objective: to make movies, lots of movies. Not just any movies, but a different type of Western movie for the era. Once read about here and sought out afterward and viewed for oneself, the attraction that these unique films held over their viewing audiences of that era-and continues to do so with fans even now—will become quite apparent. Enjoy one and all . . .

The Author

WALTER BARNES

(1918–1998)

SHOOT THE PASS, MY FRIEND!

West Virginian Walter Lee Barnes was born in Parkersburg, W.VA. on June 26, 1918. According to *entertainment.msn.com*, they claimed casting directors described him as an "outdoor action type" actor. That he was a huge, burly man with the type of face that could be pleasant one instance and downright mean the next. At 6' and 1" tall, 240 lb in his prime, he could very well have been a source to be reckoned with. His mother, though, thought the sun arose and set on her baby boy; however, others probably didn't share her feelings.

He admitted to being just one of those ornery kids per his one-on-one interview with *Spaghetti Cinema* fanzine editor William Connolly for his no. 46 issue, of which excerpts have been included below. The guys he said got to calling him Piggy after an incident that happened while growing up in the Depression era. For the interview, he related, "I stole a pig. A cop saw us. That was during the Depression. We stole the pig and we ate him. We ate the evidence," he said, "so they couldn't prove anything, but the guy (cop) always kept calling me, 'You little pig thief. You pig thief.' And my mother found out about it, and the chief of police lived next door." His mother didn't like it one bit when she find out since she thought he was the perfect little angel.

The chief sort of looked out for him since he and Walter's father had been real close friends before he died. He once told Walter, "You're either going into the *CCC's (Civilian Conservation Corps)* or reform school. Take your pick." While in the *CCC* doing that manual labor, hauling logs and the like up and down those hilly West Virginia trails he tended to put on a lot muscle on an already-growing large frame. After a couple of stints with this *CCC*, he was finally sent back to regular school and found he was now a year or two older than the other kids of his classes.

It was there that the coach noticed him during his sideline watching during the afternoon football practices. They all started calling him names and the like. So Walter decided he'd show them and take a run at the seven-man sled they were trying to push about. When he took his turn, he hit it and spun it around like it was nothing. Afterward, when the coach apologized for his teasing before and offered him a chance to play a football with them, Walter says, "I sold my soul to the devil right there: beef was cheap. And so it went from there."

He continued to play football throughout his high school, even going out for track. He also was a HS champion wrestler during these years as well. His real big chance came later when he got an offer to play football in college at *LSU (Louisiana State University)*. They wanted him bad, and after a tour of the campus, Walter himself had fallen in love with it. As he spoke of those years, he said about how it was such a great time in his life, even though he'd gotten kicked out for fighting. Barnes was best known during those grit-iron years by that same nickname his friends had tagged on him, "Piggy" Barnes, *the* linebacker.*.

---

* Barnes, in his prime, was the ultimate lean machine; a linebacker an all-conference (Mason-Dixon) sixty-minute lineman (simply meant one could stay in a game, toe to toe for sixty minutes). Looking back, reminiscent of more recent times in NFL history, the likes of *Chicago Bears* lineman Dick Butkus comes to mind. He played nine seasons in the NFL for the *Chicago Bears*. In his prime Butkus was billed as 6 ft and 3 in, 245 lb and was considered one of the most feared and intimidating linebackers.

Another was Bob Kuechenberg, a former NFL *offensive lineman* who played for the *Miami Dolphins* for fourteen seasons between 1970 and 1983.

Prior to his professional years, he had been a former all-conference pro-athlete and weightlifter while at *LSU.* By 1943 and near the breakout of WWII, Walter had been working for *Standard Oil Company,* but after he'd seen that the war had indeed begun, like many others of the day, he immediately went to join up, taking a shot at the air force. Previously, he had been in the army having been ordered to do so after being expelled from school, but one of the guys he'd whooped up on in the fight, his dad was some local high monk to monk, and so pulled some strings getting him discharged for having a perforated eardrum.

While in service, he continued to play ball for the service, as the general's favorite star player. Walter's regular job there was as a C-47 crew chief with the Third Air Force in North Carolina. It was there he'd hurt his arm and was disabled and laid up for a spell. The service was lots of fun 'n' games for Walter, but trouble always seemed to follow pretty close behind him.

After the war was over, he returned to *LSU* so as to finish his schooling, continuing his football career as well. After graduation his was picked to go with the *Philadelphia Eagles*, he was then thirty years old, being the oldest pro-rookie. He played with them only four years, but during that period he'd helped them win the newly established Pro-Bowl Games twice, which included the inaugural game.

Once unofficially, of course, he was accused of spying in a *University of Oklahoma* training session prior to a game between them and *LSU*. We say accused since he wasn't actually apprehended, but was supposedly caught from the rear (a butt shot) by the photographer of a six-man posse sent to reel the culprit in. It had been said that he was spotted, supposedly now, red-handed, hiding under a tarp on a scaffold board betwixt two ladders, with notebook and field glasses in hand, recording plays of the opposing team. Supposedly, this all happened just prior to the big 1950 Sugar Bowl game in Biloxi, Mississippi. However, nothing was ever proven, and *LSU* vehemently denied it, as did Barnes. Even to his death in 1998, he still maintained his innocence on the matter. All in all we believe it didn't matter much anyway 'cause Oklahoma won.

After the bowl win and all the spying commotion, he decided he'd stop playing and go into coaching. He went on to coach *Miami*, *Arizona State*, and *Columbia University*. He figures he was in demand then because they all wanted to find out all they could about the Eagles defense. It was during this period in time he got into acting, or so they called it. With him being a wrestler, he was he was asked to join in with the new live telecast show being

---

In his prime he was billed as 6 ft and 2 in, 253 lb. All these guys could certainly toe the mark and did throughout their pro-football years.

produced there in Philly at *WCAU-TV*. It would include some wild fight scenes, and he was asked to help with the coordination as well as act in them. He accepted the challenge and commenced to act from that time forward.

This was his first acting stint for television. The show was a Western done live with all the errors and mistakes intact. The audiences loved it, and he wound up doing some one hundred episodes for the show, *Action in the Afternoon*. It evidently was a riot; "mistakes were always the norm," he said. "Horses that were to stop would wander away. Planes would fly overhead, so a signal was given for the actors to speak louder." In one episode, he was on his horse galloping into town for a shootout with the hero when, after dismounting, then grabbing for his gun, he found it had fallen out of its holster while riding in. Save for his embarrassment, all went well when a sound effect gunshot saved the day. He was always getting ahead of himself, getting mixed up and saying the wrong words of his script, like the time he related in the interview, "One time I was talking about leaving Nigeria, and on this boat, we had a whoring time at sea (instead of) harrowing. I never even knew I said it, I just kept on talking." He certainly heard about it after the letters began rolling in though.

During the show's off-season, he continued to coach there at *Columbia University* and began taking acting classes at night with teacher Kirk Conway. Early in 1950, he got his own TV show there at *WCAU-TV*; it was called *The Adventurer,* a half hour show with Barnes as the main character Captain Nemo, an adventurer who traveled to exotic areas of the globe, fishing, hunting, and exploring. He said, "They believed everything (the public). I never left Philadelphia." It seems they took stock footage of Barnes in and around Philly and spliced in out of the way worldwide segments so it seemed he was actually in a remote area of the world. This show ran for some thirty-five episodes for forty weeks, five a week, he claimed. Making more doing that than, he was coaching football, he decided to go to Hollywood and tried his luck there. He borrowed some money, and off he went. The rest is history for Walter Barnes, an actor.

His first roles were in some of the *Warner Bros* weekly Western shows like *Sugarfoot,* his first doing another fight scene with actor Alan Hale and ex-footballer Red Morgan, the stuntman, for the scene. To help advance his now-budding career in acting (we're sure at the suggestion of *Warner* executives), he took some classes studying with Jeff Hayden, then head of *Actor's Studio* and husband of Eva Maria Saint. Afterward, there were other *Warner* shows like *Colt .45*; *Cheyenne*; *Zane Grey Theater*; *Have Gun, Will Travel*; *Gunsmoke*; *and Bronco* (a spin-off of the *Cheyenne* show). He also had a smattering of other show parts beside just the Westerns under his belt by the end of the 1950s and a few movie roles as well. One of his first films had been as Sgt. Jed Erschick for *The Oregon Passage* (1957). Others were

Revolt in the Big House (1958), *Westbound* (1959), and the now-classic Howard Hawks film with John Wayne, Dean Martin, and Ricky Nelson called *Rio Bravo* (1959). Barnes's role was that of Charlie the bartender. For this *Bravo* Hawks Western and in addition to its three star leads was an all-star supporting cast, which included Angie Dickinson, Walter Brennan, and Ward Bond. Also was an early stand-in part for future *Spaghetti* actor Chuck Pendleton (Gordon Mitchell).

For Walter's upcoming Euro film career, one might say Kirk Douglas gave that a push. Douglas was looking for big, burly guys in the business, willing to relocate for his early TV show spin-off of his successful *The Vikings* film of 1960. This was probably Walter's main reason for winding up in Europe to begin with. Later, he would relocate there and stay awhile, going on to big-screen success across the big pond. Remember now that our Walter Barnes was just a fun-loving guy at heart, and he was pretty much up for most anything in those days. So Europe wasn't really that far off the wall for him to consider.

Shortly after the theater showings began of the *Vikings* (1960) film, Douglas and his production company *Bryna* decided to cash in on its success with a new television series called *Tales of the Vikings*. Barnes also was quick to point out in the interview with *Spaghetti Cinema* fanzine: "The only thing wrong is that they didn't do it in color." It was produced in Germany where most of the original *Vikings* film had been shot, other than other locales down in Spain and some in California, USA. Barnes now was pushing forty years old (and unmarried up to that point), he was about to meet his future wife on this TV show set. After a short courtship, he married the German actress Britta Wendel* who had a small role in the series.

Barnes went on to say that the show only lasted for some thirty-nine episodes, and after the close of production, he made his way down to Rome for a visit. There he met up with old pal Lex Barker. Barnes got his lifelong

---

* Britta Wendel Barnes, an aspiring actress at the time of meeting Walter Barnes, went on to appear in a few other European films of the era. One of note was in *Fellini's Roma* (1972) and later in *Senza Ragione (Without Reason)* a.k.a. *Red Neck* (1973) as a German mother. This film, from director Silvio Narizzano, starred Franco Nero and American Telly Savalas. It was an Italian / UK coproduction. Britta in real life was a mother of two of Walter's children, both having become actors following in the footsteps of their parents. Both were girls, Lara Wendel and Michel Barnes. We bet with a household of three women in the house, they could surely put our actor / father on the defensive, and we don't mean football lines either!

ambition answered at that meeting when he had a chance to talk with Italian director Federico Fellini in person, although he didn't realize it until Barker explained who it was he was referring to as a "bullshit artist." At any rate, Lex Barker had been there in Europe for a while now since clearing out of the USA following his divorce to Lana Turner.

When Barker bailed off into his new European film career with gusto, eventually he settled there in Germany for the long term. It was during the early 1960s that the film industry in Europe had begun to revamp the old Western film genre. Prior to that, those old films of the genre that came from Hollywood had been less action yarns with lots of talky coming into their country from the States. Their new versions, however, first from the Germans, tended to follow stories written by German novelist Karl May. His Indian stories gave a new meaning to the old term *Cowboys and Indians* as was previously set by Hollywood standards.

The first of these unique German Westerns was to star Lex Barker and was called *The Treasure of Silver Lake* (1962/3). Evidently, after his meeting with old friend Walter Barnes there in Rome, they no doubt had talked up the potentials of this new type of film work aimed at the American households, the younger set in particular. Barnes who had continued to work steady in adventure films after his first Euro TV series venture with Douglas, was a bit put off by now concerning his range of offers so far, being somewhat stymied with always the action/adventure type films. His roles then had been mainly those of pirates, Vikings, or period costume dramas of a bygone era, was what he had been offered by the Euro producers to date. His being associated from the start in Westerns, from way back in his college years, he longed for a return to that genre and a change of venue.

After doing another adventure yarn (sort of a Western in kind) called *The Sign of Zorro* (1963)—in which Errol Flynn's son, Sean Flynn starred as Zorro, and Walter Barnes in a lesser role portraying one of the house guards Mario—he got his wish later in '63. For his first German Western (actually second of the genre for Lex Barker) and a 1964 release was called, *Winnetou—1.Teil (*a.k.a. *Apache Gold).* Once again Barker reprised his role of old Shatterhand as in the first film. His on-screen partner Chief Winnetou was again portrayed by French actor Pierre Brice. Although in some of the later series films, the Shatterhand character would take a backseat to other leads on occasion, but the Winnetou role would always be played by Brice right to the end of the series in '68 and some ten films in total.

By that time though, Barnes would have become deeply involved in the Italian westerns of the era, affectionately dubbed, the *Spaghetti* Westerns. When Barnes came on the scene to join with Barker for *Apache Gold* film, he didn't totally quit the *Adventure* genre since he probably had signed contacts back to back in the wings. Even as he continued to make these other films, he signed-on for three more of the German genre.

For Barnes's second film he portrayed Baumann Sr., in *Among Vultures* (a.k.a. *Frontier Hellcat)* (1964) with European beauty Elke Sommer and Stewart Grainger as the Old Surehand character replacing the Barker's Shatterhand character for this go around. Pierre Brice remained though in his regular Chief Winnetou role. For his third German Western Barnes would portray Bill Campbell in *The Oil Prince* (a.k.a. *Rampage at Apache Wells)* (1965). For this film, Stewart Grainger returned as Old Surehand along with Pierre Brice (Chief Winnetou).

Barnes began his *Spaghetti* fever with *Killer Kid* (1965). The film stars Mario Girotti (Terence Hill) in an early role, along with Peter Van Eyck as the two McGow brothers working for their evil town boss father, McGow Sr. With the old man attempting to hood wink the Parker ranch owners out of their land, Don (Van Eyck) seems to have fallen for the gal who runs the place, Nancy. Eventually comes down to brother against brother for a shootout at sundown.

For his fourth *Winnetou* film Barnes portrayed one Mac Haller in *Half-Breed* (1966). For this outing Lex Barker returns and reprised his Shatterhand's role once again with Pierre Brice as Chief Winnetou. Barnes went on to do another genre Western called *Clint the Stranger* (1967) where he was cast as Walter Shannon another greedy land-grabbing SOB. The film's star was the prolific Spanish actor George Martin who was a strong contender within the genre. His costar was German actress Marianne Koch who Leone's cast in his first Western with Clint Eastwood, *a Fistful of Dollars* (1964). Ms Koch was also a prolific actress and here again had her heels dug in for the duration of the genres.

From there Barnes went on to make *The Greatest Robbery in the West* (1967) where his role was that of Key Jarret (a.k.a. Clay Thomas) leader of an outlaw gang. He played alongside two other mainstream *Spaghetti* actors, George (Jorge) Hilton as David and Hunt Powers (actually American Jack Betts) as gunman Billy Rum. Both actors had good footholds in the genre and would have for a longtime to come. Jarret and his gang get hitched up with David who plans a robbery. The loot however gets crossed up by Billy and the three now square-off to see who will get the loot and keep it. Good film, enjoyable with action to boot.

By this time in his career Walter Barnes had eased on into the *Spaghetti* Western genre of Italy and found a niche, so to speak. The year was 1967, and the Sergio Leone *Dollar* trilogy of films that had originally kicked off the Phenomenon events of those Italian westerns was beginning to show back in the States. The *Spaghetti* Western film genre was in full bloom now with planes, and boatloads of Americans coming to the Italian shores looking for a chance to make it big in these unique Westerns.

Many actors from the States were already there and more coming every day. Other career actors from elsewhere in European had already jumped on the bandwagon. Our "Piggy" Barnes was no exception, he was there as well, shootin', fightin' and ridin' hard. Walter Barnes loved every minute of it. He related in the *Spaghetti Cinema* interview, "To live in Italy during the '60s was like living in heaven," Back on August 4, 1991, he said, "They had lots of parties. You had Guy Madison, Gordon Scott, Lang Jeffries, Brett Halsey, the guy who did *Colt .45;* Wayde Preston . . . and then the divorces start."

With the Adventure films now given way to the Westerns, our Walter Barnes took on other genres of film during this period in time, The Spy and Crime genres just now coming out of their infant stages and were beginning to stretch their legs at the cinemas. Following the solid runs of the James Bond films, the copycat spy films were coming out of the wood work. Crime films were also around beating the genre bushes, and would begin to go full tilt after 1970.

For 1968 Barnes turns out another Western, *The Moment to Kill.* His role was that of Bull for this tongue 'n' cheek slam bam shoot 'em up starring George Hilton as Lord with sidekick Bull, two notorious gunmen hot after Confederate gold. This was a great little film outing for both Hilton and Barnes, from director Anthony Ascott (Giuliano Carmineo). Then there was a little ditty called *Garter Colt* (1968).

Italian actress Nicoletta Machiavelli has the lead as Lulu, a female spy for factions (Benito Juarez, Mexican Revolutionary) attempting to overthrow the Emperor Maximilian. Barnes role here is that of the general trying to protect his Emperor. The film regarded by some as junk was an Italian/ Spanish/ German coproduction, if that helps any to resolve the issue any. Directed by unheard of Gian Andrea Rocco, in his only genre film, which might also be a reason in itself. I would normally in my collections classify this film as a spin-off of the *Spaghetti* genre I call *Tortilla* Westerns, a place where I like to put those films that are more related to the Mexican revolutionary type.

A more popular film for Barnes and of the genre was his next one, the *Big Gundown* (1968)—here appearing with the great Lee Van Cleef who in character is Jonathan Corbett, a man-hunter with political aspirations fueled by a healthy push from wealthy landowner Brokston (Barnes), who has ulterior motives. From director Sergio Sollima, this is an Ital/Spanish co production with music to match its violent feel from Ennio Morricone maestro of the genre.

Making his last Euro film in 1969, it was called *Colpo di Stato* (*Hit of State*), another Italian crime film about internal political unrest in Italy with opposing communist factions. A rare film that was unfortunately unable to be obtained for review. Having begun to have medical problems, it seems, after completing this film, he pulled up stakes and headed back home to the United States. Once back on the American soil again, he soon found the root of his problems: he had diabetes and a slowdown was in order now for our mainstream genre star. He eased his way back into American television and began appearing on several of the popular show spots of that era. At first they were only bit parts once again, but that was fine, with Barnes needed the slowdown anyway. Some of those shows were *High Chaparral*, *Alias Smith and Jones*, and *Bonanza*.

Barnes first US film after returning from Europe was a Western Black comedy called *The Traveling Executioner* with Stacey Keach and Marianne Hill. Barnes portrayed the town sheriff. A man travels though the west in 1918 with a new item for executions, the electric chair! From there Barnes continued doing TV work, but began to delve more into the feature films again, although never receiving the status he'd gained in Europe as an international star.

One of his more popular films back in the States was with Clint Eastwood in *High Plains Drifter* (1973). Barnes role here was that of town sheriff Sam Shaw. He went on to make a couple of other films with ex-*Spaghetti* Western star, Eastwood now a popular mainstream producer and director. Those other films were *Every Which Way but Loose* (1978) where Barnes portrays bare-knuckles fighter Tank Murdock. Next was in Eastwood's *Bronco Billy* (1980) as Sheriff Dix. Barnes then managed a good run with a popular TV series from the film *Walking Tall* (1981). Here he portrayed Sheriff Pusser's father Carl Pusser. He did seven episodes for this show in all.

Slowing down more, Barnes eased out of acting onscreen and retired. With his diabetes continually getting worse, he later moved into the *Motion Picture & Television Retirement Home* there in Woodland Hills, California. He did, however, resumed his career to an extent, but mainly doing voice-overs for European cartoon television shows that were recorded there in California. We have four of these features listed in his filmo section thanks to *www.IMDb.com.*

After topping off his career with some addition of sixteen films after his return to the States, he finally settled into full-retirement life from 1991 and onward. Visits from his longtime friend Wayde Preston, who was now living in Reno, Nevada, close to the *VA Hospital* there, were as numerous as could be expected since both men weren't in the best of health during this period in their lives. Walter with diabetes that was continually pulling him down daily, and Preston fighting his early stages of colon cancer—they must have been a pair. A couple of old men now, meeting together and talking about those good old days when in Europe together, they made those fabulous

Spaghetti films. Preston cancer seemed to develop rather quickly after the diagnosis was confirmed, as most time it does. He was finally stricken to the hospital early in 1992 and, later, sent home to await the inevitable. He passed away on February 6, 1992.

We can imagine after losing his good friend, Walter was no doubt devastated. Alas, he still had his daughters to help console him, and at times, there would *Spaghetti* Western fans that would drop by for visits and have an information gathering session or two with Walter on the making of those unique Westerns films of Europe back in the day. The following years after Preston passing probably dragged by for Walter; he also became increasingly ill from the diabetes. He finally surrendered, and it took him. He passed away on September 6, 1998.

> ***Note:*** It looks like for a period of thirty-one years in the business, Walter Barnes compiled a repertoire of film work from 1956 to retirement in 1987 of forty-five features. Of those, his Euro Westerns consisted of ten, plus another French / US coproduction made late in the genre for a 1977 release. It was unusual in that it was filmed on locations in Tucson, Arizona, USA. For his role, he never had to leave the States. That picture was called *Another Man, another Chance* and starred James Caan (in his only genre role) and the French actress Genevieve Bujold. Walter's role was that of character Foster. The director was Claude Lelouch, an Academy Award winner for a previous film he turned out in 1966 called *A Man, and a Woman*. This newer *Chance* film we feel was not a sequel to his original, but similarities were nevertheless there.

In addition to his Euro films, Walter turned out three for the *Peplum* (Sword 'n' Sandal) genre. Those titles were *Romulus and the Sabines* (1961) with British actor Roger Moore in one of his early pre–*James Bond* roles. Walter's part was that of Stilicone. His next for the genre was *Slave Girls of Sheba* (1963). This one was a Yugoslavian / Italian coproduction, and its stars were mainly European actors with the exception of Walter. Others recognizable to fans of the genre were José Suarez, Linda Cristal, Mimmo Palmara (a.k.a. Dick Palmer of the Westerns genre), and French actress Helene Chanel. For Walter's third of the genre was *Challenge of the Gladiator* (1965). It starred America Peter Lupus in one of his pre–*Mission Impossible,* TV series roles (that beginning 1966 role would be as associate Willie Armitage to stars Steven Hill and Peter Graves). In this *Gladiator*, Barnes portrayed the evil Nero, the depraved emperor of Rome attempting to ward a revolt against his regime led by Spartacus (Lupus).

> ***Note*:** Of interest to the *Spaghetti* Western fans, here among the credited writers for the story of this film, we find Sergio Leone's name. This time frame understand was now after his first *Dollar* Western. Leone was previously a second unit director of the *Peplums* and is credited with at least one previous film of genre as director, which was called *The Colossus of Rhodes* (1961), starring American Rory Calhoun. So it's with good reason we understand that Leone certainly had deep ties in this genre and would continue to contribute in some manner or another.

Walter also turned out a couple of spy films for 1967 release: *Target Frankie,* his role here was that of Col. O'Connor. And *Code Name Kill,* with Walter as Jurij. He also managed a couple of Euro crime films prior to his German Westerns period, both for 1968: *The Magnificent Tony Carrera,* which starred American Thomas Hunter and with the lovely Erika Blanc. Walter's role was that of Barnes (imagine that!). And his other film was *The Long Day of inspector Blomfield,* (a.k.a. *Mad Jo*) Walter's role here was that of Insp. Fred Lancaster.

Our man Barnes certainly seemed prolific enough in his film career, being all over the various European genres. No doubt his thirty-one years of service to the worldwide entertainment industry should well be remembered for his sprawling accomplishments. We Walter Barnes fans will always hold a soft place in our hearts for the big man with the simple nickname of Piggy, RIP Walter Barnes.

End.

- Below is a complete filmography of Walter Barnes Euro Westerns. The dates are aligned as close as possible with information currently at hand, plus international release dates included. **Pictures and posters are accredited to the Sebastian Haselbeck collection via his website www.spaghetti-western.net. Thanks, Sebastian.*

WALTER BARNES
EURO WESTERNS

1962

The Sign of Zorro, *IL Segno di Zorro;* a.k.a. *Duel at the Rio Grande;* Ital/ Spa/ Fr, Director Mario Caiano (Barnes in lesser role as Mario) 3/28/63

1964

Apache Gold, a.k.a. *Winnetou the Warrior; Winnetou I. Teil;* Fr/Ital/W.Ger, D: Harald Reinl (Barnes as Bill Jones) 1/15/64

Among Vultures, a.k.a. *La Dove Scende Il Sole; a.k.a. Frontier Hellcat;* W.Ger/ Ital/ Fr/ Yugo, D: Alfred Vohrer (Barnes as Baumann Sr.) 12/8/64; Stars Stewart Grainger as Old Surehand, Elke Sommer as Lisa and Gotz George

1965

Rampage at Apache Wells, a.k.a. *Uccidere a Apache Wells;* a.k.a. *the Oil Prince;* W. Ger/ Yugo, D: Harald Phillip (Barnes as Bill Campbell) 1965

Duel at Sundown, a.k.a. *Killer Kid: Shoot on Sight (Sparate a vista su Killer Kid);* a.k.a. *Killer Kid;* Fr/ W. Ger, D: Leopoldo Lahola (Barnes as McGow Sr.) 1965

1966

Half-Breed, a.k.a. *Winnetou und das Halbblut Apanatschi (Winnetou and the Half-breed Apache);* W. Ger/ Yugo/ Ital, D: Harald Phillip (Barnes as Mac Haller) 8/17/66

1967

Clint the Stranger, *Clint el solitaro;* a.k.a. *Clint, the Lonely Nevadan;* Ital/ Spa/ W. Ger, D: Alfonso Balcazar (Barnes as Walter Shannon) 2/2/67

Greatest Robbery in the West, *La Piu Grande Rapina Del West;* a.k.a. *The Greatest kidnapping in the West;* Ital, D: Maurizio Lucidi (Barnes as Key Jarret a.k.a. Clay Thomas) 10/28/67

1968

The Moment to Kill, *Il Momente di Uccidere;* Ital/ W. Ger, D: Anthony Ascott (Giuliano Carmineo) (Barnes as Bull) 4/8/68

Garter Colt, *Giarrettiera Colt;* Ital/ Spa/ W. Ger, D: Gian Andrea Rocco (Barnes as the general) 5/19/68

Big Gundown; *La Resa dei Conti;* a.k.a. *Account Rendered;* Ital/Spa, D: Sergio Sollima (Barnes as Brokston) 8/29/68

1977

Another Man, another Chance, *Un Autre Homme, Une Autre Chance;* a.k.a. *Another Man, another Woman;* Fr/ US, D: Claude Lelouch (Barnes as Foster) 9/28/77

- Dubbing roles below for Euro-TV cartoon features, thanks to *Internet* source *IMDb.com*

1988

Kido keisatsu Patoreba (Barnes as Patlabor) listed as Walter Barney

1989

Garaga (Barnes as Jay)
Rhea Gall Force (Barnes as Vikal) again listed as Barney Barnes.

1991

Soryuden a.k.a. *Sohryuden: Legend of the Dragon Kings* (Barnes as Tsuzuku Ryudo)

2002

Western, Italian Style (documentary)

A wonderfully informative piece of film work conceived and directed by Patrick Morin on the popular European Western movies so appropriately dubbed *Spaghetti* Westerns. This *WKW Production* contained one segment that included American recording artists, *John & Wayne,* who recorded live at their home-away-from-home hangout in central Rome, the *Bunkhouse Saloon.* This Roman club was mainly patronized by Americans during their Rome stay. Sometimes on party nights the service was boosted along by American actor, Walter Barnes. Via film clip shows the actor serving from the bar then later enjoying the music along with the patrons of another clip. Barnes was unaccredited for his appearances here.

This documentary had not been commercially issued prior to this 2002, *Blue-Underground* Western DVD four-pack, which was a compilation of *Spaghetti* Westerns—including the film *Run, Man, Run* (1967) in which this documentary was included in the disc *Extras.*

End.

BIBLIOGRAPHY
(W. Barnes)

Betts, Tom, editor *WAI! (Westerns . . . All'Italiana)* Fanzine articles/information on Walter Barnes:

Issue no. 36, winter 1992–'93; Interview plus Filmography Tom Betts and William Connolly;

Issue no. 40, Spec 10 Anniversary: *Man, Pride and Vengeance* Review by Carl Morano;

Issue no. 51, Boot Hill obituary for Walter Barnes

Connolly, Bill, editor *Spaghetti Cinema* Fanzine articles/information on Walter Barnes:

Issue no. 46, Sept 1991, W. Barnes part 1.

Issue no. 56, May 1994, W. Barnes part 2.

Issue no. 69, July 1998, W. Barnes part 3, plus obituary.

Haselbeck, Sebastian, owner/curator for Internet website: *www.spaghetti-western.net.*

Internet via *www.IMDB.com.* Complete Film and TV listings, plus "Mini biography for Walter Barnes" by Blythe379.

Weisser, Thomas, *Spaghetti Westerns: the Good, the Bad, and the Violent*, (1992) *McFarland*, Jefferson NC.

Western: All'Italiana (books II and III) by Antonio Bruschini and Federico de Zigno, *Glittering Images,* Firenze, Italy; book II, 2001 and book III, 2006.

The Western: the Complete Film Sourcebook (the Film Encyclopedia) (1983) by Phil Hardy, *William Morrow and Co, Inc.,* NY. Appendix no. 8, pp 379–395.

WILLIAM BERGER

(1928–1993)

EHI CISCO . . . HAI EHI PONCHO

Wilhelm Berger's heritage at birth was that of a more astute bourgeois class of professional families that resided in the town of Innsbruck, nestled in and surrounded by some of Austria's most magnificent mountain ranges. His parents, both being doctors, were in a better position than most during Europe's harder times to afford some of the finer things in life for their newborn infant son and daughter Rosemary slightly older than Wilhelm.

Born on June 20, 1928, young Wilhelm would grow up in the love and devotion of his parents as an only son. He would spend his first twelve years living under the German regime where he would be inducted into the Hitler Youth whilst attending the super strict Catholic school systems there in Germany. His father who had excelled in his profession had been appointed to the *University Medical Clinic* in Graz as director.

While there was much happiness to experience while growing up, he and his sister would experience much discipline of an enduring childhood until suddenly thing happened. Young Wilhelm Berger was but twelve when he and his sister were uprooted from their home when the war broke out. Germany, having already occupied Austria since early 1938, was now on the move. Hitler announced to the world a war was on with his invasion of Poland on September 1, 1939.

The Berger family had all been away on holiday at the time in Northern Italy. Their father opted to make a move before things worsened any further. Having chosen his options suddenly but with care and consideration for the family, he would attempt to relocate them to the United States. Berger's parents did not return home and abruptly left all behind taking only the young children with them. It was a long, treacherous trek across Europe, one that Wilhelm would not soon forget. The trip only worsened by an even longer, more arduous boat trip, until they finally landed and sequentially resettled in New York City.

His Parents, being the professionals they were, had made a quick, unabashed decision never to return home again, leaving the relatives, friends, and neighbors in exchange for a difficult but outside chance to emigration into American. At any cost, they wanted to avoid the war and the persecution of the different races. Making NYC their new home wasn't much of a problem for two young professionals with two young children. Wilhelm and Rosemary would complete their schooling years in the city, and later, Wilhelm would go on to attend *Columbia University*, where he would major in engineering. Coming from a prosperous family who at one time had money and position, he now soon found himself just another one of the boys at school. He claimed later that he would have never imagined himself becoming an actor.

Actually, he was rather unsure of his future and of thoughts of what he might wish to become in life—career wise were still a bit jumbled at this time in his life. His former objectives were no longer as clear as they once had been within the strict disciplined structure of life he was used to as a boy. The thoughts of failure and cause of disappointment for his parents was never far from the back of his mind, so he strived to do his best at whatever challenge he took up. At twenty years of age, and being a good all-around athlete, he was soon picked for the running team at *Columbia*. He was probably one of the better prospects on the team and set out to attempt a run for the 1948 *Olympics*. He made it to the finals without a problem, but during the actual race, he literally froze up, saying he could hardly walk much less run a satisfactory time. The next year, as time grew near, his prospects again seemed good; but again, when that time came, he had developed some sort of leg pains, which his doctors had a difficult time diagnosing (probably psychosomatic, as in trying too hard). At any rate, he was forced to end thoughts of ever continuing an athletic career.

In 1950, when the Korean war broke out, Berger was drafted into the armed forces and was soon sent over to the air force side to act as protégé to *Wright Field*. In this capacity, he found that he sort of liked this bit of the service and turned his thoughts to the possibility of having an extended career with the military. With his high aptitude, he was soon sent to flight school. There he found he could adapt to flying easily. Later on, he was suddenly plagued with strange attacks of nerves, and things went downhill for him after that. They kicked him from flight school returning him to his regular enlisted duties. Somewhat disinterested with the military, he wound up finding girls were much more interesting. Soon while still in the service, and on leave about 1951, he found himself married to steady gal friend Marjorie, who he simply called Marj. Berger ended up serving out only his dutiful three-year stint then exited the service.

It was during this period in time that he worked some for *IBM* but, eventually, just lost interest with that job all together after a while. Berger's early ambitions aside from all else was writing. He even took a night course in script writing. Later on, when taking a course on directing, so as to better understand the business, he was accidentally exposed to realm of stage work.

His professor had asked him to do a stand-in role for him as a favor. It seems the man's wife was a drama instructor for the *Rhode Island Theatre* group; they were in a pinch for an actor, it seems. The play's premier performance was scheduled for the following evening, and the leading man had come up extremely ill. With no other substitute available for the part in such a short notice, she was desperate. Berger took up the challenge and did the favor, pretending to be the professional actor he actually wasn't at the time.

He commented later on the subject saying that at the time he knew practically nothing about being an actor on the stage. However, the premier of the play *Gigi* came off very well and as planned. All were so relieved that this "professional actor," from New York City had come there to help them all out. Berger had played his part well that evening (acting the part of an actor) all were impressed. He found that he had actually enjoyed the surroundings, the people and the total atmosphere of the stage. It was there and then that he decided he might like to continue in stage work as an actor.

Back in the city, he immediately took up studies with the *Actor's Studio*. He later managed to work his way into some of the local off-Broadway productions there so he could learn more about applying himself with this newly acquired acting trade. Some of his early stage works were *Misalliance* and *Look After, Lulu* both for 1955. One of his more successful plays was *Silent Night, Lonely Night* later in 1959. The more successful the play (which also added greatly to his repertoire) the more they helped out in the ready cash department. The year was 1957, and remembering back to 1951 when he had ventured into marriage early on with Marj, things had been extremely tight when she had given birth to their first daughter Carin in '52. Now, it seemed Carin might now have a sister. Thankfully things were much better for them now. His second daughter Debra was born on March 17, 1957.

Billy, as he was known to his fellow actors, continued his work on the stage and hit with another good one run in 1960 called *The Cherry Orchard*. Finally, he would hit the big one in '62, with a Broadway hit called *Who's Afraid of Virginia Woolf?* He had a good run with this play, which lasted some two years. In his off-hours, he had begun to work on his own in the *Actor's Workshop,* helping to train other aspiring souls to get their feet wet on the boards. All the while he continued to hone his craft to perfection. He then advanced into stage productions of his own, doing the scripts, then acting them out along with a troupe of want-a-be followers from a hip New York artistic crowd.

By this time in his career, though, having a wife and two little girls to care for was becoming a heavy burden. He was also getting tired of the repetition of the *Virginia Woolf* play. He longed for something different, perhaps something a tad better for him and his family. Now with the show's run ending soon, and at the time, his *Actor's workshop* really wasn't going all that well, he was once again becoming more than a little unsure about his future, wanting only the very best for his family.

There were other problems, though, plaguing Billy Berger. Something was happening to his marriage, it was beginning to unravel. He would later say that it was like all of a sudden Marj had gone completely nuts. He couldn't, nor could anyone else they knew, understand why or just what was happening with her. Actually, as he looked back on things, everything around him seemed to be coming unraveled. With Marj pushing him, he finally made up his mind to make a move and quickly. So he closed up the workshop and left the theater behind for the summer hiatus to try his luck with the more lucrative movie business.

Taking the family, they left for the bright lights of Hollywood, California. They made the move lock, stock, and barrel at the insistence of Marj. After resettling there in LA, Billy proceeded to search for work. No Internet back then, just pounding the sidewalk from one place to another was the gig. Things were slow for a stage actor on hiatus with a family to feed. He couldn't help but hear the rumors of how popular the employment opportunities were for out-of-work actors across the ocean with the *Italian Cinema*. Worst of all, though, was the added strain on his already unstable marriage, which hadn't seemed to ease any with the relocation. Soon afterward it would completely come to unravel, and divorce followed shortly.

With still nothing popping on this coast, and his hiatus from the NY Stage company come and gone, he would now have to leave his family there and return alone to New York for completion of his contractual obligations. Back on his own in the Big Apple, he resumed teaching at the *Actor's workshop*. He also returned to something else that would change things as he knew them forever. A young woman was there by the name of Carol Lobravico had been hanging around and attending his classes at the shop. An artist of her own volition, she was at times an aspiring want-a-be actress—though other times she would seem content just to busy herself painting and decorating sets.

Back during the previous year, Bill had seen her a few other times at stage parties and/or other craft functions. He had already felt a strange attraction for her but tended to look over it because she appeared to rebuff him at every turn. Now Carol was there within his realm working beside him in his workshop. Carol was a jet-setter in the true sense of the word. A native New Yorker, she had run away, leaving home, Paris bound, alone, and at the age of seventeen so she could attend art school classes there among the elite. Her grandparents had actually been emigrates from Italy, and she would rather be known and associated with that family connection than to be just a Brooklyn girl with no special ties. At times she would drift between Paris, New York, and Rome, living on whatever she could earn from portrait painting and fashion drawing.

She had existed at times not unlike many young people of that era did when visiting foreign countries, receiving little or nothing in the way of pay, just sort of living off the environment and/or others around them. Back in NYC, the parties of the artistic-cultured classes were ablaze with all the latest of fads: braless, reefer, LSD, and of course free love. Flower Power was the in thing. The fight against the establishment and the rebuke of authority were the challenges of the day.

Evidently Carol and Billy had first gotten together late in 1962 at an LSD bash with mutual friends of the arts circuit. Could it possibly have been that this woman and her intervention into another woman's realm of life was what had suddenly changed Marj's feelings toward her husband so abruptly? This then may have prompted at her insistence that the family leave NY and relocate to California so suddenly. After Billy's return he resumed work there at the *Actor's workshop,* he and Carol resumed pretty much where they had left off, but without the burden of Billy's family. This unfortunately led to his divorce, and for the next two years, he continued working both the theater and the workshop, while actually living with Carol in her New York apartment.

During this arrangement, they would break all bonds with love and were partying frequently with their crowd. Promiscuity on the part of both would erupt in harsh arguments and near-constant fighting. This evolved into a love-hate relationship where soon after a fight they would severely regret their fight and then turn to being the all forgiving, loving couple toward one another. The intrinsic nature of their relationship was probably due to the fact that Carol was truly a wild thing in bloom. She was outspoken, brash, and hard to handle. She was not about to be held by bonds of any relationship in any form, especially that as in matrimonial bondage such as being a wife. This meant for her that children were out of the question.

Carol was not unlike a wild filly horse to Billy in that he was deeply attracted to her and had to have her at any cost, but once he got her, he was having hell holding on to her. She would take off for weeks at a time, leaving Billy alone to his theater work and workshop only to return on a whim, or when he'd actually wind up going, searching her out, and bringing her back home again. Both were promiscuous people by nature and were demanding in their desires. Experimentation with sex and/or drugs often led to overindulging, sometimes to the extremes whether alone or during sessions with others. After all, it was a sign of the times, the signature of an era. The sexual revolution was in and all that jazz.

Berger would, it appears in all due respect, just looked over most of it, like water running off a duck where Carol was concerned. He'd just go on about engrossing himself within his work and would forever look the other way, possibly to a fault that would eventually come to a bitter climax. His love and devotion toward Carol would grow to near idolism, as he would remember her later. A tragic love story to be sure but, surely, reminiscent of yet some our own Hollywood actors and their personal lives the tabloids have been obliged to be followed over the years.

Still undecided about whether to try Hollywood again or Rome, Bill wanted to reinvestigate his options to find if things were really hopping throughout the European circuit as he had heard when in California. During this period, the Euro film industry was fast becoming a hot spot in the world of cinema. First, the *Peplums* (sword and sandal) epics, and now, the Westerns were beginning to settle in for a good run it appeared. He considered all and then decided on a vacation trip to Europe. While his show was once again in hiatus for the summer, he took Carol and they visited the UK, then Munich, West Germany, and ended in Paris. The two of them seemed very happy during this period in their lives together. During a stopover in Rome, and after a short visiting tour through *Cinecitta Studio* watching the nonstop filming action going on there, he decided, yes, this was the place for him to start into this attractive film business.

Rome, Italy, of 1964 was an extremely busy place. Welcoming this newly found hustle and bustle, Berger—now thirty-six years old—would fall right in with the current chain of events. With his *Austrian-German* heritage looks, with longish redish blond hair and icy-blue eyes, he looked

American enough to pass off as their newest find in their never-ending barrage of imitation gringo actors (mostly Italians from Northern Italy) with the American pseudonyms.

During this time in his career, he was more like a vacationing tourist, not worrying about his stage career back in NYC. He and Carol both enjoyed all the attention the American actors were getting in Rome at that time. Also, there were film crews busy filming the exterior shots for a new action war film, *Von Ryan's Express*, by American director Mark Robson. It was to be an exciting WW2 film, starring Frank Sinatra as a POW colonel who leads a daring escape from the Germans by taking over a freight train. Other stars were Trevor Howard, Raffaelia Carra, Edward Mulhare, Adolfo Celi, and James Brolin. Somehow, during the ensuing nightlife that followed the day's shoot, Berger got hooked up with some of the cast and, finally, with the director Robson himself. He was offered a small part in the film, a scene at the railway station as one of two German undercover Gestapo agents. He accepted the role.

When teaching at the workshop, he had always been quick to remind his peers of the difference between stage and film work. Now he found out firsthand as he would later relate about when he was brought before the cameras for the first time and how he had to be told not to look directly into the cameras.

His scenes take place at the *Verona train depot* where Sinatra and Mulhare are portraying a couple of German officers. They are attempting to use forged documentation and a train transport order from a higher German official. Then while attempting to use these orders as legit in order to transport prisoners of war across the border into Zurich, who shows up but two Gestapo Agents snooping about. The one agent seemed awfully interested in the soldier accompanying the major (Mulhare, who in fact was the only one who could really speak German). Sinatra, the soldier, could not. The agent (Berger) seems deeply interested in Sinatra's wristwatch. Mulhare, in his banter with the agents, succeeds in belaying the intense mode of the situation.

After boarding the train, but before it can pull out, the same two agents come snooping about the train. They flash their credentials and board the train entering the very car where they all are. The one agent (Berger) goes directly to the soldier (Sinatra) and again starts commenting about the watch in German. Mulhare carefully motions for Frank to remove the watch and let the agent see it. When he does, the agent whips open his coat and produces several inner pockets full of contraband. He offers Sinatra some ladies nylon stockings for the watch. Sinatra shakes his head no! The tension builds. All are on the alert to kill these two agents and depart in a hurry. But Berger goes back inside his coat and produces one, two and then a third pack of American cigarettes. While Mulhare, behind the agent's back, out of his view, frets, praying with his hands, Frank says, "Ya, ya." And the deal is made. Berger takes the watch and quickly departs the train, leaving the crew in relief over the tense incident. (Evidently, the agent was really only interested in just the watch all the time). After his filming sequences were completed, Billy and Carol returned to the States.

> Their fighting by now was becoming renown from continent to continent. Later, when reminiscing about their first trip to Europe together, he spoke of being in a Paris hotel during one of their infamous arguments and, that when he had left, leaving her in the room. He had barely cleared the door when she slammed it shut, actually catching his left thumb in the doorjamb. He had to bang and plead with her to open up so he could get his thumb out. He went on to add that while filming the train station sequence in *Von Ryan* soon after that, his oversized "blue" thumb was plainly visible for all to see.

Billy returned to NYC with Carol then made a quick side trip back to the West Coast to Hollywood where he rejoined the *Von Ryan* group to resume clean-up shots of the interior scenes and dub the film. He claimed that during this period he was offered some television work on a series, but it never transpired. Then other projects were also promised—which, in turn, fell through. He had by now made up his mind to take his best shot. He would return to NYC, sew up his current obligations with the theater, close the workshop, and return to Italy.

He did just that, returning to Italy at first by himself. Billy Berger hit the shores of Italy at the right time. His having acting experience, and now with the *Von Ryan* scenes under his belt, coupled with his looks certainly helped to sell his case. While getting a start as one of the new guys in town, he teamed up with acquaintance Keith Richards of the soon to become a part of the rock singing group of Mick Jagger's, the *Rolling Stones*. They would become fast friends, even staying at Richards's place until he could get his own abode. Surviving years of rock 'n' roll, Keith Richards seems still seemingly in good health even nowadays of the twenty-first century. The aged rocker can still be seen frequenting clubs in places like Miami, New York, and others abroad. Who was it that said, "Rock 'n' roll is forever." Maybe they were right.

Berger fell right in the with the rock 'n' roll, hippie bohemians of Rome of the era. He worked by day and would party by night. The free love scene was full of loud music, new interesting babes, and of course drugs, lots of drugs. Berger was going through another of life's changes within his new surroundings, his career, and now even his love life would give in to situations found within his newfound environment. To put it bluntly, Billy Berger was running wild. Meanwhile, he was even to endure a professional name change to William instead of Wilhelm as suggested to sound more American for the Italian directors who were busy courting those American film audiences abroad.

Once settled there in Rome, Berger was eventually offered the title role of Ringo in a *Spaghetti* Western film by director Mario Maffei, *Grande Notte Di Ringo (Ringo's Big Night)* (a.k.a. *The Night of the Desperado*) (1965). With the popularity of these Westerns rising, they're productions were soon coming out of the woodwork. His supporting cast members were Adrianna Ambesi, Eduardo Fajardo, and Tom Felleghy. This was an Italian / Spanish coproduction was also scripted by Maffei, with a music score was by Carlo Rustichelli. The story dealt with recent stagecoach robberies where the amount of stolen monies had now escalated to over two hundred thousand dollars. The townsfolk were up in arms over these recent crimes. Arriving in town, a drifting gunslinger Jack Bailey a.k.a. Ringo (Berger) although being innocent lands in jail accused. Eventually he is able to sort out the culprits and exposes them with the help of a federal agent (Felleghy) who befriends him. Berger really hit it big on the large screen and Euro audiences with this film. He once stated in an interview for Christian Kessler that "I always loved working, and it was really fun to do Westerns. You know, I've never chosen a Western, they've chosen me."

Eventually, Carol and Billy would get back together again. Now that his success in film work had become more evident, he and his new-found free-wheeling lifestyle was probably much more enticing to her. The year was 1965 and Carol was finally ready to come back to Billy. Somehow, when he returned to the United States to bring her back, he had persuaded her that they must get married before leaving the States. So while there in California visiting his girls, he managed to talk her into it, saying that if he ever expected to gain custody of his girls, this would be the best way, or so his divorce lawyer had led him to believe.

Carol now was totally against the whole idea of marriage. She refused to have her feet, held to a fire by the bonds of matrimony. Since together they had fought about this subject on more than one occasion. It was plain to see she was probably just overwhelmed by the upcoming trip and thoughts of settling in Rome, so she finally caved in. They were married in one of those dime-a-dozen wedding parlor places along Sunset Strip Boulevard in Los Angeles. Afterward, she would become furious over it all when she regained her senses, tore up the wedding certificate right away, and stormed off to her room. Behind the locked door, she could be heard crying herself into oblivion for the rest of the night Billy would later relate.

In Rome, they first settled in the apartment Billy had previously acquired before leaving. He then went about his new prospective career in this new land of plenty. He was gone quite a bit during those first few months leaving Carol mostly alone again, which was a trouble in itself. While Billy was in Paris filming, Carol managed to have an affair with a British actor that was near and about. Maybe she figured it sort of payback for Billy for pushing her into the marriage bit, which they seemed to fight about often anymore. They finally drifted together again early in 1966 and were back living together, and even working together, whereby Billy was now running an *Actor's workshop* there in Rome. She resumed her acting studies and seemed to be going all out in helping Billy, who was getting some recognition with his plays. Even Carol was getting to be quite the actress herself. Later that year, though, she would up and return again to NYC by herself so as to close up and vacate her apartment there. While alone and without Billy, she again began doubting their life together. She would reason that domestic life was not really for her after all; when faced with it, she had become unaccustomedly bored to the hilt. Her husband Billy, however, was fast on the road to becoming an international film star with his *Spaghetti* film projects. Now a hot commodity and was likely to get even hotter. This probably upset her as well, longing to be back again in his limelight but not entirely under his rein.

Before the year was out, Carol was back in Rome and again with her Billy. They had moved again, this time into a newer, nicer apartment, though still in the city. During this period in time, things seemed to be going somewhat better for the two. Since his success in films, the parties they went to were now all about them, and the drugs sometimes flowed freely. They did actually manage to live together in some form of harmony for a fare stint this time. Carol, actually Carolyn as she now like to call herself, seemed quite happy during this period in her life. They even took to the film circuit together on his acting jobs. It might have been Spain, then France or maybe Belgium or even Yugoslavia the next time—all was good.

Although Billy would involve himself with other Euro film genres like the *giallo*-thriller *La Lama Nel Corpo (The Blade in the Body)* (1966) better known as *Murder Clinic*, he managed to mainstream the Westerns as his biggest on-screen accomplishments throughout his career in the Italian cinema. His second Western, *El Cisco* (1966), from director Sergio Bergonzelli, would top his first with audience appeal. Berger now found himself a film star of international acclaim. The film starred Berger as the lead portraying the title role as a determined gunslinger seemingly out for only personal gain, even at the high cost of double-crossing a Mexican gang that was in league with a local sheriff's deputy. By stealing dollars from the gang themselves, it would soon force them out into the open to get back their loot and seek revenge. At that time, they would come face-to-face with the real law of *Calabasas Township*, the sheriff along with Cisco, who had actually been working undercover for the sheriff all along to expose the outlaws.

Early in 1960, the German producers had ventured into making new Westerns with their Karl May story themes of the *Winnetou* films. These scenic Westerns, mostly shot in and around Yugoslavia, seemed to have kick-started a whole new phenomenon for genre. The tall blondish American lead actor, Lex Barker, helped to firmly seat these May stories into the annals of film history with his unforgettable role as Shatterhand. Then following in their wake was this new Italian Western spin-off genre. It was now evolving from infancy, and the best was yet to come.

Sergio Leone, coming fresh from his early directorial film works of the *Peplums*, came on the scene now with some very different conceptual ideas about making pictures, especially the Westerns. It was during the year 1964 that Leone turned out his first, now classic, *Per un Pugno di Dollari (For a Fistful of Dollars)* (a.k.a. *A Fistful of Dollars*). Using American TV actor Clint Eastwood, things would really begin to roll for them both. Seeing how the international theatergoing public was swarming over these newly founded, violent horse operas, the Italians began what would evolve into a ten-year stint of virtual nonstop mass production of these films affectionately dubbed the *Spaghetti* Westerns. Obviously targeted at the American audiences across the Atlantic, it would not be until later about 1967 that these films finally would begin to filter over into the American theaters. Not unlike the Italians, the Americans seemed to take to them almost as much. Although most critics of the day said not, but what do they know! Most moviegoers couldn't seem to get enough of them. For the most part, the majority of theatergoers throughout the world seemed to welcome these unusually strong versions rather the old conventional Western. These were totally unlike their talkative, sparse-on-action counterparts usually seen from Hollywood productions. These were indeed operatic works of violence in action, put to music.

American actors now in Rome were multiplying, but in the same token, foreign actors, some already accomplished, were also heavily involved in the film work as well. Klaus Kinski (a.k.a. Kinsky),* for example, a Polish-born

---

* Berger once commented on Kinski when interviewed by Christian Kessler, saying, "Klaus is, well . . . unfortunately I have to say, was quite a crazy guy." He went on to add further, "I always got along well with him. Kinski is quite incalculable." In other words, an extremely talented actor but he was by all reports a squirrelly kind of guy.

blue-eyed blond himself, would break into this new genre with great gusto that would only serve to embellish his career and finances. He was about to have a significant role in the next upcoming Leone Western *For a Few Dollars More* (1966).

William Berger was now also a part of that same *Spaghetti* bandwagon. He found himself increasingly in demand by the Italian filmmakers well into the next decade and beyond. His film listings are extremely impressive containing not only work in the Westerns but also films from many of the other great genres of the era. His next Western, for a 1967 release, was from director Sergio Sollima and was called *Faccia a Faccia (Face to Face).* It starred Cuban-born actor Tomas Milian. Second-billed was Italian Gian Maria Volonte, a previous Leone lead villain in both his earlier *Dollar* films. Berger was third-billed of these main stars. Others of the cast who enjoyed prominent roles were Nicoletta Machiavelli, José Torres, Rick Boyd, and Aldo Sambrell. The film had to do with an outlaw band leader (Milian) and a former history professor (Volonte) who team together causing a great deal of turmoil across the land with robberies and acts of violence. They are being chased, as it were by an astute *Pinkerton* agent called Siringo (Berger). Having second thoughts over the brutal actions of his partner, soon the professor joins with the agent to bring his friend to justice, halting the violence being brought upon his fellow man.

Berger then did some out of genre productions, for director friends of his, *The Day the Fish came out.* A US / Greek coproduction film was by director Michael Cacoyannis and held for a '67 release. Another lesser-important piece of the era by director Mario (Mark) Ferreri called *L' Uomo Delle Cinque Palle (The Man of the Five Balls* a.k.a. *L' Uomo Dai Cinque Palluncini (The Man with the Balloons).* Produced by Carlo Ponti, Ferreri scripted and directed the film, which was a combination of three short stories. Berger's role was that of Benny. Post-production woes from '65 however, forced its being shelved until a later premiere in 1967.

By now it seemed Billy and Carolyn's home life had been going too well. Even to the point of having Billy's two daughters over for a summers visit. Carolyn's now famous actor / hubby had finally acquired a different home, a place they could call their own down on the Costa Amalfi, near Naples. Although some distance outside Rome, it was still near the Auto-Starda and hitching a ride into Rome seemed to never be a problem. His usual workplace when in town was *Cinecitta.*

> The *Casa* Berger as this new home was nicknamed was fast becoming well known on the party circuit about Rome. Nearly isolated on the coast and with Berger away much of the time,

> since becoming more in demand and somewhat buried in his forthcoming film work. Carolyn now being left to her own devices, which was probably the majority of time, had now taken up with party friends who were into a new type of stage productions called *The Living Theatre.* Things were fine until she got a new burr in her bonnet, and off she'd go again to some exotic places with the theater bunch!

Billy would not find out about her leaving until he returned home and found her gone. They would sometimes viciously fuss and fight when she did return, most of those times Bill had to go fetch her. Then in February of 1968, she left again—this time she was intent on joining the group for a European tour of their play. Carolyn and Billy was truly a pair of people who could neither live together for any length of time, nor live apart for any substantial length of time either. Their existence together was true "living theater" in itself. She, however, instead temporarily postponed this troupe tour, opting for a cruise with Talida, Paul Getty Jr., on the Onassis yacht, the *Christina*, instead. Remember all, Carolyn was truly of the jet-set crowd, and she was friendly with all that wealthy class of peoples within that realm.

Evidently, changing her mind again, after the voyage began, she up and took a flight back to NYC leaving them all on the yachting adventure somewhere down in Jamaica. Not long afterward, she called Billy wanting him to fly her back to Rome to be with him. Burning the candle at both ends was taking its toll on Carolyn. She was looking bad and was in dire need of rest and refueling. Evidently, when the ticket didn't arrive, she contacted him again telling him she wanted to come home for a while to rest. Bill made the trip to NY himself to get her. When he arrived, she revealed to him exactly what her problems had really been! She'd been having pains in her stomach for some time and had finally gone to see the doctor in New York. They had found a cancer in her uterus and had stripped her insides doing a hysterectomy. She would spend her recovery time back in Rome since Billy agreed to take her back with him. Saying about their on-again, off-again relationship, Billy remarked once on the subject, saying they were together some eight years and never a dull moment.

By May, though, after her recovery, she decided to join back up with the *Living Theatre* group again. She was to meet them in Paris, France, this time and participate in an ongoing street revolution (or so it seemed) which was in progress during the time of those live performances of their play, *Paradise Now*. In reality all this was really about was rebelling against the establishment, none in particular, just any governmental establishment would do. Their reasoning was, because in their minds, it needed to be done. A quest it would seem was to tear down old world standards and practices as we knew them and replace them with woeful disrespect and pandemonium for one and all. Could this have come full circle today and possibly be the backbone of some of our governmental issues of the day? A good case in point we may all have to consider.

This *Living Theatre* group,* formed by friends of Carolyn, had supposedly been made up of stage actors, but of course, there were groupies apparently looking for a cause other than just acting. However, they seemed to double as protesters against the 1960's bureaucracy systems of a given country. Their demonstrations would begin similar in fashion to a staged *Green Peace* type rally. Eventually, these groups had filtered into the United States first forming on street corners, back lots, and abandoned buildings in and around NYC. Certain strains of the original groups probably still exist in somewhat of a lower profile somewhere out there today.

By this time, Billy Berger was finding his villa life in much turmoil and seemed not to really matter if she was there or not. Somehow though, his home was always the hosted meeting place for the group. This group, as it were, was usually a mixture of professionals from the film business, some others actors much like himself, but always a hippie entourage that following the nightlife who were mostly friends of Carolyn's. The string of parties and partygoers at *Casa* Berger had become almost nonstop. Berger continued his film work though, with a vigor, having become increasingly popular at least on screen and in the streets of Rome, if not with the producers, and within his own villa.

His next Western, a release for 1968, was another entry called *Oggi A Me, Domani A Te (Today We Kill, Tomorrow We Die!)*, which starred Brett Halsey,† billed as Montgomery Ford in the lead role as Bill. Also, starred

---

* Surfacing in Europe about this time, spreading their so-called word to the people of the world was slammed at every turn by local authorities for their efforts. First in France, then in Italy, they tried any place where the law seemed somewhat lax to their cause. However, the Italian government wasn't at all lax and took a particular affront to their actions taking a bold stand against such carryings-on. In 1969 they formed a special taskforce strictly to observe these group types and to come down hard and fast on them with arrests and imprisonment.

Drogas E Capelli Lunghi (druggies and long hairs) they called them. They seemed to exist off the environment and were intent on stirring up the public with their drug-induced ideals. That was how the authorities viewed this new type of vaudevillian barn storming.

† According to Halsey's bio for 2008, "Brett Halsey: Art or Instinct in the Movies" by John B. Murray for *Midnight Marquee Press, Inc.* claimed he retained warm memories of working with costar William Berger. Murray states

were popular Italian actor Bud Spencer (Carlo Pedersoli), William Berger, and American Wayde Preston. It was a superb casting and shot from a well-written script, coupled with direction by Tonino Cervi. The rousing music score was done by Angelo Lavagnino. The story has character Bill (Halsey) rounding up gunmen so as to use them in a track down to avenge the senseless killing of his wife.

Another astute source of information on our actor was the now-deceased Gordon Mitchell (Chuck Pendleton). He and Berger did some six pictures together. But with Mitchell being into the healthful, bodybuilders way of life would never in a million years have condoned Berger's way of living his personal life during that era. However, he did respect his acting ability and professionalism and told this author so personally on occasion when asked about the various films they had done together.

Berger's next Western was called *Se Incontri Sartana Prega per La Tua Morte! (If You Meet Sartana . . . Pray for Your Death!)* (a.k.a. *Sartana*) (1968). A real jam-up Italian / West German coproduction starring John Garko (Gianni Garko) in the title role of Sartana, bounty hunter / gunman extraordinaire. Also, starring in this jam-up Western is Klaus Kinski, Fernando Sancho, and William Berger. This film actually started a whole string of Sartana copycat films, but only four are legit sequels, which actually starred Garko in the lead role. Berger portrays the bad guy Lansky, who, with his gang, has lifted a gold shipment. Lansky and his partner Kinski double-cross the gang and then kill all of them with a type of *Gatling* gun. Sartana, who was also after the gold, begins to zero in on our two culprits, and the real action begins. This film is certainly Western action at its best from director Frank Kramer (Gianfranco Parolini). Kramer also co scripted with Renato Izzo. The Music score was by Piero Piccioni.

Also that year, Berger turned out another Western, *Il Suo Nome Gridava Vendetta (His Name Spells Vengeance)* (a.k.a. *The Man Who Cried for Revenge*) (1969) from director William Hawkins (Mario Caiano), this

---

here that "Halsey deemed him a fine actor who would have become a big star but for a drug problem."

He goes on to relate one incident in particular making this film, "William Berger rode into the lights. He turned the wrong way on his horse. We all went left, he went right." He continues saying, "He was an intellectual. One time he went out into the woods with a book. I went out to find him. He was sitting there with the book. I picked it up. It was upside-down. He was stoned."

one also starred Anthony Steffen* (Antonio De Teffe) as Drake out for vengeance against three men for the rape and murder of his wife. William Berger costars in the role of Sam Kellogg. Eventually, Drake finds them all, killing them one by one.

The year 1969 would prove to be a banner year for the Berger's and *Cinecitta*. His most popular release of the year was without a doubt another Frank Kramer (Parolini) Western called *Ehi Amico, C'E Sabata . . . Hai Chiuso! (Hey, Friend, There Is Sabata . . . You're dead!),* that starred *Mr. Badman* himself Lee Van Cleef as Sabata. William Berger costars as Banjo, Sabata's partner per se. This film actually spawned a series of *Sabata* films just like the previous *Sartana* films had. There actually were only three legit *Sabata* sequels by Kramer, and only two of those (the first and the last) starred LVC.

Inspired by the *CBS* television series of 1965 called *The Wild, Wild West*, with Robert Conrad as James West, which in turn it had been originally inspired by the earlier 007 James Bond films of the era. This was a truly unique and entertaining film. Van Cleef's character Sabata "The Man with the Gunsight Eyes" (or so the ad mat read) was a super marksman with a whole array of gadgetry and killing ideas. The film was truly a marvel to watch. Berger does a superb job as Sabata's sly partnered alliance in crime with the hidden gun in the banjo that sprays bullets out of the end at the flip of the lever action. Good supporting cast with Pedro Sanchez, Robert Hundar (Claudio Undari), Linda Veras, Ken Wood (Giovanni Cianfriglia) Romano Puppo, Gianni Rizzo and Alan Collins (Luciano Pigozzi).

Then another Western called *Una Lunga Fila Di Croci (A Long Line of Crosses)* (a.k.a. *No Room to Die*) (1969) from director Willy S. Regan (Sergio Garrone) and starred Anthony Steffen (Antonio De Teffe) in the role of Brandon. Berger co stars, his role was as Everett Murdock, a Bible-thumping, gun-slinging preacher. They are actually two bounty hunters involved with trying to stop the outlaw Fargo portrayed by Riccardo Garrone (brother to the director Sergio) who are smuggling Mexican peasants across the border and selling them as slaves.

---

* In Berger's last known 1992 interview with German Journalist Christian Kessler, translated for *European Trash Cinema,* issue no. 13 by Peter Blumenstock, Berger makes a point of letting the whole world know just how he felt about Steffen (De Teffe) and his acting abilities. Evidently, there was no love lost between them. He stated at the end of a fairly long dissertation on the guy that he should have waited and done the Sergio Sollima film *Run Man Run* instead. It had been offered to him, but the shooting schedule wasn't quite ready when this one was.

Also, for '69 film release, Berger tried his hand at doing some more screenwriting, producing, and directing of his own. He turned out a film called *Agosto '68 (August '68)*. From what we can learn, since it hasn't been readily available for review, it was actually a *Living Theatre** documentary having to do with the demonstrations that resulted from the group's live performances in Avignon, France, of August 1968, which Carol had planned to attend. Supposedly Billy edited the film that was taken live and added in his scripted narrations voiced over by Carol. Via Internet accounts of the film *www.nytimes.com,* the cinematographer had been Igor Luther, who, along with Billy himself, had shot most of the film.

With filming well under way prior to its 1970 release, we find yet another significant amount of work for Berger's film repertoire. His Westerns continued to add up with *Sartana, Nella Valle Dei Avvoltoi (Sartana, In the Valley of Vultures)* a.k.a. *The Ballad of Death Valley* from director Robert Mauri. Berger's starring role (supposedly Sartana, if we believe the title) is that of Lee Galloway who is hired to help breakout three brothers in exchange for half of their stolen gold. Wayde Preston stars as the leader of the three who instigates a double cross on Galloway by playing cat 'n' mouse with him and leaving him for dead out in the desert.

Here again, by incorporating the popular Sartana motif in the title, then using subsequent dubbing of the Berger character, he would now become Sartana for certain film releases. This was not an uncommon practice among the Italian filmmakers. Following this film, Berger managed to slip into another war film credit called *La Colomba Non Dove Volare (The Dove Does Not Have to Fly)* (a.k.a. *Skyriders Attack*), another film from director Sergio Garrone. This one starred Horst Bucholz, Sylvia Koscina,

---

* As stated by Dan Pavlides, *Rovi* for the *NY Times* account, the legendary theater group used an innovative technique that involved audience participation on stage during their live performances. The play stories always relate to the virtues of a nonviolence and resistance of governmental authority in any form. The film supposedly gave the viewer an inside look at the performance and its philosophy. Berger himself was also a member of this group.

Carolyn, from the looks of it, was really beginning to get into the groove of the acting bit. She would soon after be seen in the mainstream thriller *Le Ombre Roventi (The Red Hot Shades)* (a.k.a. *Shadow of Illusion*) (1970). The film starred Daniela Giordano, a young professional unintentionally caught up in the voodoo escapades of a cult. William Berger costars as cult leader Caleb; also, Carol Lobravico as the voodoo witch. It was directed by Mario Caiano.

and William Berger as the Air Force Colonel. No doubt this film probably brought back memories of his old air force training days.

Another Western popped, coming late in the year not to be released until 1971. It was called *Gli Fumavano Le Colt . . . Lo Chiamavano Camposanto! (His Pistols Smoked . . . They Called Him Cemetery!)* This was yet another action Western from director Anthony Ascott (Giuliano Carmineo). Starring was John Garko (Gianni Garko) as the mysterious stranger / bounty hunter. Berger is bad guy Duke, who, with his gang of gunman, terrorizes the countryside grabbing up land as the homesteaders sellout and leave. The stranger arrives on the scene in time to help two farmers fend off an attack from Duke's gang. This in turn helps the others to follow suit and puts Duke on the defensive with the farmers fighting back. Finally, a showdown between the two ensues.

Berger ventured away from the Westerns many times throughout his career, opting for other genres like the popular *Giallo* (Pronounced Yallo) thrillers. One for a late 1970 release was called *Cinque Bambole per La Luna D'Agosto (Five Dolls for an August Moon)* from director Mario Brava,* filmed on locations near the now war famous Anzio beach. William Berger portrays Professor Fritz Farrell in this tale of Island terror, murder, and mayhem.

Later on after a last split with Carolyn, the two were finally back together again for the umpteenth time, but barely, since he was getting very tired of Carol's antics. Now he found she was recovering from a bout of hepatitis (dirty needles, no doubt) and was now having to take medication. Seemingly this had settled her down once again for a time, and she was thrilled to be back again with her beloved Billy. He had to feel much responsibility for her health care, but even then, while he was off working his film roles, she still wouldn't stay home much in those days. It seems the parties were again raving on at *Casa* Berger. By now Carolyn was having huge problems with

---

* When he was asked about this film during the Christian Kessler interview, he stated that he could hardly remember it. However, he did enlighten those of us who read the interview in *ETC* with some interesting tidbits about Mario Bava and some of his cinematography techniques. Here he told the interviewer that Bava loved to play with special effects while filming.

Berger admitted that Bava was the first director he'd worked with that did his own matte-shot technique himself. He would paint a scene on glass plates, like a house on the hill beyond. He'd set up the shot and shoot. In the finish film, it would all look real, he said. The house on the hill surrounded by all the real trees and/or with actors standing within the shot being taken, et cetera. On the screen, one could not tell it was a set up, as it looked real.

the drugs. Berger the so-called guru of this hippie community, and being the party animal he was known to be, although it does appear, he seems to have preferred his acting life now over this rather bizarre home life, if you will. And to the outside world, it was certainly no secret to what when on inside *Casa* Berger, to the law or anyone else for that matter.

The Italian *Antidrug Taskforce** was going full steam by 1970, when unfortunately, the airhead "crazy carol" (as she was sometimes known) had bailed off into this group with both feet and eyes wide shut! Within the cloak of this theater group and its weird sense of expressionism, sometimes fueled on drugs, she excelled. Her acting and stage persona exemplified her inner feelings. She threw herself into her work, daring to go beyond where no one else had gone before. She is even credited as the first to have removed all of her clothes while on stage during one of these live performances.

That one scene startled the world and started a whole new stage revolution where it was duplicating itself over, and over again. Even legit actors of the stage got into the act. Robert Culp was one that comes to mind just off hand. Carolyn was said to have been in a drug-induced trance during her performance and thought of herself as a real actress working for a cause! In reality she just came out onto stage, saying her lines, such as they were, dropped her clothes, and pranced about naked. The audiences loved it. It eventually caught on elsewhere and led to a wave of similar carrying-on in other places.

Here, we will continue to offer our purely speculative scenario in Berger's defense. We feel that you can bet he probably looked the other way much of the time not wanting to hurt her further, or upset her more. We can only imagine the hurt and guilty feelings he must've had over the fact that here again his two daughters Carin and Debbie were coming from American for the Easter Holidays. Evidently, they had huge fights at times over his girls with Carolyn not wanting to be a mother figure. It was probably a bad situation all the way around.

The following account is now a matter of record and is public knowledge for the most part, at least overseas in Italy. No speculation here has been offered or implied. A review below from the Euro Italian publication *Amacord: Il*

* We speculate that naturally the *taskforce* had *Casa* Berger staked out during this period in time. With all the goings and comings, would arouse the simplest of interests. Yes, they could see well enough, there was the 'crazy one', the wife of that long hair actor Berger, just returned from that horrid theater group that had been raising so much unrest among the people there in France, and now Italy with their talk against the government and the establishment!

lato oscuro del cinema (The Dark Side of the Cinema) article, *Tra cinema e Tragedia (Between Cinema and Tragedy)* by Federico de Zigno:

> On the night of August 4, 1970 per an operation of the Municipal Anti-Drug Department of the Neapolitan Zone of Rome where the actor William Berger resided with his wife was raided. The police broke in at Villa Berger where they apprehended Berger, his wife, Carolyn, and seven other persons claiming to be only visitors. It was discovered in the house several grams of hashish—of which none claimed responsibility for or ownership. Actor Berger swore to this fact.
>
> The seven-member group of actors—all were of the long-haired types, being rebellious in their ways as eccentric persons can be—were considered by the Neapolitan Judges as self-incriminating, and the whole nine of them were deemed persons socially reprehensible. Much of their statements are still harbored on file within the *Criminal Insane Asylum of Pozzuoli*, despite the fact they were not given certain tests that could have proven their guilt or innocence.
>
> The actors were found guilty, and despite the viral hepatitis of which Carol suffered, and needed medication for, their illnesses were deemed "mental," and William and Carolyn both lost out and were to be allowed to suffer their withdrawals while incarcerated. It was stated that no amount of desperate intervention or surgery could be done deemed the officials for what was probably only an acute peritonitis, as prescribed on a final report, dated October 14, 1970.

Carolyn's ravings and stomach pains were given to being only the sufferings of one that had been drugged, a "crazy junta" they called her. William being her husband, while his only true crime had probably been to just keeping the peace within the realms of their marriage, and while trying to protect her from her self but to no avail, it just wasn't meant to be.

He was finally allowed to visit her in the jail infirmary, under guard and handcuffed. The actor related, "It was a cold room. She had only her one undergarment. She didn't recognize me." She passed away on October 9, 1970. He was not even able to embrace her in an agonizing good-bye. That autopsy, if really was done, should have immediately followed her passing and could have officially clarified the causes, but this all was tied up politically by the *Judicial Authorities* there at Pozzuoli and probably never will be released for review. She was buried in Vienna, Austria. Berger, when asked about attending the funeral since the others involved that were still in jail would also be there, declined, preferring to remain in jail.

Berger was later moved to the Salerno jail from where he stayed alone and incarcerated until March of 1971. This was mainly because he did not, and would never admit to (as the judicial suggested) that it was his wife, Carol, who alone was solely responsible for the drug crimes. The paparazzi had a field day. Films of day like his earlier '66 called *La Lama Nel Corpo (Your Blade in the Body)* were dug out and re shown to the public with added tidbits inserted where the title appeared. He was after all portraying Dr. Robert Vance, a doctor suspected of murder. The tidbits they added read, "Berger, Guilty or Innocent?"

All of this constant ridicule of him on and on, and the constant investigations were all provoked by the distain of his kind by the *judicial governmental authorities,* which we might add had still failed to bring forth any concrete evidence for keeping him incarcerated. After nearly a year of this insane incarceration, his trial finally came about. His old friend and director Marco Ferreri came to his rescue (out of the blue) without even being asked. Evidently, he had been keeping track of the forthcoming trial date. Berger was shocked when his friend took the stand to testify in his defense. He stated in the Kessler interview that he thought the kindness that he did says everything about the character of this admirable person, Ferreri.

By August 1971, a year would have come and gone, but he was finally free to come and go again. Alas, all of us have our own personal waterloos to deal with, and we know actors are no different. Even with all having transpired, once he finally was back on his own, he returned to his precious film work, and never stopped loving Italy or the Italian cinema. That in itself was truly amazing and gives us a bit of look into the character of one William Berger himself.

Upon his release, he was inundated with friends and fans who had not forgotten the William Berger of the silver screen. Oh, he had visitors while incarcerated. His mother came, as well his daughters and few friends like Pat and Henry and Igor. Not long after his release, he would fall back into the groove again, no doubt trying to forget the circumstances of his last forced hiatus from the business. He was quick to delve into the work at hand in an attempt to leave the lingering bad memories behind. It seems that about this time he'd taken up with Pat, and she had given him his first son, Wendell, to be born in the USA, December 1972.

Billy's first film following his incarnation was another *giallo* thriller called *Mio Caro Assassino (My Dear Assassin)* (a.k.a. *My Dear Killer*) (1971) by director Tonino Valerii is a superb example of the genre at its best. Here Berger stars as Giorgio Canavese. His next film, which we sincerely wonder about since it was a film about freeing women held in prison where they were likely being kept for release to a slave trader as a drug swap.

Alas, he'd agreed to do this one called *Io, tre Bastardi e sette Peccatrici* (a.k.a. *The Big Bust Out*), a.k.a. *The Crucified Girls of San Ramon* from director Richard Jackson (Sergio Garrone). Berger stars here with Vonetta McGee and featured Gordon Mitchell* as El Kaderia the slave runner. Also, included in the cast was Tony Kendall (Luciano Stella). *(Shot in 1971, not released till 1972)*

It was sometime in the early 1970s when Hanja Kochansky returned to Rome from the UK, with her was her young daughter Katya. The youngster took quite a fancy to Billy Berger when they all met. Her mom and Billy would become an item, and she would become his main squeeze. The child would grow up to later take the surname of Berger, in her teens, not because he was her father, because he wasn't, but because she felt such an ongoing attraction to him from their first meeting. "Like mother, like daughter," we'd say.

Hanja and Katya were there along with Bill's other daughter Debra. Carin, his oldest we believe had since returned to the United States after her father's release and was back with her mom, Marj, in LA. The three being there now would be the supportive bonding family Billy needed. Some facsimile of family life would once again reappear for Billy Berger. The girls soon would gather an interest in the cinema, not unlike their talented father. Both Debra and Katya would eventually venture into film work, even at an early age. Carin became a costume designer for films back in Hollywood, but also did a smattering of acting in them as well. She was even married to director Tobe Hooper of *Texas Chainsaw Massacre* fame for a while. No children though.

Berger's work, however, was changing, the previous popularity of the *Spaghetti* Westerns was beginning to wane, now being replaced with a comedic spawned likeness that begun in part from the *Trinity* film from director E. B. Clutcher (Enzo Barboni). It seemed that most of the Westerns released after the first *Trinity* film hit the scene in 1970, opened the door for more to come of the same vein. The era of the straight *Spaghetti* Western was now truly in its twilight. There were only a few others out there still to come and Berger was vowed to get his share.

---

* Berger and Mitchell would appear together in some six films during the 1970s, not all Westerns, some not unlike the above *Bust Out* film. Mitchell spoke very highly of Berger's talents, but not of his lifestyle. He claimed to have later met his wife once (meaning Hanja, although not his wife) and had commented to this author on how nice a person she was. But he didn't seem to remember meeting either his daughters Carin, Debra or Katya.

He continued in this realm of yesteryear with another "straight" Western called *Un Colt in Mano Del Diavol! (A Colt in the Hands of the Devil!)* (1972) directed by Frank G. Carroll (Gianfranco Baldanello). It starred Robert Woods as Wilton the *Texas Ranger* hot on the trail of Butch Brown (Berger) and his gang. Berger portrays a rather nasty character for this film, which is a bit unusual to his other previous roles. Another also on the agenda was *Lo Chiamavano Requiescat Fasthand (Fasthand Is Still My Name)* (1973). This *Italian* production from Mario Bianchi is yet another good one to have on one's collection shelf. William Berger costars as Machedo the villain to the hero character of Captain Jeff Madison / Fasthand portrayed by the film star Alan Steel (a.k.a. John Wyler) (Sergio Ciani).

Then we show listed a rather obscure Western called *Il Giustiziere Di Dio (The Executioner of God)* (1972). This was another of those rare, poorly distributed films that has only recently come to light via Internet video sources. It starred William Berger as Tony Lang / Father Lanthony with costars Irish actor Donal O'Brien as Frank the bounty hunter out for Lang's stolen gold. It begins with a prologue segment showing Lang, a notorious gunman and bank robber from Arizona loses his child by accident, when he falls into a well and dies. Thinking God is punishing him for his wrongdoings, he abandons the wife, his guns, and his past way of living to become a man of God.

We had previously learned further information about this film from another great Christian Kessler interview with the actor Donal O'Brien. There O'Brien mentioned the director for the above *Executioner* film, Franco Lattanzi, was also accredited with another Western during that same period. It also co starred O'Brien, but this time as an evil town boss, pitted against a revenge-hungry killer, portrayed by popular Colorado-born American actor Robert Woods who was starred. The film was called *Sei Bounty Killers per Una Strage (Six-Bounty Killers for a Massacre)* (1973). In the interview, Kessler comments on the two, saying, "Both films were incredibly shoddy, but real Italo aficionados will want to see them anyway!"

> Donal O'Brien commented on his costar William Berger for same interview via Kessler's website, *www.christiankessler.de/inhalt.htm* "This was a guy who had everything. He was handsome, knew how to act. He could have gone all the way to the top. But he got mixed up with drugs."

Berger ended out the year with yet another Western called *E IL Terzo Giorno Arrivo IL Corvo (And the Third Day Arrived the Crow)* (a.k.a. *On the Third Day arrived the Crow*)(1973). This one from director Gianni Crea; it starred Lincoln Tate as Link on the side of the good guys. Berger portrays a dual role for this film, both as notorious gunmen brothers. A mining company owner is pilfering all the loot for himself and hires gunslinger Crow who soon meets his maker via Link (Tate) a mining detective, who, along with his two brothers, were sent by the governor to investigate the mines problem. After killing Crow, then the gunslinger's brother shows up in the town later looking for revenge. He's another evil, proficient gunslinger (also Berger), but in the final showdown, he is also brought down by Link the hero.

From this time forward, during these waning years of the *Spaghetti* Westerns, Berger would only be credited with a few others to come. One that comes to mind was *Fratelli Del Kung Fu Nel Pazzo West (The Kung Fu Brothers in the Wild, Wild West)* (1973). This was a Western takeoff, in the realm of the East meets West* vein of the genre. Not nearly as good as some, but still a watch able effort by director Yeo Ban Yee for *Golden Harvest Film* an Italian / Hong Kong coproduction. The film starred Jason Pai-Pico and Po Chih Leo as two brothers reunited in the American West. Berger stars as a gunman, who, having just arrived in town, goes to bat for the immigrants who are being persecuted by the bad guys. Enter Irishman Donal O'Brien as the gang leader.

Next for Berger is a comedic Western called *Il Figlio Di Zorro (Son of Zorro)* (1973) from director Frank G. Carroll (Gianfranco Baldanello). It starred Robert Widmark (Alberto Dell'Acqua) in the Zorro's role. Costarring here is a prolific Spanish actor named Fernando Sancho as the Mexican colonel, Michel LeBlanche. Elisa Ramirez as Conchita and William Berger as gringo gun-runner called Boyd. It was a rather insignificant effort for the genre. It was actually re issued under the title *Man with the Golden Winchester.*

William Berger went on to do another Western that year, a German / Spanish coproduction which has also been a rarity to obtain until recently. It was called *Verflucht Dies Amerika (Curse This America)* (1973)(a.k.a. *Yankee Dudler / Jaider's Gang*). This one stars Geraldine Chaplin in the role of Kate Elder. (Remembering big-nosed Kate of Doc Holiday fame? She doesn't look the part though). William Berger portrays the gunman /

---

* The "East meets West" spin-off westerns followed closely with other films of the same vein—some better, others worse. A few of those more popular ones were *Red Sun* (1971) with Charles Bronson, Toshiro Mifune, and Alain Delon; *Blood Money* (a.k.a. *Stranger and the Gunfighter*) (1973) with Lee Van Cleef; and *Fighting Fists of Shanghai Joe* (1973) with Chen Lee, Klaus Kinski, and Gordon Mitchell.

dentist Doc Holiday. The intended stars of the film are Arthur Brauss as Bastian, Francisco Algor, Sigi Graue, and Kinoto. The storyline has to do with a family of Bavarian woodcutter prisoners relocated to our lawless west where they attempt to settle and fend off outlaws.

Berger's oldest daughter, Debra, while still only sixteen was about to make her screen debut alongside her father in *The Marvelous Visit* for a 1974 release. This was a French / Italian coproduction and starring Gilles Kohler and Roland Lesaffre along with Debra as Deliah (she was billed as Deborah Berger*). Berger was listed here only as an associate cast member with others. Slated as a sort of fantasy film directed by Marcel Carne, it was nonetheless a starting effort for the film starlet and a springboard for her successes that would follow.

During the latter part of 1973 Berger's main squeeze, Hanja was seen as being pregnant with a child that wouldn't be born until fall of the following year. Then back in London, Hanja Kochansky would give birth to another son for Billy Berger, born on October 3, 1974. She named him Kasmir. Hanja was a busy career woman and had been writing a book on and off during the past year with Billy. Finally, she had gotten it published by *Mayflower Publishers*, and it was being distributed by *Munn Books, UK*. It was called *Freely Female: The Sexual Fantasies of Women*. It was, we're told, an honest writing attempt to convey the female sexual needs of the modern woman to the reading public. At only 122 pages and paperback bound, it was a handy quick read and pocket reference for the woman of the world.

> Seemingly after Hanja left to return to London but prior to her giving birth to Kasimir, Berger had resumed hanging around the old group with the Getty's, J. Paul Jr., and wife, Gisela. That was probably when he was first introduced to Gisela's friend Dorte, a German gal who worked in films as an editor. Actually, the two women were on the same project together, her on the

* Deborah went on to do another film the following year. This one also was with her famous Dad. It was called *Parasycho: Spektrum Der Angst (Parasycho: Spectrum of Fear)*. Even today, it still was considered still a fairly obscure horror film done in '74 for a 1975 release. Berger is Professor Dr. Carl Nicklas. His daughter Debbie Nicklas is portrayed by Debra Berger. That father-daughter combo along with other cast members: Leon Askin, Mascha Gonska as Anna, Karl Heinz Martell and Signe Seidal are the listed stars. The film is actually a three-part segment, each with its own title, cast, and separate storyline. The Berger's segment title is "Metempsychosis." All segments are directed by Peter Patzak for this West-German / Austrian film coproduction.

> editing and Gisela as the script girl for a film called *The Sensuous Three* (1972), a German film. It was later in 1975 when Dorte (also Dorthe) gave birth to another son for Billy Berger. He was born back in Berlin, 1975. She named him Alexander (Alex).

By the time 1975 rolled around, there were only a few efforts attempting to curb the now-steady decline of interest in those Westerns and their dwindling box office appeal. The genre was actually being replaced by the more-modern wave of the crime films inspired by the American *Dirty Harry* (good cop / bad cop type) and the *Death Wish* (vigilante films). A revival effort of sorts was put forth by director Enzo G. Castellari (Enzo Girolami) for this failing genre. His film was called *Keoma IL Vendicatore (The Vengeance of Keoma)* (a.k.a. *Keoma*) and is a fine example of quality from the genre. The film starred Franco Nero (Francesco Sparanero) as Keoma, the half-breed who comes home from the war to find only a burned-out ghost town still smoldering instead. There he meets an old Indian woman who reveals his past to him in flashbacks from being rescued by this woman from death when their Indian village is razed and destroyed. Keoma travels from town to town in search for his roots and the whys to the fact that there is so much violence surrounding his life.

The haunting mystical musical score is most effective here from brothers, Guido and Maurizio De Angelis. Castellari cast Berger for the role of ex-gunman William Shannon, portraying the Keoma father figure from out of the past. Others of this fine cast were Donal O'Brien, Olga Karlatos, and Woody Strode. It was written by Italian actor / writer George Eastman (Luigi Montefiori) who acted in numerous genre films himself. It has now made classic status, at least for the fans and collectors of the genre.

Berger's next film about this time was *Oil . . . Dimensione Giganti* (a.k.a. *Oil: The Billion Dollar Fire / a.k.a. Oil*) (1976). An Italian / Romanian adventure yarn from director Mircea Dragan and starred by Stuart Whitman as oilman John Carter. Other cast members read like a Euro who's who. There were Woody Strode, Ray Milland, and William Berger as Mr. Mann from the corporate office who was involved in selling the company down the river. Others were Tony Kendall as Rashild, and with Gordon Mitchell as his rowdy partner Gordon. From 1976 to 1981, Berger would turn over some twenty additional films for his repertoire. They were mostly of the crime and giallo genres with some adventures sprinkled in like the above *Oil* film.

Berger's next Western was *California Goodbye* (a.k.a. *California*) (1977) from director Michele Lupo. The star was Giuliana Gemma portraying a displaced Southern soldier back from war, roaming through Missouri, searching for new purpose in life. Berger is costarred as Mr. Preston; others on board were Malisa Longo, Raimond Harmstorf, Chris Avram, Robert Hundar, among others. For the year 1981, Berger would watch with pride as his Hanja along with their fifteen-year-old daughter Katya* and a very young Kasimir would all three be in a film together with friend George Eastman (Luigi Montefiori). The film was called *Rosso Sangue* (a.k.a. *Absurd*). The film starred Montefiori as Mikos Stenopolis, Katya as Katja Bennett, and Kasimir as Willy Bennett. Hanja was the mother, Anja Bennett. Producer / director Aristide Massaccesi recalled the difficulty he had trying to get the young Kasimir to smile for him, as he was holding up the decapitated head of Stenopolis (Montefiori) at the conclusion of the film.

The family is talented we can certainly give them that. Even the youngest, Kasimir,† would go on to do a couple of films as a child star. In 1984 he was Gacel's son in the film *Tuareg: the Desert Warrior*. His other film part was in the television miniseries called *Christopher Columbus* (1985). He would portray Diego, son of Columbus. His real father, William Berger, was also in this *RAI* (Ital-TV) miniseries production as Francisco DeBobadilla. The film director was Alberto Lattuada. It starred Gabriel Byrne, Faye Dunaway, Oliver Reed, Nicol Williamson, Eli Wallach, Max Von Sydow, Charles Borromel, Jose Ferrer, to name a few. Berger and Reed were particularly great to watch in their roles as villains. Riz Ortolani furnishes the film

---

* Film work was nothing new even to young Katya or Katia (pronounced "Kocha") as she was known on screen. She had been working in the film industry since her debut at the young age of twelve when she starred in the film *Piccole Labbra (Little Lips)* (1978) for director Mimmo Cattarinich and his Italian / Spanish coproduction film. Katya since had been acquiring quite a film repertoire of her own until 1983. After this next film *The Moon in the Cutter,* a French / Italian coproduced film from Jacques Beineix. She decided to give up the acting for good and so, at seventeen-years old, retired from the cinema altogether and got married. From last reports, she was indeed happily married with two children, a boy and a girl all living in the NY area.

† When approached about his film career several years ago via e-mail contact, a modest Kasimir admitted to this author as having been in a couple of films during his preteen years, but went on to add that he was never a star and nowadays can hardly remember them. His profession of choice has been that of journalism, working for magazines there in the UK and in ad sales. His forte is that of being an expert in Africa and African cultures. Sounds as if he's now a man of extreme accomplishment already, and things will undoubtedly lead to acclaim and recognition later in life. A true family member, within a family of artists, the Berger name continues to ride on.

with a rousing music score that accents the film and its surrounding of the European countryside.

Another film for William Berger's slate was one called *Tex and the Lord of the Deep* (1985) from director Duccio Tessari. This was a fantasy Western adapted from an Italian comic book story. Once again the director casts Giuliana Gemma in the lead—this time as Tex Willer. William Berger is back on board as a famous character of the old west, Kit Carson. Others of cast were Carlo Mucari, Isabel Russunova, and long a staple of the Westerns, Spanish actor Aldo Sambrell. This would be very near to the last Western we would find William Berger and were mostly cameo roles at that. He would continue his films but television work would become more of a mainstay at this point in his career. Plus, there was the fact that audience taste for the genres of the past were changing. A new breed of public was out there now. There would only be a couple of more Westerns left for him before they would expire indefinitely from the silver screen.

> In 1985, it was about this date in time when our William Berger is found to have caught himself another lady. It seems, through a source from within the family, he had married a lady by the name of Linda about the mid-1980. Little is known of this mystery woman other than they were only together for just a few years before divorcing sometime between 1989 and 1991. Probably not wanting to burden the lady after finding out about his illness, we speculate he pulled the plug on the marriage, then retreated to Valencia, Spain, where he lived with his daughter Debra for a year or so before relocating back to LA with her, so as to join the other daughter Carin living there while he underwent chemo treatments.

Berger again was called for another western. This one would be a remake of the Sergio Corbucci original 1966 film, *Django,* which had starred originally a young Franco Nero in the title role. This new film would be a true revival for one much-duplicated which certainly doesn't go down in the annals of *Spaghetti* Western history without certain merit. This remake by director Ted Archer (Nello Rossati) (who also scripted with Franco Reggiani) would be called simply *Django Strikes Again* (1987). Franco Nero would again revive the now-famous Django's character from the first film. Unfortunately, William Berger's narration scenes were to be chopped from every version it seems, except for the one released in Germany.

The film sported an unusual cast for a western, and more resembled an Amazon Jungle flick instead, as was related by Thomas Weisser in his book called *Spaghetti Westerns*—the Good, the Bad, and the Violent; *558 Euro Westerns and Their Personnel, 1961–1977* published by *McFarland (1992*). The film could very well have been inspired by Sylvester Stallone's *Rambo* films of about this same period. Along for the boat ride through the jungles are Donald Pleasance and Christopher Connolly along with Lici Lee Lyon among others. Having learned his daughter had been kidnapped and was a prisoner of slave traders was enough to bring Django back from his ten-year stint at the Monastery. There he'd been trying to make amends for and forget his bloody past. Before going though, he seeks out the hiding place and digs up the *Gatling* like machine gun he used so efficiently ten years earlier.

Some three years later, Berger would be offered another cameo role for his last western of the genre. Actually, it was a Yukon spin-off of the genre, which is a place where we like to include all of the *White Fang* dog movies and others that took place in the Klondike regions of the Alaskan north. The film was called *Buck ai Confine Del Cielo* (a.k.a. *Buck at the Edge of Heaven / Buck's Greatest Adventure* (1991). Berger has an early cameo role as the boy's grandfather Thomas. He and the dumb scout Matt are soon murdered when the cabin is set upon by poachers while young Tim and his father Wintrop, a trapper and dog Buck, were off hunting and checking the traps.

Credited to a takeoff on the Jack London *White Fang* story, this Italian production was from director Anthony Richmond (Tonino Ricci) who also is credited with the story /script along with Tito Carpi and Sheila Goldberg. Others of the cast were John Savage Wintrop, Jesse Alexander Tim, David Hess Padre Dan, Jennifer Youngs as Corinne, and Rick Battaglia evil town boss Bauman who sent the gang out to rob Wintrop's hides.

With this *Buck* title, we bring William Berger's Westerns to a close. Later, from a Lucas Balbo compiled filmography, we learned that for the year 1993 (meaning, Berger's participation was some earlier), there were only two listings of film work for the actor: *Babylon* by Director Peter Patzak and another *Jungle of Fear (Devil's Riddle)* by Director Jesus Franco; then there was nothing more. It had been rumored that something was up with William Berger, health wise. Some said he had fallen severely ill. But alas, rumors from Italy have always been difficult to confirm.

It wasn't until August 1993 there in Valencia, Spain, when *WAI! (Westerns All'Italiana),* fanzine Spanish correspondent Emilio Tortajada set out to do an interview with Berger that he found out he was dying of cancer. His death came later that year, on October 2, 1993. Amazingly, it didn't happen in Europe at all but rather on US soil in Los Angeles, with his family near. William Berger passed away in silence, much as he had lived the last couple of years of his life. His cancer, we are now certain of, was prostrate. Perhaps one evening, while looking to the stars, we may see him riding across the vast expanse of the sky, heading toward the wild (not so wild anymore) distant west.

While working in earnest compiling this man's film works, we tracked some twenty-two of these unique Westerns to his credit. Noting that sometimes, within the tracking process of these Euro film titles, which can be hit and miss at best, it is then possible there may be even more out there yet to be added to this man's repertoire—that is, if and when they were to ever surface. It may have taken a monumental catastrophe to shake some sense into him, but he appears to have come round, got a haircut, and went to work big-time. May you rest in peace, Cisco!

Other films and television roles credited to this actor consisted of many in other various European genres, like crime, war, horror, and of course the *giallo*-thrillers—which all have amounted to over 110 plus. Then we must also include his accomplishments of the Theater Arts, from his work dates of the early 1950s for a total career span of some thirty-eight years. Not too shabby for an Austrian immigrant who suddenly had a yen to act on the Stage.

Because of the lack of information on this actor years ago, when I began this project, things could have been a lot different for this write-up had it not been for the Timothy Wilson book about Bill and Carol's life together. The book was *The House of Angels* published by *Michael Joseph Ltd., London* (1973). Here's to you, Tim Wilson. We fans, thank you.

Even on certain things, Berger himself wasn't of much help. When asked how many children he had during that 1992 Kessler interview, he stated, "A son in Berlin, one in Rome, one in Santa Fe, and a daughter in LA." Could he have just been confused or, more likely, just protective as fathers tend to be, counting the two blood-related daughters we know of, Carin and Debra* (not to forget Katya, who did take his surname since a teenager), then three the sons—Wendell, Kasimir, and the youngest Alex—for an even five. Even Alex Berger is credited with one film we know of. His debut was in *Sheer*

---

* Debra was probably the Berger who turned out the most films to her credit during her career, which includes TV and a 2002 documentary as herself. We count some fifteen to date. One of those films she claimed to be exceptionally proud of was with her being associated with actor Mickey Rooney in *the White Stallion* (1986), a *USA* production. Her role was that of Lili Castle. Other later credits included a stint in the US soap, *The Young and the Restless* (1986) and one last film credit, *Born* (1988), which seems to have been her last, then retiring to Valencia, Spain, to pursue other interests. Back about the time of her film debut with her father in *The Marvelous Visit* (1974), she married an Italian prince, Alessandro Dado Ruspoli. They had two sons—Tao, born in 1975, and later, Bartolomeo Ruspoli, born in 1978. The father Ruspoli Sr. passed away in early 2005.

Madness (1983) at age eight. Could it be there are others of the Berger clan out there related to our William? If so, I'm afraid we'll have to leave that question up to the next generation of genre fans to delve into. Good luck, my friends.

End.

- Below is a complete filmography of Berger's Euro Westerns. The dates are aligned as close as possible with information currently at hand, plus international release dates included. **Picture and posters are accredited to the Sebastian Haselbeck collection via his website www.spaghetti-westerns.net. Thanks, Sebastian.*

WILLIAM BERGER'S *SPAGHETTI* WESTERN FILMS

1965

Ringo's Big Night, *La Grande Notte Di Ringo;* Ital, Director Mario Maffei (Berger stars as Jack Balman) (10/21/66). *(May have been released only in Italy prior to international release so as to feel out his popularity, this being his first film.)*

1966
El Cisco; Ital, Director Sergio Bergonzelli (Berger is Cisco) (10/13/66)

1967
Face to Face a.k.a. *Faccia A Faccia;* Ital, Director Sergio Sollima (Berger as Charlie Sirringo) (11/23/67)

1968
Today We Kill, Tomorrow We Die, *Oggi a Me, Domani a Te;* a.k.a. *Today It's Me, Tomorrow It's You;* Ital, Director Tonino Cervi (Berger as costars Francis "Colt" Moran) (3/28/68)

The Man Who Cried for Revenge, *IL Suo Nome Gridava Vendetta;* Ital, Director William Hawkins (Mario Caiano) (Berger costars as Sam Kellogg) (7/28/68)

If You Meet Sartana . . . Pray for Your Death, *Se Incontri Sartana Prega per La Tua Morte; a.k.a. Sartana;* Ital, Director Frank Kramer (Granfranco Parolini) (Berger as Lasky) (8/14/68)

1969
No Room to Die, a.k.a. *Una Lunga Fila Di Croci;* Ital, Director Sergio Garrone (Berger as Murdock) (4/18/69)

Sabata, a.k.a. *Ehi Amico, C'E' Sabata . . . Hai Chiuso;* Ital, Director Frank Kramer (Granfranco Parolini) (Berger as Banjo) (9/16/69)

1970

***The Ballad of Death Valley**, Sartana Nella Valle Dei Avvoltoi;* Ital, Director Roberto Mauri (Berger stars as Lee Galloway) (8/15/1970)

1971

***His Pistols Smoked . . . They Called Him Cemetery**, Gli Fumavano Le Colt . . . Lo Chiamavano Camposanto; a.k.a A Bullet for a Stranger;* Ital, Director Anthony Ascott (Giuliano Carnimeo) (Berger as Duke) (9/23/71)

1973

***A Colt in the Devil's Hand,** Una Colt in Mano Al Diavolo;* Ital, Director Frank G. Carroll (Gianfranco Baldanello) (Berger as Butch Brown) (1/15/73)

Curse This America a.k.a. *Verflucht Dies Amerika! Jaider's Gang;* Ger/Spa, Director Volker Vogeler (Berger as Doc Holiday) 1973

The Executioner of God, *Il Giustiziere Di Dio;* Ital, Director Franco Lattanzi (Berger stars as Tony Lang) (6/2/73)

On the Third Day, Arrived the Crow, *E Il Terzo Giorno Arrivo IL Corvo; a.k.a. A Fistful of Death;* Ital, Director Gianni Crea (Berger as the crow/crow brother *dual roles*) (7/21/73)

Fast-Hand Is Still My Name, *Lo Chiamavano Requiescant Fasthand;* Ital, Director Mario Bianchi (Berger as Machedo) (1973)

Kung Fu Brothers in the Wild West*; Kung Fu nel Pazzo West; Master Killers;* Ital/Hong Kong, Director George Bange (Yeo Ban Yee) (Berger as Gunman) (1973)

Son of Zorro, *IL Fuglio Di Zorro;* Ital/Spa, Director Frank G. Carroll (Gianfranco Baldanello) (Berger as Boyd) (12/30/73)

1976

Keoma, a.k.a. *The Violent Breed;* Ital, Director Enzo G. Castellari (Enzo Girolami) (Berger costars as William Shannon) 11/25/76

1977

California Goodbye, *California Addio; a.k.a. California*; Ital/ Spa, Director Michele Lupo (Berger as Mr. Preston) (7/16/77)

1979

Closed Circuit, a.k.a. *Circuito Chiuso; a.k.a. Control;* Ital/Fr, Directed by Giuliano Montaldo; *An experimental film project for RAI (Italian TV). Is actual a film within a film that utilizes spliced in scenes from other films such as the William Berger gunfight scene in California with the film's star Giuliano Gemma. (1979)*

1985

Tex and the Lord of the Deep, a.k.a. *Tex E IL Signore Degli Abissi; a.k.a. Tex Willer and the Lord of the Deep;* Ital, Director Duccio Tessari (Berger costars as Kit Carson) (9/6/85)

1987

Django Strikes Again, a.k.a. *Django's Grande Ritorno; a.k.a. Django 2;* Ital, Director Ted Archer (Nello Rossati) (Berger as Old Timer / narrator) *Berger's narration scenes were cut out of all versions, except German, although he was paid for his part, but was not credited as being in it. (12/3/87)*

1991

Buck at the Edge of Heaven, a.k.a. *Buck ai Confine Del Cielo* a.k.a. *Buck's Greatest Adventure;* Ital, Director Anthony Richmond (Tonino Ricci) (Berger as Grandfather Thomas) (1991)

End.

BIBLIOGRAPHY
(W. BERGER)

Balbo, Lucas, A completed researched William Berger filmology for *WAI!* (1964–1993)

Betts, Tom, editor *WAI! (Westerns . . . All'Italiana)* Fanzine articles/information on William Berger:

Issue no. 3/4 November 1984, "Keoma, the Avenger" a review;
Issue no. 3, September/October 1985, "Tessari Westerns";
Issue no. 6, March/April 1986, "Tex, the Film" plus Review;
Issue vol. 3, no. 17, spring 1988, *Django Strikes Again,* plus *Keoma* reviews;
Issue no. 50, *Son of Zorro,* Tom Betts

Berger, Debra, two-part interview with Devin Kelly, posted on *www.cinema-nocturna.com,* reviewed on 2/29/2004

Connolly, Bill, editor, *Spaghetti Cinema* Fanzine, information tidbits on actor William Berger

Issue no. 58, Duccio Tessari Addio, filmology

Haynes, Jim, *Thanks for Coming* (1982), *Faber & Faber Ltd.,* London; with Hanja Kochansky name-dropping

Haselbeck, Sebastian, owner/curator for Internet website: *www.spaghetti-western.net*

Internet via: *www.IMDB.com*; 114 film listing references for William Berger from 2002; *latest TV listings entry for early 1950s of one Bill Berger are not of the same actor and are bogus.*

Ledbetter, Craig, editor of now-defunct *ETC (European Trash Cinema)* Fanzine: Interview with William Berger plus filmology by Christian Kessler with translation by Peter Blumenstock posted in *ETC* Issue no. 13, pp 8-13

Obituary from a stage productions release (in Italian) flyer for *Teatro alla Scala* (*Staircase to the Theater*), translated by Tom Prickette for *WAI!* Memorial issue 2004 (6/12/04)

Spaghetti Web-board posting (1/30/2002) of translated William Berger; interview by *Ephedrino*

Weisser, Thomas, *Spaghetti Westerns: the Good, the Bad, and the Violent*, (1992) *McFarland*, Jefferson NC.

"Western: All'Italiana" (books I, II, and III), by Antonio Bruschini and Federico de Zigno, *Glittering Images,* Firenze, Italy; book I, 1998; book II, 2001 and book III, 2006

The Western: The Complete Film Sourcebook (The Film Encyclopedia) (1983); by Phil Hardy, *William Morrow and Co, Inc.*, NY., Appendix no. 8, pp: 381-395

Wikipedia, the free encyclopedia informational on William Berger

Wilson, Timothy, *House of Angels* (1973) *Michael Joseph Ltd.,* London

RORY CALHOUN

(1922-1999)

BLACKIE IS THE MAN!

Born August 8, 1922, as Francis Timothy McCown Los Angeles, California. Long before young Francis's acting career took off, the six feet and three inches Irish/Spanish descended McCown, working stints as a boxer, a lumberjack, a truck driver, and a cowpuncher. Originally, he grew up in the Santa Cruz region of California. His father had been a gambler and was raised mostly by his mother. She later remarried to one Nathan Durgin. Young Frank was a bad boy from an early age; he seemed to be drawn to trouble. Nicknamed Smoky, he stole a gun at thirteen, was caught and sent to California Youth Reform School, but escaped. After robbing a couple of jewelry stores, then stealing a car and driving it across the state line, a Federal offense, he was caught and sentenced to serve three years in Springfield, Missouri. He was then transferred to San Quentin on the jewelry store thief charges and was finally released on his twenty-first birthday. Calhoun always attributed his getting back to the straight 'n' narrow to a priest, one Father Donald Kanally, who, in his words, had changed his life.

For his career in acting, an original screen test can be attributed to one Sue Carol Ladd, a Hollywood agent and wife of Alan Ladd, who is credited to first spotting Calhoun as the three were out riding horses one day. She got him set up with a stand-in part on the 1941 film *Sundown*, a Henry Hathaway film about WWII in North Africa. His film debut actually came later in 1944 with Carmen Miranda, with him using a combination of his real name, Frank McCown. The film was called *Something for the Boys* by director Lewis Seiler. Unaccredited in this first film, it starred Miranda, Michael O'Shea, Vivian Blaine, Phil Silvers, and Perry Como, to name just a few. McCown's first credited role with a name change of Rory Calhoun (thanks to David D. Selznick) was in the 1947 film *The Red House* from director Delmer Daves. His first starring role was in *Adventure Island*, the same year by director Peter Stewart. It starred along with him in this remake of *Ebb Tide* (1937, a James Hogan film) Rhonda Fleming, Paul Kelly, and John Abbott.

It seems to have been all downhill from there it seems, for this good-looking, fit six-foot actor. He went on to make films with great stars like Marilyn Monroe, Robert Mitchum, Lauren Bacall, Betty Grable, Susan Haywood, and young actor Guy Madison. Guy and Blackie, as Calhoun was known, became good friends. The young actor enjoyed Calhoun's company, and they hung around—often riding, fishing, and competing in archery together. Calhoun took him under his wing, so to speak, and nurtured him through those beginning years of his film work. Some thirty-four films later about 1958, Calhoun debuted in a *CBS* television series called *The Texan.*

It starred Rory Calhoun as Bill Langley: the Texan. This was another one of the so-called adult Westerns that hit small screens about this period in time. Great little series, which ran weekly featuring Calhoun along with other guest actors in weekly situations in the old west. This production ran from 1958/1960, which in turn helped add to Calhoun's TV credit history of over one thousand episodes as we scan back on his long, astute acting career.

Afterward, he branched out to Europe and got involved with one of those popular *Peplum* genre films of the era. This one was called *The Colossus of Rhodes* (1961). This epic Sword and Sandal film was just one of many the Italian films that were churned out about this era in Europe. Rory Calhoun ventured over after a job offer from the movie producer Michele Scaglione, who was an acquaintance of the Guy Madison's, and who at the time, had in some way been responsible for Guy Madison's jump onto the Euro band wagon during that same period in time.

As star of this epic film, Calhoun portrayed Darios, a Greek military hero who comes to visit his uncle in Rhodes, circa 280 BC. He becomes involved with a woman and a group of rebels who plan to overthrow the tyrannical King Serse and his second in command, the evil, Thar. This plan fails, and all are force into the arenas for the courts amusement and games. However, an untimely earthquake erupts and levels all including the king's reign of terror.

Although the film's up-and-coming director, Sergio Leone, had directed other films of this nature in Rome (mostly second unit work), this was his first with full credit given this aspiring filmmaker. Its history from here on as Leone's name has since gone down in the history books as one the greatest directors of all time. The film's costars were Lea Massari as Diala, Georges Marchal as Peliocles, and Conrado San Martin as Thar. Others often cast in the Italian films were Mimmo Palmara, Carlo Tamberlani, and Alfio Caltabiano. The film was produced by Michele Scaglione with music score by Angelo Francesco Lavagnino. This was Spanish/ Italian/ French large-budget co production and normally ran some 127 uncut.

About this time he also did a film called *The Treasure of Monte Cristo* (1960), a British adventure film remake of a 1949 original from William Berke. This film was an effort of the Robert S. Baker and Monty Berman team. It turned out to be a good Dumas tale reworking, but not much in the action department.

Then in 1961, while still in Europe, he wrapped up an adventure remake called *Marco Polo* from the Italian directors Piero Pierotti and Hugo Fregonese. This film was a great spectacle and got rave reviews even from the American shores. It starred Calhoun as the Marco Polo character along with Yoko Tani, Camillo Pilotto, and Pierre Cressoy, among others. A story here of various sagas of the Italian explorer / adventurer who, along the way in his travels, manages to rescue the daughter of the *Mongol* leader Kublai Khan. He also crosses paths with a hermit who has invented gunpowder! He then proceeds, with much effort, to build himself a Cannon.

Calhoun would venture into all genres of film work during his career, and even sometimes had been given partial credit, along with displaced producer/ director / promoter Sidney Pink* in claiming that they predated

* Sidney Pink, an entrepreneurial independent filmmaker from the old school, wound up in Spain shooting a television commercial for *Bubble-Up*, a new soft drink being introduced by *Pespi Cola* with actor Buster Keaton. Keaton in Madrid, Spain, at the time was unable to return to America to do the commercial

the *Spaghetti* Western era of film work with one they filmed in Spain back in '64 called *Finger on the Trigger* (1965). He liked to say on occasion he made the first Western in Spain. However, film work in Spain was just breaking at the time and being looked at hard for a cheap location to make quality Westerns by not only by Pink but others as well. He decided on the southern Spain area, a look-alike American southwest. It was similar to the US terrain and sets were mostly already there. The animals (horses) and the help was dirt cheap in those days. Credited as a US / Spanish coproduction Pink later claimed for his biography, *So You Want to Make Movies: My Life as an Independent Film Producer* (1989) that "he helped to popularize the *Spaghetti* Western by shooting a number of productions in Europe."

From our film history, though, the Brits got there first with a 1961 Western called *Savage Guns* with Richard Basehart. This film was a first for the genre, an Ital/ Spa/ British co production from film make Michael Carreras of the *Hammer* horror films of England. The film was coscripted

---

takes due to pending obligations. Pink was offered the producer and interpreter job for Keaton. From there he hooked up with the Spanish division of the *Mole Richardson Equipment Leasing Co. /* film producer himself Mole Richardson.

They eventually agreed on a contract to make a Spanish / US coproduction picture, a Western to be shot there in the south of Spain in an area called Almeria. The film's script was a co effort by Pink and the story author, Luis de los Arcos, who called his work *El dedo en el Gatillo*, which roughly translates to the films new title, *Finger on the Trigger.* After, contracts were all arranged and signed, which also consisted of forming a Spanish film-producing company under Spanish law called *FISA (Films Internacionales Sociedad Anonyma).* The owner of this production company was Mole Richardson / Antonio Recoder (Spanish Attorney), and Sid Pink's own Spanish representative Pepe Lopez Moreno.

With that under their belts, they proceeded to scout out filming locales. The writer Luis took them down into desert country near the south coast of Spain, Almeria. In his book, Pink quoted Rory Calhoun as saying about the area that it was, "acres and acres of nothing but acres." Other than the previous British made film *Savage Guns* (1961) film, there had been only another, more recent to this point in time filmed there and that was *Lawrence of Arabia* (1962).

After numerous star problems, since the main lead was to have been Victor Mature, who voided his contractual obligations by not showing up for filming, it put Pink between a rock and a hard place, forced his call upon his old friend Rory Calhoun who kindly agreed to fly over and went to work immediately, thus pulling Pink's tit out of the preverbal ringer. Pink would remain in Spain several more years knocking out the films. Of interest to *Spaghetti* Western fans, he would churn out five more Euro Westerns.

by ex-*Hammer* main writer from those years Jimmy Sangster. This film broke all bounds by being first to be filmed there in southern Spain. It not only starred Basehart but also Alex Nicol, Don Taylor, and Paquita Rico. Others were Fernando Rey, Maria Granada, José Nieto, and Victor Israel who would all go on to Euro Western fame in the genre.

Soon, other foreign filmmakers like Pink would venture into the genre and follow their path but usually with lesser-known films. Sergio Leone, however, is credited with the breathing a new life into this Italian film genre with his blockbuster *For a Fistful of Dollars* (1964). He then continued on to complete the *Dollar* trilogy, which starred American actor Clint Eastwood and several other well-known and well-liked American actors from a seemingly unlimited stable of top-notch performers.

Interestingly, after finishing the *Trigger* film and it began showing there in the European theaters, Pink claimed he received a phone call from Italian director Sergio Leone. It seems Leone had asked him if he'd care to help co produce a Western of his, since he had been now deemed the most knowledgeable Western film producer in Europe at that time. His Western would star the American television series actor, Clint Eastwood, and was to be called at that time, *The Magnificent Stranger,* later to be changed to *A Fistful of Dollars* (1964). Pink claims he made the ultimate mistake in turning Leone down flat, a mistake he lived to regret for sure.

We feel that Mr. Pink may have been somewhat mistaken on this as being a request for him to help coproduce Leone's *first Dollar* film. He may have very well meant Leone's second effort which would come to be called *For a Few Dollars More* (1965). Reason being, we feel this assumption would be the connection between the film's actual release dates according to current records via up-to-date Internet sources. It seems that *A Fistful of Dollars* first European release in Italy was September 12, 1964. It's Spanish release wasn't until September 27, 1965, and for it's US release not until January 18, 1967.

For Pink's *Trigger* film, it was first released in Spain on March 22, 1965. The US release didn't happen until May 1, 1965. Therefore, we feel Leone couldn't have yet seen Pink's film in the Italian theaters until at least after the Spanish release date of March 1965. Nevertheless, in the book inside flyleaf cover stated he did after all, help to popularize the *Spaghetti* Westerns of the era by shooting a total of five of these Euro Westerns films.

Although Rory Calhoun did not make any others of the *Spaghetti* Western genre, he did however venture back and forth to Rome on occasions making films of other genres. In 1966 he returned to Europe for an Italian Spy film called *IL Gioco Delle Spie (The Spies Game)* and another in 1967 called *Opercion Dilila (Operation Dilila).* Later that year, he did two others

Las Virgenes Del La Nueva Ola (Virgins of the New Order) and, lastly, *La Machacha Del Nilo (The Machacha of the Nile)*. He didn't seem to be particularly avoiding these Euro Westerns, but his television obligations pretty much kept him back on the American shores mostly during this period in time.

Calhoun and his hot-blooded Mexican songstress Lita Baron were married in 1948. They finally divorced in 1970 officially, after many trials and tribulations of a steamy relationship. During their marriage, they had three daughters, Cindy, Tami, and Lorri. A year later, our man about town, Calhoun, was remarried all ready, this time to an Australian journalist Sue Roades (he'd met her during a London interview) in 1971. The marriage lasted five years ending in divorce. They had one daughter, Rory Patricia. The couple settled their differences and later remarried again in 1982, still together at his passing, April 28, 1999.

He died from complications of advanced stage emphysema (always had been a heavy smoker in life) and also diabetes. Back in 1970, when results of the on-again, off-again trials of his marriage to Baron* was brought to a close, and he was finally sued for divorce by the fiery Lita, she named some seventy-nine women (among them Betty Grable) that he supposedly had adulterous relationships with during their marriage. Calhoun replied promptly to the charges, saying, "Heck, she didn't even include half of them."

Later in his career after various adventure films along with other Westerns (though no more of the *Spaghetti* variety), he tried once again for the television markets and signed on for a five-year stint as Judge Judson Tyler on the daytime soap serial called *Capitol* in 1982. Then at seventy year old, he made his last film, the 1992 *Pure Country* with old friend and fellow actor Forest Tucker. Just for the record, Rory Calhoun has not one but two stars on the famous *Hollywood Walk of Fame*. (One for motion pictures and the other is for television.)

---

* Back during his marriage to Baron, there had been another daughter credited to our actor from a relationship with actress Vitina Marcus, also while still legally married to Baron, we might add. This affair abruptly came to an end in 1966 when Marcus brought forth a paternity suit against the actor Calhoun. It was then settled in LA Superior Court for an undisclosed amount on monies. According to the article retrieved from *www.wikipedia.org* on Calhoun, it further stated he was forty-three years old at the time and Marcus was only twenty-eight. The seven-year-old daughter result of the relationship later went on to become "The Most Beautiful Showgirl" in Las Vegas and received the key to the city in a ceremony back in 1987 as proud parents looked on.

So as we tally up the children for our actor Calhoun, it seems he had a total of five daughters, and no boys. But seemingly he did have a string of women that wouldn't quit until hell froze over. It would certainly appear that our man Blackie was indeed the man! RIP, Rory Calhoun.

End.

- Below is a filmography of Rory Calhoun Euro Westerns. The dates are aligned as close as possible with information currently at hand, plus international release date. **Poster pictures are accredited to the Sebastian Haselbeck collection via his website www.spaghetti-westerns.net.*
- *Rory Calhoun top "Texan" photo is accredited to Brian J. Walker collection via his superb action website www.briansdriveintheater.com.*

RORY CALHOUN'S *SPAGHETTI* WESTERN FILM

1965

Finger on The Trigger, *a.k.a. Sentiero Dell'Oro (The Golden Horse Shoes);* US / Spa, Director Sidney Pink (Calhoun as Larry Winton) (3/22/65)

In the above film Winton (Calhoun) is leading a band of Union soldiers traveling westward looking for homesteading land suitable for settling down in after the end of the Civil War. Being Yankees they find themselves forced to join up with the Southerners to ward off Indian attacks and further insults of having to melt down gold to make bullets. Unfortunately, this film was Rory Calhoun's only venture into the Euro Western better known to some of us affectionarios as *Spaghetti* Westerns.

Calhoun's Other Euro Films
(A Quick List)

1961
The Colossus of Rhodes, IL Colosso de Rhodes, (*Peplum*) by director Sergio Leone

1966
The Spies Game, IL Gioco Delle Spie, (Spy)

1967:
Operation Dilila, Operacion Dilila, (Spy)

Virgins of the Last Order, Las Virgenes de la Nueva Ola, (Horror)
The Machacha of the Nile, La Machacha Del Nilo, (Adventure)

End.

BIBLIOGRAPHY
(R. Calhoun)

Agan, Patrick, *Whatever Happened to . . . ?* (1974) *Ace Books,* pp 26-7.

Betts, Tom, editor *WAI! (Westerns . . . All'Italiana)* Fanzine articles/ information on Rory Calhoun:
Issue no. 54, Boot Hill obituary for Rory Calhoun
Issue no. 60, Boot Hill obituary for Sidney Pink

Brian J. Walker, owner/curator for Internet website: *www.briansdriveintheater.com*, info on Rory Calhoun, *Beefcake* section

The BFI Companion to the Western (1993) (ref) by Edward Buscombe, *Andre Deutsch Ltd.,* London, 1988 / BFI—1993, pp 327

Connolly, Bill, editor *Spaghetti Cinema* Fanzine: article on Sid Pink, issue no. 5, February 1985

Halliwell, Leslie, *The Filmgoer's Companion* (1975) (ref), *Avon Books,* NY., pp 128.

Haselbeck, Sebastian, owner/curator for Internet website: *www.spaghetti-western.net*

Internet, via *www.IMDB.com* complete film and TV listing, plus mini bio for Rory Calhoun by Bill Takacs

Lamparski, Richard, *Lamparski's Whatever Became of . . . ?* (1976) *Bantam Books,* NY. pp 74

Obituary for Rory Calhoun, *Los Angeles Times* Friday, April 30, 1999 Home Edition, Part A, p 32, Metro Section

Pink, Sidney, *So You Want to Make Movies* (1989), *Pineapple Press,* Sarasota, FL.

Quinlan's Illustrated Registry of Film Stars (1987) by Davis Quinlan, *Henry Holt Reference Books,* NY., pp 75-6

Video Hound's Golden Retriever (1994 edition) *Visible Ink Press,* a division of *Gale Research Inc.*, Detroit, MI, pp 1139

Weisser, Thomas, *Spaghetti Westerns: the Good, the Bad, and the Violent,* (1992) *McFarland*, Jefferson NC.

Western: All'Italiana (book 3) by Antonio Bruschini e Federico de Zigno, *Glittering Images,* Firenze, Italy; book 3, 2006, pp 93

The Western: The Complete Film Sourcebook (The Film Encyclopedia) (1983); by Phil Hardy, *William Morrow and Co, Inc.,* NY., Appendix no. 8, pp 380

The World Almanac Who's who of Film (1987) by Thomas G Aylesworth and John S. Bowman, *Bison Books,* pp 84

JAMES COBURN

(1928-2002)

CAT-MAN TAMES THE ITALIAN WEST

James Harrison Coburn III was born in Laurel, Nebraska, August 31, 1928. It seems per an interview with Coburn and Timothy Rhys about 1997 revealed to us fans that he had been an only child. His father had been a motor mechanic and his mother a schoolteacher. The family had relocated to California during those terrible Depression years about 1930/31. The family, he remembered had a Model-A Ford, which they made the four- or five-day trip in. Eventually, they settled there in Compton, a suburb of Los Angeles. He remembered having his fifth birthday at the new place and recalled that he had "vivid memories of traveling out here; it was great," he said.

Having grown up there in Compton, California, he was uprooted by the army draft and sent off to basic training at Fort Dix, New Jersey. While serving his time in the service, he did early stints in New York City working part-time with stage productions there, in and behind the scenes we understand, although we're still a bit sketchy since our elusive actor seems rather reluctant to talk much about that era much, his service career as a whole or the balance of it thereof. It does seem though he worked and studied some with the renowned *Stella Adler & Jeff Corey group* there in the city.

Later, after his separation from the army, he returned back to LA. There he enrolled at the *Los Angeles City College* in order to earn more grade points for his entry into the *USC (University of Southern California).* He had at that time a yen to direct productions and thus began work there at the college with the drama department. He claims he was having so much fun doing that he dropped all the other classes and concentrated mainly on the plays and such.

While attending *USC* majoring in acting, he'd met a young lady also enrolled there. Her name was Beverly Kelly. Not much came of this first initial relationship until much later. A couple of years after his college sessions ended there at *USC,* he returned to New York City for a while. There he worked behind the scenes on television commercials and did live performing stints and such for the *Studio One* (1957). There were others as well like the *Suspicion* show and later on a *General Electric Playhouse* where productions were taped programs not to air on the tube until later in 1958. It was there while on the *GE* show set that he met Hume Cronyn and Eva Gabor. Cronyn, he added, "was a marvelous person and a superior actor." He took Coburn under his wing, and within only a few days had taught him the basic techniques of acting that would stay with him the rest of his career.

Returning to LA, he would get his *Equity Guild* card and make his Stage debut at the *La Jolla Playhouse,* La Jolla, California, in the play adaptation of the Herman Melville novel *Billy Budd* along with *La Jolla* cast regular Vincent Price. It was during this time, late in 1957, that his relationship with the now-live-in gal pal Beverly Kelly would heat up. Their firstborn daughter Lisa arrived that same year. He finally married his live-in love on November 11, 1959. They later had another child, a son James Harrison Coburn IV, born on May 22, 1961.

His official acting career appears to have begun about this 1957 era with the television bit parts there in New York. At first they were only small roles, but later back in LA, television would nearly dominate of his vast talents for years to come before he really got a good foothold in the movies. His first recorded Western efforts came upon his return to LA on the popular TV series *Wagon Train* (1958) with Ward Bond and Robert Horton. This episode was called "The Millie Davis Story," and his role was that of Ike. When he did finally break into films, it was also in a Western called *Ride*

Lonesome (1959), starring Randolph Scott. Here he portrayed Whit another of the bad guys attempting to steal away Scott's prisoner and claim the bounty for themselves. Other popular bad men of the movies also associated with this film were Lee Van Cleef and James Best. After this first film break in 1959, he again returned to the television almost entirely until the 1960s. During those years, he could be seen almost constantly on the small screen in various roles of the popular weekly shows. The Westerns, as we well know, were an extremely popular pastime for viewers during this era in time, and James Coburn appeared in his fair share of them.

Coburn's early life there in Southern California during the 1950's era has given us our first glimpse of the man and his career beginnings in New York and Hollywood. Easily recognizable on screen during that era as the tall man (six feet and three inches), lean, mean-looking as well, if the part warranted it—otherwise just a gangly-looking wrangler type that fit the Westerns to a T. But his on-screen, cat-like movements when off the horse always did lead us to believe there was a lot more to this guy than meets the eye. His intense eyes, chiseled, weather-beaten facial appearance tells us to be wary of this man. He emitted the persona of danger until that big toothy grin erupted and changed his whole appearance into a likable, watch able, carefree, fun-loving character that we all loved in his super spy *Our Man Flint* movies.

He returned to the big screen for another Western that year in *The Magnificent Seven* (1960) Starring Yul Brynner, Steve McQueen, and old college buddy Robert Vaughn. It was directed by the great John Sturges. Coburn's role was that of Britt the deadly knife-thrower of the gang. We fans will always remember the great knife fight between Britt (Coburn) and the Robert Wilke character Wallace. After this film, Coburn was back again in the comfort and complacency of the weekly television shows. His amount of his TV work during these few years was staggering to say the least. We calculate he had some eighty-four episode parts between 1957 and 1964 alone. Compared to his film work during that same time frame, of which there were only nine movies total. Most of those movies came during the early 1960s. He was in a word, a very busy actor during this period in time.

The reason that we highlight how busy he was during this 1964 period is because this was the era that Italian director Sergio Leone was in the process of attempting to cast a lead actor for his upcoming new Western called *The Magnificent Stranger*. He viewed Coburn as the man of his dreams, the ultimate actor and wanted him badly for this first Western production. His budget though was slim for this first-time genre effort, and when he and the producers send word to Coburn inviting him to star in the film for a lump-sum dollar amount of $15,000. Coburn, we understand, had requested a much higher, unreachable sum for Leone as had been rumored at $25,000.

Later, the title was subject to a distribution name change from the working *Stranger* and would be called *Per un Pugno di Dollari (For a Fistful of Dollars)* for its 1964 release.

> This $25,000 sum being out of Leone's reach at the time, they all then turned to another American actor already working there in Italy on Italian movies, Richard Harrison.* Harrison, having done a couple of these Euro genre Westerns, already thought they were not at all like what Leone had envisioned for his first outing in the genre. However, Leone felt he could work with him, and he would do nicely if he would do it. Harrison, unfortunately (or rather fortunately as things played out), was already backed up with work and bowed out, so he later claimed.

Coburn went on to be acclaimed for his superb work on *The Great Escape* (1963), which starred Steve McQueen, James Garner, and Charles Bronson. For this film, he portrayed a war POW among a similar captured group that had been sent to a special German camp. Coburn portrayed captured Australian fly officer, Louis Sedgwick, affectionately nicknamed by the guys in the camp as the manufacturer. His character could make or come up with anything they needed to further advance their plans for an escape. Another John Sturges, film this blockbuster broke all box office records at the time.

It was shot from a script reworking by James Clavell and W. R. Burnett of a Paul Brickhill's novel of the same name, which was based on actual accounts of a true story of an international cache of POWs being kept in an elite German prison. They surprised all by tunneling under the fenced compounds to the woods beyond. From what we understand, some three

---

* Richard Harrison having previously starred in a few of the popular Italian *Peplums* (Sword and Sandal) genre films was now under contract to do four more of the same vein starting immediately. Harrison suggested that Leone and his group contact the Roman branch of the *William Morris Agency* there in Rome. They did just that and later returned to him, with Leone's producers presenting him a list of three actors names that could be available and could be under consideration for the part. Leone wanted him to pick one of them. First off, all of them were Americans, either already living there or visiting in Rome. Harrison thought perhaps one might just be the better of the three, at least in his opinion. "He could ride a horse well," so stated Harrison in a much later interview. That man's name was Clint Eastwood, and the rest is history about his association with the Italian Westerns of that mid-1960's era.

hundred actually was to attempt the escape, but were caught in mid-act, and only seventy made it through the woods and beyond. Of that seventy, there were only two in the end that completely escaped scot-free. An exciting, moving film, a credit for all who appeared in it as well as a credit to the bravery of all the actual prisoners, regardless of their nationality confined in those World War II POW camps.* The film had been nominated for several awards, but only Steve McQueen actually won anything at the Awards Ceremony, that being a Best Actor at the *Moscow International Film Festival* and again as second place at the *Laurel Awards* for Top Action Performance.

Also, in the year 1964, Coburn went on to get involved in a comedic crime film called *Charade* as a nasty character called Tex Panthollow of a threesome of crooks. The film stars were Cary Grant, Audrey Hepburn, Walter Matthau, and also George Kennedy. The film has Grant's character helping a beautiful, newly widowed woman retrieve a fortune her late husband has squirreled away somewhere before a band of small-time crooks get to it first. Even as we mention, the films Coburn did during this period in time, he was, mind you, continuing to revert back to television work now and again, but was still able to turn out five more films before his career really hit the big-time. Another of his major films of that era was his portrayal of an Indian scout, Samuel Potts, a sidekick to Major Dundee (Charleston Heston) and Anthony Quinn in the Western *Major Dundee* (1965).

By 1966 the attraction of the Ian Fleming's novels being converted to film by director Terence Young had taken Fleming's fictitious super spy character James Bond (along with actor Sean Connery) and turned it all into a major box office extravaganza of the spy genre of films for that era. Connery's first venture for Young was the *Dr. No* film of ('62). His second was *From Russia with Love* ('63), and then *Goldfinger* ('64). Connery's last for a while was *Thunderball of* ('65). These popular films were soon being cloned by a whole slew of spin-off/copycat films, mostly coming out

---

* While we folks back here in the States, seem to go about our daily lives without regard as to how much, or to whom we might owe our immediate freedom to or at what cost, but those who were actually there and lived it, and lived to tell about it certainly do know. Several years ago for the 2008 presidential elections run, one of our senators stood up and ran for this post. The senator from Arizona, John McCain, was a downed fighter pilot who was captured and had to spend the remaining years of the Vietnam War in a POW camp and lived to tell of it. All though Senator McCain didn't make the presidency bid, he did give it a hard run and is still a highly respected member of our Congress.

of Europe. Some of those were eventually made into comical spoofs* that spoofed not only that spy genre of film but others as well.

Coburn soon found himself also associated within this genre of films with one of these uniquely spoof-related ventures for the big screen. Actually, it was a pair of films with a sequel following directly on the heels of the original. They were *Our Man Flint* (1966) and then *In Like Flint* (1967). These two Coburn films were far more successful than most of their counterpart copycat versions coming out of Europe. Although still a comedic spoof of the Bond films, in its own right, the successes of these two films can only be attributed to its star, James Coburn. This likeable, on-screen rogue portrays secret government agent, Derek Flint. Coburn's character of both films was supposedly *the* best at everything one could possibly be or conceive to be. A wiz at computers and electronics, he was a man of many talents and, in particular, that art of loving women. He was secretly at work to save the world from madmen and their various schemes from taking over world dominance. These were fun films for the era, and the audiences loved them.

Back in the saddle again, Coburn went on to make another Western in 1967. Although with it, being a comedy Western didn't seem to hurt his booming career in the least. It was a Blake Edwards production (of Pink Panther fame). This film called *Waterhole no. 3* was also a big box office hit. It starred Coburn as Lewton Cole along with Carroll O'Connor, Margaret Blye, Claude Akins, Bruce Dern, Joan Blondell, and James Whitmore.

---

* Popular "Spoofers", as it were, was the Italian duo who simply went by *Franco e Ciccio* of the 1960's era. Franco Franchi played the dunce of the pair who suffered in each film a multitude of humiliations in one form or another. His partner, Ciccio Ingrassia, was the straight man of the pair similar to the old Bud Abbott straight man to Lou Costello (*Abbott and Costello*) American comedy team of years gone by. Or another, if we remember, was Dean Martin (who wasn't always the crooner/singer) was the straight man to Jerry Lewis and his slapstick antics that were so popular years ago of *Martin and Lewis* fame.

Franco e Ciccio began their European antics with the spy genre *002 Agenti Segretissimi* (64) and continued with a moonwalk jaunt in space with *002 Operazione Luna* (65). These were so popular in Europe they continued to spoof other genres of filmmaking several of the Italian Westerns, which were extremely popular. Franco would constantly jabber in Italian throughout the film, but no, never mind, because their antics spoke for themselves. They make a fabulous career out of these onscreen antics and are still laughable today if the films are obtained via Internet.

Great casting for a superb film. The storyline concerned three Confederate soldiers who rob a transport load of gold from the army and hide it in the desert watering hole, thus the title Waterhole no. 3.

For Coburn's next venture in the movies, he would this time try his hand at producing and starring in a film. The picture was called *The Presidents Annalist* ('67). His role was that of Dr. Sidney Schaefer (a purely fictitious role) as analyst for the president of the United States. His costars were Godfrey Cambridge, Severn Darden, Joan Delaney, Pat Harrington, Will Geer, and William Daniels. Written and directed by Theodore J. Flicker, it was a real gas at the theaters. Nothing was sacred, and all things of the government here was subject to being spoofed, big and small alike. This was another box office success for Coburn who could now be officially classified as a producer among his many hats to wear.

His next film, however, didn't fare all that well at the box office. A US / British coproduction filmed in the UK called *Duffy*. Coburn portrayed the title character along with the likes of James Mason, James Fox, Susannah York, and John Alderton. The story was about a planned heist by two half brothers of monies belonging to their father that is being transported by ship. It was directed by Robert Parrish and really was an example of talent wasted of all those involved.

It was February of 1970 when the new monthly issue of *Playboy* magazine hit the newsstands. Coburn was involved with a nine-man panel of professionals holding discussions concerning the Drug Revolution that had hit a wave in this country during that era in time. His fellow panelists from lawyer / civil servant Harry J. Anslinger, to Literary Critic, Lesie Fiedler and included the eminent Psychologist Bada Ran Dass. Also, there was Author William S. Burroughs and John Finator, director of the *Food and Drug Administration Bureau of Drug Abuse Control*, which had merged with the *Federal Bureau of Narcotics* back in 1968 to help put a lid on illegal drug use in this country. Another was *Berkeley* professor and faculty member Joel Fort and lawyer Joseph S. Oteri of Boston's *Crane, Inker and Oteri*—also, Alan Watts an Episcopal minister and doctor of Divinity with degrees in theology as well as an authority on Zen Buddhism. Quite a prestigious group *Playboy* had pulled together for this session, and here was our actor James Coburn right in the middle of it.

Here in front of God and every *Playboy* reader here and abroad Coburn confronts the hands of fate and admits before all that he'd tried LSD and liked it! He freely admitted that he, "Coburn had experimented with LSD, under medical supervision, in the years before it was made illegal and remained convinced of its potential value to many users." He went on to add when the discussion got around to the benefits of LSD (tripper) vs. peyote cactus and other so-called psychedelic drugs. "I took both LSD and Peyote several times under the supervision of a psychologist, in order to find out if it was possible to attain the religious experience associated with these drugs. I found it an exciting enrichment of my awareness and one that I would never have thought possible before in my ordinary life."

Rocking on now, as we continue into the 1970s with more of Coburn's film work, though many were of lesser significance than others, especially to his Western fans, they were nevertheless just that many more added to his repertoire of film work achievements. That is, until we arrive at a one significant change in 1971. This was the highlight of his career as far as we, his fans, are concerned. During this period in time, we find that Italian director Sergio Leone, now off his unforgettable *Dollar* trilogy that had starred Clint Eastwood, would once again attempt to commandeer James Coburn for one of his films. His persuasion efforts this time wouldn't all be for naught as Coburn this time accepted the role. The film's title was to be called *Duck You Sucker* ('71). James Coburn would star as Irishman John H. Mallory. His costar would be none other than Rod Steiger as Mexican revolutionary Juan Miranda. Even as many of Leone's more successful predecessors had successfully involved themselves with politically motivated films of the era, Leone would now become a part of that throng himself.

It was actually to be a Leone film project, but for the direction, they had assigned Giancarlo Santi, a veteran director of the genre to fill in for the maestro Leone. (Possibly the big man, now a major filmmaker had too many other irons in the pot to keep him occupied, so the direction was to be farmed out). However, it seems that when Coburn and Steiger both found this out, they balked at working and claimed they had signed on to do a Leone film, and they wouldn't work until Leone direct them himself. He would, they assumed, be their director when they had signed on. Unwilling, but caught here between a rock and a hard place about to lose both his stars at the eleventh hour, Leone took over the film direction, pushing Santi into the already vastly bulging workload of the second-unit director position.

Set in 1913 Mexico, passing through Irish mercenary fighter, Mallory gets involved with the revolution and sides with Juan Mirandi (Steiger) who fights for *Viva Revolution* along with Pancho Villa after the assassination of people-favored Francisco Madero. This latest revolt was against the current dictator Huerta who stepped into power after the death of Madero. Revolution is a messy situation in any language to be sure.

Duck You Sucker, the films working title, would be changed for the US distribution to *A Fistful of Dynamite*. We can only assume so as to cash in or coincide with the Leone/ Eastwood *Dollar* film trilogy popularity. Coburn's next Italo-Western was to follow in quick session and was to be called *Una Ragione per Vivere . . . una Ragione per Morire! (A Reason to Live . . . A Reason to Die!)* (a.k.a. *Massacre at Fort Holman*) ('72). Coburn's role was that of Union Colonel Pembroke. Directed by Tonino Valerii one of the better Italian mainstream directors of the era, taken from a scripting by Valerii and Ernesto Gastaldi, which actually had been a liberal rework obviously inspired by the war film *The Dirty Dozen*, here put to a Civil War setting circa 1865 as the war is finally drawing to a close. Coburn's costars were Telly Savalas as Confederate major ward and Bud Spencer (Carlo Pedersoli) as condemned Yankee soldier Eli Sampson. Plot was similar to the war film as the colonel handpicked a seven-man squad of prisoners of war in hopes to recapture his fallen Fort Holman now held by the Confederates under control of major ward. It seems, all of Europe had money in this film project as it was an Ital/ Fr/ Spa and West-German coproduction.

Coburn's adventure into those wonderful *Spaghetti* Westerns of the day ended with this *Fort Holman* film. He returned back to the States, his wife of some thirteen years and his two children. His next film, another Western was *Pat Garrett and Billy the Kid* (1973). It starred Coburn as a lawman Garrett and Kris Kristofferson as the Kid. With direction by the noted Sam Peckinpah and a jam-up cast of favorites still couldn't seem to rescue this tired rendition of the old story of rivalry between the law and the outlaw. Seemingly so, it flopped at the box office.

The year 1976 was to be significant for Coburn, one to this marriage, and the other was a temporary end to his making of movies for a while. His last venture in film of that era would be with director Sam Peckinpah, where Coburn's starring role was that of a disgruntled German soldier at the Russian front in *Cross of Iron* (1977). It was about this time that he and longtime wife, Beverly, was going through trying times for the whole family when he up and deserted them in 1977 for a new live-in relationship with singer-songwriter Lynsey De Paul. For his career in films, he managed to stay in the limelight during this era by being constantly in the tabloids and also by writing two popular songs with De Paul called "Melancholy Melon" and "Losing the Blues for You." Both of these appeared in her then latest album called *Tigers and Fireflies*. The Coburn's official divorce came later in 1979, April 12 to be exact.

It was during this time in his life he began real sufferings of bouts with his rheumatoid arthritis. As it had worsened over the recent years, he found some of these sessions with the affliction would leave him completely drained and too weak even to work. For long periods, he would nearly be immobilized because any sort of movement or just standing even was a severe challenge. For ten years or more, he suffered through conventional treatments, which seemed to lead him nowhere. Finally, as a last resort, he then tried a holistic type of therapy, which seemed to make real improvements in his way of life. It was only then when he returned to small television roles, bit parts at first, even venturing into television commercials for the first time in his career.

One of his most noted was for the *Schlitz Brewing Company*, advertising their brand of beer. Later, he admitted on a talk show that he really didn't care for beer's taste.

> Coburn, we can only imagine, tried many a cure or relief giver over the years battling that terrible crippler rheumatoid arthritis. Back in the fall of 1991, he stated for a brief interview seen in *Westerns . . . All'Italiana!* A fanzine of the film genre, that he had only recently tried holistic medicines for his arthritis and that he now felt good again. He went on to add a couple of lines below about a new venture he was involved with at that time.

It was during this period that he had begun to look at possible alternatives to acting. He had thought long and hard about it, and since the 1980s, he had slacked off on his appearances as best he could doing mostly MTV movies, which weren't much more than cameo shots for various films and, of course, always falling back on his regular television appearances kept the wolves away from the door, so to speak. He also would continue his TV commercial work as well. Possibly fans can remember not only the *Schlitz Beer* but also he was now doing *UPS* and *Acura Legend* car track voice-over commercials as well. Coburn said about these: "It's interesting work, a whole new technique. I had to learn to do the nuances. But the money's good." Hell, it seemed all the actors were doing something similar. After all, during this era in time, Lee Van Cleef was now back from Italy and was on the TV selling *Bavaria Beer*, *Suntory Old Whisky*, and *Cheetos* to snack on. All the while, continuing to do those cute *Midas Muffler* commercials with other stars like George Kennedy, Jack Palance, John Philip Law, and Bo Hopkins. They were indeed lucrative ventures that took little or no effort for an experienced actor.

Another lucrative venture he finally got involved with was the animated feature voice-overs. Similar in type, not at all unlike the old language dubbing but in many a mind's eye was much easier. Actor Henry Silva, after returning to the States from Europe, had gotten involved with these in the early 1990s himself with *Batman: The Animated Series* (cartoon). Coburn's main venture along these lines were with the cartoon series, *Captain Planet and the Planeteers* (1990-'92). His role for the series was that of Looten Plunder.

> After his long hiatus from his craft in movie work during the 1980s, Coburn had now resumed making films again with *The Young Guns II* ('90) as John Simpson Chisum. The film starred

> Emilio Estavez as Billy the Kid. Kiefer Sutherland was Doc and Lou Diamond Phillips as José Chavez. After the capture of two of the Kid's gang, Chisum offers up a solution to end the Kid's reign of terror for good. A $1,000 bounty for the death of the Kid! His next one was called *Hudson Hawk* ('91) with Bruce Willis who stars as Eddie Hawk. It seems Hawk a career criminal just released from prison plans on going straight. Then he is hoodwinked into committing just one more job, this time stealing some Leonardo da Vinci Art works, or they will kill his friend.

In 1992 he began his movie work in earnest with a new crime film called *The Hit List* ('93). It starred Jeff Fahey as Charlie Pike, a pro-hit man who instead of killing a target, his business was to infiltrate by whatever means necessary to eliminate those high-powered, white-collar criminals that the law normally doesn't, or won't touch. Pike worked for his friend and mentor Peter Mayhew (Coburn), who was a prominent attorney at law, and secretly headed a task force committee fully intent on wiping out certain organized crime factions throughout the countryside.

Back in the chips once again, or so it would appear, and with his last live-in love long gone, he now settled into a new relationship with one Paula O'Hara. Friends for a while, they finally decided to do the right thing and married on October 22, 1993. His son James Jr., born in 1961, was now working in the industry as a sound mixer. The daughter, Lisa, born in 1957, was now a website designer. All things were clicking right along. He loved just sitting back at home listening to music and playing his flute, which was exactly how he died, of a heart attack there in his Beverly Hills home on November 18, 2002. He was but seventy-four years old. Catman, or so we like to remember him as, will be sorely missed, not only for his film achievements, but his constant television work as well. RIP, Catman.

End.

- *Below is a listing of Coburn's European Westerns. Actually, we calculate his total movie involvement since the beginning was in the neighborhood of some 140 (+/−). With his TV work included for a grand total amount of 173, as was documented by IMDb.com. *Posters and the title picture are accredited to the Sebastian Haselbeck collection via his website www.spaghetti-westerns.net. Many thanks, Sebastian.*

JAMES COBURN'S *SPAGHETTI* WESTERNS

1971

Duck You Sucker, *(Giu La Testa);* a.k.a. *C'era una Volta . . . La Rivoluzione, (Once upon a Time . . . the Revolution);* a.k.a. *A Fistful of Dynamite*; Ital / Spa, Director Sergio Leone (Coburn as John Mallory) (10/29/71)

1972

A Reason to Live, a Reason to Die; *Una Ragione per Vivere, E Una per Morire)* a.k.a. *Massacre at Fort Holman*; Ital/Fr/Spa/W. Ger, Director Tonino Valerii (Coburn as Union Colonel Pembroke) (10/27/72)

This brings to a close James Coburn's *Spaghetti* Western credits for his European film work. Not monumental for sure, but are indeed lasting. As we think back, he could have been the actor that starred in Leone's first Western instead of Clint Eastwood. We often wonder, what would have been the outcome of the *Fistful of Dollars* film had that actually happened? It is entirely possible that the era of the *Spaghetti* Western may never have even gotten off the ground. Or it is equally quite possible it may have even surpassed its current status in the history archives of film. That is truly something to think about as we plop another DVD issue Western favorite form that era into our players, as we sit back and enjoy those wonderful years of the *Spaghetti* west.

End.

BIBLIOGRAPHY
(J. COBURN)

Betts, Tom, editor *WAI! (Westerns . . . All'Italiana)* Fanzine articles/ information on James Coburn:

Issue no. 3/4, vol. 1: *Massacre at Fort Holman* review by Rob Hale; "Record Checklist no. 4" *Duck you Sucker* by Don Trunick

Issue no. 17, vol. 3: "Once Upon a Time: Films of Sergio Leone" by Randall Larson

Issue no. 31, "Whatever Became of James Coburn" by Tom Betts

Issue no. 43, *Massacre at Fort Holman* by Mike McQuarrie; "The Critics Say!" A review of the film

Issue no. 54, "A Brief Chat with James Coburn" by Ernest Farino; *A Fistful of Dynamite* film review by Lee Broughton

BFI Companion to the Western, the (1993) (ref), edited by Edward Buscombe, *British Film Institute,* UK. Originally published by *Andr`e Deutsch Ltd.,* London, 1988; pp. 332

Connolly, Bill, editor *Spaghetti Cinema* Fanzine: Tidbits on Coburn and/or his Euro films.

Cumbow, Robert C., *Once Upon a Time: The Films of Sergio Leone*, (1987) published by *Scarecrow Press inc.,* NJ and London

Frayling, Christopher, *Something to Do with Death* (2000) *Faber & Faber Ltd.,* London, UK., Information on James Coburn and related films by S. Leone

Halliwell, Leslie, *The Filmgoer's Companion* (1975)(ref), *Avon Book Publishers,* NY.

Haselbeck, Sebastian, owner/curator for Internet website: *www.spaghetti-western.net*

Internet, via: *www.anica.it* Ref: Film-production and date confirmation

Internet, via: *www.IMDB.com* Complete Films and TV listing for the actor plus trivia; also "Mini bio for James Coburn" by Firehouse

Interview via Internet website posting 1/30/2008: *www.celticcafe.com* ; "James Coburn: The Quintessential Cool" by Timothy Rhys with photos by Deverill Weekes

Lambert, Gilles, *The Good, the Dirty, and the Mean of Sergio Leone* (1976), *Solar Publishing,* Paris. French language printing, heavily illustrated with pictures in black and white.

Parish, James Robert, *Actors' Television Credits 1950-1972* (1973) (Ref) *Scarecrow Press, Inc.,* NJ.

Playboy magazine, February of 1970 issue: Panelist "Discussion on the Drug Revolution in America," J. Coburn as one of the prodigious members of this panel of professionals.

Quinlan's Illustrated Registry of Film Stars (1987) by Davis Quinlan, *Henry Holt Reference Books,* NY., pp 94

Tribute to James Coburn, by Alan Waldman via posting on *www.films42.com*

Video Hound's Golden Retriever (1994 edition) (ref) *Visible Ink Press,* a division of *Gale Research Inc.,* Detroit, MI. pp 1155

Weisser, Thomas, *Spaghetti Westerns: the Good, the Bad, and the Violent,* (1992) *McFarland,* Jefferson NC.

Western: All'Italiana (1998) (book I), by Antonio Bruschini and Federico de Zigno, *Glittering Images,* Firenze, Italy

The Western: The Complete Film Sourcebook (The Film Encyclopedia) (1983); by Phil Hardy, *William Morrow and Co, Inc.,* NY. Appendix no. 8, pp 331; 340-1

The World Almanac Who's who of Film (1987) by Thomas G Aylesworth and John S. Bowman, *Bison Books,* pp 98

CHUCK CONNORS

(1921-1992)

TALL MAN, WITH RIFLE

The opening scenes give way to the sound of sharp reports from a *Winchester* rifle. The rifle can be seen being levered rapidly as six shots ring out, fired simultaneously. With the smoke clearing, we see the spin of the rifle as it is twirled forward, then back cocking the big gun once again. The music then signals the start of the yet another episode of the long-running television series *The Rifleman.*

A success from its opening debut in 1958, this weekly series ran on into 1963 and starred Chuck Connors as the "tall man, with the rifle." His character was that of Lucas McCain, who acted as father, teacher, rancher, and well-known throughout the territory as the rifleman. With the season drawing to an end in 1963, it was promptly snapped up into syndication and was constantly replayed as reruns for years thereafter. Even today, it can still be seen on some cable/satellite networks that specialize in this type of vintage programming. In addition nowadays, complete season episode packs can be purchase for home video / DVD and the pleasure of watching an entire season at once or at one's leisure without commercials.

The tall man behind that rifle was in reality, Kevin Joseph Aloysius Connors, born on April 10, 1921, in Brooklyn, New York. His parents were immigrants that hailed from Newfoundland and, after arriving in New York, settled there in the borough of Brooklyn. Young Connors, along with a sister Gloria a couple of years younger, grew up on Brooklyn's west side. The father worked the New York docks as a longshoreman to put food on the table. After a formal childhood, he graduated from the *Adelphi Academy,* a private school his father had worked hard to see that he was able to attend.

As a youngster, he served as an altar boy and regular parishioner at *Our Lady of Perpetual Help Church* there in Bay Ridge, Brooklyn. Later, after finishing his high schooling, he went on to attend *Seton Hall College,* a Catholic college in South Orange, New Jersey. He entered the college on one of several scholarships that had been offered to him due to his amazing athletic abilities.

As a kid growing up from the depths of the dirt, sandlot playing field near his home to the superior athlete he would become, he would always attribute his successes in sports to one man who had helped steer him along and develop that confidence he needed to succeed in pro Sports. That man was John Flynn. Flynn took the young Connors under his wing during those sand-lot days and honed him into a superb recipient of an honored athletic scholarship.

His first pro game was with the *New York Yankees*, but this would only last one season before being called to duty during WWII. It was wartime and all able-bodied young man were egger to serve and fight for their country. Connors was no exception. He joined up with the army instead of awaiting the draft and was accepted on October 20, 1942. His occupation was then listed as a ski-instructor. However, after basic training at Fort Knox, as an infantryman, he would moonlight some by playing semipro basketball during his off-hours.

Later on, his was transferred to *West Point.* There he served out the balance of his tenure in the army as a tank warfare instructor to the many cadets at the academy. After his discharge from the service in 1946, he signed on with the *Boston Celtics* to play pro basketball. He is to be noted as the first player to ever shatter a backboard while playing in a game with the *Celtics* during this period.

After little more than one year with the *Celtics*, he decided to quit basketball and give baseball a try. He signed on with the *Brooklyn Dodgers*, as an amateur free agent player. It was during a game in Montreal, Canada, late in 1946 that he met the young lady who would become his wife and eventually the mother of his four sons. Her name was Betty Riddell, and they married in 1948. Connors remained with the *Dodgers* for five seasons, but unfortunately, he never made the major league roster and found himself being traded by the club he so loved.

He was officially traded in 1950 to the *Chicago Cubs*, where he resumed playing major league baseball with them during the first season of 1951. It was during this period in time, after having traveling the sport circles around the country for a decade now that he found himself changing in his way of thinking toward the games that he loved. Obviously coming to grips with himself, he found with his connections that by just looking a bit, he could pick up a few minor acting parts here and there that paid very well in deed. As always before, he had been a show-off type of guy, who loved doing crazy things that would sometimes get him in trouble with an angry umpire during games. Sometimes this fun would be severe enough causing him grief as he would find himself sent to the bench where he would sit out the rest of the game. Actually, this was how he had originally come about his nickname of Chuck.* It has been said that during games back when he was playing first base, he had this habit of hollering at the pitcher to "chuck it to me, baby, chuck it to me!"

Even back as far as when he was with the *Boston Celtics*, he had become sort of their public relation's "man at large." He would do the honors at all the after-dinner speeches and locker room publicity interviews. He loved that type being in charge, the man out front, the man who could talk that talk. The fans loved seeing and hearing him. After finally deciding that this show business was indeed for him, he went after it with zeal. In Hollywood, they welcomed him. His sports background and his outgoing personality—along with his tall, lean good looks—paid off as the parts began to roll in.

His very first bit part in a film was in *Pat and Mike* (1952) where he portrayed a police captain. Another film called *South Sea Woman* (1953)

* This was brought to the attention of the public when author David Fury wrote about this phenomenon acquiring of Connors nickname in his 1997 biography on Connors called, *The Man behind the Rifle* published by *Artist's Press*. Lord knows he had enough names already by birth, but we all knew none of those were Chuck!

cast him as Private Davey White. In this film, he got to work with stars Burt Lancaster and Virginia Mayo. Later on came *Target Zero* (1954) and then *Designing Woman* (1957). These were only a smattering of his work. By the time this '57 film hit the theaters, he was already an established name and present in both movies and television work.

With his thin smile and tall, lanky frame, he could easily be cast as the hero or the villain. Connors big break in films actually came in 1958 when the famous director William Wyler chose him over actors Richard Widmark and Van Heflin for a part in his new picture *The Big Country*. The film starred longstanding star-favorite Gregory Peck as the Terrill Ranch foreman, James McKay. Peck also co produced the project. It was an epic Western of some scale for 1958 that grossed well over $4 million intakes its first year in American release.

It was a bitter story of feuding and bloodshed between rival cattleman over water rights. The two families, one headed by Charles Bickford as Major Henry Terrill and the other by Burl Ives, as Rufus Hannassey (who won an Oscar) portrayed a hard-bitten rancher who forces his sons to take sides with him in this bitter battle between the two factions. Charlton Heston is Steve Leech the quick-tempered ranch foreman for the Hannassey bunch. Chuck Connors was cast as Buck Hannassey the one vicious son of Ives (for which he received critical acclaim as one of his best roles to date) that has the old man's temperament personified. Other supporting cast members included Jean Simmons and Carroll Baker.

During this time, in Connors early-acting years, he was also busy doing whatever television shows would come his way. He could be seen in such shows of the era like *City Detective*, *Superman* and the popular Westerns, *Gunsmoke* and *Wagon Train*. While he was in Denver, Colorado, during a 1958 promotion event for the just finished the *Big Country* film, Connors told reporters that he would soon be starring in a weekly series to be called *The Rifleman*.

It seems that a show that had aired earlier that year on the *Dick Powell's Zane Grey Theater* called *The Sharpshooter* had cast Connors as a proficient rifleman/rancher. His name was Lucas McCain. This show now considered a pilot show was so popular that before the year was out, the weekly series began in production. Simply called *The Rifleman*, it was an instant hit with young and old alike. Chuck Connors was on the road to fame now as an actor. The show ran through until the 1963 season ended with some 168 episodes under its belt. The show's storyline concerned a New Mexico rancher and recent widower, who, while homesteading this tough land, was trying to raise his son despite the many things against them. The son Mark was portrayed by young actor Johnny Crawford.

Courtesy of personal collection

As Connors's character went, Lucas McCain was a man certainly not to be reckoned with. At two hundred pounds plus and standing six feet and five inches tall, Connors's image was impressive. He could be seen carrying his modified *Winchester* rifle that had been altered for rapid fire. It sported a ring lever with which he could twirl the gun as he cocked it. This along with his imposing appearance alone would be enough to send the most ardent villain down the trail.

Every week they battled new and sometimes even old foes. They did battle with outlaws, Indians, and the weather. They battled sickness of both man and animal, but the next week, they were back for more. Some of the weekly guest stars were the likes of Claude Akins, James Coburn, and Sammy Davis Jr. who would appear from time to time on these episode shows.

One of these guest actors, yet mostly unknown other than being in character roles would soon become one of the noted international film stars of the European cinema. His name was Lee Van Cleef. LVC and Connors got along famously, and he would return again and again on the show averaging at least one episode a year from 1959 through 1962—four in all. The episodes were done for the *ABC Television* network. During the five years the show ran, Connors continued to ply his acting trade in the films marketplace and was quite popular in the movies as well.

It was in 1962, and the film was called *Geronimo* when Connors was bashed by the critics as being badly cast in the title role as the legendary Indian Chief Geronimo. Although the film was widely acclaimed as an outstanding film of its kind, Connors still received negative reviews. The film set in the 1880's deals with the surrender of the Indian chief and his followers to corrupt officials, which would eventually lead to a near-complete massacre of the entire Apache Indian race when they were forced to rebel against gruel and inhuman treatment while in captivity.

The great supporting cast included Adam West, Ross Martin, and Denver Pyle as the US senator who comes to the aid of the Indians by trying to prevent a brutal massacre by the Cavalry. Connors's costar in this film was Kamala Devi. She would later become his wife for his second venture into matrimony. They were married on April 10, 1963. (Connors's first marriage had ended in divorce back in 1961)

During the 1963 season run of *The Rifleman*, producer Dick Powell passed away from cancer. His contraction of this fatal death dealing disease was suspected as coming from his exposure to the desert fallout from the first atomic blasts of the early 1953. Powell had since used that desert area as a filming location for the John Wayne epic film called *The Conqueror.** This provocative subject and assumption would later be rehashed and discussed at length in a much later TV special in 1981 called "Did American Kill John Wayne?"

Befitting his Western image, Connors loved his horses as much as he loved the art of acting itself. From his horse ranch in the foothills of the Sierra Mountains of California, he raised breeding and training horses. He also kept busy during his off-acting hours with pet projects such as *The United Way* organization. Another of his pet projects over the years was his *Chuck Connors Invitational Golf Tournaments*, which sponsored the *Angel View Crippled Children's Foundation* of Hot Springs, California.

In addition to all this, he still found time to try his hand at writing some of the series scripts and teleplays over the years as well. We may also remember seeing him doing respected cowboy segments for *McDonald's* Hamburger commercials. All of this, though, would soon come to pass.

With the passing Dick Powell, Connors saw the beginning of the end. Knowing the end of this long-running series was now in sight, Connors

* This yet unconfirmed television special supposedly aired on *NBC* on March 7, 1981. It was narrated by Chuck Connors along with special guests Allison Powell, wife of the famed director Dick Powell. Others as guest were Bob Hope and Lee Van Cleef (who was also in the film), among others. The subject matter of this special was a discussion stemming from the 1955 filming of *The Conqueror*, which was filmed almost entirely on location in Utah near the old atom bomb testing range in Nevada.

would try his hand at a different type of weekly series next time around. The show called *Arrest and Trial* featured him as he portrayed an attorney Jim Egan was picked up, but only ran for one season. It was then back to the saddle again for Connors in a new Western series for television called *Branded.* This new show proved to be a hit with the audiences and had a successful run of some forty-eight episodes from 1964 until '66.

It was 1964 when Connors starred in the McEveety TV movie called *The Broken Saber.* A Western and actually a pilot for the purposed new and upcoming *Branded* TV show. It also starred longtime established actor MacDonald Carey. Its storyline concerned an embittered soldier, Jason McCord (Connors) who had been falsely tried and publicly denounced (branded) as a coward by the army. His dress saber broken in half; he was stripped of his rank and evicted from Calvary service.

The character Jason McCord would spend the rest of his life (run of the series) attempting to redeem himself in the eyes of the world and, moreover, himself. Actually, Jason McCord (Connors), as it turns out, the disgraced soldier, was working uncover for President Grant. The original series was directed by Bernard McEveety and had the type of story theme that could be branched off into an endless array of stories just fit for a weekly series. His friend Lee Van Cleef would appear in a couple of these show episodes as well. One such was called "The Richest Man in Boot Hill" for (*NBC*). Another in 1966 was "Call to Glory." Starring Connors as Jason McCord this episode contained segments, which also starred Van Cleef as Charlie Yates. It was shown in three parts, continued episodes on 2/27, 3/6, and 3/13 of 1966.

> **Note:* An interesting item here is that the first two parts of this "Call to Glory" episode was later compiled by *NBC* television for the overseas film markets. This compiled film was called "Ride to Glory." It consisted of using archive film segments from four different television episodes of the popular *Branded* weekly series that starred Chuck Connors as Jason McCord.
>
> Part one called "Call to Glory" (was aired originally on 2/27/1966). Part two called "Call to Glory II" (was aired 3/6/1966). A segment from a third episode was also used was from an earlier two-part episode called "Fill no Glass for Me" (part 1 aired on 11/7/65), which starred Robert Lansing in the role of General George Armstrong Custer.
>
> The fourth and final segments used for the movie also came from an earlier episode called "Now Join the Human Race," which starred Burt Reynolds. (This one had originally aired on 9/19/65.)

By 1966, actor Lee Van Cleef had already been to Italy and costarred with Clint Eastwood in director Sergio Leone's second of his trilogy of Westerns soon to be dubbed *Spaghetti* Westerns. Van Cleef was well on his way now as an international film star, and it appears that *NBC* was bound to cash in on his European popularity by compiling these segments of archived episodes for European distribution.

While this European publicity surely didn't hurt Connors any in the least, Van Cleef's rise to fame and popularity was probably the motive behind this hurried compilation efforts. Alas, the old style "romance-filled talkie" American formula Western we once knew was steadily being replaced by this new breed of Western movies from Europe. Operatic and stylish but most always violent in their content coupled with blaring music scores like none ever heard before. These films would from now on have a lasting effect on how Westerns of the future would be made.

Even one of our television series Westerns, like *The Virginian*, would test a variation of the *Spaghetti* formula for mature audiences of American primetime television. Another was the show called *The Wild, Wild West*, which starred Robert Conrad and Ross Martin and ran from the 1965 to 1969 seasons. It seems this series had also been compiled for feature shown overseas as well. Later, producers, seeing the popularity it had spawned in European film markets, took another run at a series with the TVM released of 1979 called *The Wild, Wild West Revisited*. They tried again for the another 1980 MTV called *More Wild, Wild West*. However, both of these after-the-series films failed to get a rise out of the older viewers who were now rapidly being replaced with a new, younger audience. Neither of these two follow-up MTV pilot shows was ever picked up for a season series.

Another popular compilation, this one from the *Branded* series was brought out by the end of 1966. This one was called *Blade Rider: Revenge of the Indian Nations*. This effort included segments derived from the same "Call to Glory" episodes, but used only parts 1 and 3. Segments were also used from the "Now Join the Human Race" episode. This feature appears to have delved into the friendly relationship between a black man (Gregg Morris), an Indian called Red Hand (Burt Reynolds), and the Charlie Yates character (Van Cleef). Intertwined here with the mediator between the three factions, Jason McCord character, who, working for President Grant (from the *Branded* series theme), was pushing the "live and let live" theory, which was being exploited here so as to offset an Indian uprising.

> *Note:* Connors's old buddy Lee Van Cleef was not in either of the two "Fill no glass for me" episodes or the one "Now Join the Human Race" episode. However, it is interesting to note that they had remained good friends and occasional drinking buddies since

> the early *Rifleman* days. They would resume their friendship while in Europe together and would remain friends long after returning to the States.

Before the end of the '66 season and the *Branded* TV series itself, Connors did another film with director McEveety. This one was called *Ride beyond Vengeance*. Scripted by Andrew J. Fenady of *Fenady and Associates*, the story had been taken from the novel *Night of the Tiger* written by Al Dewlen. With McEveety directing this film, it was said to have been the American response to the Italian Western of the day. The reference here made directly as to the film's violent content. In its entirety, the film ran some 110 minutes but was cut by 10 to 100 minutes for the American showings because of its excessive violence.

The film was in reality a dark and gloomy piece of work that starred Connors as one Jonas Trapp. Some eleven years earlier in the story Trapp, a trapper and hunter had left his young bride at the homestead he had built and went off to earn his stake by buffalo hunting. Trapped in a war and years since gone by, Trapp finally returns to the area and the nearby town only to be attacked by outlaws and relived of the $17,000 he had accumulated and was carrying with him. He was robbed, beaten, and physically branded (with a hot branding iron) by some of the local baddies. Upon pulling himself together, he then sets out to avenge his assailants and retrieve his stolen grubstake he had intended to buy cattle with. The film carried a good supporting cast with the likes of Michael Rennie as the town banker Brooks Durham, Joan Blondell, Bill Bixby, and Claude Akins. The movie introduced newcomer Kathryn Hays as Jessie Trapp's bride, who now is about to marry banker Durham. However, during the course of the film, she realizes she still loves Trapp. Action is aplenty, but the film seems thwarted by a script that's too complex.

Afterward, Connors once again delves back into another weekly television series. This time with a new show called *Cowboy in Africa*. This new weekly series would run successfully for two seasons from 1967-1968. Connors portrayed one Jim Sinclair, a Texan who runs a Western-style ranch in Africa. The series was seemingly a takeoff from the 1967 movie called *Africa, Texas Style*, that starred Hugh O'Brien.

As the 1968 season was coming to an end, Connors began to consider other options of acting work. With Clint Eastwood now gone from Europe after completing four films for the Italian directors, his friend Lee Van Cleef was by now the reigning star of the *Spaghetti* Westerns. Other Americans were also in Italy churning out these popular new Western movies. Burt Reynolds had just returned from making his one and only of the genre called *Navajo Joe* for Italian director Sergio Corbucci.

Others still in Europe and going strong at this time were Guy Madison, Richard Harrison, Wayde Preston, and Walter Barnes, to mention just a few. These unique Italian made Westerns were by now the rage. These original coproduced films by Italian, Spanish, West German, and French production teams would begin to involve other European countries and money to fuel this newest vein of the international film industry. Soon Yugoslavian, Israel, Hong Kong, and eventually British and U.S. companies as well as Mexican film moguls would get into this lucrative market. Chuck Connors was not different—after all, this was where the money was, no doubt, about it.

Connors's first *Spaghetti* Western was a 1968 release called *Kill Them All and Come Back Alone*, an Italian / Spanish film coproduction from Italian director Enzo G. Castellari (Enzo Girolami), a veteran of the Italian cinema. Produced by Edmondo Amati, it was film in color and scope with a running time of some one hundred minutes. It also co starred American expatriate actor Frank Wolff and bevy of accomplished genre regulars of multi nationalities. The music score was by genre-favorite Francesco De Masi obscuring his Italian origin behind his Anglo pseudonym of Frank Mason.

By the time this film aired in the European cinema, their audiences had already been privy to the compilation reruns of the old *The Rifleman* TV series shows as well as compilation movies like *Ride to Glory* and the more recent movie *Ride Beyond Vengeance.* This ensured Connors a large following of the Euro public. This new film concerned a band of Confederate mercenaries, among them Clyde Link who leads an assault on a Union Army fort during the Civil War in search of a known stashed gold shipment.

His next film was a Dino De Laurentiis production called *The Deserter* (1970). This Italian/ US/ Yugoslavian coproduction contained an all-star cast of favorites. Chuck Connors, though not the film's star, definitely had a presence in the film. Directed by Burt Kennedy and scripted by Clair Huffaker, this action-packed feature is still worth seeing even by today's standards. The film starred Bekim Fehmin as Captain Carter and Connors as Reynolds along with other favorites Richard Crenna as the captain and major adversary of Carters. Others were Slim Pickins, Woody Strode, John Huston as the colonel and Ricardo Montalban as Natchai the Indian scout. The storyline deals with a handpicked team of elite fighting men. All killers were brought together to work undercover for the government and help quell the serious Indian uprising throughout a certain Western territory. Carter has an underlying reason for being on the force, a revenge wish against the Apache since the savages had previously tortured, skinned, and killed his wife. Even the Cavalry of which he is a part of is against him until they find they need his services and experiences in tracking and killing the red devils.

In 1971, Connors again went with the Italian filmmakers with yet another Western, a Spanish / British coproduction from *Granada Films* called, *Pancho Villa.* Telly Savalas starring in the title role that deals with the life and times of the legendary and controversial revolutionary leader of Mexico. A strong supporting cast included Clint Walker (in his one and only genre film) who during the 1950s starred in his own long-running television series for *Warner Bros* called *Cheyenne.* Others included in this *Villa* film was Chuck Connors as Colonel Wilcox and Anne Frances (also in her only genre film). The movie was a peek into the life and era of the bandit turned revolutionary, told and truthfully interpreted by the actor Savalas, who, with screenwriter Julian Halevy, co scripting actual accounts especially for the movie. The film was directed by Eugenio Martin and was produced by Bernard Gordon.

> *Note:* Of interest here is that this is the film renowned for one scene that goes down in film history as it depicts a massive train wreck when two oncoming trains on the same track collide head-on. In addition, trivia for our Chuck Connors reports that it was during this year that he and second wife, Kamala Devi, was divorced after approximately eight-plus years of marriage.

Another Western Connors was involved with about this era in time was *The Proud and the Damned* (1973). This film starred Chuck Connors as Will Hansen. Other starring were Jose Greco, Cesar Romero, Arron Kincaid, and Anita Quinn. The storyline deals with a couple of ex-soldiers from the Civil War turned mercenaries, seeking more fighting and gold, drifting down into South Central America and getting involved with the people there and their local revolutions. Connors continued to make other films in Europe from time to time afterward, but would continue to drift back to the United States resuming his television career. It was in 1973 when he embarked upon another TV series. This short-lived show one was called *The Thrill Seekers.* Connors acted as narrator and host for this documentary about stuntmen who defy death in some instances to perform in the movies for public recognition.

It was about this time that Connors decided to become a Restaurateur and was involved opening a chain of Western-style eating establishment about California and in Florida. During this era we already had eateries like *Arthur Treacher's Fish 'n' Chips* and *Roy Rogers Hamburgers.* Now the grand opening of the US-1 Highway, Eau Galle / Melbourne, Florida, edition of the chain called *Chuck Connors Steakhouse and Lounge* was a gala affair with Connors doing the honors that night himself, serving up baked beans and cold slaw buffet style for his patrons of the evening. The checkout area of the wooden-paneled foyer contained framed autographed picture of the actor in films and in baseball uniform of the *Brooklyn Dodgers* and *Chicago*

Cubs. As I remember, the meals were great and prices reasonable. However, this restaurant adventure for Connors seemed short-lived, and it disappeared entirely a year or so later.

During the year 1976, Connors was nominated for an *Emmy* for his television miniseries role as Tom Moore, the white slaver in *Roots*. It was during the next year 1977 that Chuck Connors remarried once again. This time her name was Faith Quabius, an aspiring actress he had met while during of the 1973 film *Soylent Green*. She portrayed an attendant while his was a starring role as tab fielding. Recently divorced from second wife Kamala in '72, we assume he struck up an acquaintance with the lovely Miss Quabius. They resumed working together on Connors latest film of 1973 called *The Mad Bomber*, starring as William Dorn the sicko bomber. Her role was that of Martha. They made two other films together, one a TVM called *Banjo Hackett: Roamn' Free* (1976) in which he portrayed Sam Ivory and her role was that of Ruttles. Their next and last movie together was called *Standing Tall*. This Quinn-Martin MTV movie starred Robert Forester as Luke Shasta and Will Sampson as Lonny Moon in key roles. Others were L. Q. Jones, Buck Taylor, Linda Evans as Jill Shasta, Chuck Connors as Major Roland Hartline and Connors's then wife, Faith Quabius, as Annie Klinger. The story has to do with a rancher in 1934 Montana, who is constantly being harassed by a land baron and his gang of gunsuls trying to persuade him into selling out and leaving. Thus, he is forced to dig in and stand against them.

Connors did another MTV film about this time in 1979 called *Tourist Trap* in which he was renowned as stating at the time as the reason he took this role as Mr. Slausen was because he wanted to become the Boris Karloff of the '80s. That all may very well have been; however, he and Faith, his third wife after only a couple of years together, was ending their relationship in another divorce for our actor.

All the while, Connors was involved with American television; he continued to keep up his presence in the movie world with movies around the world like *Day of the Assassin* (1979) from director Brian Trenchard-Smith. This action film starred Richard Roundtree as Fessler and Chuck Connors as Fleming. Also starred was Glenn Ford in a cameo appearance as Christakis and Henry Silva in a small cameo part as well. Next we have *The Virus* (1980). This was a big-budgeted Japanese production filmed on locations in Alaska, USA, Antarctic, Canada, Peru, and Japan. A large supporting cast of Americans included George Kennedy, Bo Svenson, Edward James Olmos, and Glenn Ford—again, in cameo portraying the US president Richardson. Also included were Chuck Connors as *HMS Nereid* nuclear submarine Captain McCloud and Henry Silva as General Garland. A story about our world in turmoil after a man-made military virus gets loose when a private plane, transporting the germ, crashes and spreads like wildfire throughout the entire world's population, killing all it comes in contact with.

Another film Connors was associated with during this era was called *The Women of Jeremia*, A Mexican / Spanish coproduction for a released of 1979. This film was actually toned down from its borderline soft-porn original release and later after dubbing was shown to American theaters/ video and television and purported as a reissued Mexican production. This comedic Western starred popular Mexican actor Jorge Rivero as Jeremia's Sanchez. Rivero was a huge hit in Europe during this era. He made loads of Italian and Spanish films as well as those of his homeland, with some South American movies as well. This film originally was a racy little story about a minister, Sanchez, who has four virgin daughters. Then he inherits an across the border, bordello in Mexico. The film also starred Chuck Connors as Jonathan Dalton, Michael Conrad as Spencer Dalton, and American / European favorite actor John Ireland in cameo as the judge. It was reported as being filmed in Durango, Mexico, with primarily a Mexican supporting cast. It was directed by Spaniard Ramon Fernandez, but when shown to the US audiences re titled as *Bordello* in the reworked dubbed edition, the director took on the pseudonym of Ray Fellows. Alfredo Manas is credited with the story and screenplay. Amazing what a little dubbing can do, isn't it?

Other box office hit for Connors during this era was *Airplane 2: The Sequel* (1982) with Connors as the Sarge. Another was *The Hit Man* (1982) which Connors starred in as Sam Fuller, assassin for hire. And the same year, he starred in *The Vals* (a.k.a. *The Valley Girls*), in which he portrayed the father of one of the girls named Trish. The story concerns four young Valley girls from affluent Hollywood families who, being bored with the shopping and mall crawling / party life, get involved with John Carradine as Mr. Stanton who runs a home for orphaned boys. About to lose funding for the institution, the girls go to work finding their worth and proceed to save the orphanage at the same time, involved in their own personal war against sleazy drug dealers. As fans of Chuck Connors, this was not one our favorite movies to have seen him in.

Later during the year 1983, once again, Connors could be found in another TV series. This time in a short-lived soap series in which he portrayed the cantankerous head of household, Jeb Hollister, for the show called *The Yellow Rose*. This show actually ran only one season and twenty-two episodes. Though Connors was deemed a regular for the show, he actually wasn't in every episode.

Back to the movies again for *Hell's Heroes* ('87) was more to our liking as this Italian war drama brings back the action this actor is noted for. It starred American (ex-*Tarzan* star) Miles O'Keeffe as Sergeant Darkin who leads a ban of mercenaries behind the lines on an ill-fated rescue mission. It also starred Fred Williamson as Feather, Gabriele Gori as Bronx, and Chuck Connors as the US Senator Morris. This *Spaghetti* war film was directed by Stelvio Massi. Massi also acted as cinematographer for the film using the pseudonym of Stefano Catalano. Maurizio Mattei was the film acting executive producer. The story and script were credited to Roberto Leoni. Also, in 1987, we find Connors in yet another television series. This characterization for Connors was somewhat offbeat to any of his previous roles but, nevertheless, a fair show in this author's opinion. This pilot show was simply called *Werewolf*. Connors portrays Captain Janos Skorzeny, an older master werewolf. This TVM was picked up as a series and ran for twenty-nine episodes, one season (1987-'88) for the *FOX* network. Other than the original pilot, Connors actually appeared in only two of the succeeding weekly episodes. No. 2 called "Nightwatch" and no. 4 called "The Black Ship." This interesting series, to my discontent, only ran for one season ending in '88.

For 1989 Connors's began the year with a new series for *FOX* called *Paradise* where he portrayed an older Gideon McKay. This series ran into the 1990s with its last season. In one of these episodes, they featured a now-grown Johnny Crawford. This episode reunited the two for the first time since the close of the old *The Rifleman* series back in 1963. Since those *The Rifleman* years, Connors had been almost constantly in demand for (MC) projects, narration or show host projects. Television guest spots were numerous as was award shows, which he was either host or recipient. He had been a frequent visitor to the White House during the tenure of the Nixon administration and was considered a friend by then President Richard Nixon. He had already received his star on *Hollywood's Walk of Fame* early on back in 1958. During the year 1990 began a year or two of his receiving honorary awards at specific function throughout the country. In 1990, at a Western film festival in Sheridan, Wyoming, he received a *Lifetime Achievement Award.*

A year later, he was inducted into the *Hall of great Western performers of the National Cowboy and Western Heritage Museum* in 1991. During that same year, he also was elected into the *Cowboy Hall of Fame* there in Oklahoma City, Oklahoma, as well. Many, many nationally known stars now belonged to this very prestigious group of honor. Among some of the better-known names are John Wayne, Henry Fonda, Gregory Peck, and Gary Cooper, just to mention a few.

> *Note*: Interesting tidbit to point out here was that while employed as a part-time commentator for a live televised "Monday Night Baseball" game on television, he will go down in the annals

of Baseball as the only person who ever used the f-word while commenting on any game that was on the air. Needless to say, this pretty much ended his commentating / acting career in television.

After having been in mostly good health throughout his life, it was somewhat of a shock to friends and family when he was admitted to *Cedar-Sinai Medical Center* there in Los Angeles during the early days of November 1992. He had, we understand, been suffering from the lingering symptoms of pneumonia. However, when admitted, and after going through a bank of tests, he was later diagnosed with having advanced stages of lung cancer. Approximately one week later, at 2:00 p.m., November 10, 1992, Chuck Connors passed away.

Over his lifespan of seventy-one years, he had ventured into matrimony three different times and was thrice divorced. He is survived by four sons, Michael, Jeffery, Steven, and Kevin. The mother of these four boys, Connors's first wife, Elizabeth Jane Riddell, was who he had married back in 1948 while on the Baseball circuit with the *Dodgers.* This marriage lasted some thirteen years, but ended in 1961 in a divorce.

Note: Jeff Connors took an interest in his father's trade of acting. It seemed he had small parts as an adolescent youngster in three different episodes of the *The Rifleman* series. His first was in "Tension" (1959), then "The Schoolmaster" (1960) and last was "First Wages" (1961). Probably due to the divorce and the father's separation from the immediate family caused a twelve-year lull in young Jeff's acting career. Then we find he was again involved with his father in a film called *The Mad Bomber* (1973) where his part was that of a teenager on the street. Again, after this one-shot film as a teen, he wouldn't be involved in films again until the 1980s. Then we find him back on the big screen for another film called *A Bridge to Hell* (1987). Jeff's role in this film is yet unconfirmed. Since this Italian / Yugoslavian coproduced film by Umberto Lenzi, no other films have surfaced for him in recent years.

Connors remained very close with his offspring throughout his career despite his constant travel due to demands of his career. The boys will surely miss their father as he was not only a big man to look up to, but also an accomplished career actor as well. Also, he will be missed greatly by his longtime devoted secretary of many years, Rosie Grumley. We his fans, also feel their loss. For years, hardly a day went by while skimming pages of the local *TV Guide* that our eyes didn't glance and lock onto the words *The*

Rifleman, indicating it was to be shown somewhere on one of the many cable / satellite channels as reruns for that week. "The tall man, with rifle" has now been laid to rest, but in our hearts and minds, we will always remember "This big man with his long gun."

End.

- Below is a complete filmography of Connors Euro Westerns. The dates are aligned as close as possible with information currently at hand, plus international release dates included. **Posters and title picture are accredited to the Sebastian Haselbeck collection via his website www.spaghetti-westerns.net. Many thanks, Sebastian.*

CHUCK CONNORS
SPAGHETTI WESTERNS

1967
Kill Them All and Come Back Alone *(Ammazza Tutti E Torna Solo)*; Ital / Spa, Director Enzo G. Castellari (Enzo Girolami) (Connors as Clyde Link) (12/31/68)

1968/2002
- ***Western, Italian Style***; Ital (documentary); Director Patrick Morin.

A wonderfully informative piece of film work on the popular European-Western movies so affectionately dubbed the *Spaghetti* Westerns. This 1968 filmed insight into the genre greets us with an all inspiring look behind the entry walls at the then active, now defunct *Cinecitta Studios* there in Rome. There we visit stuntman as he readies himself for a scene take in his full Western garb. A quick visit to studio armory, where we find an impressive collection of guns and rifles of all types ready for action, including a demonstration of how destructive the waxed bullets used in some of the shooting scenes, can be in real life, shown breaking a saloon window.

Viewers are subjected to the world of the *Spaghetti* Western containing interviews with such artists as Chuck Connors on set of his *Kill them All and Come Back Alone* (1967) film and by the director Enzo G. Castellari (Enzo Girolami). This documentary had never been commercially issued prior to this, a 2002 *Blue-Underground* Western DVD four pack, which was a compilation of *Spaghetti* Westerns, including one popular film *Run, Man Run* (1967) on which this documentary was included in the disc *Extras.*

1970

The Devil's Backbone; *La Spina Dorsale Del Diavolo* a.k.a. *Deserter*; US/ Ital/ Yugo, Director Niska Fulgizzi / Burt Kennedy (Connors as Reynolds) (12/4/70)

1971

The Challenge of Pancho Villa, *EL Desafio De Pancho Villa* a.k.a., *Pancho Villa*; Spa / US, Director Eugenio Martin (Connors as the general) (1971)

1979

- ***The Women of Jeremias;*** *Las Mujeres De Jeremias* a.k.a. *Bordello*; Spa/ Mex/ US (MTV-Western); Director Ray Fellows (Amadeo Alvarez) and Ramon Fernandez (Chuck Connors as the elder Jonathan Dalton) (1979)

End.

BIBLIOGRAPHY
(C. CONNORS)

Betts, Tom, editor *WAI! (Westerns . . . All'Italiana)* Fanzine articles/ information on Chuck Connors;

Issue no. 35 fall 1992, *Boot Hill*: Chuck Connors obituary

Issue no. 37 Article: "In remembrance, Tall Man, with Rifle" by Tom Prickette; "Chuck Connors *Italo*-filmography" by Tom Betts

BFI Companion to the Western, The (1993) (Ref), Edited by Edward Buscombe, *British Film Institute,* UK. Originally published by *Andr`e Deutsch Ltd.,* London, 1988; pp. 355-356

Connolly, Bill, editor *Spaghetti Cinema* Fanzine articles/info on Chuck Connors and/or his films:

Issue no. 33 December 1988, Interview with Connors director, Enzo G. Castellari and a *Go Kill and Come back Alone* review by Bill Connolly

Fury, David, *Chuck Connors: The Man Behind the Rifle* (1997) *Artists Press,* MN.

Halliwell, Leslie, *The Filmgoer's Companion* (1975) (Ref), *Avon Book Publishers,* NY.

Haselbeck, Sebastian, owner/curator for Internet website: *www.spaghetti-western.net*

Internet, via: *www.anica.it* Ref: Film-production and date confirmation

Internet, via: *www.IMDB.com* "Mini biography for Chuck Connors" plus film listing review

Prickette, Tom, *Tall Man, with Rifle* previously unpublished manuscript of 1992, partially used in *WAI! Memorial issue* no. 37 with filmology reworked by Tom Betts

Quinlan's Illustrated Registry of Film Stars (1987) by Davis Quinlan, *Henry Holt Reference Books,* NY., pp: 97

Video Hound's Golden Retriever (1994 edition) *Visible Ink Press,* a division of *Gale Research Inc.,* Detroit, MI. pp 1158

Weisser, Thomas, *Spaghetti Westerns: the Good, the Bad, and the Violent,* (1992) *McFarland*, Jefferson NC.

Western: All'Italiana (books I, II, and III), by Antonio Bruschini and Federico de Zigno, *Glittering Images,* Firenze, Italy; book I, 1998; book II, 2001 and book III, 2006

The Western: The Complete Film Sourcebook (The Film Encyclopedia) (1983); by Phil Hardy, *William Morrow and Co, Inc.,* NY. Appendix no. 8, pp

The World Almanac Who's who of Film (1987) by Thomas G Aylesworth and John S. Bowman, *Bison Books,* pp: 102

CLINT EASTWOOD

(1930—)

FROM DROVER TO MOVIE MOGUL

The words "Head 'em up, Move 'em out!" brings to mind the popular *CBS* television series called *Rawhide*. This series costar character of Rowdy Yates was portrayed by bit contract player Clint Eastwood. His name however, will forever be associated with this long-running series as one of the ultimate primetime TV Westerns hits of all time.

Clint Eastwood's life in Hollywood and his career jump from television to international film star, then director, and eventually movie mogul status has been played to death in the various media accountings, and rightfully so. This man's meager beginnings in Hollywood, first as a contract bit player for *Universal International Film Studios*, he would go on to become one of most renowned and celebrated moviemakers of all time. He was schooled early in his craft by the top names of the business. Along with a keen eye for what makes a movie tick, he has parlayed his years of experience and knowledge into an award-winning career that has so far lasted for some five decades to date. He has, without a doubt, learned his craft well.

He was born as Clinton Eastwood Jr., San Francisco, California, on May 31, 1930. He came from a mixed stock of Dutch, Scottish, Irish, and English heritages. His father Clinton Eastwood Sr., a steel worker, always advised his son to "Show 'em what you can do, and don't worry about what you're gonna get." We as fans of this fine actor / filmmaker can certainly testify to that. A big baby at birth, eleven pounds and six ounce, his beloved mother Margaret Ruth Runner Eastwood lived a long fruitful life basking in the glow of her son's career accomplishments. She passed away on February 7, 2006, at the ripe old age of ninety-seven. She was a proud grandmother to her son's eight children and great-grandmother to at least one daughter born in 1994 to Clint's son Kyle Eastwood.

Mostly during the war years when his mom and dad worked in the factories, he and his younger sister Jean stayed off and on with his grandmother out in a rural mountain area on her chicken ranch outside of Sunol, California. There he learned to appreciate the out of doors, hunting and fishing. He had a cousin that had some horses, so they rode quite a bit.

During his high school years he was involved with at least one play that he sort of blew by not being very interested at the time. He said then he would never act. He was interested in other things at the time like sports, girls, and tinkering with old cars. He had no interest back then of standing up in front of a class of peers who were giggling at him from the back rows, while he made an ass out of himself. To help his family bring in money, he baled hay for a while. Also, he did some logging in and around Paradise, California, and later worked for a while with the Forestry Service fighting fires.

After his graduation from *Oakland High School* in 1948, his dad and mom had made the decision to move the family down into Texas looking for work. Clint decided he'd stay there in California and parted on friendly terms with the family. He had always got along great with his parents and respected them very much. He took his rattletrap old car and his entire belongings in a small bag and was off to work in Oregon at a lumber camp. Afterward, he wandered around California working at odd jobs when and where he could find them.

About a year later, he did work his way down Texas way so as to could visit with the family for awhile. He got a job there working for the local *Bethlehem Steel Mill.* His job was as the general clean-up / maintenance guy around the huge blast furnace. He remembered later how the heat was so super intense. Another thing was, he hated the job at the time but said the pay was good. His next venture was down in Renton, Texas, where he worked for the county there as a lifeguard and swimming instructor.

Always on the move, not staying in one place too long was kind of a trend he had adapted from his folks. His being born during those Depression years sometimes haunted him in his early formative years, since they were traveling quite a bit as his dad's work took him from town to town, and job to job.

Times had picked up since those earlier depressed years of his birth. Since WWII jobs had gotten much easier to find, and Eastwood forged around, kind alike of squirrel forging for nuts, as he sought out his niche in the new markets available. Soon he found himself up in Washington State working at a Boeing plant near Seattle in the parts department.

It was during this period in time he was making plans to return to school to major in music, but he was drafted in 1950. His armed forces tenure ran through 1954 for the army during the Korean War years. During his service stint, however, he was assigned to Special Services where those earlier years lifeguard was soon paying off. They stationed him there in California at Fort Ord as the swimming instructor. During his off-hours at the pool, while in the service, he began working part-time at a sugar factory to earn extra spending money. This was all well and good, but the army soon made him quit this little extracurricular activity.

While stationed there, he also had met a young college student whom he dated and later would marry. Her name was Maggie Johnson, an independent young woman that not only had brains but was lovely as well. While he was on leave, they married on December 19, 1953. After finishing his stint with the army, he attended Los Angeles City College studying for a business degree while Maggie modeled swimsuits for catalogs and magazines. Later, he would drop out, though, opting for a tryout for some acting parts that supposedly paid really well.

Encouraged by some of his army buddies to try acting, he decided to give it a shot. Later, he signed on as a contract bit player for *Universal Studios.* While there he took some acting courses from *Michael Chekhov* there in Hollywood. These, he claimed later, tended to help him adjust in many ways.

His early bit parts as a walk-ons and stand-ins were in some of the early B-grade movies that earned him a big $75 a week during those *Universal* years. Some of his early work credits were on films likes of *The Revenge of the Creature* (1955) as a seemingly absentminded young lab technician with his white rats. Also, in 1955 was *Francis in the Navy* with Clint as Jonesy. *Tarantula* was another 1955 horror film in which he got screen time including lines when he portrayed a jet fighter squadron leader. In all of the above-mentioned titles he was mostly unaccredited which continued for the majority of his *Universal* work. The slowness of work as it trickled in bothered him, though, as did the lack of money. Maggie worked and Clint helped to dig swimming pools there in and around Hollywood to help facilitate their meager lifestyle. They persevered, though, and Clint stuck to his guns. Toward the late 1950s, the quality and quantity of the parts had picked up. Things were beginning to look a little better for the Eastwoods.

There were always bit parts with the primetime television shows like *Highway Patrol*, *Death Valley Days*, *Navy Log*, and *Maverick*—which tended to ease the financial and marriage tensions. Then while he was visiting a friend at the *CBS* studios, he was seen and approached by a network executive, who saw him there and thought he was perfect for a cowboy type he was casting. He wanted to hire him as a cattle drover for a new weekly television series. It was to be called *Rawhide*. Eric Fleming would star as Gil Favor, Trail Boss. Clint Eastwood among other regulars would be cast as drover called Rowdy Yates. The show began January 9, 1959, and ended season 8, January 4, 1966.

Eastwood's firstborn, daughter Kimber was born during those *Rawhide* years on June 17, 1964. The child was the result of an affair outside wedlock with another woman that ended shortly thereafter. Although he has and still is very supportive of this daughter, he managed to keep it all a secret for quite a while. Although very private of his personal life, it was learned that Clint and Maggie had decided they wouldn't have any children of their own. This may have been derived in part, from the fact that Maggie had been very ill early on in their marriage with a severe case of hepatitis. They did however change this way of thinking and after some ten years when their firstborn son Kyle came into this world on May 19, 1968. A daughter Alison followed along some years later on May 22, 1972.

Due to the fact that the Eastwoods had this seemingly opening marital arrangement between them, each having their own space, an eventual divorce of the pair after some twenty-five years of marriage came as no surprise to most around Hollywood. An amicable arrangement and divorce settlement was quietly obtained, and the split was a done deal. They both admitted to the news media that they had just grown apart from one another over the years, which does seem to be the case with most early marriages unfortunately. They both moved on in life and are still good friends, parents, and grandparents today.

Near the end of *Rawhide's* sixth season, Star Eric Fleming and *CBS* producers were having problems from longtime contract disputes. This led to his eventual firing from the long-running series. Rowdy Yates (Eastwood) then took up the reins of the show filling in, but the end was plainly in sight. Early on, during the show's final season 8 of 1966, it was finally cancelled. The actors, most of whom by now had become complacent, all went their separate ways.

Fleming and Eastwood had in the past somewhat of a testy onset relationship. *CBS* finally dismissed Fleming halfway through the seventh season. Eastwood then took the lead and continued until the last show, which aired on January 4, 1966. It was later they learned while Fleming was in South America doing a two-part adventure series called *High Jungle* for an *MGM* TV movie he had drowned on September 28, 1966. Seemingly while filming a sequence on the Huallaga River, Peru he had gotten caught up in the rapids and was swept under. They later found his body downstream in a basin pool.

Eastwood, it was now learned, had been contacted earlier back in 1964 by Italian production executives going through his agent about the possibility of him appearing in an Italian-made film during a summer visit to Italy. His personal disputes with *CBS* was no doubt similar to that of Fleming's, in that they hadn't let either actor take on any outside offered movie roles since the series had begun. They were, in essence, like stuck in their immediate roles until the end of their contract with no branching out room.

This in part is understandable when looking at it through eyes of the producers. Things just like what had happened to Fleming in Peru could very well have happened while he was still under their contractual wing. That would have been devastating to the series. Which however, in a word, Fleming's firing had actually had nearly the same results.

Eastwood's earlier bouts with the producers had been somewhat quelled when they agreed to let him go and make this film for the Italians that was to be shot in Spain. After all, he wasn't the star per se, Fleming was at that time. For Eastwood, it would be a chance to do a starring role, plus coupled with a short-shooting schedule in Europe and cash money was all a very interesting offer. Who wouldn't jump at the chance, while enjoying a vacation trip to Italy and Spain to boot?

According to Eastwood, he understood that James Coburn had been offered the film but wanted too much money (it's said he wanted $25,000), but it seems the Italians were on a shoestring budget and could only afford $15,000 US. Eastwood agreed to do the film for that amount. All other factions so agreed and a deal was struck and signed. He and Maggie had often talked about taking a trip to Europe but could never afford it. Now was their chance. With the *Rawhide* show entering its summer hiatus schedule, this offer came at an ideal time.

Besides, it would give him the opportunity to get out from under the wing of *CBS* for a while and show not only to himself but his wife and others his independence, if not the chance to do other characterizations unlike the Rowdy Yates's role that he had become tired with. He had stuck it out mainly because of the shows' success and the steady income.

Grabbing a new pair of Levis, his boots, hat, gun and holster outfit he used in the *Rawhide* series and away Eastwood went. Later, we would find out that Richard Harrison* supposedly had been the one who had suggested his name for Sergio Leone from a list of three. Harrison figured that Eastwood might just be persuaded to take on the short-shooting role for cash since Coburn had turned them down. Besides, he picked him (as he later stated in an interview), "because he could ride a horse well."

The success of *Fistful of Dollars*, first of the Sergio Leone action Western trilogy, is by now well-known and documented in every type of media possible. A film classic now that in its own way helped turn the tide of the Italian cinema from the *Peplum* (Sword and Sandal) era of films into a phenomenon of the Western genre for the next ten years to come. At its peak, it is said that some five hundred to six hundred more or less films of this nature were churned out from the Italians and co producers throughout Europe. Even the Americans got into the act with actors coming nonstop to the shores of Italy to cash in on this lucrative filmmaking opportunity.

Clint Eastwood wasn't the first American actor to hit the shores of Italy, but his persona in this film alone prompted the making of a second, then a third. By the time these films finally reached the shores of the United States

* Funny thing here is, according to Mark Damon's latest autobiography (recently out in the book stores 2007), he was the one that was in actual contact with Sergio Leone and says he had suggested Clint Eastwood for the role. Be that as it may, we're quite sure Leone was in contact with lots of directors, producers, actors, and agents alike in an attempt to snare a more reasonably priced American actor (one that would willingly accept the role, I might add) to star in his new Western. Eastwood's name may very well have popped up in several of the nightly mogul fetes that transpired prior to the actual start of filming.

later in 1967, Eastwood's name was already a household name in Europe. He and his fellow actors were now international film stars of the first order.

After this first film, Eastwood later returned to Europe and stayed there long enough to pump out another two of Leone's trilogy. In addition, he agreed to another totally unrelated film called *Le Streghe* (*The Witches*) (1967). It has been an obscure Italian title for us here in the States at least for a number of years. Finally, surfacing here since the 1980s it's a strange little film that included five segments. Italian beauty Silvana Mangano stars in all five segments, Eastwood appears in one of these with her.

All during his filmmaking adventures in Europe, Eastwood watched, listened, and learned; and eventually, when he returned back to the States, it would be his turn then to turn the tides of how Hollywood films were being made. His European popularity would afford him now those opportunities back in America. There he could try out his ideas of filmmaking, the way he wanted to do them and how he thought they ought to be made. Efficient cost, prohibitive productions, not cheap per se, but with a progressive approach and a no-nonsense attitude toward filmmaking. He formed his own production company *Malpaso Productions* in 1968. The rest is pure entertainment history.

A man of many accomplishments besides filmmaking—fluent in Italian; licensed helicopter pilot for over thirty years; avid golfer; owner of the exclusive *Tehama Golf Club* in Carmel Valley, California; successful restaurateur with his *Hog's Breath Inn* restaurant and tavern, also in Carmel—he is also an equally accomplished musician (piano) and songwriter.

He is married now to present wife, Dina Ruiz Eastwood, since March 31, 1996. They have one daughter together, Morgan, who was born on December 12, 1996. His wife, Dina, loves golf and appears to be the perfect match for our lanky man of action. She was once a co host of the popular TV show *Candid Camera* and, before that, was a former local Hollywood California television news anchor/reporter. All toll our man of men has seven children with five different women, quite an accomplishment within itself.

This award-winning actor/ director/ producer filmmaker is top-notch in his field and remains at the top even today while he continues to churn out successful films for audiences the world over. In the year 2004, at seventy-four years old, he won an Oscar for *Best Director* for the film *Million Dollar Baby*. That win made him the oldest person to ever achieve that prestigious award.

If a name was ever meant to be associated with accomplishment, even while tagged with a Man with No Name" image, we tend to think of *Spaghetti* Westerns, but foremost to come in mind would be the man Clint Eastwood. *Long may you live on, Manco!*

End.

- Below is a complete *Euro* filmography for Clint Eastwood. Dates here are aligned as close as possible with information currently at hand, with international release dates included. **Posters and title picture are accredited to Sebastian Haselbeck collection via his website www.spaghetti-westerns.net. Many thanks, Sebastian.*

CLINT EASTWOOD'S *SPAGHETTI* WESTERNS

1964

For a Fistful of Dollars, *Per un Pugno di Dollari;* a.k.a. *A Fistful of Dollars*; Ital/ Spa/ W. Ger, Director Sergio Leone (Eastwood as Joe/ Man with No Name) 9/12/64

This film was a new experience for the moviegoers. A stylish operatic Western, full of violence, clichés, and references to, without reservations, the older Hollywood type of Westerns it was soon to replace. This one-time shot for director Leone would evolve into one of the most significant pieces of film work to date. A genre of film work that would soon explode across the oceans with a phenomenon effect that would sweep Europe, the Middle East, the Far East, and eventually settle here in the States as a truly exciting and dramatic experience for the movie going audiences of the world.

This young director, Sergio Leone hot from the *Peplums* (Sword and Sandal films) of Rome with only one such cinema achievement under his belt (*The Colossus of Rhodes*), would now venture into his personal dreamland of the Westerns as he remembered them from his own childhood trips to the cinema. Using the pseudonym of Bob Robertson, Leone would gather a spaghetti bowl of cast members from all over Europe for this film. Low on initial monies, he sought cheap financing from where he could. The storyline he liberally borrowed from the film *Yojimbo* (a popular 1961 Japanese samurai movie) would eventually get him into trouble over the rights of the film work. But nevertheless, he plowed ahead. The scripting evolved between Leone himself and Duccio Tessari from an original reworked story by Luciano Vincenzoni. The films working title was called *The Magnificent Stranger*.

For his lead actor, he wanted an American if he could get one. Having an extremely low budget, he was limited. Some actors already there in Rome were working on other films, he tried those to no avail. One such actor, who was already doing these Italian made Westerns, was Richard Harrison. Harrison, however, turned him down citing other obligations.

Harrison had seemingly picked Eastwood's name from a list of three actors; afterward, he suggested they contact the Roman office of the *William Morris Agency* there in Rome. Evidently, Leone did just that, and after viewing some of the old *Rawhide* reruns, he decided Clint Eastwood would probably do. When they contacted Eastwood and agent with the deal, they accepted.

Eastwood's role would be that of a laconic stranger, a bounty hunter that was extremely proficient at his profession. Constantly after the almighty dollar, he fed off the scum of the earth collecting cold hard cash for his efforts. A twofold job, if you will, cleaning up the territory of those unwanted outlaws and killers that ravaged the countryside, planting fear in the good people of the this new wild west. Judge, jury, and executioner, this man took no quarter and gave none in return. He was a deadly adversary to the point of evil. Quick and deadly as a rattlesnake with his fists, but he was far quicker and more accurate with his gun. This deadly antihero would become known as the "Man with No Name".

An Italian/ German/ Spanish coproduction filmed on locations in and around Almeria, southern Spain. Almeria was an area in southern Spain that closely resembled our American Southwest. The town scenes would be shot a few kilometers north of Midrid in a town site called Hojo de Manzanares. Horses furnished here were mostly of Spanish or Yugoslavian breeds. The stuntmen were the best Italy had to offer. They would seemingly kill themselves on screen for a chance to be in a film. The extras used, resembled those of the Southwestern Mexicans and Indians of the United States—and still worked cheap as well. Weather was mostly accommodating but brutally hot at times. Accommodations were limited at best, though; however, they would get better in years to come.

Clint Eastwood's role would soon propel him to international stardom. He was fast becoming an icon in Europe and a role model for the many copycat films that were to follow. This style of film work set the table, as it were, for things to come. This new type of antihero screen violence appealed to the theater audiences; they loved it and cried out for more. And more is just what they got with Sergio Leone's second film in the same vein, but more of it.

A young maestro Ennio Morricone was commissioned by Leone to come up with an unusual yet vibrant brand of music score for this, his first Western. Additional stars were Marianne Koch (German Actress), Gian Maria Volonte, Jose Calvo, Wolfgang Lukschy, Sieghart Rupp, and Daniel Martin. Interestingly, when this film now called *A Fistful of Dollars* was finally acquired for television rights to be shown in the States for home viewing during the early 1970s, though most of the extremely violent scenes were already cut, *ABC* still worried it still had too violent a concept for its picky audiences. Thus, *ABC* contacted independent director Monty Hellman.*

Director Monty Hellman

The Mexican actor which Hellman used, was a look-alike in size (although not as tall) and similar in actions only. His facial features remained hidden from the audiences view throughout the entire segment. A similar type poncho was used as close Hellman states, as he could find across the border at the time. Filmed in an old monastery, that would suffice as a Mexican prison of the era, along with plenty of cast shadows, and then a pouring rain sequence, the story prologue was effective to say the least. One of Hellman's stock players from more recent film work at the time was Harry Dean Stanton. He was contracted to portray the prison warden.

The Warden would offer up a pardon to Joe, if he would leave immediately for San Miguel and attempt to quell the violence taking place there between town gangs of banditos. It seems everyman the government had tried sending into this border town to try and correct the problems wound up dead. The warden went on to say in short, he could handle it in his own way. (Which meant, we can assume, killing them all if necessary!)

Hellman admits he was involved with this project between June and September of 1974. He wrote the script himself, finally leaving for Mexico late July of that year. The sequence was finally shown for the first time on TV, August 29, 1977. Funny, we understand that when Clint Eastwood happened to see the television showing, he admitted he really didn't remember doing that scene, not realizing right off it had been post-added without him. Although he was fully aware of how cagey the Italians could be with their movie making ways.

---

* They tasked Hellman with the job of developing and filming a prologue portion to be shown before the actual film began. This vignette segment Hellman decided was to be filmed in Mexico and was meant to only soften the violent and malicious indirectness of the stranger's actions. To give his actions more purpose, if you will.

A definitive issue DVD was brought out February 2006. Among its many perks, such as added missing scenes, is a showing of this archive prologue sequence along with a one-on-one interview with director Monty Hellman himself on screen. (A must-see for all fans of the genre and film)

1965

For a Few Dollars More, *Per qualche dollaro in piu`*; Ital/ Spa/ W. Ger, Director Sergio Leone (Eastwood as Manco / the stranger / Man with No Name) (12/18/65)

Starring Clint Eastwood, Lee Van Cleef, Gian Maria Volonte, Luigi Pistilli, Mario Brega, Klaus Kinski, and Aldo Sambrell. For this, the second of Sergio Leone's Horse Opera trilogy, Clint Eastwood returns as the Man with No Name, but this time around, he seemingly has acquired an original handle of *Manco* the bounty killer *(in the English translated version this was pronounced as Monco).* The storyline was originally developed by Luciano Vincenzoni, but underwent extensive changes, which involved both Leone and Fulvio Morsella.

Leone not having a sequel particularly in mind was eventually warmed to the subject by producer Alberto Grimaldi. Even though the first film *A Fistful of Dollars* had failed to make back its production costs upon the initial release, it had been extremely popular with the European audiences. Grimaldi reasoned to satisfy his own mind as to whether this had merely been just a fluke picture or perhaps it was the beginning of something bigger. Grimaldi pressured Leone into doing a second film in the same vein as the first, a sequel if you will.

With Leone given a larger budget for this film, and not having the financial worries per se bogging him down was given his head to carry on with the film as he saw fit. The script, originally written by Vincenzoni right after the film *FODs* had come out in Italy, had been previously sold and deposited with the producer Grimaldi. When the second film was decided on, the script was found, dusted off, and Leone went to work on it. Originally, the working title of this film was called *The Magnificent Strangers*.

This time, though, in addition, a partner, as it were, was added in that of an older, wiser bounty hunter character. Cold, calculating, and deadly to the point of finesse, he was portrayed by American veteran badman actor, Lee Van Cleef. His character, that of Colonel Douglas Mortimer from the Carolinas, tended to add certain depth and a more challenging vigor to Eastwood's "lone stranger" role. These two bounty killers eventually parlayed the bad guys into fortune as well as sweet revenge for Mortimer in the end.

The character of Wild the crazy hunchback was portrayed by Polish-born actor Klaus Kinski and was perfectly correlated to clash with Mortimer in a long remember scenes when during their first meeting, Mortimer antagonizes the hunchback by striking a match on his hump so as to light up his pipe as shown in the coupled scene segments below thanks to another Internet website, *www.fatmandan.com.*

Later after the bank robbery in a below-the-border Mexican saloon, the tables are reversed when this time Wild (Kinski*) accosts Mortimer during his meal and goads him into a gunfight in which (while the stranger watches with interest in the background) Mortimer kills him.

Musical maestro Ennio Morricone would score the superb music adapted specifically for this new film, with conducting credits going to Bruno Nicolai. These two would pair musically many more times to follow in much the same tradition collaborating on Euro films throughout much of the 1960's era until a falling out between the two would erupt, splitting the pair, never to rejoin one another in collaborations of music again.

> Sergio Leone's box office successes of this film and his previous *Fistful,* also with Clint Eastwood, portraying the lone gunslinger now warranted a third film in the same vein by popular demand. Clint Eastwood and Lee Van Cleef both would again return one last time for Leone in a big-budgeted extravaganza for a 1966 release.
>
> When Van Cleef was asked some years later about the working relationship between himself and Clint Eastwood, he replied, "We got along famously. Not everyone likes his style, but everyone's got their own thing, and he sure as hell has been successful."

**Below are some deleted scene views from Leone's cutting room editing, showing Eastwood's stranger character with hotel owner's wife (portrayed by Mara Krup). Many thanks to WAI! Editor Tom Betts for putting me onto these www.youtube.com site pictures.*

* Klaus Kinski would go down in film history as one of the most prolific of actors of his time with probably some five-hundred-plus film credits over a lifetime of cinematic achievements.

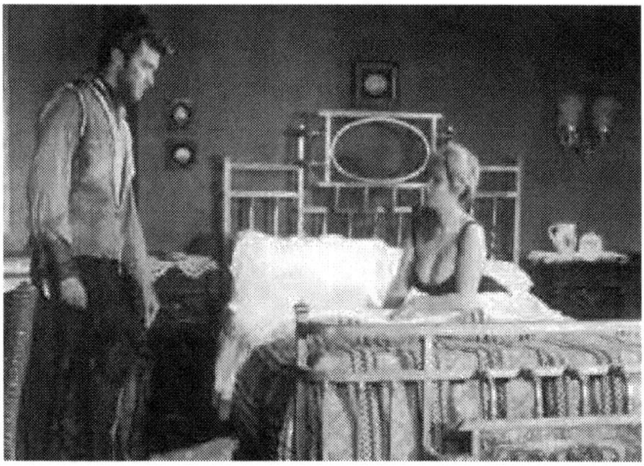

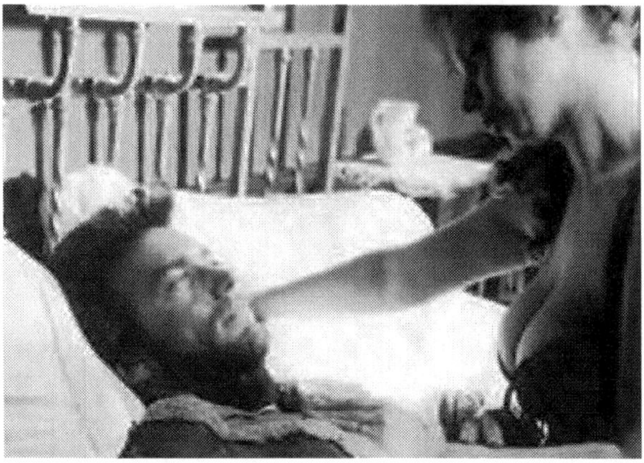

1966

The Good, the Bad, and the Ugly; *Il buono, il brutto, il cattivo;* a.k.a. *The Magnificent Rogues*; Ital/ Spa/ W. Ger, Director Sergio Leone (Eastwood as the Stranger / blondie / Man with No Name) (12/23/66)

Clint Eastwood, Lee Van Cleef, and Eli Wallach star in the third and last of the Leone trilogy Westerns. Unfortunately, this group of individuals would never again return as a team, although the trilogy and its bounty-killer theme would be duplicated many times by copycat productions that continued to pour out of Europe.

This film, third in the trilogy, has for its style and authenticity is represented here as the primo of Leone's film work. It has been considered by many as being the ultimate of the Euro, "Horse Operas". This we feel is totally up to the individual viewer as most I've found seem to prefer the second *FFDM* film with Eastwood and Van Cleef playing off one another. Returning were many of the same actors, but in different characterizations. Leone lays down a story of greed and lawlessness during Civil War times in our American Southwest, which is torn between the North and the South, in which now enters the bounty hunter!

The three weave in and out of the war-torn South along with the fighting, the bloodshed, and the sorrow of war in search of buried gold coins. *Mucho Dinero!* Which has been the downfall of many a man. The story and scripting credits for this massive reproduction of the era goes to Agenore (Age) Incrocci, Furio Scrapelli, Luciano Vincenzoni, Sergio Leone, and an unaccredited Sergio Donati.

> Interestingly, Van Cleef's nickname of Angel Eyes was supposedly coined by Eastwood during shooting. Leone liked it and actually had it kept in the script.

Although the below title is not a Western, it is, however, Eastwood's only other Euro film to date. His segment scenes were filmed prior to his leaving Italy on his last return trip to the States.

1966

The Witches; *Le Streghe*; Ital / Fr, Director Vittorio De Sica (for Eastwood's scenes) (Eastwood as Charlie) (1966)

A fourth entry for Eastwood, was a coproduction from producer *Dino De Laurentiis.* This strange surreal kind of comedy drama is an anthology of segments, which has been mostly left for the likes of those Federico Fellini fans. It appears to have been a screen vehicle for Italian star Silvana Mangano (also producer De Laurentiis's wife) in which she stars as an overbearing female protagonist (Witch), but not particularly in the literal form of a witch per se. She stars in all five film segments that are listed below along with her role in each:

> ***Strega Bruciata*** ("Witch Burn") a.k.a. "Witch Burned Alive"; as Gloria; director: Luchino Visconti
>
> ***Senso Civico*** ("Civic Sense); as a lady that's in a hurry. Director: Mauro Bolognini
>
> ***La Terra Vista Dalla Luna*** ("The Earth Seen by the Moon") as Assurdina Cal; written and directed by Pier Pasolini
>
> ***La Siciliana*** ("The Sicilian"); a.k.a. "The Girl from Sicily" as Nunzia; director: Franco Rossi

Una sera come le Altre ("An Evening like Any Other"); a.k.a. "A Night Like Any Other" as Giovanna. Dir: Vittorio De Sica. The title meaning references: just another, "same old" dull evening at home with her (once great hunk of a man) husband.

In this last segment, "An Evening Like Any Other," Clint Eastwood portrays Charlie, the once hunk of a man, now just another dull hubby of a flamboyant wife, Giovanna (Mangano), who dreams of better things in life, along with past and future sexual fun sessions. This segment was written by Fabio Carpi and Enzo Muzii and was directed by Vittorio De Sica.

The brother of De Laurentiis, Alfredo acted as executive producer for the film. The original music scores for the picture were done by Ennio Morricone and Piero Piccioni. Cut US color versions for limited showings have recently been released on DVD's with run times ranging anywhere from 121 to 105 minutes.

1967

The Magnificent Stranger, *L'Estraneo di Magificent;* a.k.a. *Maledetto Gringo*; Ital / West Ger, much to the disappointment of Eastwood fans this was not another new Euro film for his credit. Evidently with the success of the *Dollar* films that were finally being shown here in the United States about this era in time, Italian producers deciding to cash in on their new Stateside popularity of actor Clint Eastwood.

It seems they figured that by reviving a couple of the old *Rawhide* (1959-'66) series episodes. They could combine a couple of these old TV episodes and reissued them with the old *Stranger* working script title for the *Fistful of Dollars* film. By doing this, they would be marketing a new film featuring, the now internationally popular Clint Eastwood. Its first public showing graced the West German theaters on July 7, 1967. The *Rawhide* episodes that were used to compile this particular feature were "Incident of the Running Man" from season 3 (1960-'61). Also, the other called "The Backshooter" from season 7 (1964-'65). When Eastwood and his agent got wind of these happenings, they immediately sued, and the feature was withdrawn, and supposedly has been destroyed.

End.

BIBLIOGRAPHY
(C. Eastwood)

Betts, Tom, editor *WAI! (Westerns . . . All'Italiana)* Fanzine, articles/info on Clint Eastwood:

Issue no. 1, vol. 1 (1983): *A Fistful of Dollars;* and *For a few Dollars More* a record ck.

Issue no. 3/4 (November 1984): Missing scenes of Sergio Leone by Keith Hall Jr.; *The Good, the Bad, and the Ugly* a record by Don Trunick

Issue no. 3, vol. 2 (September / October 1985): More missing scenes from *A Fistful of Dollars* by Keith Hall Jr.

Issue no. 10 (November / December 1986): "Spaghetti Showdown" *For a Few Dollars More* by Keith Hall Jr.

Issue no. 12 (March / April 1987): "For a Few Critics" *For a Few Dollars More* by Tom Betts

Issue no. 17 (Spring 1988): Book review "Once Upon a Time: Films of Sergio Leone" by Randall Larson

Sergio Leone Memorial Issue

Issue no. 22 (Summer 1989): Leone: The Good, Bad and Memorable" an appreciation by Sheila Benson

Issue no. 37: Book review: "Sergio Leone: Something to do with Death" by Lee Broughton

Issue no. 39: Book review: "Clint Eastwood: A Cultural Production" by Tony Williams

BFI Companion to the Western, The (1993) (ref) edited by Edward Buscombe, *British Film Institute,* UK. Originally published by *Andr`e Deutsch Ltd.,* London, 1988; pp 339

Connolly, Bill, editor *Spaghetti Cinema* Fanzine articles, Clint Eastwood info and/or his films:

Issue no. 1 May 1984: Film *Yojimbo* by Bill Connolly

Issue no. 7 July 1985: *A Fistful of Dollars* by Bill Connolly

Issue no. 55 January 1994: The TV Prologue for *A Fistful of Dollars*

Cumbow, Robert C., *Once Upon a Time: The Films of Sergio Leone* (1987) by *Scarcrow Press inc.,* NJ and London

The Films of Clint Eastwood (1993) Filmology Booklet by Boris Zmijewsky and Lee Pfeiffer, *A Citadel Press Book* by *Carol Publishing Group,* NJ.

Frayling, Christopher, *Something to Do with Death* (2000), *Faber & Faber Ltd.*, London, UK. Information on Clint Eastwood

Halliwell, Leslie, *The Filmgoer's Companion* (1975) (ref), *Avon Book Publishers*, NY. 1975

Haselbeck, Sebastian, owner/curator for Internet website: *www.spaghetti-western.net*

Internet via *www.anica.it* ref: Film production and date confirmation

Internet via *www.IMDB.com* complete film and TV listings, plus trivia and personal quotes; also mini biography for Clint Eastwood by Scott-msa0510

Lambert, Gilles, *The Good, the Dirty, and the Mean of Sergio Leone* (1976) *Solar Publishing*, Paris. French language printing, heavily illustrated with pictures in black and white.

Quinlan's Illustrated Registry of Film Stars (1987) by Davis Quinlan, *Henry Holt Reference Books*, NY. pp 144

Thompson, Douglas, *Clint Eastwood Riding High* (1992) *Contemporary Books*, Chicago

Video Hound's Golden Retriever (1994 edition) *Visible Ink Press*, a division of *Gale Research Inc.*, Detroit, MI. pp 1187

Weisser, Thomas, *Spaghetti Westerns: the Good, the Bad, and the Violent*, (1992) *McFarland*, Jefferson NC.

Western: All'Italiana (1998) (Book one), by Antonio Bruschini and Federico de Zigno, *Glittering Images*, Firenze, Italy

The Western: The Complete Film Sourcebook (The Film Encyclopedia) (1983); by Phil Hardy, *William Morrow and Co, Inc.*, NY., pp 286; 290; 295-6

The World Almanac Who's who of Film (1987) by Thomas G Aylesworth and John S. Bowman, *Bison Books*, pp 135-6

JACK ELAM

(1919-2003)

OLD SLY-EYE SHOOTS STRAIGHT!

According to the obituary account given by the *USA Today News* on Thursday the twenty-third of 2003, our veteran villain actor Jack Elam passed away on Monday, October 20 at his home in Ashland, Oregon, of congestive heart failure. The obituary went on to say that contrary to most of his biographical listings, he was actually eighty-four years old instead of the eighty-six usually reported. He is survived by his wife, Jenny, one son (Scott) and two daughters Jeri and Jacqueline from a previous marriage.

Jack Elam will always be remembered for his one crazy eye, which appeared to do what he wanted it to in his films. He once said laughingly of this eye that he had no control over it. It just did what it wanted to. In actuality it had been the result of an unfortunate accident as a youngster during a Boy Scout meeting of all places. Another kid threw a pencil sticking in the eye resulting from a fight of course, and a sightless eye was Elam's for the rest of his life.

William Scott "Jack" Elam was born on November 13, 1919, in Miami, Arizona. He was raised and finished his high schooling though in Phoenix, Arizona. He later moved to Southern California for work while he busied himself working his way through junior college. He found work at many jobs while in school, one such as a hotel manager for the *Bel-Air Hotel* during the 1940s. After leaving business school, his work took a turn toward a career move to becoming a Hollywood accountant where he later found work as an auditor for the Samuel Goldwyn studios.

He was also sometimes involved in working with some of the independent film companies around Hollywood and also helped in the arrangement for their film financing. This working within the realm of the cinema eventually gave him the opportunity to ease his way into acting. Especially since his one good eye was under so much strain doing his present accounting jobs that a doctor he had seen recommended he change his line of work before he went totally blind. Elam started out doing bit-part acting work at first, mainly just for the thrill of it and as a supplement to his income. That was until he latched on to the role of a sex-crazed killer in the *Rawhide* (1951) for director Henry Hathaway.

For Elam's next role in one film that I was a particular fan of was the now-classic Gary Cooper film *High Noon* (1952) directed by Fred Zinnemann. The film sets standards for the Western films that followed after that like watching the clock, the buildup of tension, the train (never a good Western without a train involved), and the gunslingers. The four it brings to mind were Ian MacDonald as Frank Miller, his brother Ben (Sheb Wooley), Robert Wilke as Jim Pierce, and one badman who would go on to *Spaghetti* Western fame and fortune through the genre, Lee Van Cleef as Jack Colby. Our Jack Elam was also in this film, if we remember. He was Charlie the loveable drunk in the jail cell. He was unaccredited for this film.

Elam was more regularly seen on American television during the 1950s, but mostly always in that of a "heavy"' villain-type character role for the majority in Westerns. He was on a good roll though by '63 when he could then be seen weekly on the TV series *The Dakotas*. There he portrayed Deputy J. D. Smith to the town marshal, Frank Ragan, played by Larry Ward. The hour-long show only ran for one season from January 7 to September 9 of that year.

It was during the late 1960s, and the clutch of the *Spaghetti* Westerns, when both actors Elam and Ward would venture across the ocean to Italy and take a shot at making some quick dollars and possibly fame to go with it as well. Anything to further a now-slowed film career would work they felt. While Ward would only make two of these popular Euro horse operas, both for releases in 1968 (*Kill the Wicked, (a.k.a. I'll Die for Vengeance*) Elam would return off and on to compile an even four over the next few years.

Jack Elam didn't let the fall of *The Dakotas* TV show slow him down much as he soon returned to the small screen again for the 1963-'64 season of *Temple Houston*, which starred Jeffrey Hunter as Houston and Jack Elam as the gunfighter / traveling marshal George Taggart. This show also ran only one season, though, from September 19, 1963, to September 19, 1964. Hunter, having already ventured overseas a time or two before had, by this time, already done one of the early *Spaghetti* Westerns and would now return for a couple of more films.

For Jack Elam's first of four Westerns he did for the genre was, *Sartana Does Not Forgive* (1968), it starred George Martin as the hero character Sartana. Gilbert Roland was gunslinger for hire Kirchner. Roland a popular Mexican / American actor rekindled his faltering film career with five *Spaghetti* Westerns of the era. He became quite popular again as a Euro box office draw during this period in his life. Jack Elam portrays another gunsul, Slim Kovacs gang member of the town boss.

It seems Sam (Gerard Tichy) had sent his gang out to kill an entire family so as to gain their land. Little do they realize that the man José and family they have just murdered is the brother of the notorious Sartana (Martin), gunman / bounty hunter. When Sartana hears of the murders, he comes seeking revenge.

A *Spaghetti* film authority and regular information contributor to genre *Fanzines* was writer Mr. Keith Hall Jr. Several years back, he wrote about how Elam had been finishing up his first *Spaghetti* Western film in Spain (the above-mentioned *Sartana)* and was on a quickie vacation in Switzerland with his wife, Jenny, when he received a phone call at the hotel from his good friend and longtime acting buddy Henry Fonda. Fonda was in Italy, also with his wife, but on the set of another *Spaghetti* Western called *Once Upon a Time in the West.*

What Fonda actually wanted was for Jack to come around and do a cameo sequence for the film. He pointed out that it was only a week's shooting and that the money was great as well. He figured it would also be a great time for the two families to get together for the week. In sunny Spain, eh! They admitted later that it was very hot there and the train rails were around 150 degrees. So hot, in fact, that Jack couldn't walk on 'em without burning his feet through his boots.

It was in this film, by now renowned Italian director Sergio Leone, that the infamous "fly scene" was shot with Snaky (Elam), as one of three gunslingers who were awaiting the train arrival at the station, along with Woody Strode (Stony) and Al Mulock (Knuckles) to kill Harmonica (Charles Bronson's character) as he disembarked the train. They finally completed the scenes by finishing that one difficult scene, and it was accomplished, not by using fake flies, nor having jam smeared on Elam's face, or any amount of fly coaxing that didn't work, as all of these were tried and tried. The camera-shy, flying pest finally did the ideal shot sequence later when Leone accidentally decided to rub watermelon on Elam's face. Whoa, the flies came in by the droves, so many in fact that Elam was having a time fighting them all off until Leone's crew could set up and get the shot. It worked, though, and all were overjoyed, especially Elam. For him the ordeal was finally over with.

Interesting to note here is that Strode's Stony character is sporting a sawn-off carbine similar to the *Mares Leg,* carried by the Josh Randall character portrayed by Steve McQueen in the popular 1950's *CBS* television show *Wanted Dead or Alive.* This Italian version of the sawn off .44-40 caliber *Mares Leg* is different in that it did have certain similarities to that of the rifle carried by the Lucas McCain character (Chuck Connors) in the long-running *The Rifleman* series for the 1950's *ABC* television series. That being the adjustable bolt that ran through the trigger ring-guard, which (when tightened up to the trigger and a tidbit beyond) allowed the rifle to be fired every time the cocking lever was jacked back up into firing position. The faster McCain jacked it, the faster it would shoot, whereas the *Mares Leg* did not have this devise.

For the stony carbine, it seems the ingenious Italian gunsmiths have installed what looks similar to a bent nail (rod) on the trigger ring-guard that would also allow the gun to fire every time the lever was jacked up as well. The exception to this would be it was not adjustable as the *The Rifleman* was. The shoulder stock had also been chopped off as was the carbine barrel shortened With the short butt stock it could be held back tightly against one's gun belt when firing the contraption as seen in the photo below, borrowed for explanation purposes only from the website, *www.afistfulofwesterns*, via the section on guns/winchester.htm

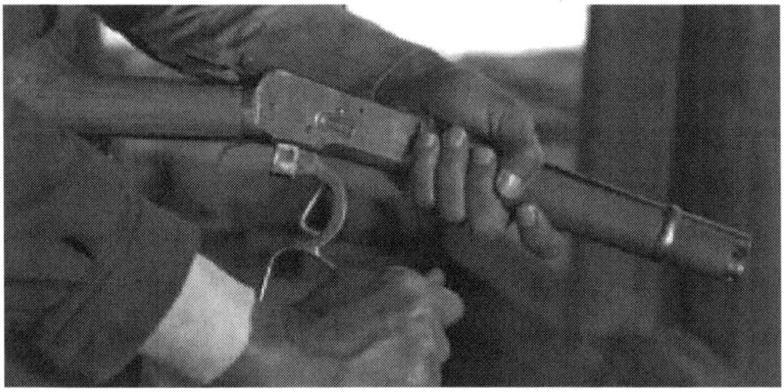

Jack Elam would continue in the realm of the *Spaghetti* Western for another couple of films yet before leaving the genre altogether. He would return to Spain for his next film called *The Last Rebel* (1971). The film starred ex-*New York Jets* football hero, Joe Namath, in one of his rare and limited big-screen appearances as a fresh from the Civil War, Burnside Hollis. Jack Elam here portrays his Confederate buddy Matt Graves. Riding through the war-torn southwest, they happen upon a lynching and save a former slave Duncan (Woody Strode). The three ride out together after and get tangled up in a crooked pool shooting scheme, which when Hollis tries his luck at the pool game for $1,000 a game and wins. They decide to keep at this game scam and split the money three ways. Graves, however, soon tires of sharing his winnings with the ex-slave. It's then their companionship all goes south after that. The film was held together solely by the good supporting cast of *Spaghetti* Western favorites like Strode and one Ty Hardin who portrays the hard-bitten sheriff.

For Jack Elam next and last for the genre, he gets to costar with beauty Raquel Welch as the star of the film, *Hannie Caulder* (1971). Welch as Hannie Caulder is a rancher's wife who has been subjected to beatings, gang rape, and the horror of seeing her husband brutally murdered in front of her eyes. Plus, her home is burned to the ground and the culprits leave her for dead.

She is saved by a passing lone gunman Thomas Luther Price (Robert Culp, in his only genre outing) who happens upon the scene in time to make a difference. He takes her to the safety and his friend, Bailey, the gunsmith at his ocean-side workshop/home to recover. Bailey is portrayed by Christopher Lee, a popular British horror film star in his only genre venture.

The three idiot killers are the Clemens brothers. The oldest and leader is Emmett (Ernest Borgnine, veteran of two other genre films), Frank (Jack Elam), and Rufus (Strother Martin in his only genre Western). As Hannie recovers, she seeks her revenge on these three who wish they'd never laid eyes on the likes of her before she's done killing them.

With Jack Elam being in so much demand for film work, he would continued portraying the tough-guy roles, and mostly on-screen villains with a sprinkling of hard-line gunslingers of Westerns. Then later in life, he changed horses and began doing mostly comedic roles for films and television. These would come about during the waning years of his career. One such effort was a 1986 situation comedy called *Easy Street*, which starred Loni Anderson as L. K. McGuire and Jack Elam was her costar Uncle Alvin "Bully" Stevenson. This thirty-minute weekly TV series ran from September 15, 1986, to May 27, 1987.

Elam was by then in his seventies and, by his own admission, still drank alcohol and smoked. He admitted to a news reporter at the time that he was indeed having trouble on the show's set with its star Loni Anderson. He stated that "I play poker, I swear a lot, I drink a lot. But Loni doesn't do any of those things. Smoking is not allowed on our stage." He admitted, though, that he respected her wishes. After all, she was the star. He said that he went outside to smoke.

Whatever faults or idiosyncrasies our *Spaghetti* actor had, we will surely forgive him. As we are probably some of this actor's more ardent fans of his screen work, we will forever miss his unique cinematic presence. Old Sly-eye, where have you gone?

End.

- Below is a complete *Euro* filmography for Jack Elam. Dates here are aligned as close as possible with information currently at hand, with international release dates included. **Posters and the title picture are accredited to the Sebastian Haselbeck collection via his website www.spaghetti-westerns.net.*

JACK ELAM
SPAGHETTI WESTERNS

1968

Sartana Does Not Forgive; *Sartana Non Perdona* a.k.a. *Sonora/ Three-Gun Showdown*; Spa / Ital; Director Alfonso Balaczar (Elam as Slim Kovacs) (10/25/68)

1968

Once Upon a Time in the West; *C'era una Volta IL West*; Ital, Director Sergio Leone (Elam as Snaky) (12/21/68)

Note: According to Christopher Frayling via his *Spaghetti Westerns* book of 1981, he states of the prologue shootout scene at Cattle Station with Frank's men, Elam, Strode, and Al Mulock was deleted from the Italian release, but later reinstated for the international release. Leone's reasoning being in the first bar scene with Lionel Stander; it was apparent that Harmonica (Bronson) had survived his assassination attempt by Frank's gunslingers. So he didn't feel the prologue was necessary.

Elam's role took place at the train depot where he and two other gunslingers await Harmonica (Bronson) to arrive. The scene picture above within the poster actually reveals the action here as Harmonica doesn't disembark the train at the dock, but instead jumps off on the other side and patiently waits for the train to again pull out, then revealing himself already getting the drop on the three killers, which he makes quick work of disposing.

Note: According to Christopher Fralying's book *Something to do with Death* (2000), Jack Elam was originally supposed to have had a part in the *GBU* film as well. His was to have been the scene as the one-armed gunslinger goes up against Sentenza (LVC). This part was eventually done by Al Mulock instead. It all had to do with timing and previous commitments so Elam had said.

1971
The Last Rebel, *a.k.a. L' Ultimo Pistolero*; Ital/ US/ Spa, Director Denys McCoy (Larry Spankler) (Elam as Matt Graves) (1971)

1971
Hannie Caulder, a.k.a. *La Texana e I fratelli Penitenza* a.k.a. *Colt pour Trois Salopards* (Fr); US/ UK/ Spa, Director Burt Kennedy (Elam as Frank Clemens) The French title roughly translates to *A Gun for Three Idiots.*

Note: The above film was actually a US / *Patrick Curtis Productions / British Tigon* coproduction film, primarily shot on locations in Spain. Supposedly it had some French influence, but nothing to confirm this was ever found. So here we have another film that even though was filmed in Spain is not actually of the Euro *Spaghetti* Western genre.

We now bring this Euro genre of Westerns for our Jack Elam to a close. RIP, ye olde one-eye.

End.

BIBLIOGRAPHY
(J. ELAM)

Betts, Tom, editor *WAI! (Westerns . . . All'Italiana)* Fanzine articles/ information on Jack Elam;

Issue no. 6, vol. 1-2: "Behind the Scenes" by Keith Hall Jr.

Memorial Issue for Charles Bronson: *Once Upon a Time in the West* review

Memorial Issue for Sergio Leone: Complete Filmography

"BFI Companion to the Western, The" (Ref), edited by Edward Buscombe, *British Film Institute,* UK, 1993; originally published by *Andr`e Deutsch Ltd.,* London, 1988; pp 254, 339

Connolly, Bill, editor *Spaghetti Cinema* Fanzine article/info on Jack Elam and/or his films:

Spaghetti Cinema Blogspot: (Tuesday, October 27, 2009): Screenwriter Dario Argento talks about Sergio Leone and the scripting of *Once Upon a Time in the West*

Cox, Alex, *10,000 Ways to Die* (2009) *Kamera Books,* UK. ; pp 199

Cumbow, Robert C., *Once Upon a Time: The Films of Sergio Leone* (1987) by *Scarcrow Press inc.,* NJ and London

Frayling, Christopher, *Something to do with Death* (2000), *Faber & Faber Ltd.,* London, UK. 2000, Information on Jack Elam, pp 221, 266, 269, 282, 300

Frayling, Christopher, *Spaghetti Westerns: Cowboys and Europeans from Karl May to Sergio Leone* (1981) (ref), *Routledge & Kegan Paul Ltd.,* London; pp 279

Haselbeck, Sebastian, owner/curator for Internet website: *www.spaghetti-western.net*

Horner, William R., *Bad at the Bijou* (1982) (Ref), *McFarland & Co., Inc., Publishers,* NC, and London; pp 13-21

Internet, via: *www.IMDB.com* Film and TV listings, plus trivia and quotes; "Mini biography for Jack Elam" by Jim Beaver

Lambert, Gilles, *The Good, the Dirty, and the Mean of Sergio Leone* (1976) *Solar Publishing,* Paris. French language printing, heavily illustrated with pictures in black and white.

National Enquirer Fanzine (1986, Issue?) Article: "Dying is a Way of Life for Easy Street Star: Jack Elam" by Cliff Barr

Quinlan, David, *The Illustrated Encyclopedia of Movie Characters* (1985) (Ref), *Harmony Books,* NY. ; pp 95-6

"Video Hound's Golden Retriever" (1994 edition) *Visible Ink Press,* a division of *Gale Research Inc.,* Detroit, MI. pp 1411

Weisser, Thomas, *Spaghetti Westerns: the Good, the Bad, and the Violent,* (1992) *McFarland*, Jefferson NC.

"Western: All'Italiana" (books I, II, and III), by Antonio Bruschini and Federico de Zigno, *Glittering Images,* Firenze, Italy; book I, 1998; book II, 2001 and book III, 2006

"The Western: The Complete Film Sourcebook" (The Film Encyclopedia); by Phil Hardy, *William Morrow and Co, Inc.,* NY, 1983, Appendix no. 8, pp 309-311

"The World Almanac Who's who of Film" by Thomas G Aylesworth and John S. Bowman, *Bison Books,* 1987; pp 138

MICHAEL FOREST

(1929—)

NO BOOTS OR GUNS FOR THIS COWBOY, EARPHONES AND MIKE WILL DO!

This American actor was born Gerald Michael Charlebois on April 17, 1929. Born and raised in Harvey, North Dakota. His family relocated out to the West Coast before he would finish high school; they settled in the Seattle, Washington, area. There he complete HS and even began college at the *University of Washington* for his first year. But, after that he relocated further south to the warmer climate of Southern California where he resumed his college studies at *San Jose State University*. He graduated with BA in English and drama. During and for a while after college, he worked his dream job, the stage. He was in numerous Shakespearean plays as well as other productions in beginning his career in stage work.

Relocating once again, he worked the boards (as those in the business affectionately refer to the stage) at the *Players Ring* in Hollywood for a while. Then little by little he began acting, doing bit parts, walk-ons, and roles for television. He began taking additional acting classes from the renowned teacher, Jeff Corey (who had been an early victim of the *Hollywood Black Listing* from the HUAC). It was there in classes with Corey where he first met Roger Corman; he was also taking classes to help him better understand the art of acting. They seemed to hit it off from the start and went on to do several films together. Later, Forest starred in three films for Corman, none of which could consider him a candidate as one of Corman's stock players like fellow actors Frank Wolff or Wally Campo. Actually, there was no vying for actor leadership in Forest's films. After all, at 6' and 3" and 215 lb his size alone kind a determined that.

To keep in shape over the years, Forest has been an amateur boxer and an avid tennis player. As a hobby, he began taking flying lessons and now holds a pilot license. He continued his stage work, juggling it, with a noted increase in his film work, specifically with the Corman troop of players wound up back in Forest's old stomping grounds, the Dakotas (during the winter months), for the filming of the *Corman and Corman, Beast form Haunted Cave* (1959). This had been Forest's first starring role in a film to date. His participation was primarily upon the request by the director Monte Hellman* who went to bat for Forest. They had been friends since Forest's earlier stage workdays. Actually they had an apartment in the same building during that era.

Here Forest portrays Gil Jackson/cowboy, a ski instructor, which the plot characters were using as a guide and gets involved with gangster Frank Wolff (as bad guy Alexander Ward) who is looking for a cache of gold bars to steal that's hidden in an old mine. Things start to fall apart when people are killed in the mine explosion, and they come upon a blood drinking beast from within the mine. For this early sci-fi thriller, Roger Corman was the executive producer, his brother Gene was the producer.

---

* Hellman (Monte Himmelbaum) was not actually involved in the *Spaghetti* Westerns of Europe per se, however for the US television 1977 release of Sergio Leone's *A Fistful of Dollars* (1964) film. He was tasked by the studio executives, under contract to film a prologue sequence with the objective of softening Eastwood's Joe character, explaining some of the super violent content of the main films storyline prior to the opening credits. The sequence was used to create a reason for him going head to head with the gangs of this border town. That being he would be pardoned and released for committing to this objective.

> For Roger Corman's first war picture called *Ski Troop Attack* (1960), it was also filmed in the Dakotas and back to back with the above *Haunted Cave.* Forest stars here as Lieutenant Factor; Frank Wolff costarred as Sergeant Potter. Roger Corman not only produced and directed but also portrayed a Nazi leader for one walk-on scene in the film. Others were Richard Sinatra, Wally Campo, and Sheila Carol (Sheila Noonan). The storyline has to do with an American commando unit sent in cross country on skis behind enemy German lines to blow a main transport route railroad bridge during WWII. Portions of this film were shot in South Dakota.

Prior to the above films, Forest had been doing mostly television bit parts and roles as they became available. His TV debut had been on *Death Valley Days* (1953) for an episode called "One in a Hundred" where he portrayed Larry Brooks. Since then he went on to play in many popular shows of the era including *Rin Tin Tin*; *Have Gun, Will Travel*; *Yancy Derringer and The Rifleman*; just to name a few. During those years, he'd also been associated with two early films. One as about a man named Slade (an unaccredited part) in *Shoot-Out at Medicine Bend* (1957) a Randolph Scott Western with Angie Dickinson and James Garner.

The other was an early entry for Roger Corman and Michael Forest's first feature film of his career. A Viking adventure called *The Saga of the Viking Women, and their Voyage to the Waters of the Great Sea Serpent* (1957) (Wow, an unmercifully long title). Forest's role was that of Zarko. The film starred Abby Dalton, Susan Cabot, June Kenney, and Betsy Jones-Moreland. Also, starring was Bradford Jackson and Gary Conway, one of Corman's stock actors of the day.

Forest went on to do a total of four films with Corman. The last film they did together was called *Atlas* (1961). Michael Forest stars here as the mighty Atlas. Frank Wolff costars as "Proximates the tyrant" who attempts to persuade Atlas to fight for him against a rebel uprising within his land. Also there was Barboura Morris as Candia. Roger Corman, the director made, an appearance as a Greek Soldier as did Dick Miller.

Forest continued his stage work appearing at *San Diego Globe Theater* where he actually played Othello three times and once as Petruchio in *Taming of the Shrew*. Juggling this and his television work continued on until about 1968 just prior to his leaving for Italy. Some of his more remembered appearances on TV and fan favorite Westerns shows were like *Maverick* for three episodes, *Cheyenne* for five episodes, *Laramie* for four episodes, *Gunsmoke* for three episodes, *The Virginian* for four episodes, *Bonanza* for three episodes, and one episode for *Rawhide* (1965). In addition, there was another more recognizable piece, but not for a Western at all, but a *Star Trek* episode called "Who Mourns for Adonis" (1967). His role was that of the god Apollo. Actually, Forest enjoyed staying close to home in the United States where he could enjoy his flying and concentrate doing his television roles—that is, until he made his big jump to Europe in the late 1960s for his first venture into the realm of the Euro Western, although not really considered one per se!

This *US* production called *100 Rifles* (1969) starred Jim Brown, an ex-footballer, now actor, is Sheriff Lyedecker. His costar was beauty Raquel Welch as Sarita. Also, along for the ride was Burt Reynolds as Yaqui Joe Herrera. Also, starred Dan O'Herlihy, Eric Braeden, and Michael Forest as Humara, another Indian role, of which he'd certainly portrayed a serious number for his work in films and television. The storyline here has to do with the sheriff chasing down Indian Joe who has just robbed a bank intending on using the monies to buy arms (*100 Rifles*) for his people so as to rebel against the US government who, he feels, is oppressing his people with cruel and unjust treatment.

This film wasn't actually considered one of the Euro genre films (the so-called a *Spaghetti* Westerns) though in fact it had been shot in Almeria, Spain—and with cast members of which many were currently or had been recently associated within that Euro Western genre. Some of those folks were Soledad Miranda, Aldo Sambrell as Sergeant Paletes, Alberto Dalbes, and José Manuel Martin. After shooting wrapped for Forest, it was back to the America and the TV roles until his next overseas venture, which was this time around a bonafide *Spaghetti* Western film.

For this, his second overseas Western was an Italian/ US/ Spanish coproduction called *The Last Rebel* (1971). It starred ex-footballer / prize quarterback of the *NY Jets*, Joe Namath, as Burnside Hollis in his first and only of the genre. It co starred Jack Elam as Matt Graves, Woody Strode as Duncan, and Ty Hardin as the sheriff—also with Victoria George as Pearl and Mike Forest as the cowboy pool hustler. It was directed by Denys McCoy (Larry G. Spangler) who also produced the film.

Storyline takes place circa 1865 in southwest Missouri at the end of the Civil War with two Confederate ex-soldiers now roaming town to town, again searching for their place in society. They have an ex-slave (Strode) with them that they rescued from a lynching party. Now considered one of the boys, he will do anything for Hollis since his rescue and does his all to help and protect the headstrong young ex-soldier as they attempt to hustle pool games for big money.

Forest's next film was *Requiem for a Bounty Hunter* (1972). This was an Italian production from director Angelo Pannacio. It was filmed outside Rome with some scenes being done at *Cava Studio,* Gordon Mitchell's old one-man-built Western town set. The film's stars per the credits are as follows: Ray O'Connor (Reno Capitani) as Cameron, Laurence Bien (Lorenzo Bien) as the sheriff and Thomas Rudy (Tomas Rudi). Also starring are Michael Forrest as Burton, Steven Tedd (Giuseppe Cardillo) as Kimble the bounty hunter, and Susanna Levi as Suzy Burton. Actually, Forest, Cardillo, and Levi are probably the main characters. Why the promotion of the gang members ahead of the main cast is bewildering and somewhat unclear? But alas, that's the *Spaghetti* Westerns for you.

The storyline has to do with the revenge for the slaughtered family theme that was so popular among these genre filmmakers. Here Barton returns home from the range to find his place has been attacked by the renegade outlaws. Among the devastation and death, he finds his wife, raped and brutally killed. His daughter was raped, but still alive in a severe state of shock. Afterward, depositing Suzy at a neighboring ranch with friends, he sets off to track the killers.

He runs upon a lone man in a burned-out structure not far away, playing a flute. When asked if he's seen the gang, the guy claims he did see some riding by the day before and knew them. His name is Kimble and he'd be glad to help find them, so they take off together. Come to find out, this Kimble was one of the attackers, but supposedly didn't take part in the rapes or murders. However, eventually Burton's daughter sees him, recognizes him and, when he leaves, follows him, baits him, and then shoots him dead.

After wrapping that Western, he stayed there in Italy and turned out a couple of other films before returning to the States this time, kind a got his bearings a bit we might say. The film *Hector the Mighty* (1972) was a *Peplum* adventure with Forest portraying Achilles. It starred Caterina Boratto, Rosanna Schiaffino as Helen, and Giancarlo Giannini as Ulysses. This was an Italian/ French/ Spanish coproduction, directed by Enzo G. Castellari. The film is seemingly a rehash, a comedy style of Helen of Troy.

Forest's next one was a historic drama/thriller called *The Assassination of Trotsky* (1972). It starred Richard Burton as Leon Trotsky Alain Delon as Frank Jackson Romy Schneider, Valenina Cortese and Enrico Maria Salerno. Michael Forest's character is Jim. Also, Hunt Powers (Jack Betts) as Lou. This was an Italian/ French/ UK coproduction from *Dino de Laurentiis* and directed by Joseph Losey, also victim of the blacklisting era in Hollywood.

At a certain time in his career, actually about now, during his ten-year European acting period, he got involved in voice dubbing for the many multi language actors who were involved in these European films. He wound up based there in Rome where he settled into a groove within this business, which has become an extremely profitable career move that has followed him from Italy back to the States. There and working in Italy, he made it a point to learn the language and today speaks fluent Italian. His dubbing work has continued to last even into the millennium, keeping him busy for much of the time. He's managed to stay fit by seeking out local gyms in the various areas he worked over the years. He said sometimes he was the only English-speaking patron in those establishments.

Forest did his first feature film dubbing, it appears, for the 1972 film *Don't Torture a Duckling.* An Italian production of what is known as a *Giallo* thriller from director Lucio Fulci, an early master and groundbreaker of that genre of films. The stars are Florinda Bolkan, as Maciara, Barbara Bouchet as Patrizia, and Tomas Milian as Andrea Martelli a reporter. As the missing girls' well-off parents were Irene Papas as Dona Aurelia Avallone and Marc Poli as Don Alberto Avallone. The police commissioner was Virgilio Gazzolo. Michael Forest dubbing was for the Milian reporter character, Andrea Martelli. The storyline has a reporter, and his gal friend attempts to investigate a child killing in a small southern Italian village where residents there are suspicious of everyone and everything.

In the dubbing business there in Rome according to actor Robert Mark (Rod Dana) (for the *WAI!* Issue no. 62) who worked the trade himself stated that in the beginning it all started with Mike and Rhoda Billingsley. It was called during that era the *Billingsley Organization.* Nowadays, he says it's called the *ELDA* (*English Language Dubbers Association*). Mickey Knox was in charge of the Rome division for years. Actors Robert Woods did dubbing for a while, as did Larry Ward. Even Henry Silva also learned dubbing while there in Rome, then back in the States went on to do some cartoon work for television along those same techniques.

Down in Spain, Barcelona, and Madrid way per Dana, Sidney Pink was the big dubbing producer there of the early 1960s. Then it fell to Mel Welles later known as the dubbing king they called him. We always got to stay in the best of hotels, ate the best foods, he said. They treated us well, I recall. The need was there, and the opportunity couldn't be missed. The need is probably more so today with film technology advances in cartoon characterization and with the acceptance of 3-D versions in both television and movies here in America. A few like Forest have stamped out a real lucrative business during and since the 1960's *Spaghetti* Westerns were coming out of Europe. More power to them.

It seems that after completing the *Duckling* film, he returned for a few commitments back in the States before returning to Rome for his long one-time stay. Back in the United States, he worked on a motorcycle gang flick called *The Dirt Gang* (1972). His part was that of biker Zeno. It seems the gang happens upon a movie crew filming in the desert, and they raise havoc with them menacing all there, destroying the equipment, but mostly, the women get the worse end of things. Not a pleasant thing to watch.

Next film was an Indian story called *Cotter* (1973). Don Murray stars as Cotter, a Sioux Indian who gets to drinking bad, thus hindering his job in the rodeo as a clown/protector to the riders. This all goes south when a bull ravages a young rider on his watch. He leaves the ring a broken man, consumed with guilt, and his continued drinking causes him even more problems when he's implicated in a murder, and nearly lynched. It seems all his old friends have now rejected him, but for one. Forest portrays an Indian who tries to help the downtrodden former rodeo clown. Interestingly, Forest claims in his genealogy searches that he is an eighth Sioux and Chippewa Indian himself.

For a 1972 release, Forest was requested for a Spanish/Italian coproduction of a comedic Western to be shot in Yugoslavia called *Now They Call Him Sacramento.* He agreed and returned to Italy to go along with director Alfonso Balcazar and crew for his production *(Balcazar Producciones Cinematograficas)* of a story he'd written about three partners who set out to rob a shipment of monies on its way to a small town. However, the crooked banker has plans for robbing it as well, and they hit as the same time. A mess ensues, and after the robbery, they all split up and go separate ways. Sacramento (Forest) along the way comes to the aid of farmer being attacked by men of an evil land baron. Back in town the women folk rise up against all the bad guys, thus another mess ensues. Sacramento soon falls for a young widow Jenny (Malisa Longo). Others of the cast were Fernando Bilbao (Fred Harrison) as Jim, Paolo Gozlino as the sheriff, and Luigi Bonos as Tequilla to name a few. Trivia report claims the Barcelona town set used was destroyed during various scenes and with the finale by the fires and all the explosives used.

Back pretty much to stay now this go around he was in for a new 1973 release of another *Helen, yes . . . Helen of Troy* film. This was an Italian production and directed by Alfonso Brescia. The stars were Don Backy, Peter Landers, Pupo De Luca, Barbara Betti, and Andrea Scotti as Enea. Michael Forest is Agamemnon and Christa Linder as Helen, with Lea Lander and Howard Ross as Paride. A more serious Italian rehash of for the love of a woman, Troy falls to Greece legendary story.

During his long stay this time in Rome, nearly ten years, he was mostly involved from here on out with film dubbing work. He did some twenty-five films of this nature dubbing English in all. The films were mostly for the crime / *Polizia* genre of films that were so extremely popular during that period in time. Forest did manage a sprinkling of acting parts in a few films during this period in time, though they were few. He was pretty much in demand with his dubbing projects that were coming out of left field as the Italians kept churning them out.

It does look like he may have taken a home trip about 1976 because he's credited with one episode of the TV show called *The Rookies* with

William Shatner and Heather Locklear. That episode was "From Out of the Darkness" (Forest as Novak). Then it was back to Rome and more *Polizia* film dubbing. It appears that he was nearly extensive in dubbing one Maurizio Merli, popular Italian actor of the era, doing about eight of his characters. Merli actually churned out some thirty plus films within his short career in films, mostly of the *Polizia* genre. Amazingly Merli*, a health nut to the core died in 1989 while involved in a tennis match collapsing at the age of only forty-nine.

Some of the films in which Forest acted in during this period were *The Magnificent Daredevil* (1973), which starred Giuliano Gemma (Forest as Bauner), *The Loves and Times of Scaramouche* (1976) (Forest as Dangler); next was a religious film outing film in North Africa called *The Message* (1977) (Forest as Kjalid). The film starred Anthony Quinn as Hamza, Irene Papas as Hind, Michael Ansara as Abu Sofyan, Johnny Sekka as Bilal among a cast of hundreds. Directed by Moustapha, Akkad tells here an historic accounting of the birth of the Islamic faith and the story of its prophet Mohammed and his part in the Islam religion. It was released in France July 1977 under death threats. Forest claimed it took a year to make this film and that he and others, even amid some threats to their personage, for their involvement was proud to have been associated in the making of this well-told epic.

Before leaving Europe for the States, Forest went on to do a *Jaws* rehash with one called *The Shark Hunter* for a 1979 release. It starred Franco Nero, Werner Pochath, Jorge Luke, and Mike Forest as Donovan. The film direction was by Enzo G. Castellari (Enzo Girolami) popular Euro filmmaker of the era. Forest, now back in the States shortly after wrapping the above *Hunter* film, he bailed off almost immediately in a TV soap series called *the Young*

---

* One of Merli's films that Michael Forest dubbed was called *Man Called Blade* (1977), a late entry *Spaghetti* Western that starred Merli as the character Blade, also costarring John Steiner as Theo Waller, Irishman Donal O'Brien as Burt Craven, and Philippe Leroy as the town boss McGowan, among others. It was directed by Sergio Martino. Storyline concerns Blade, a bounty hunter who is deadly with his tomahawk like hatchet. He captures bandit Craven with an axe-throw chopping off his hand. Later turns him loose when no monies could be collected from the oppressed town. Crossing McGowan man, Waller is a mistake. The sadistic Waller captures him, beats him, and buries him up to his neck, forces his eyes open and leaves him for dead in the glaring sun. Craven helps him escape this death sentence. Blade is now obsessed with rage and is after Waller for leaving him to die. He's back now, and his hatchet is razor sharp!

and the Restless as Jim Davis (1979); his next venture similar to this was on another soap series called *Days of Our Lives* as Corey Maxwell from (1979-'80). Later, while in NYC, he did another soap series called *As The World Turns* as Nick Andropoulos, a leading role from (1980-'82).

While there in NYC, he resumed his stage appearances and wound up on a Broadway production "Breakfast with Les and Bes." Later, for shooting in Atlanta, he did a few years on yet another soap show called *The Catlins.* As member of an *Equity-Waiver* theater company, he was nominated for his performance in "Painting Churches" as Outstanding Male Actor in a Drama.

Mostly retiring from acting after his leaving that he settled in for the long haul with mostly character dubbing for animated cartoon series for both here and aboard. The Japanese was a big user of this produce for their commercial video games and such. Forest has continued to work pretty much at his leisure now doing this work. With his home in the Seattle, Washington area, he commutes by his private plane to and from Los Angeles for his dubbing sessions. He's contented there at home now with wife, Diana, and their cat Puffy. He once stated about his European career, "I did a lot of work in Europe . . . I never regretted a moment of that over there. It gave me an opportunity to go places and see things and meet people, and I would never have had those opportunities had I not been in the acting profession."

Our actor / voice dubber was in attendance at the first ever, one-day only, Saturday, March 19, 2011, Los Angeles held *Spaghetti* Western Film Festival. Included with the World Premiere Screening of *Wild East Productions* latest DVD release of *Dead Men Don't Count* (1968) with star Mark Damon, who was also in attendance. A showing was of Leone's *A Fistful of Dollars* (1964), and the Quentin Tarantino favorite *Gatling gun* (1968), courtesy of *Dorado Films* with star Robert Woods, who was also in attendance. Also, they showed an ultra-rare *Spaghetti* Western trailer DVD especially compiled by *Wild East Productions* for the occasion.

A Special Guest Panel was held with for a panel discussion with the actor attending: Robert Woods, Michael Forest, Brett Halsey, Dan Van Husen, Richard Harrison, Jack Betts (Hunt Powers), and Neil Summers. They shared with the audience story, experiences, reminisces, and conversations all moderated by Tom Betts of *WAI! Westerns . . . All'Italiana!* internet blogspot.

Michael Forest enjoyed this experience so much he also made himself available for a cameo shot in a new Western film *The Scarlet Worm* (2011) by producer / director Michael Fredianelli and executive producer: Gerald Herman. This film was already in production in California at the time of the festival. Mike Forest's cameo role was as Judge Hanchett. Other actors of the Italian Westerns who were also involved in this film were Dan Van Husen as Heinrich Kley and Brett Halsey (as Montgomery Ford, the pseudonym he'd used in his Euro films).

Storyline concerns an aging gunman training a young gun for hire in a plot to kill a brothel owner who's been performing his own barbaric abortions on his girls. Other noted people associated with this film were associate producer Eric Zaldivar as Gus, associate producer Mike Malloy as Love Cowboy, and coproducer / cinematographer Michael A. Martinez.

Even as our actor Forest is now in his eighties, there doesn't appear to be much slowing down for him as he is healthy and appears fit as a fiddle. We can assume he'll continue in his voice-over work as a field of choice, as well as the occasional cameo opportunity should it arise, such as the last aforementioned film for some time to come. It's nice to know the man is still active and in such good spirits. We all wish him the continued best. Carry on there, big guy, and keep those earphones and mike handy.

End.

- Below is a complete filmography listing of Michael Forest's Euro Westerns. The dates are aligned as close as possible with information currently at hand, plus international release dates included. **Poster pictures are accredited to the Sebastian Haselbeck collection via his website. Actor's photo courtesy of the First LA Spaghetti Western Festival advertisements and postings accessed via www.spaghetti-western.net website. Thanks again, Sebastian.*

MICHAEL FOREST'S EURO WESTERNS FILMOLOGY

Note: This first film title although filmed in Spain, was not considered a Spaghetti Western at all since it was found to have been strictly a US production. Even though, many of the actors used in this film were or had been previously associated with those films of that European genre.

1969

100-Rifles (not considered a true *Spaghetti* Western); was a *US* production (although was filmed in and around Almeria, Spain) Director Tom Gries (ex-*Rat Patrol* director), Forest as Mara (the silent Indian scout) (3/26/69) It starred Jim Brown as Sheriff Lyedeck, Raquel Welch as guerrilla band leader Sarita, and Burt Reynolds as Yaqui Joe. Others: Eric Braeden (ex star as German tank commander of the "Rat Patrol" TV series that Gries directed). Also starring Aldo Sambrell, José Manuel Martin and Soledad Miranda (the girl in opening sequences with Joe)

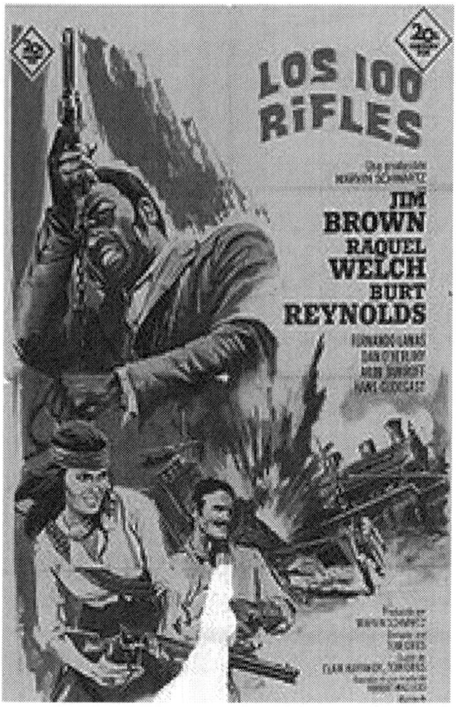

1971

The Last Rebel, *L'Ultimo Pistolero*; Spa/ US/ Ital, Producer/ Director Denys McCoy (Larry G. Sprangler) (Forest as Cowboy); 9/24/71; It starred Joe Namath (all star ex-*NY Jets* footballer) as Burnside Hollis; Jack Elam as gunman Matt Graves; Woody Strode as ex-slave Duncan; Ty Hardin as sheriff, and Victoria George as Pearl.

1972

Requiem for a Bounty Hunter *(*a.k.a. *Requiem for a Bounty Killer); Lo Ammazzo come un cane ma Lui Rideva Ancora;* a.k.a. *Death Played a Flute*; Ital, Director Angelo (Elo) Panaccio (Forest as John Barton); 1/2/72; Per the credits it starred Ray O'Connor (Reno Capitani) as Cameron, Laurence Bien (Lorenzo Bien) as the sheriff and Thomas Rudy (Tomas Rudi). Actually the main stars were Michael Forrest, Steven Tedd (Giuseppe Cardillo) as Kimble/ Whistle; and Susanna Levi as Suzy Barton.

Now They call him Sacramento; a.k.a. *The Twelve Bandoleros, I Bandoleros Della Dodicesima* a.k.a. *Now They Call Him Amen*; Spa / Ital, Director Al Bagrain (Alfonso Balcazar) (Forest stars as Sacramento/Amen); 12/23/72; It costarred Fred Harrison (Fernando Bilbao) as Big Jim; Malisa Longo as Barbara / Jenny McKinley; Luigi Bonos as old Tequila, and Paolo Gozlino as the sheriff.

1976

Man Called Blade, a.k.a. *Mannaja (Hatchet);* a.k.a. *Mannaja: A Man Called Blade/ Blade*; Ital, Director Sergio Martino (**Forest was not** actually in this film, but was the *English dubber* for Merli's "Blade" character); 8/13/72; Stars Maurizio Merli as Blade; John Steiner as Theo Woller, Donal O'Brien as Burt Craven, Martine Brochard as Angela, and Philippe Leroy as McGowan.

End.

BIBLIOGRAPHY
(M. Forest)

Betts, Tom, editor *WAI! (Westerns . . . All'Italiana)* Fanzine and currently owner / curator of the *WAI! Blogspot* via the Internet; Tom's personal information, and contact with the actor has been invaluable to this chapter on Forest.

Connolly, Bill, editor *Spaghetti Cinema* Fanzine article for Issue no. 62, posted film work of Woody Strode via article and film listings for "Farewell Woody" by Keith Hall Jr.

Haselbeck, Sebastian, owner / curator for Internet website: *www.spaghetti-western.net*

Internet, via: *www.IMDB.com* (informational link for "LA First Spaghetti Western Festival")

Internet, via: *www.IMDB.com* ; posted film / TV listings for the actor, plus Personal Quotes; "Mini Bio for Michael Forest" by Tom Weaver.

Internet, via: *www.yesweekly.com* ; posted article of August 5, 2009 for *YES! Weekly*: "Western Film Fair Corrals Actor Michael Forest" by Mark Burger.

Weisser, Thomas, *Spaghetti Westerns: the Good, the Bad, and the Violent*, (1992) *McFarland*, Jefferson NC.

Western: All'Italiana (2001) (Book two), by Antonio Bruschini and Federico de Zigno, *Glittering Images,* Firenze, Italy

The Western: The Complete Film Sourcebook (The Film Encyclopedia) (1983); by Phil Hardy, *William Morrow and Co, Inc.,* NY., pp 333 (*The Last Rebel)*

Wikipedia, the free encyclopedia; Posted bio report on the actor Michael Forest

FRANCO E CICCIO

THE ABBOTT & COSTELLO OF THE ITALO WEST

Photo courtesy of ETC no. 11

FRANCO FRANCHI
(Francesco Benenato)
(1922-1992)

CICCIO INGRASSIA
(Francesco Ingrassia)
(1922-2003)

Ciccio Ingrassia first met Franco Franchi in 1954. Later, they formed the terrific comedy team duo of Franco e Ciccio. During their peak career times of the 1960s and after, they wound up making some 130 films together into the 1990s. Franco was the shorter of the two and the Italian slapstick version, cross between Lou Costello and Jerry Lewis fame. All the while Ciccio was more of the straight man, not unlike the taller Bud Abbott, or even the Dean Martin character of their respective comedy teams during their era of fame in America.

The year was 1962 when they made their first film together as a comedy duo, it—and similar like it—soon became a screen sensation. It was called *I Due Della Legione Straniera;* a.k.a. *Two Idiots of the Foreign Legion.* It was directed by Lucio Fulci. The producers *Titanus* then saw at that time there was potential in these two comics when teamed together. They then came on the idea of making a series of parody films, mimicking (spoofing) the popular movies of the various Italian genres of the day. Hereby, the joining of the two comedians Franco Franchi and Ciccio Ingrassia would now be known as the comedy duo *Franco e Ciccio,* names that would go down in history of the Italian cinema.

Actually for the spoofing duo, their first genre Western was one called *Two Gangsters in the Wild West,* a.k.a. *Dos Pistoleros* (1964). From the title, one would think this was a Chicago gangster film, but alas, fans are familiar enough with the Italian titles to know that may not really be the case. Also along for the ride in this film were solid genre favorites like Fernando Sancho as Rio, and Helene Chanel as Betty Blanc. Others were Aldo Giuffre and José Torres. The storyline has these two Sicilians in prison for stealing a couple of mules circa 1800s. They are helped to escape by an American, who helps them so he can get them to come with him to the American west to claim a gold mine left to them by their grandfather's will, who had been killed by a gang of bandits. The guys needed to go over and take claim to the mine as rightful kin. Obviously, the American helping them has ulterior motives looking at the mine himself.

Then for 1964, the guys would be seen in another film, not of the Western genre but a Jayne Mansfield publicity vehicle called *Primitive Love.* It starred Jayne of course as Dr. Jane. The guys were both Hotel Porters, working under the Hotel Bell Captain portrayed by Mickey Hargitay (Jane's real life hubby at the time). It was a fun outing for the pair, an Italian production directed by Luigi Scattini. The beautiful duo, Jane and Mickey were both fresh from their earlier Italian *Peplum* adventure called *Hercules against the Hydra,* a.k.a. *The loves of Hercules* (1960) from director Carlo Ludovico.

Of course, when Sergio Leone finally got around to releasing his blockbuster *Spaghetti* Western, *A Fistful of Dollars* (1964), then later *For a Few Dollars More* (1965) and finally *The Good, the Bad, the Ugly* (1966), these films sent the Italian film industry skyrocketing into orbit of Western filmmaking history. Our two comics were right along for ride with their films spoofing each of the above mentioned Leone films and many more besides.

I Due Figli di Ringo (The Two Sons of Ringo) (1966) was an Italian production directed by Giorgio Simonelli and Giuliano Carnimeo. The film stars Franco as Django, and Ciccio as Gringo. It costars Gloria Paul as Dorothy and George (Jorge) Hilton (popular South American actor of the genre). Others include: Pedro Sanchez (Ignazio Spalla) and Dick Palmer

(Mimmo Palmara) as the sheriff. The film is in part, similar of sorts to the hugely popular Leone Western, *A Fistful of Dollars*. But for the beginning first five to ten minutes as a slick little parody mimicking Leone second Western, *For a Few Dollars More* with Franco acting his crazy best for the Eastwood part, and Ciccio ties his best to mimic the Van Cleef part as a villain bounty hunter for this film. Now that the duo has made their entrance in the film, the bounty hunter Joe (Hilton) arrives. After much posturing and some gun playing by the funny men, they take off with Joe as a threesome.

Its here when the film sort of takes a turn and changes directions? Now our two arrive in another town from parts unknown. They are mistakenly welcomed as the two sons of the now deceased Ringo, the town's ex-sheriff, was the top gun around the territory. The two play up their mistaken identity as Ringo's two sons for all its worth, and about to get them in deep trouble, their guardian angel Joe arrives just in time to take up for them, doing some fancy shooting in the meantime.

Later when a stage arrives from parts unknown, two women Dorothy and Marisol get off and claim in secret that they are actually the two sons of Ringo (him not knowing they were females instead of males) they are however content to allow our two would be heroes to take the heat as the two sons, while they are looking for their Pa's stolen gold, and the culprits that stole it. All well, that ends well!

> This was kind a how basically their films went, with the guys using their parody mimicking of the various genres as a staging for their wild, sometime unbelievable antics and carryings-on such as they did. Funny to some, irritating maybe to others, but they sure made a lot of them as they were extremely popular with the European audiences. When the James Bond 007 spy films hit the screens early in the 1960s like *Goldfinger* (1964) our two beloved comics came out with comedic versions as well, *Due Mafiosi vs. Goldginger.* They also mimicked the *Peplums*; the *Mafioso* gangster films, the Jungle films, *Giallo* thrillers and the Action film genres of the era. All genres of film were subjects of their comedic trials and tribulations with their special brand of slapstick comedy added in. Not unlike some of the old *Abbott and Costello / Martin and Lewis* routine sketches of the older American films of the 1940-'50s.
>
> Other Italian comics of their day like Toto and Peppino De Filippo were all great in their own right. However, as parody kings of genre movies, this team of *Franco and Ciccio* should probably have won Oscars hands down, if not for a particular film, at for volume, because they sure starred in a lot of them.

For the guy's next Western, they turned in *Two Idiots at Fort Alamo,* a.k.a. *Two Sergeants of General Custer* (1965). This one was an Italian / Spanish coproduction from *Fida Cinematografica* and *Balcazar Producciones.* Once again, this one was also directed by Giorgio Simonelli. It stars Franco and Ciccio as the two La Pera brothers. Also starring was Margaret Lee as Beth Smith / the Lynx. Others along for the ride were Moira Orfei as Baby O'Connor; Fernando Sancho as Serg Fidhouse, Ernesto Calindri as Northern States Colonel, Franco Giacobini as Cochise, Ricardo Garrone as *The Specialist* (here giving a spoofing-nod to Sergio Corbucci's Western of the same name); and Dina Loy as Mary. Also, there was actor/producer Alfio Caltabiano as Nervous Buffalo. It could be assumed his Buffalo character was a spoofing of the Gordon Mitchell character Chief Sitting (Silly) Buffalo of *Little Rita of the Far West* (1966) the first musical *Spaghetti* Western! Alas, we fans know how some of these *Spaghetti* films can be. The storyline here we find (as we're never been able to acquire this film for viewing) has to do with a lighthearted rehashing of Custer's last stand, of sorts!

Then for their next Western we call up *Per un Pugno nell'Occhio (For a Fist in the Eye;* a.k.a. *Fistful of Knuckles* (1965). This was a Spanish / Italian coproduction, directed by Michele Lupo this time around. It starred of course Franco and Ciccio along with Paco Moran as Ramon Cocos, Lina Rosales as Consuelo, Carmen Esbri as Marisol, and Monica Randall as Carmencita. Wow, all girls! This film doesn't spoof any one film in particular, but rather the genre in general, along with all the tongue-in-cheek clichés, and expanded humor played upon by these two idiots of filmdom.

Their next Western as called *Il Bello, Il Brutto, Il Cretino,* a.k.a. *The Handsome, the Ugly, and the Stupid* (1967). Here we have an Italian production, directed by Giovanni Grimaldi. This one is defiantly a spoof-nod to Leone's blockbuster Western epic *The Good, the Bad, and the Ugly* (1966). It stars Franco (Il Brutto) and Ciccio as (Il Cretino) and Dick Palmer (Mimmo Palmara) (Il Bello). Also stars Brigitt Petry as La Donna, Lothar Gunther as Capt. Imbriatella, Enzo Andronica as sheriff no. 2 and the Buxom Myra Krupp as a Saloon Girl (Remember, she was the hotel owner's wife who made it with Manco in Leone's second film FFDM.

The storyline had to do with a couple of idiots (guess who?) who are in a prisoner of war camp at the close of the Civil War. They learn of a hidden cache of gold in a cemetery from a dying prisoner, or just the cemetery name to Il Stupid, and the grave name to Il Ugly. But now with the partner, Il Bello they seem to have acquired causes them trouble while looking for the box of gold coins.

The guys then showed up in another Italian production for a 1967 release called *Due R-R-Ringos nel Texas (Two R-R-Ringos from Texas).* This little ditty was directed by Frank Martin (Marino Girolami) and again stars the duo along with genre favorites Ennio Girolami as Bruce, Gloria Paul as Evelyn, Livio Lorenzon is Captain Nordista, and Helene Chanel as Sentenza Jane (as the *female* Bad, a nod to Leone's LVC character of his GBU film). Also in this Western for his film debut was an unaccredited Maurizio Merli,* soon to become Italy's top grossing film crime fighter commissioner of that genre of films. Here his role is that of the sergeant to the Captain Nordista (Lorenzon) character.

The storyline of the *R-R-Ringos* film is mainly another spoofing of Leone's *The Good, the Bad and the Ugly* (1966) film. It takes place during the Civil War, as our two heroes while drunk, volunteer for service in the army. Sergeant Stevens (Ciccio) has a horse that talks to him (similar to the popular *Mr. Ed* American TV show) it tells him where a treasure is buried. But in order to get to the treasure they have to get behind enemy lines where all sorts of carrying-on is going on involving the two lovable clowns.

Moving right along here on the Westerns, the next one was called *Ciccio Forgives, I Don't* (1968). This Italian production was directed by Marcello Ciorciolini. Once again it stars our favorite comedic duo France and Ciccio. Also costars Fernando Sancho as El Dablo / El Pantera. Others were Adriano Micantoni as Angel face (a spoof of Angel Eyes), and the lovely Gia Sandri as Calamity Jane. This film is (other than the nod to Leone's GBU for Angel Eyes) mainly a spoof of the 1966 film, *God Forgives, I Don't* which starred Terence Hill (Mario Girotti) as Cat Stevens, the Giuseppi Colizzi film, of s trilogy he made for the Stevens character. Since we have not located this film for review, we can only gather it mimics the action (with the added carryings on by our duo) of a train holdup, as was the plot line of the original Colizzi film.

---

* This film was not only Maurizio Merli's debut movie, but also the first of three only *Spaghetti* Westerns he did for the genre. His second Western here, classified as of a Yukon film (a spin-off of the Western genre) was called *Zanna Biance IL Protettore (White Fang, the Protector, a.k.a. White Fang to the Rescue)* (1972). An Italian production directed by Tonino Ricci. It starred Merli as Ben Dover / Burt Halloway and Gisela Hahn as Katy. Also along for this ride was Henry Silva as the evil Mr. Nelson, and of course, Saccha as their dog White Fang/Fang.

Merli's only other for the genre was *Mannaja: A Man Called Blade* (1976). This late issue for the genre stars Merli as Blade a bounty hunter. The title *Mannaja* translates to Hatchet, which is his choice of weapons. Also stars John Steiner, Donal O'Brien and Martine Brochard.

For the guy's next Western adventure, we find one called *Franco e Ciccio sul Sentiero Di Guerra (France and Ciccio on the War Path)* (1969). For this Italian production, we find the producer Giovanni (Aldo) Grimaldi once again directs the guys in another spoof, this time involving Indians against the White Man, which along with the guy's bumbling help becomes a glorious victory for the Red Man! A generalization spoofing of Cowboy/Indians as only the guys could do it. Here again stars Franco and Ciccio with costars Renato Baldini as Jeff; Adler Gray as Lucy; Joseph Persaud as Indian Chief, Stelvio Rossi as Martin. The story was by Bruno Corbucci, written along with Grimaldi who did the scripting.

Their next Western was called *I Nipoti di Zorro (The Nephews of Zorro)* (1968). An Italian production was actually a spoof of the *Zorro* (spin-off) Western genre in general, and not specifically spoofing any one *Zorro* film in particular. Besides Franco and Ciccio, it costars American ex-patriot/singer/activist/actor and defector to the communist bloc of West Germany, Dean Reed in his only film outing here with the famous duo. Unfortunately this elusive title has not been obtained for viewing. But according to reports we learn it concerns Raphael (Reed) (son of Don Dieego, the original Zorro) who secretly poses as Zorro. The guys enter the picture posing as Zorro Nephews in order to impress a girl Carmencita (Agata Flori), who unbeknownst to them is actually Raphael's girl. Included in their antics, the guys even attempt to borrow money from Don Dieego (old Zorro). Probably a cute film if it could be obtained.

Down to the wire now for the last Western listing of the famous duo is one called *I Due Figli Di Trinita (Two Sons of Trinity)* (1972). Here it seems we're spoofing those comedic *Trinity* films. An Italian production directed by Richard Kean (Osvaldo Civirani). The Trinita brothers (Franco and Ciccio) star. It seems from the reports they run some sort of refueling station for cowboys, you know pit stop during the cattle drive, etc. Fresh horses, plenty to eat and drink and girls, whoa the girls! Co starring Anna Degli Uberti* as Calamity Jane, who takes care of the guys light work, like killing! Also stars Lucretia Love as Lola, and Franco Ressel as Armstrong. Others favorite of the genre along for the ride are; Fortunato Arena, Goffredo (Freddy) Unger, and Andrea Scotti.

---

* We wonder if possibly this actress Anna Degli Uberti is any relation to the *Uberti* replica gun manufacturers of northern Italy. We already know the *Uberti* family has been heavily involved in furnishing of the replica/period firearms for the *Spaghetti* Western movies since their inception back in the early 1960s. Not only the replicas period pieces, but also specialty firearms/cannons and *Gatling* gun like replicas for the various films.

At any rate, it seems the plot of this duo-fueled storyline we understand, has to do with Calamity Jane, the guy's aunt comes to their aid bailing them out of jail (for whatever reason they were in?). She then gives over to them a long secret treasure map with an X marks the spot for buried loot. They set off in search of this secret treasure trove.

Some members of the theater going public simply loved these comedic versions, especially the European folks. Others like the Americans, when they were finally given the opportunity of seeing these parodies (dubbed into English) were at best a hit 'n' miss audience. Some seemed to like them while some evoked a "take 'em or leave 'em" attitude toward the comedic efforts. Remembering of course, the Americans of the 1980s and '90s had evolved into a harder class of peoples of that era, more devoted to work and sports than to any sort of screen pleasures. Not being able to let their hair down, so to speak, and relax enough to enjoy this type of film. Most would rather watch football or baseball in their spare time, than an old slapstick movie for Europe. Personally I would take a straight Euro Western any day. However, I guess as I've gotten older, I tend to relax differently now, and do enjoy seeing the Italian duo's antics as they spoof the various films of that era.

Alas, some fans of the Italian genres still love to watch their favorite film types and actors of their choice, even if they sometimes are in such a film where mimicking/spoofing their respective genres. Some of those favorite genre actors like Fernando Sancho or Maurizio Merli, or even Dean Reed are sometime a pleasure to watch, regardless of the film type.

We do have one last Western to add to the repertoire for a 1975 release. Yet another Italian production, this one is unique in that the duo are *not* together for this one. Franco Franchi goes it alone in this *Zorro* rehash as Paco/Zorro for *IL Sogno di Zorro (Dream of Zorro)* a.k.a. *Grandson of Zorro* (1975). The film was directed by Mariano Laurenti, produced and written by Mario Mariani. Franco's costars are Mario Colli as Don Diego, Gianni Musy as General Ruarte, Pedro Sanchez (Ignazio Spalla) as Sergeant Garcia, and Paola Tedesco as Zaira. Also, there's a Friar Miguel (Maurizio Arena).

The storyline deals with an inept individual Paco who dreams of becoming Zorro. The fact that the general is now hitting on his fiancée Zaira, is only one of his immediate problems. Another one is that his servants are aware of his dreams and devise a plan to help him along as it were. They give him a sleeping concoction that while asleep, he's actually in a sleep-walking mode and become the crime-fighting Zorro, an undefeatable hero of the people! Doesn't sound too bad, but alas we never know about these films until they are viewed.

This pretty well brings to a close the Western genre film work for this comic duo of the Italian cinema. Below we'll include some of their other genre films just to give the reader an opportunity to see a partial volume of films they were actually involved with. It is staggering, to say the least. After all we have a total of ten for the duo pair, and the last one above was just for Franco Franchi which would make him eleven. Some of the other films they made were the following:

The 002 Secret Agents (1964) (spy)
Two Mafiosi (1964)
Two Prisoners Escape Sing, Sing (1964)
Due Mafioso Contro Goldginger (1965) (spy)
002 Operation Moon (1965) (sci-fi)
Two Mafiosi Contro Al Capone (1966)
Two Marines and a General (1966) with Buster Keaton seen here in his last film.
Dr. Goldfoot and the Girl Bombs (1967) (spy) with Vincent Price
Two Champions (1967)
The Two Pirates (1967)
Two Italians in America (1967)
Agent 008 Alive after three Death Tries (1967)
The Two Escaped Men (1967)
Two Crazy Persons and a Parrot (1967)
The Barbers of Sicily (1967)
The Two Gladiators (1968)
The Two Detectives (1968)
The Two Deputies (1968)
The Two Crusaders (1968)
Two Sicilians in the Court of Grande Khan (1968)
Two Sicilians in Africa (1970)
Two Whites in Black Africa (1970)
Two Magicians of the Ball (1971)
The Adventures of Pinocchio (1972)
Kung Fu, From Sicily with Fury (1973)

With the twenty-five listed above, we can clearly see the volume of their films was staggering of all genres, not just isolated in just the Westerns—although ten in that alone was a lot. We would like to bring this write-up on the pair to a close with these parting words of these two actors of the Italian cinema. Some of us will remember and never forget the likes of Buster Keaton, Bud Abbott, and Lou Costello or Dean Martin and Jerry Lewis of our time. While others, will remember and think back with a smile of the Franco e Ciccio era of film. Long may they be remembered, ye olde great duo . . .

Collage courtesy of ETC issue no. 11 back cover art

End.

- Below is a complete filmography of Franco e Ciccio's Euro Westerns. The dates are aligned as close as possible with information currently at hand, plus international release dates included. **Poster pictures are accredited to the Sebastian Haselbeck collection via his website www.spaghetti-westerns.net. Many thanks, Sebastian.*

FRANCO E CICCIO SPAGHETTI WESTERN FILMS . . .

1965

For a Fist in the Eye, *Per un Pugno Nell'Occhio;* a.k.a. *Fistful of Knuckles*; Spa / Ital, Director Michele Lupo (Stars Franco and Ciccio); 5/14/65; Costars Paco Moran as Ramon Cocos, Lina Rosales as Consuelo, Carmen Esbri as Marisol, Monica Randall as Carmencita, and Jesus Puente as Captain Hernandez.

1965

Two Gangsters in the Wild West, *Due Mafiosi Nel Far West* (Western); Spa / Ital, Director Giorgio Simonelli (Stars Franco and Ciccio as Capone brothers); 10/16/65; Costars Fernando Sancho as Rio and Helene Chanel as Betty Blanc.

1966

Two Sergeants of General Custer, *I due Sergenti Del Generale Custer;* a.k.a. *Two Idiots at Fort Alamo*; Ital / Spa, Director Giorgio Simonelli (Stars Franco and Ciccio as the La Pera brothers); 7/11/66; It costarred Margaret Lee as Beth Smith, Moira Orfei as Baby O'Connor, Fernando Sancho as Serg Fidhouse and Alfio Caltabiano as Nervous Buffalo.

1966

The Two Sons of Ringo, *I Due Figli Di Ringo;* a.k.a. *The Sons of Ringo*; Ital, Director Giorgio Simonelli and Giuliano Carnimeo (Stars Franco as Django and Ciccio as Gringo); 5/18/67; Spoofing the films *A Fistful of Dollars*, and *For a Few Dollars More* in the beginning sequences. Costars George Hilton as Joe, Gloria Paul as Dorothy and Mimmo Palmara as the Sheriff.

1967

The Handsome, the Ugly, and the Stupid, *IL Bello, Il Brutto, Il Cretino*; Ital, Giovanni (Aldo) Grimaldi (Stars Franco as Il Brutto and Ciccio as Il Cretino); 8/13/67; Costars Dick Palmer (Mimmo Palmara) as Il Bello, Brigitt Petry as La Donna, Giovanni Ivan Scratuglia as the "confessing Sergeant", Fortunato Arena as Mexican and Mara Krupp as Saloon Girl.

1967

Two R-R-Ringos from Texas, *Due R-R-Ringos nel Texas*; Ital, Director Frank Martin (Marino Girolami) (Stars Franco as Caterina and Ciccio as Stevens); 8/25/67; Costars Livio Lorenson stars as the drunken Captain Nordista. His sergeant is played by debuting Maurizio Merli who is a spy for the confederates. Also stars Helene Chanel as Sentenza.

1970

Ciccio Forgives, I Don't! ; *Ciccio Perdona . . . Io No!* ; Ital, Director Marcello Ciorciolini (Stars Franco e Ciccio); 9/26/68. Costars Fernando Sancho as El Diablo / El Pantera, Adriano Micantoni as Angel Face, Mario Maranzana as Baleno and Gia Sandri as Calamity Jane. Others were Renato Baldini, Rossella Bergamonti as Betty Jane and Giuseppe Castellano as sheriff.

1968

The Nephews of Zorro, *I Nipoti di Zorro*; Ital, Director Marcello Ciorciolini (stars Franco e Ciccio as La Vacca brothers); 12/12/68. Costars Dean Reed as Raphael de La Vega / Zorro Jr., Agata Flori as Carmencita, Pedro Sanchez as Sgt. Alvarez, and Franco Fantasia as Don Diego de la Vega/Zorro Sr.

1969

Franco e Ciccio on the War Path, *Franco e Ciccio sul Sentiero di Guerra*; Ital, Director Giovanni (Aldo) Grimaldi (Stars Franco e Ciccio); 11/20/69. Costars Renato Baldini as Jeff, Adler Gray as Lucy Foster, Joseph Persaud as Indian Chief, Stelvio Rossi as Martin, Lino Banfi as the Mormon and Fulvio Mingozzi as sheriff.

1972
Two Sons of Trinity, *I Due Figli di Trinita*; Ital, Director Richard Kean (Osvaldo Civirani) (Stars Franco e Ciccio as Trinita brothers); 7/26/72. Costars Anna Degli Uberti as Calamity Jane, Lucretia Love as Lola and Franco Ressel as Armstrong. Others were Fortunato Arena, Goffredo (Freddy) Unger, and Andrea Scotti.

1975
The Dream of Zorro, *Il Sogno di Zorro;* a.k.a. *Grandson of Zorro*; Ital, Director Mariano Laurenti (Stars Franco Franchi as Paco/Zorro); 8/16/75. Costars Mario Colli as Don Diego, Gianni Musi as General Ruarte, Pedro Sanchez (Ignazio Spalla) as Sgt. Garcia, Paola Tedesco as Zaira, and also with Maurizio Arena as Friar Miguel.

End.

BIBLIOGRAPHY
(Franco e Ciccio)

Betts, Tom, editor *WAI! (Westerns . . . All'Italiana)* Fanzine articles and Blogspot: Posted entry: *The Grandson of Zorro,* 5/17/2011

Connolly, Bill, editor *Spaghetti Cinema* Fanzine articles and Blogspot: Posted entry: "Zorro Films" 8/12/2010

Haselbeck, Sebastian, owner/curator for Internet website: *www.spaghetti-western.net*

Internet, via: *www.IMDB.com* title listings for F. Franchi (Benenato); Ciccio Ingrassia

Internet, via: *www.ioffer.com* DVD movie listings sale and summery for *Franco e Ciccio Films*

Ledbetter, Craig, editor of now defunct *ETC (European Trash Cinema)* Fanzine, Issue no. 11 with *Franco Ciccio* "Euro trash Collage" cover designs by Tim and Donna Lucas of *Video Watchdog*

Weisser, Thomas, *Spaghetti Westerns: the Good, the Bad, and the Violent*, (1992) *McFarland*, Jefferson NC.

Western: All'Italiana (Book three), by Antonio Bruschini and Federico de Zigno, *Glittering Images,* Firenze, Italy; book III, 2006, Most of the films listed in Euro Western Filmography Index section pp 88-119, *but are not actually discussed within any if the three book volumes per se.*

Zorro Unmasked (1998) by Sandra Curtis; Appendix C: Zorro Film foreign listings 1952-'75

MICKEY HARGITAY

(1926-2006)

STRONGMAN SHOOTS FIRST!

Mickey Hargitay, ex-*Mr. Universe* of 1955 was yet another of our *Spaghetti* Western film stars. While some folks believe that Mickey's only claim to fame was the known fact that he was once married to the world-renowned sex goddess of film and Hollywood, Jayne Mansfield, however, Mickey Hargitay was in fact a rare talent on his own.

Born as Miklos Hargitay of Budapest, Hungary 1926, he left his native country after WWII immigrating to the United States as a young man of eighteen to avoid the mandatory draft of the Soviet military. Stateside, he would settle in Indianapolis, Indiana. A young Mick found work as a dancer and soon married Mary Birge, his adagio* dance partner. Soon, Mary found herself with a child and later a baby girl. Tina was born in 1949. Mick, however, had other ideas about his fatherhood and of marriage at this time in his life.

Now that he had decided to follow in the footsteps of his newly found idol of the bodybuilding arena, Steve Reeves caught his attention again when he captured the new *Mr. Universe* title of 1950 after already holding the *Mr. America* title since 1947. All the while working Mick dreamed. He became more and more interested in this bodybuilding business. Another of his newfound idols was Reg Park, the British-born bodybuilder, also impressed him. Park would soon capture the *Mr. Universe* title himself from Reeves for 1951. Then not long afterward, Steve Reeves was whisked off to stardom during those early filmmaking years in Europe. Those were the years of the epics, the *Peplums* (the Sword 'n' Sandal) movies, a genre of film all their own.

> By the late 1950s, Steve Reeves had become Italy's biggest *Peplum* star, with the Italian *Hercules* (1959); *Hercules Unchained* (1960) films in Europe. By the time they hit the American theaters, he was on top of the heap. The Italian producers of the era were churning out those *Peplum* films out like spaghetti. Later as that film genre gave way to the rise of the up and coming Italian version of the Hollywood western, Reeves enjoyed a long lucrative career in Europe but would only make one contribution to the so-called *Spaghetti* Westerns that were to follow the fading *Peplums* of the mid-1960s. His one entry was called *Long Ride from Hell* (1970).

---

* Adagio dancing is a combination using strength and agility of gymnastics with the art of classical dance numbers. Mick's father had excelled in sports and always pushed his son to maintain good health and stay fit by his challenging himself in sports. He was an early soccer player and was on the Hungarian Junior National Team. Mick went on to tell *Celebrity Interview* that he became a very good gymnast, "I was such a good speed skater that before I came to America, they were about to recruit me for the Olympic team."

In America, by 1947, he worked all sort of menial jobs such as carpenter and plumber. He'd actually begun a construction business for himself and once found himself at a private country club there in Indianapolis with a friend. A lifeguard there had been watching him doing handstands, back flips, push ups, etc. He said the guy had a new magazine, and on the cover was a photo of Steve Reeves. Mick said he couldn't get over how good he looked all muscular and physically fit. He figured from then on that look was for him.

While Mick was increasingly impressed and maybe even a tad envious with those bodybuilders like Reeves, Park, and another one hot from California's Muscle Beach area, Brad Harris also joined the crowd en route to Europe and screen success in the *Peplums*. Mick, however, seemed to hold no particular visions of entering into film work, at least at that point in time. He had continued to work hard within the *World* held bodybuilding competitions and went on to claim such titles as *Mr. World* AAU of the *Tall* division in fourth place for 1952. Then he took, *Mr. World*-AAU of the *Overall* division in seventh place, that same year. Later, when in New York City, he'd gone out for another competition in which he'd captured ninth place for *Mr. America*-AAU. Again, in 1954, he etched on up the ladder to capture eighth place for the same NYC title. Now while in his prime, at age twenty-four he came in statistically as being 6' and 2" tall and weighing in at a pumped 230 lb. He moved away from the construction business and began to seek out work in avenues that would bring him more to the attention of the public's eye.

It was also during those early to mid-1950's years when actress Mae West, famous for not only her bawdy past films, but also her infamous quips like, "Come up and see me sometime!" She had a famous nightclub act in those days that she took on tour throughout the hotspots of American. For a few weeks every season, they would hit the biggies like Las Vegas, Los Angeles, Chicago, and NYC. Back in 1954, they were touring some of NYC's more trendy and flashy nightspots. West, always having her eye out for new talent, as it were, noticed Hargitay's picture-perfect pose on the cover of an older October 1953 issue of *Strength and Health* magazine. She sent her people out to find him and set up a meet with this gorgeous hunk a man. Soon Mickey's career was off and running. Fortunately, he had landed a chorus line part in what had become known as *La West's* male entourage show of 1955. Now, he was be able to get the exposure he needed to advance his popularity, while strutting his stuff out there on stage with other like young men clad in nothing but loincloths, hovering, and buzzing around the queen bee herself, Mae West.

By the years end of 1955, Mickey's bodybuilding perseverance had paid off big-time when he captured the *NABBA* title of *Mr. Universe* as a first place contender for the *Tall* division, and then again later for the *NABBA*-Overall division. He was off his circuit still doing the shows with West and her boys. As Mick stayed on tour that year with the troupe as they made the rounds out west to LA where West picked of a few more Muscle Beach bodybuilder types for her entourage, one fellow in particular stood out, he was Chuck Pendleton, a schoolteacher by profession, and an active bodybuilder who had a inkling to get ahead in this world. He joined the all-male revue in 1956, and he and Mick hit it off from the start as good friends. They were both hard into their training, and it paid off for both of them in the years to come.

When West popular *Latin Quarter* show hit NYC in 1956, both Mick and Chuck were on board. It was at this dinner show touted about town as Mae West's *Latin Quarter Review,* it was where Mick first met the lovely and stunning Jayne Mansfield. Jayne was recently separated from her first hubby Paul Mansfield, whom she had married while still in high school back in 1950. As Jayne had once put it about the marriage, "We had a baby nine months and ten seconds later." That child was named Jayne Marie and born on November 8, 1950. Now loose from her marital bounds, at least out of sight, Jayne would constantly exclaim to her public that she was always on the prowl looking for a big, muscle-bound man to satisfy her needs, and as she put it (the insinuation being sexual of course). Now she had spotted the gorgeous, blond-haired Adonis (Mickey) who she'd set her sights for and quipped over to Mae West, "I want two things here tonight, a steak for my dog and an introduction to *Mr. Universe.*" Hmm or as "The beefsteak on the end" as I've also heard it reported.

Jayne, who was readily within eyeshot of this handsome hunk of a man, proclaimed he was hers. Already she was the talk of the publicity hounds, and this just added fuel to the fires with a new romance in the wings. Mickey's big number within Mae's review was "Everything, I have is yours." Jayne took it to heart. The very next day, they attended a public function together where she was being crowned Blossom Queen. Later, they were spotted doing all the trendy nightspots, and fire flew between Mae West and Jayne Mansfield.

Not to stand still for Jayne stealing one from her stable West demanded that Mickey make a public statement proclaiming that he and Jayne were only together for publicity reasons. Instead, during a press conference in Washington DC, Mickey did just the opposite when he proclaimed his true feelings for Jayne. There was a scene, as one might figure, another member of Mae's entourage, another huge twenty-four-year-old Adonis named Chuck Krauser (accidentally, he claimed, but on purpose it would seem) caught Mickey off guard, knocking him to the floor. Afterward, Mickey would explain, "Krauser had a tremendous jealously for me because Miss West showed affection for me. Miss West has been very upset since I am with Jayne. All of a sudden, he hit me like a train three times. I get knocked out. I get a cut in the eye and lips, and I hurt my knee when I fell down unexpectedly."

Chuck rushed over to his friend, and when it arrived helped to get him in the ambulance, as it was pulling out taking him to the hospital, West could be heard calling after it, "Get him back early. We got another show to do." The June seventh newspaper headlines proclaimed: "Mae West's Strong Men in Battle." The press loved it, though Jayne was somewhat dismayed at all the press reports that seemed to be more aligned with West and her entourage than with her. West, however, really did seem to be enjoying all the attention.

Not long after Mickey had left the show, West brought to the press's attention that he was still married in Indianapolis and had been only an upholsterer when she found him. She claimed that, she had been the one who had put him up on a pedestal so the world could see him and that it all had gone to his head. After all, she quipped. "He's the old *Mr. Universe*, last year's model. They've already named a new one." And that they had, Mr. Reg Park.

Mae went on to say to the press, "He said that I fired him because of Mansfield, but that's not true. The show winds up this week, and I go into summer stock. He started making remarks about how I was Jealous of him, and Krauser,* who's sort of a boy friend of mine, just knocked him down and beat him up." Then Mae went on to give the press and the world her opinion of Miss Jayne Mansfield. "As for this Mansfield, I think she's a dangerous publicity seeker. Maybe if she went to school and learned how to act, she wouldn't have to do that." After that what little bit of friendship that had been in the wings for Jayne, Mickey and Mae, was now all over to be sure! The two lovebirds could now move on with their romance.

During this early period when Mickey had met Jayne, she had been appearing on Broadway in *Will Success Spoil Rock Hunter.* Mickey's bodybuilding career was beginning to wane after his meeting up with Jayne, although he would still continue to be popular on magazine covers. Only now, his being with Jayne tended to uplift and strengthen his popularity even more with both genders.

> Other early, popular magazine cover stints for that era of Mickey were October 1953—*Strength and Health.*
>
> May 1954 he appeared on *IronMan* vol. 13, no. 6.
>
> September 1955 while still the ranking *Mr. Universe* he appeared on another *IronMan* vol. 15, number 2.
>
> November 1955 he appeared on *Muscle Power* vol. 18, number 10.
>
> And again on *Strength and Health*, for the November issue of 1955.

---

* When Hargitay recovered, he pressed charges and Krauser wound up paying a $300 fine for his part in the incident. This brought Krauser a certain amount of notoriety and per the wishes of Mae West he underwent an official name change to Paul Novak.

> His last cover appearance this era was on that of *Muscle Builder*, vol. 5, number 5 of 1955 while still holding the title of Mr. *Universe.*
>
> Interestingly, Mickey would not appear again on any covers until nine years later, January 1964, for *Strength and Health* magazine. Then some seven months later, Mickey and Jayne would be divorced on August 26, 1964.

As Jayne had learned from West, Mick readily admitted to her that yes, he had indeed been married to a woman in Indianapolis before and was now getting divorced by that woman. He was also quick to assure Jayne that it hadn't been because of her that had brought upon the separation.* He went on to explain that he and his wife had been a dance act together. It was during those early marriage years to with Mary that he'd gotten interested in bodybuilding and later after years of hard work had captured himself the *Mr. World* title within the Amateur division, then on to *Mr. America* and later *Mr. Olympia* and finally the pinnacle championship, *Mr. Universe* (1955).

Jayne was absolutely taken with Mickey. He was just what the doctor ordered. A giant of a man who with those melon-size biceps and a chest so big they rivaled only her own forty inch chest. His being from Hungary, Mickey still had a heavy accent which gave way to an air of aristocracy in his voice. Jayne loved being with him and loved being seen with him even better. During one of the many press conferences Mickey not only proclaimed his undying love for Jane but he elaborated on his feelings aimed at the constant throng of females that were so very much interested in him as a man. With his heavy accent he stated, "The women wait for you and grab you and kiss you. Some nights I get so aggravated at them. They say, 'Let me feel your muscles.' They give you phone numbers. I always felt it should be a man who does those things. One woman wants me to pose in her house for five days she give me $3,000, but I must pose in no clothes. She says she's a schoolteacher!"

Some of Mick's other credits during this era was with a stage touring company and *Gentlemen Prefer Blondes* and later as a stage costar in

* Ironically, Jayne's own divorce would not come through from Mansfield until much later on January 8, 1958. Mick would have received his divorce from first wife, Mary Birge, that September 6, 1956. Now they would have to wait until Jayne's final decree through before the two beautiful people were able go through with their marriage. That finally came about on January 13, 1958, in Palos Verde, California.

Promises! Promises! Not to be confused with the 1963 film in which Jayne starred. After leaving NYC, they made the move to Hollywood. Jayne purchased the old Rudy Vallee mansion on Sunset Boulevard that had been built back in the 1930s. With extensive remodeling Mickey would soon have his Jayne Palace fit for his Queen. She had somehow decided that Pink was to be her trademark color. So pink it was! All went pink, the house, the car (a Jaguar, which *MGM Studios* had bought for her) and lots of pink outfits.

Since the move to Hollywood with Jayne, Mickey was having some new opportunities put before him within the film industry as well. Being holder of the *Mr. Universe* title tended to open a few doors for him as well, especially now that he was teamed with the beautiful and extremely popular Jayne Mansfield. One of these opportunities for Mickey's was an early screen part in the 1957 film *Slaughter on Tenth Avenue,* where his screen character was that of Big John. There was also a remake of the stage production *Will Success Spoil Rock Hunter* with a part in it reserved for Mick as well. Jayne portrayed Rita Marlowe and was costarred with Tony Randall for the 1957 film. Mick's Part was that of Bobo Braniganskу. A cute comedy / satire mix about an ad-man who tries virtually everything to get a glamorous star to endorse his new brand of Stay-put Lipstick.

When Chuck Pendleton made it back around to LA, he'd naturally visit his old haunts Muscle Beach and the guys. Sometimes, he would invite Mick and Jayne to come down and work out there with him with the overgrown makeshift *Jungle-Jim* setup near the boardwalk. Mickey was the envy of all those other monsters there at the beach. Chuck and Mick would remain friends for a lifetime. Chuck would hitch his pony up with his buddy, Joe Gold and later between the two began a workout training facility called *Gold's Gym*, which went big-time in franchises all over the country. That brand name was later sold off, and they returned with a new facility (with new equipment mostly of Joe's design/build type) called *World Gym.*

> As Chuck continued to watching other bodybuilder friends like Steve Reeves, Reg Park, and now Brad Harris go and make good in the European cinema of the late 50's, he also would get the burr in his trunks to take off to Europe and be in the movies as well. He sent out feeler letters with photos, and before long, he too had producers banging on his door with offers to come to Rome and join the *Peplum* party. Chuck first went to Europe in December of 1960 and underwent first a name change to Gordon Mitchell, which we fans recognize today and he carried with him until he passed back in 2003. His first *Peplum* for a 1961 release was called *Atlas, in the Land of the Cyclops.* From that point on, it's all history.

As for Jayne and her divorce from Paul, the final decree would finally come on January 8, 1958. Mickey then presented her with a ten-carat diamond ring and an offering of marriage along with his undying love. She accepted, and on January 13, 1958, they had a typical Hollywood marriage with all the press and the fans, held in a glass window-encased church. Jayne's studio, *FOX* at the time pitched in to make it a super event. Jayne's dress was a tight fitting pink-laced bell-bottom outfit, which *Fox* had wardrobe turn out special for the occasion. The attendance was kept to one hundred of the couple's closest friends, which were mainly reporters, agents and studio executives, and so on. They honeymooned in Miami before setting out to do a six-week stint at the *Tropicana* in Las Vegas.

Mickey and Jayne made headlines as "The World's Most Beautiful Animals" and enjoyed a fairy-tale lifestyle not unlike a modern-day Tarzan and Jane. Their act was called the House of Love and consisted mainly of Mickey revamping old dance routines that amounted mainly of lifting Jayne high over his head and tossing her about, while both wore nearly nothing but the barest of leopard skin outfits. The public's love for them was surpassed only by the media's attention and love of a story. The couple's togetherness in marriage was so much to the extent that it seemed almost destined to fail.

The Pink Palace in which the beautiful duo lived was indeed a mansion. It sported eight bedrooms and thirteen bathrooms. There was even an impressive electric gate and a heart-shaped swimming pool that Mickey had himself done much of the work on. It included a tiled bottom of twenty-two-carat gold mosaic, saying, "I Love You Jaynie." Inside the mansion, there was also a living room area done with pink mink. The master bedroom was wild with a heart-shaped bed and fireplace. Something to behold for sure!

After giving birth to their first son, Miklos (Mickey Jeffery Palmer Hargitay Jr.), on December 21, 1958, and while still at the Vegas, *Tropicana* Mick presented Jayne with a brand-new Pink Cadillac. During their nightly engagements there in Vegas, Mickey and Jane were now making headlines using their baby son Miklos in their act. It seems he would hold baby Mick upright, standing in the palm of his hand. Mickey proudly proclaimed, "When he is seventeen, he will be *Mr. Universe*."

However great the Vegas act was going, it also had a downside. Mickey and Jayne both loved to gamble. Jayne always figured that while she and Mickey was a house draw, the house should also pick up the tab for their losses. Not so! Later, this same era, they would be publicly accused of faking a missing at sea incident that supposedly happen while water skiing when their small boat capsized off Nassau, the Bahamas. There were three of them supposedly lost, Mickey, Jayne and her press agent Jack Drury. Evidently they had spent the night in only bathing suits on a rock about forty feet wide in the ocean. Afraid of sharks and of not being found, Mickey retorted afterward to the press, "I know what you are going to say. I love this woman. Do you think I would be damn fool enough to take a chance with her life?" During this time, Jayne and Mickey would appear in a couple of television shows mostly so as to show off the wares of the famous duo. *The Steve Allen Show,* episode of 5/22/60 in a segment portraying themselves. Then also *This Is Your Life* show honoring Jayne's life. During this time of their life, their film work now took them to Europe for the film *Gli Amori di Ercole (The Loves of Hercules)* (1960). This was an Italian/French co production *Peplum* film from director Carlo L. Bragaglia. In the United States, it was better known as *Hercules and the Hydra* or as *Hercules against the Hydra.* Jayne, who had originally been offered the role alone, agreed to take the part only if Mickey played the role of Hercules, so it was done. She had the starring role as Queen Dianira.

When filming had begun in Italy, Jayne was very much pregnant, and it wasn't long she had to leave for the birth of their second son Zoltan born on August 1, 1960. Within days of giving birth though, Jayne was already back to work on the film. Afterward, they remained in Europe to do another film called *It Happened in Athens* (1962) a major big-budgeted film about the Olympics being held in Athens. Hargitay was not associated acting-wise with this film (but we imagine was the onset babysitter) however, their firstborn Miklos Jr., who, at only twenty-three months old, did appear in cameo during an opening sequence shows a young child throwing food across a table. Of interest to *Spaghetti* fans, though, a fellow bodybuilder associate of Hargitay, now a Euro *Peplum* actor Brad Harris, was also in this film in a beefcake part, though unaccredited as Garrett.

From there, they made a quick jaunt to West Germany for a film called *Homesick for St Pauli*, which would be released only in Europe beginning in Denmark on May 4 of 1964. The film stared German Freddy Quinn, Josef Albrecht, Erna Sellmer, and Jayne as Evelyne. The directors were Werner Jacobs and Karl Vibach. It was a West German production. Not to tarry any longer in Europe at this time, they both returned now to America where Jayne still had television spot contracts to fulfill and another film waiting in the wings.

The next film, back home in America for both Jayne and Mick, was *Promises! Promises!* Mick also appeared in this film, portraying King Banner, husband to the Marie McDonald's character of Claire Banner. It was this particular film that is famous for Jayne's much-raved-about completely nude scenes. According to *Rhino's VA VA Voom! Bombshells, Pinups, Sexpots and Glamour Girls* by Steve Sullivan (1995), the film's co producer Tommy Noonan and Jayne had both agreed to allow *Playboy* magazine photographers to shoot photos from behind the scenes during the famous nude shoot. They in turn did an interview with pictorial on Mansfield for their June of 1963 newsstand edition of their magazine. The issue with headlines "The Nudest Jayne Mansfield" became the biggest seller of *Playboy** in history at that point in time. The publisher, Hugh Hefner, was even arrested on obscenity charges, which only served to sell more magazines for him. The film, however, didn't fair that well at the box office, and it wasn't long until she was back at the nightclub circuit.

Since the stink of the *Promises* film coupled with the *Playboy* issue things were cooling for Jayne here in the States. The American studios after this tended to lose interest in Jayne, so *FOX* offered to send her back to Italy on loan to make three more films. The first of the three being *Panic Button,* a.k.a. *Let's Go Bust* for an April '64 release. It starred Maurice Chevalier and Eleanor Parker. Jayne's role was that of Angela. Hargitay was not in this film. However, fans of the popular TV detective show *Tightrope* will remember its star Mike Connors here portrays Frank Pagano. Also, for fans of the Euro films, actor/director Mel Welles was also onboard.

Jayne was then zipped over to Yugoslavia to film a West Ger/ Ital/ Liechtenstein coproduction called *L'ora di Uccidere* a.k.a. *Dog Eat Dog!* This film starred Jayne as Darlene / Mrs. Smithoplis, and Cameron Mitchell as Lyle Corbett and Dodie Heath. A crime drama about a heist of monies that were being shipped to the United States and a hostage is taken. It was a co direction effort by Gustav Gavrin, Richard E Cunha, Ray Nazarro, and Albert Zugsmith. The film's Italian release was December 17, 1964. The USA release came much later on July 13, 1966.

For her third and last Italian film before leaving Europe, Jayne and Mickey would make together, *l'Amore Primitivo (Primitive Love)* (1964) by director Luigi Scattini and co scripted by Massimo Pupillo. Mickey's part in this film was that of the professor / hotel manager / bell captain a comedic farce of a film with Italian comic's, *Franco e Ciccio.* Dick Randall was also an associate producer on this film.

Randall during this period in time was busy as the film was wrapping up, doing quick documentary segments (on *FOX* dollars no less) about the wild nightlife of Europe. He was using Jayne as our tour guide who visited on-camera, sleazy night spots abroad. He had shelved this film and later would splice in scenes from Jayne's fatal accident and final segments would

* Jayne had previously done an interview/ article with photos for *Playboy* back in 1955 for their February issue. As the then elected Playmate of the Month, she was then seen clad in red skintight bathing suit for the shots associated with an interview done in Florida.

be filmed back in LA with Mick showing off the Pink Palace home he remodeled for Jayne.

Returning to the States, it was now apparent that it was still 1963, and that while for years earlier the press had glorified the fairy tale marriage publicly, now the news media seemed bored with reporting about Mickey and Jayne's sometime outlandish public actions. It seems that since 1962 this fairy tale marriage between the two exceptions of the male/female form had been on a steady path for destruction. After they returned from Europe, Jayne up and left for Mexico dragging the boys with her. She returned with a divorce pronouncement of May 1, 1963. However, this didn't last long and she soon returned to Mickey, reconciling when learning of her next pregnancy. On January 23, 1964, they were blessed with a daughter, Mariska Magdolina Hargitay* in San Monica, California.

Although, even with all the happiness a baby can bring a couple, the reconciliation between Mickey and Jayne just wasn't meant to be. All would again be in turmoil not long after giving birth to Mariska. Jayne having resumed her thoughts on divorce, returned to Juarez, Mexico, this time divorcing Mickey for a second time in August of '64. The California Superior Court recognized the Mexican decree as official date of August 26, 1964, was upheld.

It was during this year of 1964, when Mick would pack up and return to Europe burying himself in his new career, making movies abroad. His first upon his return and waiting in the wings for him was another *Peplum* called *La Vendetta dei Gladiatori (Revenge of the Gladiators)* (1964) It starred Mickey Hargitay as Fabius's son of highly respected Roman General. Livio Lorenzon portrays the evil Barbarian leader Moniki. He attempts to take over Rome, not by a massive battle effort, but by using the Emperor's own daughter against him and the forces of Rome. Pricilla (Adriana Paul) daughter of the Emperor, being tired of all the violence around her, has now rejected her palace life and has become overwhelmed by an underground Christianity movement, and thus a prime target for Moniki kidnappers.

---

* Today daughter Mariska is a headliner herself. An EMMY Award winner of 2006, she has starred since 2000 in the police crime show drama, *Law and Order: Special Victims Unit* program from its inception. This program is still on the air for the *NBC* TV network. She had also been more or less a regular with recurring roles on the old *NBC ER*, soap drama during the 1997-'98 season shows. The *Special Victims Units* programs are still as popular now as ever. Her acting counterparts had previously nominated her for an EMMY back in 2004, but that time it didn't come to pass.

Although Mick appeared in many other popular genres of the era while in Europe, one that mostly stands out more with us fans was his *Spaghetti* Westerns. One of these, his first for a 1965 release was called *Stranger in Sacramento.* It was directed by Serge Bergon (Sergio Bergonzelli). The film was based on a novel by one Jay Murphy called "I Will Kill You Tomorrow." The storyline set in the Sacramento valley of California and concerns an immigrant family of a father and three brothers driving their herd of cattle across unfamiliar land to a railhead. While the eldest rides off to look for a better-grazing place to camp, rustlers sweep in and murder his family and steal the herd. The elder son Mike Jordan (Hargitay) our hero, now sets out to avenge his father and brother's recent deaths and find who's responsible. With the help of a friend Liza (Barbara Fey) he meets, he learns that a local land baron called Lefty Barrett is behind the whole scheme. He sets to work trying to prove to an unwilling to listen sheriff of Barnett's guilt. Liza helps to trick Barnett into a gunfight finale where Mike kills him.

For Jayne during this time, due to the off-color publicity from the *Playboy* spread coupled with the film *Promises, Promises*, the American studios were now frowning upon their blond bombshell. "Many of her American friends also fell away from her. They didn't like to see her drop Mickey, who was doglike in his devotion to her." It was during this period in time that she up and decided to get marriage again, this time to film producer Matt Cimber, so on September 24, 1964, they married in Aereo Mulege, Mexico. Probably she somehow figured he could help reengineer her now failed career. Damage control, he attempted to do, but alas, it didn't happen, nothing seemed to work, was it too far gone? As time wore on she found she was pregnant again, this time with Cimber's child, she gave birth on October 18, 1965, a boy baby, Antonio Raphael Ottaviano (Tony) Cimber. Soon she was back again being friendly with Mickey or at least it would appear that way for the children's sake. Jayne leaving on a tour of South America was leaving four of her five children with Jayne Marie and Mickey. Cimber took the youngest boy off to live with his mother, but Jayne left for the tour with him.

While Mick continued trips back 'n' forth across the Atlantic to be with his kids, he continued to bang out the work. His next film another Western called *Lo Sceriffo non Spara (The Sheriff won't shoot!)* (1965). Via Internet sources this rare film finally surfaced several years back. It was an Italian / Spanish coproduction, with evidently extremely poor cinematic distribution. It starred Hargitay as Allan, outlaw leader and brother of the town Sheriff Stephen portrayed by Dan Clark (Marco Mariani). As the title suggests, *family* matters could be the reason the sheriff has refused to put on his guns again, or then is it, as the trailer would suggest? It seems family is truly the reason. A gunfight between a gang of outlaws and the sheriff resulted in him killing his own father by mistake. He has since hung up his guns. The brother Allan is now steady beating a path down the wrong side of the law and having a heyday since he knows his brother can or will do nothing about it. A great find for Mick fans.

> *Note*: Back on November 28, 2000, for a film festival in Laughlin, Nevada, the wife and I joined with other fans of Hargitay and Gordon Mitchell attended the function so as to meet the two actors in person. A great time was had by all. During the questions asked of the two, I asked Mick about his time spent in Italy making those *Spaghetti* Westerns. He told me, "I have always wanted to be a cowboy, watching them in the movies when I was young. When I was making those movies I was just having fun." We can say, "Ah yes, no doubt he was as we watch him ridin' hard across the screen, from point A to point B (always seemed to have his horse on a dead run), shootin' his guns and the fightin' all sure looked like great fun to us as well."

He continued to take time out between his Euro films taking jaunts back across the Atlantic for local work back home, and of course the kids always whenever possible. Back on one such trip, he filmed a documentary piece called *Hollywood My Home Town* for a 1965 release. Then it was off again, back to Rome for his next Euro film. This time he would venture into the horror genre for a one called *IL Boia Scarlatto (The Scarlet Executioner)* (1965). Directed and produced by Max Hunter (Massimo Pupillo) this film was a bit off the beaten path for Mick, but being game for most anything now after his split with Jayne, he'd signed on. A weirdo horror film for sure, it starred Hargitay as Travis Anderson.

It was during this period in time that Jayne, finally returned from South America, with Lawyer Sam Brody. She had contacted him to help in getting her and her finances back out of that country. It seems their customs had seized her assets, and refused to let her go because she was refusing to pay exit charges on monies she'd earned while in their country for the past couple months performing during the summer. He helped her get out with her monies mostly intact, but there after the two began a wild affair* together.

---

* From *Rhino's* biography write-up on Jayne Mansfield, we again learn that it was sometime after her divorce from Cimber that her daughter Jayne Marie ran away from home, when found by the police she asked for protection against the two, Brody and her mother citing abuse charges. The wild drinking and

For Mick's third Western of the genre and his most memorable to fans called *Tre Colpi de Winchester per Ringo,* a.k.a. *Three Graves for a Winchester per Ringo* would be for an early January 1966 release. This film presents us with a dual partnership between the star Gordon Mitchell,* and Mickey Hargitay. Both ex-bodybuilders from the USA and both ex-Mae West troupe members were now *Spaghetti* Western movie gunslingers together. And they worked well together, these two old friends. The film's story was supposedly from a suggestion by James Wilde Jr., and was directed by Erminio (sometimes Ermmino) Salvi who coscripted with Amborgio Molteni. It was an Italian production filmed in locations near Almeria, Spain and in Rome.

With these two popular Euro stars together in the same film the audiences went crazy. The words, *Più, più, più* (More, more, more) was shouted from the cinema balconies of Rome as two appeared on the screen, the fans loved them. GM here portrays Frank Kendal sometimes gun-for-hire badman, and sometimes lawman. Mickey's role is that of Ringo Carson, drifter and also gunman for hire. For the English language video releases the title was later changed to *Three Bullets for Ringo.* Although these two screen gunmen never made another Western together, each would become prolific in their own way and continued to be popular within the European cinema.

While Mick had been hard at work in Europe, Jayne back in the States seems to have gone totally off the deep end in opposite directions. Now she had taken up with the Occult and was well on her way to becoming an avid devil worshiper. It was friend Sammy Davis Jr., who at a party one evening introduced Jayne to one Anton LaVey, High Priest in the *Church of Satan.* His cult of Satanists was the latest fad of the day, a passing fancy of the rich and famous. Jayne's life and career really seemed to escalate downward after this meeting. Although others have been known to take an interest in these church rituals, Jayne seemed to have went head over heels.

---

abusive fighting, and just general carrying-on didn't go over well at the trial that followed later. Her public what few she had left after all that was not at all happy with the buxom blonde or her pick of men. Jayne wouldn't file for divorce from Cimber until July of 1966.

* Mick's old friend Chuck Pendleton (Gordon Mitchell) from their days of the Mae West troupe had already been there in Rome since January of 1961 banging out *Peplum* features. Mitchell (GM as we'll call him from here on out) turned in an impressive amount of film work from his first release of 1961 to 1965 with sixteen *Peplums.* Now in 1965 the two friends would finally make a film together, a *Spaghetti* Western.

The negative publicity alone hurt her popularity severely, coupled with her split from Mickey, her film work had dried up. With no studio work available Jayne was eventually forced to return to the nightclub circuit. Mickey, on the other hand, was steady banking out the films in Europe and was busy as ever. Although Mick only contributed to five of our beloved *Spaghetti* Westerns, he would leave a lasting impression with his fans. His parting from Jayne was probably one of his better moves in the right direction toward a new life. Although, a steady stream of poor luck would shortly follow in her wake.

For Mick's next film, another Western, his fourth an Italian production called *Cjamango* (1967). It starred Sean Todd (Ivan Rassimov) as Cjamango, Mick Hargitay as Clinton, and Helene Chanel as Helen, Cjamango's girlfriend. The evil character of the film is portrayed by Livio Lorenzon as Mexican bandit El Tigre. The film directed by Edward G. Muller (Edoardo Mulargia) was from a scripting by Glen Vincent Davis (Vincenzo Musolino). It seems El Tigre has stolen some dollars from our hero Cjamango and with the help of his friend Clinton they are intent to get it all back from the bandit. In the process Clinton pulls a double cross and makes off with the loot himself, but is killed in an ensuing gunfight. Only Cjamango now without his gun is left with Helen to face El Tigre. She, however, saves his skin but is fatally wounded for her trouble. He in turn kills El Tigre and we guess after all that trouble, lead flying and men dying, Cjamango finally got back his dollars!

For 1966 and a fifth Western from director Peter Launders (Mario Pinzuti) was next in line called *Ringo, Tempo Di Massacro (Ringo, its Massacre Time).* It was another Italian production starring Mike (Mick) Hargitay as Mike Woods / Stranton, Jean Louis, Lucy Bomez and Anna Cerreto. Actually with filming just begun and we find the star Stranton (Hargitay) has taken a few days off while they shot scenes without him so as to attend a family reunion back in LA. It seems that while on this family outing with the kids to the *Jungleland Zoo* in the San Fernando Valley, a freak accident occurred. As pictures were being taken of Mick's son Zoltan with what was purported as a tame lion, the boy then six, was suddenly mauled by the beast during the session. The boy thankfully recovered rapidly and in full by December that year, Jayne, already deeply into the Occult by now believed it had been those powers that had actually sped up the healing process.

As for Mick's Western, he never returned in time to complete it. His contract was voided and the Producers contingency plan for just such an occasion was put into action. French actor Jean Luis stepped into the limelight for the film as the star. They revamped the script some now using a storyline that had to do with Stranton (Luis) hunting for his brother Mike whom he would never find. And so goes the rest of the movie. From the version I've seen, it was a pretty chopped up editing job which then the film came across as more of a weird voodoo mystery than what we'd expect to see in a Western.

According to *Rhino's* bio, Jayne's contract for a British show tour was also in jeopardy because of her wild carryings on with Brody.* It seems she could not wear the short, skimpy outfits that were expected of her because of all the black 'n' blue marks on her legs and body in general. She had to cancel. Blonde bombshell, Mamie Van Doren was also on tour during this period in time with her show which was being held over in NYC. She'd ask Jayne if she would take her place doing her Supper Club show in Mississippi, and she would take Jayne's next show giving her a break. So Jayne agreed.

Next, the worst of the worst finally happened on a dismal foggy night of June 29, 1967, around 2:15 a.m. when a tragic automobile accident that took Jayne's life, and in which all three of their children were also involved (in the back seat with four Chihuahuas dogs) all were asleep and were spared. In the front was the driver Ronald B. Harrison, Jayne in the middle and her lawyer/boyfriend Sam Brody. All three were pronounced dead at the scene. Jayne's platinum blond wig was thrown on to the dash, what was left of it. Rumors that she had been decapitated were vicious and untrue. According to the *Rhino* bio, the *NY Times* had contacted the undertaker there in Mississippi, one James Roberts, and verified that her body had been completely intact when he received it.

Mickey was starring in *Follies Burlesque 1967* at the time of the tragedy. He was granted custody of all three children, Miklos (eight); Zoltan (six) and Mariska (three) and remarried within a year of Jayne's death to an airline stewardess from Long Island named Ellen Jean Evans. Mickey sued the Mansfield estate in September of 1967 for over $275,000 for support of their three children. According to the 1964 divorce settlement Jayne had agreed to pay him child support. After her tragic death, Mickey arranged to have a heart-shaped headstone erected for her at her at the place of burial. It is well perceived that he could have still carried a soft spot in his heart for the *Woman in Pink*.

Early in 1967 Mickey, while on hiatus from his Euro film work and after finishing up the film *Spree,* he consented to complete another documentary that had previously been in progress since about 1964. The film, *The Wild, Wild World of Jayne Mansfield* was a documentary from producer Dick Randall. It would not be released now until 1968. It certainly began on a more appreciative note of the late star's life and lifestyle than was most

* Of interest here is that Jayne's Occult leader Anton LaVey, the one she had put so much stock in up to this point in her life had tried to warn her to steer clear of Brody for her own good, but she chose to ignored the warning.

sensationalistic pieces that had plagued the media right after her accident. It was a light, as-you-go tour of the hot, nightlife and nightclub circuits of Rome, Paris and London among other places with Jayne leading us on tour.

Suddenly, all hell broke loose as we were greeted on-screen by screeching tires and massive crashing sounds as the tour film now reverted over to the tragic scene of Jayne's accident that had been spliced in. Afterward, Mickey's newly done segment came to the screen for another tour now given by Mick himself of their previous home, showing off the famous pool, fireplace and all the wall-to-wall pink.

That part with Mickey showing off the house that love built was the most interesting of the entire film which unfortunately in its entirety had turn out to be another sensationalistic piece of film work directed by a threesome of filmmakers, Arthur Knight, Joel Holt and Charles W. Broun Jr. The film boosted such clips as Jayne twisting to sounds of pop artist *Rocky Roberts and the Airdales,* and an All Girl Topless Band called *The Ladybirds*.

Mick did move onto better things afterward as he now eased into the horror genre again with *Lady Frankenstein* a 1972 entry with Joseph Cotton and the lovely Rosalba Neri directed by displaced American filmmaker/ dubber Mel Welles. During the remainder of Mickey's subsequent filmmaking, the Hargitay's as a family, Mickey, Ellen and the children had split their lives between Hollywood, and Rome. In later years the family enjoyed a summer retreat in Fort Lauderdale, Florida.

Mick continued to make films in Europe until about mid 1972. He did not return to the screen of more recent years but did return to the Hollywood scene as he starred in the *Follies Burlesque of 1972* with Denise Darcel. Then later a family segment, for a *Bob Hope Overseas Christmas Tour: Around the World with the Troops—1941-1972*. But after that he was rarely seen at any other Hollywood functions.

Mariska, as a tribute to her father did a film drama / documentary of Hungary with him back in 1987 entitled, *Mr. Universe*. It was directed by Gyorgy Szomjas who also co scripted along with Ibolya Fekete and Ferenc Grunwalsky. This ninety-six-minute / color film was released only in Hungary in 1988 and was only in the Hungarian language. Mariska* and

* Mariska Hargitay now married, to Peter Hermann since August of 2004, was also a mother now herself. Son, August Miklos Friedrich Hermann was born on June 28, 2006, and weighted in at ten pound and nine ounce. The family currently lives in the Los Angeles, California area. The five-foot-and-seven-and-a-half-inch actress (her hubby Peter is six feet and five inches) continues to divide her time between LA and NYC. When in college, Mariska majored in theater at *UCLA,* and speaks fluent Hungarian, French and Italian languages.

her Dad along with her step mom, Ellen and her brother Zoltan was also onboard portraying themselves.

Through the years following his European film work Mickey tended to keep himself busy and continually fit as well, even in later years his fitness was a major part of his life. Much of his time then, was devoted to a profitable Real estate business and since 1980 he had opened an expansive nursery/landscaping business with his son Zoltan. It is known locally in the West Hollywood, California area as *Mickey Hargitay Plants.* He and Ellen both love working with their plants and trees, a relaxing pastime for an ex-badman of the Westerns and a man found to have been blessed with the knack and a real green thumb.

In the year 1999, Mickey was the recipient of a *Joe Weider Lifetime Achievement Award* at a Los Angeles, California Body-Building Association function. His pal Gordon Mitchell also was in attendance. Mickey at that time in his life was also acting President of *Graphic Muscle*, an Internet site devoted to bodybuilding. Both men still were very much active in the art of bodybuilding at that time of their lives.

> Mickey was invited to appear in a film segment with daughter on her popular television series, *Law and Order: Special Victims Unit.* It was on a 2003 episode called "Control" where he portrayed a Grandfather in a walk-on bit part shown conversing with his daughter in character as Detective Olivia Benson on an escalator. Fortunately her father, with failing health was able to live long to see both, the Great Grandson and the EMMY Award received by his beloved daughter.

We genre fans all had high hopes that Mick and pal Gordon Mitchell would one day join forces again with others like Rod Dana (Robert Mark), Franco Nero and possibly even Tony Anthony so as to treat us all to another jam-up *Spaghetti* (like) Western. But alas, with the sudden passing of his eighty-year-old friend Gordon on September 20 of 2003, and with Mickey's continuing bout with bone cancer and heart problems of more recent years we all had put this pipe dream behind us. Mickey Hargitay finally succumbed to his ills and passed away on September 14, 2006, he was also eighty years old. As we bring this write-up to a close, I'd like to offer up a personal quote of Mickey's, "I enjoyed my career. I never wanted to be any more than what I was and I had fun doing it."

> We know he was forever grateful for all he had received in life. Even that on-again, off-again marriage and subsequent wild

> world of Jayne Mansfield that had ended in her tragic death is now over, but those three lovely children, results of that early bond, had seemingly overcome all odds. That and with the help of a loving Dad and a loving new woman, Ellen who welcomed not only Mick in her life, but also these three children as her own. RIP big guy.

In the previous waning years of Mick's life, some LA residents had gotten use to seeing the real estate agent with the turned-up collar, driving that convertible Cadillac automobile around Hollywood, is yet burned into our memory. Just as is that image of the gunslinger riding off into the sunset. These are all memories that we, as fans will not soon forget. We can only believe that he and pal Gordon are once again riding the range up yonder, with pistols drawn, shootin' for the gold as the "Strong Man, Shoots First!"

End.

- Below is a complete *Euro* filmography for Mickey Hargitay. Dates here are aligned as close as possible with information currently at hand, with international release dates included. **Poster pictures are accredited to the Sebastian Haselbeck collection via his website www.spaghetti-westerns.net. Thanks a big bucket of bullets, Sebastian.*

MICKEY HARGITAY'S EUROPEAN FILMOLOGY

1960
The Loves of Hercules; *Gli Amori di Ercole* a.k.a. *Hercules against the Hydra* (fantasy *Peplum*); Ital/ Fr, Director Carlo Ludovico (Hargitay as Hercules) 1960; Starred Jayne Mansfield as Queen Dianira/ Hippolyta.

1963
Promises, Promises! *Promesse, promesse;* US; Director King Donovan (Hargitay as King Banner); 1963; Mansfield stars as Sandy Brooks; Locale: Onboard *SS Independence* cruise ship.

1964
Primitive Love; L'Amore Primitivo (Comedy); Ital; Director Luigi Scattini (Hargitay in role as the Bell Captain) (8/17/64 in Italy, and 11/03/66 in San Francisco, California, USA); A Franco e Ciccio comedy team film, here as two Hotel Porters; Jayne Mansfield as Dr. Jane; Locale: Rome, Lazio, Italy. Dick Randall was also a coproducer of this film

Revenge of the Gladiators; La Vendetta dei Gladiatori *(Peplum)*; Ital, Director Luigi Capuano (Hargitay as Fabio/Fabius); 12/31/64

1965

A Stranger in Sacramento, *Uno Straniero a Sacramento*; Ial; Director Serge Bergon (Sergio Bergonzelli) (Hargitay as Mike Jordan); 6/15/65; *Hargitay's first film for the Western genre.*

The Wild, Wild World of Jayne Mansfield;—Incomplete documentary/ unreleased until 1968

1965

The Sheriff won't Shoot!, *Lo Sceriffo che non Spara!*; (Western) Ital/ Spa/ Fr/ British coproduction. Codirected by J. L. Monter (José Luis Monter) *(credited),* and Lionel A. Prestol (Renato Polselli); (Hargitay as Allan, the outlaw bandit leader) 9/9/65

The Bloody Pit of Horror, a.k.a. *The Scarlet Executioner; Il Bola Scarlatto;* a.k.a. *Crimson Executioner;* a.k.a. *The Red Hangman (Horror),* Ital/ US, Dir/ Prod: Max Hunter (Massimo Pupillo) (Hargitay as Travis Anderson / the executioner) 1966; others in the cast were, Walter Brandt (W. Bigari), Luisa Baratto and Femi Benussi.

Seven Golden Women Against Two Agents; *Sette Donne D'Oro contro due 07*; (Comedic-Spy); Ital, Dir/ Prod: Vincent Cashino (Vincenzo Casino) (Mickey Hargitay as Agent Mark Davis) 1966; Also stars Maria Vincent as Marie Dupont. Luciana Paoli as Miranda and director Vincent Cashino (Vincenzo Casino) as agent Barbikian. Cute little film effort as they go. Another addition within the clutch of the mid 1960's spy films set off by the success of the 1962/'63 James Bond films.

Three Graves for a Winchester; *a.k.a. Per Ringo Tre Colpi de Winchester, per Ringo;* a.k.a. *Three Bullets for Ringo* (Western); Ital, Director Emimmo Salvi (Hargitay as Ringo Carson) 3/16/66; Filmed in locations near Almeria, Spain and in Rome.

1967

Cjamango (Western); Ital, Director Edward G. Muller (Edoardo Mulargia) (Hargitay as Clinton); 8/9/67

1968

The Wild, Wild World of Jayne Mansfield, (Documentary). Mentioned in above main text body was a 1964 film effort having been shelved as incomplete was now completed and released for '68. A co directed film by Charles W. Broun Jr., Joel Holt and Arthur Knight. It was written by Charles Ross II, and produced by Dick Randall. Robert Jason was the Narrator.

1970

Ringo, It's Massacre Time; *Ringo Tempo di Massacro;* a.k.a. *Wanted Ringo;* a.k.a. *Revenge of Ringo;* (Western); Ital, Director Mario Pinzauti (Mike Hargitay as Mike (Wood) / Stranton); 8/2/70; *(Mick Hargitay never completed this film. Jean Louis took over the lead role searching for his brother Mike) Note: Euro-Americanized nickname for Mik, Mick or Mickey is Mike.*

1971

The Daughter of Frankenstein; *a.k.a. La Figlia di Frankenstein;* a.k.a. *Madame Frankenstein* (sexy-horror); Ital, Dir/ Prod: Mel Welles; (Hargitay as Police Captain Harris); 1971; Stars Sarah Bay (Rosalba Neri) as his daughter, Tanya Frankenstein. Joseph Cotton is the senior Dr. Frankenstein. Script by Edward Di Lorenzo was from a story by Canadian film producer Dick Randall.

1972
Delirium; *Delirio Caldo;* (sexy-horror); Ital, Director Ralph Brown (Renato Polselli) (Hargitay as Dr. Herbert Lewtak); 1972; Stars Rita Calderoni, as Marcia Lewtak. Also stars: Tano Cimatosa and Krista Barrymore as Joaquine, lesbian lover of Rita.

1973
The Reincarnation of Isabel; a.k.a. *Rita's Magic: Black and Secret Orgies in Three Hundred! (Rita Magie Nere e Segrete Orge nel Trecento)* (sexy-horror); Ital, Directed by Ralph Brown (Renato Polselli) (Hargitay co-stars as the vampire sorcerer, Nelson); 1973; Stars Rita Calderoni here in dual roles as Laureen/Isabella. Also stars Krista Barrymore, Raoul Traucher, Max Dorian and Katia Cardinali.

Note: It was a.k.a. ***The Ghastly Orgies of Count Dracula,*** *(Le Orge Orribili di Conte Dracula)* this title was issued as the original uncut, Italian version for the above film which supposedly contained a cameo appearance by Mick Hargitay's eight-year-old daughter Mariska.

1987
Mr. Universe (Documentary); Hungary; Director Gyorgy Szomjas; S: Ibolya Fekete; Mick Hargitay was invited to appear along with his then twenty-three-year-old daughter Mariska portraying themselves. *Also included in the cast were, wife, Ellen, and son Zoltan; others were George Pinter and Laszio Szabo; 1988; not released outside of Hungary.* (Run time: ninety-six minutes in color)

End.

BIBLIOGRAPHY
(M. HARGITAY)

Agan, Patrick, *Whatever Happened to . . . ?* (1974), Mickey Hargitay, *Ace Books*; A Div. of *Charter Communications Inc.* NY.

Betts, Tom, editor *WAI! (Westerns . . . All'Italiana)* Fanzine *Memorial* issue Mickey Hargitay 2006

Celebrity Interview: Heath Quest Magazine, Journal of Longevity, vol. 11, issue 11 for 2005 by Bob Delmonteque, ND,

Connolly, Bill, editor *Spaghetti Cinema* Fanzine

Connolly, John "The Life in Her Men" *Premiere,* July 2001

Keeps, David "Mariska Hargitay of Law and Order: SVU" *Redbook,* December 2005

Keeps, David "Mariska Hargitay on Motherhood," *TV Guide,* pp. 20-23, April, 2006

The Show Business Nobody Knows by Ear Wilson, *Cowles Book Co, Inc.,* Subsidiary of *The Henry Regnery Co.* Chapter; "The Making of a Sex Symbol" pp. 209-217.

Haselbeck, Sebastian, owner/curator for Internet website: *www. spaghetti-westerns.net*

Internet, via *www.bellsouth.net* "Actor Mickey Hargitay Dies at 80" *BellSouth* News Flash article LA *AP,* Jennifer Graylock, Thursday, September 14, 2006

Internet, via: *www.briansdriveintheater.com* "Muscles in Hollywood" section on M. Hargitay

Internet, via *www.IMDB.com* "Biography of Jayne Mansfield" and Filmography listings

Internet, via *www.IMDB.com* "Biography of Mickey Hargitay" and Filmography listings

Internet via, *www.nationalenquirer.com* ; *Celebrity News,* article: "Mariska Hargitay's Dad watches her win an EMMY, falls gravely Ill," 9/18/2006

Sullivan, Steve, *Va Va Voom! Bombshells, Pinups, Sexpots and Glamour Girls* (1995) *Rhino Press*

Prickette, Tom, *Mr. Strong Man Shoots First!* Previously unpublished manuscript of 2002

Robinson Robert, "Behind the Scenes on the Today Show"; Article: "What kind of a question was that for Jayne Mansfield?" *Daily Mail* Newspaper article Mon. November 11, 1996, pp. 23

Tabloid Article: "Was Jayne Mansfield Satan's Sex Slave" *National Enquirer*

Tabloid Article: "Did Satan Lure Mansfield into Death Trap?" *National Enquirer*

Walker, Brian J., owner/curator for Internet website: *www.briansdriveintheater.com*

Weisser, Thomas, *Spaghetti Westerns: the Good, the Bad, and the Violent*, (1992) *McFarland*, Jefferson NC.

RICHARD HARRISON

(1936—)

PEPLUM HERO, TURNS GUNSLINGER

Richard Harrison arrived in this world on May 26, 1936. He was born and raised there in Salt Lake City, Utah. After finishing high school, he ventured out into the world finally relocating to Los Angeles, then Hollywood, California area at a young age of seventeen. There he found work, although often as not was only part-time work as a male model on the catwalk, as well as a few magazine stints. Well-built, blond-headed, his chiseled good looks often confused others that took him for movie star Guy Madison of whom he had a close resemblance. Joining the *Athletic Model Guild*, he posed for such popular magazines of the era as *Physique Pictorial, Tomorrow's Man,* and *Body Beautiful* posing both with other males and female models as well.

Harrison had dreams of possibly becoming a movie star in the back of his mind, although he had to eventually settled for other work and found it at a local *Vic Tanny Gym*. He noticed that many of the patrons and clients with whom he worked with in this establishment worked in the movie industry. The mover and shakers of the industry, these people he saw almost daily. Their talks were encouraging to him. They urged him to take classes, to study, and to give acting a try. They all felt he had the looks, the persona, and the appeal that it takes to make it in Hollywood. He would eventually heed their advice as Hollywood agents soon snapped up this young beefcake and put him to work in the industry.

His film debut was in *Jeanne Eagels* (1957) starring Kim Kovak and Jeff Chandler. He went on to other bit parts in films such as *Kronos* (1957) with Jeff Morrow and Barbara Lawrence, *Too Much, Too Soon* (1958) starring Dorothy Malone and Errol Flynn. Also there was *South Pacific** that same year starring Rossano Brazzi and Mitzi Gaynor; Then *Battle Flame* (1959) with Scott Brady and Robert Blake. Harrison's next film *Master of the World* (1961) starring Vincent price and Charles Bronson. This film part gave him opportunity for an extended role as Alistair the Airship's helmsman. It was on the set of this film that he was introduced to the producer James H. Nicholson's daughter, Loretta. After a whirlwind courtship, they married some six months later.

It was through this Nicholson relationship and marriage that he was offered a chance to go to Europe and take a first time leading role in an Italian sea yarn called *IL Giustiziere Dei Mari* (*Avenger of the Seven Seas*) (1961). It was a swashbuckling adventure with Harrison starred as David Robinson, Michele Mercier as Jennifer, and Roldano Lupi as Redway. Also listed in the cast was American Walter Barnes portraying Van Artz. Barnes like other American had come to the European shores in search of work and found plenty of it. He also stayed through into the 1970s settling in at first with the West German *Winnetou* films of the renown German novelist Karl May.

* Interesting is the fact that also within the cast of the 1958 *South Pacific* picture, besides Richard Harrison, there was one Ken Clark as well. Both men later in time would see one another while in Europe during those unforgettable years of the *Spaghetti* Westerns. Both men when there would become international film stars for their great work in the various Euro genres. Harrison would be involved with some fourteen Westerns, while Clark (like Eastwood) would only do three Westerns. However, both men would be prolific in making *Peplum* and spy adventure films of that same era in time.

Afterward, Harrison was offered a contract to do a string of *Peplum* epic features with Italian producer Italo Zingerelli. The first of two to begin with was called *Il Gladiatore Invincible* (*The Invincible Gladiator*) (1962). It was to be directed by Alberto De Martino. Harrison jumped at this opportunity signing with the producer. He wound up staying in Europe some twenty years making eight of these *Peplum* (Sword 'n' Sandal) films in all. Plus, a slew of other Italian genre films along the way.

His second *Peplum* was *The Seven Gladiators* (1962) in the role of Darius leader of the seven. As the luster of the Herculean *Peplum* era began to wane he began to branch off into the realm of other Italian genres of films. One such genre was affectionately being dubbed by fans as the *Spaghetti* Westerns. These were more his cup of tea anyway and he excelled in these new and popular horse operas.

> Even as he managed to further branch off in other genre directions such as adventure films, spy intrigue, and war genres, he would never again regain the impact we feel that he initially made with these extremely popular Italian Westerns of the era. As the entire Italian cinema seemed to waning after the first initial phenomenon years, from about the mid-1970s, he like others found themselves somewhat on the outside looking in.
>
> It was then he began to apply himself to other areas of the European film industry. He tried his hand at writing, producing and directing films. Eventually, his successes in these areas though the years, coupled with some good investments have afforded him a decent retirement from film work altogether of more recent years. With exception of an occasional script-writing project now and again, the seventy-six-year-old former *Spaghetti* star Richard Harrison Sr. is pretty much absent from the big theater screens of today. He claimed in later years aside from actor Gordon Mitchell, most of his friends were Italians who were mostly in the business. GM passed away in 2004 at 80.

Harrison during his heyday years was one of the first Americans to enjoy the limelight of the Italian made *Spaghetti* Westerns. Harrison was fresh from the *Peplum* epics when he settled in with his first Western of the era called *I Tre Spietati* (*Three Ruthless Ones*) later changed to *Gunfight at High Noon* (1963) a.k.a. *Sons of Vengeance* with Raf Baldassare, and Gloria Milland (Maria Fie).

His role here was that of one of three brothers, Jeff Walker. Each goes their separate way when grown except for Jeff who stays near the homestead eventually becoming sheriff of Silver City. It's then when he must become judge and jury between brothers. This Spanish / Italian effort from Joaquin Romero Marchent would seemingly open the door as one of the first of the new era Westerns. However, with it being primarily a Spanish production and accompanied by poor distribution it wasn't released even in Italy until late in 1966.

His second Western the same year was called *Duell Nel Texas* (*Duel in Texas)* later changed to *Gunfight at Red Sands* (1963). This was an Italian / Spanish coproduction by from Giorgio Papi and Arrigo Colombo, Ricardo Blasco was the director. This one being primarily an Italian production it was bound to go further than did his first venture of the genre. Incidentally, this film was musically scored by Ennio Morricone (using the pseudonym of Dan Salvo) for this his first acknowledged effort for the genre. Harrison's role was that Gringo Martinez adopted son of a Mexican family. Mexican haters, of this border town attack the father beating him near death while robbing him, and wounding Ringo's stepbrother Ricardo. Gringo now seeks to avenge the misdeeds to his adoptive family.

> *Note*: The Spanish filmmakers of the era, as did the West Germans seemed to have had a good hold on the Western genre early on. Even the Brits had gotten into the genre early for a Spanish co production called *Tierra Brutal (Brutal Lands)* a.k.a. *Savage Guns* (1961) with Richard Basehart, Pacquita Rico and Don Taylor.
>
> However, with the advent of the above two Harrison films, basically this last one *Duello nel Texas* was the true predecessor to the Leone/Eastwood hits for the mainstream cinema from 1964. The Italians soon had it going full steam ahead for the genre. There was no stopping the bandwagon after Leone's third film of his *Dollar* trilogy hit the markets. The Italians commenced to churn out hundreds, five hundred to six hundred films until about 1974 when then the whole genre seemed to abruptly run out of steam and would begin to cave in upon itself.

Harrison's two films, along with Morricone's musical renditions, would play huge significant roles in the progression of these new Italian made films. Their early involvement came just prior to the main phenomenon era that would soon grip this new vein of Western movies and become their driving force. At first, as their popularity grew across Europe, the demand for more of them grew as well. Some Americans were already here like Rod Cameron and Cameron Mitchell. Others now were arriving almost daily to throw in their chips to become a part of the phenomenon. Actors like James Mitchum (son of actor Robert) who brought us the earlier *Massacre at Grand Canyon* (1963) from first-time genre directing effort by Sergio

Corbucci in his pre-Leone outing. Mitchum would return later with *The Tramplers* (1965).

Also, that same year another actor hot from the *Peplum* epics was muscleman/actor, Brad Harris, who already a part of the German Western with an earlier *Pirates of the Mississippi* (1963) now would entertain us with others Westerns of more Italian based involvement like, *Black Eagle of Santa Fe* (1965). Those early entries of the genre were but a pimple on the budding phenomenon about to be unleashed on the European cinema market.

Harrison's significant involvement in the birthing of this genre phenomenon was in itself all inspiring. However, of interest to fans of the genre, Harrison being offered the role of the gun-slinging bounty hunter Joe for *The Magnificent Stranger* is a valued point of interest. For distribution, the film would later be called *Per un Pugno di Dollari* (*For a Fistful of Dollars*) (1964). This film by young director, Sergio Leone, himself hot from the *Peplum*s was mostly a second-unit assistant director during his *Peplum* tenure. Finally made full director for one film and he was now jumping ship, as it were, for a new breed of fantasy Westerns, which he was mostly developing from ideas within his own mind.

As the story goes, Harrison, who, at the time, was within producers Papi and Colombo's stable of actors. They were now going to produce the Leone Western, *The Magnificent Stranger,* but above all specifically wanted an American as the lead, one of their actors of course. The monies to be offered was in the $20,000 range but Leone, according to Frayling's book, *Something to Do with Death*, (2000) wasn't all that interested in Harrison, he had more envisioned actor Henry Fonda. However, Fonda never saw the script that was sent to his agent, who returned it, saying, "that his client couldn't possible do it."

Leone then reverted to a couple of younger choices his second seemed to be James Coburn. Again, according to Frayling's book, Coburn had initially agreed to do it, but for $25,000 citing the $20,000 wasn't enough. Too rich for all concerned and Leone then moved on to Charles Bronson, whom he'd already been considering even as they had talked of Fonda. But when Bronson saw the script, he didn't think much of it and turned it down citing it was the worse script he'd ever seen. Others then came to mind like actor Cliff Robinson, another good American was being considered, but he would also be way too expensive. Rod Cameron could do it, as he was already doing *Bullets Don't Argue* for Papi and Columbo, but here again it would have stretched the budgets way too thin.

It was in fact according to Frayling, actually a woman Claudia Sartori of the Rome branch of the *William Morris Acency* who when Papi and a coproducer *Jolly Film*, (Rome) had first sent out their feelers for an actor to be considered for their new film, Sartori came up with this young American television actor Clint Eastwood. She contacted them to all come in for a showing of an episode clip from the popular *CBS* show *Rawhide.* Leone seemed to be hung up on Coburn, but agreed to sit and watch the episode clip. About midway through, Leone and group got up to leave. The price at that time for Eastwood was at a low $15,000. The price was right according to all concerned, which seemed to be driving the bargain. Leone, however, was still unsure, but if he was to get this picture made, Eastwood would have to be the man. Leone would later comment on the actor, something to the effect that it was his underlying *laziness* was where his most appeal was, like a snake seemingly asleep, but looming in the grass awaiting to uncoil itself and striking out at a moment's notice! Yes, if we think back, to the stranger / Joe in the gunfight mode, whipping up the poncho the eyes squinted / the strike/ the gunfire, then gun was lightly spin back into its holster, down comes the poncho and all is back to normal in a few seconds, now he's moving off. Yep, Leone had it down pat no doubt.

So from what we found previously rumored of Harrison's claim that he was the one who had suggested that Eastwood would be good for the part was in actuality Claudia Sartori who pushed for the young Eastwood's initial consideration. The price being right though, and the producers were all in agreement, thus Leone would have to follow and later would come around to their way of thinking. The claim of Harrisons was somewhat substantiated in part by an interview given to John Nanar, who posted it on his website *www.nanarland.com.* In that article, Harrison claimed he had declined the part due to other pressing obligations probably wasn't quite accurate, or not the whole truth at least. However, his claim to have suggested that his producers Papi, Columbo and *Jolly* along with Leone's people contact the Roman branch of the *William Morris Agency* may very well have been viable. After all, most any actor would have been interested in broadening his horizons with a new international project, coupled with the combination of work and pleasure on a Roman holiday might very well have appealed to most American actors at that time. That is, of course, if the money was right, and evidently, the $15,000 was all right with Eastwood.

Nadar had offered up that after Harrison initially turned down the offering, he was later presented with a three name list of actors and was asked to pick the one he would choose for the film. He claims to have picked the name of Clint Eastwood, mainly he said, "Because he could ride a horse well." This may have been an off-the-cuff thing between him and his producers, but at any rate, the Italians it would appear had themselves an actor, and Eastwood was on his way to Rome. The rest of the story is pure history, and the outcome of this collaboration efforts between actor

Eastwood and director Leone would tend to change filmmaking of not only by European standards but would eventually hit home back here in our own Hollywood filmdom backyard.

Harrison left the Western genre for a while after completing *Gunfight at Red Sands* reverting to several films he had already waiting in the wings. He now continued with *Messalina against the Son of Hercules* (1964). Harrison stars here as Glaucua, son of Hercules for this Roman-Saxon romp with lovely Marilou Tolo as Ena and Lisa Gastoni as the tyrant ruler, Messalina. Also, he would turn out *Two Gladiators* (1964) starring as Centurion Lucius Crassus, against his evil twin brother and Emperor Commodus (Mimmo Palmera). Another film later called *Revolt of the Praetorians* (1964). He stars here as Centurion Velerio Rufo of the Praetorian Guard who lead the revolt against the standing Emperor Domitian (Piero Lulli). Then there was another, seemingly his last for the genre called *Giants of Rome* (1964) as Claudius Marcellus leader of Emperor Julius Caesar's best commando-type squad of soldiers into the eerie land of the Druids to wipe them out.

It was about this point in time that Harrison became associated with a couple of adventure films, both for director Umberto Lenzi. One was called *Three Sergeants of Bengal* (1964) a.k.a. *Adventures of the Bengal Lancers*. Here he starred as Sgt. Frankie Ross, costarring were Wandisa Guida, Ugo Sasso, Aldo Sambrell, and Dakar. This a Spanish / Italian coproduction with a storyline concerning three British soldiers stationed in Malaysia who are sent to Fort Madras to help the fort commandant and recruits fight off a Thuggie band terrorizing the area. The other was *Temple of a Thousand Lights* (1965) with Harrison as Alan Foster in for a tight little Jungle Adventure. Director Lenzi's better-known efforts came later on in his career for the crime genre films he made. No *Tarzan* film to be sure, but entertaining all the same.

> Late in 1964, for an early '65 release, Harrison was involved with his first of several spy action films starting with *Secret Agent Fireball* (1965) as one of his better and more popular efforts of the genre. Another one he did for a February '65 release was, *Killers are Challenged* as agent, Bob Fleming, 077. Others of these type actioners were soon to follow in the wake of the popular James Bond's films of the day. The Italians being an enterprising people were busy churning these out as well. Hot 'n' heavy, thus the market gets cold, was their motto. Actors like Harrison, was ready, willing and available to help push the genre popularity along. Being an international film star wasn't all fun and games, but it sure beat the unemployment lines of Hollywood, and in general, just being out of work in the States.

For nearly a year after Harrison made the popular pre-Leone Western *Duello nel Texas*, he finally returned to the genre for a late 1965 release of one called *One Hundred-Thousand Dollars for Ringo*. This was an Italian / Spanish coproduction from producer *Balcazar* of Barcelona, and was directed by Alberto De Martino. Harrison here is the star as the protagonist gunslinger Ringo who working secretly undercover as a *Texas Ranger* attempts to clean up and restore law and order to a border town where two separate gangs are at war with one another. If we notice, this storyline is not at all unlike that of the Sergio Leone / Eastwood blockbuster film *A Fistful of Dollars* (1964).*

Harrison's next Western would be simply called *El Rojo.* For this Italian / Spanish coproduction, he portrays a revenge-seeking Donald Sorenson, a.k.a. Rojo. The film was a first time effort for director Leopoldo Savona using the pseudonym of Leo Coleman. The story has Rojo setting out to avenge his murdered family, killed for a gold mine they had been working. It seems he's after four men of power and influence. One, he learns is even the town sheriff (Carter). Eventually, Rojo eliminates them all and quells his anger and vengeance.

For his next one called *Joko, Invoke God . . . and you die!;* a.k.a. *Vengeance!* An Italian / West German coproduction by Renato Savino, and directed by Anthony M. Dawson (Antonio Margheriti). Margheriti was an all-around moviemaker, he came up with the story, and co scripted with producer Savino. The music score for this western was by Carlo Savina, and it starred Richard Harrison as Joko Barrett.

The storyline revolves around Joko who comes upon the body of his friend, who has been drawn and quartered, a brutal way to die, and even more grisly to come upon. He vowed to seek out those responsible and avenge his friend's death. Before leaving he takes along five pieces of bloody rope from the body, these he intends to return to each of the rightful owners before he takes his brand of vengeance out on them.

---

* As more and more of these Westerns were churned out, the more some would be similar in content to other previously more successful films. An effort to cash in on the reputations of those other films of the era was commonplace. Even Zane Grey had only a certain amount of ideas for his novels. Same with these movies coming nonstop out of Europe, some would obviously step on others. They would rehash even certain events throughout the world (like the assassination of US President Robert F. Kennedy, a replayed theme for the film *Price of Power* (1969); politics, and even love stories (Shakespeare). Nothing was sacred to these Italian storywriters. All was fair game to them.

Harrison's next Western was called *Uno dopo l'altro (One after another)* a.k.a. *Day after Tomorrow* (1968). This was an Italian production with direction from Nick Howard (Paolo Bianchi). The storyline concerns life after a bank robbery a mysterious gunman nosing about is actually an insurance investigator called Sam Ross (Harrison). He shows up and commences to get to the bottom of what was obviously an inside job. The guilty banker turns squeamish and nervous when confronted by the bespectacled, near-sighted field man, and the ensuing gun battles begin. Pamela Tudor costars along with Paolo Gozlino, and José Bodalo.

Harrison takes a backseat for his next Western involvement to actor Gilbert Roland who now stars in *Between God, the Devil and the Winchester* for a late '68 release. This was an *Italian/Spanish* coproduction. The direction was strangely credited to Dario Silvestri (who in actuality was the production Manager). Instead it was really directed by Marino Girolami.* His son, actor/stuntman Ennio portrays Marco Serraldo in the film. The story evolves about a mission treasure stolen from a Texas church. Harrison costars as the church's priest Pat Jordan disguised as a gunman (that's a twist)? Roland portrays Juan Chasquisdo a scout who is also looking for the stolen treasure. With Juan, Father Jordan, plus another gang led by Bob Ford (Folco Lulli) all searching for the same treasure, keeps the action waters plenty muddied.

This is about the time when Harrison now got involved with the Euro war film genre. His first was called *Thirty-Six Hours to Hell* (1969). Harrison stars here as Captain Stern, along with Pamela Tudor, Alain Gerard and George Wang. It was directed by Roberto Montero. Storyline concerns a band of Marines that land on a small Pacific island, and were being held by the Japs during WWII. They are prepared to fight to the death, to clean out the fanatical Japs who are dug in surprisingly well for what at first seemed like a nonessential man post.

Later Harrison did another that probably was a bit more popular to fans of the genre called *Churchill's Leopards* (1970). This one starred Klaus

---

* Interesting to the Western fans of the genre is that director Marino Girolami also has another son Enzo, an ex-boxer turned director himself who goes by the handle of Enzo G. (for Girolami) Castellari who had turned out many really good Westerns, while mainstreaming the crime/action film genre as more of his forte.

If we fast-forward a bit in Harrison's career we bring the attention to a blip in Bill Connolly's super *Spaghetti Cinema* Fanzine no. 35 (which is devoted to the European film industry and its participants) that about 1988, Harrison had set up a film company called *Crossbow Entertainment Group* to produce feature films for the US markets with the director Marino Girolami.

Kinski as the Nazi German SS captain that suspects a dam officer of being other than a loyal German at the time when this dam is of vital need as a supply route directly to Normandy. Alas, he's correct in his assumption since Harrison as Lt. Hans Muller, is actually Lt. Richard Benson a British commando with a snap French resistance group set to blow the dam days before D-Day. From director Maurizio Pradeaux, and taken from a co scripting with one Federico De Urrutia.

> Also, about this time, Harrison ventured to do his first crime film for the genre called *C'era una Volta un Gangster (Once Upon a Time, a Gangster)* a.k.a. *There Was Once a Gangster* (1969). Here Harrison stars as hood Larry Alfieri. Others in this rather obscure and currently unattainable Italian film were Ingrid Schoeller, Beth Warren, and Attilio Dottesio. The director was Marco Masi. Evidently, the title may have been an attempt to cash in on Leone's *Once Upon a Time* . . . title theme, which obviously didn't work and it turned out to be lost in film in the onslaught that never got beyond its first initial theater showings in Italy.

For his next film, he reverted to the Westerns for a late 1970 release of *I'll forgive you . . . Before I kill you!* a.k.a. *Stagecoach of the Condemned.* Here Harrison stars as Robert Walton (ex-gunman Wayne Sonnier). His costar was the prolific Spanish actor, Fernando Sancho as bandit Leon Pomparo (a.k.a. Ramon Sartana). Sancho seen in hundreds of these *Spaghetti* Westerns was quite popular though this Italian film era. The large, mostly reliable Internet database website *www.IMDB.com* lists Sancho the actor as having some 244 pieces of film work. That is staggering to say the least. Not all were Westerns by any means, although a good portion of them were.

This film was a Spanish/Italian coproduction from director Juan Bosch (Ignacio Iquino). Harrison's other costars was Erika Blanc as Walton's wife, Martha. Also were Gaspar "Indio" Gonzalez, Florencio Calpe and Maria Cinta among others. The storyline has to do with a stagecoach depot run by the Walton's. Bandits rob the stage wanting to kill the only witness that will hang fellow members of a gang now being held in jail for the trial. They, however, be freed if no witness shows for the trail. Problem though is identifying the correct one so they keep the whole stage depot hostage until the rest of the gang is freed. Ex-gunman Sonnier takes about all he can handle and finally he decides to pick up that hidden gun again and straighten this mess out once and for all.

Harrison's next film effort for a December 24, 1970, release was one called *Reverendo Colt (Reverend Colt).* This was an Italian/Spanish coproduction directed by Leon Klimovsky. *(Here again we may have a misconnection of directors since it is wildly believed now that Marino Girolami (Frank Martin) was the actual director of this film)* The musical score was by Gianni Ferrio.

The film stars Guy Madison as ex-gunman Colt (Madison). Harrison costars here as the town sheriff Donovan of Tucson, Arizona. Colt having experienced his calling has attempted to mend his fences and now goes by the name Miller, Reverend Miller. Coming to Tucson he stumbles onto an old friend Sheriff Donovan (Harrison). He's a friend from the days gone by when they both were slinging guns for hire. Complication develops upon his arrival when the town bank is robbed. Colt caught up in the middle is nearly lynched by angry townsfolk. Harrison saves the day, but has to jail him. Things get better for Colt as his being a man of the cloth now, is able to persuade the sheriff to let him escape, and track the outlaws himself. Harrison figures he can come out only on the top of this deal and agrees.

After Richard Harrison finally got to meet American actor Guy Madison for the first time, they hit it off like old buddies. They both had been there in and out of Rome since the early 1960s making those great Italian films. It couldn't have been too hard to not run into one another since the Americans kept to a pretty tight circle of friends while in Rome. Alas though, during the mid to late '60s a foreigner had to be very careful during those days around the bigger cities of Rome. Harrison offered up once that he was mugged and robbed there once.

The two developed a lasting friendship, and with the Madison family who were in and out visiting on occasion. Some years afterward when both men had finally returned to the LA area they still remained good family friends. Actually Harrison had been given the honor of being named Godfather to Madison's daughter Bridget's firstborn son, Spencer. Years later at Guy Madison's funeral service in 1996, Harrison delivered a stirring eulogy for the actor and friend who will forever be remembered for his 1950's television character portrayal of Wild Bill Hickok.

> Richard Harrison's own son, his youngest of two, was Sebastian born and educated in Rome would eventually venture in the footsteps of his father for a while. He was still in his early '20s when he was starred in one film that still remains a somewhat popular *Spaghetti* Western to date. It was called *White Apache* (1984) from director Vincent Dawn (Bruno Mattei). This late entry, far from the main phenomenon years of the genre is nevertheless one for the books.
>
> Mattei, a director of mostly offbeat (mostly of inferior quality) films of various genres actually had a hit here. Mattei cast Sebastian in the lead role as a young man that was an Irish baby

> that had been taken in by an Apache Chief and raised as his own as Shining Sky. This was a successful film for both Sebastian and Mattei, however, Sebastian's film career never really took off and currently he remains out of the limelight, running a technological business service there in LA which he and his father started several years back in the 1990s.

About this time Harrison also turned in another Western called *Dig Your Grave Friend . . . Sabata's Coming!* (1971). This an Ital/ Spa/ French coproduction film from director John Wood (Ignacio Iquino). Harrison is Steve McGowan who's out to avenge his father's death, joins up with a Mexican bandit called Pompero (Fernando Sancho) in order to seek out the killer. This culprit seems to be a land baron going by the name of Miller (Indio Gonzales). Miller finds out from his spies that McGowan is coming for him and he's hired supposedly the best gunman around, Sabata (Raf Baldassare) who now stands between Miller and the two oncoming avengers prepared to clash with them head-on to protect Miller. Actually in the long term, Millers own girlfriend Helen (Joan Rubin) betrays him setting him up for Steve to quench his thirst for vengeance.

Harrison was without a doubt rather prolific himself on these Westerns having turned in some seventeen as an actor with mostly lead roles to boot. Now with only a few more to go, we'll list here one for a mid-1971 release called *Lo Chiamavano King (His Name was King)* an Italian production from Antonio Lugatelli. It was directed by Don Reynolds (Renato Savino) who also wrote the story and script. The music score was by the popular Luis Enrique Bacalov. This film stars Richard Harrison as bounty hunter John King Marley. Home for a spell and working at the family ranch he returns from off the range to discover that his brother and wife have been attacked by a gang, killed his brother, beat and raped his wife. He takes his sister-in-law Carol (Anne Puskin) to his friend Sheriff Foster (Kinski in cameo) to take care of her while he takes off to seek out the gang responsible. He suspects the Benson bunch has been dealing trafficking illegal guns (stolen Gatling-guns) across the border selling them to the Mexicans. He's has had bad dealings with that same bunch before on his land, this was meant to be a warning to stay out of their business.

Harrison turned in two more Westerns for 1971 releases, both later but before Christmas that year. The earliest was *Acquasanta Joe,* a.k.a. *Holy Water Joe.* This was an Italian production from director Mario Gariazzo. Here we have Harrison doing a cameo role in this film co starring as Charlie a lowly member of the Donovan gang. Ty Hardin stars here as Jeff Donovan, an outlaw with a very bad reputation. Another American (three in one film, wow!), Lincoln Tate (as Acquasanta Joe) also costars here as a notorious bounty hunter who has just deposited a certain amount of *his* cash in the local bank, only to hear later that it has been robbed and his, among others monies are now gone. He takes off to track this bunch and retrieve his money. Meanwhile, rival gang member Charlie has taken off on his own with everybody's loot. All are now after Charlie.

The bandit lovely Estella (Silvia Monelli) who first is Jeff's gal, then later she sided up to Charlie who had the loot. But, Charlie was caught by a sheriff in another town and hanged (good-bye, Harrison). The money is now in the hands of the authorities. She finally has taken up now with Butch (Lee Banner) who has taken over as gang leader since Jeff's been gone looking for the loot. A real mess here at the end, after the ensuing gun battle with the two rival factions and the dust settles it leaves Joe unscathed, but also empty handed. Jeff although shot, does get the girl again in the end. As for the money, well that's anybody's guess?

Harrison's next was *Sheriff of Rock Spring* (1971). Another Italian Western, which tries to be more of a comedy with a cliché driven story resulting in us fans pulling our hair if we managed to last until the end of the film. This mess was directed by Anthony Green (Primo Zeglio). This film seems a real slap in the face of both lead actors we feel, and the genre as well. The entire genre was now beginning to change as result of a few comedic efforts already on the market by this time. Things really began to go south in the genre when E. B. Clucher (Enzo Barboni) first came out with his *They Call me Trinity* (1970) film. More stupidity than plot, but the Italian audiences seemed to love it, thus others began to follow in the same vein afterward. The year of the straight *Spaghetti* Western was now in its decline.

Back to the film, Harrison stars here as a former gunslinger, now reformed and settled in as sheriff of this Rock Spring. Others along for the ride are Cosetta Greco as the sheriff's gal friend and Irish actor Donal (Donald) O'Brien who made a good living within the genre for years. We have enjoyed seeing O'Brien in many Western, some comedic versions and his characters have always done him justice, as in this film although the script isn't good enough to hold an eight year olds attention much less an adult audience some of us feel.

Before the end 1971, Harrison had dropped in on the crime genre once again for another film outing and an early release in January of '72. This little ditty called *You can do a Lot with Seven Women* was promoted as a comedic crime film. It was directed by Fabio Piccioni, and starred Harrison as one Mike Spencer a cop who, posing as a photographer for a modeling agency is actually investigating a drug trafficking scheme, using

> the agency as a front. His girlfriend was killed by drug dealers involved in this scheme. Supposedly, this was a comedy but in actuality not so much. Harrison's costars are mostly women, Marcella Michelangeli as Danny, Marie Louise Sinclair as Betty Simmons and also with Aldo Bufi Landi as Marchese.
>
> From 1969-1979 our man Richard Harrison turned in some ten of these crime films we'r aware of. He was quite the work alcoholic churning out multiple genre films during his long European stay. In one statement he made in the www.*nanarland.com* interview, I knew I didn't have the tools to be a great actor, nor the desire, but I had what was needed to have a career." To repeat a phrase coined by Bill Connolly for one of his older *Spaghetti Cinema* Fanzine issue no. 2, articles for this actor he says, "The titles are many and his output steady." We'll certainly drink to that!

Then just when we thought we were clear, along comes another comedic substitution for a straight Western plot with *Due Fratelli I un posto chiamato Trinita (Two Brothers in a Place called Trinity)* a.k.a. *Jesse and Lester* (1972). Following in the footsteps of the *Trinity* film theme that seems to have been so popular during this era of the *Spaghetti* Western, was this Italian production from coproducer / director James London (Richard Harrison) in time for an early release in '72. This film however, was a bit different for actor Richard Harrison in that he actually was involved with it as co producer along with Fernando Piazzo, *HP (Harrison and Piazzo) International Film, Italy.* In addition he also coscripted along with Renzo Genta, and was the film's director for this, his first attempt along this avenue for film work.

> An interesting item here for the fans recognize that Harrison told Bill Connolly of *Spaghetti Cinema* Fanzine, and Tom Betts of *WAI!* Fanzine in conversation that yes, he did direct this film using the James London pseudonym. However, being said that I do have a firm listing from *www.anica.it.com* that the director was Renzo Genta. We all feel that even as Genta was listed as the co script writer with RH, he may very well have been the Italian co director of the film that probably helped to direct the Italian actors. When the credits were handed out, being it was an Italian film he was naturally credited over Harrison, regardless of who was actually doing the job. Bill says Harrison was quite proud of his directorial debut and in later years when back in LA taught an acting class there at *UCLA* and sometimes showed this film to the class.

The plot for this film's story has two step-brothers Jesse (Harrison) a gadabout and Lester (Donal O'Brien) a gruff Mormon preacher have now inherited land and money from their uncle. The one brother Jesse wants to build a whorehouse on the property, but the brother Lester wants to use the land to build a Mormon church. A major problem here, other than their big disagreement now going on between the two, is that the entire town where the land is located seems to be overrun with crooks of all walks of life. The monies it seems that went with the land inheritance has been stolen, now they must join together to catch the culprits and get back their loot. Although, still comedic in content) much better than the *Rock Spring* film.

> Note: Another interesting item for fans who may remember one John Dulaney. Early in his film career he actually was in the film *Jesse e Lester* (1972) with Harrison and O'Brien as an extra, a Miner. He said he and Richard became close while doing the *Long Ride to Vengeance* (1972) *see below*, where his part was that of a gambler. He is probably best remembered though, for his later part as the judge in the *Return of Sabata* also a 1972 film, with him handing Lee Van Cleef (as Sabata) a pistol. John P. Dulaney and wife, Jojo, now live in West Hollywood, California.

For Harrison next film he turned in *Joe Dakota Shoot . . . and* Shoot *again! (Joe Dakota Spare . . . E Cosi Sia)* a.k.a. *Joe Dakota.* An Italian production from director Hal Brady (Emilio P. Miraglia) who also credited with writing the script, but using his real name. The film stars Richard Harrison as Joe Dakota. As the story goes, Joe character is hot on the trail of stolen loot by means of a map that supposedly shows where it's hidden. The hell he goes through reminds us a Bruce Willis action movie. First, he's betrayed by a woman Rosy (Franca Polesello). Later he's temporarily blinded by outlaws who are torturing him. Somehow he manages to bounce back regaining his sight just in time for the big shootout with the gang. The loot is uncovered and the outlaws are all taken care of shortly thereafter. Others of the cast were José Torres and Indio Gonzales.

Only two more left to go, one was for a late '72 release called *Long Cavalcade of Vengeance* (*La Lunga Cavalcata Della Vendetta*) a.k.a. *The Long Ride of Revenge/ The Deadly Trackers*; an Italian production and directed by Amerigo Anton (Tanio Boccia) who also wrote the script crediting his real name. Richard Harrison stars here as James Luke acting as a guide for a wagon train of settlers making their way west through Wyoming. Bandits attack the train killing mostly everyone but him, including his sister, after they rape and beat her. They left Luke for dead and make off with his gal Anita Ekberg. Luke and a partner are now hot on a trail of vengeance.

Others genre favorites of the cast were Rik Battaglia, George Wang and Men Fury (Furio Meniconi).

Now we finally come to the end of Harrison's Westerns for a late '72 release called *Los Fabulosos de Trinidad (The Fabulous Trinity)* a.k.a., *With Friends . . . Nothing is Ever Easy!* This was a Spanish / Italian coproduction, in the comedic *Trinity* style. It was directed by Steve McCohy (Ignacio Iquino) who also scripted along with Jackie Kelly. Music for this romp through old Mexico was by Enrique Escobar.

Harrison here stars as a bounty hunter called Scott. His costar is Fernando Sancho as Col. Jimenez. According to the storyline, it seems Scott has helped out a gal Nora (Fanny Grey), who wants to proceed down into Mexico so as to free her three uncles from prison there. Supposedly they have been jailed there for gun-trafficking and now imprisoned at the St. Augustine facility run by a Colonel Jimenez. Nora, however, actually has an ulterior motive, that being, collecting all the bounty on her uncles herself once she's back across the border on US soil again. Scott baits him with the offering of him receiving $1,000 each, and he goes along with her plan helping to free them. The Colonel, however, seems to always be just one step behind them foiling their plan at every turn. Although in the comedic vein, it really doesn't sound too bad for a *Trinity* type film, but until seen in person, it all remains to be seen. With Richard Harrison now finished with the Western genre, he moved on to make films in various other parts of the world. He worked with pal Gordon Mitchell outside of Rome first though on the film *The Sewer Rats* (1974) as the cripple (no name) drifter. This film was actually made at Gordon Mitchell's own *Cava* studio and at the town set he'd built. Harrison went on to make a couple of action films in Turkey with GM one was called *Jolando e Margherito* (1975) a.k.a. *Four for All.* Harrison stars here as Jolando, and GM as the Margherito character; And later they were in Yugoslavia for *Black Gold Dossier* (1979) again starring Harrison here as Richard Benson; After that came a Germany film with GM called *Natascha: The Deadly Drop* (1977); And then a war film with GM called *Kaput Lager, Gli Ultimi Giorno Delle SS (Hell Camp: The Last Days of the SS)* a.k.a. *Achtung: The Desert Tigers** (1977) Harrison starred

* This was the film GM (Gordon Mitchell) used to reminisce about being in with Richard Harrison who played the good American officer while he the bad German officer. In Harrison's *nanarland.com* interview he was asked about working there at *Cinecitta studios.* The interviewer had heard stories about what it was like there during its heyday, liken to a factory, turning out multiple films at once almost with actors doing scenes in more than one picture during a given workday. He went on to reply about his and GM's experiences saying,

here as an American prisoner of war Major Lexman. GM was the evil camp Commandant, Captain Von Stalts/Stern. They were a group of allied tank commandos captured, and held in this brutal Nazi POW camp. They succeed in a daring escape plan, but the storm troopers are near behind them.

Harrison also did films in the Philippines, and Hong Kong with the *Shaw Brothers,* for one of two entrys called *Marco Polo* (1975). Another in Hong Kong with filmmaker Godfrey Ho called *Inferno Thunderbolt,* a low budget martial arts film, in which Ho later altered the editing into about nine different films, all claiming to have Harrison in them, but actually was only spliced in segments from the one, all done solely without Harrison's knowledge or permission.

Harrison has mostly retired now from the cinema world since the '90s, when he returned to the States. After a couple of bids for mayor of Palm Springs, he finally settled back to later life contentment. He however was around for a cameo in *Jerks* (2000). Married twice he is the father of three sons from first wife, Loretta Nicholson, from the 1961 marriage, now dissolved in divorced. His other sons are as follows: Robert Harrison; Richard Harrison II, and Sebastian all grown up now and out on their own. Presently, Senior has married again to the former Italian film actress Maria Francesca Pomentale since 1978, and they have one daughter.

His lovely wife, Francesca, is more commonly known through the cinema by several pseudonyms she used while working in films: Sarah Harrison, Daria Norman or Francesca Whaight. Amazing, all these film artists during this era seemed to be using those pseudonyms, it's a wonder any of them got their pay checks cashed! Alas facts being though, most did not trust their employers in Europe and demanded to be paid in cash only, which I'm sure was just as soon as possible changed into US bank drafts and/or monies transferred to other overseas accounts. If not that would surely have been a good policy to follow we feel. Certainly with the instability of those years abroad, the radical times would still put those from all walks of life; stars, locals or tourists alike with a lot of cash on them in an extremely vulnerable position, possibly even life threatening to say the least. We're quite sure that muggings off the *Via Veneto* side streets of Rome, was no doubt commonplace there as it would be here in certain darken alleys of America.

"When you are the lead actor you were required to stay there on the set, or available at all times. GM, on the other hand often would play a short part then go on to another film. On the set I usually stayed to myself." Harrison's favorite pastime he said was reading, so he read when not in front of the camera.

The whole place was a ticking time-bomb of internal unrest, which is reflected in some of the more politically inspired films that was shot during this era. This was one reason the majority of the working class of American actors did pretty much stay to themselves, in groups and tried not to involve themselves in any way with local politics. A fun place for tourists we understand, but to live there day to day we're sure was another state of affairs.

We fans of the genre had long thought perhaps maybe some of the old *Spaghetti* Western actors still with us today, being fairly healthy and all around the first of the Millennium would be able to get together for one last shoot 'em up session. Richard Harrison and buddy Gordon along with his pal Mick Hargitay were said to have been strong supporters of that idea. But alas, that chance has come and gone as have those faithful stars with exception of Richard Harrison. Alas, we fans will just have to replenish our dreams once in a while by popping in a new DVD release of some our old favorites. To be sure, that left-handed, blond cowboy ex-*Peplum* hero, now turned gunslinger, will have his films right up there on the top of our play list ready for watching again and again. Meanwhile, all the best to you Richard in your years to come, and May they be many Sir.

End.

- Below is a complete filmography of Richard Harrison Euro Westerns. The dates are aligned as close as possible with information currently at hand, plus international release dates included. **Actor photo and poster pictures are accredited to the Sebastian Haselbeck collection via his website www.spaghetti-westerns.net. Thanks again, Sebastian.*

RICHARD HARRISON
EURO WESTERN FILMS

1963

Gunfight at High Noon; *I Tre Spietati (Three Ruthless Ones)* a.k.a. *Sons of Vengeance*; Spa / Ital, Director Joaquin Romero Marchent (Harrison as Jeff Walker) (1963)

Gunfight at Red Sands; *Duell nel Texas (Duel in Texas)*; Ital / Spa, Director Ricardo Blasco (Harrison as Ricardo Martinez) 9/19/63

1965

One-Hundred Thousand Dollars for Ringo, *100.000 Dollari per Ringo*; Ital / Spa, Director Alberto De Martino (Harrison as Ringo / the Texas Ranger) 11/18/65

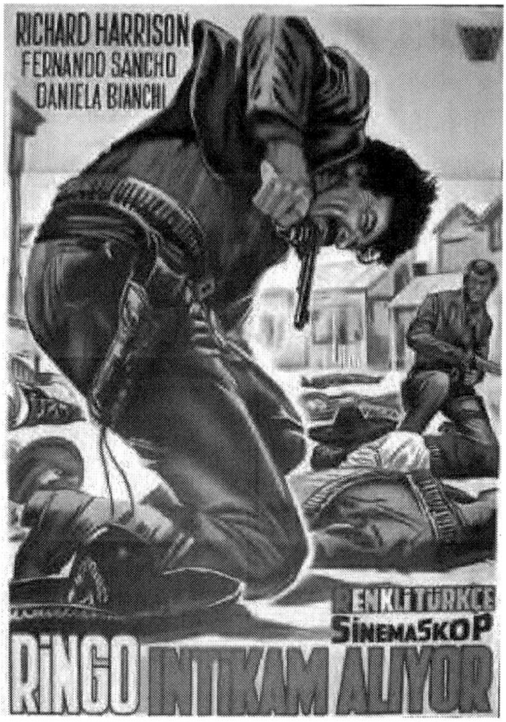

1966

ROJO; *El Rojo* a.k.a. *Texas El Rojo*; Ital / Spa, Director Leo Coleman (Leopoldo Savona) (Harrison as Donald Sorenson / Rojo) (9/1/66)

1968

Joko, Invoke God . . . and you die! *Joko, Invoca Dio . . . e Muori* a.k.a. *Vengeance*; Ital / W. Germ, Director Anthony M. Dawson (Antonio Margheriti) (Harrison as Joko Barrett) 4/19/68

One After Another, *Uno Dopo L'Altro* a.k.a. *Day after Tomorrow*; Ital, Director Nick Howard (Paolo Bianchi) (Harrison as gunman/insurance investigator Sam Ross); 8/13/68

Also in the West, There Was Once a God, *Anche Nel West, C'Era una Volta Dio* a.k.a. *Between God, the Devil and a Winchester*; Ital / Spa, Director Marino Girolami (Harrison as priest, Father Pat Jordan); 10/7/68

1970

I'll Forgive You . . . Before I Kill You. *Prima ti perdono . . . poi t'ammazzo* a.k.a. *Stagecoach of the Condemned*; Spa / Ital, Director John Wood (Juan Bosch) (Ignacio Iquino) (Harrison as Robert Walton / ex-gunman Wayne Sonnier); 8/6/70 *Note*: Not to be confused with the '71 film also by Bosch (Iquino), *Dig your grave Friend . . . Sabata's coming!*

1970

Reverend Colt. *Reverendo Colt;* a.k.a. *The Reverend's Colt*; Ital / Spa, Director Leon Klimovsky (Harrison as Sheriff Donovan); 12/24/70

1971

Dig Your Grave Friend . . . Sabata's Coming! *Vanghi Il Suo Amico Grave . . . Sabata Sta Venendo*; Ital/ Spa/ Fra, Director John Wood (Juan Bosch) (Ignacio Iquino) (Harrison as Steve McGowan); 4/2/71

His Name Was King. *Lo Chiamavano King*; Ital, Director Don Reynolds (Renato Savino) (Harrison as John "King" Marley); 5/18/71

Holy Water Joe, *a.k.a. Acquasanta Joe*; Ital, Director Mario Gariazzo (Harrison in cameo, as gang member Charlie); 12/11/71

The Sheriff of Rock Springs, *Lo Sceriffo di Rock Spring*; Ital, Director Anthony Green (Primo Zeglio) (Harrison as the sheriff); 12/17/71

1972

Two Brothers in a Place Called Trinity, *Due Fratelli I un posto chiamato Trinita;* a.k.a. *Jesse and Lester: Two Brothers in Trinity;* a.k.a. *Jesse and Lester*; Ital, Director James London (Richard Harrison) / Renzo Genta (Harrison as Jesse Smith); 4/27/72

Joe Dakota Shoot . . . And Shoot Again! *Joe Dakota Spare . . . E Cosi Sia;* a.k.a. *Joe Dakota*; Ital, Director Hal Brady (Emilio P. Miraglia) (Harrison as Joe Dakota); 5/10/72

Long Cavalcade of Vengeance, *La Lunga Cavalcata Della Vendetta;* a.k.a. *The Deadly Trackers*; Ital, Director Amerigo Anton (Tanio Boccia) (Harrison as wagon train escort James Luke); 9/4/72

With Friends . . . Nothing Is Ever Easy! *Alla Larga Amigos . . .Oggi ho Il Grilletto Facile* a.k.a. *The Fabulous Trinity*; Spa / Ital, Director Ignacio F. Iquino (Harrison as Scott); 11/9/72

This pretty much finishes up Harrison's involvement as an actor of the *Spaghetti* Westerns. Afterward, it seems he went on to more of the crime and action genres of film. He did, however, continue to write for his films and doing other contract script projects on other movies, one of these he was associated with was another Western, but not as an actor.

The film was called ***Scalps*** (1987); Ital/W. Ger/Spa, Director Werner Knox (Vincent Dawn) (Bruno Mattei); For this film Harrison not only wrote the story, but also helped to cowrite the script along with director Mattei, and Producer José Maria Cunnilles. Below is a copy of a German VHS video cover. *Note: The director's Werner Knox pseudonym used for this video. The Indian girl pictured was a newcomer to films, Mapi Galan as Yani.*

The film starred Vassili Karis, veteran actor of the Euro Western era stars as Matt. Basically, this is an Indian love story with a violent twist thanks to director Mattei who actually is the film's co director along with Italian director Claudio Fragasso.

Before we close this filmography for Richard Harrison completely, I'd like to address this one last film that his son Sebastian did well after close of the initial phenomenon years was over. After about 1975, several Westerns were still made, but they came out only sporadically. A sort of revival tactic was attempted by a select few directors, which unfortunately never really took off again. This was one of those movies . . .

White Apache, *Bianco Apache* (1987); Ital / Spa, Director Claudio Fragasso / Bruno Mattei (Sebastian Harrison as Shining Star) 8/26/87; Costarring Lola Forner as Rising Sun. Others also starring were Alberto Farnese and Charly Bravo. The story was taken for a true-life happening about an Irish baby taken during a raid and raised by the Colorado Apaches. Script adaptation was by Jose Maria Cunilles / Franco Prosperi.

End.

BIBLIOGRAPHY
(R. Harrison)

Betts, Tom, editor *WAI! (Westerns . . . All'Italiana)* Fanzine articles / information on Richard Harrison

Connolly, Bill, editor *Spaghetti Cinema* Fanzine articles / info on Actor Richard Harrison

Frayling, Christopher, *Something to do with Death* (2000) *Faber & Faber Ltd.,* London, UK., Chapter 5, pp. 134-136

Haselbeck, Sebastian, owner/curator for Internet website: *www.spaghetti-westerns.net*

Hughes, Howard, *Cinema Italiano: The complete Guide from Classics to Cult* (2011) *L. B. Tauris and Co. Ltd,* London; New York

Internet, via: *www.anica.it* Ref: Film production and date confirmation

Internet, via: *www.briansdriveintheater.com* "Muscles in Hollywood" section on Richard Harrison

Internet, via: *www.fortunecity.com* Ref: "The John Dulaney Pages" on Richard Harrison

Internet, via: *www.IMDB.com* "Mini biography of Richard Harrison" plus film listing review

Nanar, John, owner / curator for Internet website: *www.nanarland.com* Ref: Richard Harrison info bits culled from posted interview 2007

Prickette, Tom, *Peplum Hero, Turns Gunslinger,* Previously unpublished manuscript of 2002

Walker, Brian J., owner / curator for Internet website: *www.briansdriveintheater.com* Ref: Info on R. Harrison plus film listing review

Weisser, Thomas, *Spaghetti Westerns: the Good, the Bad, and the Violent*, (1992) *McFarland*, Jefferson NC.

JOHN IRELAND

(1914-1992)

IN SEARCH OF *THAT* ROLE

The name of John Ireland has been associated with Westerns, drama and action films now for well over the six decades. As a dedicated internationally known artist in the field of acting, he has definitively made his mark in the film archives of the world. He was born as John Benjamin Ireland, January 30, 1914. His birth place was Vancouver, British Columbia, Canada. From there he immigrated with his parents while still a small boy to the United States.

His father, John Benjamin Sr. by profession was a rancher and after settling found work there in the San Francisco valley lands as a ranch hand. His mother Katherine was an educator and was immediately accepted into the local school system as a teacher. John Jr. attended his lower schooling classes there until the family, now with another child, a daughter they named Catherine decided on another move, this time all the way to New York City where they finally settled for good and where John Jr. was formally raised.

It was here while attending Commerce High School that he was first introduced to the fine Arts. This also included stage acting through various skits and plays that were being performed throughout the school year. It was during these unbridled years of learning and experimenting with the various performing arts that he decided on show business as a career move. Already a top-notch swimmer from his years on the swimming team, he joined with a water carnival as a professional.

Later in 1939 he left the pro-swimming circuit and opted for work on the Stage. Stage work he found was more his cup of tea. He made his debut on the boards at the Robin Hood Theater there in Arden, Delaware. Later his off-Broadway debut was with the *Irish Repertory Players* group at the Cherry Lane Theater there in NYC. He loved the excitement of the live challenging audiences. He went on tour with such major groups as the *Clare Tree Children's Theater* in which he portrayed the Captain Hook character for Peter Pan which toured major cities during the early 1940s.

Married life for John Ireland began during these stage years. While he studied acting at the *Davenport Free Theater* there in NYC he met another young stage actor, Elaine Sheldon Gudman. They struck up an acquaintance, then after a whorl win courtship they married in 1940. She would later bear him two sons John Jr., and Peter Ireland. Peter would years later become a successful writer, actor and producer of films himself. John Jr., went on to do some acting through the years but found he preferred being behind the scenes rather than in front of the camera. Both are successful in the business today.

During this period in time, Ireland's career and family seemed to be progressing along very well. He went on to receive notable recognition in such Shakespearean plays as "Hamlet", "Macbeth" and "Othello". His Broadway debut was with "Macbeth" back in the NYC at the *National Theater* in 1941. These roles of Shakespeare only seem to moisten his growing appetite for acting.

It was later in 1945 that he made his film debut. It was a significant role in the Lewis Milestone's WWII war drama, *Windy, A Walk in the Sun,* a.k.a. *Salerno Beachhead* for *20th Century Fox.* It starred Dana Andrews and Richard Conte. John Ireland's role was that of Pvt. Windy Craven. Ironically all three of his coactors would later venture into Europe and join in on the *Spaghetti* Western craze themselves. This was a black-and-white picture, with outdoor segments shot for the most part in Southern California Parks. It's been acclaimed as one of the best war films ever made and would stand up to scrutiny even by today's standards. It was actually filmed during the war but was not released until after its end.

During those war years Ireland was already too old for the draft and at thirty-one he was off the roles. In the years to follow, even as his film career began to blossom, he would continue to do a smattering of stage work now and again. In film work though, he began to find more and more pleasure, even further recognition in the various supporting roles that film work afforded. Some of his more noted roles were As Billy Clanton in *My Darling Clementine* for *20th Century Fox* (1946); the role of Karty in *The Gangster* for *Allied Artists* (1947); and as Reno in *I Love Trouble* for *Columbia Pictures* (1947).

It was later though, about 1947 when things seem to take a turn for the worse. While under contract to famed director Howard Hawks, it is said that is where most of Ireland's problems really began. It seems while portraying gunman Cherry Valance during the filming of the John Wayne movie *Red River* that trouble brewed. Rumors have it that John Ireland still a married man had fallen in love with the film's leading lady, Joanne Dru. To make matters worse, the film's director Hawks, himself was also smitten with her. In attempt to keep them apart Hawks kept cutting Ireland's parts. This eventually led to Ireland's loosing face as well as him loosing other acting roles for future film work yet to come by Hawks who was taking a stand against him.

Be that as it may, after all that a split between him and Elaine was inevitable. They were divorced in 1948. Less than a year later, he and the actress Joanne Dru were married on May 16, 1949. He and wife, Joanne, would go on that year to work an Oscar winning film for *Columbia Pictures*. It was called *All the King's Men* and starred Broderick Crawford as the Senator Willie Stark and John Ireland was newspaper man Jack Burden. The leading lady was none other than Joanne Dru. The film's director Robert Rossen was widely acclaimed for his talent. Crawford received an Oscar for Best Actor, and the picture won for Best Picture of the year. John Ireland had received a nomination for Best Supporting Actor, via his role adapted from the prize-winning novel by Robert Penn Warren.

Although many fine supporting roles would follow, John Ireland never could seem to latch on to *that* one role that would make him a top box office star. It seems that he spent the remainder of his career doing mostly B-grade movies and playing second fiddle heroes or villains. His talents, however, were not solely in the field of acting and swimming alone. From time to time he would occasionally lend his hand to script writing and directing. His first attempts at this can be seen in *Hannah Lee*, a.k.a. *Outlaw Territory* (1953). This was a coproduction effort with wife, Joanne Dru, and their son Peter. John Ireland also co directed the film along with Lee Grimes. The film starred Macdonald Carey and Joanne Dru. John Ireland portrayed the Marshall, Sam Rochelle.

Another co directing credit for Ireland was later along with Edward Sampson in the film, *The Fast and the Furious* (1954) a low-budget *juvenile thriller* for producer Roger Corman. During these early 1950s, Ireland continued to expand his acting by involving himself with the acclaimed media, television. His boob tube debut was for *NBC* in 1950 on the *Starlight Theater* in "The Last Kiss." Throughout the 1950s, he would continue in television work, while doing an occasional play and a movie or two as the opportunities arose.

The name of John Ireland has been associated in credits of many fine films of the 1950's era. A few were more widely acclaimed than others. One role that stands out with fans of the Western genre of films was his role of Johnny Ringo the fabled gunslinger in the now classic *Gunfight at the OK Corral* (1957). Directed by John Sturges it starred Burt Lancaster as the famous lawman Wyatt Earp. It co starred Kirk Douglas in the role of Doc Holliday the infamous dentist / gambler and gunman. Also, there was the lovely Rhonda Fleming. The film also starred Jo Van Fleet, John Ireland and Lee Van Cleef among many others. Also, Frankie Lane would make a hit record singing the title song for the film.

Trouble though, was brewing behind the scenes about this time in the Ireland household. He and Joanne Dru were divorced by 1957. Later on as some would call it just a midlife crisis, others were probably just rumors, whatever, but during the years to follow John Ireland's name had been romantically linked in the tabloids with many aspiring young actresses of the day like Natalie Wood or Sue Lyon.* He was fast building a subversive reputation as a rounder, a type to stay away from. Those reports not only came to hurt him personally, but also in the long run professionally as well.

---

* Tuesday Weld later was actually offered the leading role in Stanley Kubrick upcoming blockbuster film *Lolita* (1962), she turned it down. Up and coming actress Sue Lyon accepted the part and starred in dual personages as Dolores / Lolita Haze and later in the film as the Mrs. Richard Schiller. This Academy Award winning film listed an impressive cast of James Mason doubled as Prof. Humbert and as story narrator; Shelly Winters was the mother Charlotte Haze Humbert; Gary Cockrell as Richard Schiller; and Lois Maxwell as Nurse Mary Lore.

Ironically, John Ireland had supposedly been romantically involved with both Weld and Lyon. Sue Lyon would later also venture into the Spaghetti Westerns for one film outing called *Four Rode Out* (1971). A film from director John Peyser it was a US / Spanish coproduction that was filmed in Almeria, Spain. It starred Miss Lyon as Myra Polsen and costarred Pernell Roberts as US Marshall Ross along with another American Leslie Nielsen as Mr. Brown a Pinkerton Agent. This was their only *Spaghetti* film of era. It seems Myra (Lyon) and her Mexican boyfriend bandit Frenando Nunez (Julian Mateos) were on the run from the law for the murder of her father with Roberts and Nielsen hot on their trail.

The one association with young starlets that the tabloids really went wild over was the still unsubstantiated claims that he had been having an affair with child-star actress Tuesday Weld,* who at that time was only sixteen years old. A wild child, no doubt but in the eye of the public this was not excuse. It was now 1959 and filming of the Elvis Presley vehicle, *Wild in the Country* had begun. From what it appeared to most everyone on the set, including Presley right down to the lowly stagehands, Ireland was head over heels with the impish young actress Weld from the start. John Ireland's role was that of Phil Macy one of the films main characters was no exception as he seemed totally engrossed with her. The Tabloids were having a field day, selling millions of copies of their slander zines at Ireland's expense and loving every minute of it.

Miss Weld at the time attempted to downplay the whole thing telling the reporters something to the effect that everyone had the wrong idea when a girl goes out with an older man, they all immediately jump to the wrong conclusions. They were just friends in the same business together and that was all nothing more. Later it was said that Ireland admitted that probably the only reason he didn't ask her to marry him at the time was the big different between their ages (he was 45) and her mother Aileen whom he had never gotten along with from the start. The film wasn't released until 1961, why? We can only imagine it was for fear of conflicting with other Presley pictures already being shown at theaters, or could it have been the gossip?

Well into the 1960s, though all the gossip had pretty much blown over, it seemed career-wise at least for John Ireland, he was back to success again at the box office with the 1960 epic release of *Spartacus*. Kirk Douglas starred

---

* John Ireland's first film venture overseas was for a war film called *Dirty Heroes* for a '67 release. It was an *Italian* production from director Alberto De Martino. Shot from a scripting mainly by Dino Verde and Luciano Vincenzoni for the story and with director De Martino and some six other writers in all were involved directly or indirectly in the scripting (yep, far too many fingers in the pie I'd say). It takes place in Holland, the spring of 1944 when allied forces meet German armies coming face-to-face in the final battle conflict of WWII. The underlying plot was a heist of diamonds from Amsterdam by a select group of gangsters during wartime. Great story though, but it is a little too long. It preempts Eastwood's later *Kelly's Heroes* of 1970 also about a heist during wartime.

It starred Frederick Stafford as safecracker Joe Mortimer, Daniela Bianchi (Erika Blanc) as Kristina von Keist, and Curd Jurgens as General Edwin von Keist. John Ireland portrays Captain O'Connor and Michel Constantin as Sgt. Rudolph Petoskey among others of an impressive cast.

as the lead character Spartacus, he also produced the film. A surprisingly good film even by today's standards even though it's been said that directorial interventions by the star / producer kept the entire shooting schedule on edge and in turmoil. An all-star cast with the likes of Laurence Olivier, Jean Simmons, Charles Laughton, Peter Ustinov, and John Ireland as Crixus and Herbert Lom, the list goes on.

Another fine film venture for John Ireland was *55 Days at Peking* (1962). It starred Charlton Heston as company Commander of the US marines force. Heston's second in command was John Ireland in the role of Harry a Marine NCO. These forces were defending the International Compound there in Peking, China against the *Boxer Rebels* during the 1900 rebellion that took place there.

By this time, some years had passed since his divorce from Joanne Dru in '57. He hadn't been quite so eager to jump back into matrimony after all that business. However, smitten again as they say, during this year of 1962 he did indeed once again delve into marriage. This time though, amazingly she wasn't an actress. Daphine Cameron Myrick was born to be the wife of John Ireland. This time around, it was indeed a marriage made in heaven and lasted his remaining thirty years.

In the years that followed he continued to work steady doing lots of television. He could be seen on such popular weekly shows of the era as *The Cheaters* (1960); *Rawhide* (1965-'66); *Zane Grey Theater*; *Fireside Theater*; *General Electric Theater* ; *Schlitz Playhouse of the Stars*; and the *Kraft Suspense Theater*. Despite this amount of frequency work of this entertainment media, it didn't seem to help his film career any which was still in steady decline from 1960 on.

He was a prolific artist of his trade. A workaholic that wasn't happy unless he was working. He continued to searched for work, whatever the media, be it stage, television or the movies, he continually was searching for *that* one special role that would put him over the top. Soon he found himself in Europe as this was indeed the place to be at the time. The moviemaking here was going full steam and the recent influx of European films coming out of Italy of the day would boggle the mind. He may have arrived somewhat late for the era of the *Spaghetti* Westerns, but that was no never mind, he dug in for the long haul doing all he could. In 1967 he was already fifty-three and time was a wasting.

John Ireland's first *Spaghetti* Western was called *Odio per Odio (Hate for Hate)* (1967) an Italian production, directed by Domenico Paolella. It stars Antonio Sabato as Miguel a hard working Mexican miner whose money was taken in a bank robbery. Here Sabato is co billed with John Ireland as James (Jim) Cooper a part of a band of bandits who knock over the local bank, thus taking Miguel's life savings with them. Cooper's partner bandit Moxon (Mirko Ellis) is a psycho and during the escape tried to kill Cooper and get the loot. In the gunfight, Moxon is wounded not dead as all think. Meantime Cooper and Miguel are both captured and jailed. Miguel only gave chase to get his money back, all $512.00 worth.

While Cooper is in jail, Moxon recovered now, kidnaps Cooper's wife and daughter and finds the money's hiding place takes it as well. Miguel has been let loose, and Cooper wants him to go tell his wife what has happened and take her and the daughter down into Mexico and safety from Moxon. Too late, Moxon already has them, now Cooper breaks out of jail, he and Miguel set off after them to a final showdown. Fernando Sancho listed as being in the film, was in cameo, as the bandit Coyote with the broken leg. Actually, we learn Sancho really did have a broken leg during filming, and probably explains his limited appearance.

After the early 1960 influx of the Italian Sword 'n' Sandal (*Peplums*) began to fade about in the mid-'60s, on the cusp rode in the Westerns. Hundreds of them would be made, cloned in part by the box office successes of the Sergio Leone/Clint Eastwood films that broke all box office records in Europe before finally hitting the American shores about 1967. Called the phenomenon years (1964-1974), what brought these unique Westerns to worldwide acclaim was mainly through these *Dollar* films by Leone. They lit the fuse they would blow these action films throughout the Italian cinema. This new dimension of Western is still with us today and, in some respect, much stronger now with the advent of the DVD media for the home.

John Ireland's name association with the American Westerns was background enough for the Italians. Ireland fell right in with pride helping to churn out these new operatic Western films that tickled the fancy of cinema fans. In many a critical eye the best ones of the genre were considered far superior in many ways to the old Hollywood efforts prior to this period. Here, once again, Ireland lent his hand to writing and directing with the new zeal one gets when he is finally given a freehand to do his work. Actually going by strictly by release dates, from about mid-1967 to early1970 Ireland turned out some ten Westerns. It was here during these years that his fans can honestly say John Ireland definitely made his star status.

His next Western was, *Tutto per Tutto;* a.k.a. *All Out! a.k.a. Go for Broke* (1968). This Italian / Spanish coproduction* was directed by Umberto

* The coproduction of these many films was usually a gathering of monies for a film project involving other factions which in most cases, but not always included the Spanish since the majority of these films were being shot in Spain, Almeria in particular. Also filming took place in other surrounding areas like

Lenzi for one of his three only genre films. It starred John Ireland as the bounty hunter called Owl. Mark Damon is the outlaw Copper Face who Owl is chasing. Throw in the mix, a cache of gold bars that seems as though everyone from all around is also after, and bam, we have us a *Spaghetti* Western. Not a unique story by any means although it is entertaining with Ireland and Damon who are constantly playing off one another. Other genre regulars were Raf Baldassarre, Fernando Sancho, Monica Randall, Eduardo Fajardo, and Jose Torres, among the many listed.

For a May 1968 release, we find Ireland joined with Americans filming in Spain for a remake of the Pancho Villa films. This one was called *Villa Rides* starring Yul Brynner as famed revolutionary Pancho Villa.* Others of the cast were Robert Mitchum, Charles Bronson, and Jill Ireland (no relation to John). Although this is not considered among the true *Spaghetti* Westerns, even though it was filmed in Spain, it is, however, significant in that during John Ireland's heaviest workload time while making these Euro Westerns, he was able to take time out to do a cameo for this film. His part takes place to a town barbershop where his character Dave is a client and Villa walks in.

Vendetta per Vendetta (Revenge for Revenge) (1968) was Ireland's next Western. Here he starred as Major Bower. His costars are as follows: John Hamilton (Gianni Medici) as Chaliko, Conny Caracciolo as Mrs. Clara Bower, Loredana Nusciak, and Lemmy Carson. This was an Italian production that was directed by Ray Calloway (Mario Colucci). It was an interesting film but a brutal tale even for a *Spaghetti* Western. The storyline has to do with the Major's wife, Clara, in that while he's away she takes a lover (Hamilton). Then adding insult to injury tells him where the Major's gold cache is hidden. Naturally, Chaliko then dumps the woman and takes off with the gold. When the Major returns and finds out what has happened,

---

one north of Madrid called *Colmenar Viejo* of the San Pedro region, was found to be even more accommodating for production crews. The people of these regions seemingly favored the Mexican people somewhat in appearance and cultures. The countryside closely resembled the southwestern United States during the mid- to late-1800's circa time frame that most of these films were set in.

* This film predates the 1972 *Spaghetti* Western version which starred Telly Savalas, Clint Walker, Chuck Connors, and Anne Francis in a similar tale co written by Savalas and Julian Halevy. This was a Spanish / British coproduction film from Bernard Gordon and directed by Eugenio Martin. The film was taunted as being the "true" story of Pancho Villa, at least by Savalas at any rate.

first off he kills the wife dead. Then he takes off tracking Chaliko. They eventually come to terms in a desert hideout where a finale shootout will settle all. Both men are now dead and the gold dust is lost to the wind and the desert sands.

Now we come to *Trusting Is good . . . Shooting Is Better* a.k.a. *Dead for a Dollar* (1968). An *Italian* production directed by Osvaldo Civirani. The scripting was credited to Tito Carpi, Luciano Gregoretti, and director Civirani. It starred George Hilton as bandit Glenn portraying a Priest. Gordon Mitchell here as Roy Fulton; Piero Vida as Porgy, the Portuguese, Monica Pardo as Liz, and John Ireland as the Colonel are the main characters. A threesome of bank robbers leads to a story full of double-crosses, twists and turns, stolen loot, and a mad colonel hot on their tails. It all results in Liz the prostitute, outwitting the guys at every turn, now making off with the loot. Music score was by Angelo Francesco Lavagnino.

Next for Ireland is *A Gun for One-Hundred Graves* a.k.a. *A Pistol for a Hundred Coffins* (1968). Another of director Umberto Lenzi Westerns, a prolific action and subgenre horror director, he only did three Westerns and two of them were with John Ireland. This was an Italian / Spanish coproduction that stars this time genre regular Peter Lee Lawrence (Karl Hirenbach) in the lead as the Jim (Kid) Slade. John Ireland co stars as Gariff Douglas a gun-toting preacher seemingly with his own agenda. Slade returns home from the war to find his parents had been murdered and the ranch nearly destroyed in the spree. While searching for the killers he finds three of the gang and eliminates them, the fourth man whom he has only a name, Texas Corbett (Piero Lulli) he later finds he is the leader of a new gang that plans to rob the local bank. He's asked by the sheriff to help fend off these robbers and agrees to help. He sides up with preacher Gariff who seems to have his own underlying reasons for wanting the gang stopped dead in their tracks.

For Ireland's next Western adventure, he turned in *Run, Man Run* (1968). A sequel, in fact, by director Sergio Sollima to his earlier blockbuster hit called *The Big Gundown* (1966). For this later sequel by Sollima, Tomas Milian returns as the same scoundrel Cuchillo, again, still running from the law and bounty hunters throughout border towns of Texas and Mexico territories. This time, however, the bounty hunter is portrayed by Donal O'Brien, a fine Irish actor, (born in France of Irish parentage but raised back in Ireland) who was well established in the genre. Our John Ireland is costarred here and takes on the role of Santillana a Mexican revolutionary leader who befriends the bandit Cuchillo. Our bandit soon finds out he is about to be embroiled in the bitter conflicts of governmental change, and opts to leave for higher ground with Cassidy (O'Brien) and go looking for gold bars.

> Also for another of Ireland's roles in yet another 1968 film release, he also portrays a guerilla revolutionary in the film called *El Che Guevara,* a.k.a. *Bloody Che Contra.* An Italian production, although *not* of the *Spaghetti* Western genre, was about the infamous guerilla fighter of Bolivia, SA, who was caught, tried and executed. Francisco Rabel portrayed the Che Guevara character, and Ireland portrays Stuart his second in command. This film was directed by Paolo Heusch.

His next film was called *The Cost of Dying* a.k.a. *A Taste of Death* (1968). This was an Italian / French coproduction film from director Sergio Merolle. Story/script was by Biagio Proietti with the music score done by Francesco De Masi. It stars Andrea Giordana as Tony. Costars are as follows: John Ireland as Dan El; Raymond Pellegrino as Sheriff Bill Ramson, and Bruno Conrazzari as Scaife outlaw leader. Others were Betsy Bell and Giovanni Petrucci. As winter hits, an outlaw gang coming out of the mountains unable to drive stolen cattle, come into a small village and decide to take over the town, they kill the sheriff first. Then his son Tony along with El wants revenge and their town back.

Ireland's next Western for the genre, the last for 1968 was *The Damn Hot Day of Fire,* a.k.a. *The Gatlin Gun, a.k.a. Machine Gun Killers.* American Robert Woods stars here as Chris Tanner, along with: John Ireland as Tapas, Roberto Camardiel as Dr. Allen Curtis, and Ennio Balbo as Richard Gatlin. Also stars Evelyn Stewart (Ida Galli), Candice Lagen and Gerard Herter as Mr. Bishop among others. Gatlin first introduces his deadly invention to the Union army, but in transport, it and Gatlin are besieged by Mexican banditos led by Tapas (Ireland). Now the only man they feel can get it all back before it falls into Confederate hands, is in jail to be hanged for three murders, his name is Captain Chris Tanner, a.k.a. Django. Working undercover US Security agent Pinkerton (Tom Felleghy) arranges for him to escape so he can go get back this deadly weapon that can shoot three hundred rounds per minute. Good film from director Paolo Bianchini for an Italian / Spanish coproduction. Another earlier film that addresses George Thompson's machine gun invention was *Thompson 1880* (1966).

While there in Europe, Ireland also ventured on occasion out of the Western genre into other avenues of film work. His first of two only war films was called *War Devils* (1969). John Ireland in cameo here as the general in command responsible for implementing codename: Red Devil plot and its execution. Guy Madison stars here as Captain George Vincent who is tasked with carrying out the sabotage plan by night, taking out the German big guns that are secret, but strategically located overlooking the beach head prior to the allied invasion on D-Day. This was an Italian /

Spanish coproduction film, from director Bert Albert (Bitto Albertini) who also wrote the script.

For Irelands next came a couple of Italian sex-farce comedies with an old buddy from the States Lionel Stander* who had made quite a name for himself while in Europe as an international star by this time. The films were called *The Perversion Story* (1969) with Ireland as Inspector Wald. The other *Zenabel* (1969) has Ireland as Don Alonso Imolne. His pal Stander was in both films as well.

Stander, after his so called blacklisting had opted for Europe in order to continue to work, and while there, by 1969, had carved out a fairly successful career in the Euro cinema. Ireland and Stander had been friends from those early Stage years back in NYC. They were very pleased to now make each other's acquaintance once again after all those years gone by. Both being fine actors in their own right, were now equally widely acclaimed film stars, if only in the eyes of the Europeans. They would meet up for one last time back in America in 1981 for one of Ireland's many television outings. It was on the show called *Hart to Hart* of which Stander was co starred as the butler / houseman, Max to the show's main two stars, Robert Wagner as Jonathan Hart and Stephanie Powers as Jennifer Hart. The show ran from 1979 to 1983 a more than a five-season run for this popular adventure series about a wealthy husband and wife team of amateur detectives. John Ireland's one show episode was called "Murder in the Saddle" and his role was that of Zeke Ballinger.

---

* Lionel Stander was one of those actors, who while born in NYC, 1908 was of Jewish/American heritage. While working in the film Hollywood industry circa 1953 he soon found himself the subject of an investigation and was blacklisted from work. He was subjected to hearings by Senator Joseph McCarthy's dreaded *House Un-American Activities Committee.* It seems during this era, the Performing Arts Community on a whole had been besieged by this sub-committee, formed solely to weed out those thought to have any communistic affiliations whatsoever.

In those days, even a family member still overseas, where letters or packages were being sent to or from, or any type of communications for that matter could be misconstrued as a show of guilt. Soon all foreign born citizens of that era were living in fear of this dreaded subcommittee and their decisions. Stander was but one of many fine immigrant actors who were 'dropped from the roles' for what was in actuality unsubstantiated charges of subversive activity, and the communist association charges were mostly based solely on whatever nationality a person was descended from.

With Ireland starring in so many of these unique films in such a short period of time, it was no doubt helping him to hone his craft further. Now, with this next film, another Western he evidently would have a chance to unleash his vibrant writing and directorial skills, to unwind and develop their potential. The film was called *The Challenge of the Mackennas* (1969) here he teams up again with Robert Woods. Ireland not only stars in this film as Jones/ Jonas MacKenna but also helped co write the script* with Wolf Mankowitz for this exciting Spanish / Italian co production. Scripting credit, however, went to one José L. Navarro a common Italian misinformation error of which Ireland paid no never mind to, he was happy nevertheless. Probably just happy to be working his craft again, and doing his best at what he was best at.

Robert Woods costars here as Chris. Also starring was Annabella Incontrera as Maggie, Mariano Vidal Molina as Ed Grey, Roberto Camardiel as Don Diego, and Daniela Giordano as Barbara. Directed by Leon Klimovsky and it is believed, that an unaccredited John Ireland also helped to direct† this film as well. The storyline concerns a drifter and former priest (Jones) who gets caught up in a range war between two valley ranchers, one an evil man (Don Diego) with an equally evil, spoiled son (Chris) of which

---

* Story credits for other film versions of this same film list neither, Brit Mankowitz, or Ireland. Instead, they do list, Antonio Viader and Edoardo Mulargia. This is yet another reason these films have been so hard to track, the information on them coming out of European has always been scrambled to a certain degree on most all of these genre films. The fact that, according to an article on this film by one Phil H. staff member of *www.spaghetti-westerns.net* stated that at the time of this films production, *Variety* a Hollywood reporter trade-paper supposedly reported in a blip that, John Ireland along with British screenwriter Wolf Mankowiz had supplied the story.

† When *WAI!* Fanzine editor asked actor Robert Woods (who's still around today) if John Ireland was responsible for any of the directing done on this film? That we had heard that Ireland and Woods had done most of the dramatic scenes themselves, since Klimovsky had said very little to the actors throughout the entire film. His reply was very informative. "Yes, we also had heavy hands in the shoot as he (J. Ireland) owned this one for American and Canada (minus the Maritime Provinces). It was one of a two-picture deal we made with Alex Hacohen of *Filmar* . . . the MacKennas and the one I did after it, called 'El Puro' (that John got out of shooting with me, because of a previous, higher paying engagement . . .) We did many rewrites before and during the shoot of *MacKennas* and I know that John worked hard on editing, reediting and the sale of the movie he called 'the thing' when he returned to Los Angeles."

Jones runs afoul of both as they view him more as a continuing threat to their local authority as it were.

Soon after making the *Mackennas*, Ireland ventured back to the States where he could be seen in a couple of then popular television shows like *The Virginian*, and *Mission: Impossible*. Then he went for a Canadian film called *Graveyard Story* (MTV). It was finally released for theaters in Germany on July 29, 1991; otherwise, it went straight to video. Ireland stars in it as a rich man, Dr. McGregor who stumbles upon a grave of a young girl. Some unforeseen force persuades him to dig deeper into the cause of the child's death. He even hires a private detective to investigate further, and thus discovers a whole lot more that he would ever imagine. One ad taunted the films as, "When a lonely man adopts a deceased child . . . life becomes deadly!"

While back in the State in 1968 Ireland squeezed in a role on the TV series *Planet of the Apes* which starred Rowdy McDowell. Ireland's episode was called "The Liberator," and only aired briefly for a limited time on select TV stations back in 1974. Later, we also had a brief cameo in the *Adventurers* (1970), taken from the Harold Robbins popular novel, and which contained an all-star cast. It was directed by Lewis Gilbert. When Ireland returned to the States again in the '70s he would continue with his television work, and spot appearances, but still managing to do a few other film parts sprinkled in the mix for good measure. This all meant that John Ireland was working fairly regular again, even here in the States and was diligent about his craft. With his popularity now regained, things were moving along well in the right direction for him and his family.

Occasionally after that he would venture back overseas for a film or two, but mostly he would stay back home in LA. On one of his overseas trips he pulled a stopover in Vienna for a *BBC-TV* telecast episode called *Assignment Vienna** (1972) His one episode was called "Hot Potato." This

* *Assignment Vienna* series with a cast of regulars, Robert Conrad stars as the American expatriate spy hunter Jake Webster. It co starred Charles Cioffi as Major Bernard Caldwell. Anton Diffring returns to the mini screen to reprise his roll as the German Chief, Inspector Hoffman. The music composition for the weekly series was done by Dave Grusin, John Carl Parker and Isaac Hayes with his theme part called "The Men." The show ran seven episodes at sixty minutes each for only one season. Some of the special weekly guest stars were Richard Basehart, Roy Scheider, Lesley Warren, John Ireland, and Werner Von Klemperer. It was directed by David Lowell Rich, but its stories missed the intrigue of the plot of the original film.

show was unfortunately only a one season-run effort taken from a previously successful espionage film of the same name, which starred Anton Diffring.

After the *Vienna* appearance he zoomed back to Italy for another *Spaghetti* Western effort that popped for him there called *Ten Whites Killed by a Small Indian* a.k.a. *Blood River** (1974). The film starred Fabio Testi as Ringo. John Ireland co stars as Abel Webster, and the lovely Rosalba Neri as Webster's daughter Katherine. Others were Spanish actor Daniel Martin as Condor, and Luis Induni as John. The part of now grown up Indian hitman, revenge killer we believe was an unaccredited part for Giovanni Cianfriglia. Also, there was Luisa Rivelli always lurking in the background as the witchlike Indian gal. This has been a rather obscure film even today, which seems to have had little promotion and poor distribution. Primarily it was released in Italy, 1974 and later '77 in Spain. Only as recent as 2011 has a decent viewable copy of the film came to light, in Italian with English subs via Internet sources.

Later in 1975 Ireland, we find was involved with another of the Euro war genre films, actually a spin-off exploitation of the war genre called *Salon Kitty* (1976). For many years, it was thought to have been a Western, until a VHS copy was obtained from the UK. Directed by Tinto Brass, this was a brutal depiction of sexual depravity of war torn Germany by men of Hitler's Third Reich. Toward the end of the war, star Helmut Berger as Helmut Wallenberg was task with setting up a brothel for German officers, coming in from the field, for a little R&R as it were. The film costarred Ingrid Thulin as Kitty Kellermann house Madame who falls for one of her own girls Margherita (Teresa Ann Savoy).

---

* The *Blood River* video title refers to a massacre of an Indian village some ten years before. A gang of ten white outlaws were the culprits. They killed all the inhabitants outright, except the women who they raped and beat before killing, and the river beside the village ran red with their blood. In their hurry to leave though, they had missed seeing a small boy, left alive and hiding. This boy now grown will bring about the Indians revenge upon those white killers. There's also a separate sideline plot running that actually involves Webster (he's one of the ten men) who now wants his half-breed daughter (Neri) to wed a wealthy, white landowner. This it seems is the spark that sets off the revenge cycle. She, however, is pregnant and in love with Ringo (the father) and wants only to be with him and no wealthy white man. Sorry, but a poor example of the genre on a whole, and probably is a good one to skip over.

Also, it starred John Steiner in his most provocative roles yet as Biondo a sex-crazed German General left in charge of this, Germany's most expansive and elaborate bordello. A truly depraved individual portrayed by Steiner, in a role that couldn't have done his career any good, but on the other hand shows the versatility of range this actor really is capable of. Others were John Ireland as Cliff, in what seems mostly an insignificant cameo part. Western fans will remember Dan Van Husen as Rause, along John Bartha and Tom Felleghy, both unaccredited as Gestapo Agents. Also we remember Helga (Sara Sperati) the brutal house mom under Kitty who keeps the girls in line, and whipped into shape. Not much to watch here that won't turn ones stomach.

Next, we find Ireland in a top-notch Euro spy drama called *The Swiss Conspiracy* (1976) with David Janssen portraying the American banking investigator David Christopher. A cast of lovelies like Senta Berger and Elke Sommer, and John Ireland as Texas businessman Dwight McGowan; John Saxon is the Chicago gangster, Robert Hayes; Ray Milland is the Swiss Bank's frazzled President Johann Hurtil, and Franz Benninger vice president was portrayed by Anton Diffring. A thrilling crime drama filmed on locations in Switzerland that is riddled with many twist and turns of a truly intriguing plot. John Ireland could be proud to have been affiliated with such an exciting film with such a renowned cast of actors.

Later for a 1977 release, a Spanish feature called *The Perfect Killer*,* a.k.a. *The Killers* he would once again have the opportunity to appear with another fine actor from the *Spaghetti* Westerns, old buddy Lee Van Cleef. The two had been friends from their stage acting days of the NYC / New Jersey circuits. They thoroughly enjoyed themselves during their segments shot for this film, it had been years and they had a lot to catch-up on. Both men by this time were on their third wives, and as times were changing rapidly in their careers, both were pressed to change right along with them. Van Cleef during his *Spaghetti* Western years had now parlayed his career into a satisfying

* *The Perfect Killer,* a.k.a. *Bye, bye Darling* was actually shot as a Spanish MTV film. Obscure for years, it was finally seen here in the States as a video feature. Van Cleef stars as Harry Chapman, who with partner Krista (Tita Barker) attempts a hold up of a dog track. She double crosses him and he is caught and spends time in prison where he as his cellmate Luc (Robert Widmark [Alberto dell'Acqua]) makes contact with an unnamed secretive mob organization. They are broke out of jail and now work for the mob as contract killers. In another cameo role for John Ireland, is Benny the forger, an old friend who sets the two up with new passport papers. Harry meets up with Krista again, at first intent on killing her, then falls under her charms again, and thus allowing her another chance to double cross him again. This time, however, he does kill her.

niche in the film world with his name being internationally known throughout the world. Ireland at this time in his life was sixty-three years old and had no intentions of slowing down on his career. Van Cleef on the other hand was but forty-nine with several more productive years yet ahead of him.

While both men, Ireland and Van Cleef were fine actors and enjoyed their European popularity as stars, Van Cleef could already sense his superstar status cooling all the same. Although Ireland's Euro career never reached Van Cleef's magnitude, he could nevertheless feel the cooling as well. With the dwindling of the Western film genre in Europe now, Ireland returned to American and back to television for work. The occasional movie was still the norm, but even those were getting scarcer by the year.

As John Ireland's career began to slip back in the slumps again, he resorted to doing low-budget horror films in both Europe and the United States. He also turned in such quickies as the Mexican film, *Guyana: Cult of the Damned* (1979) about the mass suicides of the Reverend Jim Jones and his cult following of some nine-hundred back in the earlier '70s. From the popular Mexican director Rene Cardona Jr., it starred Stuart Whitman as the infamous Reverend. Actor Gene Barry portrayed the Congressman Lee O'Brien; John Ireland's role was that of Dave Cole; Joseph Cotton as Richard Gable and Yvonne De Carlo as Susan Ames. An impressive cast as the story revolves around an independent religious cult church society in Guyana, South America.

He signed on for another Spanish / Mexican release of a MTV movie called *Garden of Venus,* a.k.a. *Women of Jeremiah/Bordello* (1981). A comedic Western that starred Jorge Rivero as Jeremiah Sanchez, Chuck Connors, Michael Conrad, Andes Garcia, and John Ireland portraying the judge. Cute little story about a Minister with four daughters who inherits a bordello. Connors portrays the corrupt sheriff who attempts to close them down and make them leave or all be jailed.

Grabbing at what work that could be had during this era Ireland landed another sweet television role in the 1980 MTV feature *Marilyn: The Untold Story.* The story taken from the Norman Mailer novel tells the Norma Jean Baker story from her meager beginning as an orphan in Hollywood to the famed movie actress, turned sex goddess of filmdom. It starred Catherine Hicks as Marilyn; Richard Basehart as Johnny Hyde; Frank Converse as Joe DiMaggio and Jason Miller as Arthur Miller. John Ireland's role was as John Huston, and Sheree North was Gladys Baker her mother.

Still unable to perpetuate that winning combination of role versus experience, he worked when he could, which was mostly television work that kept him somewhat busy. He and his wife, Daphne, even open and operated a classy *Tony* restaurant for a while called *Ireland's* there in Santa Barbara near where they lived. He occasionally worked on a few films in the years to follow but nothing regular was coming down the pike for him. He had always pride himself as a professional. An actor, a stand-up member in good standing with the *Screen Actors Guild; Actors Equity Association; Directors Guild of America and the Writers Guild of America.*

Times were now bad again for this movie actor and getting worse it appeared. He went so far as to even advertise in a trade paper in 1987 asking for acting work of any kind. This in itself was demeaning but it did seem to work as some started to trickle in here and there after that. What would have become another great boon for him and his career was a 1988 MTV pilot called *Bonanza: the Next Generation.* Ireland was picked to portray the Ponderosa Patriarch in the continuing role of Captain Aaron Cartwright a younger brother of the now deceased Loren Greene's old Ben Cartwright character. A new cast had to be developed entirely since the Hoss Cartwright character (Dan Blocker) was also now deceased and Little Joe, Michael Landon was not around, but his son of twenty-four years rode in for the part of Benji Cartwright. It just wasn't the same and unfortunately the audiences thought the same way. It was never picked up for any season run, thus squashing Irelands renewed hope of its success.

A new movie role came along for 1988. It was a Charles Bronson film called *Messenger of Death.* John Ireland's role was that of Zenas Beecham part of a family where the wife and children are murdered in what police believe to have been for religious reasons. Bronson, however having other ideas takes matters into his own hands and gets to the bottom of this action thriller in short order. Ireland's next film was a horror comedy from director Anthony Hickok. It was called *Sundown: Vampire in Retreat* (1989). Ireland co stars with longtime friend John Carradine's eldest son David Carradine who was stars. Ireland's role was that of the aged patriarch vampire, Jefferson for this contemporary horror Western spoof. It was interesting to watch Ireland perform horseback at the age of seventy-five. I guess the old adage is true, like riding a bicycle once learned, one never forgets.

Ireland and the young director Hickok seems to have gotten along well. At least good enough that he was invited on a second film outing called *Waxwork II: Lost in Time.* Written and directed by Hickok, this horror fantasy comedy tells a story about a couple of who uses a time machine portal to go back and defeat evil happenings throughout the world. Zach Galligan stars as Mark Loftmore and costars Monika Schnarre as Sarah Brightman. Others were Martin Kemp as Baron Von Frankenstein; Bruce Campbell as John Loftmore; John Ireland's cameo was as portraying King Arthur; Patrick Macnee was Sir Wilfred, and David Carradine as the beggar. Unfortunately this film didn't make it too far, going mostly straight to video. In between there had been several more TV show spots like, *Murder She Wrote* with Ireland as Sheriff Hainer for one episode called "Murder, Plain, and Simple" (1991). Also, the *Christine Cromwell Show*, for one episode called "In Vino Veritas" (1990).

> Actually, the *Waxwork II* film by Hickok appears to have been his last movie. Having been diagnosed for some time with Leukemia, he lost his battle with the terrible disease and passed away March 21, 1992, there in Santa Barbara, California. It has been speculated that prior knowledge of this devastating disease is what had actually prompted him to having placed that ad in the trade-paper looking for as much work as possible before his end of days. It's quite possible the desire to work all he could, and by his doing so for those remaining years would help ease the burden of family obligations which would befall his loved ones, to which he was sorely devoted. He was seventy-eight years old when he succumbed to the disease.

He was survived by wife, Daphine Ireland, of thirty years. A daughter Daphine Ireland Whelahan and three sons: John Jr. and Peter Ireland and Cameron Cameron from Daphine's first marriage. He also had a sister, Katherine who was still living at the time and two grandchildren that surely missed their snow-white bearded grandpa very much. We're quite sure he was the ideal Santa Claus during Christmas's passed around the Ireland household. Memories of his many screen roles still ring out in the archives of films and will for many years yet to come. It seems that for some fifty-three years John Ireland had honed his craft in search of *that* one role that might put him up there over the top for the annals of screen history. Alas, in the eyes of his fans he has already found that pinnacle role, back during his *Spaghetti* Western years. The years of enjoyment watching this world class actor do his work, proves to us his fans, that we will never really forget John Ireland, the actor.

End.

- Below is first an overview of the Stage plays, then a complete filmography of Ireland's Euro Westerns. The dates are aligned as close as possible with information currently at hand, plus international release dates included. **Posters and pictures are accredited to the Sebastian Haselbeck collection via his website www.spaghetti-western.net.*

STAGE CREDITS FOR JOHN IRELAND

Debut: 1939 at the *Robin Hood Theater* in Arden, Delaware.

Off-Broadway debut 1940, was with the Irish Repertory Players group at the *Cherry Lane Theater,* NYC., NY

Studied and acted on stage for a time at the *Davenport Free Theater,* NYC., NY (Met and married first wife, Elaine)

Early 1940's East Coast tour: with *Clare Tree Children's Theater* as the Peter Pan character, Captain Hook.

Broadway debut 1941 in "Macbeth" with the *National Theater* group in NYC., NY

"Hamlet" and "Othello" Shakespearean plays with impressive runs on Broadway also with the *National Theater* group in NYC., NY

JOHN IRELAND'S *SPAGHETTI* WESTERNS . . .

1967

Odio per Odio, *(Hate for Hate)*; Ital, Director Domenico Paolella (Ireland as Cooper) 8/18/67

1968

Tutto per Tutto; a.k.a. *All Out! a.k.a. Go for Broke*; Ital/ Spa, Director Umberto Lenzi (Ireland as Owl) 3/27/68

Run, Man Run, *Corri, Uomo, Corri*; Ital/ Fr, Director Sergio Sollima (Ireland as Santillana, a Mexican revolutionary) 8/29/68

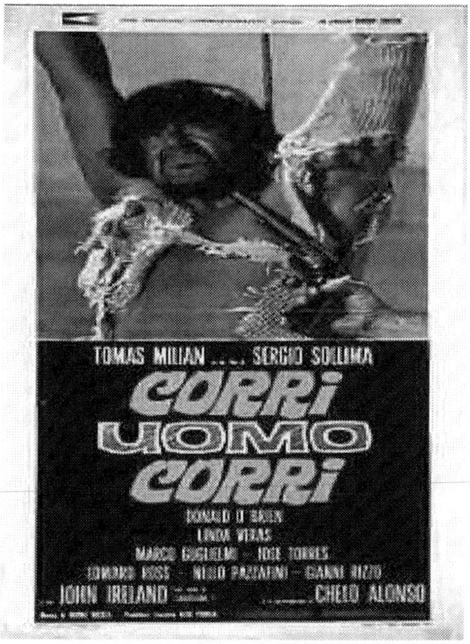

Dead for a Dollar; *a.k.a. Fidarsi e Bene, Sparare e Meglio (Trusting is Good . . . Shooting is Better)*; Ital, Director Osvaldo Civirani (Ireland as the Colonel) 8/17/68

A Pistol for a Hundred Coffins, *Una Pistole per Cento Bare* Ital/ Spa, Director Umberto Lenzi (Ireland as Gariff Douglas) 8/24/68

Cost of Dying, *Quanto Costa Morire*; Ital/ Fr, Director Sergio Merolle (Ireland as Dan El) 9/14/68

Revenge for Revenge, *Vendetta per Vendetta*; Ital, Director Ray Calloway (Mario Colucci) (Ireland as Major Bower) 8/10/68

That Damned Hot Day of Fire, *Quel Caldo Maleditto Giorno di Fuoco;* a.k.a. *Machine Gun Killers; a.k.a. Gatling Gun*; Ital/ Spa, Director Paolo Bianchini (Ireland as Mexican bandit Tapos) 12/13/68

1970

Challenge of the MacKennas, *La Sfida Dei MacKennas;* a.k.a. *Badlands Drifter*; Ital/ Spa, Director Leon Klimovsky (credited) (Ireland stars as drifter Jones); A coproduction from *Filmar Compagnia Cinematografica, Roma / Atlantide Film, Spain*; 3/21/70

1974

Ten Whites Killed by Small Indian, *Dieci Bianchi Uccisi da un Piccolo Indiano;* a.k.a. *Blood River;* Ital, Director Gianfranco Baldenello (Ireland as Abel Webster) 8/18/74

> *This pretty much completes our filmology of John Ireland's Euro Westerns. Another film that countless times has been previously associated with the Western genre, although it is not but a turn of the century comedy that Ireland was in. I will it list below for the record.

1975

We are No Angels, *Noi Non Siamo Angeli*; Ital, Director Frank Kramer (Gianfranco Parolini); Storyline circa early 1900s, a contemporary comedy stars Paul L. Smith and Michael Colby (Antonio Cantafora) (pair of actors are similar in style and antics of Terence Hill and Bud Spencer (Carlo Pedersoli) of the renowned Trinity films). Also, stars Woody Strode as Black

Bill and John Ireland as Mr. Shark. Others were Evelin Kaye, Renato Cestie, and Fiona Florence. An Italian farce about a black prizefighter (Strode) and his promoter Mr. Shark, take on the Smith / Colby team. Not all that bad, but not particularly a Western either. 9/26/75

1979

How The West Was Fun (*A Brad Marks Primetime* TV-Special) Featuring the best remembered TV and film cowboy stars. The program was dedicated to actor John Wayne, who, at the time, was bedridden with lung and stomach cancer, later he succumbed on 6/11/1979. It was a sixty-minute tribute to the actor showing clips and interviews. There were some forty-eight actors that turned out for this special among them were Chuck Connors, **John Ireland**, Guy Madison, Keenan Wynn, George Montgomery, Rod Cameron, Jack Kelly, Ty Hardin, Lee Van Cleef, and Doug McClure.

Note: The above ten listed actors of the forty-eight, like Ireland actually had Euro involvement with the Spaghetti genre of films that came out of Europe during that era of nonstop filmmaking.

> *Now we must bring this filmology to a close on our actor John Ireland a truly accomplished actor in his field, no one can doubt that for a fact, R.I.P. John Ireland.

End.

BIBLIOGRAPHY
(J. IRELAND)

Betts, Tom, editor *WAI! (Westerns . . . All'Italiana)* Fanzine articles/ information on J. Ireland

The BFI Companion to the Western (1993) edited by Edward Buscombe, *British Film Institute,* UK. Originally published by *Andr`e Deutsch Ltd.,* London, 1988; pp. 355-356

Connolly, Bill, editor *Spaghetti Cinema* Fanzine articles / "Dead for a Dollar" film review by William Connolly. Fanzine and general informational articles on J. Ireland, like SC no. 22, pp. 49 "The Luck of the Irelands" from the *LA Times* August 1987; also SC no. 38 pp. 43, Letter discussions on the *Blood River* film

Haselbeck, Sebastian, owner/curator for Internet website: *www.spaghetti-western.net*

Internet, via: *www.anica.it* Ref: Film production and date confirmation

Internet, via: *www.IMDB.com* "Mini biography on John Ireland" plus film listing review

Ledbetter, Craig, editor of now defunct *ETC (European Trash Cinema)* Fanzine, with bits on films of John Ireland, pp.19, 1969 *Zenabel* listed as a *Sexy Adventure.*

Prickette, Tom, *In Search of the Role* previously unpublished manuscript, 1987; partially used in the *WAI!* Memorial issue for John Ireland after his death for 1992; Reworked 2007

Quinlan's Illustrated Registry of Film Stars (1987) by Davis Quinlan, *Henry Holt Reference Books,* NY., pp. 240

Video Hound's Golden Retriever (1994 edition) *Visible Ink Press,* a division of *Gale Research Inc.,* Detroit, MI.

Weisser, Thomas, *Spaghetti Westerns: the Good, the Bad, and the Violent,* (1992) *McFarland*, Jefferson NC.

Western: All'Italiana (books I, II, and III) by Antonio Bruschini and Federico de Zigno, *Glittering Images,* Firenze, Italy; book I, 1998; book II, 2001 and book III, 2006

The Western: The Complete Film Sourcebook (The Film Encyclopedia) (1983); by Phil Hardy, *William Morrow and Co, Inc.,* NY.

The World Almanac Who's who of Film (1987) by Thomas G Aylesworth and John S. Bowman, *Bison Books,* pp. 218-219

KLAUS KINSKI

(1926-1991)

GUNSLINGER FALLEN, FROM THE HORSE OPERA

The Polish actor Nikolaus Günther Nakszynski better know to his fans as Klaus Kinski (a.k.a. Kinsky) was a veteran of virtually hundreds of films throughout the world cinema. He died apparently from natural causes at his home in Lagunitas, Marin County, California, on November 23, 1991. Later they claim a heart attack. It was all rather unexpected without him being ill prior to, his ranting and raving will be missed in the theaters of the world for sure.

Born October 18, 1926, in Zopot, an old seaside town situated on the Baltic Sea near Danzig. Nowadays Zopot and Danzig are both incorporated in a tri-city area called Gdansk, Poland. His parents relocated to Berlin,

Germany some five hundred miles to the southwest, in hope of getting work there in a bigger city. Young Klaus was quite young yet then, and it was there in Berlin as a child he grew up in extreme poverty.* As a boy he worked with the *Cabaret* doing poetry recitals, they even went on tour into his native country Poland. At sixteen and 1944, he was drafted into the German army. This resulted in his capture and his being held prisoner of war by the British. After his release, he began his acting career in the postwar *Berlin Theater.* He made his film debut in 1948 with *I Morituri* a German production directed by Eugene York.

He married for the first time to a German girl named Gislinde Kuhbeck on June 11, 1952. They met at an Art Academy carnival in Munich during Mardi gras time. She and another girl Therese were together and he claims during the course of the day and evening after that meeting he did both girls. Therese's parents made her get an abortion, but Gislinde carried her baby to term. The baby girl they named Pola was born there in a clinic in Munich. The next day he sent her and the baby home to her mother in Berlin. During these years Kinski was heavy into the theater work, and was a rounder chasing the girls to no end. This marriage only lasted to 1955 when it ended in divorce. Daughter Pola would bring much joy to the father when she decided later in her life to take up acting as her father had done.

Kinski continued to work fairly steady during the 1950s perfecting his skills as an actor. He was truly a driven individual to watch in action. What, with his cold expressions and sinister appearance led him to continued work throughout Europe, but here again he was always looking out for his well being and insisting on being paid very well for his talents. It was from the early 1960s that Kinski got involved in doing several of the Edgar Wallace novels made to film mostly by the German producers. He also did one for the

---

* His being brought up in such poverty alone may have given him the excessive drive to succeed, and the almost inexplicable hard-nosed tactics he used in picking and choosing his acting roles based solely on the money. In one article he had told a reporter that he lived a very expensive lifestyle and that the opportunity to do even the best film role in the world, he would not do without the money being there. It went on to said that during the 1960s he did like ten films a years, sometimes not even reading the scripts, just counting the lines that equaled the amount of monies he would receive.

Evidently, during his career, he'd turned down quite a few film offers. Some of these offers came from such great filmmakers as Federico Fellini, and even Stephen Spielberg. He drove himself as a man obsessed, making some 170 films throughout Europe and the United States during his long career.

Brits during this period for *Hammer Films* called *The Traitors Gate* (1964) a British release. Mostly though they were German and he made several for the genre. Some of his later supporting roles would go down in history for films like *Dr. Zhivago* (1965) and *The Little Drummer Girl* (1984)

Kinski's second marriage was to Ruth Brigitte Tocki, they met in Berlin after he spotted her working in store that sold gloves. They were married on October 30, 1960. He affectionately nicknamed her Biggi. This marriage also produced another daughter for Kinski, which to his delight when in her teens was also very much interested in becoming an actress. Her name was Nastassja* and is probably the better known of the two Kinski daughters, which in this day and time she is rather well known for not only her film acting, but also as a producer.

For Kinski's next film which is considered his first of his many *Spaghetti* Westerns to follow, was called *The Last Ride to Santa Cruz* for an early 1964 West German release. It starred ex-*Peplum* (sword 'n' sandal) hero Edmund Purdom as Rex Kelly. Also starring was Mario Adorf as Pedro Ortiz, Marianne Koch as Elizabeth Kelly, and Klaus Kinski as José. This genre effort is an Austria / West German coproduction, directed by Rolf Olsen. The storyline here concerns a man who was sentenced to prison for a crime he didn't commit, although finally released, and is now looking to avenge his unjust incarnation.

Those German filmmakers had been producing the Karl May, *Winnetou* Westerns since 1962/63 with American Lex Barker and French actor Pierre Brice. Among this series of May novels converted to film was, *Winnetou: Last of the Renegades* for a September 1964 release. This beautifully filmed *West* German / Yugoslavia coproduction was directed by Harald Reinl. Barker returns in the role of Shatterhand, and Brice continues his Chief Winnetou's role.

The storyline has to with a gang of outlaws who attack a wagon train (disguised as Indians) in an attempt to implicate a certain tribe of Indians that have settled nearby on open cattle lands. Shatterhand and Winnetou come to the rescue to solve the crime before an all out Indian war erupts. Klaus Kinski's role here is Luke a henchman Indian scout for the gang.

Although a few *Spaghetti* Westerns were already coming out of Italy prior to Sergio Leone's first genre effort, none really got a good foothold in the genre until his blockbuster film *A Fistful of Dollars* (1964) hit the scene. Now for 1965 this unique horse opera would have a sequel that came to be called *For a Few dollars More* (1965). This second film of an eventual trilogy brings back American star Clint Eastwood reprising his role as the magnificent stranger (not as Joe this time) but now called Manco (a.k.a. Monco). Once again he's the anti-hero, no-name bounty hunter known only by the handle Mexicans have given him. Included for this Leone outing as co star is another American, veteran actor Lee Van Cleef portraying another bounty hunter Colonel Douglas Mortimer.

For Kinski's role in the film he portrays the hunchback gunslinger called Wild of the Indio gang of cutthroat outlaws who are planning to rob the *El Paso Bank*. In an unforgettable scene with Kinski and LVC, as the gang are scoping out the town prior to the robbery, Wild encounters Mortimer in the saloon. Having his back turned, Mortimer calmly strides over and strikes a match on Wild's rough suspenders (crisscrossing his hunched back) so as to light up his pipe. Wild immediately comes to a boil, but the looks he gets from gang members caution him to quell his anger. Kinski's reactions of the quivering lip and beaded sweat will never be matched. The hatred and disbelief Kinski shows in his eyes will long be remembered. One can just feel the animosity and the pent-up aggressive frustration he relates for the camera, fueled by the raging assurance that for their next meeting, death will obviously be the only end result.

For a ten year period between 1965 and '75 during those phenomenon years of these European Westerns that Kinski was at his most prolific in the eyes of his fans. He worked on some the best films of the era during this period which amounted to twenty-three including the two German Westerns mentioned above. His roles were usually of severe extremes, a type of no-holds-barred, downright mean or dirty character types that made him such a highly sought after actor, regardless of his attitudes about money. As avid fans of the genre would exclaim, we have spent many a pleasurable hour watching this man in action. These films no doubt boosted not only his own monetary worth, but also his acting skills were being finely honed for the bigger and better roles of the future coming his way.

Moving from the Western genre, he would bounce back and forth with roles varying from mystery and intrigue to that of the horror genre. One such part he would play was an Italian remake of the famous vampire film now called *Count Dracula* (1970) and starred Mr. Evil himself, Christopher Lee in the title role as the count. This was a Spanish/ Italian/ German coproduction, with direction by the Spanish maestro of horror Jesus Franco. Klaus Kinski's role was that of R. M. Renfield (the ex-estate agent nutcase in the asylum who is under Dracula's powers). Cool film, follows the story very closely. Kinski is his usual great self in this.

Another film of this genre type was called *Web of the Spider* (1971) where Kinski portrays Edgar Allen Poe. His bouncing back 'n' forth could have been his searching for a genre niche, but we feel it probably was more money orientated in his case. Meanwhile according to Kinski's own autobiography "Kinski Uncut" *Bloomsbury Publishing* PLc, London 1996, due to the extent of his whoring around, he and wife, Biggi, were history in the marriage department by 1971. She and Nastassja (10) were back in Rome in their dream house *castello,* as he called it. He's had it remodeled especially for them. Now with this talk of divorce they are all leaving for Berlin never to return she says. He was still in Spain on a shoot down in Almeria.

His women it seems were a lot like his automobiles, he used to tell of never keeping one for long either. He said he'd swap it for just a door rattle, or maybe he didn't like the color after a week. Hundreds or thousands of dollars he managed to squander away on autos alone. *Silver Clouds, Jaguars, Mercedes* he's had them all at one time or another. Now we can kind a see why he had to have the big bucks all the time. He went through money like he did women, like water through his fingers.

A driven man he was, on one such firsthand account of his demonology was dropped upon us when actor Tony Anthony was interviewed by Tom Betts of *WAI* and Bill Connolly of *Spaghetti Cinema* fanzines. Anthony related that while Kinski was picking out a horse to ride for one of the Westerns, he naturally picked the finest looking animal in the corral. When told the horse he wanted was still a bit wild (green broke) and was strictly a stuntman's horse, he flew into one of his famous rages hollering "Nobody tells me what horse I want. I am a horseman and I've been on horses all my life." Needless to say, after mounting the animal, taking him from the corral all the while trying to rein him in, the horse retaliated by rearing up, and flipped over backward over a saloon step prop. As one would know, it broke the horse's back and he had to be put down. Although Kinski didn't appear to be hurt at the time, the whole incident didn't sit well with any of his fellow workers on the set. We understand he left from the picture and another actor was brought in to take his place.

We don't know if this was the same incident, but in his autobiography he tells in a passage (pp 186-187) about making a Western at *Cinecitta,* and on the films first day of shooting the horse he was dozing on suddenly does a back flip, squeezing him against a wall, and falls on top of him with its entire body weight. He says he manages to kick free and avoid being trampled to death. Afterward, he claimed he couldn't stand, sit up or kneel. After a visit to the hospital and x-rays they tell him his backbone is fractured, but the spinal cord is intact. He just needs time to mend. Soon he's back on his feet again after twelve days and back to his old way even with the nurse in hospital. He claims he got no salary from the picture or insurance for a claim since the Producer didn't carry any policy at all. Like we say, this may not have been the same incident, but it gives an idea of his tough arrogance of the situation.

It was later in 1971 that he meets the *Vietnamese* woman Minhoi Genevieve Loanic. He's throwing a party at his *castello* and among the guests, she just shows up. She fascinates him to the point where soon he's married again. This time it lasted until February 1979 before the divorce came. By this woman he had a son, Nickolai, born on July 30, 1976. The boy would eventually grow into a fine young man who also took an interest in acting as had his two step sisters.

For Kinski's first film outing with German filmmaker Werner Herzog they took to the swamps of Brazil, and from looks of the film it had to have been indeed a challenging piece of work. Kinski now moves from the Westerns to more appreciative arenas, his coup de grace, as it were, that came to light with his accomplished film work under the direction of Herzog. For this film *Aguirre: The Wrath of God* (1972) Kinski's starring character role was that of a demented Spanish Conquistador who slowly goes mad in the jungles of South America. (We ask you now, what better actor was there to play this role?) Yet this Aquirre was a heroic figure, but yes, of an obsessed mind. Obsessed with the crossing of this jungle, regardless of the hell he must endure, and whatever the cost in lives, animal or man. This role was a marvelous portrayal and is attributed not only to the star's acting kudos, but also the fine direction by Herzog himself.

By this 1972 date, Kinski had since 1965 turned in some sixteen Westerns. Actually seventeen if we count the one 1968 release called *Man, His Pride, and His Vengeance,* a.k.a. *Pride and Vengeance.* Actually this film was more circa late nineteenth century, perhaps taking place in and around Valencia, Spain, and not Mexico as it would seem. It is similar to another similar type that Terence Hill did back in the early '70s called *Trinity Sees Red.* I have that one classed as *Tortilla* Western. However, this one above *Pride and Vengeance* does not seem to concern any revolution which is the criteria I was using for this type of classification.

I understand from associates that in Germany for example, this *Pride and Vengeance* film was being marketed as a Western. With it being dubbed into German, makes it all sound more like a Western I'm told, with talk of El Paso and Mexico instead of Spain. The outfits and it being shot outside the city in the open countryside also adds to the feel of a Western. The film's star was Franco Nero as Don José (Django in the German dubbed version), the gypsy girl Carmen he falls in love with (also dubbed as Conchita) is played by Tina Almont. Her husband is none other than Klaus Kinski as Lt. Miguel Garcia. Don Jose knows nothing of Garcia until he shows up and they fight, and Garcia dies. Don Jose thinking he's got it made now with Carmen finds he's wrong as she leaves him flat holding the bag as she did with Garcia, time and again to the poor sap who loved her.

Out of those seventeen films Kinski had some strong titles for the support of the genre while in others he gave merely cameo appearances. Some of his better ones were *A Bullet for the General* (1966). An Italian production, directed by: Damiano Damiani. It starred Gian Maria Volonte as a Mexican Bandit/revolutionary El Chuncho. We have Lou Castel as the

Blond Gringo Bill Tate aboard the train loaded with armaments that the gang robs, seemingly to sell over to General Elias revolutionaries. But this gringo Tate, just who is this guy? An opportunist, a mercenary, perhaps, but actually he's found to be a mere bounty hunter after he collects the $100,000 reward for killing General Elias. Klaus Kinski is Chuncho's brother and right hand (psychopath) man El Santo and in rare form, although brief his appearances are. Also, there is the beautiful ex-*Bond* / ex-*Hammer* girl, Martine Beswick as Adelita Chunchio's female gang member who claims she would die for the revolution, but in reality is just out to feather her own nest as she steals Tate's dollars and splits to parts unknown. The ending has quite a twist and worth seeing as Tate is killed by Chunchio, who then is off in search of another revolution.

If You Meet Sartana, Pray for Your Death, a.k.a. *Sartana* (1968) is another great Western Kinski is in. Gianni (John) Garko stars as Sartana sure shot bounty hunter extraordinaire. This an Italian / West German coproduction directed by Frank Kramer (Gianfranco Parolini). Klaus Kinski co stars as Morgan sidekick of William Berger's Lasky role. All concerns a robbed gold shipment that Lasky and crew lifts with the help of a stolen *Gatling* gun. Others like the Banker and the deceased Mayor's widow are also involved at the higher end. Lasky and Morgan are busy working a double-cross on all factions involved. However, Sartana is also working, behind the scenes though setting a trap for all the bad guys, even the Mayor's widow who has his coffin stuffed full of gold bars instead of the Mayor. This is the original *Sartana*, of the series. Lots of twists and turns here, others were sure to follow but this one was the best in my opinion.

Another of Kinski's good ones as it were was *The Grand Silence;* a.k.a. *The Big Silence* (1968). An Italian production directed by Sergio Corbucci. It stars Frenchman Jean-Louis Trintignant as the hero mute bounty hunter Silence (as a boy has his vocal cords cut); Klaus Kinski as the lead bounty hunter Loco/Tigero. Silence is offered $1,000 to kill him by the widow whom Tigero killed. Also along for the chilling snow jaunt is American Frank Wolff as the sadistic sheriff of Snow Hill, brought in to clean out all the bounty hunters the town seems to be plagued with. Luigi Pistilli is Policutt bounty hunter sidekick of Tigero; Also with Vonetta McGee and Mario Brega. Film supposedly takes place in Utah, but appears to have been shot in the Italian high country during the dead of winter.

Next as a sucker for the *Sartana* films, we offer up *I Am Sartana, Your Angel of Death,* a.k.a. *Sartana the Gravedigger* (1969). Here we have an Italian / French coproduction directed by Anthony Ascott (Giuliano Carmino). Gianfranco Parolini initially created the Sartana character in his 1968 film, but Carmino took it and carried the torch for three film sequels starring Gianni (John) Garko in his continuing character role he originated in the Parolini film. Carmino did another one for 1972, but used actor George Hilton for the lead in that one. In all there were seventeen of these sequels/copycat films, as the case may be, that evolved from the Parolini original. All are quite entertaining and usually well made, even though from a variety of directors.

For this *Gravedigger* film the storyline has a bank robber disguised as Sartana and puts the robbery blame on the real Sartana. Now he has bounty hunters from all over after his hide while he attempts to clear his name. Also on board for this film were Frank Wolff as Buddy Ben; Klaus Kinski here as hot head Holden. Others were Gordon Mitchell as Deguego, Ettore Manni as Red Baxter and Sal Borgese as Sheriff Fisher.

In yet another Western for a late 1972 release Kinski co starred with the prolific Spanish actor George Martin in *The Return of Clint the Stranger* (1972). This was an Italian / Spanish coproduction directed by actor, George Martin. Martin stars as Clint Harrison in a sequel of sorts to his first *Clint the Stranger* film of 1968. Here that same gunman wishing to leave his past behind and return to his wife and young son. She employs him as a ranch hand on the condition he never touch his gun again. All well and good, he enjoys being home with his son. However, Klaus Kinski in the role of Scott a local land baron is trying to buy up all the area ranches and when refused by the owners, he hangs them. Going without a gun doesn't last long here before he's forced to use it again. Others of the cast were Marina Malfatti as the wife, Norma, Augusto Pesarini as son Jimmy, and Daniel Martin as Slim.

Kinski turns in a starring role in his next Western *The Fighting Fists of Shanghai Joe* (1973). This Italian production directed by Mario Caiano is an early East meets West spin-off theme films of the Western genre. Klaus Kinski stars here as Scalper Jack. Kung Fu artist Chen Lee co stars as Joe. Others along for the ride are Robert Hundar as Pedro, and Gordon Mitchell as Burying Sam, Carla Romanelli and George Wang. Lots of violence here makes for an interesting film. Storyline has a Chinese immigrant coming to America seeking a new life. In Texas gets a job as a cowboy and observes Mexicans from across the border are being transported in to be used as slaves. A much better film that its sequel by Bitto Albertini.

The sequel *The Return of Shanghai Joe* (1974) was a West German / Italian coproduction. It also starred Kinski as Pat Barnes the evil stogie smoking town boss. Chen Lee continues to take a back seat here as costarring as Joe who in this one befriends a shyster called Bill Caren portrayed by Tommy Polgar together they set out to clean up the town. Not one of the better films of spin-off genre. However, Kinski does do a nice job in his role.

Coming to end of Kinski's Westerns, his last was *A Genius, Two Partners and a Dupe,* a.k.a. *Nobody's the Greatest / The Genius* (1975). This film was a French/ West German/ Italian coproduction of another (comedic Western) directed by Damiano Damiani. Terence Hill stars as the Joe the Genius, Miou-Miou as Lucy, Robert Charlebois as Bill, Patrick McGoohan as Mayor Cabot, Klaus Kinski as Doc Foster and Mario Brega as the coach driver. The mayor turns out to be the bad guy here as he wants to cope no. 300,000 dollars the Government is sending in for Indian relief monies. Joe plans to foil this attempt taking it all himself. By this date in time the comedy Westerns had pretty much taken over the *Spaghetti* Western genre as we once knew it. The era of the straight shoot'em ups were becoming few and far between. Seeing the hand writing on the wall we imagine with his film opportunities in the genre slowing to a crawl, we find our Klaus Kinski branching out again into other more lucrative avenues of film work.

For a 1976 release Kinski ventures over to the Horror genre once again for another Jess (Jesus) Franco film called *Jack the Ripper.* Here is a stylish rehash of the legendary fiend of London town with Kinski starring portrayal as Dr. Dennis Orloff / the Ripper. Tight little atmospheric film here from one of the Italian masters of gore. This Swiss / German coproduction classified as a *Giallo* thriller is neatly done up in brilliant color and wide-screen. Others of the cast were Josephine Chaplin as Cynthia, Andreas Mannkopff as the Inspector Selby, Herbert Fux and Lina Romay as one of the victims. Well worth the watch, can be obtained, via Internet.

It seems once Kinski returned into the fold with director Werner Herzog once again, he had enough sense this time to stick it out awhile. Although they were both driven men and were too much alike to get along good, they did manage to make it though several more films together without actually killing one another. I can just imagine some of the brutal exchanges that went on between them while filming it had to have been an ordeal for sure.

For their next film together was a horror yarn called *Nosferatu the Vampyre* (1978). This is a German / French coproduction directed by Werner Herzog. Kinski's starring role here was as the infamous Count Dracula / the Vampire. His co stars were Isabella Adjani, Bruno Ganz and Jacques Dufhilo. Truly a creepy, but inspiring film remake of the old 1922 classic German silent film called *Nosferatu* from director F. W. Murnau and starred Max Schreck as the ghost like creature of the night. This '78 film credits "Dracula" literary work as basis for the script. However, the creature's makeup resembles the one of the earlier 1922 film. The storyline is a bit of a Dracula rehash, but is set in the Black Seaside town of Varna. Instead of the tall suave Chris Lee type, we have here a frail looking old man destined to search for blood from the living to continue his vile existence. Atmospheric and spooky, Kinski's role is classic but not scary.

For Kinski, yet a third venture in filmdom with Herzog for the 1978 film *Woyzeck.* This a German production directed by Werner Herzog who once again unleashes Kinski in another fabulous role as a broken soldier Friedrich Johann Franz Woyzeck. The man's sanity is broken, and he is driven to uncontrolled violence. His co stars were Eva Mattes and Wolfgang Reichmann. It was said that Herzog shot most of the scenes with a fixed camera.

It would seem that Herzog has at last brought out the best in the actor Klaus Kinski, but not withstanding a certain amount of stress on the part of Herzog himself. One his many problems in working, was with his actor Kinski of course. With Kinski being so well known for his love of money, was equally well known for his not being the easiest of actors to direct and control while in production. When shooting was under way, they seemed to advance daily into fits of screaming rage at one another. Finally it all came to an end one day with the two of them threatening to kill one another, there on the spot. (I believe that incident actually happened during the shooting of the *Aquirre* film of '72. Probably one reason they stayed apart so long between films).

Still yet Herzog had one more endeavor to accomplish between them. It would include another romp into the Jungles of Brazil, South America where they commenced to shoot their next film, *Fitzcarraldo* (1982). For this West German / Peruvian co production directed by Werner Herzog it starred Klaus Kinski as Brian Sweeney Fitzgerald/Fitzcarraldo. It also starred the lovely Claudia Cardinale, and José Lewgoy. I have had some people tell me this was a boring film, wow, how could it be with the toting a huge paddlewheel riverboat up and over and back down a mountain and through jungles on both sides, is anything but boring. Plus, with the beautiful Claudia Cardinale to look at throughout the movie, get outta here!

This Fitzgerald is evidently a very demented and disturbed individual, but all the more determined to build an opera house in the middle of a damn jungle. It was filmed on locations in Peru; the Amazon Basin, Brazil; the Amazon Rainforest, Amazonas, Brazil; Manaus Landing, Manaus, Amazonas, Brazil; and the *Teatro Amazonas Opera House,* Praca Sao Sebastiao, Manaus among other locales in and around Peru and Brazil. Amazingly an Opera House is truly there.

Also during Kinski's prolific career in films, he managed to turn in several from the late 1960s of the popular War genre of films coming mostly out of Italy during that era. While these got fairly hot for a certain period of time, they never really took over the failing Western genre. Some of these films were *Five for Hell* (1967) Dir: Gianfranco Parolini. The film starred Gianni (John) Garko. Kinski co stars as SS Colonel Hans Mueller; *Churchill's Leopards* (1968) Dir: Tonino Ricci. Kinski stars as an SS Captain,

Richard Harrison co stars as British Commando leader. *Salt in the Wound* (1968) Dir: Tonino Ricci; Stars Klaus Kinski, George Hilton; *Heroes in Hell* (1974) Dir: Michael Wotruba; Stars Lars Block Major Carter, Klaus Kinski in cameo as Gen Kaufmann; *Codename Wildgeese* (1984) Dir: Antonio Margheriti; Lewis Collins, Lee Van Cleef, Ernest Borgnine and Klaus Kinski as Charleton; *Kommando Leopard* (1985) Dir: Antonio Margheriti; Stars Lewis Collins, Klaus Kinski as Silvera and John Steiner. All come to a total of six of this war/action genre.

For a late 1987 release, Kinski returned for another ravaging with director Werner Herzog. This next film was called *Cobra Verde,* a.k.a. *Slave Coast.* A German production directed by Werner Herzog. Here again it stars Klaus Kinski as Francisco Manoel da Silva/ Cobra Verde, José Lewgoy, King Ampaw and Peter Berling. Filmed partially in Africa, with a storyline about an Island plantation owner who having hired a feared bandit (Cobra Verde) to oversee the slaves working on his land. As we might have know, Verde is caught messing around with the man's two young daughters and now he wants him gone, but not entirely dead gone. He sends him into Africa as a punishment. There Verde is subjected to all sorts of tortures and humiliations until he begins to train an army of rebels for his retribution.

It was about this period in time when our Mr. Kinski has run upon the lovely Debora Caprioglio; a beautiful buxom Italian actress. Kinski makes sure she is involved in his next picture called *White Hunter,* an Italian adventure for an early 1988 release. The film's storyline has to do with the wife of a White Hunter is mauled to death by a panther. Upset and mad over the incident that took his love from him, he goes off the deep end searching for revenge which eventually consumes his being. Here again, not a better actor picked for this part I'd say.

It starred Kinski as Klaus Naginsky, Harvey Keitel as Thomas, Yorgo Voyagis as Guide/leader and newcomer Debora Caprioglio as Deborah. Directed by Augusto Caminito, (plus as director unaccredited is Mario Caiano). According to my source book "Disorder and Genius: The Complete Klaus Kinski" by Lucas Balbo and Laurent Aknin it revealed that Kinski was only in it as a cameo for the first thirty minutes, then disappeared for the rest of the film. They really didn't make it clear whether or not he left with his future bride Debora?

Possibly he left so as to get married to this lovely Debora. All we know for sure is for his long awaited personal film achievement called *Klaus Kinski Paganini* (1987-'88) film, an Italian/ French/ Spanish coproduction which he directed and starred in as Nicco Paganini the so-called Devil Violinist of Nineteenth Century Europe. Here we find the lovely *Debora* (Caprioglio) *Kinski* credited as Antonia Bianchi Paganini, as his wife. Also Kinski's son by Minhoi (who would have been eleven) Nikolai Kinski is also in the film as Paganini's young son Achille Paganini.

Officially I haven't found her listed as his wife other than this one credit, the informational source website *www.IMBd.com* lists her only by her name, between the dates of 1987-1989, which is prior to his death. At any rate, rest in peace ye olde horseman from hell. Possibly one day we'll see old Klaus back up on another steed, pistol in hand, riding hell bent for leather across the stormy skies. In our dreams right!

End.

- Below is a complete filmography of Klaus Kinski's Euro Westerns. The dates are aligned as close as possible with information currently at hand, plus international release dates included. What storyline breakdowns were not addressed in main text body, they are herein. **Posters and title picture are accredited to the Sebastian Haselbeck collection via his website www.spaghetti-western.net. Many thanks, Sebastian.*

KLAUS KINSKI
EURO WESTERNS . . .

1963

***The Last Ride to Santa Cruz*;** W.Ger/ Fr, Director Rolf Olsen (Kinski as José); 1963

1964

Winnetou: Last of the Renegades; a.k.a. *Giorni di Fuoco*; *Last of the Renegades*; Fr/ Ital/ W. Ger./ Yugo, Director Harald Reinl (Kinski as David Luke Lucas, the Scout); 9/17/64

1965

***For a Few Dollars More*;** *Per Qualche Dollaro in Piu* a.k.a. *The Magnificent Strangers*; Ital/ Spa/ West German, Director Sergio Leone (Kinski as Juan Wild the hunchback); 12/18/65 (Ital)

The famous strike of the match scene with Wild and Mortimer, courtesy of Author's collection

1966

A Bullet for the General, a.k.a. *Quien Sabe?* ; Ital, Director Damiano Damiani (Kinski as El Santo General El Chuncho's assistant); 2/7/66

1967
Man: His Pride and his Vengeance; *L'Uomo, I'Orgoglio, la Vendetta* a.k.a. *Pride and Vengeance*; Ital/ West German, Director Luigi Bazzoni (Kinski costars as Lt. Miguel Garcia) 12/22/67; *Found to not really be a Western, however has been promoted as one in more than one country, and most listings carry it as such is why it is included here.

1968
The Ruthless Four, *IL Spietato Quattro;* a.k.a. *Sam Cooper's Gold*; Ital, Director Giorgio Capitani (Kinski costars as Brent / *El Biondo* (the Blond); 2/9/68; Stars Gilbert Roland, George Hilton and American, Van Heflin as Sam Cooper in his only Spaghetti Western. A man strikes gold only to find his ruthless son (Hilton) and his two partners (Hilton, Roland and Kinski) intend to take his find from him.

If You Meet Sartana . . . Pray for Your Death, *Se Incontri Sartana Prega per la Tua Morte;* a.k.a. *Sartana* a.k.a. *Gunfighters Die Harder*; Ital/ West Ger., Director Frank Kramer (Gianfranco Parolini) (Kinski costars as Morgan); 8/14/68

The Big Silence, *IL Grande Silenzio;* a.k.a. *Great Silence*; Ital/ Fr, Director Sergio Corbucci (Kinski costars as Tigero / Loco); 11/19/68

1969

Twice a Judas, *Due Volte Giuda;* a.k.a. *They were Called Graveyard* a.k.a. *Shoot Twice*; Spa/ Ital, Director Nando Cicero (Kinski stars as land baron Victor Barrett / Dingus); 1/9/69; Also stars apparent brother of Barrett, Antonio Sabato, who find Victor is running Mexican slaves across the border to work on confiscated land he's acquired illegally.

I am Sartana, Your Angel of Death, *Sono Sartana, IL Vostro Becchino;* a.k.a. *Sartana the Gravedigger*; Ital/ Fr, Director Anthony Ascott (Giuliano Carmino) (Kinski costars as Holden the hothead in poker game); 11/20/69

1970

And God Said to Cain, *E Dio Disse a Caino*; Ital, Director Anthony M. Dawson (Antonio Margheriti) (Kinski stars as Gary Hamilton); 2/5/70; Also stars Peter Carsten, Cella Michelangeli and Lee Burton (Guido Lollobrigida). Hamilton serving time for something he didn't commit is blessed when because of some judicial/presidential pardoning is now free. He immediately goes after the man who arranged to have him arrested so as to abscond with his land. The local Land Baron we find is none other than Acombar (Carsten).

The Bell, *La Belva;* a.k.a. *The Beast* a.k.a. *Rough Justice*; Ital, Director Mario Costa (Kinski as Johnny Laster / Machete, a sex-crazy outlaw); 9/12/70; Cast included: Gabriella Giorgelli, Lee Burton (Guido Lollobrigida), and Luisa Rivelli among others. According to Kinski's book, *Kinski Uncut*, he considered Costa to be a lousy director and they had a major falling out during this film over difference of opinion while directing Kinski. It became a huge disappointment to Producers West Devon, Italy, and at the box office.

1971

Strange Tale of Minnesota Stinky, *Doppia Taglia per Minnesota Stinky;* a.k.a. *Fistful of Death* a.k.a. *Giu la Testa . . . Hombre (Down the Head . . . Hombre)*; Ital, Director Miles Deem (Demofilo Fidani) (Kinski costars here as the Rev. Cotton, in a good guy role); 4/17/71; Stars Hunt Powers (Jack Betts) as Butch Cassidy. Gordon Mitchell is in a cameo as Ironhead. A lone gunman, Macho Callaghan (Jeff Cameron) tracks down members of a gang that killed friends.

A Coffin Full of Dollars, *Per una Bara Piena di Dollari;* a.k.a. *Showdown for a Badman*; Ital, Director Miles Deem (Demofilo Fidani) (Kinski costars as Dan Hagen / Slander); 4/1/71; Hunt Powers (Jack Betts) stars as bounty hunter Tamayo, Gordon Mitchell as John Hamilton; Jeff Cameron (Geoffredo Scarciofolo) is the Hamilton brother a.k.a. "Nevada Kid" home from the war, and finds his family has been slaughtered. He set out with Tamayo to track down the perpetrators. They find out badman Hagen ordered the killings of course.

His Name was King, *Lo Chiamavano King*; Ital, Director Don Reynolds (Renato Savino) (Kinski costars as Sheriff Brian Foster); 5/18/71; Stars Richard Harrison as John "King" Marley. King returns from the range to find most of his family murdered by Benson's gang of gunrunners and outlaws.

Vengeance is a Dish Served Cold, *La Vendetta E un Piatto Che Si Serve Freddo;* a.k.a. *Death's Dealer* a.k.a. *Vengeance Trail*; Ital/ Spa, Director William Redford (Pasquale Squittieri) (Kinski as Dentist Virgil Prescott) 8/13/71; Stars Leonard Mann as Jeremiah Bridger, Ivan Rassimov as Perkins. Lone survivor of a vicious Indian attack on his family, Bridger become a wild Indian killer, later he finds out Land Baron Perkins had orchestrated the attacks to acquire the land. When Bridger finds out he gets to the bottom of it in quickly. He's aided by town dentist Prescott.

Pray to Kill and Return Alive, *Prega per il Morto e Ammazza il Vivo;* a.k.a. *Shoot the Living, Pray for the Dead*; Ital, Director Joseph Warren (Giuseppe Vari) (Kinski stars as Dan Hogan); 8/13/71; Story deals with the internal leadership issues between a holdup gang leader Reed (co stars Dean Stratford[Dino Strano]).

The Price of Death, *IL Venditore de Morte;* a.k.a. *Last Gunfight*; Ital, Director Vincent Thomas (Enzo Gicca Palli) (Kinski costars as Chester Conway local troublemaker / killer); 9/17/71; Stars John Garko as retired bounty hunter called Silver. Also with Franco Abbiana as Conway's attorney Jeff Plumber. Conway is a black sheep town nuisance who gets railroaded for something he really didn't do. However, come to find out he is guilty of murder, but was never found out before this happening.

Black Killer; Ital/ West German, Directed by Lucky Moore (Carlo Croccolo) (Kinski stars as sharp-shooting stranger in black, who actually is frontier Lawyer James Webb); 11/27/71; Also stars Fred Robsahm, Antonio Cantafora and Marina Mulligan among others. Webb goes to the aid of a town plagued by a wild bunch gang of Mexican killers called the O'Hara Brothers and corrupt Judge on the bench. All men who have taken up the post of sheriff have been killed, twenty-six in all within two years. Now when rancher Collins is killed and his wife beaten and gang-raped by the bunch, his brother a bounty hunter Bud Collins (Robsahm) plans to clean the place out with the help of sure-shot Webb.

The Return of Clint the Stranger, *IL Ritorno di Clint IL Solitario*; Ital/ Spa, Directory George Martin (Kinski costars as Scott); 12/14/72; Stars George Martin as Clint

My Name is Shanghai Joe, *IL Mio Nome E Shanghai Joe;* a.k.a. *the Fighting Fists of Shanghai Joe* a.k.a. *Shanghai Joe*; Ital, Directory Mario Caiano (Kinski costars as Scalper Jack); 12/28/73

The Return of Shanghai Joe, *IL Ritorno di Shanghai Joe*; W. Ger/ Ital, Directory Bitto Albertini (Kinski stars as town boss Pat Barnes); 2/28/75

A Genius, Two Friends, and an Idiot; *Un Genio, Due Compari, Un Pollo;* a.k.a. *Genius* a.k.a. *Nobody is the Greatest*; Fr/W. Ger/ Ital, Director was Damiano Damiani (Kinski as Doc Foster); 12/16/75

This brings to a close the Spaghetti Western credits for Klaus Kinski.

End.

BIBLIOGRAPHY
(K. Kinski)

Amacord Italian Film Fanzine article, Issue no. 13, 1998; "Klaus Kinski: Delirious, Chaotic . . . A Genius" by Giorgio Navarro and Igor Molino Padovan; *Translation by James Prickette*

Amacord Italian Film Fanzine article, Issue, vol. 2 no. 7, April 1997; "Jess Franco Special: Dignore of the Incunis" by Gian Luca Castoldi, Main pgs btw 32/33 pp. 1-19;

Also article on *Gli Specialist,* A Western di Sergio Corbucci" by Federico de Zigno Section a.k.a. *IL Grande Silence* pp. 47

Betts, Tom, editor *WAI! (Westerns . . . All'Italiana)* Fanzine articles/ informational tidbit on Klaus Kinski; Plus the *WAI! Memorial* Issue for Klaus Kinski no. 33

Connolly, Bill, editor *Spaghetti Cinema* Fanzine articles / informational tidbits on the actor Klaus Kinski; Plus article reprint from: *Variety* 1989 on *Scena Film* (Augusto Caminito film Co.) law suit of January 19, 1987 against Kinski and their three-picture deal. Pp 49, I

Cox, Alex, *10,000 Ways to Die* (2009), *Kamera Books,* UK. pp 65, 326; 119-126; 185-192,193; 295-299; 257-261

Disorder and Genius: The Complete Films of Klaus Kinski (1997) by Lucas Balbo and Laurent Aknin; *Midnight Media Publishing*

Haselbeck, Sebastian, owner/curator for Internet website: *www. spaghetti-western.net*

Hughes, Howard, *Once Upon a Time in The Italian West* (2006) by Howard Hughes, Publishers *I.B. Tauris,* London, NY. ; pp: 44; 94-105; 193-204

Internet, via: *www.IMDB.com* "Mini-bio on Klaus Kinski", plus film listing review

Kinski, Klaus, *Kinski Uncut: The Autobiography of Klaus Kinski* (1996) by: Klaus Kinski and Wilhelm Heyne Verlag, GmbH; Publisher: *Bloomsbury Publishing* PLc. Translated from German by: Joachim Neugroschel

Ledbetter, Craig, former editor of *ETC (European Trash Cinema)* Fanzine, Reprint of Christian Kessler Interview with William Berger, *Translated by Peter Blumenstock.* Issue no. 13, pp 10 on Berger working with Kinski.

Prickette, Tom, *Fallen, From the Horse Opera* previously unpublished manuscript of 1992, partially used in the *WAI!* Memorial issue for Klaus Kinski after his death for 1991

Quinlan, David, *The Illustrated Encyclopedia of Movie Character Actors* (1985-6); Pub. *Harmony Books,* NY., pp 172

Weisser, Thomas, *Spaghetti Westerns: the Good, the Bad, and the Violent,* (1992) *McFarland*, Jefferson NC.

Western: All'Italiana (books I, II, and III) by Antonio Bruschini and Federico de Zigno, *Glittering Images,* Firenze, Italy; book I, 1998; book II, 2001 and book III, 2006

Who's Who of Film: The World Almanac (1987); Publisher: *Bison Books,* A Division of *Random House* Canada, Ltd., pp 243

MICKEY KNOX

(1922—)

ACTOR, WRITER, DIALOGUE DIRECTOR, PRODUCER

THE PEN, MIGHTIER THAN THE SIX-GUN!

Born on the first of January 1922 of Russian/Jewish heritage, life for young Mickey began in the Coney Island area of Brooklyn, New York. His mother, originally from Odessa, Russia, had this baby out of wedlock. The father, also a Russian immigrant was known about the area as kind of a Poet. Mickey remembers very little about this man, his father and would grow up hating him because he had left them. Evidently, he would return for visits occasionally, of which Mickey could barely remember, but does remember his mother relating stories to him, and on occasion he would send back poems he had published in the newspapers.

His mother alone raised the family of three—Mickey the youngest, a half-brother, and a sister from a previous marriage back in Russia. She remarried about 1928, this time to a local man of Polish/Jewish descent. The new stepfather was a good man and a good provider. Later, the family would relocate, first to a small farm in a more rural area. After the Depression years hit, they wound up moving down to the Washington DC area about 1937.

Mickey by that time was a *rough-and-tumble* lad of fifteen. After growing up on the streets and boroughs of the Brooklyn area, he became well in tune to the rough side of city dwelling. Washington DC of that era was more or less much the same in that respect. His primary schooling had been in Brooklyn during his early teens, and finished there in the DC area. His mom had always been an active person in local politics and was no less active there in DC, the heartbeat of the United States. Trying to keep his nose clean, so to speak, and keep at his studies was sometimes a major issue for young Mickey. He grew up hard and tough in a world that seem to take, but didn't give much in return. It was here in DC that he had a revelation that becoming an actor was what he wanted to do in life.

Knox, however, was a man born to wear many hats in his long career. His role models at that time were the likes of John Garfield (an outsider, much as he was there in DC, but full of passion) and James Cagney (also, much like Mickey, a smaller man, but tough that took no shit). To be an actor was his choice and he applied himself therefore not only in school, but later at a Catholic university where he studied speech and drama.

Eventually, he would return to New York City while attempting to find work there on the Broadway circuit. He picked up work here and there where he could, working on sets, painting and repairing them. He managed to get small parts to play occasionally. He also worked with the summer stock stage companies, one in Maryland and one in Virginia. Some years later, after establishing himself as a competent stage actor, he relocated to the Hollywood, California, area where he planned to give acting in films a try.

Those days in Hollywood of the late 1940s was not unlike today (just the names have been changed over the years) a brutal, dog-eat-dog place to live and work. One had to be tough in order to survive in the arena, or limelight as it was called. Making a successful transition from stage to film work coupled with his previous years of hard work and perseverance would finally pay off for Mickey. His repertoire of film works was mounting since his debut as Johnny Martin in the 1947 gangster film, *Killer McCoy* by director Roy Rowland, a film about corruption in the fight game leading to murder. It starred Mickey Rooney and Brian Donlevy.

Others that followed were similar roles for Mickey like, *I Walk Alone* (1948), *The Accused* (1949), *White Heat,* and *Angels in Disguise* both of 1949. The 1950s brought more roles but with an even wider-acting range. By 1951, he had even branched out into the new television media, obtaining many parts on various shows thereafter. By the mid 1950's he had branch out further and pursued his interests and goals in dialogue work, story, and script writing. He continued with bit parts and screen roles, but by this time in his career, he was leaning more with the dialogue work. His last film of that era was the *Singing in the Dark* (1956) in which he portrayed Harry the handsome tough. On this film, he was also the film's dialogue director.

Then it happened, like a nightmare in the dead of night. The place in time was called the "McCarthy Era," as was the public's nickname of those terrible years. All of Hollywood was in an uproar over the accusations of communistic affiliations among the acting community. During the early 1950's tensions had grown because of the so-called Cold War and the European Iron Curtain, which separated the good guys from the bad guys.

Back across the ocean here in the States, our own Congress began to investigate its own US citizens, questioning whether or not they had any ties to peoples of these communistic communities behind the Iron Curtain. A subcommittee was formed and headed by Senator Joseph R. McCarthy. It was called the *House Un-American Activities Committee*. It would soon put the fear into the hearts of all foreign-born citizens.

Things began happening within the Performing Arts communities as well. Actors, performers of the New York theater groups, the Broadway circuit were all now at siege with these investigations. It soon filtered into the television groups and out into the Hollywood film studios of California. The movie capital of the United States had at that time come up with what was called the "Black List." If you were an actor, either know or even suspected of commie affiliations, or for that matter had a family member thought to have had, and/or of the Jewish faith, you were deemed a suspect! Thus, you were "Blacklisted."

Mickey's first wife, Georgette, a French gal could see the hand writing on the wall and broke off with him. For nearly a year after that, he could find no work, very little if any. He kept going, though, migrating back and forth between New York and Los Angeles finding small jobs here and there with a few roles at the *Actor's Studio* run by his friend Norman Mailer. Many a fine actor suffered this fate during that era. "McCarthyism" had struck home for Mickey Knox. He readily admits that his mother was a political Left-winger and she had brought him up in that way of thinking from an early beginning. As his acting projects would fissile out, slowly at first, and then eventually drying up after 1956. He managed to hang on awhile longer though, seeing how his dialogue work as director and screenwriting abilities were not wholly affected by this squeeze early on.

In actuality, his last film the 1956 *Singing in the Dark* was an Indie film shot in New York by independent director Max Nosseck. There in New York, the full effects of the McCarthy shake-up had hit hard. This film being an Independent was outside the Actors Guild loop, so to speak. There under the "Blacklist" wire, Mickey worked his last film of the era.

> *Helpful politician that he was, Joseph R. McCarthy also began to wage war on the rock 'n' rollers, and youth toughs of that era as well. His venture to stamp out motorcycle gangs, and juvenile delinquency in towns across America was going all out. This one-man task force was going to clean up the United States single-handedly. He put out a ban on switchblade knives, their sale, possession, and import into the United States from foreign countries. Even now during the millennium era, these bans in most States throughout the United States are still on the books and still in effect.
>
> There was soon a silver lining though. He was publicly denounced after being first member censured and then condemned by the US Senate in 1954 for his radical behavior on the subcommittee. He was in a word, mostly "blackballed" from the world. He died May 2, 1957, a broken man he was only forty-eight years old. A real barnstormer in his day, but in his short lifespan he managed to turn the Americas of that era into a literal turmoil for all those who live here.
>
> Unfortunately, his rousting of the entertainment world would linger on (much like that of the band on the knives) well into the late 1950s before really easing up. However, like Knox and others in the business, they had already begun new careers in Europe by that time and most were still leery of venturing back on US soil for work.

Another major shift in Mickey's lifestyle would come yet again. Not long after his last film of 1956 this accomplished. Even though he was a dedicated actor and writer of the industry, he also was finally forced into relocating to Europe for work. Rome, Italy, was where fortunately by the 1960's film work there was booming. With his first wife having been French, he was fluent by now in that language. Also, having some Italian language skills himself, he quickly adapted to life in the strange new world of the Italian cinema. Further developing his language skills over the next few years, Mickey would become a master at reworking the Italian film scripts and dubbing them into English.

He worked closely with the Italian directors and sometimes his American counterpart actors, who, by that time, were beginning to migrate to Italy from the States during those early years of 1960. Mickey had by now become an essential part of that system. The films then being made during that era were primarily aimed directly at the US film markets. His talents had become invaluable to the Italian producers, and distributors.

Being the hard man he was, with tough scruples, it's been said he would fight at the drop of a hat, and tangle with anyone who would threaten his existence in the business or, for that matter, just plain rubbed him the wrong way. He was in a word, a dubbing master and acted the part and was a shrewd businessman to boot, Mick as he was known by his friends and associates, parlayed his talents into an impressive amount of credits for a lifetime of being in the business. For a man that started from scratch, then going from popular actor of the 1950s, to having to uproot everything, and start all over again in Europe, this man is the ultimate of the word *accomplishment.* Widely accepted by his peers as top-notch in his field, he is admired and even revered by some for his work.

His friend Norman Mailer's wife, Adele, had a younger sister Joan. Mickey had first laid eyes on her back in 1951 while sharing Thanksgiving dinner with the Mailer's back in Brooklyn. She was only sixteen then. He only ran into her once again later in 1959. By then she had become a fashion model, mature and was a beauty to behold. By the time in 1962, when he was in Paris working on the film production *View from the Bridge,* he would take along his new wife, Joan, with him. Later that same year, still in Paris he worked on *The Longest Day* (1962) and then went directly onto a new *Marco Polo* film, which wouldn't be released until much later as *Marco the Magnificent* (1966). For both films, he had been the acting dialogue director.

The *Polo* film from Producer Raoul Levy was directed by Denys De La Patelliere. It starred Noel Howard, Horst Buchholz, Anthony Quinn, Omar Sharif, Elsa Martinelli, Akim Tamiroff, and Orson Welles. The film was to have starred one Alain Delon, a popular French movie star in the title role. Mickey likes to relate the story that Delon at their first meeting decided to put the make on his new wife, Joan. With her being pregnant at the time, she wasn't having any of it and let him know in no uncertain terms. Delon didn't really get the message of the abrupt rejection, but we figure he had a little help from Mickey on the subject and it finally must've hit home because he was never in the film when the shooting started. It was later in 1964 when their daughter Valentina was born. Then following a short recovery Joan was pregnant again with Melissa, who was born late in 1965.

Also, in 1965, the Knox family had by now relocated back to Italy for shooting of the new John Frankenheimer film, *Grand Prix* which starred

James Garner (of American TV *Maverick* fame); Also starring was Italian actor Antonio Sabato, and the popular Japanese actor, Toshiro Mifune. This fine Japanese actor was for Mickey, a major problem in seeing how he didn't speak any English at all. They managed though, and having reviewed this film for the first time only a few years ago, I can testify that it all came out fine.

Although many of his accomplishments were as an actor, Mickey was associated in that respect with one film, a comedic gangster quickie he and Norman Mailer threw together working from their loft in NYC. It also involved George Plimpton and ex-boxer José Torres who brought his dog along. It was called *Beyond the Law* (1967), but not to be confused with the *Spaghetti* Western often associated with the same name that was made in Italy with Western screen legend Lee Van Cleef. That cast they had for that film besides Van Cleef, did include another fine actor though, who had also suffered from those infamous "blacklisting" days of Hollywood during that same "McCarthy Era," his name was Lionel Stander.*

Both men, by now were neither young any longer, but certainly far from old by any means. They were like others of the trade, zapped in the prime of their careers and forced to relocate for similar reasons beyond their control. There were others who had come to Europe so as to revitalize sagging careers in acting from back in the States. Lee Van Cleef had himself been one of those seemingly washed up actors. His new screen image and persona which he conveyed across the screens of those European cinema houses with those Leone films had made him an instant international star. He became known and still is considered an icon of the Italian *Spaghetti* Western era.

In the middle of all the excitement of this new era of cinematic history in the making, led by director Sergio Leone with his new breed of Horse Operas was none other than Mickey Knox. A valuable asset to the Italian filmmakers he was soon affectionately dubbed the "Mayor of Rome." By the time Mickey made his one and only entry of the Italian Western film

* Lionel Stander, Mickey reminisces about in his biography, that when he had been called before the *House Un-American Activities Committee* for questioning, according to Mickey, he was probably the only person to ever stand up to, and even overpower the committee's aggressive attempts at intimidation. Mickey states in his book, that Stander "Using his heavy, buzzsaw voice, he accused the Committee of being un-American" themselves. He went on to quote them certain amendments of the US Constitution that they were violating. As he rambled on and on, they couldn't seem to shut him up so they dismissed him. Mickey goes on to add, "On the stand, Lionel was a marvel; he beat them at their own game."

genre, he had already been affiliated with one of the most popular *Spaghetti* Western films of the era. *Il Buono, Il Brutto, Il Cattivo (The Good, the Bad, and the Ugly).* This was the 1966 film by Sergio Leone that broke all box office records in Europe and eventually would astound record keepers here when it finally showed in the States after 1967.

It was Leone's third and final installment of his "Man with No Name" trilogy that began in 1964 with *A Fistful of Dollars* and then *For a Few Dollars More* (1965). All three films starred the previously little know American television actor Clint Eastwood as the laconic, cigar chomping gunslinging bounty hunter. Originally cast with the character ID known only as Joe; then Manco for the second film. These were quickly forgotten as the distribution of the three films, were being promoted for the United States film market as being "the Man with No Name" trilogy. They were unique in content and sound. Whoever was affiliated with them became either extremely popular or at least very well known worldwide.

For *The Good, the Bad, and the Ugly* (1966), the last installment by Leone, Mickey was the dubbing director for the English language version of the film that would be distributed for all English speaking countries, primarily the United States. After spending many months on locations in Spain for this film, he along the cast and crews finally again retuned to Rome where Leone threw a lavish party for all concerned. Knox was to meet Leone again a few months later in New York City at a voice-recording studio in Manhattan. There along with Lee Van Cleef and Eli Wallach they were there to do the English language dubbing for the film from the cue track. Eastwood wasn't at this particular session, but came sometime later after all the others had already been dismissed.

> Evidently there was some sort of problem with Eastwood and him bringing with him to the dubbing session the original first shooting script, and was insisting on using that one to read and not the newer reworked one that Mickey had worked on and was so approved by *United Artists.* Seemingly the disagreement was between then *UA Vice-President* Chris Mankiewicz and Eastwood himself. We understand that Eastwood did eventually cave and did the approved script after all reading it alone without any other live counter dialogue since Mickey was no longer there.
>
> The above quip about the disagreement was derived in part from an Internet posted interview with Mr. Knox from 1997/'98 by Cenk Kiral for his website *www.fistful-of-leone.com*

Eli Wallach later related in his book, *The Good, the Bad, and Me* that Mickey labored over all those spoken lines like a master detective. He remembered one scene in particular in which he was sitting on a horse, in the desert yelling out his lines. The horses he said, hated the hot sand and his wasn't very cooperative. Wallach let us readers know that it wasn't an easy scene to dub in a closed room later, while sitting atop a stool in the studio there in New York City. He said Mickey yelled out some encouragement though, "Just yell the goddamn line. We'll take care to match your yelling with what's on the screen."

Mickey also went on to do the dialogue for the English language version of Leone's next blockbuster Western called *C'Era una Volta Il West (Once Upon a Time in the West)* for its 1968 release. Through his own admission, Mickey also acted as interpreter for Leone while on the Monument Valley, Arizona, United States, shooting locales. This bang-up tribute to the American West was actually taken right to the Western Americas for its superb location shots. This Monument Valley locale had become an American staple for shooting locations since director John Ford had made it famous with his 1939 film starring John Wayne called *Stagecoach*. Ford being an idol of Leone, he relished the idea of coming to the USA and shooting his film on the same ground that Ford had made so popular to the Western genre of yesteryear.

For Leone's *Once Upon a Time . . .* he starred Charles Bronson as Harmonica, another laconic gunman type, "a man of few words", who is set on revenge since his youth. An endeavor triggered by his father's unwarranted hanging by an outlaw / gunman called Frank portrayed by another old friend of Mickey's, Henry Fonda. The Frank character was quite a role switch from the mostly good-guy roles of Fonda's many previous films. This portrayal alone is well worth the watch. The music score was yet another of Italian composer Ennio Morricone's most popular adventures in theme music.

Later on Mickey would even venture into film producing for himself with a newly formed production company called *Hercules,* Italy. He first would be a coproduction effort along with *Tritone* of Spain and *Terra* of West Germany. For this Executive Producer role we believe this was his first and only producing venture to our knowledge. The film was called *Viva La Muerte . . . Tua! (Long live you're Death!);* a.k.a. *Don't Turn the Other Cheek* (1971). This was a tongue 'n' cheek, comedic style Western which was just beginning to become popular with the genre. This theme would eventually become a lot more popular following the successes of the *Trinity* films,* which followed later.

* The *Trinity* films relate to the popular E.B. Clucher [Enzo Barboni] films of 1970's of which numerous cloned versions were made afterwards following in

No doubt popular with the throngs of moviegoers in Europe during this era, but when shown in America this film of Mickey's didn't fair all that well at the box office. It's unfortunate in that it had a superb cast of three main leads as partners. There was Italian star Franco Nero portraying a Russian Prince; Eli Wallach (now also an international star thanks to Leone's *GBU*) as the Mexican bandit and the third was popular British actress Lynn Redgrave portraying an Irish News journalist/activist. All three are joined at the hip, so to speak, so as to retrieve a large cache of gold. Although Mary O'Donnell, the journalist appears to want the gold only to fire up the revolution and make more headlines.

To quote actor Walter Barnes during his stay in Rome he related, "I'm having fun. This is great," he reminisced, "Something I've never done before, you know? Living in Europe, doing all these damn films in these different countries, with marvelous actors from England, from Germany, From France, from Spain and Italy, and you're just sitting there gobbling it up? Then the divorces start!"

Mickey Knox was no less vulnerable and while he was away from his spouse Joan, an Italian neighbor, only an acquaintance made off with his

---

the footsteps much as was the case of the Italian western phenomenon Sergio Leone had started back in 1964 with his *Dollar* films.

Unlike the *Dollar* films, these particular versions of the genre, *They Call Me Trinity* (1970) and *Trinity is Still My Name* (1974) were, while still being westerns per say, were more in the comedy vein. Not spoofs like the *Franco e Ciccio* Italian westerns of that era were, but never-the-less, the sly 'tongue-in-cheek' humor of the *Dollar* type was now replaced with rousing, buffoon style fighting, and even slap-stick comedy like routines. This important series of this new phenomenon era, even starred an Eastwood look-alike, Terence Hill [Mario Griotti] an already adapt actor of the western genre from Northern Italy. Tall, blond and blue-eyed who went on to fame and fortune thanks in part to these two films alone?

Sergio Leone even got into the act himself, first with *My Name is Nobody* (1973) in which he was an unaccredited director behind the scenes assisting director Tonino Valerii. He was also credited with the original story idea as well. In yet another entry he was behind the scenes again, as the unaccredited director assisting Damiano Damiani for *Genius: Two Friends and an Idiot* (1975). Of the two, *Nobody* was by far the better film with Henry Fonda playing opposite Terence Hill's character of nobody. There was also an interesting array of American actors thrown into the mix for the fun. Plus, another rousing musical score by Ennio Morricone as well.

bride. Taking the girls she left about mid-1969. They went their separate ways eventually divorcing. He has, however, over the years retained a close relationship with his two daughters.

While Mickey Knox continued to act in a few films mostly by choice only, while in Europe, back in the States he found he no longer had that luxury to pick and choose any longer. He later appeared in a few American documentaries on which he worked well into the new Millennia. Lately though of more recent years, very little has been heard from him. It has been reported that after spending some thirty-three years in Italy, he had finally returned to the United States taking up residency in the Los Angeles, California, area near his beloved daughters Valentina and Melissa.

Prompted by old friend Norman Mailer, he combined his memoirs into an autobiography published some years back called *The Good, the Bad, and the Dolce Vita: The Adventures of an Actor in Hollywood, Paris and Rome,* for *Nation Books* 2004.

Note:*("The Dolce Vita" translates to "The Sweet Life").*

Hopefully, he is now settled back enjoying the fruits of his long derserved labors during those wonderful, often tense and trying times of those wild, *Spaghetti* cinema years. Being born in 1922 would now make him 90 years old at this time. Still revered by his peers he will be long remembered for his contributions in the era of the *Spaghetti* films. Indeed, "The Pen is Mightier than the Sword" or in our case mightier than the six-gun!

End.

- Below is a Euro filmography for Mickey Knox. Dates here are aligned as close as possible with information currently at hand, including international release dates. **Poster pictures are accredited to the Sebastian Haselbeck collection via his website www.spaghetti-western.net. The M. Knox title photo was courtesy of interviewer Cent Kiral via his website www.fistful-of-leone.com*

MICKEY KNOX
EURO WESTERNS

1966

The Good, the Bad, and the Ugly, *Il Buono, Il Brutto, Il Cattivo*; Ital, Directed by Sergio Leone, it starred Clint Eastwood (as Blonde), Lee Van Cleef (as Angel Eyes) and Eli Wallach as (Tuco); **Mickey Knox** was credited as dubbing director for the English language version of this film that would eventually be distributed to the United States 12/23/67; Italian release was 12/29/66

1968

Once Upon a Time in the West, *C'Era una Volta Il West (There was once the West)*; Ital, Director Sergio Leone (Starring Charles Bronson, Henry Fonda, and Claudia Cardinale. Also starring were Jason Robards, Frank Wolff, and Lionel Stander; **Mickey Knox** did the dialogue for the film's English language version plus acted as the English interpreter for Leone while on set at Monument Valley, AZ, United States; Released 12/21/68 Ital; 5/28/69 USA.

1971

Long live You're Death! *Lungo Viva La Sua Morte!* ; a.k.a. *Don't Turn the Other Cheek;* a.k.a. *Long Live the Revolution*; Ital/ Spa/ West German; Director was Duccio Tessari (Starring Franco Nero, Eli Wallach, Lynn Redgrave, and Horst Janson); this film was produced by Mickey Knox and to our knowledge was his only production effort along those lines; 12/22/71 Ital; Oct/1974 USA

End.

BIBLIOGRAPHY
(M. Knox)

Betts, Tom, editor *WAI! (Westerns . . . All'Italiana)* Fanzine articles/ information on films of Mickey Knox

Connolly, Bill, editor *Spaghetti Cinema* Fanzine articles / info bits on Mickey Knox

Frayling, Christopher, *Something to do with Death* (2000) *Faber & Faber Ltd.,* London, UK. Information on Mickey Knox, pp. 219, 269-70, 272, 273, 290, 294-5, 399, 400

Haselbeck, Sebastian, owner/curator for Internet website: *www.spaghetti-western.net*

Internet, via: *www.anica.it* Ref: Film production and dates.

Internet, via: *www.IMDB.com* film listing review plus dates

Kiral, Cenk, owner/curator of *www.fistful-of-leone.com* website, Mickey Know interview of 1997/98 published on his site with one color photo of Knox.

Knox, Mickey, *The Good, the Bad, and the Dolce Vita (The Good Life)* (2004); Preface by Norman Mailer, publisher: *Nation Books,* NY.

Tender Comrades (1997) by Patrick McGilligan & Paul Buhle, Publisher *St. Martin's Griffin,* NY., pp. 351-388

Weisser, Thomas, *Spaghetti Westerns: the Good, the Bad, and the Violent,* (1992) *McFarland*, Jefferson NC.

GUY MADISON

(1922-1996)

FROM MATINEE IDOL, TO COMMAND PERFORMANCE

Matinee idol, to be sure, the bobby-sox generation of the mid-1940s definitely had someone other than Frankie Sinatra to swoon over. One of the most sought after and talked about of the handsome young heartthrobs of that era was Guy Madison. Even before his commitment to Uncle Sam and the United States Navy was over, he was already a face to be remembered and long talked about for decades to come.

He was born Robert Ozell Moseley, of devout Baptist family stock on January 19, 1922. His birthplace was the small community of Pumpkin Center, northern California, east of popular ski resort, Mt. Shasta. Later the family relocated again further south to the Bakersville area where young Moseley was raised and schooled. His parents Ben Moseley had eventually found work there (*Santa Fe Railroad,* thirty-five years) and between that and his ranch work (which he'd done most of his life) they settled in to stay. Originally the family hailed from the Ozark Mountains of Missouri. Grandfathers on both sides of Robert's family had been Baptist Ministers and ranchers.

Ben Moseley and wife strived hard to raise their family of five (four boys, David the oldest, Harold, Robert, Wayne and one sister, Rosemary) in the depressed era when hard times hit the county with the great Depression of the late 1920s. Young Robert's childhood was extremely tough, filled with hardships. Money was very scarce and food was slim for most they, were fortunate in what they could grow. The youngsters grew up never forgetting the hardships.

People that knew young Robert in his youth would say that he was always a bit tight-lipped about himself and his family life. We his fans can also appreciate that fact as well as we attempt to reveal some light into the life and times of this man we call hero of the silver screen. Those folks that knew him claim that even as a young man he had always been as straight arrow about life as anyone could be. Also, we learn that he could also be stubborn to a fault, unswerving and determined in whatever endeavor to would attempt to pursue.

Growing older, he longed to be a commercial fisherman. But still just a young boy he would have to curb those ambitions and settle for more realistic options like cattle ranching. As a prelude to this endeavor he had joined the *FFA* (*Future farmers of America*) while still young and in school, he would now have the opportunity to raise and show cattle at the local County Fairs.

During these Depression years, this was indeed a problem trying to obtain money to get a start in this cattle business. To show how determined to succeed he was at this, we learn that somehow he had talked the owner of a prize calf (he had been eying) into letting him have it to raise, and repay him later when he took it to auction. He did just that, resulting in a prize-winning bull that he had raised himself. He paid back every last penny of the deal, with interest. This sort of determination would stand throughout his career and life.

> When Robert was but fifteen, a friend of the family Jim Murphy made a bow for him from lemonwood. He cherished this magnificent piece of workmanship. He continued to bow-hunt whenever he could find the time, though time was precious in those days for the Moseley's, just trying to scratch out a living. He

continued to help with the ranch chores and also worked through his formative years fairly steady at cattle ranching as a hand.

Older now he worked a stint as a telephone lineman prior to his navy enlistment days. In his off-time what there was of it, he busied himself taking classes at the *Bakersfield Junior College* on Animal Husbandry, which was unfortunately cut short when the World War II broke out. Like so many other young men of day (including his older brother David) eager to defend their home country in this time of peril, Robert enlisted to serve his country.

To Robert's good fortune, he was stationed in the San Diego area. At the time, the war department had a massive promotion for the armed forces under way. Moseley had previously acquired his lifesaving methods and water sports accommodations back while in school and summer camp, he was an ideal choice for doing a stint as a lifeguard for naval duty at North Island. For nearly a year he helmed this job for the navy when one day, their publicity department asked him to do some photographs for their Monthly Service Magazine publication called "The North Islander." He was happy to oblige them and did so without fanfare as he would enjoy the little diversion from his normal routine job. He appeared on the back cover of the next issue posing aboard a decommissioned naval ship, "The Star of India."

While sitting at a drugstore counter, sipping a cup of coffee, Hollywood talent agent Helen Ainsworth leafed through this very same publication. Coming to the last page, she turned the magazine over and placed it back on the counter so as to resume her coffee and donut. She then noticed the picture on the back and the great looking young man that was in it. This, she thought to herself, was a very photogenic young man. She knew, almost without thinking, how much in demand at that time Hollywood was for a young man with his looks and appeal.

Ms. Ainsworth began writing letters until contact with this Robert Moseley was made. Afterward, a meeting was set up so he could be introduced to the then young *Selznick Studios* executive, Henry Wilson. Wilson in turn would then introduce this young Moseley to David O. Selznick himself head of the Studio. Although he had to return to his duties for the navy almost immediately, Ainsworth on the other hand having him as her signed client, went to work badgering *Selznick Studios* about her newest find. Her persistence eventually paid off. This was 1944 and the Studio was about to go into production on a new film to be called *Since You Went Away.* Starring Claudette Colbert, Jennifer Jones and Joseph Cotton, Selznick himself went so far as to have new scenes written into the script for our young Robert. He also sought special permission that allowed him to use Moseley (on a prearranged seven-day pass) while he was still active to the navy.

Moseley's part was that of a Sailor named Harold Smith. The setting was a quick scene shot in a bowling alley and another one at a train station where he is depicted as a departing GI saying good-bye to his sweetheart. Needless to say, when this film hit the movie houses, the audiences, especially the bobby soxers went wild over the new face of Bob Moseley. Now, having returned back to his regular navy duties, and trying to keep a low profile about all this movie business, his fan mail began piling up as his popularity began to rise.

It was also in 1944 that he met another hunter, Howard Hill. With Howard he learned how to make a laminated bamboo bow and also the art of arrow making. Fast friends with similar interests, they hunted together for some 20 years after that initial meeting. It was an age when quality workmanship counted and fine craftsmen turned out exceedingly supreme hunting bows for wild game taking. Types varied from the laminated bamboo types to the Osage orange long bows. These combined with finely crafted cedar arrow shafts and homemade arrowheads produced some of most accurate, and the finest quality of bow-hunting equipment around. Although Robert's career seems to be moving fast or would be soon, he would always try and make time for his hunting trips.

Almost a year later and while he was still on active duty in the navy, Mr. Selznick once again stepped in between Moseley and the navy. This time though, Selznick saw to an early out of Moseley's military commitment to the navy. Immediately following Robert's service discharge, Selznick sent Henry Willson* to find Bob and sign him to a film contract with the Studio. Wilson was also given orders to enroll him into a crash course of drama and acting.

With all this going on, a name change seemed now in order. Ms. Ainsworth came to the rescue here as she is the one credited with coming up with the name, Guy Madison. The guy part was taken from a real life friend of Bob's that he so admired a great deal. The Madison half was borrowed

---

* Henry Willson, it was a known at the time that Willson was a closet gay according to rumors, and had a habit of incorporating his work and pleasures as one. It was understood, although never discussed widely that any young aspiring male actors being placed in his charge *could* fall victim to his lecherous advances that usually began under the pretext of helping said young protégé.

Being straight arrow, our young Moseley wasn't going for this type of help and evidently made that clear from the start. Consequently, we believe that Willson's involvement in helping Moseley had cooled considerably after that. This may have helped in the later decision by Selznick Studios to loan out the Moseley's contract indiffintely.

from a billboard sign advertisement for *Dolly Madison Cupcakes,* and so the name Guy Madison, we notice that Willson had actually taken credit for this, but it wasn't true.

David Selznick realizing the public's demand for a new good-looking, screen image was solely responsible for rushing this still green young actor into the limelight. He was set for a starring role opposite actress Dorothy McGuire for the 1946 film entitled *Till the End of Time.* Some of the more popular and experienced supporting cast members of this film included Robert Mitchum and Bill Williams.

Later *Selznick Studios* began a strategic move, previously done on new beginner stars. That strategy was of loaning out of the particular individual to other studios so as to make other films for them so as to acquire further acting experience. They seemed to be vying for time in hopes that he would eventually learn his craft well enough and/or become popular enough that in time they would again exercise their contractual rights and pull him in for one of their films once again. Madison's popularity though, continued to rise and with the help of his very capable agent Ms. Ainsworth, Madison would continue making films seemingly one after another.

Although by 1946 he had studied hard and was adamant about his acting, he figured that stage work was where the learning should begin. Thus he devoted much of his off time toward that endeavor. His stage debut came at the *Laguna Playhouse* for the play "Dear Ruth." The next season found him at the *La Jolla Playhouse.* Next year he began a tour with "John Loves Mary."

Meanwhile renting a modest house from an enlisted buddy, who was still in the service, his younger brother Wayne, still in school, was out for the summer came to live with him. Wayne was soon to become a navy man himself, but for the time being he would help his older brother enjoy some fruits of his recent labors. They enjoyed fishing together with a new sixteen foot skiff that Guy had built himself. In addition there was always the occasional hunting trip, so Guy could continue pursuing his interests in the art of Archery that he so loved.

As a much liked young actor about Hollywood, Madison would enjoy the friendship of many other young talented actors of the day. Probably one of his closest friends during this period in time was Rory Calhoun. Calhoun spoke once in interview on Madison saying, "I call Guy Madison, Tiger because that is what he reminds me of, a sleeping tiger. He's quiet, but all the time he knows what's going on and just how to handle it."

Calhoun and Madison met during those early years at *Selznick Studios.* They liked one another's company from the start, and had similar interests. When the six-foot-one Madison first met and sized up the 6'-3" Calhoun with the jet-black hair he called him Blackie. Calhoun also as avid archer, and along with newfound friend Madison they enjoyed many a great time together during those early years in their off-hours, fishing and hunting small game. Years later Rory Calhoun and then wife, Lita Baron Calhoun, continued to remain true-blue and loyal friends to Madison.

It was while studying drama at *Luther Lester's Drama School* at *Paramount Studios* that Madison met a young actress soon to become his wife. Her name was Gail Russell. Already an established young actress, the extremely beautiful Miss Russell had in turn taken a liking our young Mr. Madison as well. He was falling in love and it was apparent the feelings were mutual. For nearly four years he courted Miss Russell before finally popping the question to which she readily accepted his hand in marriage, that was 1949.

Courtesy of personal collection

Meanwhile, during those years Madison continued to churn out films like, *Texas, Brooklyn and Heaven* (1948) and *Honeymoon* (1949) all while still on loan to other Studios. Selznick still owned his contract and he was still obligated to *Selznick Studios* while under that contract. He got to thinking that possibly he was being used and that he could do better out from under this Selznick umbrella. So with this feeling of being used still bearing on his mind, he sought to buy up his own contract from the Studio and then struck off on his own.

With things slowing down for our Guy Madison almost as fast as they had begun, he began doing stints on the radio. One of the shows he was involved in at that time was a 1949 airing of "Wild Bill Hickok" with Madison voicing the lead as Hickok. Madison took to his new role and thought perhaps this might just be the thing for a new market in home entertainment called television. Working under this assumption that audiences might just approve of this type of show, he and agent Ms Ainsworth began to lay the ground work to set this idea in motion, bringing this revamped radio show into the homes and TV screens across America. According to Madison they did some 300 shows which spanned a period of three years. Meanwhile he continued to work and make other films as were offered to him.

Guy Madison soon was under contract with *Monogram Studios*. The *William Brody Production Company* was the executive producers for the new show. It was to be called *The Adventures of Wild Bill Hickok* and it would consist of 120 episodes at approximately 26 to 28 minutes each. Half of the shows were filmed in black and white while the other half were in color. The show sponsors for the entire run into the future year of 1959 was *Kellogg's Breakfast Cereals Company.*

Madison would star in the role of US Marshall James Butler Hickok. He commented years later during a magazine interview that he'd been advised against taking this role for television, but that he had stuck to his guns." Speaking for his many fans out there, we're certainly glad he did. He went on to say that, "For some time since I came to Hollywood, I felt completely at ease from the minute we started shooting."

For his on-screen partner, it had been prearranged to use actor Burl Ives. However, here again agent Helen Ainsworth had stepped in with her advice, worth and wisdom and suggested using actor Andy Devine for the part instead. Devine would portray Jingles B. Jones, Hickok's comical sidekick. These two would team up every week for the viewing audience while riding the ranges and righting the wrongs of the badmen who would cross their paths. Long will be remembered was Devine's classic line as the gravel-voiced Jingles hollered after Hickok as they rode off into the sunset, "Hey! Wild Bill, wait for me!"

Courtesy of personal collection

Andy Devine once interviewed said, "When I first meet Guy, I found it extremely hard to get along with him. As far as our work was concerned there was no problem. But I'm the kind of fellow who loves to talk to people, get to know them real well. Call it nosey, call it chummy, call it what you want . . . but it didn't get me anywhere with him. Most subjects he wouldn't discuss at all. About the rest he was hesitant. The only exception was hunting and fishing."

The character of Bill Hickok on his fine Appaloosa horse named Buckshot along with partner Jingles on his trusty steed, Joker easily won the hearts of many a youngster growing up during this period in time. We might also add here that it was not all boys who were avid fans of the show and its pair of hard riding, defenders of law and order, but young girls of the era were also considered huge fans as well.

During the early 1950s saw a new realm of entertainment that had come on the scene called 3-D pictures, short for three-dimensional. This type of sensationalism on screen was becoming the rage. During preproduction of a new Western film soon to be released in this new mode of cinema viewing achievement called *Natural Vision 3-D* by *Warner Brothers.* Steve Trilling the manager for productions at the time had an eleven-year-old daughter named Susan who was well aware of her father's recent problem of trying to pick a leading man for this new film. Being a big fan of the Madison's television show she suggested to her father, "Why don't you use Wild Bill Hickok?"

This suggestion resulted in Trilling borrowing some film footage from the weekly series and showing it to Jack Warner. Warner immediately responded by saying, "Go get him!" Thus it came to pass, Guy Madison was accepted for the role in the film just from his presence seen on the film clips alone and no screen test was even made. This film would become Madison's second big chance to rejuvenate his already faltered movie career.

When Guy Madison emerged before the audiences in the feature showing of this first of its kind 3-D Western called *Charge at Feather River*, he came across as calm and cool as any other of the great actors of the day would have. The film was a tremendous success. Critically acclaimed for its special effects and sharp crisp *Warner Bros* color, this film was definitely the one that put Guy Madison's movie career back up in lights. Warner had already signed him for his next picture that was to go into production within the next few months it was to be called *The Command* another 3-D Western.

It was during this period in time that Madison and agent Ms Ainsworth had formed their own production company, *Romson Productions*. Along with his brother Wayne in the background they began taking some of the old *Wild Bill Hickok* shows reediting them and compiling them into feature films that would now be sold to overseas markets and shown to audiences abroad. This meant another good thing for Madison in that now he would be getting European exposure, and unbeknownst to him at the time, this would eventually come as another advantage to him in his later career.

The year was now 1954 which not only brought him his second feature film with *Warner Bros* but also his *Wild Bill Hickok* television series had been nominated for an EMMY Award for the Best Western Adventure Series. This brought joy on one hand but on the other a sadder note, also a divorce would be in the cards from his actress wife, Gail Russell, after only five years. After having been separated for over a year, Madison once stated that for various reasons they just couldn't seem to make a go of it. He went on to add, "I have only appreciation for the wonderful years she made possible. I have no regrets."

During those *Wild Bill Hickok* television years, Madison also made some fifteen movies as well during that period. Shortly after completion of *The Command* picture, he was signed to do a long-term contract with *20th Century Fox*. During his predivorce separation from Gail Russell, and prior to the divorce final period, Guy began to open up a bit to enjoy some of the fruits of his labors. After all, he was back on top again. The pickup truck he used to sport around Hollywood in was now gone and a sleek new *Lincoln* Capri automobile took its place. He was seen around town now wearing tailor made suits. Joined a golf club in *Lakeside* and ordered himself a custom-made .375 Magnum rifle for a big game hunt trip to Africa with friend Howard Hill.

During that separation period and while dating some of the more prominent women of Hollywood during that time, none seem to really strike a chord with him. One of the more impressive women he dated had been Barbara Warner, daughter of producer Jack Warner. However, a much better match for him was yet another woman who seemed to share his love of the out of doors and of sports. Her name was Sheila Connolly.

This aspiring film starlet turned actress was born in 1930 of Irish stock parents living in Brooklyn, New York. Due to the illegal immigration status of her father at the time, some two years later the family of five girls and one brother would return to Ireland in 1932. Her father was eventually to become the well-known Irish Jockey, Timothy Connolly. They wouldn't return again to New York until 1946. It was then that the young Sheila would attempt to break into modeling as a career which eventually led her to Hollywood as an aspiring actress. Getting her bearings in Hollywood had been hard at first for a country girl raised around horses and animals for most of her formative years. Sheila and Guy met at a Sportsman's Boat Show being held at the *Pan Pacific Auditorium* there in Los Angeles.

The tall, good-looking Madison, Sheila found was quite different from most men she had met, especially of the Hollywood type. He was more down to earth, a serious type of "man's man" that relished his off time and adored the out of doors and a completely professional actor who worked hard for his place in the industry.

Courtesy of personal collection

After a whirlwind courtship which ensued, there was the usual meeting of the family and friends (actor Rory Calhoun and his wife, Lita, were still very much the greatest of friends) the romance blossomed. Later in October of 1954, with Guy's signed waver for divorce in his hand finally signed from Gail, he invited Sheila to a celebration dinner date at the famous *La Rue Restaurant,* there on Sunset Boulevard. Frequented by the stars it was a posh place and they managed to sit at a table next to Grace Kelly and Clark Gable. It was an exciting night for the two young lovers and it was here that Guy purposed to Sheila for her hand in marriage. She accepted as they were by that time madly in love.

This impromptu proposal led to a sudden elopement. They flew to Juarez, Mexico, where the divorce papers were finalized on record and then minutes later they were married on October 26, 1954. No one knew of their intentions or of their whereabouts except Madison's business manager Charlie Trezona, who had quietly kept their plans all to himself. This was a marriage seemingly made in heaven for the two lovebirds. Sheila loved mostly the same things in life as did Guy. They both loved being out of doors and she came to enjoy the many hunting and fishing trips they took together. Eventually their marriage was blessed with children. First came along Bridget Catherine in October 1955 (Rory Calhoun was named the Godfather). Erin Patricia followed the next year being born on July of 1956. Last but not least to be sure would be Dolly Anne Madison, although her birth would come later in May, 1957.

After the birth of Erin in 1956, good things continued to transpire for the joyous Madison household. After some twelve years of being the dreamy "bobbysoxer" box office idol now turned into the steely-eyed Wild Bill Hickok / actor turned businessman, we find that Madison had seemingly sprouted his own formula for success. This in turn led him on a long, stable career by systematically separating himself from the Hollywood scene and his working environment, from his home life, his family and his hobbies, which of course was hunting and fishing. In addition, he also enjoyed making things out of wood. Not only pieces of furniture but also the arrows he used for hunting trips. Even to his first boat, the sixteen-foot skiff he'd built himself.

Courtesy of Bridget Madison

His own production company *Romson* was finished filming its latest movie, *The Hard Man* soon to be released in the theaters. Forming his own company several years back had been his decision that incorporated his longtime friend and agent Helen Ainsworth who was now head producer for the company. *The Hard Man* picture was the fourth of a six-picture deal for *Columbia Pictures* and one of three of the six that he had agreed to star in himself. A success in life, at the age of thirty-five years old and a hard and fast veteran of the Hollywood machine, he was sometimes still standoffish to others and seemed hard to get to know.

Madison had a general philosophy about life in general, that was equally as straightforward as his attitudes were. He once stated, "I believe in the Golden Rule, and I always do to others as I would like them to do to me." His goals were always clear-cut and out in the open. He only wanted the utmost for his family, wife and children. He always intended to remain in the field of acting and provide diversity for the pleasure of his audiences and fans. However, at the same time he continued to provide any measures that would keep his independent productions rolling on an even keel. One of his most enthusiastic supporters, always rooting in the wings was his wife, Sheila. Having been a model herself before becoming an actress still continued to model on occasion. First and foremost, though, she was always the devoted mother and wife.

Guy and young Bridget courtesy of Bridget Madison

She went on to explain that, Guy was always a bit too serious about life in general, but with the children around in years to come, he seemed to take on a sense of humor he didn't have before. This teamed with his overflowing generosity, even coupled with his own unique style of keep-to-himself personality he was always extremely well liked as a performer and deeply thought of by his close-knit circle of family and friends.

We fans could certainly testify as to his unique style of standoffish personality where his past film work was concerned. In as much as Andy Devine once said about Guy, "While Guy is generous, he hates to accept thanks." This would hold true and seemingly is what probably prompted fanzine magazine Editor, Tim Ferrante of his popular *Westerns all'Italiana!,* of years later to make a few comments about Guy's attitude toward his past European film work, during a luncheon interview of November 1986 with the actor. Tim wrote, "As this interview and lunch drew to a close, I couldn't help but marvel at the man who has supplied so many, many hours of enjoyment. I get the feeling that Guy Madison does not grasp the entire impact he has had on the movie and television public. He has been admired for over three decades. The folks here at *Westerns all'Italiana!* Will forever hold him in their highest esteem?"

But alas, film work for our Guy Madison failed to remain all peaches and cream. As things began to fade out for Guy once again in the late 1950s, with his last US film *Jet over the Atlantic* (1960). It starred Virginia Mayo and George Raft. Madison's role was that of Brett Murphy, but not a starring role by any means. Now he was facing a slipping film career once again. Things had been going great guns so long, was about to erupt. Yet another dilemma, his long-running popular television series contract was up for renewal. It, however, was being dropped by the original sponsor, the *Kellogg's Cereal Company.*

It was hard to believe, let alone imagine that the pictured characters of Wild Bill and Jingles would no longer grace the boxes of *Sugar Pop's* brand cereals. Taken completely by surprise at this newest career junction, he claimed there was nothing waiting in the wings at the time. For the first time in a decade, he was now faced with having to go out and find acting jobs. From the other producers/directors he was getting a cold shoulder from Hollywood. He had seemingly developed a reputation for being hard to work with, since he had a session with a director who supposedly he told off after the director cursed at him. A certain amount of jealously had to be figured in there with his rapid successful advance from matinee idol to mogul. Now on the way down once again, he was probably subject of all manner of ridicule from others in the business.

Madison's wife, Sheila, and her sister had just recently returned from a European tour that included Rome and surrounding cities with friends. While there in Rome, they had met an agent whom she felt might do Guy's collapsing career some good as a prospect for work there in Europe. Still having this agent's card, she offered it to Guy. With his *Wild Bill Hickok* feature film compilations having been shown in the European theaters for quite some time, the name Guy Madison was nearly as popular there then as it once had been back in the States.

A meet was set up in Rome with those to be involved. Guy had asked Sheila if she and the girls would join him for this trip to Rome, since he'd never been there before. She agreed and they all flew over settling in at the *Excelsior Hotel.* Sheila promptly moved out after only a week citing it was no place for children. Guy found them accommodations at a villa outside the city owned by a Contessa who often rented out to film stars. She and the children remained there while Guy went with cast and crew to Yugoslavia for the shoot. He had asked but she refused to go with them citing once again it was no place for children.

Things had been a might touchy in their family life for some time as Guy seemed to be more insistent on things being his way much of the time, which often seemed to leave poor Sheila in a world of her own, just her and the children. She had desired for some time to resume her acting, possibly to do a film with Guy. But he wouldn't hear of it and flatly refused. Thing had been different before the girls came, since his ideals in upbringing had taught him from an early age that the woman's place was there in the home taking care of the children. This however wasn't sitting well with a career-minded wife. Guy would always ask her to join them on the ever frequent hunting/fishing trips, but she felt he had no more interests in such things other than the children in her world. Much too often she was left alone with her thoughts as she had been this time in Rome.

The work was indeed the opening Guy needed. The year was 1960 and after the necessary contacts were signed, he was off to Yugoslavia for filming of his first Euro movie. Once there much of his off-time was spent rambling through the woods and mountains with his bow and arrows, hunting. When traveling abroad, he always took along his hunting gear as he never knew when that chance opportunity of a lifetime might happen his way. The film was called *The Slave of Rome*. The star was Italian beauty Rosanna Podesta. Storyline has to do with Valerio (Madison) leading Roman troops invade Gallia by order of Julius Caesar because of a broken treaty. They capture Anthea (Podesta) Gaul princess who eventually falls for her captor Valerio. When released it well received throughout internationally. It was soon to become one of the then biggest box office draws of the *Peplum* (Sword and Sandal) epic productions that era.

When Madison returned to Rome to collect the family for their trip home he found Sheila by then had made up her mind in triplicate. That trial separation once they had talked about was now on for sure, and she was filing legally. He remained there in Rome while she and the girls set off for home. Madison was immediately given another picture contract while there. It was called *The Women Prisoners of Devils Island* (1962). Storyline deals with women brought from France to a Penal colony on an island off the coast of South American. Madison stars as ship's Captain Henri Valliere as the new overseer and tries to stop the abuse. One woman (Mercier) just brought in is there looking for her sister, she and Valliere eventually fall in love. Also, another subplot about hidden gold is at the root of it all.

Later returning home shortly after the shoot was done, he was hopeful in doing a new *Zane Grey Theater* episode that was being produced by his agent Helen Ainsworth. Since he was and had been her main marketable star, having to resort now to Europe for work, she had been doing her level best to find her actor a steady television series that would again bring him home again to the States to stay. She had quickly churned out a new story, which she felt would fit him to a tee.

Guy and agent Helen Ainsworth from personal collection

She had high hopes for Guy when she submitted the new story for production reviews. Actually, it was accepted and underwent a teleplay sprucing up by Herb Meadows, and was to be directed by Harry Keller. The MTV show pilot was to be called *Jericho*. Ms. Ainsworth had at this time become very ill and wasn't up to her usual fighting self for her clients. However, this episode pilot did get made and while Madison was in town for the filming she tried not to let on that anything was wrong.

Back home here in the States, things seemed to continue to falling apart for our actor. His home life, had if anything had gotten worse. Sheila claims that upon his return she had tried to make things work but to no avail. With him away working abroad, his once happy home life had ceased. The trial separation for Sheila and Guy, who both had jointly agreed was still in effect prior to his returning to Rome. That separation unfortunately would only lead eventually to their divorce. But for the time being, pending obligations forced his immediate return to Europe and another *Peplum* film for which the contracts had already been signed. This next film would star American lead actor Jack Palance. The film was called *Sword of the Conqueror* (1961) with Palance as Alboino, Eleanora Rossi-Drago as Rosmunda, and Guy Madison was Amalchi the evil backstabber second in command who lusted after Rosmundo for himself as they both vie for her heart and hand in marriage.

Seemingly to make matters worse yet, Madison now found out that his longtime agent, loyal friend, confidant and co producer within his own production company was in ill health. Helen Ainsworth, who had believed in him so much as a young, aspiring actor, was now found to be stricken with cancer. Ms. Ainsworth had been an inspiration to many up and coming young actors in Hollywood. She had, up to now, been an extremely active person, full of life and ready to fight the studio moguls at the drop of a hat for her clients. Married late in life, Mrs. Helen Ainsworth Shumate was suffering; her health had deteriorated to the point that she finally was bedridden at the age of 59. Madison was summoned home again. Regretfully she passed away on August 18, 1961.

Unfortunately, Guy and Ms. Ainsworth's hopes for the success of the *Jericho* TV pilot failed to blossom and Madison had to return once again to Rome, this time with an apprehensible feeling gnawing at his insides, back in Europe he did have a few more new picture contracts awaiting his return, which was some relief. Other than his three lovely, school-age daughters, there wasn't much left in Hollywood for him at this time.

Madison already having contracts signed, turned in another two period dramas before jumping ship for the Westerns one being, *The Executioner of Venice* (1963) Lex Barker stars as San Ricco's son of the Venice Doge; Guy Madison costars as Don Rodrigo Zeno, the evil Grand Inquisitor (Master) of Venice who is eventually overthrown and publicly beheaded. The other was, *Gentlemen of the Night* (1963) Madison stars as Massimo a war lord returning to Venice from fighting with Turks discovers a new evil Doge of Venice has now married his former love, Katarina. All hell is about to break loose.

During this period in time the once one-picture trips he had previously been taking back in the earlier 1960s, were now over. His stay soon evolved into a twelve-year long stint. During this long stay he did exceptionally well in the international film market. His films were always well received and he was and still is extremely well remembered as a fine person and great actor.

During this period in time and unbeknownst to Madison, he would become one of the main actors instrumental in the success of the newest rage of film phenomenon so affectionately dubbed by its many fans as the *Spaghetti* Westerns film genre of Europe. The name *Spaghetti* specifically pertaining to the origin of the Italian Western film genre was gradually taking the place of the now slipping, once highly regarded *Peplum* epics. These *Peplums* had dominated the overseas film markets since mid-1950.

Now this new Western genre of film, still in its infant stages, that seemingly began with earlier European attempts at bringing somewhat of a semblance to our US-made Westerns, to the European audiences. Some of the early attempts were British, some Spanish, others of mixture of input of European origin, these were called co productions. Meaning they might have

German, Italian, Spanish or Yugoslavian, or some even US monies involved to form coproduction values to get these movies made and distributed to not only European, but also aimed for US markets. This type of production values we can directly attribute to Alberto Grimaldi, friend and one time Lawyer of director Sergio Leone. Grimaldi would soon become coproducing executive extrodinare in the years to come with his *PEA* Company.

Once in Europe, figuring to stay awhile, Guy Madison joined with the likes of ex-*Tarzen* star Lex Barker and others on this newfound Euro bandwagon of films. Madison costarred in his first German Euro Western opposite Barker for the film called *Apaches Last Battle* (1963). With this film Barker portrays character Old Shatterhand, and co stars with his Indian sidekick Chief Winnetou portrayed by Frenchman, Pierre Brice. Madison's role was that of a trouble-making cavalry officer who is trying to undermine peace attempts between the Comanche and the Apache Indians.

Before the new Westerns genre could shift into high gear, Madison fell back with making a few other period dramas before he would totally immerse himself in the Westerns. Madison also team up with actor Ray Danton and costarred with him in two films of the East Indian adventure variety. Both films were released for 1964 and called *Sandokan against the Leopard of Sarawak* and *Sandokan Fights Back*. In both films Danton* starred as the hero Sandokan with his friend and sidekick Captain Yanez (Madison). These *Indie* Thuggie sect films were quite popular of that era, although not readily seen in the United States, the European audiences were quite taken with them all the same, and Guy Madison's international popularity continued to grow in that respect.

Madison would now officially embark on this new *Spaghetti* phenomenon trail during the year of 1964 with his starring role as Wyatt Earp in *Duel at Rio Bravo* a.k.a. *Gunman of the Rio Grande*. This film was a Spanish/ French/ Italian coproduction. This movie would put Madison's name back on top of the billboards as he now returned to his leading character roles. The storyline dealt with lawman Earp who goes undercover as a gunslinger called Laramie to clean up a corrupted Mexican American border mining town.

---

* Ray Danton had been extremely popular and a frequently seen face on American TV during the late 1950s. He is probably best known on the big screen as the star of the bio/film, *The Rise and fall of Legs Diamond* (1960). A 1930's style gangster film and another called *The George Raft Story* released in 1961. Danton having a yen to direct and to produce films of his own wound up in Italy during the early '60s and eventually started his own production company there in Rome.

It was also that year, when Italian director Sergio Leone coming directly from the *Peplum* era himself would team up with American TV actor, Clint Eastwood. Together they would be the pair that would launch the *Spaghetti* Western genre of film into a proper orbit all its own. Other American actors would join the throng, some having been victims of slipping career problems, others with hopes of newfound stardom within the international film industry. Then there were others who were just seeking work, be it whatever, they would come flocking to the European shores.

Even Madison's old friend Rory Calhoun even ventured over to get involved with one of these Westerns, as a favor mainly to displaced American filmmaker Sidney Pink. That film was *Finger on the Trigger* (1965). It starred Calhoun and James Philbrook, directed by Pink and filmed in Spain with Spanish/ Italian/ US coproduction backing. Earlier in the '60s Calhoun had been involved in one *Peplum* epic called *The Colossus of Rhodes* (1961). His director at that time had been a young Italian named Sergio Leone, believe it!

Also during the latter part of 1964 and early '65 Madison would return to the adventure genre making another of the *Indie* Thuggie films called *Mystery of Thug Island,* a.k.a. *Snake Hunter Strangler*. It starred Madison as Souyadhana who was leading a band of mercenaries sent into India to exterminate a vicious sect. This film went through several title changes also being called *Mysteries of the Black Jungle,*(1965) *actually was found to be the same film*, it costarred Inge Schoner as Ada and Giacomo Rossi Stuart as Tremal-Naik (the snake hunter), also with Peter Van Eyck as the British Captain MacPearson. This was an Ital/ Monaco/ W. Ger coproduction was directed by Luigi Capuano. The Music score sometime credited to Carlo Rustichelli was found to be wrong, as researched by music Guru Don Trunick who found it to actually be Pino Donaggio.

Madison's next adventure film was called *The Adventurer of Tortuga,* a.k.a. *Cold Steel for Tortuga,* a.k.a. *Kidnapped to Mystery Island* (1965). Madison stars here as Alfonso di Montelimar, the evil Governor of Santa Cruz. Rik Battaglia costars as Pirate Pedro Valverde, and Nadia Gray as Rosita. Landing Spaniards are battling with North American Indians on the isle of Tortuga. It was directed by Luigi Capuano. Actually a subplot is going on here more suited to the latter title *Kidnapped.* It seems Pirate Valverde is kidnapping wealthy women for ransoming their Dowries so as to finance trips to Tortuga, but has now fallen for an Indian Princess.

Madison broke off for a while now with Europe and went for another German Western early in 1965 called *Viva Gringo,* a.k.a. *Legacy of the Incas* This was one of those West German/ Italian/ Spanish coproductions that was more in the adventure mode, although nevertheless still a Western by genre. Like the *Winnetou* films, this one was based on another of German novelist Karl May's stories. It was filmed on locations in Cuzo, Peru, SA, and Spain. Finally a great DVD issue (English dubbed) of this film has been issued from *Koch Media*, Germany.

Back again to Italy and Madison's next Western called *Five Giants from Texas* (1965). This was an Italian/ Spanish coproduction and a true Western in every sense of the word. Back in the saddle again, Madison starred as John Latimore obviously a Texan and brother to one Jim Latimore who had married into a wealthy ancestral ranching family in Mexico. His brother has turned up dead and John has arrived with help to avenge his brother and care for the widow Rosaria (Monica Randall [Randel]). A basic revenge theme here, dished up quite well. While working his European stint, Madison would only venture home to the States once a year and that being at Christmas time. He then would return back to Italy for more work while things were hopping.

Hopping, they were indeed! During those ten years from 1965 through to 1975, the European filmmakers would churn out hundreds of these hot-off-the-press *Spaghetti* Western films. Entertaining, some were but unfortunately others were bad copies of others and the genre became extremely repetitious after a while as it began to fade by the early '70s. Also by 1970, the basic Western were reverting to comedic spoofs of its original self. Though still entertaining in some respect to some, the older standard versions were always the best in my humble opinion.

Madison continued to endure his off-time away from family and moviemaking by engrossing himself with his bow hunting, and also in the bow and arrow making, for which he had set up a small shop there in his rooms in Rome. Occasionally, he would venture out but not often, choosing to keep more to himself studying his scripts and working on his hobbies. A blessed call from his daughters would cheer him up but then the emptiness would set in afterward.

> By the mid-1960s, while there in Rome, Madison had made acquaintance with a beautiful Italian lady. This friendly liaison soon turned to romance and as the feelings were mutual it blossomed. Madison, however, tended to steer clear of any matrimonial involvement fearing that this might once again bring an end to the current happiness they both were experiencing. On September 19, 1967, they were blessed with a fine baby boy. They named him Robert (Roberto) Madison. Finally, a son was brought into the world for our Guy Madison. We're quite sure he was beaming with joy from the bottom of his heart.

The new Western genre seemed to have given some a chance at things they probably never would have had, or the opportunity to do back in the

States. Opportunities like writing a story or script, doing technical advising, directing, voice dubbing, and / or the art and craft of just being able to try different aspects of acting was a huge learning experience and playing field. For many it simple made better actors out of those who were border line before. For others it taught them how to hone their craft and make their lives better for it. But for others, unfortunately and there were a few, that had gone the wrong way and tended to let the good life get the best of them, eventually paying dearly for it as some did. Too much, too soon, some even lost their lives for it in the end. Mostly though, I can honestly say were better for their experiences in Europe, and Guy Madison we feel was one of those.

Even for an experienced actor such as Madison who had mostly always portrayed the hero, a good guy in the majority of his film work, now had the opportunity to let his hair down and become the bad guy for a change if he so desired. Much encouragement was given these experienced actors, much like dealing with thoroughbred horses, the Italian directors tended to give them their head as it were. They recognized the fact that most of these actors came with a vast knowledge about making these Western films and relied much on their knowledge and skills to improve their own techniques and style. A hand in hand effort on everyone's part was used and the results were sometimes tremendous. To some it was just another job. To others possibly the money wasn't quite up to what they felt was their standard. But each actor's popularity grew through cinema audience appeal and we're quite sure their monetary box office values grew respectively as well. Besides, the opportunity to live and work and enjoy the European culture firsthand would have been an enormous plus during those years. It seems that of those actors that did go and did get involved, their fans still treated them with as much respect if not more but without the clique-orientated regime of the "make or break" Hollywood sect watchdogs.

During past interviews and according to one set made during the *WAI! (Westerns . . . All'Italiana!)* Fanzine interview, Madison claimed to have done quite a bit of technical advising, even some second-unit work while on some of these films he was involved with. It seems the Italians loved to see their American actors performing their own stunts, just to observe their technique and style (also to see if these past pampered movie stars from the United States could cut the mustard) This should however, while not take anything away from the Italian and Spanish stuntmen themselves, who as far as the work goes, those stuntmen would do virtually anything for money. Borderline crazy would more justly some it up.

Also we've read from several interview sources that Madison claimed to have never dubbed his own voice for the Italian films he worked in. We do find this very much the case for most of the actors in these Italian / Spanish films. Only mainstream films were likely to go through a NYC dubbing session. However, we might add the filmmakers did seem to go out of their way in an attempt to locate a dubbing artist who did sound very much like him for the majority of his Euro films.

According to the *WAI!* Madison article, when an "All Quiet" was called for on the set, it was near about an impossible thing to happen. He said the Italians, Spaniards and Germans just couldn't stop shouting at one another long enough to cinch a good take. So the actors, such as he, would be directed to count to ten, et cetera when it was their turn to say their lines. Thus the lip movement was thusly recorded and everything they shot was post-synced afterward. Makes sense if we think about it with all those foreign actors on the set at the same time. Besides the Italians had a law on record for the Industry which allowed no direct sound recording while filming, thus the dubbing functions that would take place later.

Of the same token, the directors could use this cute little dubbing trick to their advantage with actor and actresses of multi nationalities that spoke different languages, or had heavy accents, or even those who had trouble remembering their lines was also in the clear without too severe a problem. Afterall these films were being targeted to points all over the world, so for other languages, all that had to be done was to insert the proper dialogue sync and they had a new release for that part of the world and that audience.

Another of Madison's more popular Euro Westerns was the 1967 *Winchester for Hire* a.k.a. *Payment in Blood.* The storyline wasn't a whole lot different than others of the "Don't let the war die" theme / formula that some of these Westerns followed during this period of the genre. Here Madison portrays Colonel Blake. Storyline: Has to do with marauding attacks by Blake's renegade band of ex-soldiers, but when undercover agent Stuart is sent in to investigate, he finds it's actually the lure of hidden war treasure is the real motive behind the twisted Blake attacks.

Popular television actor and teenage heartthrob (although himself a good ways past his teenage years at the time) of the 1950's show, *77 Sunset Strip,* actor Edd "Kookie" Byrnes* then freshly cut loose from *Warner Bros*

* Edd Byrnes remained in Italy only long enough to turn out three of these *Spaghetti* Westerns. Only recently he'd been cut loose from *Warner Bros* being involved in one of those contract disputes with the Studio similar to that some other actors had went through at the time like, Clint Walker and Wayde Preston. Byrnes three Euro Westerns however really didn't seem to revive his sagging career and popularity all that much.

He once made an off-the-wall statement thought, to the effect that if he and the popular Johnny Carson were to walk down the *Via Condotti* in Rome, that his autograph would be asked for ten times over that of Carson's. Evidently was not unlike so many other actors of the day coming over to Europe to cash in on the growing fame of these European films.

For the next year 1967, the worst (we feel) of Madison's three films he did was called *The Bang, Bang Kid.* It also starred the extremely versatile actor, Tom Bosley (in his only genre outing). For this Western fantasy, Madison portrays Bear Bullock a gunman, who's somehow taken over the role of the town boss or king. He's found to be an evil tyrant who drains the townsfolk of their money with exorbitant taxes, making their lives miserable at every turn, and continually bullying them to keep them in line and working at his mine by using a pack of ruthless gunslingers. An inventor character named, Merriweather T. Newberry (Bosely) enters the picture bringing with him his mechanical man invention. He proceeds to help the town by converting this robot of his into a mechanical gunslinger. With the robot he plans to exterminate all of the town's bad guys, thus giving the town back to the people.

Madison began jumping around more between the genres this year, beginning with this one Spy film (the first of three) shot in 1967 for a 1968 release called *LSD: Flesh of the Devil* this was a weird film as it incorporated a new twist for the spy genre adding the *LSD* (a chemically manufactured drug used to get high) theme that had been sweeping the world with young people during this era in time. Madison stars here as Rex Miller government secret agent hot on the trail tracking down a group that had been using LSD as a recruiting means for espionage. It was an Italian production, directed by Albert Zugsmith (Massimo Mida).

During this point in time he ventured to do two more of these spy dramas. His next one was called *The Devilman Story* (1967). Even though this film only had a later 10/22/69 French theater release, we feel it was the original film by director Paul Maxwell (Paolo Bianchini), of which his second film called out below was cut from, and used as the mainstream film with a 1/26/68 Italian release showing date. The storyline of this *Devilman* film has Guy Madison starring as Mike, a Journalist and editor of a popular Science magazine who is on a quest to locate some missing scientific papers that came up missing while doing a story about "Advanced Surgery" by a renowned author/surgeon Professor K. Block. Block has since come up missing. Mike and the Professor's daughter is intent on finding him, but believe he's been snatched.

Madison had some problems with Byrnes in the super-ego department (not saying that Madison himself didn't have a stubborn streak) and they didn't get along well together. But be it courtesy or professionalism, neither actor ever seemed to have spoken bad of the other, at least in public.

The third film of the genre (but what we believe was the second half of the above *Devilman* was called *Superargo and the Faceless Giants.* Also, a spy drama storyline has the star now as Ken Wood (Giovanni Cianfriglia) as a wrestler, superhero crime fighter (complete with the mask, cape and red tights, sort of a Red Superman). Madison's role here is more of a cameo / supporting role as one Professor Wendland. For this film, our superhero is after a mad scientist who is kidnapping wrestling champions and turning them into zombies to do his evil bidding in his quest to take over the world. Both this and the above were Italian productions directed by Paolo Bianchini.*

Back again to the Westerns and what we consider his the best of the genre called *Son of Django* (1968). The storyline concerns a young boy who grows up with his only interest is someday getting revenge for the murder of his father Django, which he had been forced to watch as a helpless little boy. Now grown into a man, Jeff (Gabriele Tinti) was befriended by a traveling, gun-toting preacher called Father Fleming (Madison). As an ex-gunman himself, Fleming attempts to steer the young man toward the path of good and righteousness, but finally the young man's cause wins him over and he agrees to help the lad find the killer and quell his pent up vengeance when he finds him and his murderous gang of killers.

Then for a mid-1968 release, Guy Madison turned up in yet another Western called *The Long Days of Hate* better known as *This Man Can't Die!* Its storyline reverts to the revenge for the murdered family theme. Madison portrays a government agent by the name of Martin Benson. While working undercover, when he returns home to the family ranch he finds the retaliation of the outlaws was to murder his parents and rape of his younger mute sister Jenny along with his younger brother, Daniel (Robert Widmark) (Alberto Dell'Acqua) they vow to get their revenge.

---

* Paolo Bianchini was responsible for another later *SuperArgo* film, a sequel in which Guy Madison did *not* appear in. This Italian / Spanish coproduction 1966 film, *Superargo Contro Diabolikus,* once again starred Ken Wood (Giovanni Cianfriglia) as the crime fighter superhero. Director was Nick Nostro (Paolo Bianchini). Actually this appears to have been the original film, and probably should be viewed first before watching the *Faceless Giants* film. Therein the storyline explains how the masked wrestler actually becomes involved in crime fighting instead of wrestling and his working for the Secret Service as an agent sent to stop Diabolikus and his evil plans to wreck on the global economy but turning uranium into gold.

Madison continued to stay busy during his career period in Europe (make it while he could seem to be his motto) he would make many films outside the Western genre whenever offered.

During the later 1960s, the war film genre had become very popular in Europe. According to his *WAI!* Interview Madison signed on to do three of these commando-type films, which seemed to be gaining in popularity. Other popular genre actors of the now full-steam-ahead *Spaghetti* phenomenon were also engaged in turning out some of these genre war films, although most of the productions would eventually just drift away into oblivion nearly as quickly as they began. The Italian filmmakers used mostly leftover WWII war equipment, tanks, trucks and jeeps that were readily available in Cairo, Egypt for these films as well as shooting locations.

Madison's actually wound up doing five confirmed of these War genre titles. They began with *Hell in Normandy* (1968) an Italian / French coproduction. Madison stars as Captain Murphy and his elite squad is sent in by the cover of night prior to D-day, to take out a big German gun installation set above Omaha Beach. Also stars Erika Blanc as Denise, and Peter Lee Lawrence. This was an Italian / French coproduction directed by Alfonso Brescia.

For his next of the genre, an early 1969 release was *Battle of the Last Panzer.* This low-budget Spanish / Italian coproduction WWII drama starred Giuli Carr, Rafael Hernandez and Stan Cooper (Stelvio Rosi) for this film about a German Tank commander caught behind enemy lines trying to get his one Panzer back to safety of German held territory. Madison's starring role for this film as Captain Lofty was mostly in name only, and is little more than a cameo. The film was scripted and directed by Jose Luis Merino.

Also for another early 1969 release we find Guy Madison is associated with yet another war title called *A Place in Hell.* Madison stars as Major Marc McGreaves war correspondent covering the action during WWII. This was an Italian production, was directed by Giuseppe Vari. Madison's costars were Monty Greenwood (Maurice Poli), Fabio Testi as Charlie and Helene Chanel (Raffaella Carra).

Madison's next war film, for a mid-1969 release was *Hell Commandos.* This time Madison stars as Major Carter. Also, an Italian / Spanish coproduction that was possibly shot back to back with the above *Last Panzer* film from the same director Jose Luis Merino. It does have a different storyline, and is somewhat of a better film bordering more on an espionage type of drama than the above *Panzer* film. It does however still incorporate some of the same war scenes from the *Panzer* flick which makes us believe that the two films were in actuality one in the same film, or perhaps shot back to back.* Music score for both films was by the popular Angelo Francesco Lavagnino. The film costarred Stan Cooper (Stelvio Rosi), Piero Lulli, Manuel Zarzo, and Carala Pravetoni. Others: Alfredo Mayo as the Professor and Giuli Carr.

For Madison's last of the war genre films and a late 1969 release was *The Devils from the War* a.k.a. *War Devils.* This one starred, Raf Baldassarre and Luis Barboo. Guy Madison stars here as "Capt George Vincent' in yet another cameo role, along with veteran American actor John Ireland also in cameo as the general. This was a Spanish / Italian coproduction, written, scripted and directed by Bitto Albertini. Another low-budget effort seen in America only as a video release called *War Devils.* Afterward, Madison returns to the Western genre once again.

Back in the Western groove for a later 1971 Spanish release we find *The Reverend's Colt.* Madison once again portrays a man of the cloth as Reverend Miller. Miller is an ex-gunman, who has mended his ways and is now on the side of good versus evil. Longtime favorite of the Euro films, Richard Harrison costars as the town sheriff Donovan. This little ditty, although a Spanish / Italian coproduction, directed by Leon Klimovsky was a pretty good film. According to a Richard Harrison interview with *WAI!* Tom Betts and Bill Connolly of *Spaghetti Cinema* Fanzines several years back, he stated that Marino Girolami, the film's producer actually did the film's direction.

This Miller in the *Colt* film would tend to be used by the sheriff who, infringing upon their friendship of years back when Miller had been a hired gun and bounty hunter. Both men had been gunman in their more formable years, now in somewhat separate ways as one a sheriff, the other a Preacher. Miller goes along with the sheriff's plan to use him to round up the band of outlaws that had robbed the town bank, and for which he'd mistakenly been accused and nearly lynched but for the sheriff stepping in. In return for his efforts, the bounty collected on the band of outlaws would be his to build the new town church and thus win back the confidence of the townsfolk. Needless we say,

* It was not uncommon for the Italian filmmakers to fool audiences by taking a long-winded film (time-wise) and while in the cutting and editing room, chopping it up, splicing segments of other films archived before. To put it quite simply, to make a separate film altogether then adding a different title, set up for distribution. Italian director Demofilo Fidani (a.k.a. Miles Deem) was one of the true masters of this art of reconstituted filmmaking. One filmmaker that regularly practiced this deception on the general viewing audiences was Luigi Batzella.

Miller does accomplish his task and went on to collect the bounty money and was able to build that fine church. A pretty good entry for the genre, and was Madison's last Western. His was a jam-up job in the role of Miller and as for Richard Harrison,* it always good to see him play once again on screen.

According to rumors sometime around 1971, Madison had informed his fans that he was putting together another film production company of his own and had planned to produce and star in several of his own productions once again, this time in Europe. This we feel never panned out, as no films to our knowledge has ever surfaced since that he starred in and/or directed since the 1950s. It would appear that this might have been one of those bad investments he had spoken of several years back in that *Westerns . . . All'Italiana!* Fanzine interview with Tim Ferrante.

Alias we find our Guy Madison's Euro film career approaching 1973, and he's trying out a different film genre called the *Giallo* (or *Gialli's*) pronounced Yallo (Thrillers). These Italian crime thrillers were becoming quite the rage for the era and have somewhat of a reoccurring popularity even now in the off market DVD's of today. This film made in 1973, but not released until the following year was called *IL Baco Da Seta (The Silkworm).* It starred Nadya (Nadja) Tiller as Emerald Amadier, Evi Marandi and George Hilton (Jorge Hilton) (popular South American actor) and Guy Madison, who does a cameo role as, Robert an old flame of Ms. Amadier.

Madison's brief appearances in a couple of film sequences are mostly one prior to, and the other actually at the ending, which unfortunately leads us to a mass of twisted misunderstandings (probably due to the chopped-up quality of the film available for viewing) where the two old lovebirds are seen together again at the very end arm in arm on a park bench. It seems the entertainer has found herself in a peck of trouble with the authorities when a jewel thief scheme (her own jewels) was being used to help get her feelings of bygone era attention back once again in the newspaper headlines. However, things go badly erupting in murder of her behind the scene partner (a much younger man) who had his eyes and thoughts not on her but on her wealth all along. This had been an Italian Production, directed by Mario Sequi (as Anthony Whiles).

For Guy Madison's last effort from Europe we have located one more for a 1973 released, called *Le Favole Erotiche Delle 1000 e una Notte (The*

---

* Guy Madison and Richard Harrison became fast friends while in Europe, specifically Rome. Harrison, through the years, has become a rather prolific filmmaker himself with jaunts all over the world, making a larger name for himself in the action film genre. Harrison as good friends of the family has remained so over the years. He also spoke on behalf of her father giving the eulogy at his funeral some years later.

Erotic Fables of the 100 and 1 Nights). This Italian fantasy production was directed by Adalberto Albertini. Another rare, elusive title that is yet to arrive into our hands, but nevertheless it is confirmed and it has been found just obtaining it for review has been the problem.

The storyline has to do with the Caliph of Baghdad who is furious with the betrayal of his wife, Jasmine. He sets forth a ruling across his land, that he will kill a virgin each night until his estranged wife has been delivered to him so he may bestow his wrath of justice upon here.

The Visir's daughter, Scheherazade volunteers to go to the Caliph and attempt to persuade him to stop the killing of these innocent maidens. He indeed falls in love with her and succumbs to her wishes. Guy Madison stars as the Caliph of Baghdad. It costars Venantino Venantini as the old Visir and Pascale Petit as his daughter Scheherazade.

With this film Guy Madison's twelve year stint in the European cinema draws to a close, at least for those films we've been able to locate and confirm at this time. During 1973 he would return to the United States anxious to rekindle his faded American career back home. He did return overseas afterward, but only on a few rare occasions. From now on he would remain true to his US citizenship for the rest of his continuing career. We feel that Madison may have begun to see the wane of the *Spaghetti* film phenomenon as we have, or at least saw a change that he knew was in the air concerning these once so popular Euro films.

Most of the Westerns were no longer of the straight kind he was used to making, but now they were mostly of the comedic variety. He may have also felt that a return to the United States at this time in his career was long overdue and might be worth another shot at attempting to renew his Stateside career. Possibly the time spent away had now calmed the Studio waters, and tempered the tides that had once been against him. Perhaps he might now have an opportunity once again for a true comeback in the business.

We first observe Madison's attempts to reenter the American television industry as being in one episode of the weekly series, *The Smith Family*. His episode was called "Winner Take All" and was aired April 19, 1972, during the show's second season. The series starred Henry Fonda as Police Detective Sergeant Chad Smith. Other regulars were Charles McGraw as Police Captain Hughes, Ron Howard as Bob Smith and Darleen Carr as Cindy Smith.

> It was during this latter part of 1973 period, while back in the States that we might have glimpsed Guy Madison's return to doing plays on the *Dinner Theater* circuit throughout the Midwest. According to past interviews though, he has readily admitted to never really enjoying any of the plays he'd ever done. We can only guess a man, has to, what a man, *has* to do! In addition he could also be

seen attending many of the Western film festival shows that were being held throughout the country during this period in time.

Madison returned overseas once again, during the year 1975. This time however, it was off to the Philippine Islands for an Italian / Filipino coproduction. Madison claimed in a later interview that he lost some twenty pounds in weight during his five month shooting stay there. He said that they even fed them dried fish and rice for breakfast. The film was called *South Pacific Connection,* however has never traceable under that title. It appears that this film had a very limited Euro Filipino cinema showing engagement and was shelved until a later release date. It was breathed new life when the Kung Fu films were revitalized again and took a new hold on the market again during the 1980s. It was revived for video, along with a different title called *Stickfighter* for its new release.

Upon his return to Hollywood, Madison was briefly visible that same year involved in a MTV movie. This, for a 1975 *ABC Sunday Night Movie* telecast called *Hatcher Bodine.* Expounded as an unsuccessful TV pilot, this yet unconfirmed film title evidently had an extremely limited television engagement during this era. It supposedly starred Guy Madison in the lead role of Hatcher Bodine, a grizzled Mountain man type* always on another quest of one thing or another which constantly involved his getting in all sorts of trouble with the criminal factions and undesirables on the wrong side of the law.

In 1976 we find Madison associated with another cameo part, this time in a Michael Winner film called *Won Ton, Ton: The Dog Who Saved Hollywood.* This film was a comedy starring Bruce Dern as one Grayson Potchuck. Others along for this all-star cast ride included some of Guy Madison's oldest friends of TV and film of the past. From his *Wild Bill Hickok* days, his old sidekick (Jingles) Andy Devine was also on the ticket, portraying a priest at the dog pound. Also, another old friend from years past in cameo as Philip Hart, was Rory Calhoun, also like Madison now an ex-spaghetti veteran film actor whose roles and parts was also becoming

* There were a couple of television shows that popped up about this time with more or less similar storylines. One as I remember, just offhand was with Dan Haggerty as *Grizzly Adams* which did make it to a series with a fairly good run. Another MTV pilot was called *Banjo Hackett: Roamin' Free* and starred Chuck Connors in a role of Sam Ivory. This "Bodine" show (if it was that, in reality) was then just one of many shows that failed to materialize and bit the dust never to be realized during that era in Television.

few and far between. Madison's cameo role for this film was that of a film star at a gala nighttime opening for a new film screening.

Next for a 1977 movie Madison turned up in another cameo role for an MTV production called *Where's Willie,* a.k.a. *Willie*. It starred Marc Gilpin as Willie along with Henry Darrow as his father and town sheriff, Charlie Wade. Katherine (Kate) Woodville portrays his mother Beth Wade. It also starred, Robert Clarke, Guy Madison was Tony Flore. John Mitchum (brother of actor Robert) and Fran Tucker portrayed Willie's grandparents. Also was a newcomer, Rick Montanio as Willie's sidekick called Tracks.

The storyline dealt with a young computer wizard who has turned his community upside down with his innocent computer meddling. Being grounded and feeling unwanted he decides he's better off leaving home and going to live with his Grandparents. Madison's cameo was that of an airplane pilot, Tony Flore who meets the young runaway Willie on a bus trip to his Grandparents home. Taking a liking to this seemingly very smart youngster, Flore takes him under his wing, so to speak, and finally talks him into returning home. He even buys him a ticket for his trip back. This story, aimed more at the younger generation of that day was directed by John Florea from a script by Alan Cassidy IV along with Ann and Frank Koomen.

Mostly retiring after this last show, Madison would spend much of his time now doing the things he loved like hunting, fishing and overseeing his various investments. He would not officially retire until 1987, when he turned 65 years old. Until then though, only certain movie bits and some light television parts, would get his attention and bring him back for the occasion. In 1979, we find him appearing in another television series, for one episode of *Fantasy Island,* the popular series of 1978 to 1984. It starred Riccardo Montalban as Mr. Roarke the Island host and his midget buddy, Herve Villechaize as Tattoo. A long-running fantasy series in where persons of obvious wealth would come to this Island paradise to live out their fantasies in a safe secure environment under controlled circumstances. Guy Madison's one of a two-part showing was either "Yesterday's Love" or "Fountain of Youth", (still unclear not having been seen to confirmed as to which episode part he was actually in) however, his character was that of one Brick Howard.

Also in 1979 we find Guy Madison was part of a ritualistic outing for an *ABC* TV Special called *How the West Was Fun* from Producer Brad Marks. This special telecast honoring film great John Wayne as one of filmdom's greatest Western stars. At the time it was of general knowledge that John Wayne having his cancer return in the form of lung and stomach cancers was on his death bed. A tribute to the actor's long endurance within the Western genre was the main theme of this sixty-minute program. Clips and interviews were included along with a slew of former Western film stars of yesteryear onboard to offer their respects to this great man of action.

Also in 1979, Madison was briefly associated with another TV series. This time, an MTV miniseries called the *Rebels* which starred Andrew Stevens as hero, Philip Kent. Other series regulars were Kim Cattrall as Anne Kent, Don Johnson as Judson Fletcher and Doug McClure as Ept Tait. This was a spin-off from a previously successful mini *The Bastard* directed by Russ Mayberry. The storyline takes place during the US / British battle for independence and was the second of a trilogy story (third was called *The Seekers*) which evolved around life and times of the popular fictional character of Philip Kent created by novelist John Jakes. This lead character of the novel was cast as a freedom fighter during the American Revolutionary War. Guy Madison was in another of his cameo roles, this one as the sadistic Lieutenant Mayo.

For a long spell afterward, we would not hear about Madison again until the year 1986 when we found he had been involved in a French/ UK coproduced MTV movie pilot called *The Adventures of William Tell.* Directed by George Mihalka who upon remembering Madison's prowess and proficiency as an archer and as a hunter had seemingly coaxed our semi retired film star into this one more outing abroad. It was filmed entirely on locations in France.

This period adventure starred Will Lyman as the adventurous William Tell. Also starring was Jeremy Clyde as his sidekick Gessler. Harry Carey Jr. as Mutino and Guy Madison is Gerrish, one of Tell's rowdy four horsemen. It was a story about a band of adventurers circa fourteenth century. Johnny Crawford is masterful as the evil Prince Ignatius and Guy Rolfe portrays the emperor. The plot revolves around their struggles and battle skirmishes against tyranny and oppression. The script was by Steven Bawol and Anthony Horowitz. The movie after its initial pilot telecasting in Europe went straight to video here in the United States and was evidently never televised on television here in this country. The video release was titled simply, *Crossbow.*

Madison's role of Gerrish was that of old friend and rival of William Tell in this revealing story depicting the rebel resistance causes and their fights for freedom during the oppressive years by dominant evil overseers and rulers of fourteenth century Europe. Real life old friend and acting buddies, Madison and Harry Carey Jr. had great time there on location while in France according to his daughter, Bridget.

This French produced MTV feature film did in fact make it as a television series which ran for two seasons from 1987-1988 in France. Madison's role however, was only his one-time appearance within the pilot film. Even though, by accounts he is shown to be associated with two other of these episodes, which apparently were mere compilations from the original movie pilot. One such episode was aired December 27, 1987, called "The Four Horsemen" by all accounts appears to be clips of the original pilot story told in flashbacks. The second episode, "The Princess" is considered just a rerun of the original pilot feature as they do have all the same cast members listed in it as did the original film of 1986.

Back in the States once again during the year 1988, Madison consented to do another on-screen cameo appearance along with several other older actors that had previously been associated with television and feature film Westerns throughout the years. This, another MTV movie was a remake of the original 1948 John Wayne film called *Red River*. It was filmed in Tucson, Arizona and it starred James Arness as Thomas Dunson, a role that John Wayne made famous. The original film debuted some forty years earlier and was the pet project of the famous director Howard Hawks. This remake costarred Bruce Boxleitner as Matthew Garth, Gregory Harrison as Cherry Valance and Laura Johnson. Among the ex-Western film stars of yesteryear who agreed to cameo spots in this film were, Ty Hardin as Cotton, Robert Horton as Mr. Melville cattle buyer. **Guy Madison** as Bill Meeker, Rancher. Others were John Lipton, Ray Walston as Groot, and L. Q. Jones portraying Sims.

Regretfully, the above appearance would be Guy Madison's the last professional one. Still in the year 1988, we understand he was involved in a near fatal automobile accident where he was critically injured. According to all accounts, he had been stopped on the Santa Monica Freeway outside Los Angeles, California, and was changing a flat tire on his *Pontiac Fire-bird.*

Courtesy of Bridget Madison

Another vehicle evidently rear-ended his car slamming it out into traffic where it was then struck by a tractor-trailer rig. Madison barely escaped with his life but suffered some severe lung damage and a dislocated shoulder as he was thrown clear of the wreck. It was some three years later first of January, 1991 that he had to have repair surgery (almost eight hours of it) again at *UCI Medical Center* there in Orange, California. The operation consisted of scar tissue removal and further lung repair of tissues damaged in the 1988 crash. Madison had also returned to the *UCI Center* in 1993, where basically he underwent virtually the same scar tissue removal and repair operations again. Evidently, it was to be a reoccurring event with the expectations of him having to periodically return and undergo further scar tissue removals.

When able, Guy Madison resumed his attendance at Western Film Festival functions throughout California, Nevada and Arizona areas. Besides receiving a *Lifetime Achievement Award*, he was also honored at the 1986 *Golden Boots Awards for Excellence* in his field of endeavor, there at the Woodland Hills, California, *Acting and Film Awards Festival.*

For years while in reasonably good health, he would attend the annual *Andy Devine Days Festivals* held in Kingman, Arizona. He had been an honored guest there yearly since returning to the States through his longtime friendship and association with their beloved hometown boy, Andy Devine. Madison, a smoker all his life, and evidently fairly heavy at times had by now taken a toll on our Western hero. For years since his near fatal accident, he had to continue suffering through those reoccurring bouts of required surgery. The lung damage from not only this accident, but years of tobacco use tended to limit his movements in his later years. Far from being the active fisherman and hunter he once was didn't sit well with a now embittered, older Guy Madison. His voice nearly gone from the smoking and bouts of emphysema he would finally succumb to the fatal disease passing away on February 6th, 1996.

Funeral Services for the actor were held on February 12, 1996, at the *Ramon Chapel* of the *Palm Springs Mortuary,* Palm Springs, California. Officiating was Pastor Ross Baidlaw of the *Palm Springs Baptist Church.* Eulogy was given by actor, longtime friend of the family Richard Harrison. Other noted friends of the actor attending were Rory Calhoun and Harry Carey Jr. as was ex-wife Sheila Connolly Danziger.

His son, Robert Madison, then twenty-nine years old, flew in from Rome, where he continues to live and work following in his father's footsteps acting within the Italian cinema there. Being in attendance, he volunteered to give an impromptu speech on behalf of his Father. We will attach here a copy of that speech, most graciously provided to me personally by his daughter Bridget for all to see.

MY SPEECH AT GUY MADISON'S FUNERAL (2/12/1996)

I just wanted to say, that I always loved my father and have been always proud of him even in the past when he was away most of the time. I have never said anything wrong against him. He was a great man. He didn't use to show his real feelings too much but he used different ways to say, "I love you." He had a very good heart. I usually came to visit him every two years and I must say I've been very lucky this time to decide to come over in January. We had a wonderful time together. He taught me many important things and gave me some very good advice that I will never forget.

He couldn't stand the fact that I can't use my hands to repair things, cut wood and so on . . . And every time he had the chance to tease me how to do something with my hands, he didn't save a word. Even if he was sick and couldn't breathe well. He paid for riding lessons for me and I accomplished very good results at the end. He wanted me to learn how to ride because he said, "If you are in a studio for an interview and the Producer and the Director ask you, "Can you ride?" What do you answer son?" I said "No" and he said, "Ok, next!"

Another sentence I will never forget was, "You will never be an actor if you can't make a table." Well, at first, I found this sentence a little ridiculous, but on second thought I realized there was some truth in what he said. *(So)* "Uncle Harold, please help me to make a table!"

Some people have been very important for me in my relationship with my father, Bridget, Erin and Dolly, Uncle Harold, Uncle Wayne, Sheila Danziger and Richard Harrison. Thank You

"I love you Dad!"

Robert Madison

Robert Ozell Moseley better known to all as Guy Madison was interred at the *Palm Springs Mausoleum* in Cathedral City, California. Divorced from actress wife, Gail Russell (deceased), and Sheilah Connolly, he was survived by her and his three daughters, Bridget, Erin and Dolly; and the one son, Robert.

Courtesy of Bridget Madison

As we bring our piece on Guy Madison to a close, I'd like to say how much we have enjoyed the researching and collecting materials on this fine actor. I might add Guy Madison has been one of my personal favorites through the years; having grown up in the 1950s, I was a part of the throng of young viewers that thought of Guy Madison as a screen hero. Wild Bill, a true hero to his fans of TV, film and in life as well. I know there are still many of us out there today, who remain devoted fans of the man. Though the years have somehow crept up on all of us, we can still look back at the man and remember who was once a matinee idol, and can see for sure, how his endeavors of work made it a Command Performance in his life. His career statements as I have set forth herein can certainly testify to that.

We'd also like to thank those of that unique Western film genre the *Spaghetti* Western for their endurance though the years. Although few are now left in this day and age, their performances are not forgotten. Most of all though, we'd like to thank his lovely daughter, Bridget who fought through thick and thin to get a star for her father on *Hollywood's Walk of Fame.* She accomplished that goal for the love and appreciation of her father, which has set a fine example of perseverance for all young women growing up in today's society. This achievement is now there for all to see, that Guy Madison, actor with his many career achievements behind him, is right up there at the top along with the other many actors, male and female alike that helped to make this exciting Western film genre possible.

Courtesy of Bridget Madison

Other genre actors like Lee Van Cleef, may have been a hero of the later *Spaghetti* Westerns, but we can honestly say Guy Madison was one of our true Western heroes, from even back when actors like LVC was still slinking behind boulders playing the bad guy on TV. The name Guy Madison may not be a Matinee idol during this day and age, but to us his fans he will always be a big screen hero. We will continue to miss that Guy Madison era in films and especially our hero who came *From Matinee Idol, to Command Performance* of life. Rest easy great hunter, as long as we have our memories we can still see him riding across badlands into a fading distance of a not so long ago.

End.

SPEC SHEET AT A GLANCE FOR GUY MADISON

Re: GUY MADISON—Real Name: Robert Ozell Moseley

Father: Ben Moseley
Mother: Mary Jane
Family: One of five, three brothers: Wayne Moseley (a.k.a. Chad Mallory); Harold Moseley (one older brother David Moseley deceased), and one sister: Rosemary *Moseley* Anderson
Born: January 19, 1922, Pumpkin Center, Bakersfield, California.

Height: 6'-1"; **Weight:** 185 lb (in his prime); **Eyes:** Hazel; **Hair:** Chestnut/brown
Family Ancestry: English, Irish, German, Scottish and American Indian
Education: Attended Bakersfield Junior College

Marital Status: Married to actress Gail Russell (1949-'54) divorced
Married to model / actress Sheila Connolly (1954-'63) divorced

Children: Bridget Catherine Madison (1955—
Erin Patricia Madison (1956—
Dolly Anne Madison (1957—
Roberto (Robert) Madison III (actor) (1967—

Died: Robert Moseley (Guy Madison) passed away February 6, 1996
Cause: Emphysema, and complications thereof.

At the time of his passing he was survived by: Three daughters: Bridget, Erin, Dolly and one son, Robert. Also one sister Rosemary Anderson of Sacramento, California, and two brothers: Wayne Moseley of Sherman-Oaks, California, and Harold Moseley of Mt. Shasta, California.

Moseley began his studies at the Luther Lester's Drama School at Paramount Studios. While there he met a young actress he really liked, her name was Gail Russell. They eventually married some four years later.

GUY MADISON STAGE CREDITS

1945
DEAR RUTH—Made his debut at the *Laguna Playhouse* with this play during the 1945 summer season.

1946
LIGHT UP THE SKY—His second summer season he could be found at the *La Jolla Playhouse* involved with this play.

1947
JOHN LOVES MARY—In his third season, he could be found on tour with this play.

**After returning to the States late in 1972 Madison would once again return to stage productions*

1972 MID-WESTERN DINNER THEATER

This concludes the available listings on Guy Madison's stage work. While undoubtedly there may be more to his credit, these have been all that were readily available to this author.

RADIO WORK

1951-'56 *THE ADVENTURES OF WILD BILL HICKOK,* Stars Guy Madison voicing the role of Marshall Hickok. During a three-year period this show boasted that it ran some three hundred broadcast episodes.

- Below is a complete filmography of Guy Madison's Euro Westerns. The dates are aligned as close as possible with information currently at hand, plus international release dates included. **Posters and title picture are accredited to the Sebastian Haselbeck collection via his website www.spaghetti-western.net. Many thanks, Sebastian*

GUY MADISON
EURO WESTERNS

1963
Battle at Fort Apache, *Battaglia Di Fort Apache;* a.k.a. *Apaches Last Battle;* a.k.a. *Old Shatterhand;* a.k.a. *Shatterhand*; W. Ger/ Yugo/ Fr/ Ital, Director Hugo Fregonese (Madison costars as the deranged Confederate Captain Bradley); 1963; Stars Lex Barker as Old Shatterhand, and Pierre Brice portraying Chief Winnetou.

1964

Jennie Lee has a New Gun, *Jennie Lee ha una Nuova Pistola;* a.k.a. *Sfida a Rio Bravo (Duel at Rio Bravo); Gunmen of Rio Grande*; Spa/ Fr/ Ital, Director Tulio Demicheli (Madison stars as Wyatt Earp / Laramie); 1964 (Ital); Costars Madelene LeBeau as Jennie Lee, Fernando Sancho as Pancho Bogan and Gerard Tichy as Zack Williams.

1965

The Legacy of the Incas; a.k.a. *Viva Gringo*; W. Ger/ Ital/ Spa, Director Georg Marischka (Madison stars as Karl Hansen / Jaguar); 1965; It costars Geula Nuni as Graziella, William Rothlein is Haukaropora the Inca Prince being groomed to be crowned King of the Inca. Carlo Tamberlani as the evil high priest Anciano; Rik Battaglia as Kampfer Perillo; Raf Baldassare as Geronomo Indian companion to Jaguar; Fernando Rey as the Peruvian Presidente Castillo.

1966

The Five for Revenge, *I Cinque Della Vendetta;* a.k.a. *Five Giants from Texas;* a.k.a. *No Drums, No Trumpets*; Ital/ Spa, Director Aldo Florio (Madison stars as John Latimore / Tex); 1966; Costars Monica Randall as Rosaria, Mariano Vidal Molina, Jose Manuel Martin, Antonio Molino Rojo, Giovanni Cianfriglia, and Guanni Solaro.

1967

Seven Winchester's for a Massacre, *Sette Winchester per un Massacro;* a.k.a. *Winchester for Hire;* a.k.a. *Payment in Blood;* a.k.a. *Blake's Marauders*; Ital, Director E. G. Rowland (Enzo G. Castellari) (Madison costars as Colonel Blake); 1967; Stars Edd Byrnes stars as Stuart, Enio Girolami, Luisa Barrato, Rick Boyd (Federico Boido) and Pedro Sanchez

Son of Django, *Figlio Di Django;* a.k.a. *the Return of Django;* a.k.a. *Vengeance is a Colt .45*; Ital, Director Osvaldo Civirani (Madison stars as Father Fleming); 1967; Costarring Gabriele Tinti as Jeff (Son of Django); Others were: Ingrid Schoeller, Daniele Bargas, and Pedro Sanchez.

The Bang, Bang Kid, *IL Bang, Bang Kid* (Western fantasy); US/ Sp/ Ital, Promoted by Sidney Pink; Director Luciano Lelli (Stanley Praeger) (Madison stars as Bear Bullock / the King); 1967; Costars Tom Bosely as Merriweather T. Newberry, Sandra Milo as Gwenda Skaggel, and Riccardo Garrone as Killer Kossock and José Caffarel.

1968

The Long Days of Hate, *I Linghi Giorni Dell'Odio;* a.k.a. *This Man Can't Die!* Ital, Director Gianfranco Baldanello (Madison stars as Martin Benson); 1968; Costars Lucienne Bridou as Suzy Benson, Robert Widmark (Alberto Dell'Acqua) as Daniel Benson and Anna Liotti as Jenny Benson. Others: Peter Martell (Pietro Martellanza) as Tony Guy, Rik Battaglia as evil town boss Vic Graham; Rosalba Neri as Maylene as Saloon owner.

1970

The Reverend's Colt, *La Reverendo Colt;* a.k.a. *Reverend Colt*; Ital/ Spa, Director Leon Klimovsky; (Madison stars as Reverend Miller (Colt); 1970; Costars Richard Harrison as Sheriff Donovan, Thomas Moore, Maria Martin, German Cobos, Pedro Sanchez and Perla Crista. Also: Stephen Tedd (Giuseppe Cardillo), Alfonso Rojas, Marino Vidal Molina and Cris Huerta.

Note: Even as Leon Klimovsky is credited as the director of this film, it is widely believed that Marino Girolami credited under pseudonym Frank Martin as the Producer was actually the film's director.

End.

BIBLIOGRAPHY
(G. Madison)

Betts, Tom, editor *WAI! (Westerns . . . All'Italiana)* Fanzine articles/ information on G. Madison;

Issue no. 11, January/February 1987 "Guy Madison: An American Actor in Rome" by Tom Ferrante;

Special Issue *Memorial*: "Wild Bill Goes to Europe" Prickette, Tom Info excerpts/ Filmography by Tom Betts;

Issue no. 47, "Boothill Zine-Obituary" by Tom Betts

The BFI Companion to the Western (1993) edited by Edward Buscombe, *British Film Institute,* UK. Originally published by *Andr`e Deutsch Ltd.,* London, 1988; pp. 366

Connolly, Bill, editor *Spaghetti Cinema* Fanzine articles/information on Guy Madison;

Issues no. 1-12 Richard Harrison Interview installments;

Issue no. 49 Film Reviews;

Issue no. 64 "Guy Madison/ Martin Balsam" March, 1996

Danziger, Connolly, Sheila, *Angel Face: A Memoir* (1999) Published by *Marino Books,* div of *Mercer Press,* Dublin, Ire., Chap.16: "Guy Madison, alias Wild Bill Hickock", pp 165-197

Haselbeck, Sebastian, owner/curator for Internet website: *www.spaghetti-western.net*

Internet, via: *www.IMDB.com,* complete film and TV listings; plus Trivia; plus "Mini-Bio of Guy Madison" by Jim Beaver

Prickette, Tom, *From Matinee Idol, to Command Performance,* previously unpublished manuscript of 1987, partially used in the *WAI!* Memorial issue for Madison after his 1996 passing; Redone in '07

Quinlan's Illustrated Registry of Film Stars (1987) by Davis Quinlan, *Henry Holt Reference Books,* NY., pp 300 (Therein contains one unconfirmed film title *Retroguardia* for 1970)

Video Hound's Golden Retriever (1994 edition) *Visible Ink Press,* a division of *Gale Research Inc.,* Detroit, MI. pp 1292

Weisser, Thomas, *Spaghetti Westerns: the Good, the Bad, and the Violent* (1992) *McFarland,* Jefferson NC.

Western: All'Italiana (2006) (book III), by Antonio Bruschini and Federico de Zigno, *Glittering Images,* Firenze, Italy; *Euro-western Filmography section* pp 92-109

The Western: The Complete Film Sourcebook (The Film Encyclopedia) (1983); by Phil Hardy, *William Morrow and Co, Inc.,* NY. Appendix 8 *Sound Westerns,* pp 375-394

The World Almanac Who's who of Film (1987) by Thomas G Aylesworth and John S. Bowman, *Bison Books,* pp. 282

GORDON MITCHELL

(1923-2003)

"MAN, WITH *THAT* LOOK!"

Charles (Chuck) Allen Pendleton was born in Denver, Colorado on July 29, 1923. Growing up in Depression era Denver during this era was no joke as he readily admitted to fans that his childhood was a difficult and mostly unhappy period in his life. His parents, Oscar (Bud) Pendleton, occupation truck driver originally from Kansas, and his mother the Colorado born Verona Meeks marriage didn't last long. Within three years or so after Chuck and his sister Elaine were born, the parents was separated by 1926, later divorced that same year. The split left a sickly Verona now with two young kids. So from an early age he had to help care for his chronically ill mother.

Chuck was enrolled for first grade classes at *Sacred Heart Catholic School* there in Denver. By the time he was eight years old, he was already into strutting about, showing off his young body and flexing his yet immature muscles. It was in 1931 when his mother met and married one Paul Leitz who worked at a local bottling plant there in Denver. At the beginning of his four grade year Chuck was expelled for peeing himself in class, he then resumed his elementary schooling at the *Mitchell Elementary* School.

While Lenitz came with baggage in that of an older daughter, she (Lucille) would leave home in 1932 to get married at around seventeen years old. That same year Chuck and his family grew by one more, when his mom gave birth in June to another boy baby they called Paul Jr., however before young Paul's next birthday he would have succumbed to pneumonia and died. Barefoot and pregnant as the saying goes, Verona again gave birth to a girl baby in November of 1935. They called her Eloise Leitz. It was later in August of 1937 when Chuck said the whole family then relocated to Hawthorne, California, where his step father worked part-time as a manager at the *7-Up Bottling Plant.* A ten year old Chuck already entered into school there remarked about how he saw the teachers trying to teach the kids about health, not to smoke or over eat, and get plenty of exercise. But all the while they themselves weren't showing their pupils any good examples, as they were continuing to do all those bad things off school grounds.

His being interested in sports and fitness from an early age, he found that fitness and health walked hand in hand and not only tended to help improve his health in general but his physical appearance as well. With him having a sickly parent at home, all this dwelled on his mind a lot. By December that same years though, they had up and again relocated, this time to Inglewood. Chuck was now fourteen years old and for the first time since the separation, he met his real father, Oscar Pendleton. A family picture snapped by Leitz showed an already tallish teenaged Chuck, and sister Elaine, with Oscar and the mother Verona. After the move Chuck would continue his junior high school education at the *George W. Crozier Intermediate School* in Inglewood. By the time he was sixteen, he'd already taken up weight training and lifting. He was determined that he wasn't going to be one those sickly ninety-pound weakling fellows.

After graduating high school in 1942, he entered college at *USC, University of Southern California.* Shortly thereafter, WWII broke out. Like a lot of young men during that era, he signed on volunteering to fight for his country. Not long afterward he was taking basic, then went on to serve out his stint with the *Army Air Corps.* While in the Hermosa Beach, California area he'd met his would be future wife, Leta. It was later during his tour of duty overseas, that he joined up with others for the Battle of the Bulge. He was also present during for the liberation of Buchenwald, helping to free the prisoners at that German Concentration Camp. It was there he was captured and held awhile as a prisoner of war until its end after April. Afterward, he was hospitalization for a bit, before being sent back to California. Subsequently, after completing his hitch, he was honorably discharged on January 21, 1946.

Almost immediately, he reentered *USC* again, to resume his college curriculum, which included anatomy, biology and physiology studying to become a teacher majoring in Physical Education. He would use his degree to pursue a job as a high schoolteacher. His ambitions were at that time, to teach and help make a difference with the young people of the day. While there had been a few girls in the wings back in those days one, Sandy in particular he'd met on the beach in 1945, but then after his discharge he succumbed to the inevitable and married his main gal pal Leta in August of 1946. They moved into the GI housing while he was in school. After graduation, receiving his BA in June of 1949, he continued on the next semester for his MA, and then bought a house in San Gabriel.

Evidently the Sandy, ex-gal friend resurfaced again during a 1950's New Year's Eve party. It was soon afterward when he and wife, Leta, separated. Chuck went on that year to receive his Masters in Guidance and Counseling then got a job teaching HS and Junior HS there in San Marino. He was also over the recreation department during that period as well. There, he was teaching handicapped students and those problem students, deemed as delinquents.

Then the Korean War broke out and Chuck was recalled to the Air Corps active duty roster in June 1951 slated for Korea. He was returned to Scott Air Base from June to Sept of 1952, then transferred to Frankfurt and reassigned for a stint in Casablanca (Neuassaur). By November 1953 he was discharged in New York at Camp Kilmer, where he was reclassified from active to inactive as a First Lieutenant.

After his return from the war, he moved into an apartment and resumed his teaching duties, however, not as content now with the situation there in San Marino he decided to go into the Los Angeles school system instead as a permanent substitute teacher. He then became sort of the roving delinquent problem solver of the LA school system, working all area schools from about 1954 until 1960.

Still technically, a member of the Armed Services Personnel he was asked to do a consulting job for a Ronald Reagan movie (on Reagan's birthday in fact, February 6, 1954) he did this willingly and enjoyed the work immensely he said. That film was called *Prisoner of War* starring Reagan, Steve Forrest and Dewey Martin. Chuck also had a small walk-on part, but was unaccredited. This was a busy year for Chuck, his divorce was finalized and he'd met bodybuilder friend Joe Gold at the beach and soon he was moved again, this time another apartment, Seaside Terraces closer to the Muscle beach area where all the bodybuilders hung out.

Of his teaching, he once commented that he was more often as not given the tough, unruly kids for his classes. He loved to relate the story about his shop class where on the first day of school, when he called role. Calling the class to order, he would then pick up a 135-pound anvil off his desk and flip it over with one hand and begin pressing it up and down above his head. That tended to get their attention. After about ten presses he would quietly put to back down on his desk still with just the one hand. He claimed he never had any student problems during those classes.

Another teaching story he loves to tell was the one about Robert Mitchum's older son James (Big Jim) as they call him now. During the year 1958, Robert's son would make his screen debut with his father portraying his younger brother Thad for the Mitchum moonshine film, *Thunder Road.* To be sure Jim was no doubt a major handful in school and thought he would run over his schoolteachers that is, until he ran across Charles Pendleton. As Chuck called the class to order Mitchum ignored him and continued eating a sandwich standing in front of his desk. Chuck tells us he walked over and took the sandwich and stuffed it back in the lunch bag. Jim proceeded to ask him if he knew who his father was, being *the* Robert Mitchum, and that he was going to tell him just what he'd done. Chuck came back with, "You and your dad and the rest of your family can come over here and I'll kick all of your buns at once." Jim just looked at him then sat down, causing no more trouble after that.

Although working as a teacher, Chuck could still utilize his free time for his sport of bodybuilding and exercise. Being of a good build now from years of lifting weights indeed had paid off. As a husky six-footer with blond hair and blue eyes, Chuck had been augmenting his teaching salary with part time jobs in the movie industry (as had some of his other weightlifting beach buddies) for some time. During this period in time, he weighted approximately 220 lb.

Another exceptional walk-on part soon crossed his path, when he and buddy Joe Gold would both be in the Charlton Heston/Yul Brynner blockbuster epic by Cecil B. Demille called *The Ten Commandments* (1955). This was truly an epic of films, still available on DVD today. It's worth the look, to see those two massive specimens of male physic (Chuck and Joe) as they escort prisoner Moses (Heston) in chains, down to Egyptian ruler Pharaoh's (Brynner) palace court. In addition there was another actor getting his big start in this film as well, his name was Woodrow (Woody) Strode. Strode actually portrayed two parts in this film, he portrayed the conquered King of Ethiopia, and that of a litter bearing slave.

Now with Chuck having come in league as a stalwart member of the bodybuilding fraternity of southern California, this would bond him a lifetime friendship with others of the sport. One especially lasting would be with Joe Gold. Gold was born in Los Angeles in 1922. He became increasingly interested in weightlifting and took to building odd looking, but practical assist machines out of junk from his brother's local scrap yard. At twelve he'd observed how his sister-in-law had designed a makeshift lifting device for strengthening her arms (a broom handle with pails of water on either end) a sort of crude barbells.

He also fell in with other like-minded individuals down at the beach where he joined in with a bodybuilding group of guys in Santa Monica. This area was known as Muscle Beach and eventually filtered on down to encompass Venice Beach as well. This area is still every bit as popular today as it in its heyday of the 1950s. At the onslaught of WWII Gold served in the Merchant Marines becoming a machinist, a trade that would be a benefit to him in his future business of bodybuilding. Unfortunately he was hospitalized for a while due to an explosion via a torpedo attack. Later in life, these old injuries would come to haunt him and eventually confine him to a wheelchair, but he would continue to be prolific in his designs, and instrumental in building of his, by now famous gym equipment. Later when recovered, he went on to do a stint for the navy in the Korean War. Joe and Chuck had a lot in common back then, and when they first met became fast friends lasting a lifetime.

> In 1963 Joe Gold eventually got together in an arrangement with the *Muscle Beach Weightlifting Club* in Santa Monica to build an indoor facility. By that time Chuck was already in Italy making *Peplum* (Sword 'n' Sandal) films. Alas the partnership with the Club faltered, so Gold went it alone, with help from friend Chuck as coowner, by 1965 he had opened his own gym. A no-frills, hardcore bodybuilding facility there in Venice, called *Gold's Gym*. Gold had designed and built all the exercise equipment therein. Eventually this one evolved into a chain of gyms all over the country until 1970 when he sold it.
>
> It was later in 1977 Gold would open another gym, first in Santa Monica, then one in Marina Del Rey, which he continued to own and operate until his death at eighty-two years old in 2004. This gym was devoted more to the fitness / exercise buffs and was called *World Gym,* a franchised chain, still in operation today. With Chuck's continued coownership help this exercise complex attracted not only the professional office worker attempting to stay fit, but also the elite rich 'n' famous, as well as movie stars alike. Arnold Schwarzenegger and *The Hulk* (Lou Ferrigno) could sometimes be seen there on a semiregular basis.

> With Chuck now being an International star of European films (he was more popularly known by his screen name) and in later years, when home and available between acting in films, one might drop by the gym facility there at Marina Del Rey and find a friendly man behind the counter with that special look that fans would readily recognize as film star Gordon Mitchell.

Also in 1954, Joe Gold had landed a stint with ex-film star and bawdy showman Mae West. Friend Chuck was also involved here in the group as well, they both managed to wrangle time for her touring shows around the country. There Chuck met another young bodybuilder Mickey Hargitay, who would become a lifetime friend as well. They both would even be in Europe during the same era of the *Spaghetti* Westerns and even got to do one of these genre films together in 1965. Other than his rather short Euro film career Hargitay is mostly known as the second husband of blond bombshell actress Jayne Mansfield. Ironically, they had met on the Mae West show. Hargitay at that time was a first class bodybuilder and *Mr. Universe* of 1955.

> From around 1954, the "Mae West Troupe" (a Muscleman Review centering on West as the object of their affections) was running the Hollywood club circuit. Fresh from NYC, the review would welcome the likes of Chuck Pendleton to become a regular member of her troupe as it toured the United States for the 1956 show. While on season tour, they would hit some of the hot spots of the country including Las Vegas, New York and Miami.
>
> Some of Chuck's other bodybuilding associates who would become renown via film careers in Europe were Mark Forest (Lou Degni), Reg Lewis, Brad Harris and Mickey Hargitay (who would join the Mae West troop for the 1956 review). Later on, a young Dan Vadis and close friend of Chuck's would join the troop for a one-city review in Las Vegas. All of those guys would eventually become involved at one time or another with the Italian *Peplum* films, and some would become quite popular, from an original kick-start by another early bodybuilder Steve Reeve, who was the first to hit the Italian (Epics) with his famous *Hercules* film of 1957.

Chuck had known Reeves well during those early years while teaching when Reeves had fallen in love with one of Chuck's former students, one Sandy Smith. Chuck remembered back when Steve's had got first involved with the Italian cinema by sending pictures of himself to some Italian producer who looking for strong looking, bodybuilder type to star in an epic, *Peplum* picture. Eventually director Pietro Francisci would contact Reeves for a leading part in his film *Hercules*. This venture for Reeves would become extremely profitable and earned him International stardom.

Meantime back in LA, Chuck continued to teacher classes when school resumed from summers vacation. The part time film parts, he continued to caulk up with such films as *Around the World in 80 Days* (1955), which starred David Niven and Shirley MacLaine. Also there was supposed to have been another for a 1955 but actually he wasn't in it. It had been the Frank Sinatra, Kim Novak blockbuster *Man with the Golden Arm*. This was a serious drama for the times about drug addiction use by Jazz musicians. An Otto Preminger film, and with a riveting Elmer Bernstein Jazz score. When asked point blank about this one in particular, Chuck didn't remember ever being in it, even though it seems to be on a lot of his film lists of achievements for that era.

Chuck's next part came along on Dick Powell's war film *The Enemy Below* (1956). Here action takes place mostly underwater in two cans (subs) for this WWII drama which has wits being matched between two submarine commanders and crew as the chase is on between US and German sub patrols. It starred Robert Mitchum, Curt Jurgens, Doug McClure and David Hedison. Shot during the summer of 1955, with Chuck on the same set, he got to meet Mitchum face-to-face. It was here he finally had the opportunity to talk with Mitchum about the incident with his son Jim back in school. Mitchum got a big laugh out of it and told Chuck that he'd done the right thing that the lad was sometimes a handful all right.

Chuck's film work, although the parts were still minuscule at best, did seem to be coming a little more frequently now, so next would be his first Western called *Rio Bravo* (1957). It starred John Wayne, Dean Martin and Ricky Nelson. For Chuck's one bit part, a barroom scene he said director Howard Hawks put him at the bar to keep his distinctive face from upstaging his leading actors; Next came *The Spirit of St. Louis* (1957) starring Jimmy Stewart and Patricia Smith; Then a swashbuckler Pirate drama called *The Buccaneer* (1957) which starred Yul Brynner and Charlton Heston, and was directed by actor Anthony Quinn. Chuck acted as one of Andrew Jackson (Heston's) men, still unaccredited though.

It was about this era in time when Joe Gold decided on building his first house, a duplex on Grand Boulevard. After they completed it Chuck and Joe moved into it early January of 1958. After that Chuck resumed with whatever films came his way like, *The Young Lions* (1958) starring Marlon Brando, Montgomery Cliff and Dean Martin. This WWII drama was directed by Edward Dmytryk. It even had a role in it for future *Spaghetti* Western econ Lee Van Cleef as the Sergeant Rickett. Also, that year Chuck had one quick scene shot where just his hands were used, for the film *Killers of Kilimanjaro*.

For his next film, he shared the limelight with bodybuilder buddy Brad Harris in a comedic film called *Li'l Abner* (1959). Finally credited for this film, they portrayed beachside hunks Luke (Harris) and Rufe (Chuck). The film starred Leslie Parrish, Stubby Kaye, Jerry Lewis (in Cameo), and Stella Stevens as Appassionata Von Climax, directed by Melvin Frank.

Next was an Independent documentary on weight training called *Project Power,* shot in 16mm and completed in 1959, basically it has been used more as an internal training video, and a staple for bodybuilding instructors since it was shot. However, never really being commercially introduced to the public it has been extremely elusive until now. Recently a Canadian version has surfaced that we are currently pursuing. One of these days we may yet get to actually view it.

Another unaccredited part popped for Chuck late in 1959. It was for the Kirk Douglas epic star maker *Spartacus.* This Stanley Kubrick film sported an all-star cast of favorites like Douglas himself as the runaway slave; Laurence Olivier, Jean Simmons, Tony Curtis, Peter Ustinov, Woody Strode, Herbert Lom and John Ireland, to name a few. One man, we now know for certain wasn't in the film, was Chuck Pendleton. He admitted when asked again point blank about this film, that yes he'd been cast as one of the extras, and supposed to work second unit. As the night wore on though, he had fallen asleep and simply missed his call. Oh well, all we can say he certainly make up for it when in Italy. He spoke of this same incident for a *cinema-nocturna.com* interview in March of 2003 along with other questions on a Sunday "Chat Session"

1960 was also the year he and Joe Gold began work on a six-unit apartment complex on Washington Way, Venice. Later about midyear while at the Vic Tanny's place/gym so deemed "the Dungeon" there in Santa Monica, he spotted an announcement from some Italian producers that were requesting guys, bodybuilders like himself to send pictures and contact information for those who might be interested in coming to Italy to playing roles in the *Peplum* (Sword 'n' Sandal) films. He already knew Steve Reeves and how he had shot to fame and fortune in Italy with those Hercules movies. He felt like, he'd give it a shot himself. Chuck said he knew a guy on the strip that did photographs and he went in to see him. They took some pictures, and he send off the materials to Italy. Thinking nothing probably would ever come of it, he resumed work there at the club teaching his weight training classes, and in off-hours still helped Joe on the six-plex apartment building.

Low and behold by December that year he was notified by a phone call from Rome, Italy that he had been chosen for the role of Maciste. Some producer wanted him there for the film *Maciste against the Cyclops.* So by the first of January they had sent him money and a plane ticket. He'd made arrangement for a six to eight week absence from his teaching duties and away he went to Italy. He said he landed in Rome January 5, 1961. Attempting to make his way through Customs and the crowds, with photographers everywhere snapping pictures, he said someone was hollering at him he finally noticed, "Gordon, Gordon Mitchell Stop!" As the big Italian assistant producer came up to him he said in pretty good English, "Excuse me, Mr. Pendleton, but we have changed your name to Gordon Mitchell!" Chuck said he nearly fell over on the spot. He just couldn't believe it. The guy claimed it was the truth and not made up for nobody, even though Chuck told him he was quite comfortable with his own name, but it was all set, Gordon Mitchell was his screen name.

The name change and all may have been a bit premature since after his arrival they did want to see what he looked like in a screen test and a sort of audition which evidently he passed all with flying colors. It seems he was taking the part of Maciste replacing Mark Forest who had been doing quite a few pictures there earlier, but had decided to take a six-month leave of absence from film work. Since his absence, production monies had come through and the film was to go into production. Mitchell would be his replacement. This little stroke of luck for Mitchell turned out to be a huge boon for him. His first picture underwent a slight name change from *Maciste . . .* to *Atlas in the Land of the Cyclops* (1961) for distribution, but in Italy he was still Maciste.

The films producer Donati Carpentieri had more waiting in the wings. They really liked Mitchell. After all, he was a serious actor now in the business. He never smoked, or drank alcohol and never did run with any of the producer's girlfriends. Mitchell commented later for a French *Nadarland.com* interview, that he was so good in fact, some even though of him as being gay, he scoffed some at that idea, and claimed he was really more of an introvert in defense of being in a situation he really knew nothing about at the time and didn't want to make any enemies in the business. According to a statement made by Joe Gold, talking of Chuck's early Muscle Beach days and his catching the girls, had become sort of a legend. "He put us all out of business." Later, he admitted when talking about women in Rome, "I didn't get too involved with any actresses, you never knew who were keeping them!"

Mitchell, as we will now continue to call him reminisced about how much of a coincidence the name of Gordon Mitchell really was to him. He said it was back in 1955, when a friend of his told him about a woman medium, a Dr. White. He spoke with her on the phone setting up a meet for a reading a couple of weeks later. When they met, right off the top she'd ask if I have a half-brother named Paul Junior, she went on to say that he had died when he was only 18 months old. With that he almost fell out of the chair. It was so, and he had never, ever told anyone about that before! She continued on saying that his name was Pendleton, but that he also would be known by the name of Gordon Mitchell. She told him that he would eventually go to Europe to work in films and that to the rest of the world, he would become well known by his acting pseudonym of Gordon Mitchell.

To top that off, he says back in 1960 after returning to school from summer vacation, one of his students admitted that his mother was an astrologist. Upon meeting and talking with her, she told him that in a few months he would be leaving the teaching business altogether and would go to Rome and work in films. That's what she told him, his chart had told her. Some weeks later just for fun, a fortune-teller friend of his told him very much the same thing by reading the cards. He himself shuffled the cards and she read them again, resulting in the same conclusions. Again he shuffled the cards and once again, the same thing cropped up.

So no wonder, when all this happen at the airport in Rome, he nearly fainted right then and there. He just couldn't believe what was happening. Fortunately, for us fans, it did happen, and we're all the more thankful for it. Some forty odd years later and more than two-hundred films under his belt, the name of Gordon Mitchell can still command attention in film circles, especially the *Spaghetti* Westerns of which we are all certainly huge fans of.

Costarring with Mitchell in his first role was the beautiful Italian heartthrob Vira Silenti. Also, there was the Afro American ex-*Mr. Universe* Paul Wynter (pronounced as winter). Afterward, with the impressions made, Mitchell was asked to continue in the Maciste role for the rest of the series. He did decline this not wanting to sign an option and thus becoming limited in his script choices and picks. But with Mark Forest* still away, the

---

* Mark Forest, real name (Lou Degni) a native New Yorker born in Brooklyn 1933. His is a third-generation Italian/American, with grandparents who immigrated over to the States from Naples. Years later after he'd relocated to the Los Angeles area, and during his early bodybuilding days he was involved in a night club act called "Strength Premise." He was also in the Venice and Muscle Beach areas of Santa Monica when he became Mr. Venice Beach of 1954. That same year he came in second place for the Mr. Muscle Beach competition. Of all the California muscle guys Forest was second recruited by Italian filmmakers to go to Italy and make movies following the earlier successes of Steve Reeve and his *Hercules* films. Forest's first film was called *Goliath and the Dragon* (1960). In all, from 1960 to 1965, he made twelve films total.

Amazing after such a prolific career beginning in film work, he walked away from it all to study opera and voice. Today he lives in Arleta, California, where he continues to sing and teach opera.

producers now teamed up with American ex-*Tarzan* actor Gordon Scott for their next *Maciste* film.

There was after all, plenty of work for Mitchell, after finally arrived and got going on the first film, then just kept coming, and coming after that. The next thing he knew he'd worked all year long and still had film work backed up. For his next film, which began just two days after finishing the first one, was called *The Giant of Metropolis* (1961) for director Umberto Scarpelli. It was more of an "Atlantis, lost continent" type of film where he portrayed Obro, a daring man of strength and courage who challenges the evil King Yotar who was threatening to destroy all. His costar was the beautiful Cuban actress Bella Cortez who would continue to star with him in his next two films, *Vulcan, Son of Jupiter* (1962), where he portrayed Pluto; *Ali Baba and the Seven Saracens* (1962), here he portrayed Omar the ruler. He says Ms. Cortez was the real life girlfriend of director Emimmo Salvi, whom Gordon made several, films together including a couple of a Western. Mitchell said they all got along very well together, that Emimmo trusted him. Until his passing in 2003, Mitchell said he had still stayed in touch with Ms. Cortez who up until that time had been living in the States.

Mitchell continued to reveal how much he enjoyed those early films he made, and that they were his favorites of all the movies he'd made over the years. During this *Peplum* career period he turned in some fourteen of this genre between 1961 and 1965 before his involvement with the Westerns. Among those films were a sprinkling of Viking and Pirate films as well as one sci-fi in which he was mainly a cameo as a video screen voice in *2+5 Mission Hydra* as Murdu. It also starred an Italian bodybuilder, Kirk Morris (Adriano Bellini).

Some of his other films in this vein were *The Return of the Son of the Sheik* costarring as Joseph mercenary leader, and *The Fury of Achilles,* stars as Achilles' directed by Marino Girolami. This movie, he said, was probably his favorite of the *Peplums* he'd done. Others of the *Peplum* vein he did during this period of his career were *The Conqueror of Corinth* costars as General Metello; *With Fire and Sword* costarred as Ulrich, and *Julius Caesar against the Pirates* as evil pirate king Hamar, Lastly was *Zeus* (1982) starred for Enimmo Salvi's last film.

Gordon Mitchell has had an astounding career well into the millennium. He worked in some of most exotic places the world had to offer during his era in the movies. He managed to turn in more than two-hundred film appearances in projects made throughout the world in places like Greece, Turkey, Yugoslavia as well as Italy and Spain. Not too shabby a career for a veteran bodybuilder and ex-schoolteacher.

It was 1965 when Mitchell first became involved with the Italian Western genre with *Three Graves for a Winchester, Per Ringo.* This, his first of more than thirty Westerns to follow was directed by his friend Emimmo Salvi. Mitchell starred here as Frank Sander, the Texan. His costar and friend/ fellow bodybuilder, and ex-*Mr. Universe,* Mickey Hargitay was also in this Western. They had a great time making this film together, so claimed both Mitchell and Hargitay. It's a shame they never made another one together. Hargitay's role here was as Ringo Carson. The film was accompanied by a rousing music score orchestrated by Armando Sciascia.

Of these thirty-plus Westerns Mitchell did during his career in Italy, he was told right off at the beginning as he was still pumped up for the *Peplums,* that the Italian audiences preferred their cowboy actors as the tall, slim wrangler type they were used to seeing in the older American films. Wanting to stay in the groove meant he'd have to conform, so he did. He said he dropped down from his normal 220 lb to about 170 lb and pretty much stayed there the rest of his life. Other actors coming to the genre from the *Peplums,* not wanting to be left behind, did the same.

About this era in time Mitchell said there in Rome, he and Mickey as well as Steve Reeves all lived next door to one another. Mitchell had built a rooftop makeshift gym for the guys and they would come up and lift weights and work out together. There were other American actors, some ex-bodybuilders there as well, all of whom were friends and associates of one another. There were Brad Harris, Ken Clark, Dan Vadis, Gordon Scott and Richard Harrison. By his own admission Mitchell said he didn't fraternize with some of the other actors and their world of partying. Those actors, some of whom were intent on chasing the girlfriends and even wives of some of the film people didn't sit well with him. Those were touchy waters especially when your livelihood depended upon those people working in the industry.

During these early years, Mitchell would branch out, feeling out the other film genres for work with such titles as *Death Danced the Twist* (1962) an obscure crime film (not yet obtained for review) spoken of by Mitchell during his French *Nadarland.com* interview, in which he says the film was actually made. It was directed by Piero Costa and starred GM, Fred Harrison (Fernando Bilbao), Roger Browne and Luisa Rivelli. Another was *At Midnight, You Throw the Body Out!* (1966). A comedy directed by Aldo Florio, GM portrays a crazed German killer. That same year, GM stars in his first horror film *called The Vendetta of Lady Morgan,* in a role as the butler Roger. Also with Erica Blanc (Enrica Maria Colombatto), and Paul Muller, directed by Massimo Pupillo. It was shot at the famous *Borghese Castle* in Artena near Ostia, Italy. The eerie musical score was by Piero Umiliani.

Throughout his career Mitchell would revert many times to this horror genre for work. He was quite prolific at times with the likes of:

Frankenstein's Castle of Freaks (1972) as Igor; *Frankenstein 1980* (1972) as Dr. Otto Frankenstein; *Skin under the Claw* (1975) as Prof. Helmut; *Dr. Jekyll Likes them Hot* (1978) as gym owner Petorius; *Blood Delirium* (1988) as manservant Hermann; *Curse of the Red Butterfly* (1982) as gang leader Brado; *Cross of the Seven Jewels* (1983) as the Black Mass Priest. Also, there is one yet unconfirmed title out there for this genre called *The Mutant* (1984) which may very well be a sci-fi entry instead of a horror. Besides the *2+5 Mission Hydra* (1966) he also did two other sci-fi films: *The Alien Within* a.k.a. *The Evil Spawn* (1987) as Dan Thorn; another called: *An Enraged New World* (2002) as Gen. Murchison directed by Mike A. Martinez.

Mitchell also turned in several for the Adventure genre during his long prolific career, some of those were *Radhapura: Terminal of the Damned* (1968) *as Slaver Alfredo; Oil: The Billion Dollar Fire* (1970) *as the disgruntled Paul; Four for All* (1975) *as Margherito; Marco Polo (a RAI TV miniseries)* (1981) *as Arnolfo;* Next was an unconfirmed title called *The Conqueror* (1982); and finally *Mines of Kilimanjaro* (1983) *as Rolf.*

Mitchell's most prolific work to date though was his Westerns. Beginning with his first in 1965, he went on to turn in some thirty more entries for the genre. His second was called *Thompson 1880* (1966) as Glenn Sheppard. This storyline has to do with a man and his machine gun invention. His next released that same year was called *Kill or Be Killed,* with Robert Mark (Rodd Dana) as the violin playing gunslinger. Here Mitchell guest-starred as a hired gunman called Baltimore Joe.

Mitchell was called home as his mother takes very ill and passes away, and soon after his stepfather also died the same year. After spending a required time dealing with family and such matters, he returned to do a spy film with Ty Hardin and Michael Rennie, a Sergio Corbucci film called *Moving Target* (1967). Mitchell as the deadly henchmen called the Albanian. Mitchell now continues after his returns to his Western work as the load gradually increases. *John the Bastard* (1967) was his next as the Mormon sect killer, Danite. For another that same year was a starring role for Mitchell called *Born to Kill.* Here Mitchell portrays gunslinger Rod Gordon/Roose who helps to rid a town of a whole slew of bad guys. They make him the town Marshall and he even gets the girl in this one, the Mayor's daughter Laurie Waldman (Femi Benussi). It was directed by Antonio Mollica.

Also 1967, we find Mitchell had done yet another Western *Rita of the West,* this one, however, was a musical Western, believe it! Yep, it starred Italian pop artist Rita Pavone with some catchy little song and dance numbers. Mitchell's role was that of an Indian Chief, Silly Bull (or Sitting Buffalo in other dubbed copies). Also stars Kirk Morris as Ringo and Terence Hill (Mario Girotti) as Black Stan. Not a bad little film seriously.

> Mitchell did turn in another Western that year, but for a *RAI* (Italian TV) production called *Toto Ciak.* This actually was a comedy vehicle for the Neapolitan comic Antonio De Curtis, professionally known as just Toto. It was actually a TV Special that was aired on *RAI* Primetime TV June 8, 1967. It presented three sketches starring the comedienne Toto in various mock roles spoofing the more popular film genres of the day. In one he was the "Secret Agent" spoofing *James Bond* Spy films; Second was "Toto vs. Ringo" a Westerns spoof with Gordon Mitchell portraying Ringo a notorious gunman; Third was "The Lieutenant" spoofing Crime films and included Ubaldo Lay as Sheridan.

For 1968 Mitchell came *Saguaro* starred Kirk Morris (Adriano Bellini), Larry Ward as Saguaro, Alan Steel (Sergio Ciani), GM guest stars as gunman Clayton. Next he gets to guest-star in a Lee Van Cleef Western called *Beyond the Law.* Here he nearly takes the show in the role of outlaw leader Burton a notorious gunman. Continuing in the genre next with *Lynching* (1968), he costarred with popular Dutch actor Glenn Saxon. Mitchell's role is that of Morgan Pitt / Mule. It was directed by Al Bradley (Alfonse Brescia). For his next Western Mitchell does another for 1968 called *Dead for a Dollar.* It starred Jorge (George) Hilton, John Ireland and GM as the wanted outlaw Roy Fulton.

It was also this year in '68 that Mitchell began his next prolific venture with the Crime film genre. For his third of the genre came, *For a Fistful of Diamonds,* in which he co stars as Al Rubino. Then there was *Phenomenal and the Treasure of Tutankamen,* a superhero/crime film with Mitchell costarring as Gregory Falco a big-time confidence man and thief. From there he would go on to make some twenty-eight of these crime films. Prolific indeed, match that to thirty-plus Westerns, and the various *Peplum* features early in his career, I'd say the man had his nose to the grindstone for sure.

> Later in the year, he had returned to the States for Christmas time. Not the same without his mom and stepdad now, but he still had his sister and her family as well Joe Gold, his family and the guys down at the gym. He had planned on attending a New Years Eve party with friends Mickey and Ellen Hargitay. But as luck would have it they would have to meet him at the airport New Years Eve instead. He'd gotten a call from director Fellini, who wanted him back the on the thirty-first for a part in his new film *Fellini Satyicon* (1969). His part would that of Il Perdone, the Highwayman. This film is not quite what we'd call a *Peplum* entry, although it was depicting that era of Rome and its internal

> decay from within from overindulgence of just about everything one could possibly imagine, mainly sex. If one has watched any of Fellini's films, they can see what his films are like. Supposedly he was one of Italy's best, but I find his films personally just weird.

Mitchell went to say about his trip home that while at Joe's gym (which he was part owner of) he got to meet Arnold Schwarzenegger and Franco Columbu the *Sardinian* Power lifter and buddy of Arnold's about that period in time. Later in the '70s Lou Ferrigno and British bodybuilder / ex-*Peplum* star Reg Park could be found there on occasion.

This year would be another first in Mitchell's career as he turned in his first War genre film called *Suicide Patrol* (1969) Here Mitchell costarred as Sgt. Smith to the lead, French actor Pierre Richard. Here again, during Mitchell's long endearing career he would turn in some eleven films of this genre. Some those were *Hell Camp: Last Days of the SS* (1977), GM as Camp Commandant Stern. This film was directed by Ivan Kathansky and also starred Richard Harrison. This is the film Mitchell had previously talked about where Harrison played the good US Officer (Major Lexman) and he plays the vicious German officer.

Some of Mitchell's other better know war films yet to come were *Black Gold Dossier,* a.k.a. *Achtung! Desert Tigers* (1978), again with Richard Harrison. Then came, *Inchon* (1982) an epic size Korean war drama from director Terence Young. Here Mitchell has an unaccredited cameo, as Marine Troops Commander (GHQ officer). The film starred Laurence Olivier, Ben Gazzara and Jacqueline Bisset; another one was *Treasure of the Lost Desert* (1984), with GM as Arms dealer; and lastly I'll mention *Commando Invasion* (1985) with Mitchell as Colonel McMoreland.

It was also 1969 when Mitchell turned out another Western that really helped keep the ball rolling for the genre called *I Am Sartana, Your Angel of Death,* a.k.a. *Sartana the Gravedigger.* It starred Gianni (John) Garko as Sartana. It was directed by Anthony Ascott (Giuliano Carmineo). Garko made five of these Sartana series films from 1968 to 1971. These made by Carmineo were probably the better of the series with the character becoming more mystical, ghost like even.

Mitchell made three of these Sartana films, another one was *Django and Sartana are Coming . . . It's the End!* (1970). It starred Hunt Powers (Jack Betts), Chet Davis and Mitchell as one Black Burt Kelly. It was directed by Miles Deem (Demofilo Fidani). Mitchell worked quite a few films of Fidani. Fidani was quite proficient at shooting lots of film that he would later splice in various other segments and scenes making several films from one editing session. Another of Fidani's efforts was *The Stranger that kneels beside the Shadow of the Corpse* (1970) starring Hunt Powers as bounty hunter Lazar, Chet Davis as Blonde and Mitchell in a cameo as Roger Murdoch. For Mitchell's last Sartana film, it was called *Lets go Kill Sartana* (1971) which starred George Martin, and costarring GM portraying Greg the crazy one, and Virginia Rodin as Lena. This elusive title is still on several wants lists, but yet remains to be obtained for review. The trailer has been out awhile.

Also for 1971, Mitchell turns in a comedic Western effort guest-starring as the bad guy Coyote. This was more of a vehicle for the blonde bombshell Mamie Van Doren and Italian comic Chiquito (Augusto Paugan) (as the Kid) called: *the Arizona Kid.* Mainly for the bulk of Mitchell's Westerns, we find this genre work was done between 1965 and 1975. For that ten year period, the main clutch of the Westerns genre phenomenon he turned in like thirty Westerns, including the one *RAI*-TV show with Toto. After that there was only a sprinkling of oaters among his other crime and horror film entries.

Many scripts that have come and gone that would have brought our man Chuck to venture into many facets of the film industry. One most folks would not even realize in their fondest imagination is the fact that, while there based in Rome, he took a parcel of land in payment for work from one of the Italian filmmakers. This piece of land lay outside Rome to the south in an area called *Cave* (pronounced Cah'-vay). Here Mitchell went about (in his spare time away from films) building himself a full-size replica Western town. A town he would largely construct from memory, in the likeness of 1866 circa Denver, Colorado, his birthplace.

With this town, he would again supplement his income by renting it out to the various film directors as set locations for their many varied films. Rome and surrounding areas were becoming more cramped by the day. The directors jumped at the opportunity to use this location with less stringent regulations toward fire codes they were more accustomed to back nearer to Rome. As I stated before, the man's accomplishments were certainly overwhelming to the imagination. Eventually, he thought one day when he would think about leaving and returning to the States, he might could leave this town for the more unfortunate and homeless families of the area. This town he felt would provide shelter from the elements and give them a fighting chance to bounce back into life's mainstream. Alas, we're afraid this never did work out quite as he had envisioned.

It seems per the *Spaghetti Cinema* no. 39 article on GM called "My Name is Chuck" by William Connolly: The building of the Western town project had been previously approved and authorized by the cave town mayor. Cave was about thirty miles / twenty-five minutes outside Rome. The film he had been working on at the time was his first comedy called, *At Midnight . . . You throw the Body Out!* (1966). It starred Brett Halsey,

Luisa Rivelli and GM as Van Himst. It was directed by Aldo Florio. He went on to say, the Producer didn't have enough money, so he took the offer of a ten acre land deal in lieu of. He surmised land, was land a good investment.

With the Mayor's approval and signed papers he figured that was all he needed and was off and running with a small bulldozer clearing land building a road. After a little bout with the small farmers there about, which he finally settle with a little money and having them work for him bringing him lumber and wood scraps for his buildings. He began to build the stores and whatnot out of this wood. He said he had spent about $30,000 in wood alone which is scarce there and a very valuable commodity.

He stated for an English, Italian news article by Nino Lo Bello, "Denver, Italian style, a building south of Rome" given to me by GM himself, in which he says "All the money I get from renting the location and most of my salary from films goes into the buying of wood, nails, cement, equipment and what have you for this mad-mad project of mine. The first year I put up four wooden buildings. Last year I managed to get up another twelve structures, and this year I hope to have five more finished." All of this work he'd pretty much done on his own which is staggering, the man had perseverance.

His first bite came from filmmaker Miles Deem (Demofilo Fidani) who told him you get me the proper permission and stamps from the government he'd work there at his studio. It seems the Government would pay him a subsidy to work in a place they approved.

After much interaction with government officials and the getting of fire insurance etc, and another year later, he finally got an in hand Occupation document including papers saying it was approved by the government. He was then ready to rock his friends couldn't believe an American had done this in Italy. The final approval documents were stamped May 16, 1975. The more prosperous the studio got though, the more things the government seemed to pick at.

He went on to say in the *Spaghetti Cinema* interview for Bill Connolly, he had a five year license and was busy with films being made, by the end of the fifth year, they sent him a notice that he would have to build a sound stage now at a cost of a million dollars. He figures they had all gotten jealous of him doing so well out there and him being an American to boot. It was then he found out that in Italy, there is no live sound recordings done, that's one of the laws. This law could have very well been the main reasoning behind all the added soundtracks after the fact, and the dubbings. Possibly, it had more to do with area overcrowding near and around Rome studios like De Paolis, Elios, or Cinecitta than we imagined.

At any rate, Mitchell went on to add, "If I had understood the law really well, I'd still probably be functioning. He then attempted to turn it into an ecological park, which turned out to be more of a bigger problem, but then nearing his goal finally, the Communist party would blow the whole thing off. It was in a word an experience I believe, but it sure kept him busy.

By 1975 Mitchell had slowed on the Western genre as the phenomenon was pretty much dried up by that time but for a few in the comedic vein of which Mitchell also had a part in. One later entry for a 1978 release was a turn of the century oater called *White Fang and the Grand kid,* a.k.a. *White Fang in the West.* This one has Mitchell, being credited under his real name Charles Pendleton, which is a rare item to come across. He costars as the town boss Mulligan, driving his big open top car through the fields and town alike. Tony Kendall (Luciano Stella) stars as Franky with the Kid Billy and Buck the dog. It was written and directed by Vito Bunschini.

Actually, the only other later entry we originally thought was a Western, turned out not to be was called *Fists, Dollars and Spinach* (1978). Supposedly a crime parody on a *Popeye* comic book character called Sammy Manna who owns a down and out Spinach farm. Mitchell portrays a mob boss Frank Stylus who's after his land. Sammy wants to keep the farm and continue helping to keep his people employed. It was directed by his old friend Emimmo Salvi. Domenico Salvi more commonly known as Emimmo was an active director and screenwriter throughout his career in the Italian cinema from the 1950s. Mitchell was fortunate to have worked for Salvi several times which no doubt was a boon for both their careers. They made seven films together, three *Peplums*; one *Viking*; one *Western*; one *Crime* Parody; and one *sci-fi* for which Salvi had some dealings, either as director, writer and/or producer. Per Mitchell, he was a great organizer on film projects.

> This sci-fi project for Emimmo Salvi came into being much later about 1982, and was called *Zeus* (1983). Per *Spaghetti Cinema* no. 59 issue interview by William Connolly and Tom Betts, of April 1, 1990, Mitchell explains that his friend Salvi committed suicide because he was found to have diabetes. According to Mitchell, Salvi had called him the day before, he was in hospital, and went on to let Mitchell know that the next morning they were meeting with the producer and we're finally going to make the film *Zeus* after all. After some six months of preparations, they were now ready. SFX man Bonati had finished the technical part, really beautiful he told GM. He said Salvi was crying on the phone he was so happy that we were going to make another film. It was the very next day that a friend called to tell him Salvi had committed suicide. The gun used though wasn't found.

Tom Betts located an Italian website to confirm the *Zeus* title and found it was actually completed and released in 1983, and was an Italian / US coproduction, *20th Century Fox* release. It starred Aaron Hichis as Zeus, Natasha Windless as Giunone, and Gordon Mitchell (in unknown role). For the direction credits, both Domingo Haman (who completed the film) and Emimmo Salvi (who had started it) are listed. Producer was Mac Rufus. So if we gather from this Salvi died sometime in 1982, not 1989 as originally thought.

There were several pictures made there at Mitchell's mock town with its many structures, some that were blown up along the way that he would later rebuild. A couple of the films in remembrance of this shooting location were *Strange Tale of Minnesota Stinky,* a.k.a. *The Western Story* (1971) another Mile Deem (Fidani) film with GM in cameo as Ironhead Donovan. Then there was a Richard Harrison* film, one called *One Woman for Seven Bastards* a.k.a. *Sewer Rats* (1974), a crime drama with Mitchell in the role of Gordon one of the seven gang members.

The guys loved it there said Mitchell in one of our phone conversations back about 2001, "If they wanted to blow up a building, they would set this up first with me, then do the effects, and blow it on film." He would then hop back on his dozer and clean up the debris. Then he would calmly rebuild the structures again later. Being far enough outside of Rome and general civilization, the special fire restrictions, et cetera didn't really apply so therefore almost anything went, as long as it was cleared through our town Marshal, Gordon Mitchell.

Then it happened, "things were going too good." Mitchell said. He'd already had been in constant turmoil with the authorities of the area for permits, exorbitant taxes and other totally unrelated erroneous charges that constituted a never ending payment of monies to the Italian bureaucracy. All of a sudden he explained, "They claimed to have rezoned the area annexing the property and just out and out took it!" He fought it as best he could, but was unsuccessful in even recouping any of his lost initial cash outlay. It was truly a shame, but a lot of investments went sour with that form of government which was the ruling class of Italy during that era.

There was another Western Mitchell was said to have been associated with according to several sources an erroneous title listing has evolved for

---

* Richard Harrison continued making films himself all over the world. Some of his film ventures were obviously shot there at Mitchell's Cave Studio. Harrison would say, "Often as not, they could even get Mitchell to climb down off his bulldozer long enough to dawn his hat and shoot a scene with them for a cameo appearance." He went on to say he was a sweetheart, great guy to be around.

a 1978/79 film called *Porno-Erotic Western;* a.k.a. *Pago Cara Si Muerte (Spa)* (*You Pay Dear for Death)* supposedly a comedy directed by Gerald B. Lennox, actually a pseudonym we find for Angelo Pannaccio. The film's cast listing is somewhat misleading and begins with Karin Well (Wilma Truccolo), Ray O'Connor (Remo Capitani), Rosemary Lindt, Tomas Rudi and Lorenz Bien. Therein we find Charles Pendleton (GM) is also listed as is Patrizia Mayer.

It is believed that this was a spliced in compilation of films by the director Pannaccio, in particular an earlier film of his called *Requiem for a Bounty Hunter* (1970) that was filmed at Mitchell's Cava Studio. If we note, per the above cast list, there was no mention of the actual lead characters of this *Requiem* film, like Steven Tedd (Whistler) or Michael Forest (Burton). Mitchell, however, at times has been listed as being in this *Requiem* film. However, in the copies currently available via European sources, he is not found to be in it as an actor, nor is he credited. It could be his scene/or scenes could have been cut out during Pannaccio's final editing.

> We speculate here that Pannaccio possibly later in the 1970s when a very erotic period had begun to evolve in European film work may have reopened his film and done some slick reediting, inserting some of these previously cutout scenes along with adding some other erotic scenes spliced in as well. There was a period in time when there were several films on the market with erotic Western themes like *The Ramrodder* (1969)*; The Erotic Adventures of Zorro* (1971)*;* and *The Virgin Cowboy* (1972) to name a few. It is quite possible Pannaccio felt he would just jump on that bandwagon wave by altering his Western and making a whole new film from scraps (talented these Italian filmmakers). Could be Chuck just happened to be in one or more of those scrapped scene pieces he used?

When asked point blank about this title, Chuck claimed he knew nothing about it and said he was never in such a film with that title. Another interesting thing here is for the music score which is listed being by Giuliano Sorgini, and not by Daniele Patucchi as on the original *Requiem* film. Back in 2006 we accidentally ran across a listing and a film poster for this film on a German website (since defunct) *www.fatmandan.de*. So evidently, this film was in the process of being made although no confirmation of that has since been found. Furthermore, since this film has never been unearthed to date for a review we will now rest our case.

Moving on now Mitchell continued to bang along in the Italian Cinema on into the 1980s with such *postwar* films as *Holocaust Part II* (1980) actually more of a crime drama with GM as Felix Oppenheimer; *Endgame* (1982) with GM as Colonel Morgan; *She* (1982), GM as Hector Commander of the Nork forces of the Nork Valley stronghold; and *Rush* (1984), here with GM as Yor, evil Ruler of the New World Order colony.

After returning home to LA and the *World Gym* business there at Marine Del Rey with partner Joe Gold, he continued to go back and forth to Europe a couple of times a year for small film projects. Once was in 1976 for an Italian film (yet to be acquired for review) called *The Killers* which stars GM in the role as the contract killer Pablo. Again, in 1980, he returns for friend producer/director Paolo Percora and a crime film shot at the *Cave Film International* studio (we believe this was Mitchell's old place) called *La Lucertola (The Lizard)*. It starred Gordon Mitchell as mob boss Don Savior, Luciano Salce and Peppe Pecora, director's son. This film by Percora has been confirmed as made, but still is yet to be acquired for review.

Later, for another Italian release of 1984, Mitchell returned to Rome for a second crime film venture with friend director Paolo Percora and called *Faida (Feud)* Peppe Pecora stars along with Gordon Mitchell as the vengeful Priest Prete. Rocking along with some television show episodes in Europe for the 1980s, we find his first was one called *Marco Polo,* a *RAI-TV* miniseries begun in 1982 with Gordon Mitchell participating in a four-part showing through '83 as Arnolfo. A period drama set in Italy. Also, for 1983, he remains in Italy to portray an Italian police commissioner for one episode of a *RAI*-TV series called *Ten Italian Directors, Ten Italian Stories.* Mitchell's starring episode was simply called "Il Commissario" (The Commissioner). For 1988, GM returns to Italy and *RAI*-TV for another miniseries called *The Betrothed* with GM as crime boss Don Gonzalo. This series ran from 1988-2001.

Lest we forget several comedies our man was involved with overseas. Some of these were quite funny like an early one called *Rompo* (1971)a Bruno Corbucci film: *The Slave* (1972) with GM as Von Thirac a former Nazi officer with a wooden arm, who runs a charter plane service; *The Domestic* (1974) GM is Gen. Von Werner, *Happy Birthday Harry* (1980), John Richardson as Harry Peterson on his fortieth birthday. GM as Sandy's muscled-up jealous boyfriend, also Terry-Thomas as Doctor Christopher; *the Umbrella Case* (1980) a French production with Pierre Richard. GM as Moskovitz the Russian killer; *Women Doctors Prefer Sailors* (1981) GM is the killer, chasing everybody about; Then lastly back in the States, for a Fred Olen Ray film called *Bikini Drive-in* (1994) a nod to the actors career with him in cameo as Goliath for a drive-in film clip of the fictional "Goliath and the Cheerleaders";

Next, for 1997, Chuck returned to Munich, Germany for director friend Clemens Keiffenheim and a TV show called *Hercules Prays in Munich.*

Later he delved into a German TV series called *Marriage before Court* for another episode called "Cybersex and the Sect trap" (1998). For the credits on both the above shows he uses his real name Charles Pendleton.

For 2001, Chuck was back in Rome and was cohost on his friend, Paolo Pecora's Television show for *RAI*-TV network, Rome. Televised early Sunday evenings (during this era in time) immediately following the afternoon football (Soccer) game. Chuck was the celebrity cohost as Gordon Mitchell a name synonymous in Italy with bodybuilding and the movies. He presented short takes of himself and friends from the *World Gym Internationals* and other like Championship events. Also weekly, they would include televised interviews of himself, and his many friends back in California near and about the Muscle Beach areas of Venice and Marina Del Rey gyms.

In later shows, Chuck with friend and traveling companion Bill Comstock showed various outtakes, including tips about actors and American cultures in Arts and the Cinema along with a weekly brief history on sports discipline. Also, as a little something for the younger fans, they introduced a crime-fighting superhero called "The Rivloc," an antidote bug zapper that works against the evils of racism which seems to affect all of us in this day an age.

For 2002, Chuck went the full yardage for a young moviemaker Michael A. Martinez and one of his full-length sci-fi / futuristic productions called *An Enraged New World*, GM as General Murchison. Great job on everyone's part, good story and great camera work, filmed on locations in Alaska. Afterward, Chuck returned to Munich, Germany for another production by his friend Clem Keiffenheim.

This time it was for a major film project called *Die to Live: Das Musikill (*a.k.a. *Music That kills),* a black comedy. It stars Chuck, here again as Gordon Mitchell as the star of a theater troupe who suddenly dies. To avoid certain failure to the whole production because of his death, they take his body to a mad taxidermist and have him stuffed. Afterward, he is reanimated so as to be operated by computer remote control. All is good now with a robotic control stage star filling the theater every night with patrons. A wild project that hopefully someday we'll get to see since it was released to German DVD back in 2004, and the English version that was promised, coming soon that still hasn't surfaced in this country or via Internet sources to date.

A trailer for the film was shown here in the States back July 6, 2003, at the "Sword and Sandal Film Festival" event held at UCLA, Los Angeles, California, on that Sunday. That event was attended by Chuck himself in character as Gordon Mitchell.

It was also 2003 when Chuck signed on again to do a last crime film cameo for Michael A. Martinez and his then coproducer, one Nick Groff The new film was called *Malevolence.* Here Chuck portrays a retired Capo Fabrizio De Martino. Also, there's a nod to the genre as retired producer Ted V. Mikels is on hand portraying director Rene Cardone Jr. This was really Chuck's last outing onscreen. He passed away apparently in his sleep September 20, 2003. Found in a peaceful setting in his apartment there in Marina Del Rey surrounded by his precious pictures he'd painted himself over the years since returning to the States. His movie memorabilia also adorned the walls as a distinct reminder to one and all of those wonderful years he spent abroad in film work.

Now bringing this bio on our man Chuck Pendleton (Gordon Mitchell) to a close leaves us somewhat exasperated to say the least. His achievements of some two-hundred-plus films and assorted television work, special appearances, et cetera tends to put this piece of work down as a feeble attempt at scratching the surface of the man's career in the Cinema. His personage is certainly immortalized by his lifetime of accomplishments, and by his following of fans that continue to follow his work.

Furthermore, it has been my astute pleasure to having met the man in person within a film benefits setting, befitting that of the Film Star he most certainly was and continues to be in the eyes of his fans. Mr. Charles (Chuck) Pendleton (Gordon Mitchell) your fans truly thank you. The Man with *That* look has certainly gone far in filmdom, RIP great warrior.

End.

- Below is a complete filmography of Gordon Mitchell's Euro Westerns. The dates are aligned as close as possible with information currently at hand, plus international release dates included. **Posters and picture are accredited to the Sebastian Haselbeck collection via his website www.spaghetti-western.net*

GORDON MITCHELL EURO WESTERNS FILMOLOGY

1965

Three Graves for a Winchester; *Per Ringo, Tre Colpi Di Winchester per Ringo;* a.k.a. *Three Bullets for Ringo*; Ital, Director Emimmo Salvi (GM stars as Frank Sanders / the Texan); 1966; Costars Mickey Hargitay as Bill (Ringo) Carson, John Heston and Milla Sannoner and Spean Covery.

1966

***Thompson 1880*;** Ital, Director Albert Moore (Guido Zurli) (GM costars as Glenn Sheppard a down and out miner); 10/13/66; It starred Jorge (George) Martin as Raymond machine gun inventor; Also Gia Sandri, José Bodalo, José Jaspe, Pedro Sanchez and Paul Muller.

Kill or be Killed, *Uccidi O Muori;* a.k.a. *Kill or Die!* A.k.a. *Ringo vs. Jerry Colt*; Ital, Director Amerigo Anton (Tanio Boccia) (GM costars as Baltimore Joe, gunman in black); 11/1/66; It stars Robert Mark (Rodd Dana) as the violin-playing gunman Jerry Colt; Elina De Witt, Albert Farley and Andrea Bosic.

1967

Born to Kill, *Nato per Uccidere*; Ital, Director Tony Mulligan (Antonio Mollica) (GM stars as Rod Gordon / Roose); 6/15/67; Costars Femi Benussi as Laurie, Aldo Berti as Dodge, and Tom Felleghi as Mr. Tyson.

Rita of the West; *Little Rita nel Far West;* a.k.a. *Li'l Rita; Crazy Westerners*; Ital, Director Ferdinando Baldi (GM as Sitting Buffalo Indian Chief); 8/11/67; Stars Rita Pavone, Kirk Morris, Fernando Sanchez, Terence Hill (Mario Girotti) and Livio Lorenzon.

1968

Saguaro; *Sapevano Solo Uccidere;* a.k.a. *I'll Die for Vengeance*; Ital, Director Amerigo Anton (Tanio Boccia) (GM costars as Clayton Foster); 3/10/68; Stars Kirk Morris (Adriano Bellini) as Jeff Smart, Larry Ward as outlaw Saguaro and Alan Steel (Sergio Ciani) as band leader. Jeff's love interest is Katy (Kim Arden).

Beyond the Law, *Al Di La Della Legge;* a.k.a. *The Good Die First; Bloodsilver*; Ital/ W. Ger, Director Giorgio Stegani (GM in cameo as gunman / gang leader Burton); 4/10/68; Stars Lee Van Cleef as Billy Joe Cudlip as gunman/ opportunist, Antonio Sabato as Ben Novak, Lionel Stander as Preacher and Bud Spencer (Carlo Pedersoli) as James Cooper silver mine owner.

Trusting is good . . . Shooting is Better, *T'ammazzo Raccomadati a Dio;* a.k.a. *Dead for a Dollar*; Ital, Director Osvaldo Civirani (GM in cameo as outlaw Roy Fulton); 8/17/68; It stars Jorge (George) Hilton as Glenn Reno, John Ireland as The Colonel, Sandro Milo as Monica Pardo, and Dick Palmer (Mimmio Palmara).

If Born a Swine . . . Kill Him!, *Sei Una Carogna . . . E T'Ammazzo!* A.k.a. *Lynching*; Ital, Director Al Bradley (Alfonso Bescia) (GM in cameo as gunman Morgan Pitt / Mule who loves a good fight); 11/21/68; Stars Glenn Saxson as US Deputy Marshall Grant; Maria Bardanzellu, Fernando Sancho, and Giovanni (Nello) Pazzafini.

1969

I Am Sartana, Your Angel of Death; a.k.a. *Sono Sartana, Il Vostro Becchino; Sartana the Gravedigger*; Ital/ Fr, Director Anthony Ascott (Giuliano Carmineo) (GM as bounty hunter Degueyo); 11/20/69; Stars Gianni (John) Garko as Sartana, Klaus Kinski as bounty hunter, Frank Wolff, Ettore Manni and José Torres.

1970

Django and Sartana are coming . . . It's the End! *Arrivano Django e Sartana . . . E La Fine!* A.k.a. *Django and Sartana . . . Showdown in the West*; Ital, Director Dick Spitfire (Demofilo Fidani) (GM costars as outlaw leader Burt Keller); 11/20/70; Stars Hunt Powers (Jack Betts) as Sartana; Also Chet Davis as Django; GM, Simone Blondell and Krista Nell.

The Stranger that Kneels beside the Shadow of a Corpse, *Inginocchiati Straiero . . . I Cadaveri Non Fanno Ombra;* a.k.a. *Dead Men don't make Shadows*; Ital, Director Miles Deem (Demofilo Fidani) (GM in cameo as outlaw Roger Murdock who has the gold); 11/27/70; It stars Hunt Powers (Jack Betts) as bounty hunter Lazar, Chet Davis, and Simone Blondell.

Seven Savage Men, *Se T'Incontro T'Ammazzo;* a.k.a. *Finders Killers*; Ital, Director Gianni Crea (GM costars as jack's brother Chris Forrest); 3/27/71; Stars Donal O'Brien as Jack Forrest, Mario Brega as Crandell / Parker, Dean Stratford (Dino Strano) as Dexter Crandell's gunman and Femi Benussi. Storyline: Has two brothers looking to avenge the murder of their parents. All things point to land baron Crandell and his gang.

For a Coffin full of Dollars, *Per Una Bara Piena Di Dollars;* a.k.a. *Showdown for a Badman*; Ital, Director Miles Deem (Demofilo Fidani) (GM costars as bounty hunter John Hamilton); 4/1/71; It stars Hunt Powers (Jack Betts) as Mexican bandit Tamayo; Klaus Kinski as Dan Hagan and Jeff Cameron as Nevada Kid / Mark Hamilton. Also Simone Blondell (Simonetta Vitelli).

Strange Tale of Minnesota Stinky, *Doppia Taggliaper Minnesota Stinky;* a.k.a. *The Western Story; A Fistful of Death*; Ital, Director Miles Deem (Demofilo Fidani) (GM co stars as iron head Donovan); 4/17/71; Starring Hunt Powers (Jack Betts)as Butch Cassidy, Jeff Cameron (Geoffredo Scarciofolo) as Lt. Macho Callaghan, and Klaus Kinski in cameo as Rev. Cotton.

Reach You Bastard, *Giu Le Mani, Carogna;* a.k.a. *The Ballad of Django; a.k.a. The Django Story*; Ital, Director Lucky Dickinson (Demofilo Fidani) (GM in cameo as the last badman on Django's hit list, Buck Bradley); 8/21/71; Stars Hunt Powers (Jack Betts) as Django, Jeff Cameron (Geoffredo Scarciofolo) as Wild Bill Hickok, Dean Stratford (Dino Strano) and Dennis Colt with Paul Crain as outlaw brothers.

Note: Fidani seems to have made this film purely out of scenes being spliced in (like cut 'n' paste).

Let's Go and Kill Sartana, *Vamos a Matar Sartana*; Ital, Dir's: Peter Launders (Mario Pinzauti) and George Martin (GM costars as Greg (Crazy Person) Matto); 9/6/71; Stars George Martin as Nebraska Clay/Tex, Isarco Ravaioli as Sheriff Chet Hammer, Virginia Rodin as Lena and Monica Taber as Carol/Lucy, and with Cris Huerta and Daniel Martin.

The Day of Judgement, *Il Giorno Del Giudizio;* a.k.a. *Drummer of Vengeance*; Brit/ Ital, Director Robert Paget (Mario Gariazzo) (GM as Deputy Sheriff Norton); 9/9/71; Stars Ty Hardin as Roger Murdock out for avenge his murdered wife and child; Costars Craig Hill as the traveling carne who hides Murdock; also with Raf Baldassarre, Lee Burton and Rosalba Nera.

His Name is Sam Wallash . . . But they call him Amen, *Era Sam Wallash . . . Lo Chiamavano Cosi Sia;* a.k.a. *Savage Guns*; Ital, Director Miles Deem (Demofilo Fidani) (GM in cameo nod to the genre as "Gordon Mitchell born to kill, with some 20 notches on his gun butt"); 11/25/71; Stars Robert Woods as Sam Wallash, Dean Stratford (Dino Strano) as Mash Flannigan/Donovan, Dennis Colt, Simone Blondell (Simonetta Vitelli), and Custer Gail.

Others in cameo as *Specialists* are: Peter Martell (Pietro Martellanza) as "Peter Martell, procurer of the dead"; and Linclon Tate as "an expert knife thrower and bank robber."

Storyline: Has all three *Specialists* being brought in to kill Wallash by Flannigan.

The Arizona Kid, *I Fratelli Di Arizona* (comedic Western) Ital/ Philippine, Director Luciano Carlos (GM in cameo as badman called Coyote); 1971; Stars Chiquito (Augusto Pangan) as the Kid, and Mamie Van Doren as Sharon Miller, Mariela Branger, Bernard Bonnin and Pilar Velazquez.

His Name was Pot . . . But they called him Allegria, *IL Sun Nome Era Pot . . . Lo Chiamavano Allegria;* a.k.a. *Lobo the Bastard/ Lobo/ Hero Called Allegria*; Ital, Director Dennis Ford (Demofilo Fidani) (GM co stars as Ray part of a pair of bank robbers); 11/26/71; Stars Peter Martell (Pietro Martellanza), as the other bank robbing partner Pot. Also stars Lincoln Tate as Lobo (Wolf), others were Daniela Giordano and Lucky MacMurray.

A Man Called Dakota, *Un Uomo Chiamato Dakota*; Ital, Director Mario Sabatini (GM stars as Deputy Sheriff John Lead); 3/5/72*;* Stars Anthony Freeman (Mario Novelli) as Dakota, ex-Union officer. Also stars Tamara Baroni, Cleo Del Cile and Bill Vanders as Sheriff Scott.

The Magnificent West, *IL Magnifico West*; Ital, Director Gianni Crea (GM as the evil landgrabbing town boss Martin); 5/27/72; It stars Vassili Karis as Texas Bill, Lorenzo Fineschi as Bill's partner Lefty Jim, Dario Pino Fred, Italo Gasperini as Pistola and Fiorella Mannoia as Mary. Storyline has Bill and partners helping a small community fight off local landgrabbers.

Stay Away! Trinity Has Arrived in Eldorado! *Scansati . . . A Trinita Arriua Eldorado!* A.k.a. *Eldorado Comes . . . Stay Away from Trinity*; a.k.a. *Pokerface*; Ital, Director Dick Spitfire (Demofilo Fidani) (GM co stars as Jonathan Duke); 11/12/72; Starring Stan Cooper (Stelvio Rosi) as Seb Carter, GM, Craig Hill as Eldorado, also with Dennis Colt and Custer Gail.

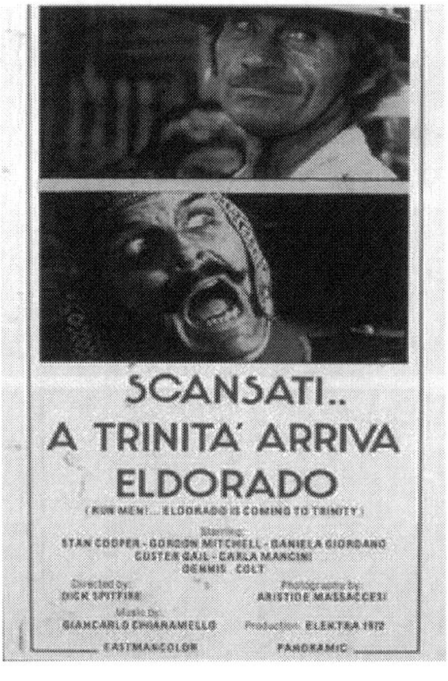

Anything for a Friend, Amico Mio . . . Frego Tu . . . Che Freo Io! (Comedic Western) Ital, Director Miles Deem (Demofilo Fidani); (GM as outlaw caked Muller); 2/18/73; Stars Red Carter (Fred Harris) as Jonas Dickerson, Bud Randall as Mark Tabor, a pair of conmen. Outlaw Muller has self-appointed himself as town boss of Denver, Also Simone Blondell is Pearl.

Once Upon a Time in the Wild, Wild West, *C'era Una Volta Questo Pazzo Pazzo West;* a.k.a. *Crazy, Crazy West* (Comedic Western) Ital, Director Enzo Matazzi (Francesco Degli Espinosa) (GM costars as Mike / Bill); 10/17/73; Stars Vincent Scott as Rico, Dennis Colt (Benito Pacifico) as Joe, Malisa Longo as Dolores, Luciano Conti, and Fiorella Magaloti as Flo.

My Name is Shanghai Joe, *IL Mio Nome E Shanghai Joe;* a.k.a. *The Fighting Fists of Shanghai Joe*; Ital, Director Mario Caiano; (GM in cameo as the town gravedigger Burying Sam); 12/28/73; Stars Chen Lee as Joe, Klaus Kinski as Scalper Jack, Carla Romenelli as Christina. *Storyline is an East meets West theme.*

Seven Devils on Horseback, *I Sette Del Gruppo Selvaggio*; Ital, Director Gianni Crea (GM costars as gang leader Cooper); 3/29/75; Starring Dean Stratford (Dino Strano) as Jeff McNeal, his sister was brutally killed and he seeks revenge from those of the gang that's responsible; Also with Mario Brega as Tornado and Femi Benussi as Rosie.

The Tiger From the River Kwai, *La Tigre Venuta Dal Fiume Kwai*; Ital, Director Franco Lattanzi (GM as ruthless gang leader Jack Mason); 9/23/75; Stars George Eastman (Luigi Montefiori) as Sheriff Sam, Krung Srivilai as Tiger, Loredana Parnese, Bruno Arie and Kam Won Lon as Won Lon. Storyline is another East meets West theme as a Thailander comes out West and encounters violence and serious racism problems.

White Fang and the Grand kid, *Zanna Bianca e Il Grand Kid;* a.k.a. *White Fang and the Kid;* a.k.a. *Billy in the West;* a.k.a. *Rusty and Joe*; Ital, Director Vito Bruschini (Charles Pendleton (GM) costars as Mulligan, the evil town boss (*In some video versions he's called Mr. Morgan*); 12/15/78; Stars Inga Alexandrova as Inga, Tony Kendall as Frankie James, Fabrizio Mariani as Billy the kid, and Buck the dog. Others were Lea Lander, Sandro Chiani and Enrico Turella.

Storyline: Laughfully has to do with Frankie (Frank) as brother of Jesse James. Now he's reformed with the help of Inga, Billy and Buck. Together they rid the town of Mulligan.

Porno Erotic Western, *Porno Erotico Western;* a.k.a. *You Pay Dear for Death*; Ital, Gerald B. Lennox (Angelo Pannaccio) (Charles Pendleton is credited, but claims he knew nothing of it?); 9/12/79; Stars Karen Well (Wilma Truccolo), Lorenzo Bien, Ray O'Connor (Remo Capitani), Rosemarie Lindt, Tomas Rudi and Patrizia Mayer. Supposedly the storyline has a father and two sons defending the oppressed against oppression?

Note: Appears to have been edited from scrap scenes of the 1970 Western by Pannaccio called *Requiem for a Bounty Hunter* that was filmed at Chuck Pendleton's *Cave Studio* outside Rome. That alone could have been the connection because he doesn't appear to have been in that film either, unless his scene / or scenes had been cut out.

End.

BIBLIOGRAPHY
(G. MITCHELL)

Betts, Tom, editor *WAI! (Westerns . . . All'Italiana)* Fanzine articles/info on actor Gordon Mitchell:

WAI! Memorial Issue, 11/2003: "GM, Good or Bad Always the Hero (bio) by Tom Betts;

Obituaries for the actor; GM Western Filmography by Tom Betts with color posters;

The *Cave Studio* Italian news photo plus article by Nino Lo Bello; Plus an extensively researched filmograpy listings, and including other genre films by Tom Prickette

The BFI Companion to the Western (1993) edited by Edward Buscombe, *British Film Institute,* UK, 1993; originally published by *Andr`e Deutsch Ltd.,* London, 1988;

Connolly, Bill, editor *Spaghetti Cinema* Fanzine articles/ interviews/ informational tidbits on the GM the actor:

Issue no. 39 (March 1990) Interview with GM by William Connolly with Davis Cotner;

Issue no. 40 (July 1990) no. 2 Interview segment with GM by Bill Connolly with David Cotner;

Issue no. 47 (December 1991) no. 3 Interview segment with GM by Bill Connolly plus *WAI!* T. Betts;

Issue no. 59 (December 1994) no. 4 Interview segment with GM by Bill Connolly plus *WAI!* T. Betts.

Haselbeck, Sebastian, owner / curator for Internet website: *www.spaghetti-western.net*

Informational materials: Article by Nino Lo Bello on GM's Western Town; plus personal filmo listings from the actor Chuck Pendleton (GM) himself, sent via e-mail to this author 1/7/2001

Internet, via: *www.briansdriveintheater.com*, Information and Filmology for the actor GM, Posting update of 4/25/2001, titled "Good or Bad, Always the Hero: Gordon Mitchell"

Internet, via: *www.GordonMitchell.net* (now defunct) website previous posting as early as 2000; Reprint of Video Watchdog Issue no. 48 article: "Gordon Mitchell: Atlas in the Land of the Cinema" by Christian Kessler posting of 5/13/01;

Internet, via: *www.IMDB.com*, an in-depth filmology plus trivia section; plus minibio on the actor GM by Gary Brunburgh.

Internet, via: *www.nadarland.com*, Interview with John Nadar posting viewed was of 2003

Internet, via: *www.paolopecora.net.* Info plus ad mat jpegs for films *Lucertola* and *Faida,* 2001; A special thanks for info/personal accounts regarding his films done with actor Gordon Mitchell.

Internet, via: *www.thewildeye.com,* Info on Gordon Mitchell/films and director Emimmo Salvi, A special thanks for the accounts therein viewed from the website.

Keiffenheim, Clemens, *Producer / filmmaker,* a special thanks for info / personal accounts regarding his TV and film productions done with actor Gordon Mitchell.

Martinez, Michael A., *Actor, SFX Professional, Producer / filmmaker,* A special thanks to Mike for films/ info / personal accounts regarding his films done with actor Gordon Mitchell.

Phone Interview with actor GM and Tom Prickette January, 2001 (unpublished)

Prickette, Tom, "Filmology for Actor Gordon Mitchell," previously unpublished partial compilations of 2000; Also "The Man with That Look", unpublished manuscript 2003

Premiere Magazine article on Mae West, "The Life in Her Men," interview segments with Mickey Hargitay and GM commenting within the article for July, 2001 issue

Video Hound's Golden Retriever (1994 edition) *Visible Ink Press,* a division of *Gale Research Inc.,* Detroit, MI. pp 1313

Video Watchdog Issue no. 48, Fanzine article, 1998; Gordon Mitchell Interviewed, Article: "Gordon Mitchell: Atlas in the Land of the Cinema" by Christian Kessler, plus brief US filmology.

Weisser, Thomas, *Spaghetti Westerns: the Good, the Bad, and the Violent* (1992) *McFarland,* Jefferson NC.

Western: All'Italiana (books II and III) by Antonio Bruschini and Federico de Zigno, *Glittering Images,* Firenze, Italy; book II, 2001 and book III, 2006

The Western: The Complete Film Sourcebook (The Film Encyclopedia) (1983); by Phil Hardy, *William Morrow and Co, Inc.,* NY., pp 301; Appendix no. 8, pp 375-393

WAYDE PRESTON

(1930-1992)

A SALESMAN, WITH GUNS!

A salesman maybe, but agent extraordinaire was the storyline plot behind the 1957 television series called *Colt .45*. As the show's star Wayde Preston portrayed Christopher Colt, a gun salesman for the new model Colt .45 revolver. Actually, the gun salesman part was just a cover. In reality he was working for the United States Government. As a secret field agent, circa 1873, Chris Colt using this cover as gun salesman was able to infiltrate the various towns and factions out west in a time of continued civil unrest, takeovers, and political revolts against the now incumbent Republican administration under the watch of President Ulysses S. Grant. This was a time still fresh in the memories of all countrymen that followed the bloodiest internal war the United States has ever seen on its shores, the Civil War, a war between states, a war that had sometimes more often as not pitted brother against brother.

At 6'-4" and 210 lb., Preston struck quite an imposing figure upon his Palomino horse, high-top black boots and white hat. This was the newest in the line of hit TV series shows called adult Westerns. They were currently being produced and marketed during this late 1950s era by Executive Producer William T. Orr and his snap production team for *Warner Brothers Television.*

A unique team of writers, directors along with other crewmembers, worked behind the scenes on several of these top-rated shows of the day. These Westerns generally ran as a thirty-minute weekly episode (approximately twenty-six minutes was the case with *Colt .45*) to the longer sixty-minute episodes such as the long-running, award-winning series called *Maverick.*

Uniquely classed as an Adult Western, this *Maverick* show aired September of 1955 preceded only by the *Life and Legend of Wyatt Earp* an earlier Orr television production, both for *CBS* network, began a long line of screen successes for Orr and his team. The *Maverick* show was a huge hit, as it turned out with the younger generation as well as the older ones they were more aimed for. The show starred talented young actor James Garner who portrayed the somewhat cowardly, card-sharking Bret Maverick. On occasions, he would be paired with an onscreen brother named Bart (Jack Kelly). These two would then comprise a unique pair of enterprisingly, unbeatable gamblers who roamed the west and allowed us to observe their weekly exploits on our home television sets.

Another of these top-rated, long-running shows of a similar beginning was the weekly *Cheyenne* series. This show starred the big man, Clint Walker (six feet, six inches) in the title role of Cheyenne Brodie. The character of Brodie was a drifter, but with morals and a strong sense of right from wrong. A kind a jack-of-all-trades and as we watched each week, he would most likely try his luck at a different job each episode.

Bronco was another of these now popular adult Westerns, originally a spin-off of the *Cheyenne* show it turned out to be nearly as popular as its predecessor. It cast yet another tall good-looking young man Ty Hardin in the title role of Bronco Lane an ex-confederate army captain. Lane also sort of drifter himself, would sometimes take on a Marshalling or Deputy job, between stints with the rodeo circuit. This spin-off was shown every second week and eventually evolved into a trio of hour-long, revolving weekly shows that ran for the 1960-1961 episode seasons that ran on the

ABC Television network by Orr's production team. The third show of this revolving trio was called *Sugarfoot*. It starred Will Hutchins in the title role as the tenderfoot cowpuncher who was (in his spare time) studying the Law via a mail correspondence course.

These were the days. The late 1950s and the era of the adult-age Western was in full bloom on the television. We're quite sure if one grew up during this era, they well remember the many different Westerns that were on during this period in time. Mostly we remember them as more talky, than action, but alas, some stood out more than others. It was hard to miss these big guys with guns traipsing across one's set of the evenings at home for some superfine entertainment. One of these was this popular *Colt .45* show which began in 1957 and ran on into the '60s with some sixty-eight episodes running approximately twenty-six minutes each.

Wayde Preston, whose real name was William (Bill) Erskine Strange, the Preston name change came via William Orr and Jack Warner of *Warner Bros*. He was born in the Steamboat Springs area of Colorado on September 10, 1930. His parents John and Bernice eventually moved on over into Laramie, Wyoming where Bill and two younger sisters Joan and Mary grew up together. Bill's high school years were spent there in Laramie, graduated from *Laramie High* in 1947. He had been an avid athlete who enjoyed football, and track along with school's great ROTC training program. He also excelled in school band training where he appeared to be quite taken with music in general. Later he would attend college there in Laramie, at the *University of Wyoming* and was studying for the pharmaceutical trade.

His induction into the military came early in 1950. His basic he took at Fort Bliss, Texas. But with his early ROTC training, he stood out among his peers and with the Korean War breakout on June 25, of that same year he saw action there serving as a First Lieutenant with the Army Artillery Corps. A counterattack by invading Korean forces caught his command by surprise and led to his capture. For the balance of the wartime, he remained a Korean prison until war's end per the proposed ceasefire on June 23, 1951. His young age, gung-ho and full of himself, then the surprise attack, the impending imprisonment, and having to watch men under his command die before his eyes had left him with a bitter taste in his mouth that would last him a lifetime.

> According to actor Brett Halsey's biography, who worked with Preston back in 1968 in Europe on the Spaghetti Western film *Today we Kill . . . Tomorrow We Die!* Halsey stated for the biography written by John B. Murray called *Art or Instinct in the Movies* (2008) *Midnight Marquee Press, Inc.*; "He was hard to get along with. He had lots of problems."

When discharged, he returned home and opted for a stint as a Park Ranger there in the wilds of Wyoming's Grand Teton mountain range and the *National Parks Service*. Later on, he would try his hand at many different jobs, mostly working the outdoor life he loved. He also worked the Rodeo circuit a couple of seasons as a bronc rider. As most young men raised in that part of the country, the rodeo was an avid pastime for them. Preston was no different, but better at it than most. (Somewhat similar to the storyline of the *Bronco* television series we previously spoke of.)

Learning to fly, however, had been one of his longtime ambitions. Taking lessons, he delved into his studies with an intense vigor. Later after acquiring his flying license, he went to work for *McDonnell-Douglas Aircraft,* as a pilot. This is a given proof of his many talents.

Afterward, he joined up with the Howard Hughes commercial airline company *TWA* where he worked for a while as one of their commercial pilots. On one of his many trips to the San Francisco area, there in a local lounge frequented by the public there at the airport, he met and befriended an entertainment agent. On another trip, visiting the same local watering hole, this agent pal of his had introduced him to the beautiful young actress he was meeting there, Carol Ohmart. Miss Ohmart was at the time working under contract to *20th Century Fox* film studios and was doing television spots on The *20th Century Fox Hour,* show.

By this time in her career, bleached blond bombshell, Armelia Carol Ohmart, had been somewhat of a hot item in and around Hollywood. A native of Salt Lake City, Utah (where from she had just arrived for the meeting) had come to public attention at only nineteen as *Miss Utah* of 1946. Later she entered the *Miss America* contest and as a runner-up, came in fourth. This prompted her to go into modeling as a career where later she picked up some commercial advertisement work and special appearances for early television late in 1949.

Having signed a contract with *Paramount Studios*, in 1955, the press releases taunted her imagine as their answer to the fabulous Marilyn Monroe. But, as it turned out, she would never quite make the grade. Before meeting Preston, she already had been associated with two prior movies for *Paramount Pictures.* In one she costarred alongside Anthony Quinn in a dramatic dud at the box office by director Harry Horner called *Wild Party* (1954).

Later in 1955 she was starred in another film, a drama called *The Scarlet Hour* by director Michael Curtiz. A film more tailored to her brash personality with her role of Pauline Nevins who taunted marital discord between her and on-screen husband Ralph Nevins (James Gregory) which eventually led to murder. Costarring with Tom Tryon as her lover wasn't a lot of help though, as this film also bottomed out at the box office.

Unfortunately with both films of *Paramount* being duds, they quickly wrote her off as a leading lady. Having to fall back on her television work, Carol dug in and worked regularly on television into the 1970s. The slinky blonde became known more for her ultimate bitch-role persona even before the likes of Joan Collins and Morgan Fairchild made that type so popular on nighttime television soap operas, during the 1980s. Miss Ohmart came out on the big screen only occasionally after that. One of her best noted roles was that of Annabelle Loren, wife of Frederick Loren portrayed by Vincent Price in William Castle's 1959 horror film called *House on Haunted Hill.*

By the time our William Strange had the pleasure of meeting this beautiful package of trouble, she had already been married once before to Ken Grayson in 1951. However, the clash of personalities led to a split and an early divorce. When Miss Ohmart finally met this big hunk of a man Bill Strange, a whirlwind courtship erupted between the two. Not long afterward, they were married on Thanksgiving Day 1956. During their courtship period, she had been working with Bill coaching him in the art of acting to the point where, when he was introduced to the people at *20th Century Fox*, they signed him on almost immediately as an acting understudy. Now, he could further his lessons and perhaps even a career in acting could follow.

As typical for an understudy at the studio, Bill worked about a year or so doing the stage circuit, playing bit parts here and there. While on the road much of the time, he gathered up a phenomenal amount of experience, and acted in plays virtually coast to coast from Maine, New York, New Jersey, down to Florida and finally back to Los Angeles to complete a season.

Back in California, and as time went by, he had become bored with all the lessons, the small bit parts, and most of all the traveling. There seemed to be nothing really for him to sink his teeth into. Once back in the LA area he wandered over to the *Warner Bros.*, studio lot. He was there to see a bit-player buddy of his, one of the first people he'd met early on there in Hollywood and who had become fast friends with for years to come. Walter Barnes* had been supplementing his income for some time working as a part-time television actor playing mostly villain parts since early in 1955. He had already been on several other TV episodes himself, a few for *Gunsmoke* of *CBS*, and also *Warner's Cheyenne* shows of *ABC.* He'd been working fairly steady within the industry since retiring from his pro-football years with the Philadelphia Eagles 1948-1951.

---

* Walter Barnes, was known best during his grit-iron years as, Piggy Barnes, linebacker. Prior to his Professional years he had been a former all-conference pro athlete and weightlifter at *LSU*. Louisiana. He went on to play pro-ball prior to his acting days both in Hollywood and Europe.

Warner Bros. at the time was probably the most prolific, if not the most profitable television production company around Hollywood during that '50's era and their hit TV Westerns became household names. Some shown in the later evening programming were the so-called adult Westerns, so named under the assumption most of the younger set was already in bed for school the following day. Although, some of the younger set did get to watch these in later years as they became syndicated rerun shows and shown earlier in afternoon and early evening timeslots. Shows like *Gunsmoke, Cheyenne, Bronco, Sugarfoot* and the relatively new *Maverick* shows were all extremely popular and *Warner* was still in the market for more.

When Bill Strange arrived on the *Warner* lot that morning, he found to his surprise that everyone welcomed him with open arms. He soon entered into a seven-year stock contract with *Warner.* Now with a name-change to Wayde Preston, slick-styled Western duds and a fancy pair of nickel-plated holstered revolvers, he was now on his way to possible TV stardom. The American television audiences would first have a glimpse of this tall, good-looking fellow as he portrayed the Christopher Colt character in the *ABC* show premier episode of *Colt .45*, on October 18, 1957.

Supposedly, as the show storyline went, he was a family member of the firearms maker *Colt,* he graciously showed off his firm's latest finery in weaponry, the *Peacemaker Colt* .45 caliber revolver. From town to frontier town Colt held exhibitions where he could flaunt his expertise with his pair of nickel-silver pistols, to the envy of all who watched. These exhibitions would serve to instill the kind of respect and town friendliness required by a man who was also serving a dual purpose.

A salesman was seemingly his game, but this was only a front as he was actually commissioned directly by then President Grant as an army intelligence agent, who in frontier territory of the mid-1870s, working under guise as a member of the *Colt Arms Co.* of New Haven Conn. He was tasked with special projects governed by the President himself and was authorized to track down notorious outlaws of the day, bringing them to justice. The idea for the series was based on the 1950 *Warner Bros.* feature film, which had the same title and starred Randolph Scott. It had been directed by Edwin L. Marin and also starred Zachary Scott and Lloyd Bridges. Later it was retitled as *Thundercloud* for the home video market.

Prior to Preston's *Colt .45* show debut, he filmed one earlier episode in 1957 for *Warner's Maverick* show called "The Saga of Waco Williams." For this preliminary episode, Preston portrayed Williams who sported a mustache and dressed all in black. Quite a contrast this was to his White-hat, clean-shaven good-guy image of the Christopher Colt character he was soon to play. Not to upstage the main *Maverick* characters of the show, it was temporarily shelved and not aired until much later on February 15 of 1959. Preston was so good in the episode the producers raved over his character. There was even talk at the time of scrapping the new *Colt .45* show and beginning another series based entirely on this Waco Williams* character Preston he'd portrayed instead.

But alas, commitments being as they were, the season's first show of *Colt .45* aired on schedule. The first episode was called "The Peacemaker" which also guest-starred a couple of *Warner's* stock actors, Peter Brown as Dave and Andrew Duggan as Jim Rexford. Also starred was Erin O'Brien in the part of Sister Helen MacGregor and Helen Brown as Sister Howard. Filming locations used were at the *Warner Bros.* back-lot and Western town set. In addition some location shots were done out on Warner's Ranch.

Sadly, though, the relationship between *Warner Bros.* and Wayde Preston (as he was now known) became strained almost from the start of the series. In later years, Preston reflected upon some of the many reasons for his dissatisfaction with *Warner* at the time. He cited the long, arduous working hours (5:00 a.m. to sometimes well into the night). The sometimes, dangerous stunts which mostly they, the actors were obliged to perform themselves. Lastly would be the low pay versus the long, erratic hours that just didn't seem to add up in the long run. After many a confrontation with the directors and producers, he finally made his move and walked off the set soon after completing the first show of the 1958-'59 season. However, he was not alone in his quest for better pay, conditions and benefits against *Warner Bros.* Clint Walker of the popular *Cheyenne* show had made his mind up as well and joined in the walkout.

Another fine actor of the day, Edd Brynes of the equally popular *Warner Bros.* famed *77 Sunset Strip* detective show also walked off. His parking lot attendant character of Kookie was soon replaced by a tall, blond-haired, surfer-type soon to be a star on his own weekly television show, Troy Donohue. As for Preston and his show, the producers sent in actor Donald May for the last shows of 1959 season to replace him. A fine, young actor, May portrayed the part of Sam Colt Jr., supposedly a cousin of the Chris character Preston had played.

Preston did eventually return to the show, but by then producers had decided to keep May's character on in the script. (Possibly, as sort of an

---

* It's been found that the story writer for this Waco Williams saga, a young Stephen J. Cannell eventually revamped his script character for actor Tom Selleck in his character of Lance White in a rereoccurring role for, *The Rockford Files* series he was involved with at the time. This show starred James Garner as a modern day ex-cop/ detective was extremely popular and turned into a long-running series of the 1970s.

insurance policy against previous antics by their unruly, star performer.) While the main show's character was still Christopher Colt, he could now be seen as a guest star on some of the other *Warner Bros.* shows as well, which had been another one of Preston's main beefs* all along.

As predicted though, and as time passed, the old problems began to rekindle themselves and boredom surfaced once again, Preston would finally leave the show for good this time. At that point in time, Donald May regained fulltime lead status for the duration of the show's run, which was soon to be finalized with the last episode aired September 27, 1960. It was then sold into syndication and reruns began running for several years afterward. In addition, all of the twenty-six show episodes were renamed and shown in the United Kingdom on *BBC Children's Television* of 1966 under the title *The Colt Cousins*. Donald May went on to star in another show, this time on his own for *Warner* called *The Roaring '20s*.

As we look back, we can remember many of the familiar faces who had guest-starred on the *Colt .45* weekly outings of yesteryear. Some would later gain renowned popularity in big screen roles that were yet to come. Some of those were the likes of Walter Barnes, Charles Bronson, Ed Brynes, Jack Elam, Adam West and veteran badman, Lee Van Cleef.

Lee Van Cleef, who was later to be skyrocketed to international film stardom with the now classic Italian *Spaghetti* Westerns of the mid-'60s, did two episodes for *Colt .45*. The first aired January 24, 1958, called "Dead Reckoning." The second was on June 21, 1960, called "The Trespasser." Although Preston was no longer around for this latter show, he and Van Cleef had hit it off very well during the earlier episode back in 1958. On the previously show they had become pals and later good friends for the remainder of their acting years.

During that 1958 year, Preston had started a sideline business of his own. A flying service called *Comanche Aero Services* that operated out of the *Van Nuys Municipal Airport* there in Van Nuys, California. He continued to rely on this business between his contractual bouts with *Warner Bros.* Even after his time with the series had ended by 1960 he was still acknowledged

---

* It seems *Warner* had previously wanted Preston and others exclusively for their one show only and nothing else on the side. This not only limited their talents and abilities, but not to mention boredom that tended to set in with the actors. Similar in fashion to the same beefs that Eric Fleming and Clint Eastwood had with producers over their *Rawhide* show series for *CBS* Television (1959-1966). That upset eventually cost Fleming his job as the producers fired him over it, citing breach of contract.

as a star with the public who could still see him in syndicated episodes of this popular series long after his departure from the show. Fans could also continue to see him in other popular TV Westerns of the day, with an occasionally guest spot on some shows like, *Sugarfoot*, or another of the *Maverick* episodes. There was even one of the *Bonanza* series shows with his off-screen pal Lorne Greene. For these show characters he might be again in his famous Colt character, or that of some heavy/villain role, which he adapting to playing very well. Even by not shaving a couple of days, he would come to certainly look the part.

Basically what he was finding out though, was there wasn't much work out there in Hollywood for an ex-TV Western series star that was now stereotyped. He tended to concentrate more and more on his flying business at that point in his career. However, even this was to be short-lived since from around 1960 things had been getting pretty strained with his marriage. Finally he and Carol would divorce by 1962, thus forcing him to sell off his Aviation business to meet the divorce creed obligations. Fortunate for the both of them, no children were involved.

Meanwhile, some of the older television Western shows were in the process of being revamped and shown to overseas audiences. Usually, distributors would have the producers compile the episodes making feature length films that could be then renamed, and remarketed to be shown to overseas. Those European fans loved the old television Western hero's of a bygone era. These Euro audiences relished the old revamped shows now seen as movies on the big screen. In Europe, television was not for the populace of that era, and these were shown at the indoor theaters throughout. The audiences that came and went daily loved them. By showing these compiled features the distributors were actually doing the actors a favor. They were bringing the names and imagines of these television actors abroad to the eyes of the general public that normally wouldn't have the opportunity of seeing these old Western television shows or actors otherwise, except through pictures and magazines.

Names like that of Guy Madison from, *The Adventures of Wild Bill Hickok* series. Others like Alex Nicol, Jeffery Hunter, Broderick Crawford, Rod Cameron and Audie Murphy all old ex-Western stars of either movies and/or television were by now becoming household names overseas.

Other actors and close friends of the Preston's such as Rory Calhoun and Gordon Scott had already been in and out of Europe finding much work there with the European film productions of the day. Old friend Walter Barnes was another from Preston's early television days in Los Angeles, who was now becoming quite the celebrity in Europe, time certainly flies. With his ties now severed in the States, Preston also took off to Europe and Italy in particular. The Italian film industry was booming there during this era. In Rome he found work plus the respect as being an accomplished actor as well. The Italian's loved him and he was now a star once again.

Being extremely talented in many fields, he learned to speak Italian and Spanish fairly easily, also other dialects of Irish and even some Russian. An accomplished athlete, he was a natural stunt man, since he had done much of that work while on the *Warner Bros.* sets. Also, his being an expert in the Art of Judo* didn't seem to hurt his reputation any to say the least.

Like many of his friends and constituents, he began to observe the opportunities of the European cinema, as a working environment. Clint Eastwood had been shot to international fame as the Man with No Name gunslinger character created by Italian Sergio Leone in his extremely popular *Spaghetti* Western *Dollar* series.

His friend Lee Van Cleef had been cast as an older bounty hunter opposite Clint Eastwood's Manco character in Leone's second film of his *Dollar* trilogy. These actors were heroes to the European audiences long before the films ever reached the shores of the United States and they all enjoyed movie star status while there in Europe. Now Wayde Preston reasoned he could become a part of that action as well. He began to make himself at home.

His friend Van Cleef who had been an unemployed actor trying to paint for a living was now a walking icon of these Euro Westerns. The Italian directors were cloning more and more of these so-called *Spaghetti Westerns* and were aiming them directly at the American audiences. Other actor friends like Edd Brynes and John Ireland were being starred in these mass-produced films. He felt that he was also ready now for Euro star trail as well.

He would gradually ease into the *Spaghetti* phenomenon years of the 1960s with his first film in 1966. His first though wasn't a Western, but a spy film clone, set much in the same vein as the earlier James Bond films. *Man on a Spying Trapeze* would be his Euro screen debut. Preston starred as secret agent Jerry Land. When Land goes to the aid of a fallen fellow spy, he finds a wrecked and burning car. Nearby he finds a hidden camera and microfilm. Then a dead man shows up at the Roman coliseum. This was a great little spy actioner that combined much the same tongue-in-cheek humor of the James Bond films of Terence Young, along with picturesque locations and nonstop action.

---

* Actor and friend Jack Kelly of some years back remembered him as, "Probably one of toughest men in Hollywood during those years, a man not to be run over easily." Which, in retrospect we speculate that, was probably how some of his initial contract problems with *Warner Bros.* had begun with his refusing to be runover on certain issues.

In 1967 he worked with some of America's finest film actors while on a film called *Anzio*. It was a US / French / Italian / Spanish coproduction war film for *Columbia Pictures,* starring Robert Mitchum, Peter Falk, Earl Holliman, Mark Damon, and upcoming American actor Thomas Hunter. Filmed on locations, some in Yugoslavia and Italy, it was under direction by veteran Edward Dmytryk. Wayde Preston portrayed Colonel Darby Hendricks in this story about the Allied invasion of the German-occupied Anzio, Italy, during WWII. The story was told as through the eyes of an American war correspondent (Mitchum) who was embedded in the action.

Soon after its release for 1968 Preston worked on his first of several *Spaghetti* Westerns that followed. His lead was ex-bodybuilder turned action star Steve Reeves for *Vivo per la Tua Morte (I Live for your Death);* a.k.a. *A Long Ride from Hell.* Steve Reeves starred as Mike who along with his brother Roy (Franco Fantasia) and the ranch foreman Bobcat (Mario Maranzana) go after a gang of horse thieves who have stolen the whole ranch herd. But, to their surprise they are blamed for the rustling and jailed in the Yuma prison for the crime they were attempting to right.

Wayde Preston is Marl Mayner an evil land-baron type and leader of the gang who are putting the squeeze on the local ranches for their land. He's now the object of Mike's revenge when he finally escapes prison, after his brother Roy died behind bars. Good film and intense vehicle for muscleman Reeves, as he was co producer along with director Alex Burkes (Luigi Bazzoni). An Italian coproduction film with a screenplay co written by Reeves and one Roberto Natale, it was taken from a novel by Gordon Shirreffs' called *The Judas Gun.*

More Westerns to follow were; *E Intorno a Lui fu Morte (Death Knows No Time)* also a 1968 film release and was an Italian / Spanish coproduction. It starred Italian actor and ex-stuntman William Bogart (Guglielmo Spoletini) as Martin Rojas who portrays an ex-Mexican landowner, now evicted by his government and seen as an outlaw. Wayde Preston in little more than a cameo role in this film as ex-town sheriff turned US Marshall Johnny Silver, who is hot on outlaw Rojas's trail.

> Preston would now remain in Rome churning out the films until sometime in the early 1970 when he decided to hang it up and return to the States. It's our understanding that the Italians on a whole were sad to see him go as he was said to have been very well liked by his Euro audiences and fans. In a quiet modest way he took his film accomplishments seriously but without much fanfare.

His next film to come that same year was *Oggi A Me Domani A Te (Today it's me . . . Tomorrow it's You!)* (1968) which starred Bret Halsey,* using the pseudonym name of Montgomery Ford. Preston's role in this film was that of Jeff Milton friend and sidekick to Halsey's starring role as Bill Kiowa eager to recruit gunmen to fight on his side while he avenges the senseless killing of his Indian wife and the burning of his home. This film also has two other fine actors that were already extremely popular in these Euro-Westerns. An Austrian born, American trained (now living in Rome) ex-stage actor from New York, William Berger. The other an Italian stuntman turned popular lead actor was Bud Spencer (Carlo Pedersoli). Spencer would later gain renowned attention as sidekick to Terence Hill's (Mario Girotti) popular Trinity character in their extremely popular Italian produced comedic Westerns of the 1970s with the *Trinity* film series.

Preston's next film and his last for 1968 was called *l' Ira di Dio (The Wrath of God)*. This was yet another Brett Halsey film. He starred here as a lone gunman known as Mike who takes off after a band of robbers who have killed his fiancé in the course of a town robbery. Wayde Preston stars here in a mere cameo role, as Logan one of seven bandits who was involved in that robbery, and the accidental murder of Mike's woman during that firefight.

During the year of 1969 came the released an Italian / Spanish coproduction crime genre film called *Cinque Figli di Cane (Five Children of Dog)* a.k.a. *The Great Gang War*. It starred Italian George Eastman (Luigi Montefiori [Montefiore]) as Irish, the wild and often unruly Irishman. Wayde Preston co stars as the cool, time-tempered Grim Doyle, undercover police agent. With story / script, and film direction by Alfio Caltabiano the storyline revolves more around Doyle, who is part of a newly formed Police Crime task force of 1928. Doyle is quick to go undercover in prison as a convicted felon in order to help breakout and free four hardened criminals for a special job that seemingly only these four men and their skills can do.

By Doyle is acting as a member of one mob, he's actually pitting one against another gang by fretting the faux takeover of yet another gang of bootleggers who are trying muscle in on their territory? Eventually the scheme comes to light, which is to bust up the entire bootleg operations

---

* Brett Halsey, Popular American 1950's bit actor who had taken a big jump coming overseas at a seemingly impasse in his career which paid off with him becoming a huge star there in the Italian films. He also ventured out of the Western genre moving in a path similar to that Preston had taken with popular Spy films of the day. Then a *Giallo*-thriller or two, even some of the Horror genre or perhaps the ever increasingly popular crime genre films would all come to bear his name in their credits as his popularity increased with European moviegoers.

from the entire area which involve various mobs who are constantly at war with one another. This was a meaty role for Preston and a shame a sequel was never made as a follow up using this Grim Doyle character. The film was quite good and a pleasure to watch.

After that genre move, Preston went back to the Westerns again, he now had a starring role this go around in *Dio Perdona la Mia Pistola (God will Forgive my Pistol!)*. This was a straight Italian production from director Mario Gariazzo who along with Leopoldo Savona also penned the story and script. Preston here as Texas Ranger, Johnny (Texas) Brennan is sent to the town of Oakland City to oversee the hanging of a convicted postal / bank robber named Prescott (Jose M Torres). While there he uncovers evidence that this man was actually innocent of the crime. The real culprit was later found out to be an evil land Baron Martin portrayed by bodybuilder / actor Dan Vadis.

It was about this time that Preston would become involved in yet another Western although he seemingly was unaccredited for the film, but was nevertheless in it all the same. For a late 1969 release the film was called *Boot Hill* from director Giuseppe Colizzi, already noted in the genre for two previous Westerns. This one however would be his last for the genre after taking ill, bedridden and passing away later in 1979. In this film we have Terence Hill (Mario Girotti) starring as Cat Stevens, Bud Spencer (Carlo Pedersoli) as Hutch Bessy, and Woody Strode as Thomas. Others were Victor Bruno and Lionel Stander also in main character roles. Wayde Preston's unaccredited role was that of McGavin who with his gang rousts the general store and its proprietor for a set of keys. (An unusual looking pistol he carries in this scene, more like a flintlock looking barrel type, which is all we see of it).

The storyline of the film has to do with Stevens getting shot on his claim by mining company men. He hides out in a traveling circus and befriends Thomas, an acrobat an ex-gunslinger, who with strongman deaf-mute Hutch help Stevens get even with the company for stealing his mine.

For Preston's next film, another Western released in 1970 he co stars this time with William Berger who took the lead role for *Sartana Nella Valle Gegli Avvoltoi (Sartana in the Valley of Vultures);* a.k.a. *The Ballad of Death Valley*. Berger is Lee Calloway a gunman hired to free the three Douglas brothers from jail, but who seems to have an underlying motive. By freeing the gang he figures they will lead him to a cache of stolen army gold. Wayde Preston portrays the older leader of the gang, Anthony Douglas who seeing through his little ploy, and after the escape pulls a double-crosse on Calloway taking his horse and leaving him for dead out in the desert.

Fortunately for him, the near-dead Calloway is found, and nursed back to health by a mystery woman. Later, when recovered this same woman Ester

(Jolanda Modio) turns him over for the bounty on his head. An Intriguing story, well acted, taken from a scripting by the director Roberto Mauri. This was an Italian production from producer Enzo Boetani.

Preston's next 1970 effort was called *Un Uomo Chiamo Slitta, (A Man Called Sledge);* a.k.a. *Sledge*. This was an Italian / US coproduction by Dino De Laurentiis and Harry Bloom. A major disagreement in direction with Producer Dino De Laurentiis got the original director, hothead ex-actor Vic Morrow* replaced for Italian director Giorgio Gentili. However, due to contractual obligations, Morrow did receive full directorial credit.

This *Sledge* film stars James Garner as Luther Sledge. Garner was, like Preston had been another ex-*Warner Bros.* stock actor from the 1950s. His show had been the popular series called *Maverick* in which he starred as the main character Bret Maverick. Others of the *Sledge* cast were mostly multi-internationals like co star Laura Antonelli (in her only Western). A few other Americans, whom the producer and Morrow had wooed into getting involved, also became part of the cast like John Marley, who was already working in Italy at the time. But others like Dennis Weaver and Claude Akins were both friends of Morrow and longtime associates in television back in the States. Also, there was another American, an already well established *Spaghetti* actor known as Ken Clark.†

---

* Vic Morrow, a born and breed New Yorker debuted on the stage circuit several years prior to his film debut in 1955 in *The Blackboard Jungle*. He would later venture to Italy as the director for this *Sledge* coproduced film of 1970, but his attitude got him crossed-up with the producer and finally got him dismissed from the production all together. Morrow continued to act and direct back in the States until a severe mishap ended his life while filming in 1982 on the Stephen Spielberg blockbuster *Twilight Zone: The Movie* ('83). The scene had to do with a helicopter rescue mission ongoing in a Viet Nam war zone rice paddy when a malfunction caused the copterto crashed on top of the film set, where Morrow was working. Several others were injured.

† Clark was another American with past experience in television acting and early sci-fi films not unlike director Morrow had been. Actually though, Clark had previously even been in one the old *Colt .45* episodes back in 1959 called "The Sage of Sam Bass." His one episode, however, had been with Donald May and not Preston. May's show character had been that of Samuel Colt Jr., and was supposedly a cousin of the Preston' Colt.

Clark had ventured into Italy for the *Peplum* (sword 'n' Sandal) roles that rose to popularity during the '50s and early 1960s prior to the wave of the Euro-Westerns. His first *Peplum* had been The *Son of Hercules in the Land of Darkness* ('63) which had starred Dan Vadis. Clark had since gotten a good

As *Sledge* storyline goes, after a robbery, Sledge and his gang having successfully escaped, and for the time being have eluded the sheriff's posse. As they take a breather near the edge of the desert, they begin to gamble with the loot and fight among themselves for the lion's share of the take, $300,000 in gold. Preston portrays Ripley, sheriff of Rockville, a small town where Sledge and his boys had paused to take on supplies before the big robbery. Already having big prices on their heads, Sheriff Ripley was quick to assess the situation and forms a posse to track the gang soon after they left town. Good film with Garner, Weaver, Akins and John Marley each in their only *Spaghetti* Western film outing.

Preston's next film and it appear to have been his last European venture, has been an extremely elusive piece of work to acquire. Only recently obtained, the film, another Western was called *Ehi Amico . . . Sei Morto (Hey Amigo . . . to your Death!)*; a.k.a. *Hey Amigo, A Toast to you Death!* (1970). This Italian production starred Wayde Preston as Postal Officer Dove Williams / Amigo. He's out tracking outlaws that had made off with a gold shipment he was responsible for. Later, with the help of an acquired friend, Loco (Marco Zuanelli) they track them into Mexico where upon coming to a small town near a desert, they overhear rumors of a gold treasure being transported somewhere in the area.

What had actually happened was a band of outlaws led by Barnet (Rik Battaglia) had come into town earlier that day, rousting Dove first as he was the only thing close to a lawman in this South Texas Border town. They take him prisoner along with the rest of the townsfolk and corral them into the saloon awaited the arrival of the stage coach that was loaded down with gold coins. After they left, leaving four dead in the street, the whole town blames Dove as he should have expected a robbery of this type with that amount of gold coins being shipped through their town. Guilt, as well as to save face he now single-handedly has set off following the trail of the coach. Several twists and turns embellish this basic robbery tale makes for a great little film that make it truly worth while waiting for to see at long last.

Upon Preston's return to the States about mid 1970, he resumed his pet peeve career of flying. Moving back to the Van Nuys, California area, he began to teach flying, and giving lessons once again. It's hard to realize the amount of film work he managed to squeeze into just the few years while in Europe. I have heard amounts (exaggerated to be sure) upward to forty

---

foothold in the Italo movie scene during that era and went on to become quite an International star in his own right. After doing several of the *Peplum* genre films he branched off into the *Spy* genre doing several of that type before venturing on into the Spaghetti Westerns about 1965.

films. Unfortunately due to the circumstances abroad and the availability of films coming out of Europe, Italy and Germany in particular, we can only confirm the titles we are actually aware of. A more in-depth filmology on this actor follows this bio segment.

Over the years Wayde Preston had invested heavily in real estate in and around the Reno, Nevada area. It was here that he eventually moved in later years dividing much of his time between there and Los Angeles, California. He had made the effort to resume his acting career once back in the States, but found things for him exceedingly slow. He even tried his hand back in Stage work again, something he had done early on in his acting career while with Carol Ohmart during his *20th Century Fox* years.

> Much like actor Guy Madison had done when he returned to the States during the mid-1970's Preston did as well. Both men had for a while, ventured into the nighttime Dinner Theater circuit in and around the Los Angeles area. This was new vein, of outlet for Stage work and was becoming quite popular.

Preston did manage to snare an unaccredited walk-on TV bit part in *The Colby's,* a *Dynasty* spin-off television series that starred Charlton Heston as the ultra rich, Jason Colby. It was a weekly, late-night soap opera run for *ABC.* Times were indeed rough and prove rougher for our ex-Western film star.

Later during the late 1970s, we understand that Preston underwent surgery to remove a cancerous skin growth by his right temple. Being of fair complexion, the ravages of the sun seemed to have taken its toll. Afterward, feeling more like his old self again he could be seen out and about. His attendance was noticed at some of the *Western Film Festival* functions about the Los Angeles, Reno and Vegas areas during this period in time.

He did later manage to make a return to the big screen, working briefly when he landed the part of Jack Rogers, father of the ex-marine, crime fighting super soldier son soon dubbed *Captain America* (1990). The film starred Matt Salinger as the transformed Marine superhero Steve Rogers. Ronny Cox portrayed the president of the United States, Tom Kinball his secretary of defense. Others highlighting the superb cast were, Ned Beatty, Darren McGavin and Melinda Dillon. For Preston, the role was little more than a cameo and to our disappointment, was his last known screen appearance.

We did learned that in his younger years, back when different jobs were the norm for him, he had worked as an Engineer with some extremely high radiation type equipment involved. Now, while not particularly common knowledge, it may be entirely possible that during that period in his life, after the service that he may have even worked a short tenure at the *Rocky Flats Nuclear Facility* there outside of Denver, Colorado. After all, it was but a short trip from Wyoming to where, in it's hey day of the early 1950s, there was much work and higher than average pay to be found at the facility.

The work done there was with plutonium as with other dangerous elements for the required machining and manufacture of trigger assemblies used by the United States on their nuclear bombs. These were stored in secret arsenal stockpiles of that era throughout the country. These triggers, as it were, had a certain diminutive lifetime that constantly required the changing and upgrading to ensure a full working assembly at all times.

Work in these types of plants during their infancy periods in the United States circa early 1950s were particular outlandish, safety-wise! According to what we have learned over the years about handling those materials, the *Rocky Flats Facility* in particular had been a huge thorn in the *D.O.E.* (Department of Energy's) side for many years. It was shut completely down in 1986. During the following few years, it was completely dismantled, torn down to the ground by specially trained groups of workers taking the highest possible precautions while in and around the old complex, which was at that time plagued with rats, rattlers and tarantulas. It has since been totally cleaned up and converted into an environmentally protected area and game preserve.

Probably unrelated but nevertheless still a possibility, the deadly cancer disease was but dormant and would strike him down again. This time when stricken he was confined to the *VA Hospital* there in Reno, Nevada early in 1992. To the shock and regret of his many fans, William (Bill) Strange (Wayde Preston) being near the end, preferred being sent home and passed away there at his Lovelock, Nevada home on February 6, 1992. It seems he had lost a major battle with colon cancer, and was only 62 years old. Longtime friend actor Walter Barnes* had visited him prior to his passing reflected upon their friendship over the years saying, "A mild-mannered, pleasant man. Well liked by all that knew him, he will long be remembered by his friends and fans alike."

Having renewed they're past friendship, since both had been in Europe during those *Spaghetti* years. Now both had long since retired at the time of Preston's passing. When Preston would visit LA from time to time over the years, he would always look up Barnes and stay awhile at his place. We

---

* Walter Barnes and Wayde Preston didn't actually make any movies together there in Europe, as each were busy going his separate ways. However, when back in Rome together, they would meet on occasion there on the Via Veneto for a good time now and then. Barnes while in Europe for some ten years churned out some twenty-nine films, with nine of those being Westerns. Barnes had also done one *Colt .45* episode back in 1957 with Preston called "Final Payment." His character was that of Mace Bluestone.

can only imagine about some of the reminiscing they did of those mad-cap years while in the Euro film business overseas. Now as we sit back and with sadness think of the many, great *Spaghetti* film actors and directors who have passed on before and since, it does tend to make us all shiver and wonder just how short a lifetime can be.

As we look back on the 1950's television show *Colt .45* remembering as we watched the big man in the high-top black boots, white hat with that pair of nickel-silver pistols strapped to his legs, I know I will always find a place in my memory for this salesman with the *Pistolas*, Wayde Preston may you R.I.P.

End.

STAGE WORK CREDITS
For WAYDE PRESTON

"The Rainmaker": as Starbuck, at the *Sombrero Playhouse,* Miami, Florida.
"The Time of Your Life": as Joe, at the *Woodstock Playhouse,* New Jersey.
"A Sound of Hunting": as Sgt. Carter at the *Greenwich Theater,* New York City.
"Mr. Roberts": as Mr. Roberts at the *Kenney-Bunkfort Playhouse,* Maine
"Detective Story": as McLeod at the *West Cahuenga Playhouse,* Los Angeles, California.

- Below is a complete filmography of Wayde Preston's Euro films. The dates are aligned as close as possible with information currently at hand, plus international release dates included. **Posters and picture are accredited to the Sebastian Haselbeck collection via his website www.spaghetti-western.net. Thanks, Sebastian.*

WAYDE PRESTON
EURO FILMS
(Mostly of the Spaghetti Western variety)

1966
Man on a Spying Trapeze (Spy); Ital, Director Juan De Orduna (Preston as secret agent Jerry Land) *Preston's first Euro film . . .*; 2/28/67 W. Ger; 4/24/67 Spa

1967
The Battle for Anzio, *Lo Sbarco Di Anzio*; a.k.a. *Anzio* (War); US/ Fr/ Ital/ Spa, Director Edward Dmytryk (Preston as Colonel Darby Hendricks) 7/24/68

1968

I Live for Your Death, *Vivo per La Tua Morte;* a.k.a. *A Long Ride from Hell;* a.k.a. *The Invasion of Fort Yuma*; (Western) Ital, Director Alex Burkes (Luigi Bazzoni) (Preston as Marl Mayner gang-leader / land baron); 5/5/68 (Ital); 2/25/70 (USA); *Preston's first Spaghetti Western.*

Death knows No Time, *E Intorno a Lui Fu Morte;* a.k.a. *Tierra Brava* (Western); Ital/ Spa, Director Luigi Mondello (Preston as Territorial Marshall); *Preston's role here is little more than a cameo . . .* 3/5/69 (Ital)

Today It's Me . . . Tomorrow You! *Oggi a me Domani a Te;* a.k.a. *Today We Kill . . . Tomorrow we Die!* (Western); Ital, Director Franco Cucca (Preston as Jeff Milton); 3/28/68 (Ital); 6/71 (USA)

The Wrath of God, *L'Ira Di Dio*; (Western); Ital/ Spa, Dir. Albert Cardiff (Alberto Cardone) (Preston as Logan); 8/24/68 (Ital)

1969

Commandment of a Gangster, *Comandanenti: Per Un Gangster;* a.k.a. *Cinque Figli Di Cane (Five Children of Dog);* a.k.a. *The Great Gang War;* a.k.a. *Bootleggers* (Crime); Ital/ Spa, Director Alfio Caltabiano (Preston as Police undercover Grim Doyle); 3/6/69 (Ital)

***God Will Forgive my Pistol! Dio Perdona La Mia Pistola*;** (Western); Ital, Dir's: Mario Gariazzo & Leopoldo Savona (Preston stars as Texas Ranger Johnny *Texas* Brennan); 8/7/69 (Ital)

Boot Hill, aka *La Collina Degli Stivali (The Hill of Boots)*; (Western) Ital/ Spa, Director Giuseppe Colizzi (Preston's role as McGavin in the general store was uncredited); 12/20/69 (Ital)

Director Colizzi did three Westerns for the genre including this one above, *God Forgives . . . I Don't* (1966) and *Ace High* (1967). This one was Colizzi's last of the genre, he died in 1979.

1970

The Ballad of Death Valley; a.k.a. *Sartana Nelle Valle Gegli Avvoltoi (Sartana in the Valley of Vultures)*; (Western); Ital, Director Roberto Mauri (Preston as bounty hunter Jason Craig); 8/15/70 (Ital)

A Man called Sledge, *Un Uomo Chiamo Slitta;* a.k.a. *Sledge*; (Western) Ital/ US, Dir's: Vic Morrow and Giorgio Gentili (Preston as Sheriff Ripley); 11/14/70 (Ital); 6/9/71 (USA)

Hey Amigo . . . To Your Death! *Ehi Amico . . . Sei Morto;* a.k.a. *Hey Amigo . . . A Toast to Your Death!* A.k.a. *Killer Amigo* (Western); Ital, Director Paul Maxwell (Paolo Bianchini); (Preston as postal officer, Dove Williams); 12/20/70 (Ital)

To our regret, the above listed film was Preston's last known *Spaghetti* Western. After relocation back to the States he managed a few other screen parts but nothing in a starring capacity for our Western action hero.

1990

Captain America (Action/ Crime); US/ Yugoslavian, Director Albert Pyun (Preston as Jack, *advance in time to present day* . . . is now the husband of our action hero Steve's former girl friend Bernice); 12/14/90 UK; 7/22/92 USA

Storyline: According to *www.Imdb.com* reads: "Frozen in the ice for decades, Captain America is freed to battle against arch-criminal, the *Red Skull*." The super soldier Steve, had been racing towards Germany to sabotage rockets of a Nazi madman *Red Skull* when he was interrupted, and frozen in the Artic Ice for decades. Now reawakened in a different age and time of the future, he finds the evil *Red Skull* is still up to no good. Although now, he has a new identity, and plans to kidnap the President of the United States. Our super soldier hero must stop this madman once and for all. Starring Matt Salinger as the ex-marine hero, Steve Rogers who become a Government crime fighter called Captain America. *(This was Wayde Preston's last known film!)*

Wayde Preston circa 1991

Preston passed away in Lovelock; Nevada on February 6, 1992, succumbing to a brief but courageous battle with colon cancer. RIP big guy.

End.

BIBLIOGRAPHY
(W. Preston)

Betts, Tom, editor *WAI! (Westerns . . . All'Italiana)* Fanzine articles for Memorial issue, 1992, "Wayde Preston" informational page by the editor; Plus reprint of page on "Wayde Preston" with permission by editor Boyd Magers of the *Big Reel* on the actor, and his films

Boston Globe, The article on Arvo Ojala via *www.boston.com* "Hollywood master of the quick draw" 7/22/2005 published *NY-Times, 2006*

Connolly, Bill, editor *Spaghetti Cinema* Fanzine articles / information on the actor, plus Wayde Preston films reviews

Cox, Alex, *10,000 Ways to Die: A Director's Take on the Spaghetti Western* (2009) *Kamera Books,* Harpenden, Herts, UK.

Haselbeck, Sebastian, owner / curator for Internet website: *www.spaghetti-western.net*

Internet, via *www.anica.it* Ref: Film production and date confirmation

Internet, via *www.IMDB.com* Mini biography of 2006 plus film listing review and dates

Prickette, Tom, *A Salesman, with a Pistol,* Previously unpublished manuscript of 1992; partially used in the *WAI! Memorial* issue for Wayde Preston after his passing of 1992; Reworked 2007

Summers, Neil, photo reference book: *The First Official TV Western Book* (1987); *Old West Shop Publishing,* W. VA. Ref: *Colt .45,* pp. 51

Weisser, Thomas, *Spaghetti Westerns: the Good, the Bad, and the Violent* (1992) *McFarland,* Jefferson NC.

Western: All'Italiana (books II and III) by Antonio Bruschini and Federico de Zigno, *Glittering Images*, Firenze, Italy; book II, 2001 and book III, 2006

DEAN REED

(1938-1986)

THE SINGER WITH SIX-GUN GOES RED!

Dean Cyril Reed was born in Denver, Colorado, on September 22, 1938. His Mom and Dad along with three other children were raised in the Wheat Ridge, area, a suburb. Raised in a farm environment, Dean had two brothers Vernon and Donny. He went to the local schools, and military academy. He was a Boy Scout and member of the *Future Farmer of America.* He excelled in sports, after school he worked at a local dairy. At school he set a record for the mile-and-half cross-country foot race. His mother Ruth Anne used to tell a story about him racing a mule once 110 miles on a bet, for a quarter. Impressive he was, but he wanted something else, he wanted to impress the girls, so he took up playing the guitar at age twelve. This was, it would appear was a good move on his part. The girls he soon found loved him, especially when he got up on stage and would mimic the pop songs of the day. He played not only at his school auditorium, but also *Philips Auditorium* there in Denver. Nowadays it's known as *Philips Arena* where they hold all sorts of sporting events like Wrestling, Hockey and Ice skating. Reed even played up in Estes Park* at the *Harmony Guest Ranch* there.

When Reed left home and ventured out California way, his already proficient singing had landed him a huge seven year recording deal with *Capitol Records*. Others like *Imperial* and *Philips* were soon to follow suit. While attempting to branch out further career wise, he found that his pop recording of "Our Summer Romance" had hit the roof down South America way. Reed figured he'd just go there and cash in on his newfound fame and possibly fortune. So he left the United States where his singing career seemed in stalemate with other top performers of the era, the year was 1959. By 1961 *Imperial* was putting out, "Once Again" and "I Forgot More Than You'll Ever Know." Later, followed by *Philips* with "Cannibal Twist" and "Ghilena" were all big hit singles. Probably due to the poverty and economy with the peoples of area down in Chile and Argentina, the singles were a much better seller there than the albums were understandably.

Upon his arrival there in South American he was mobbed by the local teens there. They loved him and they loved his music. When he played and sang rock 'n' roll hits to them they went crazy with devotion toward him. This was indeed the kind of recognition he was after. He decided to stay awhile and while getting more popular by the day since landing another recording contract there with *Odean Records,* Chile, who for their *Odean Pops* edition put out such hit singles such as "Female Hercules"; "Hummingbird"; *Pistolero*, and his version of "Hippy, Hippy Shake" which blew the charts. *Capitol Chilea* would put out such Spanish language singles as *La Nova*; *Un par de Tijeras*; Also "Don't be a Stranger" were all issued

---

* Estes Park, the home of the still standing *Stanley Hotel,* made famous by the Stanley Kubrick film with Jack Nicholson called *The Shinning* (1977) with the story taken from the thriller novel by Stephen King. We understand that now after some thirty-four years since its publication, King is writting another novel, tentatively called "Dr. Sleep" to be released in November this year. If we remember, the Jack Torrance family barely survived the ordeal of being snowed in and isolated during the winter months at the Overlook Hotel (modeled after the *Stanley*). Now in King's latest sequel, the youngster Danny, now grown up is a forty-year-old man looking after elderly in a care facility, that is until a vampire tribe shows up, and the saga continues.

on .45's. The .45 albums were out there, but the singles by themselves were by far the better sellers.

It was more than likely his seeing the poverty and the poorer masses of people that his music seemed to sway and tantalize to such a degree that he felt warmth for these people that screamed with delight when he walked into a room or onto a stage. He watched how authorities of the local governments treated them, in some cases much as cattle or like dogs even. This upset him and he felt himself right in being able to bring a certain amount of pleasure into their lives. Soon he was thinking like them, supporting their Left-wing causes, and joining in with their protests. He would sing at their rallies and after learning the language, would talk their talk, speaking out politically in public, even during his concerts.

His father Cyril had once stated that when Dean went on tour to South America, he was a normal all American boy. It was there we understand he became absorbed with radical like (not exactly communistic) but rather socialistic ideals. The old man Cyril, had been an official card carrying *John Birch Society* member since the organization was formed in 1961. For the book interview "Comrade Rockstar" by Reggie Nadelson had talked with Dean's mother at her home in Hawaii. Ruth Anna Brown said of her late husband Cyril, "he was a cantankerous creature." She mentioned that she divorced him as soon as the boys were grown. We might wonder just where Dean Reed had acquired his Leftist leaning, his hardnosed father perhaps.* Reluctantly, Reed left from South America (deported as the story goes) when the military governments came to power there in Argentina and Chile.

Relocating to Europe specifically Rome by 1965, it was while there he was invited to go and sing for the *Helsinki Peace Conference*. Later he went on to Moscow when invited and was responsible he later claimed for the introduction of rock 'n' roll firsthand (his version) to the Russian people. Then it was back to Rome and it was during this period in time when he was starred in his first *Spaghetti* Western film for a late 1967 release. It was called *Winchester Does Not Forgive,* a.k.a. *Buckaroo,* an Italian production

* Dean Reed's dad Cyril was a hard man with hard ideals himself. He had been a teacher in the local school system and by all accounts quite the womanizer. Dean mother Ruth Anna had been a student of his. According to his mother, Cyril *did* believe in whippings. But Dean she said would never cry. They tell the story of how old man Reed died, by his own hand they'd say. The problem went back to 1984 when during a combine accident he'd lost a leg. He couldn't afford a new one (artificial) it was rumored, so he just committed suicide. When a reporter asked Dean why he didn't buy a new leg for his father, he'd said he was just too proud to take it.

from director Adelchi Bianchi. Here Reed was starred as a stranger who arrives in town only known as buckaroo. His costars, already veterans of the genre like the lovely Monika Brugger, and Livio Lorenzon. Others were Ugo Sasso, Omero Gargano and French actor Jean Luis. Storyline has to do with two partners coming west so as to take claim to a silver-mine they'd recently purchased back east. It seems while in route Lasch (Lorenzon) kills his partner, now he's the sole owner of this soon to be lucrative business venture. Some five years later along comes a mysterious stranger (Reed) taking up a job as foreman at a local horse ranch. Actually he's the now grown son of the past dead partner and he's planning on taking his revenge out on this man Lasch.

Acting for Reed came relatively easy since he had been an entertainer for much of his life, singing and guitar strumming from age twelve so as to please the girls he claimed. By 1958, at age twenty he was already on his way to Hollywood, even singing on television. There he'd gotten himself a recording contract. Then one with *Warner Bros.* for which they had him taking acting classes so as to become an actor* in films. His newfound best friends were now Don and Phil Everly, the duo rock 'n' roll singers of the day with hits like "Bye, Bye Love"; "Wake up Little Susie" and "Hey Bird Dog, Get away from My Quail." So yes, an entertainer Dean Reed was and there in Italy he fell right in with these rough 'n' ready Westerns, European style. His prior popularity would afford him a certain amount of input with the scripts and his scenes, but best of all, his choice of the best-looking gals for the close-ups.

For Reed's next Western we call up *God made them . . . I kill them,* a.k.a. *I kill them . . . His Life Is Mine* (1968). For this film Reed wrote and performed the title song *La Canzone: God Creates Them, I Kill Them* recorded for the soundtrack by Marcello Gigante and issued by *Mercurio*

---

* As an actor/entertainer Reed had already wet his appetite to some degree in this arena while still in Argentina. There he had actually done three early films as a singer with other Spanish singers. For his first film, a musical comedy called *My Best Girlfriend,* and it starred Argentine pop artist Palito Ortega. Reed sang two songs for it and one became quite popular called "Wandering Girl." For his second film venture, filmed in Mexico was one called *Guadalajara en Verano* in which he portrayed singer Robert Douglas. This was another musical comedy, and it starred Elizabeth Campbell and Xavier Loya, and was released in Mexico 1/28/65. His third film adventure was called *Ritmo Nuevo y vieja Ola* filmed back in Buenos Aires, also a musical comedy this time from director Enrique Carreras.

Records, Italy. In the film Reed stars as bounty hunter Slim Corbett.* His costars were Peter Martell (Pietro Martellanza) as Don Luis / actually gang leader Rod Douglas. Piero Lulli is Sheriff Lancaster, Agnes Spaak and Lina Veras as Dolly among others. It was an Italian production from *PEA* and directed by Paolo Bianchi (Paolo Bianchini). It was shot from a scripting by Fernando Di Leo, future crime genre filmmaker.

The storyline concerns Corbett who is hired by residents of a small border town to put an end to a band of outlaws coming across the Mexican border doing havoc by looting and ravaging s the countryside, stealing the gold shipment, then scooting back to safety across the border. Soon it's found out the town's own banker is behind it all coordinating the gang attacks. Actually this film predates another similar in storyline Western called *Beyond the Law* (1968), which starred genre favorite Lee Van Cleef, and since his participation it was much more popular for the genre than Reed's venture.

Reed began to branch out further in Europe with appearances, records and even managed to get involved with other popular film genres of the day, like a comedy spoof film with the team of *Franco e Ciccio*, a popular Italian comedy pair similar in fashion to the old American *Abbott and Costello,* and *Martin and Lewis* comedians of years past. An Italian production film and a second Spoof venture from director Frank Reed (Marcello Ciorciolini) who had already done a previous spoof with the two comics. This was however just another comedy vehicle for the pair, Franco Franchi and Ciccio Ingrassia were making money at the European box offices hand over fist with these Spoof films.† This was

---

* Slim Corbett was the name of this film's bounty hunter hero, but back in Reed's youth when he first began playing out for recognition he went by the handle of Slim Reed. According to all reports, he had grown to height of six feet one.

† Spoof films as they are affectionately called by fans are actually another spin-off of the *Spaghetti* Western genre. A genre spin-off is just a place where we collectors like to place films of a certain category so as not to confuse them with those of the mainstream genre. This spin-off for example deals strictly with those comedy spoofs for that particular genre, in this case Westerns. Director Frank Reed (Marcello Ciorciolini) had done a previous spoof with Franco and Ciccio called *Ciccio Forgives, I Don't* (1968), not a Zorro film but rather just another spoofing of the Westerns in general.

The producers/distributor for these films would pick out titles of mainstream popularity at that given time and cop the title, or a portion thereof for one of their spoof films. As an example the film *God Forgives, I Don't* (1966) with Terence Hill, Bud Spencer and Frank Wolff, totally unrelated film in content to the spoof was probably extremely popular at the box office during another along the same lines for that Western genre done in a style that only they could do. This one was called *The Nephews of Zorro* and starred Franco e Ciccio along with Reed now portraying the infamous Robin Hood of the old west named Raphael de La Vega, otherwise known as Zorro. Raphael was the son of the original Zorro, Don Diego de La Vega (Franco Fantasia). Reed did, however, do the soundtrack title song of "Zorro" for the film.

No different with this Dean Reed film, it's the usual laughable farce on top of farce with these two comics and their shenanigans. Upon their arrival in the town of Las Palmas they immediately get off on the wrong foot trying to impress a beautiful girl they meet, Carmencita (Agata Flori), Raphael's gal friend. But worse yet, they are over heard by Captain Martinez (Ivano Staccioli) bragging that they are really Zorro's Nephews, and he charges them with treason and they are set to hang. Raphael, disguised as Zorro saves their butt for the sake of Carmencita, but also sends them packing down the road as well. Lots of fun and games in between though, as these two nitwits attempt to outwit the Captain and his men, especially the fat Sergeant Alvarez (Pedro Sanchez).

For Reed's next film, he ventures way away from the Westerns out into the realm of a sexy drama called *The Secret Diary of Fanny* (1969) starring Giovanni Lenzi as Fanny. It was directed by Sergio Pastore. Costars were Ivano Davoli, Mario Donen, Dean Reed (part info not available), and Anthony Steel. We can only say this appears to have been his only venture into this genre per the listings we've found on him. Afterward, he moved into the Giallio-thriller genre with *Death Knocks Twice,* a.k.a. *The Blonde Connection* (1969). A well made thriller from genre director Harald Philipp. A West German/ Italian/ Monaco coproduction film for *PAC / Maris Film,* Reed portrays private detective Bob Martin who investigates several murders of beautiful women that seeming have all the same MO Reed's costars are Fabio Testi as Francisco Villa Verde, Ini Assmann as Ellen Kent, Mario Brega, Helene Chanel, and Femi Benussi as Lois Simmons. Also starring in cameos were Nadia Tiller as Maria; Anita Ekberg as Mrs. Ferretti and

---

the time this *Ciccio* film was being made, so they latched on to a similar title in order to play the association game with theatergoers. Hell, the Euro audiences didn't mind, they loved these action orientated spoofs.

Others Western films these two comics did were *Two Gangsters in the West* (1965); *Two Sergeants of General Custer* (1965); *Sons of Ringo* (1966); *Two R-R-Ringos from Texas* (1967); *Grandson of Zorro* (1968); *Two Sons of Trinity* (1972) and the list goes on, but we feel you now have the drift. Although Giorgio Simonelli directed the majority of Franco and Ciccio films, other directors were also prevalent in the game as well.

Aldolfo Celi. Francisco is found to be the killer who strangles his female partners during sex.

Not wanting to get stereotyped by the Westerns we can assume, or perhaps he was just stretching his wings in various genres of the European film industry. Reed for his next picture stars in a crime film. This Spanish / Italian coproduction was from director Ignacio F. Iquino, called *Tre per Uccidere (Three to Kill)* (1970). It stars Reed as Owen, along with Daniel Martin as Frank and Luis Marino Dugue as Cliff Olinger three brothers from Sicily who now in Chicago, circa 1930 formed a brotherhood called "A Band of Flowers." The story is based on a novel of same name, by prolific Spanish author Lou Carrigan.* The three decide to hold up the *Gulf Bank of Chicago*, and escaped with the money. How far they get is another kettle of fish entirely as they hold up in a small town outside of Chicago on the way to Nebraska. Here they run into women troubles even as the Police are hot on their tails. Others of the cast were Fernando Sancho, Maria Martin, and Krista Nell.

Next on Reed's ever-expanding European film career he was back in the Westerns with *Adios Sabata* (1971). This Italian / Spanish coproduction was from director Frank Kramer (Gianfranco Parolini). It turned out to be Reed's most popular of the genre. He costars here alongside top draw of the era, Yul Brynner in a film originally called *Indio Black: Bounty Hunter*†

---

* Lou Carrigan (Antonio Vera Ramirez) (a.k.a. Walter Carrigan) has turned out novels of six films to date from the *Spaghetti* era of the European cinema. One was a war drama, called *The Legion of No Return*. Another, the above only crime novel called *"La Banda de Los Tres Crisantemos"* a.k.a. *Tre per Uccidere*, and the other four all became *Spaghetti* Western films: *Twenty Paces to Death* (1972); *And the Crows will Dig Your Grave* (1972); *Four Candles for Garringo,* and lastly: *Stagecoach of the Condemned.*

† The *Bounty Hunter/ Sabata Adios* film was actually the second of what would later become a Sabata trilogy with the other two made by the famous *Spaghetti* Western icon, Lee Van Cleef. All three films were the brainchild of Gianfranco Parolini. Since Van Cleef had done the extremely popular first *Sabata,* Parolini had wanted him for his second film also, but was obligated by a three-picture deal with producer Alberto Grimaldi of *PEA* and *Columbia Pictures* the International distributors. We originally thought the popularity of the first Sabata was the sole reasoning behind the addition of this *Indio Black* film to the chain of the trilogy.

However, then when Van Cleef later claimed the reason he didn't do the film at the time was he was sewn up contractually with other work (that may have been, but then reports filtered back saying he just didn't like the script which later underwent a title change seemingly to cash in on the popularity of the previous *Sabata* film of 1969 and its character of the day. Brynner as the Indio black character was now dubbed in the English language prints to Sabata. Reed's character was that of Ballantine an entrepreneur of sorts, who making what he can, doing what he can while following along in the wake of Mr. Bounty hunter extraordinaire, Sabata.

Other cast members of *Adios* included: Pedro Sanchez (Ignazio Spalla), Susan Scott (Nieves Navarro) a well-known Spanish actress within the genre. Also were Gerard Herter, Franco Fantasia, Andea Scotti, Sal Borgese and Rick Boyd (Federico Boido). The storyline has to do with a master gunfighter, who with help a his small band of men help out revolutionaries in a plot to infiltrate the Mexican gold reserve and steal a wagon load of gold out from under Emperor Maximillian's astute Austrian commandant Skimmel's (Herter) nose. First, they have it, then they don't; then Sabata has it, then Ballantine winds up with it. Good film, lot of action, twist and turns and with a great music score by Bruno Nicolai.

Reed's next was a Spanish / Italian adventure pirate film called *Los Corsarios,* a.k.a. *The Corsairs / The Pirates of Green Island* (1971). Here he stars portraying Alan Drake adventurer and pirate. He is hired by a small Caribbean island republic to protect its viceroy, the young and beautiful Isabella (Anna Bella Incontrera) from those within the realm that wished to see her harmed in a power struggle since the death of her father. It is

---

at all). Could there possibly been more to it all than we originally thought? It might be suggested here that the script he saw may not have been from this *Bounty Hunter* film at all, and within Parolini's production time frame he might not have had time to cough up another script and may have just went with the altering of Brynner's film to quickly meet his contract obligations. Then again perhaps there may even have been a problem between Parolini and LVC at the time, although they were supposedly big buddies. However, a longer running riff between LVC and Grimaldi back since his *Big Gundown* days may just have been the real culprit here. At any rate we'll never know exactly and Yul Brynner wound up in the *Sabata* trilogy seemingly just because he'd made the previous *Indio Black.*

Incidentally, this was Brynner's only Euro-Western effort although as he'd done plenty of Westerns back in the States earlier, and plenty of other European films afterward, but for different genres. Another interesting point here is the two *Magnificent Seven films* Brynner was noted for would forever be scared because LVC actually turned in one of these called *The Magnificent Seven Ride* (1972) directed by George McCowan. We guess paybacks, could have been the name of the game here.

said to have a top notch music score by Nico Fidenco, but unfortunately we have never viewed the film. Julian Esteban is the Producer. The director was Ferdinando Baldi long established film director of the Western genre, who from all reports does a fine job with this adventure film.

For a late 1971 Italian film release, Reed is back we find with another Crime film. *La Stripe di Caino.* (A literal translation is The Stripe of Cain). Supposedly a crime thriller but reports on this film are scarce and it hasn't been available to be obtained for review. Other than the cast and name of the director Lamberto Benvenuti, little else is known about the film. Reed stars as Roy Bosier. Others of the cast are as follows: Stefania Careddi, Giorgio Farretto, Margherita Horwitz, and Umberto Raho.

Another obscure film is Reed's next effort for the Euro cinema was called *Sotto a Chi Tocca!* a.k.a. *Next in Line!* (1972). It's a Spanish / Italian / West German coproduction film another adventure comedy from director Frank Kramer (Gianfranco Parolini). Dean Reed stars as Straccio, Pedro Sanchez as Pietro, Aldo Canti, Mario Brega as Fregonese, Fany Sakantany as Julie and George Wang as Indicoyocoyo. Storyline it appears has to do with a young acrobat (Reed) is out to overthrow the Tyrant Governor (Brega) in order to reestablish a small democracy in order to free his lady fair.

For Reed's next film venture, he rejoins the Western genre with *Twenty Paces to Death,* a.k.a. *Saranda* (1972) a Spanish / Italian coproduction film. It was codirected by Manuel Esteba (his first and only genre film); also Ted Mulligan (Antonio Mollica), and Jose Ulloa. (A lot of fingers in this pie!) Reed stars here as Saranda. His costars are Patty Shepard, Alberto Farnese, and Luis Induni. The storyline concerns a man called Kellaway who takes in an Indian half-breed child, the only survivor of a massacre and raises him as his own. However, the problem here is the young man, grown now has fallen in love with Kellaway's daughter (Shepard). Her father is now the Silver City town Mayor, but two past associates (Clegg and Cedric) have something they intend to hold over Kellaway's head, his involvement in a past gold robbery toward the end of the war. To make matters worse, Kellaway friend the Senator (Induni) wants to marry said daughter. This is somewhat of a forbidden fruit affair, envisioned by members of the town's upper crust at that time and Kellaway wants no part of it. First off, he banishes the young man from his ranch and forbids him to ever contact the girl again. They, however, continue to meet secretly and Saranda winds up fighting not only prejudices but also outlaws Clegg and Cedric to win his gal over from her father. Others were Maria Pia Conte and Cesar Ojinago as Clegg.

Evidently the production had problems from the start (other than too fingers in the pie?) we are unclear as to the actual problems per se and / or the extent of such but we find that popular genre director Ignacio F. Iquino who also co produced this film as well as co authored the script is said to have completed the project. Iquino, certainly more prolific at making films of this genre than any of the other previous names associated was the better bet.

For Reed's twelfth European film outing we find one called *Aus dem Leben eines Taugenichts (The life of a Ne'er-do)* a.k.a. *Life of a Good-for-Nothing* (1973). Somehow Reed got involved in this German / Italian coproduction from *DEFA (Deutsche Film),* Germany which appears to have basically been made primarily as a persuasion for tourists to come over to the Eastern block of Germany and take a look see for themselves what the country is like of that era.

The story has do with a good-for-nothing (as his father calls him) Taugenichts (Reed) who bounces from place to place and woman to woman, happy carefree as a bird, singing and in general appears to be having a ball until a Countess pulls switch on him and instead of his meeting his lady fair the young Countessa he meets the hooded, cloaked and grossly overweight old Countess instead. In another segment he meets up with a robber Rinaldo Rinaldini instead.

For Reed's last *Spaghetti* Western involvement we call up *Storia di Karate, Pugni e Fagioli (The Story of Karate, Fists and Beans)* a.k.a. *Robin Hood, Arrows, Beans and Karate* (1973). A Spanish / Italian coproduction was this time a comedic Western from director Tonino Ricci. It starred Dean Reed as Sam, and his partner Chris Huerta as buddy who are bandits at heart. Another of the era of *East meets West* spin-off films that were becoming so popular about the era in time. Some of the films along these lines were really good, while others not so good. They were in a sense enjoyable for genre fans, especially those of the Italian cinema about this era in time. A mixing, if you will, of film genres like the Kung Fu / Karate, Chop, chop films combined in an action Western circa 1880s as the trains were now rumbling through those Western railhead towns across the west. The influx of peoples from the east like the Chinese used as cheap labor combined with an era that still involved much danger from outlaws, many refusing to give in to the changing times. This was the era also of the bounty hunters, the Pinkertons and the low-lives they pursued. For this film the storyline has the banker's daughter Baby (Francesca Coluzzi) having been kidnapped. Sam and Buddy join with pal Ken (Sal Borghese) and the Colonel (Alfredo Mayo) in an attempt to get her back from Espartero (Fernando Sancho) and his gang. All this makes for a violent ending free-for-all involving Mokaiko (Iwao Yoshioka) a Japanese cook and the boys. Luis Induni portrays the sheriff. This result in much mayhem and comedy as this Western chop, chop moves through the west.

Reed must have enjoyed these comedic Western outings in film (possibly they reminded him of out west and home) for a late 1974 release we find that he was now involved with another of this type called *Kit and Co.**. This one, however, was an East German production from director Konrad Petzoid. The storyline appears to have been lifted in part from a Jack London story of the Alaskan gold fever years. This story has to do with the adventures of one Kit Bellew (Reed) and buddy Shorty Rolf Hoppe toward the end of the nineteenth century.

> *This above film was not in the *Spaghetti* Western category per se, but nevertheless, was a German made Western genre film. Its significance here is not to pick 'n' choose, but only to point out that Reed's second wife, Renate Blume, was in this picture, and probably is where they first met while on set. Miss Blume already a fine actress since her early years back in her career beginnings of 1964 when she starred as Rita at age twenty in *The Divided Heaven* by director Konrad Wolf. Since, she has accumulated some sixty-nine titles (according to *www.IMDB.com* listings) of mixed television and movies on into a film currently awaiting a 2012 release. Born in 1944, she would currently be sixty-seven years old and still going strong in the business.

Reed had become quite prolific in turning out film work during these 1970s. For a 1975 release we find he turned in another Western, this one a drama also of East German origin. It was called *Blutsbruder (Blood Brother)*. It starred Reed as Harmonika and costarred Gojko Mitic as Harter Felsen and Gisela Freudenberg as Rehkitz. Mitic was at that time an extremely popular actor behind the Iron Curtain Socialist countries. By this time in Dean Reed's film career, no longer in South America, but it still seems his political views had now advanced to the big screen in Europe as well. This film mainly about the American Indian's hardships, sufferings and relationship with the whites who are depicted as mean, overly cruel and greedy white men. The Socialistic countries ate this type of film propaganda up during this era in time. For the film Reed wrote, and performed one his most popular hit songs of the day "Love Your Brother."

The film's storyline concerns Harmonica a soldier who is forced to take part in an Indian attack/massacre. The sordid violence against women and children turn his stomach and he deserts the army. He takes up with the Indians after he is captured. He eventually becomes their friend and a brave warrior for the Indians fighting against the evil White Men.

The very last Western that Dean Reed was seen in was the 1981 release of his own pet project called *Sing, Cowboy, Sing!*, a comedic Western musical. Actually it was more of a Spoof of those old American Westerns of yesteryear. We find it was conceived, written and directed by Reed himself under the supervisory wings of his old Hollywood teacher and mentor, Paton Price. In this film, Reed stars as Joe, the lead character. It was another East German color film production that was destined to become a huge hit in those Socialist Countries. The film was a parody of the singing cowboy type films of years gone by. We do remember those years of Dale and Roy Rogers and Gene Autry to name a couple of the more popular ones.

While all the filmmaking, the singing and recordings* was going on Reed was intently going back and forth into the USSR, to Rome and even back into Chile. It was there in Chile where his first wife, Patty, had been going for their divorce. From there he was off to the *Leipzig Film Festival* also in Chile and then back to East Berlin. Next he was gone to Lebanon, West Berlin and then to Havana, Cuba. He remarried again for the third and last time in 1981 to the German actress we spoke of above, Renate Blume. They were meant for one another, she loved him dearly and him her from all reports. His first marriage back in 1964 to Patricia had produced one daughter Ramona born in Rome, now both mother and daughter live in LA., USA. His second marriage took place in Berlin to Wiebke. They also had a daughter, Natasha who still lives in Berlin today. Alexander Reed affectionately called Sasha by Reed is his adopted son and continues to live in Berlin close to his mother Wiebke.

> Our singing American defector Dean Reed for a time took up residency in Russia and would bounce back between there, Italy and Germany. A hippie war protester of the Vietnam era he was officially classed as a contentious objector. As the report went; Singer/musician turned *Spaghetti* actor who worked fairly regular in the European film industry living in East Germany was found dead under mysterious circumstances on June 12, 1986. Found dead† in a lake on his East German estate where he and wife, actress Renate Blume had been living since 1972.

---

* On his acting, singing career Reed once stated during an interview in 1985 he'd acted in some eighteen films, not counting the three he'd done while in Argentina, prior to his first *Spaghetti* Western film *Buckaroo* in Italy. As for his recordings, he claimed to have put out some thirteen albums all toll during his singing career.

† His death has been surrounded by suspicion, and probably one of the biggest promoters of this suspicion had been the East-German authorities themselves. According to his daughter Ramona (by his first wife, Pat) they changed their

It seems as though from some of his last statements made in public that he may have mellowed some with age, his being only forty-eight years old when he died.*. According to his wife, Renate, after that trip he took back to America in 1985, nothing was ever the same with him. So it seems he missed his home country, and was homesick. Could it be that the man called the "Johnny Cash of Communism," and the only American to ever receive the *Lenin Prize* for art, could have been home sick for his country land? After all we're talking of the man who denounced his citizenship to the United States, converted to Communism and moved behind the Iron Curtain to East Germany to live out his years. "Better Red Than Dead" wasn't that his motto, furthermore he readily admitted to having converted to Marxism during his years in South America. But now we hear that same man during a *60 Minutes* segment for documentary filmmaker and longtime friend Will Roberts, when Reed admitted before the camera that he'd like to return to the States because "I have a great fear of growing old and dying in country where the language is not my own." The fact of the matter is that he never really did give up his citizenship to the United States. On an interview segment for *Entertainment Tonight* that took place in February the year he died, he reaffirmed his desires to return to the States saying, "I don't think it's probably important exactly where I die. I think its important how I died." He went on to say, "I have fear of growing old in any country that's not mine. I would like to grow old in a small cabin on a mountain in Colorado, looking at the blue skies."

It is possible we feel that his death may very well have been staged and that he may have been murdered by those factions who didn't want Reed to denounce all that he'd stood for so many years within the communistic countries, dropping all and returning to his homeland again. His wife, Renate, even stated for Nadelson's book (pp. 166) on whether if Reed was to return to the States for good, would she have gone with him? She answered, "I would have no audience there. I would have no career, no job. I do not

---

stories three difference times concerning the death reports, first a heart attack, then suicide by hanging, and the last one, the drowning story. Reed according to all reports was a strong swimmer having acted as lifeguard there at the *Estes Park Municipal Pool* facility during summers while he was still in high school.

The family all showed up in Berlin for the funeral services, his mother Ruth Anna Brown; first wife, Patty, and daughter Ramona; Second wife, Wiebke, and daughter Natasha, and stepson Alexander (Stasha), and third wife, Renate Blume Reed (since both were professionals they were without children). Actually, after the birth of his second daughter Natasha, he'd gotten a vasectomy.

speak enough English, and I am not young." With that we would rather leave all speculations on Reed's death to others and will bring this write-up to a close on the singer / *Spaghetti* Western star, and activist that went Red!

End.

- Below is a complete filmography of Dean Reed's Euro-Westerns. The dates are aligned as close as possible with information currently at hand, plus international release dates included. **Posters and title picture are accredited to the Sebastian Haselbeck collection via his website www.spaghetti-western.net.* Thanks again Sebastian.

DEAN REED
SPAGHETTI WESTERNS

1967

The Winchester Does not Forgive, *Il Winchester Che Non Perdona;* a.k.a. *Buckaroo*; Ital, Director Adelchi Bianchi (Reed as buckaroo); 10/28/67

1968

God made them . . . I kill them, *Dio li Crea . . . Lo li Ammazzo;* a.k.a. *I kill them . . . His Life Is Mine*; Ital, Director Paolo Bianchi (Reed as Slim Corbett); 4/29/68

The Nephews of Zorro, *I Nipoti di Zorro* (spoof Western); Ital, Director Marcello Ciorciolini (Reed as Raphael / Zorro); 12/12/68 (Stars *Franco e Ciccio*, Italian comics noted for their spoof-films)

1971

Adios Sabata; **a.k.a.** *Indio Black: Bounty Hunter; Indio Black, Sai Che Ti Dico . . . Sei un Gran Figlio di . . .*; Ital, Director Frank Kramer (Gianfranco Parolini) (Reed as Ballantine); 3/4/71 (W. Ger); 9/22/71 (USA) *(Title officially changed to Adios Sabata.* Starred Yul Brynner in the title role of Sabata, a master gunfighter)

1972

Twenty Paces to Death, *Veinte Pasos para la Muerte (Spa);* a.k.a. *Saranda*; Spa/ Ital, Director Ignacio Iquino (others assoc: Ted Mulligan [Antonio Mollica], Manuel Estebe, and Jose Ulloa) (Reed as Saranda); 4/7/72 (W. Ger)

1973

The Story of Karate, Fists and Beans, *Storia di Karate, Pugni e Fagioli;* a.k.a. *Robin Hood, Arrows, Beans and Karate* (comedic Western); Spa/ Ital, Director Tonino Ricci (Reed as Sam); 10/19/73 (W. Ger) *(East meets West genre spin-off film)*

End.

BIBLIOGRAPHY
(D. Reed)

Article *Los Angeles Times* "The Kremlin's Shadow" by Pat H. Broeske, approx—1978

Betts, Tom, editor *WAI! (Westerns . . . All'Italiana)* Fanzine articles/ information on Dean Reed

Connolly, Bill, editor *Spaghetti Cinema* Fanzine article (SC no. 21) "Some of the Spaghetti Cinema of a Dead American Communist" by William Connolly; SC: "Retrospective!" A gathering of articles from *Newsweek* 3/20/72, "The Red Dean" and 6/8/81 "Crooning for the Kremlin"; also one included from *Village Voice* 5/86 compiled by Eric Mache and Tom Betts of *WAI!*

Haselbeck, Sebastian, owner/curator for Internet website: *www.spaghetti-western.net*

Internet, via: *www.anica.it* Ref: Film production and date confirmation

Internet, via: *www.IMDB.com* (Ref: Film listings, reviews) plus minibiography by Jennifer Dunbar Dorn

Nadelson, Reggie, *Comrade Rockstar: The Story of the Search for Dean Reed* (2004) *Arrow Books, A Div of The Random House Group Ltd.* London, UK; First publishes 1991 by *Chatto & Windus Ltd.*

Prickette, Tom, *The Singer, Shoots to Kill*, previously unpublished manuscript, 2002;

Weisser, Thomas, *Spaghetti Westerns: the Good, the Bad, and the Violent*, (1992) *McFarland,* Jefferson NC.

Western: All'Italiana (books II and III) by Antonio Bruschini and Federico de Zigno, *Glittering Images,* Firenze, Italy; book II, 2001 and book III, 2006

GILBERT ROLAND

(1905-1994)

ACROSS THE BORDER SOUTH, HIS WAY!

Gilbert Roland (Luis Antonio Damaso de Alonso) was born on December 11, 1905, in Juarez, Chihuahua, Mexico of Spanish parentage. He began his famed acting career in the early 1920s. Nicknamed Amigo he starred in an everlasting variety of film work through the '20s, '30s, '40s and into the 1950s when he popular beginning to wane, he ventured overseas to Italy and joined the noted *Spaghetti* bandwagon of European films being made there and targeted to the moviegoing audience of America.

Quite the ladies' man was the suave Gilbert Roland. He was married twice during his long career. First time, was to the gorgeous actress Constance Bennett from April 20, 1941, to June 13, 1945. They were blessed with two children, both daughters for Roland, Lorinda and Gyl. After their divorce and the dust settled, he remained a single heartthrob for millions of female fans until his next marriage to one Guillermina Cantu in 1954 and they settled in El Paso, Texas where it remained home to him from then on. This marriage seemed to be everlasting as they were still together at the time of his death on May 15, 1994, of the dreaded disease, lung cancer. Not much surprise there though, as he was forever seen on film smoking. During his *Spaghetti* Western film era in Europe, he can be remembered as always having one of those nasty looking cigarillos between his lips, and wearing his gloves, hat and gun. We often wondered if he may have slept in such an outfit.

Our darkly handsome character actor only had a seventh grade education, but was the son of a real Spanish bullfighter. He actually was trained himself from an early age for the ring. He later wound up choosing a film career instead after his family was forced to leave Juarez, Mexico, when the revolutionary Pancho Villa became active in the area. His arrival in Hollywood everyone would say was at the right time. Rudolph Valentino was at his career peak in the Silents at the time. With the advent of sound soon coming, the studios were just waiting for such an actor to arrive as the ultimate Latin lover type, "tall, dark and handsome," De Alonso was all those things, including the five-foot-and-ten-and-three-fourth-inch in height. His film debut was in *The Plastic Age* (1925). Another one called *Midshipman* (1925) he was reported as only earning $50.00 a week. But it was his role opposite Norma Talmage for *Camille* (1927) as a matinee idol Armand Duval that really put his name on the star board to success. It's hard for us to believe, especially myself of him being such a huge star back in 1927, and was still around making pictures, let alone starring roles, as it were, during those later 1960s (although he would have been only in his early '60s) in Europe during those crazy years of the *Spaghetti* Westerns we've all grown to appreciate so much.

Originally he had contrived his screen name of Gilbert Roland from two different sources both being favored films stars that he admired as a youth. From the old silent screen days, he took the Gilbert from silent star John Gilbert for one, and the Roland from actress Ruth Roland for the other. He was the brother of Mexican American Francisco Chico Day renowned Hollywood director and film producer who is noted as the first Latino / American to become a card carrying member of that elite Hollywood sect.

It was during the 1930s when Roland became involved in a touchy offscreen romance with the Hollywood legendary actress Norma Talmadge, suitable for gossip columns (the tabloids didn't exist yet). This affair resulted in her divorce from hubby producer Joe Schenck, and she and Roland were to be married soon thereafter. However, evidently she had lost interest in him and found someone new before the knot was to be tied. That new man in her life was none other than comedian George Jessel. Her and Jessel did indeed eventually marry in April of 1934, but were divorced by August of '39. Seemingly a flitty butterfly type, she didn't marry again until 1946, that time to a Doctor Carvel James. This marriage for her lasted until a fatal stroke took her on Christmas Eve 1957, while in Las Vegas, Nevada.

The first sound exhibition picture was done as far back as 1900 in Paris, France. However, slow developing technology was even slower coming across the ocean. The first major sound production motion picture (via disc recording) was *The Jazz Singer* (1927) with Al Jolson. From there on it was all downhill and by the 1930s the "talkies" as nicknamed were here to stay. Gilbert Roland made a successful transition from the Silents, but even so by 1934 the Latin Lover craze was mostly over with.

For the 1940s and '50s, he turned in several swashbucklers films like: *The Sea Hawk ('40)* and *Captain Kidd ('45).* And a very well done high profile crime drama called *Gaming on the High Seas ('40)* as Greg Morella who runs a crooked offshore gaming ship. He also turned in many Westerns, even getting onboard for a stint as the third Cisco Kid for a series of six films released in 1946 and '47. They were *The Gay Cavalier ('46); South of Monterey ('46); Beauty and the Bandit ('46); Riding the California Trail ('46); Robin Hood of Monterey ('47); Killing of Bandits ('47).* He did adventures like *The Desert Hawk ('44)* in a dual role as Kasim (desert hawk), and the evil twin Hassin. In a word Gilbert Roland was a very popular and a much sought actor during and after the 1940s. Moving in to the '50s, he continued with same, but branched out some doing the new media for home entertainment called television off and on so as to fill in between his film work which seemed to have no inclinations of slowing any time during that era.

An interesting point to bring up about here was with his early training as a bullfighter would actually come to benefit him some in the early '50s when he was co starred in a film called *The Bullfighter and the Lady* (1951) Here he portraying an older matador, El Torero Y La Dama. The film starred Robert Stack, Joy Page and Katy Jurado, just prior to her famous role as Helen Ramirez for the Fred Zinnemann classic *High Noon* (1952) opposite Gary Cooper. For *Bullfighter* a cocky American (Stack) decides he's going become a bullfighter and gets the onetime great to help him in his quest which soon results in tragedy. Produced by actor John Wayne, and directed by Budd Boetticher.

Roland's next big hit came in 1952 for *The Bad and the Beautiful* with film greats Kirk Douglas (producer), Lana Turner (actress), Dick Powell (writer), and Barry Sullivan (director). Hollywood was an open book as this film depicts, letting the viewers observe the film capital at its scummiest with the multiple affairs of a star actress with her producer, writer, director and finally her Gaucho/lover turned actor (Roland). It was directed by Vincente

Minnelli and was scripted by Charles Schnee. This picture won Five Oscars, among them for Best Supporting Actress went to Gloria Grahame.

One of Roland's most popular films, and a personal favorite of mine, being the first time I remember seeing him on the big screen, was in the sponge diving adventure picture filmed in Key West, Florida called *Beneath the 12 Mile Reef* (1953). Here he starred with a young Robert Wagner, as Greek family sponge diving team from the old country, now relocated to Florida. Roland here is Mike Petrakis with son Tony (Wagner). Actress Terry Moore is Tony's love interest, although she's from an opposing family of divers. Others were J. Carrol Nash, Richard Boone, Peter Graves and Harry Carey Jr. This was the very first Cinemascope production to hit the theaters, in vivid color eluding the beautiful ocean scenery surrounding the Florida Keys. It was a story of family feuds between procurers of the merchant based sponge accumulation business of diving for said raw product. Using the old hard hat diving rigs of the day, sometimes brother against brother would battle below the depths for area bed rights. To escalate the catch, Mike goes out to the 12 mile reef in order to double up. Danger and death lurks in this deep water and is forever a warning to young Tony.

I have fond memories of my own diving experiences of years past working marine construction in Florida. Rarely a time when I was down, that didn't I think about this movie, it was truly a great classic for those who have never seen it? The film was directed by Robert D. Webb and the story written by A. I. Bezzerides about a Romeo-Juliet-ish romance between separate members of rival families dug deep in the competition of the sponge business.

After his venturing over to Europe in the mid-1960s, he turned in some six films. His first was a crime film called *The Poppy is also a Flower* (1966) with Yul Brynner. This was great film from the James Bond film director Terence Young. It contained an all-star cast of favorites which starred Senta Berger and Stephen Boyd as Benson in a story about chasing Opium shipments all over Europe from Iran to the Euro-based distributor using a new method of tracking by injecting small amount of radioactive material in the shipment back in Iran and tracking it with Geiger Counters through the various port of call to it destination.

Buried among the many stars of this film was our Gilbert Roland as Serge Marko. Others of this well made crime thriller were Angie Dickinson, Jack Hawkins, Rita Hayworth, Trevor Howard, Marcello Martroianni, Naja Tiller, Luisa Rivelli and Bob Cunningham (who also turned in a couple of *Spaghetti* Westerns himself). Actually many of these names we'll continue to recognize from the Euro films of the era like: Marilu Tolo, Howard Vernon, Eli Wallach, Barry Sullivan and Harold Sakata, of James Bond odd Job fame is Martin. Wow, what a cast. Well worth the look see if so inclined. The director Young, if we remember, besides his accomplishments as the director of three James Bond, 007 movies would later turned in one of the best of the spin-off (East meets West) Euro-genre Westerns made, called *Red Sun* (1971). It starred Charles Bronson, Ursula Andress, Toshiro Mifune and Alain Delon.

For the rest of Gilbert Roland's European films, which were only five for the *Spaghetti* Western genre, his first being one of three Edd Byrnes made in Europe called *Go Kill and Come Back* (1967). Herein for this Italian production Roland is the bandit Monetero co starred with Byrnes to film lead George Hilton (Jorge Hill), a popular South American actor of this genre. Twist and turns galore in this story as three gunmen are out after the same hidden treasure of missing gold coins. They constantly keep double-crossing one another until they happen upon the coins in an abandoned church, then the finale shootout begins. The film begins rather violent at the first, but later changes its tune about midway to several comedic incidents which make the film all the more enjoyable to watch.

Noted for its nod to the genre, and the previously popular Leone and Corbucci film's in a prologue sequeance it showing three bad looking customers riding slowly into town looking about, and mean as hell. The townfolk split, and run to hide for the impending gun battle. The three we notice are, one in poncho, similar to the Leon's no name *Stranger*. The other man, black clad with a moustache, we gather depicting Leone's *Mortimer,* and the third has a resemblance to Corbucci's *Django* character. All three are being faced down by a lone gunman with his back to us as he draws and kills all three in the street; Bam, bam, bam! Then the credits begin to roll. Great music score by Francesco De Masi to boot make for an enjoyable piece of film work by Enzo G. Castellari (Enzo Girolami) in my humble opinion.

In between films, it appears Roland returned to the States and resumed obligations in television prior to his return and his second Euro-Western called *The Ruthless Four* (1968). This was an Italian production was directed by Giorgio Capitani. This film brings together American actor Van Heflin in his only genre venture; George Hilton, Gilbert Roland and Klaus Kinski all together in a well made film about a gold mine owner attempting to retrieve the gold without being robbed after a falling out with his partner. He brings in his son Manolo (Hilton) who he believes he can trust, but finds the son has a partner himself called Brent, the blond (Kinski) who is intent on taking the gold from the old man and his son for himself. Van Helfin here as Sam Cooper, an older prospector who has struck gold in his long overworked mine is now worried. For one thing, he's unsettled over all the no goods hanging about town watching them as they load up supplies, so he enlists the aid of an old friend and gunman Mason (Gilbert) to come along with them for protection.

For Roland's next Western, he stars as scout Juan Chasquido / Jess Guido in *Between God, the Devil and a Winchester* (1968). Richard Harrison costars as the priest, Father Pat Jordan for this an Italian / Spanish coproduction from director Mario Girolami. Good retelling of the Robert Louis Stevenson novel, *Treasure Island* reworked into a Western. The plot has to do with finding the hiding place of a treasure with several different factions searching for it. One faction is Colonel Bob Ford (Folco Lulli) and his boys who attempt to get the scout Juan to come with them to help them locate the different areas where the treasure could possibly be located. All said and done a young boy actually finds the treasure and turns in over to his uncle, the priest.

Roland's next Western while in Italy was called *Johnny Hamlet* (1968). This film is kind of a retelling of Shakespeare's "Hamlet" set in the old west for an Italian production. The adapted reworked story was written by Sergio Corbucci which he co scripted with the director Enzo G. Castellari. It stars Chip Gorman (Andrea Giordana) as Johnny Hamilton who, back from the war finds his father now dead and his mother has suddenly remarried to a not well liked uncle. He has since the marriage pretty much taken over everything, even to renaming the ranch. Johnny suspects something is not as it should be here, so he delves deep into his father's death and finds foul play involved. With the help of his old friend Horace Dazio (Roland) he finally gets to the bottom of it in short order.

For Roland's last Western of the genre, we call up *Sartana Does Not Forgive* (1968). Spanish actor George Martin stars here as Uriah / Sartana. In this Italian / Spanish coproduction Roland costars as a gunman for hire called Kirchner. Sent in to wipe out a ruthless gang ran by the land grabbing town boss Sam (Tichy). With that chore out of the way, he's offered a job protecting a killer by the name of Slim Kovacs. Kovacs wants nothing to do with Uriah, even though he had killed the man's entire family so that Sam could acquire their land. Little did he know Uriah, better known as Sartana (Martin) the notorious gunman and bounty hunter would return from the war still walking upright. Now he's back and looking for revenge. This film was co produced and directed by Alfonso Balcazar. The rousing music score was by Francesco De Masi.

After completing this last film Roland left Europe and returned home to the States in time for the holidays of 1968, it was later found that a variation on his name was being used by an Italian actor as his pseudonym. The name Gill Roland (a.k.a. Gil Roland/Rowland) being used by one Gilberto Galimberti was probably a producer ploy used in an attempt to cash in on Roland's earlier *Spaghetti* film popularity. Never a leading star, Galimberti made only three Westerns of the genre using that close resembling pseudonym: *Fasthand* (1972)*; In the Name of the Father, the Son, and the Colt* (1972) *and For a Book of Dollars* (1973).

After Roland's return to the United States, he worked mostly in television, but did however turn in a few good significant films occasionally right on up and through his last western screen effort he made for a 1982 release called, *Barbarosa.* The legendary songwriter / singer / star-performer Willie Nelson portrays the title character. Gary Busey co stars as does Gilbert Roland, here portraying Barbarosa's father-in-law Don Braulio. It seems he's a wealthy rancher whose daughter Josephine (Isela Vega) has married Barbarosa against his will.

Some of Roland's other significant films of that late era of his career was *Stickfighter* (1974) A Philippine production, filmed on locations in the Philippines and directed by Luis Nepomuceno. Quite an impressive cast of actors and one of the last films we find ex-*Spaghetti* Western star Guy Madison in. Per the storyline the about 1600, an evil Spanish governor (Alejandro Rey) has acquired an equally evil master samurai to teach martial arts to his son Miguel (Dean Stockwell). As if oppression wasn't bad enough with the Spaniards being particularly mean to the Island populace. This evil ruling class is now to be challenged by the hero Roland Dante as Ben who is now an expert in the art of *Arnis* (stickfighting) tutored by the old master himself (Madison). Gilbert Roland as Allan joins him in his quest, along with his girl friend Leni (Nancy Kwan). Lots of action coupled with sword play against the stick fighters. Nice to see all the old actors once again, especially Madison and Roland.

For Roland's next fairly significant piece of film work in the waning years of his long career was one called *Caboblanco* (1980) a US/ Spa coproduction adventure drama filmed on locations in and around the Bahamas. The story was based on the novel by Scott O'Dell. It was produced and directed by Saul Swimmer. Charles Bronson stars as Giff Hoyt, co starring Jason Robards, Dominique Sander, and Gilbert Roland as Dr. Rudolfo Ramirez. The story revolves around found sunken treasure, and an ex-Nazi (Robards) collector who acquires it via murder and intrigue. Others of the cast were Carl Anderson, Burton Burri, Perla Cristal and Aldo Sambrell.

With that we'd like to bring this piece to a close about Gilbert Roland, a fine actor that no one can dispute. More fitting here would be a couple of quotes of the actor I'd like to relate previously posted on *www.IMDb.com* in this actor's brief write-up piece. "Death comes soon enough so why kill yourself crying about it?" Another was, "I don't have any delusions about myself as an actor. I'm grateful for being able to find enough work all these years." So yes, we can all agree that our actor here defiantly did things his way from across the border south, RIP Gilbert Roland.

End.

- Below is a complete filmography of Gilbert Roland's Euro films are aligned as close as possible with information currently at hand, plus international release dates included. **Posters and title picture are accredited to the Sebastian Haselbeck collection via his website www.spaghetti-western.net. Thanks, Sebastian.*

GILBERT ROLAND
EURO FILMOLOGY

1966

The Poppy is also a Flower; a.k.a. *The Opium Connection* (international crime thriller) Fr / Aus / US, Director Terence Young (Roland as Serge Markos) 10/16/66 (US); Filmed in exotic locales like Rome and Naples, Italy; Monaco, Geneva, Switzerland; Iran, and Nice, France.

EURO-WESTERNS

1967

Go Kill and Come Back, *Vado . . . L'Ammazzo e Torno;* a.k.a. *Any Gun can Play*; Ital, Director Enzo G. Castellari (Enzo Girolami) (Roland costars as bandit Monetero); 9/26/67; Stars George (Jorge) Hilton (popular South American actor of the genre), along with Edd Brynes ex-*Warner Bros.* stock TV player.

1968

Sam Cooper's Gold, *a.k.a. Everyman for Himself, Se Per Ognuno;* a.k.a. *The Ruthless Four*; Ital, Director Georgio Capitanti (Roland costars as Mason gunman friend of Cooper's); 2/9/68

God was in the West, Too, at one Time, *Anche nel West c'era una Volta Dio;* a.k.a. *Between God, the Devil and a Winchester*; Ital / Spa, Director Marino Girolami (father of Enzo G. Girolami (Enzo G. Castellari); Roland Stars here as Juan Chasquisdo the Scout); 10/7/68

That Dirty Story of the West, *Quella Sporca Storia net West;* a.k.a. *Johnny Hamlet*; Ital, Director Enzo G. Castellari (Roland costars as Horace Dazio, friend of Hamilton's); 3/22/68

Sartana Does Not Forgive, *Sartana non perdona;* a.k.a. *Sonora;* a.k.a. *Three Gun Showdown*; Ital/ Spa, Director Alfonso Balcazar (Roland co stars as gang leader Kirchner); 10/25/68; George Martin is the star here as Uriah / Sartana; Also along for the ride was American Jack Elam

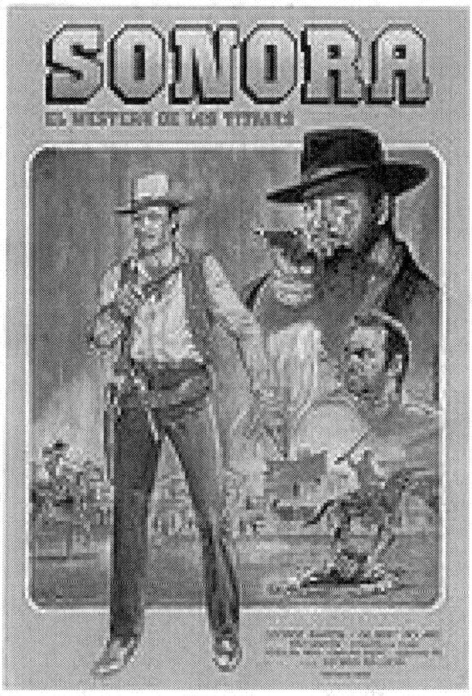

End.

BIBLIOGRAPHY
(G. ROLAND)

Betts, Tom, editor *WAI! (Westerns . . . All'Italiana)* Fanzine, 1985 articles/ info/film listing for Gilbert Roland

Buscombe, Edward, *The BFI Companion to The Western* (1988) *Andre Deutsch/BFI Publishing*, pp. 380-1

Connolly, Bill, editor *Spaghetti Cinema* Fanzine articles/tidbits on the actor Gilbert Roland and Euro films he was in

Halliwell, Leslie, *The Filmgoer's Companion* (1975) *Avon Books,* NY.; pp.660

Haselbeck, Sebastian, owner / curator for Internet website: *www.spaghetti-western.net*

Internet, via: *www.anica.it* Ref: Film production and date confirmation

Internet, via: *www.IMDB.com* posted "Mini biography of Gilbert Roland" by Guy Bellinger; plus his film listings and personal tidbit info including quotes of the actor

Prickette, Tom, *Films of Gilbert Roland* previously unpublished informational text on the man and his films, 2007

Video Hound's "Golden Movie Retriever (1994)" ref book, Publisher: *Visible Ink Press,* Detroit, MI by *Gale Research Inc.*

Hadley-Garcia, George, *Hollywood Hispano: Latinos in the Movies* (1991) published by: *A Citadel Press Book, Carol Publishing Group,* with presentation by actor Edward James Olmos

Lamparski, Richard, *Lamparski's Whatever Became of. . . ?* (1976) Publisher *Bantam Books Inc.* NY.

Weisser, Thomas, *Spaghetti Westerns: the Good, the Bad, and the Violent,* (1992) *McFarland,* Jefferson NC.

"Western: All'Italiana" (Book two) by Antonio Bruschini and Federico de Zigno, *Glittering Images,* Firenze, Italy; book II, 2001

"The World Almanac Who's who of Film" by Thomas G Aylesworth and John S. Bowman, *Bison Books,* 1987; pp. 363

MARK STEVENS

(1916-1994)

SHERIFF RUNS WILD, IN THE ITALO WEST

Richard William Stevens was born on December 13, 1916, Cleveland, Ohio. He was from Scottish and English parentage, his father at the time however, was an American aviator. An early divorce though separated the family and resulted in his having to relocate with his mother to her home country of England. They lived with his grandparents until a later move took them back across the ocean to Canada. There he grew up with an older Sister and there subsequently brought up. It's been said that he was born with a habitual chip on his shoulder. His somewhat rebellious attitude kept him in trouble both in and out of school. He managed to actually get himself removed permanently from every school system that he ever attended. A slightly built youngster he muscled himself up while enjoying extensive athletic programs. From an early school age, he excelled in his athletic abilities until, while training for the Canadian Olympic Diving Team he hurt his back on a highboard accident, an injury that would eventually keep him from returning to sports or service with the armed forces.

Talented, however, he did some singing and emcee work at nightclubs. Joining in with Radio and then his following work at the *Cleveland Playhouse* would eventually bring him to Hollywood, California where he eventually found work as a bit player in films, often unaccredited, or using the name Stephen Richards at times. Once he was contracted to *Warner Bros.* in 1943 for $100.00 a week and later he went over to *20th Century Fox,* where Daryl Zanuck suggested a name change to Mark Stevens. He was married in 1945 to Annelle Hayes an aspiring actress who was auditioning for a part when they met. During a fairly long marriage of some seventeen years they would finally divorce in 1962. They had two children together, Mark Richard and Arrelle. He was never known to have married again, but did in years past, had been associated in a brief affair with actress Hedy Lamarr.

Never really advancing past the co star stages he finally ventured into Television during the 1950s. He starred as Martin Kane in the series *Martin Kane, Private Eye* (1953-'54), and eventually went into directing and producing, forming his own company *Mark Stevens Television, Inc.* He did however continue to act in bit roles and guest spots with on many of the TV Western and drama shows of the era. His direction credits, however, were few and far between, from the early 1950s, we found one credited to him called *Cry Vengeance* (1954) in which Stevens starred as Vic Barron a framed ex-cop seeking revenge for his murdered family.

Another in 1956 with *Time Table*, in which he also starred as Charlie Norman an insurance detective who finds himself investigating a robbery that he actually was a part of. He was credited as star and also producer of this one. A third was for the 1958 Western *Gun Fever.* He starred here as gunman Luke Ram along with costars John Lipton and Larry Storch. Stevens not only directed this but also coscripted with Stanley H. Silverman from a joint story venture by Julies Evans and Harry S. Franklin. His only other accomplishments along these lines before heading off the Europe was for the film *Escape from Hell Island* (1963) in which he starred as Captain James and also directed.

For the *Spaghetti* Western fans, Stevens did *Sunscorched* (1965). Its release timing wasn't great in that it didn't hit the European West German theaters until 10/1/65 not even coming to the Italian theaters yet. The genre was in fact just on the cusp of the actual phenomenon, awaiting Leone's second film release of his Dollar film called *For a Few Dollars More* in Italy on 12/18/65. It being a Spanish/ West-German coproduction probably did benefit some from Leone's first film of the genre *A Fistful of Dollars* that was released to the Italian cinema in September of 1964 approximately one month until Germany got to see this Stevens film. There were already many pre-Leone Westerns out there: *Duello in Texas ('63); Ride and Kill ('64); Minnesota Clay ('64)* and *Gunman of the Rio Grande ('64)* were all no doubt already being well received at the box office prior to this film being released. But then again, it being made without Italian backing is probably what sent it straight to West Germany.

The film's main director was Jaime Jesus Balcazar, but the film's star Mark Stevens is also listed as codirector. Alfonso Balcazar was credited with the story and with coscripting along with Stevens; plus Irving Dennis, and Antonio De La Loma. The film's production was through Antonio Balcazar's own Spanish film company *Balcazar of Barcelona.* It starred Stevens as town Sheriff Jess Kinley, thus the film's original title *Jessy does not forgive . . . He Kills!* His costars were Mario Adorf as the badman gang leader Abel Dragna and Marianne Koch as Anna-Lisa. Others were Vivien Dodds, Oscar Pellicer, Frank Brana and Luis Induni among others.

The storyline has to do with a gang that rides into town and finds one of their old members, as it were, now the town sheriff, also a married man with a kid. Kinley doesn't want to tip his hand by them revealing his past to the townsfolk so he looks over a lot of their goings on. Even to the extent of backing down to them in public and having the town now consider him a coward unfit for the office of their sheriff and protector. It isn't long though the secrets out and the mayor takes back his star. His wife leaves him and the gang attacks the church for gold, and kills the preacher's son. Anna-Lisa who runs the stables had been a true friend to Kinley through this whole ordeal. He's has now had enough, and goes wild killing them all. This film we find was Steven's only* venture into the realm of *Spaghetti* Westerns during that prolific era of the genre.

---

* Stevens was thought to have been associated with another *Spaghetti* Western for a 1966 release. *Go with God, Gringo,* was like others of the era another Italian / Spanish coproduction, this one directed by Edward G. Muller (Edoardo Mulargia). For the film, however, we find it starred Dutch actor Glenn Saxon (a.k.a. Saxson) along with costar Lucretia Love.

Listed among the credits of the associated actors we find one Mark Stevens as character Smith, and being one the four imprisoned bandits who escape with Saxson's character Gringo. We have since found out the Stevens guy was not our actor, but actually a pseudonym being used for this film by an Italian actor, Pasquale Simeoli. So truly our Mark Stevens only did one of our favorite Euro-Westerns after all.

Among Stevens other accomplishments is an impressive listing of guest appearances on television shows stemming from the late 1940s through the late 1980s. Stevens evidentially opted for a return to the United States shortly after the above *Jessy* film was completed. Upon his return stateside he resumed doing guest appearances on television shows such as *Kojak* with Telly Savalas and *Police Story*. Afterward, about 1975, it's evident he returned to his beloved Spain settling in to operate a restaurant there in Majores for some ten years while writing novels some of which were "This, Then My Mind"; and "Run Fast, Run Far," then also "The Ex-Patriots." He evidentially returned back to the States again during 1986-'87 where he made several other appearances, one in an episode of *Murder She Wrote*. Another one was for the *Scarecrow and Mrs. King* show. He also did one episode with Tom Selleck and crew on *Magnum PI*. His last appearance listed was for a *Law and Harry McGraw* show episode called "Mr. Chapman, I Presume?" for an October 13, 1987, airing.

Steady on the move we find even at an older age, he favored returning again and again to the Spanish coast and Majores in particular and to a woman there named Hilde. Here he opted to play out his final years. He passed away there in Majores, dying of cancer at the age of 77 on September 14, 1994. We as fans would like to join with his family, his many associates and all of his Spanish friends and neighbors that mourned the lost of this class actor.

End.

- Below is a partial filmography listing of pertinent Mark Stevens Euro films. The dates are aligned as close as possible with information currently at hand, plus international release date for the Western only. Stevens photo via *LA Times* Internet posting regarding his *Hollywood Walk of Fame* Star. **Poster pictures are accredited to the Sebastian Haselbeck collection via his website www.spaghetti-western.net. Thanks, Sebastian.*

MARK STEVENS EURO FILMS

1964

Frozen Alive, a.k.a. *Fall: X-701* (sci-fi thriller); UK/ W. Ger, Director Bernard Knowles (Stevens Stars as scientist Frank Overton); 1964 (W. Ger); Dec/ '64 (UK); January/ '67 (US); Costarring: Marianne Koch, Joachim Hansen and Delphi Lawrence as Joan Overton. Storyline has a scientist, partner / assistant Dr. Helen Wieland (Koch) experimenting with suspended animation by freezing life to a near all but dead state of being, then reviving it again. Without her knowledge, he uses himself as the test subject. While the Doctor is frozen, under constant surveillance his wife is found to have been murdered. When he's awakes from his subzero sleep he's now the primary suspect. Good film, from German producer Artur Brauner, Ronald Rietti and coprod Irving Dennis. Script by Evelyn Frazer.

1965

Jessy Does Not Forgive . . . He Kills! *Jessy Non Perdona . . . Uccide!* A.k.a. *Sunscorched* (Western); Spa / W. Ger, Director Jamie Jesus Balcazar and Mark Stevens (Stevens Stars as Jess Kinley the sheriff of Fraserville); 10/1/65;

Mark Stevens not only starred here but he also cowrote the script along with Alfonso Balcazar (story), also with Jose Antonio de la Loma and Irving Dennis. In addition Stevens also codirected the film along with Jaime Jesus Balcazar, son of Alfonso with a debut helping hand from the more experienced Stevens.

1966

Go with God, Gringo, *Vajas Con Dios, Grino* (Western); Ital / Spa, Director Edward G. Muller (Eduardo Mulargia) (We found that Mark Stevens is truly *not* in this film regardless of credits)

1970

The Fury of the Wolfman, *La Furia Del Hombre Lobo;* a.k.a. *The Wolfman Never Sleeps* (Horror); Spa, Director J. M. Zabalza (Julio Perez Tabernero) (Stevens as Bill Williams); 2/7/72 (Spa); Stars Paul Naschy (Jacinto Molina) as Count Waldemar Daninsky / the Werewolf. It costars Perla Cristal as Dr. Ilona Elmann and Veronica Lujan as Karen, also with Michael Rivers and Mark Stevens.

Typical storyline of man bitten by werewolf in Tibetan Alps is now trying to rid himself of this awful curse. Fortunately, he finds a woman (Karen) that loves him enough to destroy him and his terrible curse. What separates this story from others of the same vein is that in the background an evil Doctor (Mad to the core) (Cristal) is working her own agenda collecting said monsters under the pretext of trying to help them.

The beautiful Karen (Lujan) is her assistant and her boyfriend is Mark Stevens. If Daninsky doesn't get shed of his curse, and soon by the next full moon, he is subject to change into a vicious killer werewolf. Confusing story, flow is all wrong, probably due to choppy editing. Whatever the case, it seems to have been the last entry for our actor Mark Stevens, may he RIP.

End.

BIBLIOGRAPHY
(M. STEVENS)

Betts, Tom, editor *WAI! (Westerns . . . All'Italiana)* Fanzine article/Obit on Mark Stevens Issue no. 44

Halliwell, Leslie, *The Filmgoer's Companion* (1975) *Avon Books,* NY., pp.722

Haselbeck, Sebastian, owner/curator for Internet website: *www.spaghetti-western.net*

Internet, via: *www.IMDB.com* Film listings/trivia plus posting of mini biography for "Mark Stevens" by Gary Brumburgh

Los Angeles Times, Website posting Hollywood Star Walk confirmation article on "Mark Stevens: Actor/Director/Producer" of August 5, 1956, by Walter Ames

Video Hound's Golden Retriever (1994 edition) *Visible Ink Press,* a division of *Gale Research Inc.,* Detroit, MI.; pp 1392

Weisser, Thomas, *Spaghetti Westerns: the Good, the Bad, and the Violent* (1992) *McFarland,* Jefferson, NC., pp 305; 132-3

The Western: The Complete Film Sourcebook (The Film Encyclopedia) (1983) ; by Phil Hardy, *William Morrow and Co, Inc.,* NY., pp 392

The World Almanac Who's who of Film (1987) by Thomas G Aylesworth and John S. Bowman, *Bison Books,* pp. 390-1

LEE VAN CLEEF

From his granddaughter Kate's own words:
"He was the best of the best. I love you grandpa."

DEDICATION

I would like to dedicate this chapter to our now deceased good friends Ruth and Bill Staats. Without their endearing help in relating Bill's past experiences and years of friendship with the actor, much of this chapter could not have ever been possible. May God bless and keep them both . . .

Before we delve into the main text body of this chapter on actor Lee Van Cleef, I would like to first add in a couple of items of interest for the reader. Firstly is a short piece written by my friend Tom Betts, written a longtime back for me to use as an opening for my Van Cleef piece. I thought it an appropriate time to add it in now. In addition following, I will offer up a brief Introduction piece that includes special words from my friend Bill Staats pictured above.

THE MAN IN BLACK IS WAITING

I've been a Lee Van Cleef fan since 1953 when I was 7 year-old and my grandmother took me and my sister to see *The Beast from 20,000 Fathoms*. Of course we went to see the monster dinosaur not any of the actors in the film. Near the end of the movie, after the beast has destroyed half of New York City, it wanders into an amusement park. The scientists call on the military for help and they send in a sharpshooter. Armed with a grenade launcher loaded with a radioactive isotope Professor Nesbitt asks the marksman, played by Lee Van Cleef, "Are you any good with that gun?" Lee looks him straight in the eye and says, "I can pick my teeth with one of these." Even then I said to myself, is this guy cool or what?

It was several years later after seeing him countless times on television I finally learned that the actor's name was Lee Van Cleef. Thankfully, I was a big western fan, so I saw him quite a bit, always playing the henchman, gunman and hoods. Seldom did he ever live to see the end of the TV episode or film, as he was always killed off. Still his face became very familiar to me. As I grew older I'd see him in films both at the theater and on late night movies.

In 1966/'67 a new type of Western hit the American cinema, The *Spaghetti* Western. Now in college I went to see *A Fistful of Dollars* on opening night at the local theater. There were eleven other people in the theater watching it. I was blown away by the appearance of Clint Eastwood and his "Man with No-Name" character. I didn't understand the advertising though that kept ending with, "It's the first motion picture of its kind. It won't be the last." How did they know? Well they knew because Sergio Leone's 'Man with No-Name' trilogy of films was made three years before, and a lawsuit by Akira Kurosawa, who claimed Leone had stolen the film directly from his *Yojimbo* movie and had held up the release of the films internationally. When the second film *For a Few Dollars More* was advertised it stated, "The Man with No-Name is back. The Man in Black is waiting." This man in black was none other than Lee Van Cleef. Boy, I couldn't wait to see this second film. I was even more blown away when instead of playing the villain he was another anti-hero character named 'Colonel Douglas Mortimer', and was looking great. Two scenes from that film I will always remember: when Mortimer unties his bedroll and an assortment of guns roll out. The other is when Mortimer strikes a match on Klaus Kinski's hunchback to light his pipe. Lee's character was every bit an equal to Clint's, just a shade older and wiser.

This new image of Lee was carried on through the rest of his film career. At 40 years of age, character actor Lee Van Cleef had become a star. He had become a cult star in the United States, but an International Star everywhere else in the world. In 1980 I began researching *Spaghetti* Westerns and Lee

Van Cleef. I hooked up with another fan of the genre and a great Lee Van Cleef fan. J. Tom Prickette. Together we shared information and continued our research. I found out living in Northridge, California, while attending college at nearby *Cal State*, that Lee only lived about five miles from my folks home in Tarzana. I located the address and drove by his modest ranch house multiple times over the years. Never seeing or meeting him, he was still my hero.

Tom has now put together a lifetime of collecting, researching and writing into this book form for all those *Spaghetti* Western fans. This special chapter on Van Cleef is truly for the fans that have idolized the man from *High Noon* to *The Master* TV series. Herein is the *Reel* and complete story of the real anti-hero Lee Van Cleef.

Tom Betts
Editor and Chief of *WAI!*
(Westerns All'Italiana)
Fanzine & Blogspot

INTRODUCTION

Some years after I had began writing about the actor Lee Van Cleef I was to become even more interested in him after reading about him in William R. Horner's book *Bad at the Bijou,* 1982 by *McFarland Publishers.* Back in those days, there was very little on the man, even less about his early life and career beginnings with exception of this book compiled from an actual interview with the actor. Even in those days much of his film achievements were muddled it seemed, though there were many.

As I remember during the 1950's and '60's it seems that evil looking face of his was on television a couple times a week. He was steady becoming the badman we all loved to see, but hated all the same time. When his two European films, *For a Few Dollars More,* and *The Good, the Bad and the Ugly*, finally hit our shores about 1967, they rekindled a new thrill upon seeing him now up on the big screen. This time he had much more of a presence than we had ever had the pleasure of seeing him as before.

Even though the old TV 'Rowdy Yates' character of *Rawhide*, Clint Eastwood was the main star in these two films, we fans in our minds believed LVC was truly the main attraction. Even when the first of Sergio Leone's trilogy, *Fistful of Dollars* finally came to our local drive-in, sometime after the first showings of *GBU*, and *FFDM* as I remember it, we still remained confident in our opinion that the 'Mortimer' and 'Angel Eyes' anti-hero characters were without a doubt the bigger hero, screen wise for us fans.

It was after those first viewing that piqued my interest even further in finding out more about this man. Then when I found out there was very little to be found on him that tended to fuel the fire even more. Without the Internet, we were confined to what one could dig up in the libraries of the various town and municipalities we were near at the time, and a lot of word of mouth which was sometimes very unreliable. I was fortunate in being 'on the road', as-it-were during the 1980's and was able to visit libraries not only in my home state of Florida, but others like Colorado as well. The old *Denver Public Library* was a God's send to my cravings for information.

Letters, I wrote hundreds of letters everywhere and finally tracked down the actor's home base, just outside LA not long after he'd passed away in early 1990's. By that time, I had packed in a grand amount of materials on the man that was ever growing. Collecting his movies on VHS was the mainstream of my efforts and a never ending challenge, especially those coming out of Europe, with the multiply title changes and elusive dating. Most of these had never been shown in American theatres and some never would. What few did happen to make it like, *The Big Gundown* usually hit the big screens of the larger cities like in NY, LA or Chicago. Even those were mostly limited showings at best I've been told. Other places like in my neck of the woods in Florida, we never even got the chance to see them until much later, and then it was always at a drive-in, be it raining or not we went. So the videos were by far the best way to view these elusive films, if of course, they could be tracked down, and obtained from mostly European sources.

It was during those years and mostly as the result of my huge letter writing information that I stumbled onto one of Lee's childhood friends he grew up with there in Somerville, NJ. It was retired postman, William H. Staats. Through subsequent letter correspondence and even phone calls, sometimes a couple times a month for awhile there, we became fast friends regardless of the age differences between us. Since Bill and his wife Ruth had moved to Florida from Las Vegas, and living in the Melbourne, FL. area we were able to meet in person on many occasions. My job in those days took me to lots of different States, towns and places I probably otherwise would never have seen including overseas for a period of time in the UK. The consulting firm I worked for sent me for nearly a two year period, and all the while Bill Staats and I corresponded regularly and saw each other often when I returned on home leaves on several dinner outings.

Our friendship developed into much more than just a freak acquaintance in that we were sincerely joined together with a combined interest. It was sometimes hard for me to grasp that I was actually sitting and conversing with a man who actually grew up with screen villain, LVC. But Bill was an easy man to talk to, he really sort of idolized Lee, even to the point of keeping a scrapbook on him and taking an occasional visit to Lee out in Hollywood, which he loved relating stories about his trips of the mid and late 1950's.

He and Ruth both were a wealth of information on Lee, and believe you me I was somewhat of glutton when it came to absorbing that information. Since I was a collector of Lee's films, I would continually send found copies of these films when acquired, for Bill's viewing pleasure. He loved them, the more I'd send him the more eager he became for more, and more. He couldn't believe he'd made all those films in Europe. Since Lee's mother Marion had actually lived with the Staats at their home in *Bound Brook* for a time, Ruth was a lot more prolific with stories and gossip related by Marion than one would believe. Ruth would tell about how she and Marion would go into Somerville to catch Lee's movies at the *Cort Theater*. Seems Lee's mom would want to go again and again to see the same movies while Bill worked.

It was a real pleasure knowing both Bill and Ruth, never got to meet Bill's first wife Evelyn who he married about 1955. On a couple of Bill's earlier visits to the coast to see Lee and Pat, he and Eve as he called her, would pal around Hollywood and taking in the beach together having great times I understand. Bill and Eve divorced after about 8 years of marriage, later on he met Ruth and something clicked, they married on Feb. 14th 1963. Late in our friendship I did get to met Ruth's daughter Gigi, who also lived in Florida. From what Ruth use to tell us after Bill passed away, he did have an estranged daughter who lived on Florida's west coast, but Ruth never had much to say about her. Mostly it was stories she would relate about Lee and his life, his marriages and the occasional bits concerning his drinking.

Neither Ruth nor Bill for that matter, were into drinking anything alcoholic, and she didn't really care much for those who did. We can only assume she tolerated Lee and his friends on certain occasions because of Bill. I on the other hand tended to feel quite differently about the subject. With my being a workplace person, having grown up in the heavy construction industry, I have known quite well what it's like to get involved with the guys after work hours, hitting the bars and such. In my day, that was just apart of the underlying advancement program for the business. Even the most innocent of work related successes of day, holidays and / or all special occasions warranted a bottle, or at a minimum several beers and / or a good night of drinking and rehashing of job related happenings or discussions. Yes, I can well imagine how Lee could be sucked into the Hollywood scene, as-it-were. It was however, unfortunate that he let it get the best of him to the point of also sucking the health from him. We his fans will never forgive him for that.

When I first mentioned to Bill that I was researching, and gathering materials and information on Lee for an extensive book on the actor, he was overwhelmed to say the least. Any and everything he could do to help he was all for it. I had asked Bill on one occasion to sometime write me, in his own words something I could use as an introduction for the book. He agreed to do it. As I had lots of other pressing job related priorities on my plate at the time (and not wanting to pressure him either), I had let it pass, so as to and peculate for awhile. Actually I found he had completed it not long afterward and presented it to me on our next meeting. I was thrilled to say the least. He had typed it on his old *Royal,* using his own words and had signed it.

My friend Bill passed away back on Oct.12, of 2000. In this, his Introduction piece he writes apologizing for his composing in the beginning. The typing isn't the best we'll admit, but it is still in his own words for and about his buddy Lee. I am attaching this letter in its entirety below. I certainly do hope all will enjoy it as much as I did when I first read it.

Author

Lee and Bill Staats at the Van Cleef's in CA June, 1962
From Author's personal collection

July 24, 1994

Dear Tom,

I'm not too good at writing this introduction but I'll do the best I can.

MY REMEMBERANCES OF LEE VAN CLEEF:

We grew up in the same home town of Somerville, New Jersey. Lee was born January 9, 1925 and I was born August 24, 1924. It seems we always knew each other from early years on until his death on December 16, 1989. This gave me a feeling of loss like when one loses a brother. I had no brothers and Lee was an only child. His parents Clarance and Marion Van Cleef treated me like a second son. I spent many happy hours at their home about five blocks from where I lived with my parents and my sister. We went thru school together, biked together all over town and outlining areas. We shared many confidences as we were maturing into young men. Naturally we both began to think about girls and giggled over this and other things. Both were happy the day school was out so we could get out in the open air in the spring. This was cut short as he was sent to Boy Scout camp in early summer. Next we would meet first day of school in the fall.

Lee played trombone in the high school band. He was very musically inclined and very good at this. When World War 2 started he quit high school and joined the Navy at age 17. After several jobs one of which was working on Doris Duke's farms in south Somerville, he met a man who belonged to a little theater group in Clinton, N. J. One night Lee went with him to see what this was all about. They needed an extra fill-in fellow that night and Lee was put on the stage. From this he was later ~~granted~~ given a part in the road company of Mr. Roberts. Producer Stanley Cramer saw the ~~paly~~ play one night and thought Lee would be ideal for one of the parts Cramer was casting in the upcoming movie "High Noon". Lee was tested and given the part of one of the three killers shown in the beginning of the movie. He spoke no lines in this his first movie. Later it was discovered what a wonderful speaking voice Lee had and he went on to many other parts in many movies. I visited him in Hollywood and he took me on some studio tours. We would also meet again when he would come home to Somerville to see his mother. Lee lost his father in 1948 of a heart attack. not much more except he was a good friend and always there for me. There was no one like him in real life or in the movies.

William H. Staats

LEE VAN CLEEF

(1925-1989)

Courtesy personal collection

IN REVERENCE OF A BADMAN

This well-known screen villain was born Clarence Leroy Van Cleef Jr. of Dutch parentage in Somerville, New Jersey on January 5, 1925. He grew up there spending his formative years while a youngster enjoying the four seasons of this beautiful New Jersey countryside area. He enjoyed doing what most boys did during that era in time. There was always something ongoing around the Raritan River basin, fishing, small game hunting, bike riding as well as swimming or canoeing out on the river.

Young Lee was for the most part, your average boy about town. He enjoyed those family outings with his parents, mom Marion Levina and dad Clarence Leroy Sr. He once related a tidbit of his life when he mentioned how his parents had taken him on his first canoe trip out on the Raritan when he was but two years old. He grew up to love the out-of-doors and vowed later in life he would never work indoors. But of course, due to circumstances he would have to venture from this vow from time to time.

His father, a mild-mannered gentleman from all accounts, worked at the downtown Somerville, *First National Bank* situated at Bridge and Main Streets. He wished only the best for his son's future, but little did he realize he would not live to see the dreams of success for his son come true. He emphasized to Lee time and again the importance of a good education. Toe the mark, he would tell him, so he could eventually make something of himself. Possibly Lee could take up accounting, in the business world as he had done. Later during his high school years having shown an interest in studying music and took up playing the guitar and trombone. Other school interests was working with his hands in the shop classes, which he continued to take all four years of in high school thoroughly enjoying the woodworking.

From information mostly conpiled from newpaper accounts we learn that young Lee was also full of the devilment at that young age, and enjoyed roughhousing with his friends. Some of those were, Bill Staats a neighbor who would later become a Somerville Postman. Another was John McLachian who in later times would operate an insurance, real estate / travel business on Main Street. Also, there was James (Jimmy) Miesowitz who would later become President of the local *Lion's Club*, Somerville Chapter.

Robert Vaughn Jr. remembering those years back when his parents ran the family business *Vaughn's Meat Market and Grocery* there on Main Street that his parents had once hired Lee to work there in the store during one summer vacation period, upon the request of Lee's father. Knowing Lee was a bit wild as a youth, the senior Van Cleef thought perhaps this job would teach him some responsibility and help keep him out of trouble.

Actually Lee worked there more than one summer we understand from Vaughn Jr., who had in more recent times ran *Vaughn's Deli* where he kept autographed pictures of Lee from the movies there on the walls of his shop there on Gaston Avenue. When in town visiting his mother, Lee would always stop by for a short visit. "He was a nice guy" he said. "He took care of his mother."

Sometimes on occasion when Lee was back in town for a visit, he and some of the guys would get together, have drinks, horse around a bit and talk of old times down at the *Somerville Hotel/Bar* on Main Street. Lee would be interested in the usual about old girl friends and old buddies, their whereabouts and how many kids they had now or the like. The guys, however, were much more interested in what he was doing way out there in Hollywood. The movie stars he now knew and the girls. Always they were interested in the girls. Boys wouldn't be boys if they weren't.

Mr. John McLachian once interviewed years later said of Lee, "he was a decent sort of guy, not like the tough-guy characters of his films. He was sinister as hell when you first saw him, but he was a real decent person." He remembered meeting Lee (Leroy as he was actually known back then) for the first time back before they were even classmates in school. They met at the *YMCA Retreat* in Pennsylvania one summer.

Another classmate Dick Henry who lived next door to the Van Cleef's remembered that he and Leroy as youngsters spent a lot of time together. "Lee and I were very close" said Mr. Henry. He recalled that Lee's parents maintained a cabin bungalow on the South branch of the Raritan River. "Lee and I spent summers canoeing. We had a lot of good times."

Henry remembers Lee as being quick with a smile and a joke. "He was quicker with a smile than most people would think from the parts he's played. He would be himself with me, but when he was out in public he would revert to his stage personality—people expected him to act a certain way."

> In later years some of his fellow actors when interviewed and questions were asked about how it was working with the famous badman, Lee Van Cleef. Some would give similar replies as did Mr. Henry. Actor Kurt Russell mentioned once that he enjoyed working with Lee. It was a lot of fun because Lee was the practical joker on the set and loved to play little tricks on his fellow actors. Not at all like the badman persona that comes to mind when one thinks of Lee Van Cleef, the actor.
>
> During another interview during the 1980s the interviewer said, when attempting to capture the mind set of Lee Van Cleef, the man not the actor stated that he appeared to have a hipster sense of humor and attitude. It would seem not unlike most of us in our life, we simply have mellowed with age, apparently Lee had done the same.

His having grown up in this small town, with his father being a staple of the community, Lee very much the average youngster. He had been a fine Boy Scout who loved being out doors. Very much the avid swimmer he excelled in lifesaving methods. Also, he enjoyed the hiking, camping and archery was among his favorites. Although living in a small country town where farming was commonplace, he made up his mind at an early age that the farm life wouldn't be the life for him.

Another of his classmates Ms. Jane Drake, retired Assistant Borough Clerk of Somerville, once recalled "At the time he was just another kid, a nice kid. Who would have thought he would become such a famous movie star."

It was during Lee's last year of high school that WWII War broke out. The seemingly unprovoked Japanese had set their sights on a major US Naval installation, Pearl Harbor, Honolulu, Hawaii on December 7, 1941 and proceeded to bomb it. By the next day December the Eighth Congress had declared full out war on Japan. Like many of Lee's friends as well as other young men of the day wishing to show their patriotic side, wanted to drop everything and go fight for their country as soon possible. That possibility for Lee was to quit school and join up being of the first in his school to jump at the chance, however like other students the gentle persuasions by their principal and parents to stay in school and finish the school year out before enlisting. Having signed up in a pre enlistment program for the Service, he was then willing to stay in school (suggested by his principal and backed by his father) so as to continue his education to graduation, and also continuing his latest part-time job on a local Jersey farm working for one Wilbur Everett of New Center. His job there involved helping with day to day chores, He said he pitched a lot of hay in those days. Work though involved tractor work. The plowing, cultivating and planting that were involved in the harvesting of grains and vegetables which were the main objectives. He had also learned to care for the livestock and to do both hand and machine milking according to what all he had listed on his enlistment papers.

Loving the water as he did, his Service branch choice was with the navy and on September 16 of 1942 he was officially theirs and was soon off for basic training. He was assigned to Company 344 and from there he would soon be off to see rest of the world.

After completing his basic training in Newport, Rhode Island, Lee was assigned to the *Naval Fleet Sound School* and underwent training to be a sound operator.* He was later commissioned to a subchaser and then to a

---

* It was during this schooling period at Sound School there in Key West, FL. that he was taken ill with Scarlet Fever, January 29, 1943. He was moved to the special US Naval Hospital in St Albans, New York on February 15 of that same year for treatment.

It was during this time off, as it were, from his naval schooling, while hospitalized and subsequent recuperation period that he and his childhood sweetheart Pasty Ruth Kahle really go close. Eventually, by the end of the year, they were married on December 10, 1943.

After his hospitalization, he didn't return to active duty until March 11 of 1943, as his first assignment he worked a stint on the Submarine Chaser USS *SC-681* as helm sound and radar watcher one of its initial cruises. This brand-new ship commissioned just days earlier on March 8, 1943, was 110' and minesweeper, the USS *Incredible* patrolling the Caribbean Sea. There he worked as sonarman. They would cruise the Crimean Sea during the famous Crimean Conference on December of 1944 which was attended by then president Franklin D. Roosevelt and King Aziz Ibn Saud of Saudi Arabia. Van Cleef's ship was one of six escorts making up the President's convoy traveling to this important Mission of Peace Summit talks.

The USS *Incredible's* general orders included participating in the Invasion of Southern France and including follow up operations from August 15 until October 17 of 1944. During the time period of September 9 and 10 and during normal minesweeping operations off the coast of Menton, France the ship came under heavy fire from enemy shore batteries and attack by some twelve Human (two-man operated) Torpedoes. Lee was deemed eligible for accommodations in the form of: The American Theater and African Mediterranean-European Ribbons, plus one Bronze Star for his efficient performance under fire that day. He was personally commended for his efforts by Commanding officer Admiral King for his accomplishments.

Van Cleef remained onboard the USS *Incredible* as they continued duties off the southern coast of France until January 18, 1945, when the ship was picked for a special mission to Russia, clearing mines in the Black Sea while acting as air-sea rescue patrol ship. But by February 20 they had resumed voyage on back down to Palermo, Sicily and by May 5 would once again dock back in Norfolk for an overhaul and refitting before the long trek over to Pearl Harbor arriving just 8 days after Japan surrendered. They continued to clear mines there in the harbor vicinity until August 31 when leaving now bound for the China Sea / Ryukyu Islands area southwest of Japan. There they continued sweeping operations in that area for Special Naval ops called *Operation Skagway* through Christmas that year but by February 17 of '46 the USS *Incredible* had returned to US shores, docking there in San Pedro, California.

10" long and carried a 27-man complement. The vessel had been built by the Thomas Kurtson Shipbuilding Corp. at the Halesite yard, Long Island, NY.

By February 3 of 1944 and prior to his commissioning on the USS *Incredible* he had already returned to the Naval Key West Training facility where he took a refresher Fleet Sound Course, then was transferred to the Mine craft Training Center, Little Creek, VA on March 8 then later joining with other crewmen on another new ship ready for service, the USS *Incredible AM-249* (Admirable class) by April 17, 1944. This 530 ton ship was built at Savanna, GA. shipyards, at 184' and 6" long was equipped with a barrage of heavy fighting tools of war.

Upon Van Cleef's discharged from active duty on March 6, 1946, his departure from Service left him with an impressive accumulation of metals and accommodations: Sonar-man First Class and the Mine-Sweeping Insignia plus the Bronze Star mentioned above Also he had received the Asiatic Pacific Medal, African European and Middle East One-Star Medal, American-Pacific Medal, Good Conduct Medal and the WWII Victory Medal.

His official separation from service took place in Toledo, Ohio where he was reunited with wife, Pat, who had been staying nearby in Sharon, PA with relatives. Together they returned to Somerville, where Lee's aging parent's still resided. Here they proceeded to make a home and a new life for themselves. Lee and Pat having settled there in Somerville, found work for a while as an engineer at the nearby *Singer Sewing Machine* electrical plant. Afterward, during the summer seasons Lee with Pat both worked at the *Boy Scout Camp* in Maine. Pat's Aunt and Uncle had a place there in New England no far from the camp. In previous years when Lee would be spending his summers there at camp, he and Pat would meet up and enjoy passing the time together. Now married Lee was acting assistant manager and counselor for the facility, and Pat also worked there as secretary. She would continue to work in secretarial capacities right up to quitting only just prior to giving birth to Alan in 1947. Approximately one year afterward along came Deborah (Debbie). The second son David would not come along until the early 1950s.

Lee would venture into many different fields of endeavor after that, at first egged on by his Father he had delved into accounting. For a while he even held down a job there at the same bank that Van Cleef Sr., would eventually retire from. Not particularly enjoying the indoor work his banking opportunity didn't last long especially, if dad was overseeing his work. Other jobs included his working on a cattle ranch outside Somerville which belonged to the high profile Duke family, famous for their tobacco holdings during that era in time. In later years, heiress daughter Doris Duke* continued to make headlines in the society columns of New York and Hollywood with

---

* Doris Duke was but tweleve years old when she inherited the $100 million estate from her tobacco holding rich father. Prolific in one sense, like the old song says, "Looking for love in all the wrong places," Duke twice divorced and lonely again at the age of seventy-four got hooked up with her butler late in life. Bernard Lafferty had worked for singer Peggy Lee as personal assistant before Duke hired him in the capacity as her butler and close confidante. After her death in 1993 age eighty, Lafferty wound up not only the executor of her entire $1.2 billion estate but also personally collected some $5 million outright plus another $500,000 a year for life.

her many infamous romps with a bevy of men, who ranged from Hollywood jet set circles to European playboys, some of whom had reputed mafia ties.

Lee being an avid outdoorsman tried working with the *Forestry Service* for a while, but the pay he found for those types of positions weren't all that great back then, especially for man with a young family. He picked up more aggressive pay work at a nearby factory outside Manhattan, doing time study methods and motion analyzing. Later, around 1946, we understand he did return to accounting work for a while, taking in business accounts working nights from home to earn some extra cash. All the while he was becoming more interested in a pastime that little did he realize or even imagine would eventually propel him into anything remotely resembling a movie star.

For relaxation in the evenings sometimes he and Pat along with friends would visit a *Little Theatre Group* showing there in Clinton not far from Somerville. This venture for fun and entertainment one night was actually a setup one might say, by a coworker buddy from the plant who was actually a member of the *Clinton Music Hall Players* group himself. Lee had been taking some jovial prodding from that same guy until he finally succumbed to the dare and took to the stage that night for a reading* of an available part for the upcoming play *Our Town*. Low and behold and got the part!

Lee found that he really enjoyed this type of diversion of life and so would continue to meet with the group several nights a week acting on stage as a regular along with the others on these homegrown plays. For

---

Actress Victoria Principal stated later in an Enquirer article that her hubby, Plastic Surgeon Henry Glassman received some $500,000 for a facelift procedure he performed on Duke when she was seventy-nine. The article also stated that after her death in her Beverly Hills mansion, a nurse had claimed that Lafferty and a doctor had sped up her dying by pumping her full of morphine. No concrete evidence could ever be found to back up her claim (partly because of the cremation of her remains so quickly following her death).

The article went on to say that he then moved on over to Elizabeth Taylor, comforting her in her time of need following her and Larry Fortensky's split. Fortunately he didn't live much longer to squeeze into somebody else's fortune, he died in 1996 at fifty-one years old.

* Lee stated for the *Pittsburgh Press News* edition Friday July 24, 1970, via *The North American Newspaper Alliance*: "I read some lines, very bad, and he says I'm hired and he wants me back tomorrow. I'm working at the plant and doing public accounting at night and I don't see how I can do it. But I was there Monday morning and I've been acting ever since."

his next big role, he auditioned for the part of Joe Pendleton the boxer in *Heaven Can Wait*. It was during one of these play airings that the group was having for visiting talent scouts that he lucked out. Impressed with Van Cleef's stage presence and delivery, one of the attending scouts later took him on into New York City to agent Maynard Morris of the *MCA Agency*. Morris liking what he saw in turn sent them on over to the *Alvin Theatre* on Fifty-Second Street for an audition. He wasn't by himself it seems, there were some 500 others there looking for parts as well, the play it turned out was the upcoming *Mister Roberts*.

A road company director Joshua Logan liked him right off and took Lee into his fold of young players. The play's star was to be Henry Fonda a young man who already was a seasoned veteran would portray the lead role as Lieutenant JG Roberts. Van Cleef had been given the part of Mannion one of the onboard sailors, an MP. Later on they would take this play on the road for a fifteen month tour.

From these meager beginnings, Van Cleef would experience many ups and downs during his rise to fame and fortune of years later. It was during one of these performances on stage while doing a Los Angeles engagement that he was noticed by accomplished film director Stanley Kramer who just happened to be in the audience one night. Kramer offered to take Van Cleef to Hollywood and give him a part in his upcoming film *High Noon*. His star Gary Cooper was already signed.

The choice was his now, stay with Logan and continue to beat the boards (as those in the business so affectionately called working the stage) or go with Kramer on into Hollywood and the give the movie a try. Van Cleef accepted the offer and after auditions he was cast in the role of one of three gun slinging henchmen awaiting the release of a criminal friend from jail. The train was set to arrive in town at high noon that day. The ex-con Frank Miller portrayed by Ian McDonald and his evil associates planned on taking out his vengeance for his conviction and jail time spent on the entire town, and it's Marshall Will Kane (Cooper) by killing him and treeing his town that had convicted him.

Kramer had originally wanted Van Cleef to have his somewhat distinctive hawk-like nose altered and take the Deputy Harvey Pell role, but Lee had declined opting for more of a silent role, that of the gunslinger Jack Colby. The other two gunmen roles went to Robert Wilke and Sheb Wooley. The Deputy role was eventually given to Lloyd Bridges. It wouldn't matter in this black 'n' film of Kramer's but for years rumors* had persisted that a

* We would like to put this particular fallacy to rest as total false. According to Van Cleef's naval enlistment records when he entered the service in 1942

family trait of the Van Cleef heritage was that one of his eyes was green, the other was blue and that this had been corrected in later years by the use of corrective colored contact lenses.

Van Cleef was a natural in his gunslinger role of Jack Colby. His beady eyes and high cheek bone structure and his dark seedy complexion gave off a menacing appearance that certainly fit the role. His physical appearance, stance and swagger in his walk, along with his overall general demeanor were other distinctive traits that would set this man apart from others. He just looked like trouble personified. One of Van Cleef's more noted quotes during one interview was, "Being born with a pair of beady eyes was the best thing that ever happened to me. I just look mean without trying" certainly sums it up nicely.

In other films we would notice his crisp, to the point verbal delivery of his lines that gave off a no-nonsense tone coupled with a deep voice that would emphasize the underlining aggressive demeanor that he wished to convey across to the screen. Once on the big screen, his popularity as a badman began to expand with the various viewing audiences. From this his first appearance Lee Van Cleef would continued in the business for some thirty-seven years as some of the worst, the meanest, and loveable badman characters an actor would ever wish to play. We all loved to see him in action, as somehow we all seem torn between love and hate between those on-screen characters baddies that he came to portray throughout the years.

During Lee's early years he took to his acting role like a duck does to water. He once said of his parts, "Whatever I did as a heavy, I did as *heavy* as I could, then the other guy is that much stronger." In a later statement about

---

at seventeen years old, he was 6' and 0" tall. He weighted in at 170 lb with brown hair and brown eyes (with no mention of multicolored eyes) and 'ruddy' complexion. In an old 1943 youngish, full face photo of him in his navy uniform it shows us both his eyes were indeed brown. As for his height, most reports given say 6' and 2". This may be true since at seventeen he was still at 6', could have grown a bit more? He stated once in an interview when asked about portraying violence in film, particularly like abusing women, slapping them around and the like. He was quick to say he didn't abuse women like that ever. When it was stated that he'd done it in the *GBU?* He was quicker to point out that a stuntman was used in that sequence and not him. He then claimed himself as being 6' and 2", weighting close to 200 lb.

This affirmation goes along with a previous press release on him back December 10, 1953, of an interview made the previous year, right after his screen debut in *High Noon*. It stated at that time he was twenty-seven years old and stood 6' and 2" and weighed 195 Ib. We rest our case.

1966 he virtually reiterated the same saying when asked if he minded being typecast as a movie bad guy, he then said "The way you handle the part can get the audience's sympathy for the heavy rather than for the hero."

His interest in his trade even went to the extent of writing home to the *Somerset Messenger Gazette,* the local newspaper, where he would send in columns or letters of what he believed would interest the readers of his former hometown, with all the happenings out in Hollywood the movie capitol of the United States. Past *Gazette* Editor Tony Phyrillas informed us he'd gotten in the habit of doing this as far back as while he was in the service. Keeping the hometown folks informed, he thought that was a great idea and the thing to do. He even wrote some columns for the papers while in Europe making those great *Spaghetti* Westerns.

> One of the earliest accounts of his literary interest in keeping his public informed was in an early article he sent back to the *Gazette* while in the service onboard ship, December 7, 1944. He wrote about diving some thirty feet off of the bridge of a minesweeper into the Mediterranean Sea in order to rescue the ships mascot Rusty, a Cocker Spaniel. Funny thing about this accounting was that he admitted to having his pipe smoking in his mouth when he dove over the side. "When I hit the water," he said "I heard something snap in my mouth. I don't know how my teeth escaped breaking. Luck I call it." At any rate he had saved the day rescuing the dog and all was well aboard ship once again.

There was another letter he sent to then editor Conover, back on November 10, 1953, where he stated that he had been thinking about writing a column for the paper to keep his Somerville fans in touch with the movie industry in Hollywood that he was now so much a part of. He expressed his appreciation for the townsfolk continued interest in his career and thought this might be a good way of thanking them. The letters would continue like that for several years and Mr. Conover would publish the articles in his paper whenever they arrived.

Another early account of his early writing interests was a column which appeared monthly for a while in "Screen Stars," a syndicated fan magazine. One article in particular appeared in vol. 13, no. 5, September, 1955 issue. Under the *Dear Fans* article section he writes to fans in what appears to be an open letter asking the question, "Should Married Couples take Separate Vacations." Within the article he states his personal feelings on the subject and discusses it rather in-depth. Then he asked for fans opinions on the subject. As we today, reading this and asking ourselves, could this really have been from our badman hero?

One other article done, while already a huge star in Europe during the late 1960s is which he personally tackles the subject of violence in movies in an article "Italy Accents Motion in Pictures." In another of his open letters to fans, after he recently attended a *Venice Film Festival*, he attempts to take on two subjects of thorough discussion at the time concerning the wave of European Spaghetti Western films, like those he'd been involved in up to that time. "Are critics really against the natural violence portrayed on screen, or against the European films in general" was one. Another was the standard comment, "Too long!" The films seem to just go on forever, never ending was one comment.

> Here LVC laid down an attempt at defending the subject, and violent content of these films he was now associated with. The contrast between stark realism on film to a point, on one hand and being theatrically operatic on the other was most intriguing he thought. Thus coupled with the new spine-tingling musical renditions of the Italian composers like Ennio Morricone, had sent this new wave of horse operas to a new beginning of Western genre filmmaking. He went on to speak his mind and heart on the subject saying, "These films fulfilled a need, the proof is in the box office receipts. It's only the sick that will repeat what they have seen."

With insurmountable luck on his side, LVC would parlay his acting into stardom both here and abroad with his International fame brought about from via the era of the Italian *Spaghetti* Western. At one time he had all but given up on acting and very nearly thrown in the towel, as he struggled for existence following his slow recovery after a severe automobile accident, that long hiatus from acting that tended to separate him at that time, from the business and his past dreams of success.

According to one verbal account, related to me personally by John Mitchum (actor and brother of Robert Mitchum) who seemed to be in the know (but evidently wasn't as much in tune, so we later find out) about the incident at the time. Mitchum had met Lee while filming the 1955 crime movie *The Big Combo* where they had become good friends. When I brought up the accident incident to him back during a film festival event in Sonora, California, he announced that "Hah, Lee was dead drunk at the time, and crossed the centerline into that oncoming milk truck that hit him." However, from what we've learned since of the accident, it seems actually a bit different than Mitchum's rendition. The story began following wrap-up of the final day's shooting for the film, *Ride Lonesome* shot on location up at Lone Pine, California. Van Cleef along with others had been enjoying a picture-wrap party that signaled the film shoot completion. Most were staying over the night in lew of the long grueling drive back down to the valley. The next morning Lee was also in that line heading back down to his Apple Valley home after being away several weeks on the shoot. Fortunately, he was still driving his old '52 Cadillac Series 75 Limo work car when he was involved in the head on collision with another automobile late that September of 1958.

> According to *Somerville Gazette* newspaper account reported on October 16, 1958, it stated "Police said the driver of the other car involved came across the center line of the road and hit Van Cleef head-on." Even as the actor's car was considered a tank among vehicles of the day, it was said to have been demolished.

Except for the location shoots, and his time away from home during this period in his life, Lee was still thought to be enjoying marital bliss with wife, Pasty Ruth, and the three children. Ironically, it was found out that Pat had only been a short distance ahead of Lee, with all three children onboard with her when Lee's accident happened. We speculate that she may have been taking the two older children Alan and Debbie to school that morning when the crash occurred. Or perhaps her and the kids may have been up to Lone Pine for the warp party, and were coming home with Lee following in his car.

Subsequently it has been thought for years that Lee's partying on film locations with the guys and gals after work hours had seemingly already taken a severe toll on the marriage. This may or may not have been the case at all, but if so, it may well have been the straw that "broke the camel's" back where Pasty Ruth was concerned. However, be that as it may after spending several weeks in the hospital Lee was eventually sent home to recuperate. If one might consider, we could almost feel the pins and needles that he'd be stepping on around that household if all that partying had been true. At any rate, something, would eventually lead to his moving out and staying with fellow actor Robert (Bob) Ivers, sharing a San Fernando apartment with him. Ivers and Van Cleef had much in common back in those days, both coming from *Little Theatre* backgrounds. Ivers and Lee had been pals since being together on the Randolph Scott film, *Ten Wanted Men* (1955) (Ivers passed away February 13, 2003, in Yakima, WA from cancer). With LVC moving out, whatever the reason would only lead to his eventual full-fledged divorce along with the long recovery period from the accident.

> Early the next year, and just eight days following Lee's thirty-fourth birthday, an official separation between him and Pat became common knowledge when a newspaper story leaked about his being seen with aspiring actress Barbara Armstrong. According to the blip in *The Daily Gleaner* of January 17, 1959, Lee and

wife, Pasty Ruth, had indeed separated. Alas and by 1960, the Van Cleef's would officially be divorced.

Up to that point in his career, his staple acting parts in the movies had been the Westerns. Following this accident, it was speculated that he might never again be able to mount and ride a horse. Thus, it was thought that his career in movies as an actor was now at an end. Indeed he had suffered a severely fractured left arm and a shattered left knee cap. After the casts were removed, a stainless steel rod would remain in his arm the rest of his life. Years later he would suffer extensive arthritic pain and discomfort coupled with a certain amount of physical handicaps such as the limited use of his left arm and problems walking, all the result of this near-miss accident that he almost didn't come out of.

For transportation he came to relying a lot on friends and fellow actors like Ivers, Peter Breck* or John Mitchum. Possibly Rance Howard (father of Ron Howard, the future actor/director) may have shuttled him about some as well. Howard had been the stuntman / actor who originally taught LVC to ride a horse after his first coming to Hollywood for his debut role in *High Noon.* When asked didn't he ride horses on the farm that he worked on, he would simply reply, "They used tractors, not horses."

In addition to Howard's teaching Van Cleef to ride in those early days, it seems he may have had help in other areas of expertise during that early Hollywood period. Top gunman / stuntman and bit-player Arvo Ojala back during the 1950s and '60s, was *the* man to teach the art of quick draw and shooting to any young actor coming through the mill at that time. Even as LVC and Ojala hit the scene about the same period in time, since he didn't begin working in Hollywood until 1951, and of course, LVC was just breaking into films himself with *High Noon* being shot the summer of 1952. Although totally unconfirmed, their paths may or may not have crossed on the film sets of the day. Ojala's first bit part in a film was for

* According to a story related to me by family friend Ruth Staats that friend and fellow actor Peter Breck had once given Lee some poor advice, at least according to Lee's mother Marion, who cared not for the rowdy Breck. Lee had, on a spur of the moment, followed Breck's advice firing his then agent Sid Gold. Going then with another, and the results were worse than ever. His work had nearly dried up completely after that. His new wife, Joan, was working and bringing in the food for the table, but times was mighty tough. It wasn't until Lee agreed to return to his previous agent Sid Gold that he began to work again on a semi regular basis.

Columbia Pictures in *Eight Iron Men*, which was released late in 1952. LVC also worked for *Republic Pictures* and his parts were shot on a ranch outside LA. One of Ojala's early, more-noted gun-coaching bits was with Marilyn Monroe and Robert Mitchum for the film *River of No Return* (1954). So it is entirely possible Lee may have picked his prowess pointers from Ojala, or others while on locations, possibly even in *High Noon,* or just maybe it all came natural to him.

> In any case, there were many minor actors of the day who were tutored by this expert with guns. Some of Ojala's more popular pupils of the day worked for *Warner Bros Studios*, James Arness (*Gunsmoke*), James Garner (*Maverick*), and Wayde Preston (*Colt .45*), whom he claimed were probably three of the more proficient that he had coached.

During a 1978 interview, LVC talked some on his handling of a six-gun. He began saying that, although he had been shot by the best of them, "I'm probably the fastest draw of them all." He went on to add about how during one movie the cameraman discovered it only took him three frames of film for him to draw and fire his pistol. That was purported as only an eighth of a second. He then mentioned about how even with blanks, if you mess up the draw, you can injure yourself by firing prematurely into the holster or shooting one's leg. When asked by the interviewer had he ever made that mistake and shot his pistol off in the holster, he replied. "Sure, once or twice." He said, "It's very painful."

Also during another film Van Cleef made in 1955 called *Seven Angry Men* which starred Raymond Massey, Debra Paget, Jeffrey Hunter and James Best. Best relates a tale in later years for an interview article with *Psychotronic Video* fanzine about when he actually shot Lee Van Cleef in the chest on this particular film. It seems while shooting a scene Best's character was being advanced upon by Van Cleef's character, in the script he was to shoot him with his gun, bam he did just that!

After the scene was over, Van Cleef sauntered over to him and quipped, "You're a good shot, Best. You hit me right in the heart!" Best replied something to the effect as to how did he know they'd been using blanks. It seems though, sometimes when using full blank loads, those waxed plugs will go like real bullets for quite a ways. Van Cleef then showed him the burn holes in his front coat near his heart and Best then understood.

> It was also a little-known item that during this period in time, Lee had managed a brief affair with an ex-model who later drifted into show business. Dagmar, she called herself, but her real name

was Virginia Ruth Egnor. She was an early 1950's rage as the statuesque blonde, who, after a brief modeling career, haunted the television variety show circuits through the 1950s.

Dagmar began her television career on *Broadway Open House* (1950-1951), a late-night TV variety show hosted by Jerry Lester. She was hired to appear as a dumb blonde who came out on stage early in the show to read some insane poetry lines with a deadpan delivery. She was an instant hit, then after Jerry left (seemingly involving a bitter feud had developed between the two); but by spring of 1951, she had been retained and continued to work with new show host, Jack Leonard.

Later that year, she got the opportunity to host her own TV show called *Dagmar's Canteen*, which ran from late 1951 through May 11, 1952. It had a live audience, mostly of service personnel in which she also danced with, sang to, and invited them to help her in doing various skits and the like. She was well-known for her comedy routines and, of course, her deadpan delivery of poems she'd made up. Her sister Jeanne Lewis was also on the show, acting mostly as the meek, silent assistant hostess.

For a while there, she had even become a regular on the *Milton Berle Show* from of the mid-'50's. It was also during that same period in time that she was becoming a well-known panelist of the *Masquerade Party* at that time hosted by Douglas Edwards, a popular news reporter and famed anchor of *CBS Nightly News*.

It seems that Lee's and Dagmar's paths could have criss crossed many times over the years in the darken settings across Hollywood. Their little "meets" would again pick up in later years after Lee's return to the States and just prior to the end of his second marriage. She was at the time still in a marriage of convenience to one Dick Hinds, who passed away later in 1977. She herself would live on to pass much later on October 9, 2001.

All the while, during and after Lee's divorce with Pat, his injuries still required many follow-up visits to the hospital and, of course, physical therapy treatments, which led to his meeting of divorcee Joan Miller who was working clerical at the time. They hit it right off and soon a romance was developing. Joan Marjorie Miller, now estranged from a previous marriage, had baggage of her own though, a beautiful young daughter, Denise. With Lee also having a daughter Debbie, he took right to the little girl and found he was happier now in this threesome arrangement than he'd been in years. Since the lost of his Apple Valley home in the divorce, which left him mostly with the clothes on his back, he'd been staying with his friend Bob Ivers. Not many months after the relationship with Joan had begun, he left Bob's apartment and moved over with Joan and Debbie in their Granada Hills home.

Joan Miller was an Oregon beauty born to proud parents Rex A. and Helen T. on August 25, 1929, was just four years younger than Lee and had studied to become an opera singer from an early age. However, doomed by a failed first marriage and also child to care for, the divorce tended to put those dreams of singing professionally behind her when work became the first order of business to survive with a young child.

With his agents' help, Lee continued to chase after television parts as best he could for some time after that, at least he figured until the healing of his injuries would allow him more of a rigorous work schedule. He was bound and determined that this near-miss accident wouldn't keep him down. In 1959 alone, he appeared in several popular TV shows of the era, mostly Western. *The Rifleman* episode: "The Deadly Wait," *Tombstone Territory* episode: "The Hostage," *Riverboat* episode "Strange Request," among others, was a *Lawman* episode: "The Conclave." None were ever big parts. Though it did help keep bread on the table. According to NV Marriage Registry, Lee and Joan were married in Las Vegas, Nevada, on May 9, 1960.

Lee's first movie part following the accident and initial recovery was *Posse from Hell* (1960). Herbert Coleman was director, the producer was Gordon Kay. Lee readily admitted that upon returning to work some six months after the accident, he had to use a stepladder to get on his horse. The movie parts he was getting at time though weren't much and would dwindle even further as time went by. The known fact of his leaving one family and now taking up with another didn't seem to sit well with Hollywood movie executives. His agent, Sid Gold, did the best he could to keep him working, but film opportunities for our actor seemed to be drying up.

> Ruth Staats would tell the wife and I the story of how Lee's mother Marion would relate to her about her financial difficulties during this period in time. It had now been awhile since Lee's father had passed away, back in 1948 (with a heart attack at the early age of fifty-three) and his mother having to finally give in to day-to-day pressures, up and sold the old homestead there in Somerville. With the monies she received from the sale (reportedly some $15,000) had invested it. It was however becoming apparent fast to her that she could not live entirely on the interest from her saving and investments. The facts being that Van Cleef Sr. was now gone and Marion herself had never worked a day in her life other than as a housewife. She was finding things outside the marriage bond mighty tough. To make matters worse, here was Lee now recovering from his accident and recent divorce had now up and remarried again suddenly. This time to Joan when

not even yet fully recovered! He still wasn't working full-time as he once had been, so there was little or no help for her from him at the time.

Marion Van Cleef had decided to move in with a longtime friend Reva La Fever, also a widow. Her husband had been in agriculture, living and working on the huge acreages just a couple of miles south of Somerville, owned by the Duke family. It was some two thousand acres mostly of tobacco with forty miles of intertwined roads. This same farm Lee had worked on for a while after his discharged from the army several years back. Anyway, as the story goes, although Marion and Reva had been friends before, now living in a small trailer together, Marion now found it wasn't the best of situations. Marion later told Ruth that Reva was being nasty to her. So eventually, upon the insistence of friends Bill and Ruth, she agreed to come live awhile with them until her son got back on his feet once again and could send her some extra money to live on like he used to do. According to Ruth, she and Bill had just moved from Somerville into a larger house not far away in *Bound Brook*, so they had plenty of room. "We had many long talks together, Marion and I, some were about Lee," says Ruth. Some of those stories related to Ruth by Marion I will relate here for the reader as they were related to me.

Marion Van Fleet of Dutch ancestry was born in 1897. Her father died when she was eight years old. Her mother, bless her soul, took in washing to help put food on the table. She had broken wrists, and they were crippled and deformed. This quite a chore as the ringing out of the clothes took the most time as she would ring a little and have to stop and shove her wrists back in place before continuing.

From all this, Marion learned patience early on. She had known Clarence Van Cleef (Lee's father) all her life, with him and his parents coming to visit her family's home when he was only three, and she was just an infant in her baby crib. As the kids they grew up in South Branch, a small town outside of Somerville, New Jersey. The famous Diamond Jim Brady had a large mansion there and Marion's father had worked for him. As children Clarence and Marion grew up together, friends and, eventually, sweethearts. Later on, in love, they would marry, and she now became Mrs. Clarence Leroy Van Cleef. Ruth Staats remembers her saying that her only son, Lee, didn't look like her but instead favored his father more in the looks department.

Having never worked herself, Marion was from the old school of women and thought it was a disgrace for a husband not to support his family, having to put the wife out to work. She once told her son, that he was the first Van Cleef to ever live off a woman! That, according to Ruth, was the only time she ever told him off. She also said that Marion was always a little ashamed of Lee for dropping Sid Gold, when he had stuck by him through thick and thin. Marion didn't like being disloyal, and he certainly hadn't been raised like that. But Marion said, "You know kids, they will do what they want in spite of early training!"

> Ruth went on to say, "As to Marion's character, she was different from some women, especially of today's day and time. She was a man's woman. She found men to be nice creatures and could see no fault in them. She would take up for Lee no matter what. She didn't like Lee's first wife, Pat, very much and must have shown it numerous times. After the divorce, she didn't see the three grandchildren for a longtime afterward." Pat was the type of person that would take to pouting Ruth said, neither she nor Marion could stand this about her. "The baby boy David was about twenty years old, when Marion finally met him up with him again." (Note: The fact here that Marion lived in New Jersey and the kids stayed with their mother Pasty Ruth who lived in California, probably had a great deal to do with the visiting factor.)
>
> Ruth continues, saying, "Marion would send all three children checks for Christmas, but never got any kind of a thank you from any of them. Denise, her stepgranddaughter, by Lee's second marriage to Joan, was the only one who ever thanked her." "Marion, however, seemed to take all that in stride," says Ruth. "I think in her own heart, she must have known the divorce of Lee and Pat had two sides, but all she ever told me about was Pat's shortcomings. Alas, mothers and their darlings . . . I guess you get the point! Bill and I have since lost all contact with Pat and the kids and have no idea of their whereabouts today." It was later learned that Pat had indeed remarried and was thought to have relocated some years later to somewhere in North Georgia. This, however, has never been confirmed, and we've had no wishes to pursue this tidbit of information no matter how true it might be.
>
> Ruth, in conclusion, stated, "I always thought of Marion as a Pollyanna type of person. But under all this, I feel there was a struggle for survival. She spoke only good of the second wife, Joan, that is until Lee and her divorced. Marion had told Bill that Joan took Lee for a bundle."

> Mrs. Marion Van Cleef passed away two years before her son in 1987, she was ninety years old. Ruth went on to say, "I have no idea who Lee got his acting talent from but he did get his good speaking voice from his mother. Her voice was divine, well modulated and carried well just like his."

While living with the Staats during the 1960's Marion would find an enjoyable pastime in visiting the local movie house when they showed one of Lee's latest films. She so enjoyed these trips to the movies and would remark about how sometimes, when Bill worked, she and Ruth would go take in one of Lee's movies. She would always comment, said Ruth, on how she though each and every picture they went to see was her favorite one. She would want to return to see it again and again, sometimes three and four times.

Once in a *Somerville Gazette* interview, after viewing one of her son's latest films, she stated, "And do you know he didn't die this time." She went on to comment, "He's all I have left now." She would often remarked to Ruth about how she so wished her husband could have still been around to see their son's name in lights, but that she always felt his confidence in Lee was always there.

Van Cleef's second wife, Joan, had stuck by him during those lean years, working at several different jobs herself just to keep them afloat, all the while hoping upon hopes that his career would break its current doldrums pattern and take off once again. One of Lee's other work preoccupations at home during this period had been carpentry. An actor friend of his, George Montgomery had gotten him interested in building pieces of furniture like cabinets, tables, and chairs. At first, just a hobby to keep him occupied while out of work, but once he even considered making a living from it. He even sold some, but soon found he couldn't really make a living at it and support a mother, ex-wife with three kids, and a new wife with another child.

At one time it was reported that he landed a job outside Hollywood doing house painting. Although it was outside work, he wasn't sure he'd found his forte in this field either. Another time, we understand that while building a playhouse for his daughter Denise, working with a table saw, he managed to lob off a piece of his middle finger* on his right hand at the first joint. He would now carry that distinctive mark to his grave.

---

* It's been speculated for years many times over as to how he actually lost that finger tip. Some say it was while building his studio out back of the house. Others more inclined to action/drinking association have stated he lost it in a bar fight. The version of the story we have chosen to relate is believed to have

Another sideline he had gotten involved with was picture painting. Having built the small shop out back of the house for woodworking, it was easily converted to a studio where he found he was quite good at it this little venture. He even managed to sell off a few from time to time, though mostly to friends. These pictures were mostly of the sea and landscapes and also helped keep them afloat, along with the television show residuals coming in from his past work.

Joanie as he liked to call her had dabbled some in the finer Arts herself in earlier times as singing opera. However, now she continued to work clerical and lucked out finding a better secretarial position at *IBM*. They had both, however, settled into a much simpler lifestyle than what Lee had become accustomed to with his earlier film career.

He couldn't even afford an anniversary gift for his wife much less pay the phone bill at the time, which was only about $12. Recanting the story for an interviewer years later, he retorted, "Hell, I tip more than that now." Drinking and feeling sorry for himself, supposedly, he was seen in a local restaurant/bar by an Italian movie director. As the story goes, when approached by an interpreter for the director, Van Cleef spurned him away at first, thinking they were pulling his leg. The director, by the name of Leone, had recognized him from previously viewed studio film segments of the *High Noon* film by Stanley Kramer. Evidently, Henry Fonda and Robert Ryan had been among his first choices, but for this latest film effort they had all turned him down for one reason or another, so now they approached this man.

Later on, Van Cleef would come to owe much of his return to the trades and successes of later years to this largely unknown Italian film director, Sergio Leone, who had dreams and a vision of his own. In his own mind, he had developed a visionary about our American West circa 1860s and its many wide-ranging different characters of depth and interest. One of these characters was of a man with a particular look, that man as it turned out would be Lee Van Cleef. From all reports, it seems, Van Cleef and Sergio Leone got along great both professionally and otherwise.

As the story goes, they met once again dealing through the interpreter, but this time, with Van Cleef's agent Sid Gold, and they closed the deal. Supposedly, Lee signed for the one movie, a nine-week shooting schedule for a little more than $1,500 a week plus expenses. He peeled off his agent's 10 percent right then and there. Later stating, "Believe it or not, at that point I was actually making more money than Clint Eastwood." The working title

been the truth. Whatever the case, the stubby finger was his to carry for the rest of his life.

for the movie as scripted was called *The Magnificent Strangers*, but would eventually be changed for marketing reasons to *For a Few Dollars More.*

After the meet, Van Cleef stated that he walked in the house and threw his wife an envelope on the bed. The rubber band broke and money flew everywhere. She was so excited, laughing and crying at the same time, she had to count it four times, he said. The day before had been their third wedding anniversary, and he hadn't been able to afford her even a small present. The contract was signed on April 10, 1965.

As time went by, Van Cleef's other children would join them occasional on visits. By all accounts, they were an extremely happy family during this early period. In one interview, some eight years later, Joan would even voice her opinion about this badman, actor she had married. "He has never been anything but a hero to me and kids." When asked about giving up her opera singing career years before, she calmly replied, "One ego in the family is enough."

In the same interview, when asked how they all get along together, Van Cleef quipped, "We are a united family, the words stepmother and stepfather just don't exist in this household." In addition, he was asked about how he felt toward any of his children following in his footsteps and becoming actors. He replied, "The answer is yes! If they have talent, but they'll have to prove it before I give any encouragement." He went on to add, "There are too many actors who don't have a prayer, and I don't want my kids to join the pack. It doesn't seem to me to matter much what they do as long as they do it well."

Although much of the Leone / Van Cleef story is pretty much commonplace today, some of us fans still keep an ever-ready vigilance out for any others of a lost film or two from Europe that might still surface. While most all have now been accounted for in this day and time, there still may be yet another elusive* title or two floating around yet to be tapped and seen by worldwide fans of this actor.

---

* It had been reported back in September 18, 1969, via *The Somerset Messenger Gazette* that after Lee's completion of the *Barquero* film for Aubrey Schenck he was thought to be returning to Italy for the film *Professional Gun*. This never came about since about that time Jack Palance and Franco Nero turned out a film called *A Professional Gun,* a Western that later underwent a title change to *The Mercenary* for a 1968 released.

That same article went on to state that at the time three more films were under negotiations back in the States, one of which was *Scalawag*. This one was to have been filmed in Yugoslavia. But to our disappointment, this film was later signed for by Kirk Douglas as lead actor (not only as lead, but also the

Late in 1967, on more than one of Lee's and Joan's trips back into NYC for dubbing* sessions of one of his films, they would always take that short jaunt over to Jersey and visit with his dear aging mother, Marion. The elder Mrs. Van Cleef, being alone since the passing of Clarence Leroy Sr. in 1948, was for the time being, had been living just outside Somerville in the *Bound Brook* subdivision with Lee's old pal Bill Staats and his wife, Ruth.

LVC had observed Clint Eastwood's successful return to the States and his Hollywood career, striking off on his own with his new production film company *Malpaso*. Van Cleef began to have visions something similar might be possible for him and Joanie. During a 1970 dubbing jaunt back to NYC then to LA, Lee had contacted his agent Sid Gold for a meet. They then laid the groundwork for some of his ideas. Gold formed a couple of different production companies at that time. These were mainly companies constructed on paper, and were based in Las Vegas, Nevada. One was already in use acquiring script properties that were just awaiting the master's touch.

Once, in an interview, Van Cleef stated that he had an itching to direct as well as produce movies himself. He felt that he might enjoy directing as much, if not more than acting in films. One film property acquired by one of his companies, *Falcone Productions Inc*, was an original effort by John Eglvo called "Deathwatch." In yet another blip advertisement found in one *TV-Guide* issue taunted us with a working title film he was to do called *A Legionnaire for All Wars*. At the time, this film was supposedly under production from Van Cleef's company. It was to have been a

---

producer and director). For the second film, Lee brought was under contract for the film *EL Condor* to be made in Almeria, Spain. For this one, he would be double billed with ex-footballer turned actor, Jim Brown and actor/restaurateur Patrick O'Neal.

A third film mentioned was to be called *Gaucho* to be filmed in South America. In this film Lee would have an opportunity to play his guitar and sing! Van Cleef stated for the article, "Like my nose, my singing will never be forgotten."

* After one such dubbing session and subsequent visit with his mom, he and Joanie were off again for a return trip to Los Angeles and their home. Daughter Denise, still in high school at the time, would be soon nearing her graduation period coming up in 1970. She had become the apple of Van Cleef's eye. They got along so well it was hard to believe she and he weren't blood related.

Earlier, Lee had officially adopted the little girl, and she had readily chosen to take his name as her own. A college trust had been arranged so she could continue her studies in her field of choice, later that would become veterinary medicine.

contemporary melodrama set in Africa. Van Cleef himself was to star as a jungle mercenary.

The storyline supposedly was that he was hired for his combat experience and killing expertise by a father seeking to avenge the deaths of his two children that had been previously kidnapped, held for ransom then later found murdered. It was to have been filmed in Portugal, Spain. We speculate that this may have been the basis for the later 1984 *Jungle Raiders* film by director/friend Antonio Margheriti (Anthony M. Dawson).

Unfortunately, and to the regret of his fans (for reasons not known) the *Legionnaire* or the "Deathwatch" script never did surface as movies. For that matter, we could find no evidence they were ever made by either of his companies. We feel quite sure (although unconfirmed) that probably the divorce between Joanie and Lee in 1974 more than likely had the most to do with these films never being made. It is a fact though, that one of the two production companies he had, the one called *Fleet Productions Inc.* remained in existence, on paper at least until 1978 when the Nevada Corporation License expired and it was discontinued. (Van Fleet was his mother's maiden name).

> It was observed in one interview I read some years back in the 1980s, which I wish to pass along here: LVC while in Las Vegas, Nevada, met up with Clint Eastwood at a gaming table there. Van Cleef had a script property at the time that he thought might interest Eastwood, with hopes they could possibly return and do another together film one day. Evidently, this never came about. It's quite possible this tidbit found was only a rumor and simply not true. Or possibly, Eastwood and Lee could not come to terms. At any rate, it never came about, much to our disappointment.

Van Cleef's third wife, Barbara Hevelone, didn't come on to the scene until much later, only meeting in 1973 on set during filming of a scene from *Blood Money*, a working title that eventually was changed to *The Stranger and the Gunfighter* for the US release in 1974. Barbara had been playing the accompanying piano for the saloon scene when Lee in character of Dakota, the film's main star saunters in. Barbara remembered during that first meeting, "Something just clicked, I felt as though we had always known each other." Barbara also was an extra in the film as a bar girl.

As the piano player, she'd been hired specifically for this song and dance sequence, little did Barbara Hevelone realize then that she was to become the wife of actor Lee Van Cleef. She married him following his divorce final to second wife, Joan. This marriage would be the actor's third and final.

In the film sequence LVC as character Dakota on stage, could be seen pointing at the piano player (Barbara) while he's doing a brief song and dance number called *"Rye Whiskey."* The below photo accompanied by an article late in 1974 while in the Canary Island during filming of *Take a Hard Ride* stated their intentions to marry pending his divorce final. Barbara was then thirty-four years old and our actor was forty-nine soon to be fifty at time of the photo and article. Eventually, they married July 5, 1976, and lasted until his passing on December 16, 1989.

The chance meeting of these two, where sparks flew between them would have to sit on a back burner until rekindled again about a year later. It was during this period in time that Lee was fully involved in somewhat of a messy divorce and settlement* issues with Joan; it wouldn't all be finalized until February 1974 according to *California Divorce Index*, between 1966-1984.

* Van Cleef's wife, Joan, had if we think about it, been the very backbone of our actor during his recuperation period after that near-fatal accident since 1960. She not only had nursed him but also help support the three of them (sometimes mothering his three estranged children as well who had stayed with them on many occasions, loving them as her own) during those very lean years following the divorce from his first wife, Pat. All the while, she had hoped that

Barbara was born in the farming belt of Nebraska in the 1940s. She grew up to become a multifaceted musician—in that as a musical professional, she would become a concert pianist who was comfortable with either jazz or the classics. She also, we understand, plays the harp equally well. Many an evening, in happier times, the Van Cleef's would entertain friends or just themselves with her on the piano, or harp and Lee accompanying with his guitar or trombone.

Early on in their relationship, Barbara had still very much been the professional, being the accomplished concert musician she was, she had continued to attend to her theatrical engagements, which at times involved stints of play accompaniment of theme music for films. (Like the one she was doing for music composer/director Carlo Savina when she met Lee)

Lee had himself remained very much involved with his film career during those early years when they were together, though both activities had slowed considerably with time. Whatever the activity though, be it television and/or musical ventures,* they would always find time for one another as they always traveled together.

---

things would turn around for this man she had fallen in love with. Now, it was over, Joan wasn't going quietly to be sure, and not many could blame her.

It is readily known that during the period, just after the *Return of Sabata* movie, about 1972, things had taken a turn for the worse in their marriage. When both were around one another, it came to constant arguing and bickering for all to hear, be it on the set, at a party, or in private as has been rumored by sources in the know at the time. We can only assume that things had gotten progressively worse. Possibly, rumors of the chance meeting between Barbara and Lee on the set of *Blood Money* may very well have gotten back to Joan as she languished back at home in the States pondering her next move.

* Musical ventures indeed, Lee's singing debut to the world with the two songs (which he partly sang and partly talked his way through) was title music used for the score of the 1971 film of the same name, *Captain Apache*, and its flipside of "April Morning." Van Cleef's musical interest dates back to his high school years where he studied music and learned to play trombone and guitar during band classes.

He had resumed interest in music while on the *Apache* film continuing with the "Rye Whiskey" number on the set while filming *Blood Money* (1973). He would not really continue his musical interests too seriously until after he and Barbara were married in 1976. He would on occasion resume playing the trombone while Barbara accompanied on the piano. He also had learned to master the guitar, and it was during this era in time that he had taken up songwriting.

It was during these early years with Barbara while his interest in music was peaked, he also returned to his television roots as well. He began with a brand-new MTV movie. Hoping for a weekly series with *NBC*, which unfortunately didn't pan out this go around, but he did find some success much later in the mid 1980s.

> Lee's first venture with a MTV pilot movie was back in 1977 for a ninety-minute color film for *Viacom Enterprises* called *Nowhere to Hide*. It aired on *NBC* television on June 5, 1977. Lee Van Cleef portrayed US Marshall, Ike Scanlan, who is tasked with the retrieval and protection of a former syndicate hitman turned against his former mob boss and is to testify at his trial.
>
> Due to a weakened heart from a serious early bout with scarlet fever back in 1943, then in later years the weakened heart and subsequent problems caused Van Cleef a temporary sidetracking of his busy career in 1981. Sometime after completing the John Carpenter film, *Escape from New York* (released summer of 1981), and unbeknownst to his public and fans, he underwent a

---

When the composing began, he would even try them out later in Spain while on shooting locations making later films. In one past interview, he had admitted to doing some singing in a local Flamenco Club there in Spain not far from where he supposedly had a leased cattle ranch. Not commonly known, but upon returning to Los Angeles in 1972 following the *Captain Apache* film. He had Sid Gold set up a music company for him. It was called *Lee Van Cleef Music* and a blanket recording company called *LVC Records*. Both based in LA.

It was from here he had actually cut a demo of two records in 1973, both were written/produced by *D. Lanning*. The forty-five RPM demos, a pair of which, thanks to Ruth and Bill Staats, are now in this author's personal collection. In pristine condition, they still have original labeling that contains titles and his LA-based office address stamped on the labels: *LVC Records*, 1880 Century Park E. Suite 712, Los Angeles, California, 90067.

The four songs, one each per side were "The Bad Man's Back," and on flipside, "Call the Law." The second record holds "If All I Ever Do." On flipside, "Who's Gonna Share Your Dreams." In this day and time, it's hard to understand or realize just how involved he was with his music. It was reported in 1978 that after some bickering with other record labels that he finally signed exclusively with *Blue Seagull Record Company*. After the initial signing, producer Jerry Cole recorded two singles that were to have been released in August of that year. An LP volume was said to be following in October. Other than the two original single demo cuts from *Lanning* no others have ever surfaced to our knowledge.

permanent pacemaker implant operation. He didn't fully resume his career after that until 1982/'83 when he took on another MTV pilot movie called *The Master Ninja.* This became a successful venture as was picked up for a one-season run on *NBC* with thirteen episodes at sixty minutes each.

After that, Van Cleef continued to make a film now and then, venturing back to Europe only on a couple different occasions after that to film *Codename: Wildgeese*, and the *Italian/Spanish* film called *Killing Machine*—both were set for a release of 1985. Back in the States, he sided up with David Carradine for a co starring role in a Fred Olen Ray film called *Jade Jungle* (working title) later changed to *Armed Response.* Van Cleef portrayed the father and ex-mercenary to China town bar owner Carradine. In a later interview, Fred Olen Ray gave us fans a staunch insight view of how the now older Van Cleef was to work around during filming. One of the most interesting things he spoke of was that per the script, Lee's character was to be tied down on a pool table and stuck with acupuncture needles. Van Cleef's off-the-top reply to that bit of nonsense was, "I'll be goddamned, if I'm gonna lay on a pool table with needles stuck up my ass!" I thought that was quite a comical retort by our badman hero, and I remember it to this day. I just had to include that little tidbit for the readers.

According to the article/interview,* Olen Ray said, "He liked his beer." He went on to say that when they weren't shooting his scenes, "Lee would slip off to his trailer and have a few." Olen Ray said he would venture down there to have one with him in order to head him off and get him back to the set sooner rather than later. However, Olen Ray was quick to add that he always knew his lines and never had any problems with him about his drinking on the set, other than his being a little crotchety toward the end of the day. It seems Lee preferred to work only eight hours when most actors put in at least ten and more.

Olen Ray reported that due to Van Cleef's previous injuries, which by now were really bothering him, fight scenes had to be staged differently because of his left arm with the steel rod, and running with his leg injury, was out of the question. He went on to state that in the last scene of the shoot (January 1986), he was to rapidly fire a pump shotgun, which meant he'd have to pump it with his left arm. He complained, but Olen Ray insisted, and he did it. Afterward, the cast brought him out a birthday cake. The film was released in October 1986.

*Great *Spaghetti Cinema* fanzine article, a good read. Many thanks to Editor, William Connolly and, of course, to director

Fred Olen Ray for this valued insight about our hero during the actual making of a movie.

Van Cleef would return to Europe only once after that for the shooting of *The Commander* (1987), a German / Italian film project, from producer Erwin C. Dietrich. It was to be directed by his friend Antonio Margheriti. The making of the film also reunited him with some of his past *Spaghetti* acting acquaintances Lewis Collins, Klaus Kinski and Brett Halsey. This West German film was released on April 28, 1988, and, subsequently, other European countries, but never in the United States, except per bootleg copies via the Internet. Only nowadays is it just becoming available via Amazon.com on a *PAL* DVD issue from Germany, Spain, and Italy.

Lee Van Cleef's last Western was a contemporary one adventure. The story setting begins on a remote plantation ranch in South America. With a working title of *May the Best Man Win,* it was later changed to *Thieves of Fortune* for the US video release. An old family patriarch, Sergio Danielo Christophero (Van Cleef) feels his death is near. While celebrating the year of his one-hundredth birthday, he sets a plan in action to test just who his real legitimate heir will be. He figures the man who will eventually inherit his fortunes and worth he has built up during his lifetime should be legit and not fly in send by the corporation to take over. In reality, it's but a camco role for our long-respected hero, LVC. Ironically, blunt and to the point, the storyline ends this character's career, which seems to justly correlate with that of the actor himself.

Much to the regret of Van Cleef's many fans worldwide, his untimely passing was an unwelcome disappointment that was very much unexpected when, less than a month to his sixty-fifth birthday, he passed away. Officially, a cardiac arrest befell our hero on December 16, 1989.

He was survived by his three children from the first marriage to wife, Pasty Ruth: Alan, Deborah, and David. His second marriage to Joan Miller (1960-1974) yielded only the adopted daughter Denise (from Joan's previous marriage), who, after college graduation, went on to become a veterinary professional.

His third wife, Barbara Hevelone (July 13, 1976-December 16, 1989), was by his side when the attack occured. "It was such a shock." she remembered as she recounts. "He just sat straight up in bed, then he was gone!" She called for the paramedics and, when they arrived, rushed him off to *St. John's Regional Medical Center* where he was pronounced dead at 12:04 a.m. With this marriage, there were no children involved.

With Lee and Barbara, both being an older and more eccentric couple during the late 1980s, had learned to relax with more of a philosophical look at life. They lay back in those later years, enjoying the fruits of their labor and the finer things life had to offer. When not filming or on the musical circuit, they were mostly homebodies, which when not enjoying their yacht, down in Tarzana either for short jaunts or dockside relaxing, were just enjoying the quiet life in their fine home there in Oxnard.*

Services for Van Cleef were held on December 21 at the *Old North Church* in the *Forest Lawn Mortuary* facility there in Hollywood Hills. In lieu of flowers, the family had requested that donations be made to *St. John's Regional Medical Center Foundation*, there in Oxnard, California. The service was conducted by the Reverend Robert M. Bock with the eulogy was read by life long friend Rance Howard.

There was quite a cast of celebrities who joined in the service paying homage to this astute film personage. Among the honorary pallbearers were Tom Jennings, popular Hollywood agent who took up the reins of Van Cleef's career after longtime friend and agent Sid Gold passed away in the mid-1980s.†

---

* Oxnard, California, a sleepy beach front community nestled between Malibu and Santa Barbara is really but a farming community noted for its Lima beans and kosher wines production. About an hour's drive north of Los Angeles, this quite sleepy community is not far, but far enough from the hustle and bustle of Hollywood life. It was here the Van Cleefs enjoyed settling back and enjoying their retiring years.

† It was Sid Gold's expertise and agent awareness combined with Van Cleef's own shrewd sense of business that had helped to propel his career to the magnitude it had reached prior to his unexpected heart problems of the early 1980s. As success would have it, these two men were a powerhouse of career moves. Its believed that Gold was responsible for many a contract negotiations including the one with Sergio Leone that started the whole ball rolling in the second phase of Van Cleef's career. From overseas report, it's also understood that Van Cleef had been somewhat equally successful in real estate markets here and abroad with holdings of a cattle ranch in Spain, a villa in Rome and properties in Nevada.

Besides the Oxnard home that Barbara and Lee resided in, there was also an ocean front home in Tarzana, which had been under extensive renovations for some time, in order to house his aged mother, prior to her passing on December 28, 1987. She had for years, since a relatively long stay with the Staats, been residing at the Somerset Valley Nursing Home in Bridgewater, New Jersey. Lee and Barbara had been renovating the old house in hopes of having his mother closer to them now that she had gotten older and needed more watchfulness and constant care.

Another honorary pallbearer was Romano Puppo, veteran Italian stuntman/actor of the popular *Spaghetti* Westerns. He and Lee had been friends since their first meeting on the set of *Sabata* back in 1969. Puppo had been hired as stuntman and double stand-in for Van Cleef on this film by director Gianfranco Parolini.

> For some time, Van Cleef had resorted to using a stunt double for his horseback riding and fight sequences. It seems that as the years went by the old knee injury had been giving him quite a bit of problems. Not being able to mount his horses any longer was an old doctor's speculation that indeed had come true. He had previously admitted having to resort to using a small stepladder for this purpose.

Renown Italian director, Antonio Margheriti was also there as an honorary pallbearer paying his respects. They had not only been good friends for many years, but each man highly respected one another for their past filmmaking achievements and accomplishments. Margheriti had used Van Cleef in several films since their first meeting back in 1973 when filming *Blood Money.*

Other pallbearers were longtime friends and fellow actors, Rory Calhoun, Ray (X) Brands, and Harry Carey Jr. Lee's body is interred there in the *Forest Lawn Hollywood Hills Cemetery* of Los Angeles, California. His plot is located in the *Serenity section.*

Picture below compliments of dear friend and huge fan of Lee, Valerie Lambert, who had this arrangement placed on his grave plaque and was kind enough to send me this fine picture.

We the fans continue to mourn our loss of this actor, even today as we plug into our player, a nice new HDVD reissue of one of his great Westerns. These films bring us back to another place in time—a time when the world was a much different place, as we imagine ourselves in the saddle of a fast steed riding the planes of the southwest with one of our biggest on-screen heroes, the great Lee Van Cleef.

End.

Early STAGE work for Lee Van Cleef

1947

OUR TOWN. LVC's character was that of George. This play was performed by the Music Hall Players, an amateur Little Theatre group from Clinton, New Jersey, to which Van Cleef had become a member. This town today is still considered to be the home of the Little Theatre groups in this country. This had been another adaptation of the Pulitzer Prize-winning play by Thornton Wilder about small town America centering upon conflict and strife of a small New England community and its inhabitants.

HEAVEN CAN WAIT. This was another play adaptation by the Clinton Music Hall Players group. LVC's stage character was that of Joe Pendleton the boxer who is taken to heaven prematurely. A friend of the play's director, a visiting talent scout offers Van Cleef an opportunity to come with him into New York City and try out for an audition of the upcoming stage production "Mister Roberts" along several hundred other would be stage actors. Van Cleef accepted the offer.

1949

MISTER ROBERTS. This play was directed by the then thirty-nine-year-old, but already well-known American stage director Joshua Logan. Logan had been fortunate in already obtaining established stage and film actor Henry Fonda* for the part of Mister Roberts. After LVC was awarded a

* Over the years, LVC continued to praise Henry Fonda as the one person who had most influenced his acting throughout his career. He claimed that he had watched and studied Fonda's techniques the entire length of the tour. One thing among many that he had observed was Fonda's way of speaking directly to another actor's eyes. This we can honestly say LVC learned very well in that as his audience can testify, his eyes are usually the first thing we notice and captures our attention.

part in this play by almost impossible odds, he was committed to a tour the country's stage circuit with the troop for the next fifteen months playing the part of Mannion, one of the devilish enlisted men aboard Robert's ship. This exposure to the stage audience would eventually bring him and film producer Stanley Kramer eye to eye for interviews being held for parts in one of Kramer's most successful films yet to be made, *High Noon* of 1952.

This concludes the available listings on Van Cleef's stage work. While undoubtedly there are many more to his credit, these have been all that seem to be readily available at this time.

- Below is a complete filmography of Lee Van Cleef's Euro films, mostly Westerns. The dates are aligned as close as possible with information currently at hand, plus international release dates included. **Posters and title picture are accredited to the Sebastian Haselbeck collection via his website www.spaghetti-western.net. Many thanks, Sebastian.*

LEE VAN CLEEF
EURO FILMOLOGY

1965

For A Few Dollars More, *Per Qualche Dollaro in Piu;* a.k.a. *Two Magnificent Strangers*; (Western); Ital, Director Sergio Leone (LVC co stars as Colonel Douglas Mortimer, bounty hunter); 12/18/65 (Ital); Stars Clint Eastwood as Manco (Man with No Name); Also stars: Gian Maria Volonte, Luigi Pistilli, Mario Brega, Klaus Kinski and Aldo Sambrell. (Manco, in the Ital/Eng translated version this was pronounced as Monco).

Storyline: Originally developed by Luciano Vincenzoni, but underwent extensive changes that involved Sergio Leone himself along with Fulvio Morsella.

Leone not having a sequel particularly in mind was eventually warmed to the subject by producer Alberto Grimaldi. Even though the first film *A Fistful of Dollars* had failed to make back production costs upon its initial release, it had been extremely popular with the European audiences. Grimaldi reasoned, to satisfy his own mind whether or not this had merely been a fluke picture or perhaps the beginning of something bigger. Grimaldi continued to pressure Leone for a second film done in the same vein as the first, and so the sequel came into being.

With a larger film budget and not having that financial end to bog him down, he was given his head to carry on as he saw fit. The script, originally written by Vincenzoni, was right after the film *Fistful* came out, had been deposited with an underling of producer Grimaldi. When the second film was decided on, the script was found, dusted off; and Leone went to work.

This time, though, a partner as such was to be added, that of an wiser older bounty hunter character. Cold, calculating, and deadly to the point of finesse, he would be portrayed by American veteran actor Lee Van Cleef. His colonel character added a certain depth, a more-challenging vigor to Eastwood's lone wolf role. These two bounty killers would eventually parlay the bad guys into a fortune in bounty money, and sweet revenge in the end.

Musical maestro Ennio Morricone would again score the superb music rendition specifically for the film, with conducting credits going to Bruno Nicolai. These two would continue collaborating on Euro film music throughout much of the 1960's era.

When LVC was asked some years later about the working relationship between himself and Clint Eastwood, he replied, "We got along famously. Not everyone likes his style, but everyone's got their own thing, and he sure as hell has been successful."

1966

The Good, the Bad, the Ugly, *IL Buono, Il Brutto, Il Cattivo;* a.k.a. *The Magnificent Strangers*; (Western); Ital, Director Sergio Leone (LVC costars as *The Bad*, Sentenza, the killer); 12/23/66 (Ital); Stars Clint Eastwood as Blonde (Man with No Name) returns to the role that made him famous; Also stars Eli Wallach as Tuco Ramirez (Shorty) a Mexican outlaw bandit. Others of the cast were Aldo Guiffre, Mario Brega, Luigi Pistilli, Al Mulock, Antonio Casas, Livio Lorenzon, Antonio Casale and Rada Rassimov.

Storyline: These three deadly leading characters are after a cache of gold coins worth a fortune. They weave in and out of the Civil War-torn south in search of this army gold, killing many who get in their way, they even resort to fighting among themselves.

Note: Writing and scripting credits for this massive war reproduction goes to Agenore (Age) Incrocci, Furio Scrapelli, Luciano Vincenzoni, Sergio Leone, and an unaccredited Sergio Donati.

The Big Gundown, *La Resa Dei Conti;* a.k.a. *Colorado*; (Western); Ital / Spa, Director Sergio Sollima (LVC stars as Jonathan (Colorado) Corbett noted Texas Lawman); 11/29/66 (Spa); Costars Tomas Milian as Cuchillo Mexican bandit running from a crime he didn't commit. Also: Walter Barnes as Brokston, a hard man, used to getting his own way and ready to fuel Corbett's political ambitions in order to get what he wants. Also stars Gerard Herter as the Austrian-born Baron and Captain Von Schullenburg, Brokston's bodyguard. Others: Luisa Rivelli, Fernando Sancho, Nieves Navarro, Benito Steffanelli and Maria Granada among many.

Storyline: Brokston hires famed man-hunter / lawman Corbett to hunt down and kill a young Mexican whom all are led to believe raped and killed one of his young servant girls. Actually, Brokston's own son-in-law Shep has actually done the deed, and he's intent on covering it up.

1967

Day of Anger, *I Giorni Dell'Ira;* a.k.a. *Two Enemies*; (Western); Ital / W. Ger, Director Tonino Valerii (LVC stars as gunman Frank Talby); 12/19/67 (Ital); It costars Giuliano Gemma as Scott Mary as Talby's protégé clone of himself. (Not unlike a Frankenstein monster that in the end bites his maker in the arse). Also with Walter Rilla, Crista Linder, Piero Lulli and Yvonne Sanson among others.

Storyline: Has Talby coming into a new town and taking over. He takes a young nobody, lifts him out of the gutter, and turns him into a proficient gunman like himself, a helper and bodyguard until that day comes when he steps on him; then he has all hell to pay!

From personal poster collection

1967

Death Rides a Horse, *DA Uomo a Uomo (As Man to Man);* a.k.a. *The Man from Far Away*; (Western); Ital, Director Giulio Petroni (LVC stars as gunman Ryan); 8/31/67 (Ital); Also stars as co billed John Philip Law as Bill. Others of the impressive cast were Anthony Dawson, Luigi Pistilli, William Bogart, Mario Brega and Jose Torres to name a few.

Storyline: Now grown, Bill is out to avenge the brutal killings of his parents and sister back when he was a small boy. Ryan had also been part of the same gang of thieves but not a party to the rapes and killings. He was double-crossed by the gang leaders and spent fifteen years of hard labor in an Arizona prison. He is also out for revenge, plus $1,000 for each year he spent in jail from each of the double-crossers.

1968

Beyond the Law, *AL Id La Della Legge;* a.k.a. *The Good Die First;* a.k.a. *Bloodsilver* (Western); Ital / W. Ger, Director Giorgio Stegani (LVC stars as Cudilip, a bandit/conman, turned lawman); 8/10/68 (Ital); It costars Antonio Sabato, Bud Spencer (Carlo Pedersoli) as mine owner Cooper and Lionel Stander as preacher. Gordon Mitchell in cameo, as outlaw Burton who comes to raid the mine. Master Dubber, Mickey Knox was supposedly in this film but in an unaccredited part.

Storyline: Has a young engineer Ben Novak (Sabato) bringing in payroll to mine workers, but Cudilip and his gang lift it from the stage coach before it arrives, then takes on the sheriff's job.

Commandos; a.k.a. *Sullivan's Marauders;* a.k.a. *Bite the Dust* (War); Ital/W. Ger, Director Armando Crispino (LVC stars as NCO Sullivan); 11/19/68 (Ital); Co stars equally billed was Jack Kelly as Captain Vallie. Also stars Joachim Fuchsberger as Lt. Heitzel Agen/Professor, Heinz Reincke as Officer Hans, Helmut Schmidt as Sgt Miller, and Otto Stern as Sgt Braumann. Others: Pier Luigi Anchisi as Riccio, Gianni Brezza as Marco, Duilio Del Preta as Bruno.

Storyline: A ninety-day wonder, Vallie is sent in to take charge of an elite group on a mission in Northern Africa concerning the takeover of a strategically located Oasis fueling depot in the desert currently held by Germans. This must be accomplished prior to the D-Day allied invasion.

1969

Hey, Friend, there is Sabata . . . You've Closed! *Ehi, Amico . . . C'e Sabata, Hai Chiuso!* A.k.a. *Sabata* (Western). Ital / Spa, Director Frank Kramer (Gianfranco Parolini) (LVC stars as Sabata); 1969 (Ital); 9/2/70 (US); It co stars William Berger as Banjo. Also with Pedro Sanchez as Carrincha, Franco Ressel as Stengel, Robert Hundar as Oswald, Linda Veras as Jane, Spean Covery, Ken Wood (Giovanni Cianfriglia) and Romano Puppo.

Storyline: The fast shooting accuracy of Sabata hurls this story of robbery, blackmail and greed along at a fast pace. Banjo with his gun in the banjo is a particularly interesting character in that both he and Sabata continually try to outdo one another as they find themselves between a gang of killers and a 60,000 dollar ransom.

1971

The Return of Sabata, *E' Tornato Sabato . . . Hai Chiuso Un Altra Volta*; (Western); Ital / Fr / W. Ger, Director Frank Kramer (Gianfranco Parolini) (LVC stars as Sabata); 9/3/71 (Ital); 8/9/72 (US); Costars Reiner Schone as Clyde, Annabella Incontrera, and Giampiero Albertini as McClintock Also with Pedro Sanchez and Mario Brega.

Storyline: Has to do with our expert shot now working sideshows in a Circus with pal Clyde plan on knocking over the *McClintock bank*, but find all the money therein is counterfeit?

Captain Apache; (Western); UK/ Spa, Director Alexander Singer (LVC stars as Capt. Apache); 10/27/71 (US); 1/27/75 (Spa); Costars Carroll Baker as Maude and Stuart Whitman as Griffin. Also with Percy Herbert, Elisa Montes and Hugh McDermott as General Ryland and George Margo as the sheriff. Longtime friend of LVC, Ray X Brands also had a small part.

Storyline: Captain Apache, famous Indian Scout / Intelligence investigator for Union Army is sent into Indian Territory to investigate the murder of the Indian Commissioner. Actually he finds it's an undercover plot to assassinate then President Grant.

Note: First of many pictures to follow in which LVC now wears a hair piece; Lee also resumed his singing ventures with this film, doing the title song plus "April Morning" with Dolores Claman, composer, song writer and personal singing coach to Van Cleef.

Badman's River; a.k.a. *E' Continuavano a Fregarsi Il Millone de Dollari (And . . . They go on Losing the Million Dollars!)* ; A.k.a. *Hunt The Man Down*; (Western); Spa / Ital/ Fr, Director Eugenio Martin (LVC stars as Bomba King confidence man/ex-con); 12/23/71 (Italy); 1/24/74 (United States); It co stars James Mason, Gina Lollobrigida, Eduardo Fajardo, Gianni (John) Garko, and Aldo Sambrell.

Storyline: This Western is a riverboat adventure with love and thievery abound. Also, a secret mission intent on destroying a Mexican federal arsenal that supposedly holds a million dollars.

1972

The Grand Duel, *IL Grande Duel;* a.k.a. *The Big Showdown;* a.k.a. *Storm Rider*; (Western); Ital / W. Ger/ Fr, Director Giancarlo Santi (LVC stars as Sheriff Clayton); 12/29/72 (W. Ger); 1974 (US); Costars Horst Frank as David Saxon, Peter O'Brien (Alberto Dentice) as Philippe Werner, Dominique Darel as Elizabeth Saxon, American actor Jess Hahn is along for the ride as Big Horse, the Stage driver.

Storyline: Sheriff Clayton is attempting to solve a crime, while protecting an innocent young man life with bounty hunter and vigilantes abound, closing in for the kill.

1973

Blood Money; *La, Dove Non Batte IL Sole (Where it doesn't beat the Sun);* a.k.a. *Stranger and the Gunfighter*; (Western); Spa / Ital / HK, Director Anthony M. Dawson (Antonio Margheriti) (LVC stars as Dakota); 1974 (Spa); 1/11/75 (Ital); 5/1976 (US); It co stars Lo Lieh as Ho Kiang and a bevy of beauties Karen Yeh, Femi Benussi, Erika Blanc and Patty Shepard all have a piece of a treasure map portion tattooed on their bottoms, each a different piece of the puzzle.

Storyline: Has bank thief Dakota, jailed for attempted bank robbery and murder of Wang. His son Ho Kiang comes to investigate the old man's death and finds pictures from safehold, the key to Wang's hidden fortune. He breaks Dakota out of jail for his help.

1974

Take a Hard Ride; *aka La Parola Di Un Fuorilegge . . . e Legge! (An Outlaw's word . . . and The Law!)*; (Western); Ital/ US, Director Anthony M. Dawson (Antonio Margheriti) (LVC co stars as bounty hunter Keifer); October 1975 (Aus);10/29/75 (US); It stars Jim Brown as Ranch Foreman Pike, Dana Andrews in cameo as his ill boss. Also stars Fred Williamson as Tyree. Others were Catherine Spaak, Jim Kelly, Barry Sullivan as the Marshall and Harry Carey Jr.

Storyline: Concerns after the long, hard drive, now the money that Pike is attempting to bring home after selling the herd at market, some $86,000 cash, is a problem as scavenger Kiefer is intent on taking it all for himself.

1975

Mean Frank, Crazy Tony; *IL Suo Nome Faceva Tremare . . . Intepol In Allarme (Your Name Makes Us Trimble, Call the Law!);* a.k.a. *Powerkill; Escape from Death Row*; (Crime); Ital / Fr, Director Michele Lupo (LVC stars as Frank Diomede gangster); 1973; Costars Tony Lo Bianco as Tony, Edwige Fenech as Orchidea, Fasto Tozzi, Jess Hahn and Romano Puppo.

Storyline: The young wanta-be gangster Tony Breda actually helps out the incarcerated Frankie Dio by breaking him out of jail and helping him get out of the country by boat.

God's Gun; *A Bullet from God*; (Western); Ital / Israeli, Director Frank Kramer (Gianfranco Parolini) (LVC stars in dual roles as twin brothers, one a priest Father John and a gunman Lewis); March/ 1975 (US); Costars Jack Palance as Sam Clayton, Richard Boone as the sheriff, Leif Garrett as young Johnny, Sybil Danning as his mother, and Robert Lipton as Jess Clayton. Palance's own son Cody is onboard as Zeke Clayton member of the gang. Others were Ian Sander as Red Clayton and Didi Likov as Rip

Storyline: Has young Johnny, after observing the killing of his friend Father John, goes and seeks out the man's brother, a known gunman, to avenge his friend's and his own brother's death by the vicious Clayton gang.

1976

Kid Vengeance; a.k.a. *Vendetta*; (Western); US / Israeli, Director Joe Manduke (LVC stars as McLain); August 1977 (US); It costars Jim Brown as Isaac, John Marley as Jesus, Glynnis O'Connor as Lisa and Leif Garret as young Tom.

Storyline has a young boy with his friend and parents are in harm's way when along comes a gang. While hiding, he sees them kill his parents and sister, then steals all of Isaac's hard-earned gold. The young lad Tom is determined to take vengeance on this McLain bunch of army deserters and cutthroats and gets his friend Isaac to help since it was his gold that was taken.

Video box cover personal collection

1977

The Big Rip Off; *a.k.a. L'Ultimo Colpo, (The Last Hit);* a.k.a. *Controrapina;* a.k.a. *The Squeeze;* a.k.a. *Diamond Thieves; The Heist;* a.k.a. *Rip-off* (Crime) Ital / W. Ger, Director Anthony M. Dawson (Antonio Margheriti) (LVC stars as Chris Gretchko); 10/25/78 (Swe); February 1981 (US); Costars Karen Black as Clarisse Saunders, Edward Albert as Jeff Olafsen, Lionel Stander as Sam, Robert Alda as Capt. Donati and Rudolf (Dan) Van Husen as Hans.

Storyline: An aged safecracker is contacted to do one last job for old times' sake. He fights it, but eventually goes along with it as long as things are done his way. Good film, shot in NYC locales.

Note: This film went through a multitude of title changes, no wonder some of these films have been soooo hard to track!

The Perfect Killer, *L'Assassino Perfetto;* a.k.a. *Quel Pomeriggio Maledetto (That Accursed Afternoon);* a.k.a. *The Satanic Mechanic* (Crime); Spa / Ital, Director Marlon Sirko (LVC stars as a syndicate contract man Harry Chapman); 11/30/77 (Ital); It costars Tita Baker (Carmen Cervera) as Krista, Robert Widmark (Alberto Dell'Acqua) as Luc the hired assassin; Diana

Poliakov as model Liv and Karen Well as Liz; guest-starring as Benny was John Ireland.

Storyline deal was Krista constantly double-crossing Harry to the point where the mob puts out a hit on him. On the run, Harry is dodging the law and the mob to get back even with Krista. When this film finally arrived to the United States, it went straight to video.

1979

- ***The Hardway***; (Crime-thriller); Irish/UK (a MTV prod);

Director Michael Dryhurst (LVC costars as syndicate hitman, McNeil); 1979; Stars Patrick McGoohan as John Connor, Also starring Edna O'Brien as Kathleen, Donal O'Brien as Ryan and Michael Muldoon as Hogan.

Note: This was filmed on actual locations in Ireland. Produced by John Boorman and M. Dryhurst for *ATV British Telefilm Productions Ltd.* Screenplay was a joint effort by Richard F. Tombleson and Kevin Grogan. Music score was by Brian Eno and Tommy Potts. Shown in Euro markets but went straight to video here in the USA.

Storyline: Has to do with hitman Connor who is tired of seeing people die and tired of killing. He wants out and to retire. But his people aren't going to let him go. They send another hitman, O'Neal equally the best. Now they parlay to a bitter end. Who is the better man, as this thriller does step up to the plate!

1984

Jungle Raiders; *La Leggena Del Rubino Malese (The Legendary Ruby of Malaysia);* a.k.a. *Captain Yankee* (Action); Ital, Director Anthony M. Dawson (Antonio Margheriti] (LVC co stars as Inspector Warren); August 1985/86 (US); It stars Christopher Connelly as Duke Howard / Capt. Yankee, Marina Costa as Yanez, Alan Collins (Luciano Pignozzi) as Gin Fizz. Also: Dario Pontonutti, Mike Monty, Rene Abadeza and Francesco Arcuri

Storyline: Malaysia circa 1938, our hero Captain Yankee and Museum Curator Yanez are searching the world, tracking the fabled gem called the Ruby of Gloom. LVC, in more of a cameo part, as he drifts in and out of the story leaving the plot mastery to the Captain and Yanez.

1985

Codename: Wildgeese, *Arcobaeno Selvaggio* (Action); Ital/ W. Ger, Director Anthony M. Dawson (Antonio Margheriti) (LVC co stars as Archie China

Travers); 10/5/84 (W. Ger); 9/1986 (US); Stars Lewis Collins as Capt. Robin Wesley; Ernest Borgnine as Frank Fletcher, Klaus Kinski as Charlton, Manfred Lehmann as Klein and Mimsy Farmer as Kathy Robson

Storyline: Hong Kong, a British mercenary Capt. Wesley is hired by a leader of the international drug agency to destroy an opium depot deep in the Thai Jungle, unofficially of course. This would drive up demand prices, and the agent Fletcher who hired them and henchman Charlton are found to be behind the whole plot and the opium shipments. First off, Wesley gets old friend China an ace chopper pilot out of the local jail to join him, and fly the mission.

Killing Machine; *a.k.a. Goma-2;* (Action); Spa / Fr, Director J. Antonio de la Loma (LVC stars as Maitre Julot); 5/10/84 (Spa); Costars Margaux Hemingway as Jacqueline; Mexican action star, George Rivero, is really the main character Chema. Others: Willie Ames, as Tony, Richard Jaeckel as Martin, Mimsy Farmer, as a Reporter and Aldo Sambrell as the pilot

Storyline: Concerns a brutal crime war that is choking the Euro trucking industry. Underworld crime versus independent truckers who haul fruit and vegetables from Spain across Europe into Germany. Crime lord Julot (LVC) is a retired French Major.

Note: The orig. Spanish title *Goma-2* literally means (Rubber-2) which basically relates to plastic explosives being used on caravans (Lorries/ trucks) which are being blown up. It was filmed on locations in Barcelona and Southern France. Lots of action here.

1988

The Commander; a.k.a. *IL Triangolo Della Paura (The Triangle of Fear)*; (Action); W. Ger / Ital, Director Anthony M. Dawson (Antonio Margheriti) (LVC costars as Mazzarini, a tough demolitions expert from the old school); 4/28/88 (W. Ger); Starring Lewis Collins as Jack Colby, Donald Pleasance as Carlson, John Steiner as Duclaud, Manfred Lehmann as Wild Bill Hickok and Brett Halsey* as McPherson.

---

* According to Brett Halsey, a European film star in his own right with several Spaghetti Westerns and other genre films under his belt was seen recently in LA at the first ever *Spaghetti* Western Film Festival, 03/19/2011. Afterward, when comments came around during the discussions about his being in this film with Lee back in 1988, the question arose, "Was Lee actually drinking

Storyline: A group of mercenaries led by Colby are contracted to go into the Thailand, Golden Triangle area of Southeast Asia. They came to kill a drug lord who has threatened to cut off his supplies going to the west.

Note: Antonio Margheriti directed six films with LVC. They were good friends as well. Margheriti was one of the *Honorary Casket Bearers* at Van Cleef's funeral. See Brett Halsey* statement below . . .

1989

Thieves of Fortune; a.k.a. *May the Best Man Win;* a.k.a. *The Chameleon;* (Contemporary Western adventure); US/ S. African, Director Michael MacCarthy (LVC as stars as Sergio Danielo Christophero); 1989 (US); Costars Michael Nouri, as the films true lead, as Juan Luis, plantation overseer for the Christophero's vast holdings; Shawn Weatherly as Peter, Craig Gardner as HH, Liz Torres as Big Rosa, and Russell Savadier as Miguel among others.

Storyline: Soon after celebrating his 100th birthday, Christophero passes away. Per his will, his true heir can only be ascertained as the best man to oversee his vast enterprises and holdings after the passing of a predetermined set of test trials. The real heir is a woman, not a man. She dons the masquerade as one Peter and thus is subjected to the ritualistic test trials laid down by the will, thus the *May the Best Man Win* title.

Note: LVC's entire appearance probably consumes only the first fifteen minutes of the film or less for this cameo. This ironically was his last movie project prior to taking ill suddenly and passing on December 16, 1989.

LEE VAN CLEEF FILM AWARDS

1983

LIFETIME ACHIEVEMENT AWARD: *Academy of sci-fi, Horror and Fantasy Films*

GOLDEN BOOT AWARD: *Motion Picture and Television Fund Film Festival of Los Angeles, California*

---

beers on the set of this *Commander* film as has been rumored?" He answered, "Yes and kept telling everyone he was no longer an alcoholic."

1991

SERGIO LEONE AWARD: the ***Spaghetti* Western Hall of Fame Award,** via *Westerns . . . all'Italiana* fanzine magazine.

HONOREE—4TH Annual Wild West Film Festival—Held in Tuolumne County, Sonora, California on September 27/29, 1991

All of the above were awarded posthumously and received on the actor's behalf by his surviving wife, Barbara.

End.

BIBLIOGRAPHY
(L. VAN CLEEF)

Actors and Actresses, vol. 3: The International Dictionary of Film and Filmmakers (1988) by James Vinson, Christopher Lyon & Greg S. Faller; Pub. *St. James Press,* Chicago & London, pp 629

Betts, Tom, editor W*AI! (Westerns . . . All'Italiana)* Fanzine articles/ information on LVC;

- Vol. 1, Issue no. 1 (1983) "A Pocketful of Lee Van Cleef" by Gary Dorst; *Beyond the Law* Review by Bob Hiott;
- Vol. 1, Issue no. 2 (Dec.1983) "Stage Brush Fellini" by Bob Hiott;
- Vol. 1, Issue no. 3/4, (Nov. 1984) "Missing Scenes" Reviewed by Keith Hall Jr.;
- Vol. 2, Issue no. 2 (July 1985) *Bad Man's River* Review by William Connolly;
- Vol. 2, Issue no. 5 (Jan/Feb 1986) "Movies Aboard" translated newspaper reprint from Italy, Article: "Italy Accents Motion In Pictures" by Lee Van Cleef;
- Issue no. 8 (July/Aug 1986) "More . . . Missing Scenes," Reviewed by Keith Hall Jr.;
- Issue no. 10 (Nov/Dec 1986) "Spaghetti Showdown," Films Review by Keith Hall Jr.;
- LVC *Memorial Issue* 1990;

Betts, Tom, previously unpublished manuscript partials/ filmology on LVC, July 1, 1985; Sent to Tom Prickette 12/25/1992 to join with his yet unpublished works on the actor.

"Movie and Film Collector's World" *Poster-zine,* Article: "Lee Van Cleef Interview" by Max Allan Collins, Issue no. 171, October 21, 1983; *Compliments of Tom Betts,* 1992

The BFI Companion to the Western (1993) edited by Edward Buscombe, *British Film Institute,* UK. Originally published by *Andr`e Deutsch Ltd.,* London, 1988; pp. 355-356

Connolly, Bill, editor *Spaghetti Cinema* Fanzine:

- Issue no. 10 (March 1986) "Jose Antonio de la Loma films"
- Issue no. 14 (Aug 1986) Article: "Mr. Ugly Comes to Town" by Keith Hall Jr.;
- Issue no. 38 (Mar 1990) "LVC Complete Filmology";
- Issue no. 41 (Agu 1990) Article: "1968 Cinema's Greatest Year";
- Issue no. 71 (Oct 1999) Obituaries: "LVC on Set,";
- *Spaghetti Cinema* Blogspot (May 4, 2009) Article: "Sergio Leone on Lee Van Cleef"

Cox, Alex, *10,000 Ways to Die* (2009) (Ref), *Kamera Books,* UK.

Cumbow, Robert C., *Once Upon a Time: The Films of Sergio Leone* (1987) published by *Scarcrow Press inc.,* NJ. and London.

The Films of Clint Eastwood (1993) Filmology Booklet by Boris Zmijewsky and Lee Pfeiffer, *A Citadel Press Book* by *Carol Publishing Group,* NJ. ;pp 60-69

Filmographie 1950-1989 on Lee Van Cleef, compiled by Ms. Dolores Devesa, Dept of Documentation, Ministerio De Culture, Spain via written contact with her back in 1991.

Frayling, Christopher, *Something to do with Death* (2000) *Faber & Faber Ltd.,* London, UK. ; Information gathering on Lee Van Cleef

Frayling, Christopher, *Spaghetti Westerns: Cowboy and Europeans from Karl May to Sergio Leone* (1981) (Ref), *Routledge & Kegan Paul Ltd.,* London

Halliwell, Leslie, *The Filmgoer's Companion* (1975) (Ref), *Avon Book Publishers,* NY.

Haselbeck, Sebastian, owner/ curator for Internet website: *www.spaghetti-western.net*

Horner, William R., *Bad at the Bijou* (1982) (Ref), *McFarland & Co., Inc., Publishers,* NC, and London. ; pp 43-60

Internet, via: *www.anica.it* Ref: Film production and date confirmation

Internet, via: *www.IMDB.com* "Biography of Lee Van Cleef" plus film listing review

Ledbetter, Craig, editor of now defunct *ETC (European Trash Cinema)* Fanzine; Article "Interview with Antonio Margheriti" by Peter Blumenstock and Christian Kessler also with Loris Curci's translation help. Issue vol. 2, no. 7 ; pp 26

Lambert, Gilles, *The Good, the Dirty, and the Mean of Sergio Leone* (1976) *Solar Publishing,* Paris. ; French language printing, heavily illustrated with pictures in black and white.

"Lee Van Cleef . . . The Master," article by Hal Uchida, *Tribune* May/June issue 1984, pp 24-6

Malloy, Mike, *Lee Van Cleef* (1998) *McFarland & Co., Inc., Publishers,* North Carolina, and London.

McGlasson, Michael G., *Lee Van Cleef: Best of the Bad* (2010) *BearManor Media,* Duncan, OK.

Mitchum, John, *Them Ornery Mitchum Boys* (1988) *Creatures at Large,* Pacifica, California

Monster Biz, Fanzine on Cinema Video, "Article Lee Van Cleef and complete Filmology," French Language issue no. 35, 1984

Parish, James Robert, *Actors' Television Credits* 1950-1972 (1973) (Ref) *Scarecrow Press, Inc.,* NJ.

Prickette, Tom/Betts, Tom, "Master of the Silver Screen Badmen, Mr. Ugly Lives on . . .," previously unpublished manuscript/filmology on actor LVC, ; Partially used in the *WAI! Lee Van Cleef Memorial issue* 1990; Portions reworked 1992; 1997.

Quinlan's Illustrated Registry of Film Stars (1987) by Davis Quinlan, *Henry Holt Reference Books,* NY. ; pp. 240

Screen Stars, fanzine article, NY. vol. 13, no. 5 September 1955 issue: *Dear Fans* segment, by Lee Van Cleef: "Should Married Couples Take Separate Vacations?" pp 6-7

Thompson, Douglas, *Clint Eastwood Riding High* (1992) *Contemporary Books,* Chicago. ; pp 36; 204

TV-Guide, August 31, 1957, article: "Baddies Behind Bars," pp 13

Video Hound's Golden Retriever (1994 edition) *Visible Ink Press,* a division of *Gale Research Inc.,* Detroit, MI. pp 1411

Weisser, Thomas, *Spaghetti Westerns: the Good, the Bad, and the Violent* (1992) *McFarland,* Jefferson NC.

Western: All'Italiana (books I, II, and III), by Antonio Bruschini and Federico de Zigno, *Glittering Images,* Firenze, Italy; book I, 1998; book II, 2001 and book III, 2006

The Western: The Complete Film Sourcebook (The Film Encyclopedia) (1983) by Phil Hardy, *William Morrow and Co, Inc.,* NY. ; Appendix no. 8, pp 375-393

The World Almanac Who's who of Film (1987) by Thomas G Aylesworth and John S. Bowman, *Bison Books* ; pp. 413

LARRY WARD

(1924-1985)

THE WICKED I AM, THE WICKED I BE!

Larry Ward's real name was Ward Gaynor. Little is know of his early life and family.*. He was yet another of those American actors that was to join the throngs already in Italy at the *Cinecitta film studios* during those *Spaghetti* Western years. He was born on October 3, 1924, in Columbus, Ohio, where he would grow up. His father had been a former football coach and was an Ohio State senator. After high school, he went on to study at a couple of different universities before he joined the navy and served out his obligatory three-year stint. Upon his discharge, he used his GI Bill to enroll himself in the *American Theater Wing* and went on to appear in several play productions, but later decided to turn his attention more to writing. In 1954, he appeared in the television daytime soap, *The Brighter Day*, where he played a Dr. Randy Hamilton. It didn't take him long until repetition probably got to him, and his mind was then set on Hollywood. For his part in the show, the producers arranged for his character to leave from the show by having a fatal heart attack.

> *An interesting correlation here is that another Gaynor, a Jock Gaynor born on September 14, 1929, in NYC began his acting career in Hollywood doing bit parts on TV Westerns. He finally landed a role in 1960 on the series for *NBC* called *The Outlaws* (1960-'61). Gaynor's appearances were only for the first season of 1960. His role was that of Deputy Marshall Heck Martin. The show starred Barton MacLane of US Marshall Frank Caine. Also, the cast included Don Collier as Deputy Marshall Will Foreman. As one of this three member team of lawman, Gaynor we understand was replaced later on by Wynn Pierce for the early 1961 episodes. Gaynor had completed only episodes 1-9 for the fall of 1960.
>
> In one report according to Don Collier about Gaynor being replaced he said "Jock Gaynor was a little green . . . he never should have been hired for the part. He wore his boots funny and had that goofy hat. It didn't work at all. I don't know who did the hiring, but they didn't have any—sense at all! (Laughs) Well, they had a little bit of sense they hired me and Bart (Laughs)." Evidently there wasn't any love lost there in that replacement with rest of the cast members.
>
> Funny thing, at first we thought this Jock Gaynor and our Ward could have been brothers, but after doing further research into the matter, we now believe they were not, and that it was just a last name and era in time coincidence. We later found that one of our *Spaghetti* Western favorites Jack Betts (who used the pseudonym of Hunt Powers while in his films) was starred with Jock Gaynor in an unsold pilot for 1961 called "The Jay Hawkers" about two Kansans who wander the West.

Later in Hollywood, Ward Gaynor had been chiefly writing stories / television scripts for television. It was in 1962 and strictly by chance that he was able to ease into television work as an actor. As it happened, he went visiting to *Warner Bros* studio to talk in person with producer Jules Schermer about a film script he'd been working on. There he found Schermer was dully impressed with his own voice delivery, having heard it a few times over the phone. Now that he'd finally got a glimpse of the man behind the voice, he was so impressed that he offered him straight away a small part in one of their weekly series, a Western. That show was the *Lawman* series which starred John Russell and Peter Brown. His debut episode was called "The Holdout" (aired 2/18/62). For Gaynor's particular part the Studio suggested a name change to that of Larry Ward, which he gladly took their advice and continued to use it from then on for the balance of his career. Ward's part in the episode was that of Blake Stevens.

They liked him so well in that part that they set him up with another episode which immediately went into production. It was (as we understand it, just an episode and not yet a series pilot at that time) shown on 4/23/62, and it was called "A Man Called Ragan." It guest-star was Lee Van Cleef as Johnny Wilson. This episode had to do with the Marshall (Ragan) riding into a town to see an old buddy (Wilson). He, however, is met with hostility by a cattle baron Ben Stark (Arch Cooper) who tells Ragan that Wilson has disappeared and suggests that he do the same. The show was truly a hit with the test audiences. It had been shown in the regular *Cheyenne* show timeslot of Monday nights and was so popular that it was immediately considered for a new series position* that would eventually replace the long-running *Cheyenne* show that up until recently had regularly starred Clint Walker. Walker, it seems, was at this time in some contract disputes with *Warner Bros.* along with others of similar claims, like Wayde Preston formerly of the *Colt .45* show and Ed Kookie Byrnes of *77 Sunset Strip* fame.

> *Prior to his new show starting up, his producers allowed him some acting development time, as it were, after the *Lawman* episode, he could be seen in several other *Warner* shows of that era. Shows like: *Checkmate,* Ep: "Will the Real Killer Please Stand Up?" ('62) as Mr. Trent; *77 Sunset Strip,* Ep: "Pattern For A Bomb" ('62) as Paul Landers; *Have Gun, Will Travel,* Ep: "Memories of Monica" ('62) as Ben Turner.

Ward now under full-time employment to *Warner Bros.* became a star of their new primetime Western for *ABC* called *The Dakotas.* Here Ward stars as the US Marshall Frank Ragan head of a team of lawmen attempting to uphold the law of the land throughout the badlands of the Dakota Territory circa 1866. His regular show deputies were Jack Elam as Deputy J. D. Smith (ex-gunman), Chad Everett as Deputy Del Shark, and Michael Greene as Deputy Vance Porter.

The new show premiered on January 7, 1963, with episode no. 1 called "Return to Dry Rock," which was directed by Stuart Heisler. Guest stars were Edward Binns, Richard Hale, and Natalie Trundy. JD (Elam) is in the spotlight here (for this first episode of season one*) after a friend of JD's who had stuck up for JD when he was being run out of a town years back as a gunslinger, now the man was dead and JD was intent on avenging his death with or without Marshall Ragan's approval. For the record, LVC actually guest-starred in another of these *Dakota* episodes. That one being "Thunder in Pleasant Valley" and aired on February 4, 1963. It also starred Gregory Walcott, Patricia Huston, and Karl Swenson, to name a few. LVC portrayed outlaw Slade Tucker who abducts Rancher McNeill's (Swenson) daughter and demands a ransom.

Amazingly it was cancelled just one show short the end of its first season's run on September 9, 1963,* bummer. A previously shown episode had gotten a bad rating. We know Larry Ward was sick to be sure, and we certainly hoped that it wasn't one of his scripts, but it could very well have been, although he didn't immediately leave out for Europe. Remaining there in LA through the thick and thin press coverage and continued with other TV commitments. Immediately, following his show end, he appeared on one *Gunsmoke* episode called "Louis Peeters" (aired on 1/5/63) as Bart. He would return to the show three more times until 1966 and before leaving for Europe. Some of the others were *Temple Huston* ('64), *The Outer Limits* ('64), *Rawhide* ('65) as Sgt. Morton for episode "A Time for Waiting," *The Fugitive* ('65), *I Spy* ('66), *Lost in Space* ('66), *The Rat Patrol* ('66), and *The Time Tunnel* ('66), to name a few of the more popular ones of the day.

We can well imagine, though, at this point and time he was probably thinking about a change or, at the very least, a change in locations. Having heard all the hype about all the available film work overseas is what may have prompted him to venture later over to Europe, specifically to Rome in an

---

* As I remember, it was a good show. It ran some nineteen episodes for season one, then was cancelled before the twentieth episode: "Black Gold" could be released. The reason we find it all had to do with a show episode called "Sanctuary at Crystal Springs," which was shown on May 6, 1963. Afterward, another episode slipped through the airwaves and was shown on May 13, 1963, called "A Nice Girl from Goliah" before all stop halted the show's production and airing.

It seems that on the "Crystal Springs" episode public outcry against the plot caused the cancellation of the entire series as it was then pulled completely after that. The plot line of the show was that townsfolk are incensed when Del (Everett) and JD (Elam) gun down two of the murderous Barton brothers inside a church. Then to make matters worse, the third Barton son, Stan, was holding the pastor hostage in exchange for the deputies.

attempt to right his tilted career. It doesn't appear that he stayed long there, choosing to return frequently so as to continue his television obligations.

> Larry Ward's first Euro film was of for the Crime genre from director Mario De Nardo called *A Treasure One Must Not Steal!* (translated title) for 1967. He was starred here as Bill leader of an adventurous team of young people going to Turkey in search of a treasure that turns out to be a scam, and they are all abducted and held of ransom. A rare find today; it wasn't available for review. Evidently, Ward did stay long enough this being his first trip to get in one for the Western genre and a starring role in *God Does Not Pay on Saturday.*

For a 1967 release, this Western would also be known as *Kill the Wickeds!* This was an Italian production from director Amerigo Anton (Tanio Boccia). It starred Larry Ward as the retired gunman Benny Hudson. Also starring was American Robert Mark (Rodd Dana) in the troublesome want-a-be gang leader role of Wyatt Randall. It co stars Furio Meniconi as the bandit leader Ben Braddock who was just saved from hanging by loyal members of his gang. While on the move after they lose the posse, they decide to hide out in a desolate ghost town where they come upon this rancher / retired gunman Hudson and his woman Mary (Daniela Igliozzi). The gang proceeds to take over the town, bullying what few people are left, old Molly (Vivi Giori) for one. Hudson and his wife, whom they torment until Hudson finally having enough, gets a chance to get his guns and goes to work clearing house. The dollars from the stage holdup the gang had in their procession is left burning in the street as Lam and Mary's keeping the gold dust ride on off.

Evidently, after completing the above Western, he did return back home to LA and resumed his television work for a while longer. We find from his films listings a later 1967 release in which he finally tackled a part in a US film called *Hombre* with Paul Newman, directored Martin Ritt. Ward's part was that of a soldier. Then it was back to TV acting once again until his next trip overseas for another starring role, but in a *Giallo* thriller this time called *Macabre;* a.k.a. *The Invisible Assassin* for a 1969 release. Here Ward gets to stretch his acting experiences further now portraying dual roles as Peter and John.

> The storyline of this film concerns a woman who schemes to steal her husband's wealth after she gets involved in an affair with his twin brother. They plan a scheme to drive him insane so that he'll then be committed to an institution for life, and they can then

> have access to all his wealth for their own. As you can imagine it being a *Giallo* thriller, there are a few ghastly twists and turns in the story, just to make it interesting.

Afterward, it was back across the big pond once again and a possible chance of a re occurring role associated from two episodes for the popular primetime show called *The Virginian.* Those episodes were "Lost Grave at Socorro Creek" as Bill Burton, and "No War for the Warrior" as Sheriff Grey. Alas, his hopes for a semipermanent show didn't pan out, and it was back for the balance of the year doing other television parts like in *Dan August* ('70), a detective series with Burt Reynolds and the episode "The Soldier" with Ward as Captain Kent. Next was a couple of episodes for *The FBI* one called "The Witness" as a naval commander, and the other "The Passing of a King," both for 1970.

By this time, the Italian producers were probably burning up the overseas phone lines, so he was soon on a plane heading back to Italy again for another Western. This Italian production for a 1971 release was called *Saguaro.* Only recently has a decent version of this film become available through Internet sources. Even at that, it is in German language but has English subtitles. Also known as *I'll die for Vengeance*, it has the Venetian ex-*Peplum* (sword and sandal genre) star Kirk Morris in the lead here as Jeff. He arrives back in his hometown from the Civil War just in time to watch his childhood friend gunned down by a band of Mexican. All the while a do-nothing scared sheriff hides out in his office during the bank robbery. Jeff hitches up his gun belt and takes over the lawman's duties as a deputy sheriff. Now he's intent on getting back the Banks money, along with fulfilling his pent up vengeance as well. It seems Pedro and his band of marauders, are taking their orders from an elusive evil overseer named Saguaro portrayed by Larry Ward. The music score was done by Angelo Francesco Lavagnino.

Ward did only four films aboard in all, and unfortunately, he only did two of these *Spaghetti* Westerns. Not long after completing the above *Saguaro*, he returned to the States. On his previous visit to Rome between films, he had spent some of his time learning to do voice-over work on Italian films for the industry. There were several Americans that had been associated with this trade working there at one time or another including the guru himself Mickey Knox. Others to name a couple were Rodd Dana (Robert Mark*) and Robert Woods.

---

* Robert Mark (Rodd Dana) was the star of the first Western Larry Ward did there in Italy, *Kill the Wickeds!* It only makes sense that while Dana had already

By 1971 Ward seems to have ceased going over to Italy altogether, opting to stay back here in the United States and resume his story and script writing there in LA while continuing to still do his guest spot roles for television. Also, he may have been giving his newly acquired mini career in voice dubbing a tryout as we find he was credited with one in 1976 for *Star Wars* and the character Greedo (Ward was unaccredited). Also, we find he was involved with another later in 1983 for *Star Wars IV* and the Jabba the Hutt character (Ward was unaccredited once again). From the amount of television work, we found listed for Ward, he probably managed a good living, from all the steady work, and in between filling in with his writing.

It was about 1971 when Ward would get involved with another overseas venture in films. This time he would be involved with writer/actor Jock Gaynor and become a joint venture with producers Ben Balabat and John Garwood. Gaynor whipped out an old story, dusting it off and, with Ward, polished it off, and added in a few scary parts in the script for from a new film to be shot in the Philippines. On an island vacation, as it were, the three scouted out filming locations together around the Philippine islands. Finding suitable places, they quickly rounded up a few cast members. They called for friends Norman Foster (the director) and Diane McBain to fly over, and they got it shot, wrapping in short order for all the underwater and location scenes. "Down 'n' dirty" they called it.

The film would come to be called *The Deathhead Virgin* (1974). "Chained for 100 years in a Sunken Tomb . . . ," so the poster reads. It starred Jock Gaynor as a treasure hunter who investigates a sunken Spanish galleon all but forgotten off the coast of one the Philippine islands. The ship thought to be haunted, supposedly was watched over by the spirit of an ancient *Moro* princess. Larry Ward co stars here as Frank Cutter an island expatriate from for the States who knows the spot of the legends and takes Larry Alden (Gaynor) on this thrilling expedition. From all the reports, it sounded interesting enough, so we proceeded to track the film down through our European video sources some years back in order to give it a good viewing. Not too bad was the final verdict. Especially nice to see the films co star Diane McBaine once again after so many years.

After this film, Jock Gaynor continued his acting in television until his producing career finally took off about 1979 with the *Buck Rogers in the 25th Century* television series. He produced some twenty episodes for this series from 1979-1980. Larry Ward incidentally, also became involved in

---

been involved with the dubbing and voice-overs for foreign languages there in Rome at the time, he may have taken Ward and showed him the ropes, even to letting him get his feet wet doing same.

one episode of this series doing a guest appearance for one of a two-part sequence called "Flight of the War Witch I" (and II). Ward's part was the "first Council member," which aired on 3/27/80. As for Jock (a.k.a. John) Gaynor, he continued to produce work for television and was listed as an executive producer by 1984 on a show called *The Initiation*. Unfortunately his career was brought to an untimely end when he passed away suddenly on April 2, 1998.

As for Larry Ward, after *The Deathhead Virgin*, he continued mostly writing and some voice-over work; but as time wore on, his acting appearances became less frequent until his untimely death from lung cancer came and took him away on February 16, 1985. He passed while hospitalized there in Los Angeles. He was only sixty-one years old, but had been a heavy smoker for years as friends in the business would say. He had been married once to 1950's Hollywood siren/actress Roberta Haynes. She was, according to Rodd Dana, had been a longtime friend and a past yoga student of his. He went on to say that he and Larry had spent some fun times together while making *Kill the Wickeds* in Rome and Madrid. They had also spent time together back in the States during the late '70s shortly before his death there in LA. One Larry Ward's last accomplishments for pictures was the writing of the story for a film of the same name called *Crackdown* (1988). For his efforts and appreciation, he was given a special nod in the credits as In Memory of Larry Ward, RIP. Ye olde Overseer of the Wickeds.

End.

- Below is a complete *Overseas* filmography for Larry Ward. Dates here are aligned as close as possible with information currently at hand, with international release dates included. **Posters and title picture are accredited to the Sebastian Haselbeck collection via his website www.spaghetti-western.net. Many thanks, Sebastian.*

LARRY WARD
EURO FILMOLOGY

1967

It's Not good to Steal the Treasure, *Non Sta Bene Rubare IL Tesoro;* a.k.a. *A Treasure One Must Not Steal* (Crime); Ital / W. Ger/ Fr, Director Mario De Nardo (Ward stars as Bill); 1967 (Ital); It costars Pat Nigo (Pasquale Nigo) as Mehdi, Marie-France Pisier as Flo, and Ingeborg Schoner as Germaine. Others: Elina De Witt as Madame and Norma Dugo as Li-O. The music score was by Piero Umiliani.

God Does Not Pay on Saturday, *Dio non Paga IL Sabato;* a.k.a. *Kill the Wickeds!* Ital, Director Amerigo Anton (Tanio Boccia) (Ward stars as Benny Hudson); 8/15/67; It costars Robert Mark (Rod Dana) as Wyatt Randall. Others: Maria Silva as Judy Mary, Daniela Igliozzi as Shelly, Vivi Gioi as Molly Warner, Max Dean (Massimo Righi) as Laglan' and Men Fury (Furio Meniconi) as Braddock. A rousing music score by Francesco Lavagnino.

1969

The Invisible Assassin, *Viaje Al Vacio;* a.k.a. *Macabre* a.k.a. *Shadow of Death*; (*Gallo* thriller); Spa / Ital, D's: E. and Javier Seto (Larry Ward stars in dual roles as twin brothers, Peter and John); 6/6/69 (Ital); It costars Teresa Gimpera as Denise, Giacomo Rossi-Stuart as Gert and Silvana Venrurelli as Annie.

1971

They Only Knew How to Kill! *Sapevano Solo Uccidere!* a.k.a. *I'll Die for Vengeance;* a.k.a. *Saguaro* (Western); Ital, Director Amerigo Anton (Tanio Boccia) (Ward co stars as Saguaro); 1971 (Fr); It starred Kirk Morris (Adriano Bellini) as Jeff, Alan Steel (Sergio Ciani) as Pedro and Gordon Mitchell as Clayton. Also Kim Arden as Kathy and Ana Castor.

Note: Below is not a Euro-film, but rather a Philippino coproduction entry

1974

The Deathhead Virgin (Thriller); US / Filipino, Director Norman Foster (Ward co stars as Frank Cutter); 1974 (Filipino); It starred Jock Gaynor as Larry Alden. Both actors co wrote story/script. Others of the cast were: Diane McBain as Janice Cutter and Kim Ramos as Moro Princess, and Vic Diaz.

Note: Interesting trivia facts were about Diane McBain who co starred as Daffney McDutton on the long-running *Warner Bros.* 1960-'62 US TV series *Surfside-Six.* The show starred Van Williams, Lee Patterson, and Troy Donahue as a trio of crime investigation partners. Regulars on the show were McBain and Margarita Sierra as Cha Cha O'Brien. The series action usually began for a briefing on their houseboat / office docked at the *Marina Del Rey*, California. It had begun originally as a spin-off from a story episode via another earlier *Warner Bros.* series called *77 Sunset Strip.*

End.

BIBLIOGRAPHY
(L. Ward)

Betts, Tom, editor *WAI! (Westerns . . . All'Italiana)* Fanzine: article/obituary: "Whatever Became of Larry Ward?" Issue no. 62; same issue, interview with Robert Mark, where he talks of friend Ward

Connolly, Bill, editor *Spaghetti Cinema* Fanzine articles/info on films

Haselbeck, Sebastian, owner/curator for Internet website: *www.spaghetti-western.net*

Internet, via: *www.IMDB.com* "Larry Ward" film and TV listings

Internet, via: *http://ctva.biz/US/Westerns/archives* Extensive Western TV show listings plus info

Prickette, Tom, "Larry Ward Filmo", A previously unpublished informational bit on Larry Ward the actor, 2005

Summers, Neil, *The First Official TV Western Book* (1987) published by *Old West Publishing*; a photo reference booklet from actor/stuntman Neil Summers

Weisser, Thomas, *Spaghetti Westerns: the Good, the Bad, and the Violent,* (1992) *McFarland,* Jefferson NC.

Western: All'Italiana (books II and III), by Antonio Bruschini and Federico de Zigno, *Glittering Images,* Firenze, Italy; book II, 2001 and book III, 2006

Wild East Productions, NY. Many thanks to Ally and Eric for the opportunity to see their great new 2009 DVD reissue of the *Kill the Wickeds* film starring Larry Ward

WOMEN OF THE *SPAGHETTI* WESTERNS

The names herein are a mixture of American and foreign, International movie stars and starlets that blended into Europe along with their counterpart male actors in search of that ultimate film opportunity. Most at first were used more or less as window dressing, some eventually evolved in the era with more substantial roles while others fell by the wayside. Some even delved into the soft-porno-film genre prior to giving up entirely. Whatever the case may have been, here are names of some of those female actresses that were commonly associated with these popular Italian-made 'Spaghetti' films of a bygone era . . .

Ursula Andress, (Swiss born and former Bond girl from first of the Spy genre films; Once married to actor/ director/ producer John Derek (1957-1966); Companion to actor Harry Hamlin; Also is mother of Dimitri Hamlin) two westerns; *Red Sun* 1971 as Cristina, prostitute; *Mexico in Flames* 1976 as Mabel Dodge

Laura Antonelli, (Laura Antonaz) (Italian); One western; *A Man called Sledge* 1971 as Maria

Tina Aumont, (Maria Christina Salomons) (American); Two westerns; *Man, His Pride and his Vengeance* 1968 as Carmen; *The Brothers Blue* 1971 as Polly Clay

Carroll Baker, (Karolina Pickarski) (American (Ms Baker became extremely popular in Europe as a *Scream Queen* of *giallos* & horror films); One western; *Captain Apache* 1971 as Maude

Bridget Bardot, (Bridget Anne-Marie Bardot) (French); Three westerns; *Viva Maria* 1965 as Maria O'Malley; *Shalako* 1968 as Countess Irina Lazaar; *Frenchie King* 1971 as Louise (Frenchie King (Miller)

Liz Barret (Luisa Pasqualotto Baratto (also as Barrett) (Italian); Five westerns; *Killer Kid* 1967 as Mercedes Hernandez; *Two Pistols and a Coward* 1967 as Maggie; *Requiescant* (*aka Kill and pray; Let them rest*) 1967 as Lo; *Long Day of the Massacre* 1968 as Lara; *Payment in Blood* 1968 as Manuela

Anne Baxter, (American and granddaughter of noted architect Frank Lloyd Wright; once married to actor John Hodiak (1946-1953); Also is mother of actress Katrina Hodiak); One western; *Tall Women* 1966 as Mary Anne

Femi Benussi, (Eufemia Benussi) (Italian); Ten westerns; *Rattler Kid* 1967 as Helen; *Last of the Badmen (aka Time of Vultures)* 1967 as Rubia; *Born to Kill* 1967 as Laurie/Flory Waldamore; *Death walks in Laredo* 1967 as Tula; *Zorro the Fox* 1968 as Donna Isabella; *Duel in the Eclipse* 1968 as Alma; *Quintana* 1969 as Virginia De Leon; *Finders Killers* 1971 (Saloon girl); *Stranger and the Gunfighter* 1974 (as the Italian mistress); *Seven Devils on Horseback* 1975 as Rosie;

Martine Beswick, (Jamaican born was a former Bond girl for two *007* films; also two *Hammer* films plus later Italian horror films); Two westerns; *A Bullet for the General* 1966 as Adelita; *John the Bastard* 1967 as Dona Antonia Terecico (Tenorio)

Erika Blanc (Enrica Bianchi Colombatto) (Italian); Thirteen westerns; *Colorado Charlie* 1965 (Saloon Singer); *Dequeyo* 1966 as Rosy, (Woman in Danger City); *Django Shoots First* 1966 as Jessica; *One Thousand Dollars on the Black* 1967 as Joselita; *The Greatest Kidnapping in the West* 1967 as Jenny; *Shotgun* 1968 as Jo Anne; *Shoot, Gringo . . . Shoot!* 1968—as Sally; *I'll forgive you . . . before I kill you!* 1970 as Martha Sonnier; *Fistful of Lead* 1970 as Trixie; *Run Men, Eldorado is Coming* 1972 as Ragazza; *Lobo the Bastard* 1971(Girl at Fiesta); *Thunder over El Paso* 1972 as Jenny; *Stranger and the Gunfighter* 1974 (as the American mistress);

Honor Blackman; (British) one western, *Shalako* 1968 as Lady Julia Dagget; (Once married to Maurice Kaufmann (1961-1975)

Simone Blondell, (Simonette Vitelli) (Italian and is the daughter by marriage of director Demofilo Fidani); Fourteen westerns; *Stranger Say your Prayers* 1967; *And Now make your peace with God* 1968; *Pray to God and dig your Grave* 1968 (as Don Enrique's maid); *Four came to kill Sartana* 1969 as Suzy; *El Zorro, Lawman* 1969 as Perla Dominguez; *Shadow of Sartana . . . Shadow of Death* 1969 as Trudy (Sullivan's daughter); *Django and Sartana are coming . . . It's the End* 1970 as Jessica Cobb/ Anne; *Man Called Django* 1971 as Inez; *Reach you Bastard (Aka Django Story)* 1971; *His name is Sam Walbash, but they call him Amen* 1971 as Fanny; *Stranger that kneels beside the shadow for a Corpse* 1971 as Maya; *One Damned day at Dawn . . . Django meets Sartana* 1971 (as the Sturges' widow); *A Barrel full of Dollars (Aka Showdown for a Badman)* 1972 as Monica Benson; *Anything for a Friend* 1973 as Pearl

Genevieve Bujold, (French and is mother of assistant director / actor Matt Almond); One western; *Another Man, another Chance* 1977 as Jeannie Leroy;

Capucine, (Germaine Lefebvre) (French and once married to director/ screenwriter/ actor Pierre Trabaud (1950-1950 (only 6-mos); She was found to have committed suicide later at age 62); One western; *Red Sun* 1971 as Pepita

Claudia Cardinale, (Tunisian) two westerns; *Once Upon a Time in the West* 1968 as Jill McBain; *Frenchie King* 1971 as Maria Sarrazin

Helene Chanel, (Helene Stoliaroff) (French) seven westerns; *A Dollar of Fear* 1960 as Alice Perkins; *Terror of the Black mask* 1963 as Carmencita Gomez; *Two Gangsters in the Wild West* 1965 as Betty White; *Death Rides Alone* 1967 as Dolores Talbot; *Killer Caliber* .32 1967 as Sherrill Morgan/Dolly; *Two R.R.-Ringos from Texas* 1967 as Sentenza Jane; *Cjamango* 1967 as Perla Hernandez

Geraldine Chaplin, (American and daughter of silent-screen legend Sir Charles Chaplin; She was educated in Switzerland; a dancer who studied at *The Royal Academy of Ballet,* London; Is the half-sister to actor Sidney Chaplin; Has two sons); Two westerns; *Carlos* 1971 as Lisa (A W.Ger MTV movie); *Curse this America, (a.k.a. Jaider's Gang)* 1973 as Kate Elder

Emma Cohen, (Emmanuela Beltran Rahola) (Spanish and once married to director/ screenwriter Fernando Fernan Gomez (2000-2007); Three westerns; *Frenchie King* 1971 as Virginie; *Cut-Throats Nine* 1973 as Katy (Cathy) Brown; *Cipolla Colt* (aka *Cry Onion)* 1975 as Mary Ann Pulitzer

Maria Pia Conte, (Maria Pia Vaccarezza) (Italian); Seven westerns; *Dynamite Jim* 1966 as Lupita, dancehall girl; *Five Dollars for Ringo* 1968 as Miriam Graf; *If you meet Sartana . . . Pray for your Death* 1968 as Jane Randall; *Zorro the Conqueror* 1969 as Isabel; *Twenty Paces to Death* 1970 as Clare; *And Crows Will Dig your Grave* 1971 as Susan; *God in Heaven . . . Arizona on Earth* 1972 as Kathleen (Catherine)

Perla Cristal, (Perla Cristal Lijik) (Argentinean); Seven westerns; *Two-Thousand Dollars for Coyote* 1965 as Rita; *Seven Guns for the MacGregors* 1965 as Perla; *The Tall Women* 1966 as Pilar; *Christmas Kid* 1966 as Lisa (Marie) Lefleur; *White Comanche* 1967 as White Fawn; *Reverend Colt* 1970 as Dorothy; *Dust in the Sun* 1971 as Carla

Katia Christine, (Scandinavian); Two westerns; *Greatest Robbery in the West* 1968 as Katie O'Brien; *They Still Call Me Amen* 1972 as Clementine

Sybil Danning (Sybille Johanna Danninger) (Austrian); One western; *God's Gun* 1976 as Jenny (Johnny's mom)

Carolyn Davys, (Crodin Davis); One western; *Gunmen of the Rio Grande* 1964 as Clementine Hewitt

Rosemarie Dexter, (Pakistani); Three westerns; *For a Few Dollars More* 1965 (as Mortimer's sister in flash-back); *El Desperado* 1967 as Katy/

Kathy (the outlaw's woman); *Come Together* 1971 as Ann in this a contemporary film with *Spag*-west scenes added in.

Karin Dor, (Katherose Derr) also Dorr (German and once married to German director Harald Reinl (1954-1968); Later remarried to stuntman George Robotham (1988-2007); Five westerns; *Treasure of Silver Lake* 1962 as Ellen Patterson; *Winnetou: Last of the Renegades* 1964 as Ribanna; *Winnetou: the Desperado Trail* 1965 (is in it, but unaccredited); *The Last Tomahawk* 1965 as Cora Monroe; *Winnetou and Shatterhand in the Valley of Death* 1968 as Mabel Kingsley

Anita Ekberg, (Italian and once married to British actor Anthony Steel (1956-1959); Re-married to American actor Rik Van Nutter (1963-1975); Two westerns; *The Deadly Trackers* 1972 as Manuela; *The Valley of the Widows* 1975 (For this film, an unsubstantiated rumor claims that for Ital-released version of this Spanish / West German film, director Volker Vogeler supposedly deleted all of her scenes per her request?)

Edwige Fenech, (Edwige Sfenek)(Italian) (Later she ventured into *giallo* and soft-porn roles; She later founded *Immagine e Cinema S.r.l. Productions*); One western; *Heads or Tails* 1969 as Manuela;

Agata Flori, (Tunisian and once married to producer Dario Sabatelli (196?-1992); Six westerns; *Seven Guns for the MacGregor's* 1965 as Rosita Carson; *Up the MacGregor's!* 1967 returns as Rosita Carson; *I Came, I Saw, I Shot* 1968 as Rosario; *Nephews of Zorro* 1969 as Carmencita; *Heads You Die . . . Tail I Kill You* 1971 as Anna Lee; *Return of Hallelujah* 1972 as Fleurette

Lola Fontana (Loletha Elayne Falana) (British); One western; *Black Tigress* 1967 as Lola Gate

Anne Francis, (American and former child radio personality, then model; Once married to actor Bamlet Lawrence Price Jr., (1952-1955); One western; *Pancho Villa* 1972 as Flo

Lynne Frederick (Lynne Maria Frederick) (British and once married to actor Peter Sellers (1977-1980; Then later to British TV personality David Frost (1981-1982); Two westerns; *Red Coat* 1974 as Elizabeth; *Four Gunman of the Apocalypse* 1975 as Emanuelle *Bunny* O'Neill

Susan George, (Susan Melody George) (British and married to actor Simon McCorkindale (1989-2010); One western; *Bandera Bandits* 1973 as Sonny

Daniela Giordano, (Italian); Nine westerns; *Find a Place to Die* 1968 as Juanita; *Long Day of the Massacre* 1968 as Pacquita; *Five-Man Army* 1969 as Maria; *Challenge of the MacKennas* 1969 as Barbara; *Four Gunman of the Holy Trinity* 1971 as Sarah Bowman; *Hero Called Allegria* 1971 (Mexican girl); *Have a Good Funeral, My Friend . . . Sartana will pay!* 1971 as Jasmine (Abigail Benson); *Trinity and*

Sartana are coming! 1972 as Martha; *Go Away! Trinity has arrived in Eldorado* 1972 as Juanita

Gisela Hahn, (Gisela Drenkhan) (German); Five westerns; *They call me Trinity* as Sarah; *Durango is Coming, Pay or Die!* as Margot; *Don't Turn the other Cheek* 1971 (Orlowsky's wife); *White Fang to the Rescue* 1974 as Katie; *Scaramouche* 1976

Barbara Hevelone, (American is an accomplished pianist/ musician went on to marry actor Lee Van Cleef for his third marriage (1978-1989 until his death; She is also sister of bit-actor Bob Hevelone); One western; *Stranger and the Gunfighter, a.k.a. Blood Money* 1974, (Piano player for *Rye Whiskey* song 'n dance number performed by Lee Van Cleef; Also she was seen in another saloon scene as a *bar-girl extra,* same film)

Jill Ireland, (Jill Dorothy Ireland) (American and once married to David McCallum (1957-1967); Then to Charles Bronson 1968 until her death of cancer in 1990; Is mother of actors/ composers Val McCallum and Paul McCallum); Two westerns; *Chino* 1973 as Louise; *Villa Rides* 1968 (Woman in the restaurant)

Fran Jeffries, (Francis Makris) (American and once married to singer/ actor Dick Haymes (1958-1965); then to director/ screenwriter/ actor Richard Quine (1965-1969); Also mother of actress Stephanie Haymes); One western; *A Talent for Loving* 1969 as Maria

Marianne Koch, (German); Six westerns; *Fistful of Dollars* 1964 as Marisol; *Place called Glory* 1965 as Jade Grande; *Sunscorched* 1966 as Anna-Lisa; *Who killed Johnny R.?* 1966 as Bea Bordet (Dillion's woman); *Clint the Stranger* 1968 as Julie Harrison; *Last Ride to Santa Cruz* 1969 as Elizabeth Kelly

Mara Krup, also as Maria Krup (German); Seven westerns; *For A Few Dollars More* 1965 as Mary (hotel mgr's wife); *The Handsome, the Ugly, the Stupid* 1967 (Saloon girl); *Sugar Colt* 1967 (Woman in shooting gallery with cigar); *A Man Called Amen* 1968 as Millie; *Light the Fuse . . . Sartana is Coming* 1970 (hotel owner); *Return of Halleluja* 1972 as Mary; *Return of Clint the Stranger* 1972 (brothel madam)

Janet Leigh, (American and once married to actor Tony Curtis (1951-1962); Mother of Jamie Lee Curtis, and Kelly Curtis); One western; *Kid Rodelo* 1966 as Nora

Sara Lezana, (Sara Lezana Minquez) (Spanish and a famous flamenco dancer); Three westerns; *Gunfight at Red Sands* 1963 as Lisa (Liza) Martinez; *Murieta* 1963 as Rosita Murieta; *Last of the Mohicans* 1965 as Cora Munro

Christa Linder, (Crista Linder) (German); Three westerns; *The Tall Women* 1966 as Bridget; *Day of Anger* 1967 as Gwen/ Betty; *Trinity plus the Clown and a Guitar* 1975 (the Gold sister)

Helga Line, (Helga Lena Stern) (German and former circus acrobat); Seven westerns; *Seven Hours of Gunfire 1964; Sign of Zorro* 1964 as Mercedes; *In a Colts Shadow* 1965 as Fabienne, saloon gal; *Have a Good Funeral, My Friend . . . Sartana will pay!* 1970 as Julie; *Raise your hands, dead man . . . You're under arrest* 1971 as Maybelle (Mabel); *Those Dirty Dogs* 1973 as Maria; *China 9, Liberty 37* 1978 as Cottrell's wife

Gina Lollobrigida, (Luigina Lollobrigida) (Italian and once married to producer Milka Skofic (1949-1971); Mother of actor Milka Skofic Jr.,); One western; *Bad Man's River* 1971 as Alice (Alicia)

Beba Loncar, (Desanka Loncar) (Yugoslavian); One western; *Days of Violence* 1967 as Christina (the saloon girl)

Malisa Longo, (Maria Luisa Longo) (Italian); Eleven westerns; *Zorro, Rider of Vengeance* 1968 as Carmen di Mendoza; *Once Upon a Time in the Wild, Wild West* 1969 as Dolores; *Zorro, Marquis of Navarra* 1969 returns again as Carmen di Mendoza; *More Dollars for the MacGregor's* 1970 as Yuma (the Indian witch); *Django Challenges Sartana* 1970 as Maria; *Blindman* 1971 as the bride; *Desperado* 1972 as Barbara; *Now they call him Sacramento* 1972 as Barbara (Jenny) McKinley; *White Fang and the Hunter* 1975 as Connie; *California* 1976 as Yasmin; *Macho Killers* 1977 as Helen

Sophia Loren (Sofia Villani Scicolone) (Italian and sister of screenwriter Maria Scicolone; Married twice to producer Carlo Ponti (1957-1962), and (1966-2007); Two westerns; *The Return of Pancho Villa* 1951 as the Secretary; *The Dream of Zorro* 1952 as Conchita

Diana Lorys, (Ana Maria Cazorla Vega) (Spanish); Seventeen westerns; *Shadow of Zorro* 1962 as Mestiza;*Cavalry Charge* 1964 as the Indian girl; *Tomb of the Pistolero* 1964; *Twins from Texas* 1964 as Fanny; *Gunfighters of Casa Grande* 1964 as Gitana; *Murieta* 1965 as Kate; *Three from Colorado* 1965 as Ann Sullivan; *Texican* 1966 as Kit O'Neal; *White Comanche* 1968 as the Indian squaw; *Sartana does not Forgive, aka Sonora* 1968; *Villa Rides* 1968 as Emilita; *Bad Mans River* 1971 as Dolores; *Kill Django . . . Kill First* 1971; *Chino* 1973 as the Indian girl; *Get Mean* 1975 as Princess Elizabeth Maria; *California* 1976 as Jasmine; *Crimson Night of the Hawk* 1978 as Dinah

Lucretia Love (Italian and later went into the soft-porn film genre; Once married to producer Mauro Parenti (1969-19??); Four westerns; *Go with God Gringo* 1966 as Carmen; *Colt in the hand of the Devil* 1967 as Janet; *Blindman* 1971 (as the bride); *Two Sons of Trinity* 1972 as Lola

Sue Lyon, (Suellyn Lyon) (American); One western; *Four Rode Out* 1969 as Myra Polsen; (the outlaw woman)

Nicoletta Machiavelli, (Italian); Seven westerns; *The Hills Run Reds* 1966 as Mary-Ann Milton; *Navajo Joe* 1966 as Estella; *Minute to Pray . . .*

a Second to Die 1967 as Laurinda; *Face to Face* 1967; *Garter Colt* 1967 Starred as Lulu (Garter Colt); *Hate They Neighbor* 1969 as Peggy Savalas; *No Room to Die* 1969 as Maya

Elsa Martinelli, (Elsa Tia) (French and mother of actress Cristian Mancinelli); One western; *The Belle Starr Story* 1968 as Belle Starr (Myra Belle Shirley)

Marisa Mell, (Marlies Theres Moitzi) (Austrian); Four westerns; *Call of the Wild* 1962; *Last Stage to Santa Cruz* 1964 as Juanita, (Mistress of the bandit leader); *Ben and Charlie* 1970 as Sara; *Miss Dynamite* 1972 as Miss Dynamite

Michele Mercier, (Joscelyne Yvonne Renee Mercier) (French); Two westerns; *Cemetery without Crosses* 1969 as Maria Caine; *Call of the Wild* 1972 as Calliope Laurent

Gloria Milland, (Maria Fie) (Italian); Ten westerns; *Gunfight at High Noon* 1963 as Louise Walker; *Three Swords of Zorro* 1963 as Maria (Virginia de Santa Ana, daughter of Zorro); *Seven Guns from Texas* 1964 as Mary (Maria); *Seven Hours of Gunfire* 1964 as Calamity Jane; *Hands of a Gunman* 1965 as Laura Murphy (Miriam); *Man with the Golden Pistol* 1966 as Lily (Norma O'Connor); *Hate for Hate* 1967 as Maria (Consuelo) Cooper; *Man and a Colt* 1967 as Carmencita (Beatrice); *Man who killed Billy the Kid* 1967 as Mrs. Bonney (Billy's mother); *Hour of Death* 1968 as Maria (Margot)

Jeanne Moreau, (French and once married to director Jean-Louis Richard (1949-1951); Then to producer/ director William Friedkin (1977-1979); Mother of assistant director/ actor Jerome Richard); One western; *Viva Maria* 1965 as Maria

Krista Nell, (Doris Kristanelli) (Austrian); Seven westerns; *Kitosch, the man who came from the North* 1967 as Eva; *To Hell and Back* 1968 as saloon girl; *Django and Sartana are coming . . . It's the End* 1970 as Cleo, the saloon girl; *You're Jinxed, Friend . . . You've Just met Sacramento* 1970 as Evelyn; *Kill Django . . . Kill first* 1971 as Burton's woman; *God is my Colt* .45 1972 as Mary; *Paid in Blood* 1972 as Cora

Rosalba Neri, (Italian); Nineteen westerns; *Johnny Yuma* 1966 as Samantha Felton; *Arizona Colt* 1966 as Dolores; *Dynamite Jim* 1966 as Margaret (the Dance Hall girl); *The Great Treasure Hunt* 1967 as Agnes; *Days of Violence* 1967 as Lizzy (John's girlfriend); *This Man Can't Die* 1968 as Jenny Melina (owner of the saloon); *Long Ride from Hell* 1968 as Encarnation (the prostitute); *Sartana does not forgive (Sonora)* 1968 (as the Passenger); *Killer Goodbye* 1969 as Fannie; *Arizona Colt Returns* 1970 as Paloma Morena; *The Rewards yours, the Man is mine (El Puro)* 1970 as Rosie; *Watch out Gringo . . . Sabata is coming* 1972 as La Ragazza (the Girl); *Wanted Johnny Texas* 1971; *Drummer of Vengeance*

1971 as Rising Sun, (the murdered Indian wife of hero); *And they smelled the Strange, Exciting, dangerous Scent of Dollars 1973* as Maria; *Man called Invincible* 1973 as Miss Pappalardo; *Blood River* 1974 as Catherine Hammond Webster; *Lucky Morgan won't get that Gold!* as Wauneta; *Ringo's Big Night* 1966 as Ringo's saloon gal

Loredana Nusciak (Loredana Cappelletti) (Italian and former *Miss Trieste* of 1959; Once married to actor Gianni Medici (196?-); Six westerns; *Man from Canyon City* 1965; *Django* 1966 as Maria; *Ten Thousand Dollar Blood Money* 1966 (as Django's woman); *Seven Dollars on the Red* 1968; *Revenge for Revenge* 1968; *God will forgive my Pistol* 1969

Glynnis O'Connor, (American and daughter of producer Daniel O'Connor and actress Lenka Peterson; Sister of actor Darren O'Connor); One western; *Kid Vengeance* 1976 as Lisa Thurston

Kareen O'Hara, (Stefania Careddu di Sambrese); Two westerns; *Any gun can play* 1967 as Marisol (Wapa); *Johnny Hamlet* 1968 as Eugenia

Gloria Osuna, (Spanish); Four westerns; *Gunfight at High Noon* 1963 as Suzanne (Susan Westfall); *Few Dollars for Django* 1966 as Sally Norton; *The Magnificent Texan* 1967 as Carmen Perera; *A Pistol for a Hundred Coffins* 1968 as Marjorie

Luciana Paluzzi, (Italian and former *Bond* girl went on to do *giallo* & horror genres as well as spy films; Once married to actor Brett Halsey; Mother of actor Christian Halsey Soloman); Two westerns; *Forgotten Pistolero* 1969 as Anna Carrasco; *Come Together* 1971 as Lisa (A contemporary film with *Spag*-western scenes added in)

Gloria Paul, (British and former dancer at *Lido de Paris* and member of the "Blue Belle Girls"; Companion of composer Piero Piccioni; Mother of producer Jason Piccioni); Two westerns; *For a few Dollars Less* 1966 as Juanita; *Two R.R.-Ringos from Texas* 1967 as Evelyn

Rita Pavone, (Italian singer / actress, also married to actor Teddy Reno since 1968—; Mother of actor Allesandro Reno, and singer Giorgio Reno); One western musical; *Rita of the West* (aka *Lit'l Rita*) 1969 as Rita

Maria Perschy, (Herta-Maria Perschy) (Austrian and studied acting in Vienna; Married twice, one daughter; She died in 2004 at 66 yrs old of cancer); Three westerns; *Bandits of the Rio Grande* 1965 as Helen; *The Tall Women (Aka Seven Vengeful Women)* as Ursula; *Seven for Pancho Villa* 1967 as Vera Stevens (the widow)

Pascale Petit, (Anna-Marie Petit) (French and once married to actor Gianni Esposito (196?-1969); Mother of actress Douchka); Two western; *Find a place to Die!* 1968 as Lisa Martin; *Cowboy Kid* 1972 as Maureen

Monica Randal, (Aurora Julia Sarasa, sometimes as Randel or Randall) (Spanish); Thirteen westerns; *Billy the Kid* 1963; *Heroes of the West* 1963 as Sherry; *For a Fist in the Eye* 1965 as Senora Carmencita

Benton; *Charge of the Seventh Cavalry* 1965 as Amanda; *Five Giants from Texas* 1966 as Rosaria Latimore; *Ringo and Gringo against All* 1966 as Carolina (the outlaw's gal); *One hundred thousand Dollars for Ringo* 1966; *Red Blood, Yellow Gold* 1968 as Annie; *All Out* 1968 as Maria; *Red Sun* 1971 as Maria; *A Cry of Death (Lynching)* 1971 as Lucy; *You Are Carrion, and I will kill you!* 1972 as Nancy (Saloon owner); *Pancho Villa* 1972 as Lup

Giovanna Ralli, (Italian); Three westerns; *Taste of Violence* 1961 as Maria; *The Mercenary* 1968 as Columba; *Cannon for Cordoba* 1969 as Leonora

Lynn Redgrave, (Lynn Rachel Redgrave) (British and daughter of actor Michael Redgrave and actress Rachel Kempson; Sister of actress Vanessa Redgrave and actor Colin Redgrave; Sister-in-law of genre actor Franco Nero); One western; *Don't Turn the other Cheek!* 1971 as Mary O'Donnell (The Irish Journalist/ revolutionist)

Sydne Rome, (American); Two westerns; *Alive or Preferably Dead* 1969 as Rossella (Scarlet) Scott; *A Man Called Amen* 1972 as Dorothy, school teacher;

> *Note*: Rome is credited as being in *Mexico in Flames* 1982, but *actually was not*! She *is* costarred with Franco Nero in the second installment of this "*John Reed: Journalist*" MTV mini-bio series called, *The Ten Days that Shook the World (aka Red Bells)* 1983 which is not a western at all but about the Russian Revolution.

Gia Sandri, (Gia Skalha) (India); Seven westerns; *Stranger Called Sacramento* 1965 as Emili; *Thompson 1880* 1966 as Sheila O'Connor (The town widow); *A Dollar between the Teeth* 1966 as Maruca; *John the Bastard* 1967 as Gertrude; *Two Pistols and a Coward* 1968 as Dora; *Cicco forgives, I don't* 1968 as Calamity Jane; *Wanted* 1968 as Cheryl

Olga Schoberova, (Olinka Berova) (Yugoslavian and mother of actress Sabrina Berova; Once married to bodybuilder/ genre actor Brad Harris (1967-1969); Then to producer/ actor John Calley (1972-1992); Four westerns; *Massacre at Marble City* 1964 as Mary Brendel; *Black Eagle of Santa Fe* 1965 as Lana Miller; *Count Bobby, the Terror of the West* 1965 as Milly; *Lemonade Kid* 1966 as Winifred Goodman

Karin Schubert, (Italian and later went on to become soft-porn-star of Euro-films); Two westerns; *Companeros* 1970 as Zaira Harris; *Three Musketeers of the West* 1972 as Dr. Alice

Susan Scott, (Nieves Navarro Garcia) (Spanish); Eight westerns; *A Pistol for Ringo* 1965 as Dolores; *The Return of Ringo* 1966 as Rosita; *Big Gundown* 1966 (as the wicked widow; *El Rojo* 1966 as Consuelo; *Long*

Days of Vengeance 1967 as Dolly; *Indio Black (Adios Sabata)* 1970 (as saloon singer); *Light the Fuse . . . Sartana is coming!* 1971 as Belle Manassas; *Kill the Poker Player* 1972 as Lilly (Kate)

Patty Shepard, (Patricia Moran Shepard) (Married to actor Manuel de Blas (1967—); Sister of actress Judith Shepard); Four westerns; *Twenty Paces to Death* 1970 as Deborah; *Frenchie King* 1971 as Petite Pluie; *A Man Called Noon* 1974 as Peg Cullane; *Stranger and the Gunfighter* (as the Russian mistress)

Maria Silva, (Maria Jesus Marin Rodriguez) (Spanish and married to director Jose Granena); Nine westerns; *Shadow of Zorro* 1962 as Irene; *The Terrible Sheriff* 1963 as Clementine; *Cavalry Charge* 1963 as Sara; *Shoot to Kill* 1965 as Mary; *Kill the Wickeds* 1967 as Judy Mary (Liam's woman); *Fedra West* 1968 as Isabel Alvarez; *Sartana Kills them All* 1970 as Maria; *The Black Wolf* 1980 as Marquesa; *Revenge of the Black Wolf* 1981 returns as Marquesa

Silva Solar, (Genevieve Couzain) (French and former *Miss France* of 1956; Married to producer Rugelio Madrid (19??-2011); Nine westerns; *Shoot to Kill* 1963 as Mary; *Two Gunman* 1964 as Mora Sheridan; *Heroes of the West* 1964; *Tomb of the Pistolero* 1964 as Taffy; *Man Called Gringo* 1964 as Kate; *Relevo para un Pistolero (Relief of the Gunman)* 1964 as Carmen; *Finger on the Trigger* 1965 as Violet (the widow); *Three from Colorado* 1967; *Gentleman Killer* 1969 as Jill (Vicky)

Elke Sommer, (Elke Schletz) (German and once married to actor Joe Hyams (1964-1981); Cousin of actor Gudy Sommer); One western; *Among Vultures (Frontier Hellcat)* 1964 as Annie Dillman

Agnes Spaak, (French and daughter of screenwriter Charles Spaak; sister of actress Catherine Spaak); Five westerns; *Killer Calibre .38* 1967 as Beth (Betty); *God made them, I kill them!* 1968 as Doris; *Death Knows no time* 1969 as Mrs. Rojas; *Death on High Mountain* 1969 as Daphne; *Hey Amigo . . . A Toast to your Death* 1971 (as the Farmer's wife) (also to note for this one film she used the pseudonym of Anna Malsson)

Catherine Spaak, (French and sister of actress Agnes Spaak); One western; *Take a Hard Ride* 1974

Stella Stevens, (Estelle Caro Eggleston) (American and mother of director/ actor Andrew Stevens); One western; *A Town Called Hell* 1971 as Alvira, the widow

Evelyn Stewart, (Ida Galli) (Italian); Thirteen westerns; *Blood for a Silver Dollar* 1965 as Judy O'Hara; *Adios Gringo* 1965 as Lucy Tillson; *Charge of the Seventh Cavalry* 1965 as Nelly Bonnet Patterson; *Django Shoots First* 1966 as Jessica Cluster/ Custer; *Seven guns for Timothy* 1966 as Coralie; *Blood at Sundown* 1967 as Judy McDougall (Lopez's girl); *Machine Gun Killers* 1968 as Belinda Boyd; *No graves on Boot*

Hill 1968 as Dolores; *Man who cried for Revenge* 1969 as Lisa; *Chuck Moll* 1970 as Sheila; *Four Gunman of the Holy Trinity* 1971 as Sarah (Julia); *Man Called Invincible* 1973 as Miss Marlene; *The Little Cowboy* 1973 as Mrs. Callaghn (the kid's Mother)

Pamela Tiffin (Pamela Tiffin Wonso) (American and married to producer Clay Felker); One western; *Deaf Smith and Johnny Ears* 1972 as Susie

Marilu Tolo (Maria Lucia Tolo, sometimes as Tolu) (Italian); Three westerns; *Django Kill . . . If you live, shoot!* 1967 as Lori; *Roy Colt and Winchester Jack* 1970 as Manila; *Don't turn the other Cheek* 1971 as Lupita

Pamela Tudor, (Priscilla Eddy) (French); Six westerns; *Death at Owell Rock* 1967 as Eisabeth Patterson; *Time of Vultures* 1967 as Steffy Mendoza; *Dollars for a Fast Gun* 1968 as Helen Ray (Sarah); *One after the Another* 1968 as Sabine; *Canadian Wilderness* 1969 as Ann Sullivan; *Sartana in the Valley of Death* 1970 as Clementine (Esther)

Mamie Van Doren, (Joan Lucille Olander) (American and once married to musician Ray Anthony (1955-1961); Two westerns; *Arizona Kid* 1974 as Sharon Miller; *The Sheriff was a Lady* 1965 (saloon girl)

Pilar Velazquez, (Marie del Pilar Vealzquez Llorente) (Spanish and once married to composer Miguel Gallardo (1979-19??); Eight westerns; *Awkward Hands* 1968 as Dorothy; *I Came, I Saw, I Shot* 1968; *Forgotten Pistolero* 1969 as Isabella Carrasco; *Gunman of the Rio Grande* 1969; *Dust in the Sun* 1971 as Madame Goldini; *His Name was Holy Ghost* 1972 as Juana Mendoza; *Thunder over El Paso* 1972 as Anna; *Arizona Kid* 1974

Linda Veras, (Sieglinde Veras) (Italian and companion of director Sergio Sollima); Four westerns; *Face to Face* 1967 (Fletcher's woman); *Run Man Run* 1968 as Penny Bannington; *God made them . . . I Kill them* 1968 as Suzanne; *Sabata* 1969 as Jane; *Chapaqua's Gold* 1970 as Moria Shannon

Karen Well, (Wilma Truccolo, sometimes as Carol Wells) (Italian and later went on to Italian soft-porn films); Three western; *Zorro at the Court of England* 1969; *Fasthand* 1972 as Mary Cruz; *Porno-Erotic Western* 1979

US co produced 'Counterpart' westerns most commonly filmed in a European country like Spain and/ or other countries like Mexico, South America and Canada. The more popular of these Women associated with these films are listed below . . .

Candice Bergen, (Candice Patricia Bergen) (Daughter of ventriloquist Edgar Bergen and actress Frances Bergen; Sister of actor Kris Bergen; once married to director Luis Malle (1980-1995); One US counterpart western; *The Hunting Party* 1971 as Melissa Ruger

Senta Berger, (Austrian and married to director Michael Verhoeven (1966—); Mother of actor/ director Simon Verhoeven and actor Luca Verhoeven); One US counterpart western; *The Glory Guys* 1965 as Lou Woodward

Verna Bloom, (Married to screenwriter Joy Cocks); One US counterpart western; *High Plains Drifter* 1973 as Sarah Belding

Susan Clark, (Susan Goulding Clark) (Once married to producer/ actor Robert L. Joseph (1970-1973); then pro-footballer/ actor Alex Karas (1980—); Step-sister of actress Linda Thomson); One US counterpart western; *Valdez is coming* 1971as Gay Erin

Faye Dunaway, (Dorothy Faye Dunaway) (Once married to composer Peter Wolf (1974-1979); One US counterpart western; *Doc* 1968 as Katie Elder

Mariette Hartley, (Mary Loretta Hartley) (Once married to actor (Jerry Sroka), producer/ director Patrick Bovriven (1978-1996); Two US counterpart westerns; *The Magnificent Seven Ride* 1969 as Arilla Adams; *Barquero* 1970

Marianna Hill, (Marianna Schwarzkopf) (Is cousin of noted US Army General Norman Schwarzkopf); Two US counterpart westerns; *El Condor* 1970 as Claudine (The Colonel's mistress); *High Plains Drifter* 1973 as Callie Travers

Jill Ireland, (Jill Dorothy Ireland) (British and once married to actor David McCallum (1957-1963); Then to actor Charles Bronson (1968-1990, until her death, breast-cancer); 3-children by McCallum: David Jr., Valentine and Paul; With Bronson one daughter Zuleika); Two US counterpart westerns: *Villa Rides* 1968 (girl in restaurant); *Chino* 1973 as Catherine

Shirley MacLaine, (Shirley MacLean Beaty) (Sister of actor Warren Beatty; Married to producer Steve Parker); One US counterpart western; *Two Mules for Sister Sara* 1970 as Sara, (the Nun/ whore)

Sheree North, (Dawn Shirley Crang); one US counterpart western; *Lawman* 1971 as Mrs. Laurie Shelby

Stephanie Powers, (Stefania Zofya Federkiwwicz) (American); One western; *The Magnificent Seven Ride* 1969 as Mrs. Laurie Gunn

Jean Seberg, (French and once married to director Francois Moreuil (1958-1960); Then to director Romain Gary (1962-1970); then director Dennis Berry (1972-1978); One US counterpart western; *Macho Callahan* 1970 as Alexandra Mountford

Inger Stevens, (Inger Stensland) (Swedish and married to producer Ike Tunes (1961-Apr.1970 until her death, suicide/ barbiturate overdose); One US counterpart western; *Hang 'Em High* 1968 as Rachel Warren

Raquel Welch, (Jo Raquel Tejada) of Bolivian/ British parentage (American) (Once married to producer Patrick Curtis (1967-1972); Then to director Andre Weinfeld (1980-1990); Mother of actor Damon Welch and actress Tahnee Welch); One western; *100 Rifles* 1969 as Sarita; *Hannie Caulder* 1971 as Hannie Caulder

Shelley Winters, (Shelley Schrift) (American and married to actor Vittorio Gassman (1952-1954); Then to actor Anthony Franciosa (1967-1960); One US counterpart western; *The Scalp-hunters* 1968 as Kate

End.

PSEUDONYMS

A partial listing of those use by some of the better known *Spaghetti* Actors, Directors and Producers . . .

Alphabetically Listed with Pseudonyms first

A one-time multi-listing which contains many names/ pseudonyms not previously related or found in other listings or publications

KEY: (Dir) Director; (Pro) Producer; (Scr) Screenwriter; (Cine) Cinematographer; (W) Writer

Al Bradley (Dir) (Alfonso Brescia)
Albert Band (Dir/Pro) (Antonio Alfredo)
Albert Mann (Dir) (Bitto Albertini)
Al Cliver (Pierluigi Conti)
Aldo Sambrell (Act, Dir, Pro) *sometimes as A.F. Spell* (Alfredo Sanchez Brell)
Alex Burkes (Dir) (Luigi Bazzoni)
Andrew Scott (Andrea Scotti)
Andrew Ray (Andrea Aureli)
Anna Malsson (Agnes Spaak)
Anthony Freeman *sometimes as Tony Freeman* (Mario Novelli)
Anthony Ghidra (Dragomir Gidre Bojanovic) *Croatian actor*
Anthony M. Dawson (Dir/Cine/Scr) (Antonio Margheriti)
Anthony Richmond (Dir) (Tonino Ricci)
Anthony Whiles (Dir) (Mario Sequi)
Arthur Kent (Arturo Dominici)
Arthur Scott (Dir) (Luigi Scattini)
Avi Nesher (Dir) (Rumat Gan) *Israeli director*

Barbara Simon (Bruna Simionato)
Benny Reeves (Benito Stefanelli)
Bert Woods *(sometimes Robert S. Woods)* (Robert Woods)

Bill Jackson (Gino Buzzanca)
Bob Avalone; Bob Hevilon; Robert Lone (Robert *Bob* Hevelone) *(Brother of Barbara Hevelone, wife of deceased actor/ Spaghetti western icon, Lee Van Cleef)*
Bob Collins (Dir) (Umberto Lenzi)
Bob Hunter (Dir) (Bruno Mattei) aka William Snyder; Vincent Dawn or Werner Knox
Bob Roberts (Fulvio Testi)

Calvin Jackson Padget (Dir) (Giorgio Ferroni)
Carrol Brown (Carla Calo)
Charles Otter (Carlos Otero)
Charles Quiney (Carlos Quiney)
Chet Davis also as Victoriano Gazzara (Franco Borelli)
Cole Kitosch (Alberto Dell'Acqua)
Crazy Matthews (Attilio Severini)

Dan Clark (Marco Mariani)
Dan Edwards (Dir) (Edoardo Margheriti) *(son of Dir. Antonio Margheriti)*
Dan Harrison (Bruno Piergentili)
Dan May (Dante Maggio)
Daniel Moock also as Pipolo (Giuseppe Moccia)
Dan Vadis (Daniel Vafiadis) *(China born; ex-body builder/ actor)*
Dan Jones (Dir.) (Luigi Batzella)
Donal O'Brien sometimes as Donald O'Brien *(Fr. born actor, of Irish parentage, returned to Ireland, then later back to France)*
Dean Reese (Attilio Dottesio)
Dennis Colt (Benito Pacifico)
Dirce Funari (Patrizia Funari)
Dick Hope (Scr) (Roberto Leoni)

Emil Jordan (Claudio Gora)
Erika Blanc (Enrica Bianchi Colombatto) *(sometimes as Erica White)*
Evelyn Merril (Gloria Osuna) *(sometimes Gloria Demme or Gloria Ocana)*

Franco Nero (Francesco Sparanero) *(Nero's Ital voice has been dubbed into English in several films by Anthony Russel)*
Frank Farrel (Franco Fantasia)
Frank Garfield (Dir.) (Franco Giraldi)
Frank Martin (Dir.) (Mario Girolami) *(sometimes as Fred Wilson)*
Frank Reed (Dir.) (Marcello Ciorciolini)
Frank Ressell (Franco Ressel) *(sometimes as Ray Ressel)*

Frankie Liston (Franco Lantieri)
Frank Valenti (Dir) (Pierluigi Ciriaci)
Franz Wieland (Franco Castellano)
Fred Lyons Morris (Dir) (Luigi Batzella)
Fred Harrison (Fernando Bilbao)

Gary Hudson (Gianni Garko) *(sometimes as John Garko)*
George Greenwood (Giorgio Cerioni)
George Hilton (Jorge Hill) *(South American actor from Uruguay)*
Gilbert Roland (Luis Antonio Damaso de Alonso) *(Spa/ Mex, famous as an actor in America since 40's)*
Gil Rowland *(sometimes as Roland)* (Gilberto Galimberti)
Glenn Vincent Davis (Scr) (Vincenzo Musolino)
Gordon Mitchell (Charles *Chuck* Pendleton)
Graham Sooty (Virgino Gazzolo)
Grant Laramy (Germano Congo)
Gus Stone (Romano Puppo)
Guy Madison (Robert *Bob* Ozell Moseley)

Helen Parker (Maria Luisa)
Henry Mankiewicz (Dir) (Leon Klimovsky)
Howard Ross (Luciano Rossi)
Howard Vernon (Mario Lippert)

J. Luis Monter (Dir.) (Roberto Montero)
Jack Dalmas (Dir) (Massimo Dallamano) *(sometimes Max Dillman)*
Jack Palance (Vladimir Palanuik) *(Russian born actor)*
James Harris (Dir) (Marcello Ciorciolini)
James Hill (Giulio Maschetti)
James Warren (Dir) (Minio Guerrini)
Jeff Cameron (Goffredo Scarciofolo)
Jerry Wilson (Roberto Miali)
Jill Powers (Milla Sannoner)
Jim Clay (Aldo Cecconi)
Jim Reed (Luigi Giuliano)
Joe D'Amato (Dir.) (Federico Slonisko)
John Barracuda (Massimo Sernto)
John Bartha *(sometimes as Gianni Bartha)* (Janos Barta)
John Clark (Hugo Blanco)
John Elder (Scr) (Pro) (Dir) (Anthony Hinds) *(sometimes as Tony Hinds)*
John Hamilton (Gianni Medici)
John Heston (Jvano Staccioli)

John J. Dawson (Dir) (Leandro Lucchetti)
John McDouglas (Giuseppe Addobbati)
John Old Jr. (Dir) (Lamberto Bava)
John Sansom (W/Pro/Dir.) (James *Jimmy* Sangster) *(British scriptwriter)*
John Turner (Gino Turini)
John W. Fordson (Dir.) *sometimes as J.W. Fordson* (Mario Costa)
John Wilder (Dir) (Luigi Russo)
John Wood (Dir) (Juan Bosch)
Jose Maria Zabalza (Dir/Scr.) (Julio Perez Tabernero) *(aka Harry Freeman or Joseph Trader)*
Joseph Warren (Dir) (Giuseppe Vari)
Joshua Sinclair (John Louis Loffredo) *Born in NYC. (aka John Loffredo or Johnny Loffrey)*
Judy Robbins (Giulia Rubini)

Karen Blake (Sydne Rome)
Karen Well (Wilma Truccolo) *(sometimes as Carol Wells)*
Keren Yeh (Yen Ling Chih) *(Chinese actress)*
Kirk Morris (Adriano Bellini)
Klaus Kinski *sometimes as Klas Kinsky* (Nilcolas Nakszynski) *(Polish born actor)*

Larry Ludman (Dir) (Fabrizio De Angelis)
Laura Antonelli (Laura Antonaz) *(Italian born, though area now part of Croatia)*
Laura Gemser (Moira Chen)
Lee Burton (Guido Lollobrigida)
Leonard Mann (Leonard Manzella)
Lewis Coats (Dir) (Luigi Cozzi)
Luciano Loreas (Luciano Catenacci)
Lucky Moore (Dir) (Carlo Croccolo)

Mamie Van Doren (Joan Lucille Olander)
Marc Stevens *(also as Marta Stevens)* (Pasquale Simeoli)
Maria Silva (Maria Jesus Marin Rodriguez) *(sometimes as Mary Silvers)*
Mario Costa (Dir.) *(sometimes John W. Fordson)*
Mario Darnell (Mario Dardanelli)
Mark Davis (Gianfranco Clerici)
Marlon Sirko (Dir) (Mario Siciliano)
Martha Dovan (Marta Padovan)
Maurice A Bright (Dir) (Scr) (Maurizio Lucidi)
Max Steel (Dir/Cine) (Stelvio Massi) *(sometimes as Stefano Calalano)*

Michael E. Lemick (Dir) (Michele Massimo Tarantini)
Michael Rivers (Miguel de la Riva)
Mike Ashley (Mino Roli)
Mike Hargitay (*sometimes Mik, Mick or Mickey Hargitay)* (Miklos Hargitay) *(Hungarian born actor)*
Mike Middleton (Dir) (Massimo Mida)
Mike Moore (Amedeo Trilli)
Miles Deem (Dir) (Demofilo Fidani)
Monica Randall (Aurora Julia Sarasa) *(sometimes as Randal or Randel)*
Monty Greenwood (Maurice Poli) *(French actor)*
Montgomery Clark (Dante Posani)
Montgomery Ford (Brett Halsey)
Montgomery Wood (Giuliana Gemma)

Nick Howard (Dir) (Paolo Bianchini) *(sometimes as Paul Maxwell)*
Nick Nostro (Dir) (Paolo Bianchini) *(sometimes as Nick Howard)*
Norman Clark (Pier Paolo Capponi)

Pat Greenhill (Germana Montererdi)
Paul D. Robinson (Dir) (Ignazio Dolce)
Paul Solvay (Act/Dir) (*sometimes as Paola Solvay*) (Luigi Batzella)
Paul Maxwell (Dir/Scr) (Paolo Bianchini) *(sometimes Nick Nostro/ Nick Howard)*
Paul Stevens (Paolo Gozlino)
Pedro Sanchez (Iqnazio Spalla)
Peter Barclay (Pietro Ceccarelli)
Peter Carter (Piero Lulli)
Peter Cross (Pierre Cressoy)
Peter Martell (Pietro Martellanza)
Peter Thorrys (Pietro Torrisi)
Peter White (Franco Cobianchi)
Priscilla Eddy (Pamela Tudor)

Ray Calloway (Dr) (Mario Colucci)
Red Carter (Ettore Manni)
Rick Boyd (Federico Boido) *(Italian actor)*
Rick Garrett (Riccardo Garrone)
Rick Horn (Anton Geesink) *(Netherlands born actor]*
Robert Rise (Roberto Risso)
Robert Hill (Roberto Dell'Acqua) *(Italian actor)*
Rock Stevens (Peter Lupus) *(the big guy who played in US Mission Impossible TV-series)*

Robert Stevenson (Valentino Macchi)
Robert Widmark (Alberto Dell'Acqua) *(Italian and brother to Roberto)*
Ryan Baldwin (Renato Baldini)

Sean Todd (Ivan Rassimov)
Sheryll Morgan (Helena Stoliaroff) *(often times as Helene Chanel)*
Simone Blondell (Act) (Simonette Vitelli) *(Daughter of genre director Demofilo Fidani and Mila Vitelli)*
Spean Convery (Spartaco Conversi)
Stan Cooper (Stelvio Rosi)
Stanley Kent (Stelvio Candelli)
Steele Priscila (Ida Galli) *(sometimes as Isli Oberon, but mostly as Evelyn Stewart)*
Steno (Dir) (Stefano Vanzina)
Stephen M. Andrews (Dir) *(mostly as Enzo G. Castellari)* (Enzo Girolami)
Stet Carson (Fabio Testi)
Stuart Murphy (Dir) (Mario Bianchi)

Ted Carter (Giovanni *Nello* Pazzafini)
Ted Kaplin (Dir) (Ferdinando Baldi)
Telly Savalas (Aristotle Savalas)
Thomas Clay (Franco Gulia)
Thomas Moore (Dir) (*also as Paul Solvay sometimes Paolo)* (Luigi Batzella)
Thomas Rudy (Tomas Rudy)
Tony Dry *(sometimes as Toni Dry)* (Anthony Secchi)
Tony Russel (*sometimes Tony Russell)* (Anthony Russel)
Tor Altmayr (Tullio Altamura)

Vance Lewis (Dir) (Luigi Vanzi)
Vincent Dawn (Dir) (Bruno Mattei)

Wanda Vismara (Uschi Glas)
Wayde Preston (William Erskine Strange)
Werner Knox (Dir) (Bruno Mattei)
William Bogart (Guglielmo Spoletini)
William Redford (Pasquale Squiteri)
William Snyder (Dir) (Bruno Mattei)

Yul Brynner (Taidje Khan)

Additional notations were by the author . . .

FILM DISTRIBUTION

ACKNOWLEDGEMENT AND RECOGNITION PAGES

Many thanks to those listed below, who have through the years brought us the many hours of pleasure, we the fans have had in the pursuing, acquiring, watching, collecting and owning copies of these wonderful films of yesteryear. A Toast, to all the Men and Women that were involved in bringing us those fabulous *Spaghetti* Westerns . . .

ABC*-Pictures International (formerly "ABC Pictures"); ABC-TV (American Broadcasting Corp); Abkco Films; Accadia Film; AFT Distributing Corp; Aitor Films; AJAY Films; Albatros; Alcifrance; Allied Artists (Formerly "Monogram"); The American Film Institute; American International Pictures (Formerly "American Releasing Corp"); Artistes Associes; Atlantida Film; National Telefilm Associates (Formerly called "Astor"); Artistes Associes; Atlantic Releasing Corp.; AVCO Embassy Pictures Corp.; Azteca Films; BBC-Television Enterprises/ Time-Life Warner Films; CANNON Group/Cannon Releasing; Capitol International; C/A/U Productions; C.B. Films; CBS-TV (Columbia Broadcasting System); C.C. Astro; C.C.C. (C.C. Champion); Cecchi Gori; Centauro Films; C.I.C. Films S.A.; Cine Espana; Cinefilms Zodiaco; Cinema International; Cinemaster International; Cinerama Releasing Corp.; Cineriz Distribuzione; CIO-Film; Circus Film-Fono; CIRE Films; Cobelcine; Columbia Pictures (CPT); Compass International Pictures; Compton; Compton-Cameo; Concordia Films; Constantin-Film; Copacabana Filmes; Copercines; Cosmopolis Films; C.R.C. Produzione; EKO; Embassy Pictures; Emery Pictures, Inc.; EMI Films Ltd., (Anglo-Amalgamated, Anglo-EMI, Assoc-British Pathe Ltd., British Lion Films Ltd., Lion International);Etoile Film; Euro International; Excelsior Films; Explorer Films '58; FJDA; Filmax; Film Around the World; Film Ventures International; Filmways Pictures; Filmways Inc.,("Filmways International");Flora Film; Fono Roma S.p.A.;*

Fox-Rank Distributors; Gala; Gatto Cinematografica S.r.l.; GGP; General Film Distributors; Golden Era; GSF Productions; G.V. Roma; Harlequin International Pictures; Hispamex Films; iFiSA; I.F.C.; Inex Films; Intercontinental; Interfilm; Inter-Ocean; Italcid; JF Films; Kinekor; KINO International; Le Film Trianon; Lea Films; Leone Film; Les Films; Jacques Leitienne; Libra Films Corp; Lorimar Productions; Lutecia Films; Lux Cinematographique; Magna S.p.A.; Marco Film; Mecurio Films; Mediaset; Medusa Distribuzione; Mercury Films; Metheus Films; Metropolitan Films; MGM (Metro-Goldwyn-Mayer); Midega Film; Mundial Films; National Film Board of Canada; National General Pictures; NBC-TV (National Broadcasting Corp.); N.C. Roma; New World Pictures (Film Group); New World Pictures; NTA (National Telefilm Assoc (formerly "Republic Pictures"); Nora; Orphee Productions; PAC; Panta Cinematografica Distribuzione; Paramount; Paramount (non-Theatrical Films); Parnass Film; PEA (Produzione Europee Associate); PCB (Producciones Cinematograficas Balcazar); Poli Films Mundiales; Procines; Prodimex; Promofilm; Protor Film; Rafran Films; Rank Film Distributors (Gaumount-British/General Film Distribution); Regal Film; Rizzoli Films; R.M. Films; Sanchez Ramada; Scotia-Barber Distributors; Scotia-International; Selenia Cinematografica; Seven Seas; Stellar IV Film Corp.; Sunn Classic Pictures (formerly "Sun International Pictures"); Swank Motion Pictures (Non-theatrical films of Columbia, Warner Bros, Universal, Avco-Embassy, National General and American International films); Titanus; Tobis Filmkunst; Transvue Pictures; Trans-World Entertainment; Warner Bros.,(and formerly owned films by "National General Pictures/ Cinema Center Films"); Tritone; 20th Century-Fox (formerly "Fox Film Co."); UGC; UIP; Ulyses Films; UMC Pictures; United Artists (as Premier Pictures, All MGM films since 1973); United International Pictures; United Producers; Universal Pictures (Formerly Universal-International now handled by Swank); Universal Exportation Films; Uranos Cinematografica; Variety Film; Vis Radio; Warner Bros.; Warner-Pathe Distributors . . .

Author

INDEX

A

Acquasanta Joe/ Holy Water Joe (1971), 214, 227
Adios Sabata/ Indio Black (1971), 407, 416
Adorf, Mario (Act), 260, 433
Albertini, Bitto (Dir), 243, 265, 278, 319
Alessandroni, Alessandro (M), 64
All Out / Go For Broke (1968), 239, 251
Alvarez, Amadeo (Ray Fellows) (Dir), 113
Among Vultures/ Frontier Hellcat (1964), 25, 30
And God Said to Cain (1970), 272
Another Man, Another Chance (1977), 28, 33
Anything for a Friend (1973), 371
Apache Gold / Winnetou the Warrior (1964), 24, 30
Apache's Last Battle / Old Shatterhand (1964), 311, 331
Arizona Kid (1971), 354, 368
Ascott, Anthony (Giuliano Carmineo) (Dir), 26, 31, 52, 67, 264, 272

B

Bacalov, Luis Enrique (M), 214
Bad Man's River (1971), 496
Baker, Carroll (Act), 57–58, 67–68, 86, 99, 485
Balcazar, Alfonso (Al Bagrain) (Pro/ Dir), 30, 152, 157, 163, 433, 435
Baldanello, Gianfranco (Frank G. Carrol) (Dir), 57–58, 67–68, 255, 264, 407, 484
Baldi, Ferdinando (Ted Kaplin) (Dir), 364, 409
Bang, Bang Kid, The (1967), 316, 335
Ban Yee, Yeo (Dir), 58, 68
Barboni, Enzo (E.B. Clutcher) (Cine/ Dir), 56
Barker, Lex (Act), 23–25, 45, 247, 260, 310–11, 331
Barnes, Walter (Act), 19–34, 105, 204, 380, 383–84, 392
Barret, Liz (Luisa Baratto) (Act), 197
Barton, Dee (M), 150, 156, 501, 503
Bazzoni, Luigi (Alex Burkes / Fred Lyon Morris) (Dir), 386, 394
Beast, The / Rough Justice (1970), 273
Benussi, Femi (Act), 197, 351, 363, 367, 371, 406
Berger, William (Act), 35–38, 40–44, 46, 48–71, 246–47, 387–88
Bergonzelli, Sergio (Serge Bergon) (Dir), 44, 66, 188, 196
Berti, Aldo (Act), 363
Beswick, Martine (Act), 264

Between God, the Devil and a Winchester (1968), 211, 224, 424, 427
Beyond the Law (1968), 286, 352, 365, 405, 483, 496
Bianchi, Mario Adelchi (Frank Bronston) (Dir), 57, 68
Bianchi, Paolo (Paul Maxwell) (Dir), 316, 398
Bianchini, Paolo (Nick Nostro / Nick Howard) (Dir), 211, 223, 317
Big Gundown (1968), 26, 32, 241, 408, 481
Black Killer (1971), 276
Blanc, Erika (Enrica Bianchi) (Act), 350
Blasco, Ricardo (Dir), 206, 221
Blondell, Simone (Simonette Vitelli) (Act), 366–68, 371
Blood River (1974), 246, 255
Boccia, Tanio (Amergo Anton) (Dir), 217, 228, 363, 365, 504, 508
Boot Hill (1969), 34, 79, 102, 113, 388
Bordello / the Women of Jeremias (1979), 113
Born to Kill (1967), 351, 363
Brega, Mario (Act), 126, 264, 266, 367, 371, 409
Brescia, Alfonso (Al Bradly) (Dir), 152, 318, 352
Bronson, Charles (Act), 58, 84, 138, 141–42, 144, 249
Bruschini, Vito (Dir), 34, 71, 80, 95, 114, 134
Brynner, Yul (Act), 83, 240, 342, 345, 407–8, 416
Buck at the Edge of Heaven / Buck's Greatest Adventure (1991), 63, 70
Bullet for the General (1966), 263, 270

C

Caiano, Mario (William Hawkins) (Dir), 49, 66
Calhoun, Rory (Act), 29, 73–80, 298–99, 304, 312, 322
California Goodbye / California (1977), 60
Cameron, Rod (Act), 150, 156, 206, 250, 273–74, 367
Captain Apache (1971), 471–72, 485
Capuano, Mario (Dir/M), 196, 312
Cardinale, Claudia (Act), 267, 291
Cardone, Alberto, 361, 395
Carlos, Luciano (Dir), 50, 56, 123, 126, 131, 237
Carmineo, Giuliano (Anthony Ascott) (Dir), 26, 31, 52, 67, 264, 272
Carreras, Michael (Dir) of British "*Hammer Films*" fame for one genre film., 75, 404
Cervi, Tonino (Dir), 49, 66
Challenge of the MacKennas / Badlands Drifter (1970), 244, 255, 514
Chanel, Helene (Sherill Morgan) (Act), 28, 161, 164, 169, 172, 191
Chaplin, Geraldine (Act), 58
Christine, Katia (Act), 61, 200
Ciccio Forgives, I Don't! (1968), 164, 172, 405
Cicero, Nando (Dir), 272
Ciorciolini, Marcello (Frank Reed) (Dir), 164, 172–73, 405, 415
Civirani, Osvaldo (Glenn Eastman) (Dir), 165, 174, 241, 334, 365
Cjamango (1967), 191, 198
Claman, Dolores (M), 485
Clint the Stranger (1967), 25, 30, 265, 276
Closed Circuit (1979) (film within a film), 69
Coburn, James (Act), 81–95, 100, 120, 207–8
Colizzi, Giuseppe (Dir), 164, 388, 396–97
Colucci, Mario (Ray Calloway) (Dir), 240, 254

Connolly, William, Spaghetti Cinema fanzine/Blogspot, 34, 114, 133, 200–201, 354–56, 374
Connors, Chuck (Act), 96–114, 138, 186, 240, 248, 256
Conqueror, The (1956), 101, 349, 351
Conte, Maria Pia (Act), 200, 234, 409
Cooper, Gary, 109, 238–39, 271, 318–19, 370–71, 427
Corbucci, Sergio (Stanley Corbett) (Dir), 62, 104, 163, 165, 264, 423–24
Costa, Mario, 46, 273, 350, 493, 528
Cost of Dying / Taste of Death (1968), 242
Crea, Gianni (Dir), 57, 68, 367, 369, 371, 414
Crispino, Armando (Dir), 483
Cristal, Perla (Act), 425, 436
Croccolo, Carlo (Lucky Moore/ Sobey Martin) (Dir), 276
Curse This America / Jaida's Gang (1973), 58, 67

D

Damiani, Damiano (Dir), 263, 266, 270, 278, 289
Danning, Sybil (Act), 490
Day of Anger (1967), 481
Dead for a Dollar (1968), 241, 256, 352, 365
De Angelis brothers, Guido & Maurizio (M), 60
Death Knows No Time (1969), 386
Death Rides a Horse (1967), 482
De Laurentiis, Dino (Pro), 105, 131–32, 389
De Martino, Alberto (Dir), 205, 210, 222, 237, 361
De Masi, Francesco (Frank Mason) (M), 105, 242, 423–24
Deserter, The / Devil's Backbone (1970), 105
Dexter, Rosemarie (Act), 367
Dig Your Grave Friend . . . Sabata's Coming! (1971), 214, 226, 407
Django (1966), 62–63, 70, 161, 317, 334, 366–67
Django and Sartana Are Coming . . . It's the End! (1970), 353, 366
Django Strikes Again/ Django 2 (1987), 62, 70
Douglas, Kirk (Act), 23–24, 127, 236–37, 346, 388, 404–5
Drummer of Vengeance (1971), 368
Duel at Rio Bravo (1964), 311, 332
Duel at Sundown (1965), 30
Duel at the Rio Grande/ Sign of Zorro, The (1963), 29

E

Eastwood, Clint (Act/Dir), 115–22, 124–28, 130–33, 208–10, 287, 468–69
Ekberg, Anita (Act), 217, 406
Elam, Jack (Act), 135–45, 149, 156, 383, 429, 502–3
El Cisco (1966), 44, 66
Escobar, Enrique (M), 218
Esteba, Manuel (Ted Mulligan) (Dir), 409
Executioner of God (1973), 57

F

Face to Face (1967), 46, 66
Fajardo, Eduardo (Act), 43, 240, 486
Fasthand Is Still My Name (1973), 57
Felleghy, Tom (Tomas Felleghi) (Act), 43, 242, 247
Fellini, Federico (Miles Deem) (Dir), 273–74, 319, 353, 355, 366–68, 371

Fidani, Demofilo (Miles Deem / Dick Spitfire/ Dennis Ford, 273–74, 319, 353, 355, 366–68, 371
Fidenco, Nico (M), 409
Fighting Fists of Shanghai Joe, The (1973), 265, 371
Finders Killers (1971), 367
Finger on the Trigger (1965), 75, 312
Fistful of Dollars, A (1964), 45, 76, 122, 124, 133, 161–62
Fistful of Dynamite / Duck you Sucker (1971), 88, 92, 94
Five for Revenge / Five Giants from Texas (1966), 333
Flori, Agata (Act), 165, 173, 406
Florio, Aldo (Dir), 333, 350, 355
Fonda, Henry (Act), 109, 137, 207, 288–89, 291, 477
For a Fist in the Eye (1965), 163, 168
Ford, John (Dir), 48, 81, 107, 154, 211, 288
Forest, Michael (Act), 77, 147–59, 344, 347–48, 358, 475–76
Forrest, Mark (Act), 150, 156, 341, 367
Four Rode Out (1969), 236
Francis, Anne (Act), 66, 72, 117, 240
Franco, Jess (Jesus) (Dir), 62–63, 86, 160–63, 165–75, 194–95, 405–6
Franco and Ciccio on the War Path / War Path (1969), 289
Franco e Ciccio (Italian comedy team of films), 165, 173, 175
Fregonese, Hugo (Dir), 74, 409

G

Galimberti, Gilberto (Gill Roland) (Act), 424
Gariazzo, Mario (Robert Paget) (Dir), 368
Garko, John (Gianni) (Act), 49–50, 52, 57, 68, 264, 366–67
Garrone, Sergio (Willy S. Regan) (Dir), 50
Garter Colt (1968), 26, 32
Gentili, Giorgio (Dir), 389, 397
George, Gotz (Act), 30
George, Susan (Act), 73, 148, 248, 301, 408
Gigante, Marcello (M), 404
Giordano, Daniela (Act), 51, 244, 369
Girolami, Ennio (Act), 26, 124, 128, 132, 164, 288–89
Girolami, Enzo (Enzo G. Castellari) (Dir), 60, 68, 105, 111–12, 423–24, 426–28
Girolami, Marino (Frank Martin) (Act/Dir), 163, 172, 213, 336
God Does Not Pay on Saturday / Kill the Wickeds (1967), 504, 508
God Forgives, Ciccio Don't (1968), 164, 397, 405
God Made Them . . . I Kill Them (1968), 404, 414
God's Gun (1976), 490
God Will Forgive My Pistol (1969), 388, 396
Go Kill and Come Back / Any Gun Can Play (1967), 114, 423, 426
Good, the Bad, and the Ugly, The (1966), 130, 133, 161, 163–64, 287, 290
Grand Duel, The / Big Showdown, The / Storm Rider (1972), 487
Grandson of Zorro / Dream of Zorro, The (1975), 166, 174–75, 406
Greatest Robbery in the West (1967), 25, 31
Gries, Tom (Dir), 155
Grimaldi, Alberto (Dir/Pro), 126, 407, 479
Grimaldi, Gianni (Dir), 49–50, 52, 57, 68, 264, 366–67
Grimaldi, Giovanni (Aldo) (Dir), 50, 163, 165, 171, 173, 317

Gunfight at High Noon (1963), 205, 220
Gunfight at Red Sands (1963), 206, 209, 221

H

Halsey, Brett (Montgomery Ford) (Act), 26, 48–49, 154, 378, 387, 494
Handsome, the Ugly, the Stupid, The (1967), 163, 171
Hannie Caulder (1971), 139, 143
Hardin, Ty (Act), 139, 149, 214, 256, 325, 351
Hargitay, Mickey (Act), 177, 184–89, 191, 193–201, 344, 350
Harris, Brad (Act), 179, 183, 185, 199, 207, 346
Harrison, Richard (James London) (Act/Dir), 216, 227
Haselbeck, Sebastian, *Spaghetti*-western.net website, 29, 34, 65, 70, 78, 80
Hate for Hate (1967), 238, 251
Hellman, Monty (Dir) Credited with US TV prologue for "*A Fistful of Dollars*"., 125–26, 147
Hess, David (M), 63
Heston, Charlton (Act), 85, 99, 238, 342, 345, 361
Hevelone, Barbara (M) Third wife of actor Lee Van Cleef, 151–52, 188, 204, 244, 469–72, 474–75
Hey Amigo . . . a Toast to Your Death (1970), 390, 398
High Plains Drifter (1973), 27
Hill, Craig (Act), 71, 175, 257, 279, 368, 370
Hill, Terence (Mario Girotti) (Act), 25, 85, 164, 255, 289, 387–88
Hilton, George (Act), 25–26, 161–62, 170, 271, 320, 423
His Name Was King (1971), 214, 226, 274
His Pistols Smoked . . . They Call Him Cemetery (1971), 52, 67
How the West Was Fun (1979) Doc-dedication to TV and Film Cowboys, 323
Hughes, Howard/ *RKO Pictures* (Pro), 231, 279, 321, 379
Huston, John (Act/Dir), 105, 248, 503

I

I am Sartana, Your Angel of Death (1969), 264, 272, 353, 366
If Born a Swine, Kill Him! / Lynching (1968), 365
If You Meet Sartana . . . Pray for Your Death/ Sartana (1968), 49, 66, 264, 271
I'll forgive you . . . Before I Kill You / Stagecoach of the Condemned (1970), 212, 224
Induni, Luis (Act), 246, 409–10, 433
Iquino, Ignacio (John Wood/ Juan Bosch) (Dir), 212, 214, 218, 224, 226, 409–10
Ireland, Jill (Act), 240
Ireland, John (Act), 108, 233–50, 255–57, 319, 346, 352

J

Jesse e Lester, Two brothers in a Place Called Trinity (1972), 217
Joe Dakota Shoot . . . And Shoot Again! (1972), 217, 227
Johnny Hamlet / Dirty Story of the West (1968), 424, 428
John the Bastard (1967), 351
Julian, Franco (M), 106, 236, 240, 409

N

O